Banking and Financial Systems

V. Nityananda Sarma

Delhi • Bengaluru • Mumbai • Kolkata • Chennai • Hyderabad • Pune

Published by
Cambridge University Press India Pvt. Ltd.
under the imprint of Foundation Books
Cambridge House, 4381/4 Ansari Road, Daryaganj, **New Delhi** 110 002

Cambridge University Press India Pvt. Ltd.
C-22, C-Block, Brigade M.M., K.R. Road, Jayanagar, **Bengaluru** 560 070
Plot No. 80, Service Industries, Shirvane, Sector-1, Nerul, **Navi Mumbai** 400 706
10 Raja Subodh Mullick Square, 2nd Floor, **Kolkata** 700 013
21/1 (New No. 49), 1st Floor, Model School Road, Thousand Lights,
Chennai 600 006
House No. 3-5-874/6/4, (Near Apollo Hospital), Hyderguda, **Hyderabad** 500 029
Agarwal Pride, 'A' Wing, 1308 Kasba Peth, Near Surya Hospital, **Pune** 411 011

First published 2011

ISBN 978-81-7596-637-6

Published by Manas Saikia for Cambridge University Press India Pvt. Ltd. and printed at Shree Maitrey Printech Pvt. Ltd.

Contents

Preface *v*

1. Banking Systems 1
2. Functions of Modern Commercial Banks 19
3. Nationalisation of Banks in India 84
4. Money Market 102
5. Capital Market 135
6. Development Banking 162
7. Cooperative Banks in India 209
8. Regional Rural Banks (RRBs) 232
9. Exchange Banks 244
10. The Reserve Bank of India 269
11. The State Bank of India 311
12. Financial Services 318
13. Banking Technology 351
14. Negotiable Instruments 388
15. Banker and Customer 427
16. Special Type of Customers 450
17. Paying Banker 470
18. Secured Advances – Mode of Creating Charge 493

Index *533*

Preface

The Banking industry in India has changed spectacularly since 1991 due to the Government of India policies in respect to liberalisation, privatisation and globalisation, which has stepped up the level of competition in all spheres of economic activity. The modern banking industry is characterised by extensive reorganisation, restructuring, expansion and phenomenal growth with mergers and acquisitions among the public and private sector banks. The growth of modern banking is both an innovative and creative human endeavour. Therefore, students should be aware of the ongoing changes that are taking place across the world.

This book addresses the following issues:

- Evolution of banking systems – commercial banking development in India from its inception till date
- Nationalisation of banks in India – merits and demerits; improvement in banking activities; innovations
- Money market – characteristics of Indian money markets; components; defects; working; suggestions for improvement
- Capital market – primary and secondary market; characteristics; improvement; stock exchange dealings; Securities Exchange Board of India (SEBI) operations; working of stock exchanges; different methods adopted; capital formation; improvement
- Financial systems – financial activities of major institutions like IFCI; IDBI; UTI; mutual funds; insurance companies; *nidhis*; chit funds and other non-financial banking companies, financial policies
- Cooperative banks – structure; development; activities; loan disbursement; defects; suggestions for improvement
- Regional rural banks – structure; working; defects; provision for loans toward agriculture and small scale sectors; suggestions for improvement
- Exchange banks – foreign trade; foreign exchange; domination of foreign banks over Indian banks; development of Indian banks in foreign exchange and foreign trade; foreign exchange system and control; International Monetary Fund (IMF); Special Drawing Rights (SDRs)
- Reserve Bank of India – RBI Act of 1934; functions; organisation; structure; capital; monetary policies; credit creation; credit management, etc.

- State Bank of India (SBI) – structure; organisation; capital; functions; financing of agriculture and small scale industries
- Banking technology – innovations in banking industry; ATM; credit card; computerisation; online banking; SWIFT; different techniques adopted in banks for better services to customers; housing loans, etc.
- Indigenous bankers and money lenders – their activities in villages and towns for small business, agriculture, financing, particularly in undeveloped banking areas
- Negotiable instruments – promissory note; bill of exchange; cheques; characteristics; crossing of cheques; endorsement; pass book, etc.
- Banker and customer relationship – special relationship; opening of accounts; special accounts to various types of customers; paying – banker and collecting banker
- Secured advances and mode of creating charge – banker's lien; general lien; specific lien; types of securities; creation of charge; types of charges; advances on securities; movable and immovable securities; advances against documents of title deeds and other documents, etc.

Banking is an important subject of study for commerce students in different courses like B.Com, BBA, M.Com, MBA, CA, ICWA, and other professional courses. The book is intended to serve as a standard textbook for many universities in India, offering banking courses which includes Banking theory, Law and Practice and Financial systems. Any feedback, suggestions or comments on this book would be much appreciated.

V. Nityananda Sarma

1
Banking Systems

Evolution of Banking Institutions in India

Evidence shows that ancient India was not a stranger to the concept of banking. Depositing money and lending money out of the deposits acquired from the public, rules governing the policy of loans, and rates of interest are found in the works of the ancient sage "Manu".

References were also made in the works of Kautilya's, *Arthasasthra*, *Gouthama*, and *Budhayana*. But banking in those days by and large was limited to money-lending, financing kings and their wars as in medieval Europe and England. The *hundis* (equivalent of bills of exchange) date back to the days of Mahabharatha. The Hindus had been familiar with the usage of *hundis* from time immemorial. Money lending and money changing by Hindus were two important functions of banking in ancient India.

Revilpout, a French writer, mentions about the presence of banks and bank notes in Babylon in 600 BC. Professor Marshal in his book *Money Credit and Commerce (1923)* writes about the money transactions in temples of Olympia and other sacred places in Greece around 2000 BC. To quote him, "private money changes began with the task of reducing money currencies, more or less exactly, to a common unit of value, and even to accept money on deposit at interest and to lend it out at higher interest permitting meanwhile drafts to be drawn on them." In the middle ages, in Italy, the first bank called the "Bank of Venice" was established in 1157, during the time when the authorities of the state of Venice were in financial trouble due to war.

In England, the bankers of "Lombardy" had taken the initiative to start modern banking along with their trading activities in London. Commercial banking began after 1640, when goldsmiths started receiving deposits from the public for safe custody and issued receipts for the acknowledgements which were used as bearer demand notes later on. Initially the Bank of England was established in 1694 on the lines of ancient Indian system to support government with finance. Modern joint-stock commercial banks, however, came into the picture with the ratification of the Banking Act of 1833 in England.

In India, the agency houses in Calcutta undertook banking operations along with other businesses. The Bank of Hindustan was the earliest bank started under European directions in India. Between 1809 and 1843, the

Presidency Banks (The Bank of Bengal, The Bank of Bombay, and The Bank of Madras)were given the power to issue notes but the notes were replaced by government paper money in 1862. The principle of 'limited liability' was first applied in the year 1860 to joint-stock banks. The Allahabad Bank Limited and the Punjab National Bank Limited were established as 'limited liability' banks during the period 1865–1895. Before 1860 (before the introduction of the principle of 'limited liability') many banks sprang up like mushrooms and several of them failed to survive due to mismanagement, speculation, and fraud on the one hand, and currency troubles in India during that period (1870–1893) on the other. The consequent lack of confidence in the banks resulted in the slow growth of joint-stock banks in India even though the principle of 'limited liability' was applied.

The Swadeshi movement inspired some patriotic entrepreneurs in India to start a number of joint-stock banks during the period 1906–1913. People's Bank of India Limited, Central Bank of India Limited, Indian Bank Limited, and Bank of Baroda Limited were started during the boom period of 1906–1913. The Presidency Banks were amalgamated into the Imperial Bank of India in the year 1921 by a special Act. It was not allowed to issue currency, but was allowed to hold government balances and to manage public debt and clearing houses till the establishment of Reserve Bank of India (RBI) in 1935.

After independence, RBI, the central bank in India, was nationalised in 1948 in order to effectively control inflation and to launch a programme of economic growth and development.

The Banking Companies Act, 1949 was passed to consolidate and amend the law related to banking companies. The Act was necessitated to safeguard the economic interests of the deposit holders and the country. The State Bank of India Act was passed in 1955 in order to take over the Imperial Bank of India and constitute the State Bank of India (SBI). The SBI has the largest number of branches in the country and it does large volume of business in commercial banking. In 1959, through SBI (subsidiary banks) Act, 1959, several subsidiaries viz., Bank of Bikaner, Bank of Indore, Bank of Jaipur, Bank of Mysore, Bank of Patiala, State Bank of Travancore, State Bank of Hyderabad, State Bank of Sourashtra were constituted in order to widen the area of operations of the SBI. The SBI played a very important role not only in mobilising the country's savings but also in financing of industries and rural credit.

Fourteen private sector banks were nationalised in 1969 for their strategic role in the development of commercial banking. These banks were:

(a) The Central Bank of India.
(b) The Bank of India Limited.
(c) The Punjab National Bank Limited.
(d) The Bank of Baroda Limited.

(e) The Commercial Bank Limited.
(f) The Canara Bank Limited.
(g) The United Bank of India Limited.
(h) The Dena Bank Limited.
(i) The Syndicate Bank Limited.
(j) The Union Bank of India Limited.
(k) The Allahabad Bank Limited.
(l) The Indian Bank Limited.
(m) The Bank of Maharashtra Limited.
(n) The Indian Overseas Bank Limited.

Later in 1980, six more private sector banks were nationalised. These were:

(a) The Andhra Bank Limited.
(b) The Corporation Bank Limited.
(c) The New Bank of India Limited.
(d) The Oriental Bank of Commerce Limited.
(e) Vijaya Bank.
(f) The Punjab National Bank Limited.

Nationalisation of banks was thought to be necessary to bring down inequalities of income and wealth and to ensure greater social justice. It was also felt that nationalisation would stimulate economic growth and promote core sectors of the economy.

Nationalisation of banks played a key role in improving the rate of savings in the country, which in turn has enabled it to launch massive programmes of development of industry and agriculture. India is one of the very few countries in the world which has not witnessed any major financial or banking disasters since independence due to the consistent prudent policies and right direction of the RBI and the Government of India. Under the able guidance and directions of the central Bank (RBI) and the government, both public and private sector banks flourished stimulating economic growth.

Types of Banks

Banks can be classified into various types on the basis of their functions, ownership, dominance, etc. The following are the various types of banks:

Central Bank

The Reserve Bank of India, the apex institution, is the central bank in India which controls, regulates, and supervises the monetary and credit systems of the country. Important functions of the central Bank are:

(a) It has the monopoly to issue notes.
(b) It acts as the banker, agent, and financial adviser to the state.

(c) It is the custodian of member bank's resources.
(d) It is custodian of nation's resources of international currency.
(e) It serves as the lender of the last resort.
(f) It functions as the bank of central clearance, settlement, and transfer.
(g) It acts as the controller of credit.

Besides these functions, India's central bank also performs many other functions to promote economic development in the country.

Commercial Banks

The banks which perform all kinds of banking business and generally finance trade and commerce are called commercial banks. Since their deposits are for a short period, these banks normally advance short-term loans to the businessmen and traders and avoid medium-term and long-term lending. However, recently the commercial banks have also extended their areas of operations to medium-term and long-term finance. Majority of the commercial banks in India are in the public sector. However, there are certain private sector banks operating as joint-stock companies. Hence, the commercial banks are also called as joint-stock banks.

Savings Banks

The main purpose of savings bank is to promote saving habits among the general public and mobilise their small savings. In rural India, largely postal savings bank do this job. They open accounts and issue postal cash certificates.

Industrial Banks

Industrial banks, also known as investment banks, mainly meet the medium-term and long-term financial needs of the industries. Such long-term needs cannot be met in the commercial banks which generally deal with short-term lending. The main functions of the industrial banks are:

(a) They accept long-term deposits.
(b) They grant long-term loans to the industrialists to enable them to purchase land, construct factory building, purchase heavy machinery, etc.
(c) They help saving or even underwrite the debentures and shares of industrial firms.
(d) They can also provide information regarding the general health of the economy. In India, industrial banks, like IDBI, IFCI, SFCs are playing a significant role in the industrial development of the country.

Agricultural Banks

Agriculture too requires long-term and short-term capital. Fixed or long-term capital is required to buy land and to effectively bring permanent improvements.

Short-term capital is necessary to buy seeds and to meet transplantation expenses. Cooperative banks supply short-term needs of agriculturists. India has primary credit societies at the village level. These societies are the associations of borrowers. They receive membership fees, share capital, and deposits. They lend for short period. They charge a low rate of interest on loans. They are managed by elected directors. Any ten members who are majors can start a credit society. These societies are helped by the cooperative central banks. Land development banks grant long-term loans on the security of loan. These loans can be repaid in annual installments. Loans are given for the purchase of land, tractors, other equipment, land improvement, etc.

Exchange Banks

Exchange banks finance foreign trade. They specialise in foreign exchange business. They do have branches in important parts of the world. They collect credit information regarding importers and exporters. They accept and discount foreign bills. They issue letters of credit. In foreign countries, commercial banks finance both in land and foreign trade. Indian commercial banks in the past did not undertake financing of foreign trade. Their role however, have changed in recent times. They are now undertaking those services. There are foreign exchange banks in India too. The foreign banks have branches in India's ports. They finance transportation of goods from ports to inland centres and from interior parts to ports. They accept deposits. Thus, they compete with Indian commercial banks.

Scheduled and Non-scheduled Banks in India

Banks have been broadly classified into scheduled and non-scheduled banks. Scheduled banks in India constitute those banks which have been included in the Second Schedule of RBI Act, 1934 and fulfills three conditions. (a) It has paid-up capital and resources of at least Rs 5 Lakhs (b) It ensures to RBI that its operations are not detrimental to the interest of the depositors (c) It is a corporation or a cooperative society and not a partnership or single-owner firm. The banks which are not included in the Second Schedule of RBI Act are non-scheduled banks.

Classification on the Basis of Ownership

On the basis of ownership, banks can be classified into three categories.

Public Sector Banks

These banks are owned and controlled by the government. In India, the State Bank of India and its associate banks, nationalised banks, and the regional rural banks come under these categories.

Private Sector Banks

These banks are owned by private individuals or corporations and not by the government or cooperative societies.

Cooperative Banks

Cooperative banks are operated on the cooperative lines. In India, cooperative credit institutions are organised under the Cooperative Societies Law, and play an important role in meeting financial needs in the rural areas.

Classification on the Business of Domicile

On the basis of domicile, the banks are divided into two categories.

Domestic Banks

These are registered and incorporated within the country.

Foreign Banks

These are foreign in origin and have their head office in the country of origin.

Banking in England and Germany

Banking in England

During the eighteenth and nineteenth centuries, deposit banking existed and the reason for its popularity are highly historical.

In the early nineteenth century, small-scale industries were run on individual or family basis. Trade with eastern colonies fetched enormous profit and England had surplus capital. In England, commercial revolution that preceded the industrial revolution created a class of investors with sufficient means to invest and intelligent enough to select their wise investment. There was no need for banks to finance either for promotion or expansion of a company. Investment trusts helped in the provision of long-term finance to industries. Banks were confined to the supply of working capital finance alone. The tendency of the British banks towards industries underwent a change considerably after 1914. The huge financial resources required for manufacturing industries necessitated a change in the functions of the bank. The Great Depression of 1930s had such severe adverse effect on the British industries that most of them were unable to repay the bank loans. The banks turned the advances into long-term loans by way of acquiring shares and debentures in the industrial enterprises. The concept of liquidity of assets was indeed stocked with the development of stock exchanges. The liquid assets such as shares and debentures of industries were accepted due to shiftability. The Bank of England was prepared to grant loans against industrial securities.

The Bank of England evinced greater interest in the promotion and development of industries. The Securities Management Trust, as subsidiary of Bank of England was established with the object of advising industries and examining rationalisation of schemes. In 1930, the Bankers' Industrial Development Company was set up as a private company on the same lines. In 1954, Industrial and Commercial Finance Corporation was organised to provide medium-term and long-term capital to small-scale and medium-sized industries. The Finance Corporation for Industry Limited was formed in the same year to assist quick rehabilitation and development of large-scale industries.

The above circumstances resulted in the association of banks with industries. This trend continued even after the second World War by way of direct loans to industries and subscribing to the share capital of specialised institutions. These banks in England gave greater attention on indirect finance.

Banking in Germany

In the second half of the nineteenth century, a number of banks were established in Germany whose aim was to promote industrial development through setting up of new companies and consolidating the existing concerns. They generally carried on with their own funds (capital and reserves) and were essentially of the nature of investment trusts rather than industrial banks. The most common method of promotion of companies in Germany was as follows.

If a bank was satisfied with the plans of a company, it formed a Konsortium (Consortium) or Syndicate, that is an association of various joint-stock banks and also of private men, so as to facilitate the flotation of a new company. Every member of the Konsortium pledged to accept a portion of the capital issue. The initiating bank generally became the director and constituted the central selling agency for all the securities. It kept common accounts and called upon members for contributions. The members of the Konsortium being members of the stock exchange, got the securities of the new concern listed in the stock exchange and this added marketability to the investment. The Konsortium was generally for a definite period after which it would be either terminated or renewed for a further period. Banks either kept the securities permanently or disposed them of later through the stock exchange. On the termination of the Konsortium, the total profit or loss as well as any remaining unsold securities were shared between the members in proportion to their participation.

Apart from helping the flotation of new concerns and investing funds in purchasing shares and debentures of industrial concerns, the German Credit Banks helped industrial units by the system of 'industrial current account' under which they lent to the industrial units to meet their working capital needs as well as long-term capital requirements for expansion, replacement, and reorganisation of Plant and Machinery. As PB Whale puts it, "the industrial current account is the pivot of all transactions between bank and industry, promotion and issue of transactions, direct participation in industrial undertakings and cooperation in management through a board of supervisors, these stand in very many cases in a close causal sequence with Bank Credit".

A very significant fact in the relationship between banks and industrial units in Germany was the exchange of representatives on the respective Board of Directors or Supervisors. Those banks which participated in the promotion of industrial undertaking obtained representation on the supervisory board of companies who were their customers. At the same time they invited the leaders of commerce and industry to represent on the board of supervisors of banks. Thus, there was a very close relationship between industry and banks under the system of investment banking. In the words of PB Whale, "without the vigorous and daring initiative of the banks, the present proud edifice of the German national economy could not have been erected in so relatively on a short time".

With the turn of the twentieth century, industrialisation in Germany grew rapidly and the German banks began to receive large amounts of deposits from the public and hence commercial banking, once considered a sideline and subsidiary business, began to assume greater significance. The German banks combined development banking with commercial banking and such banks are known as mixed banks.

Causes for the Success of Investment Banking in Germany

(a) The success of industrial banking was due to the judicious distribution of assets so as to minimise risk.

(b) German banks worked in collaboration with one another by forming syndicates to minimise risks and distribute them among many banks and even individuals.

(c) High proportion of owned resources of German credit banks during the nineteenth century.

(d) Efficient management made day-to-day functioning successful of the German banks.

(e) German credit banks were in a special and advantageous position to perform useful functions. They were able to advise the investors because they had full knowledge of the various concerns with which they were immediately connected.

(f) Many of the large banks engaged industrial experts to guide and advise their officials in their relations with industrial enterprises. The exchange of the representatives between industry and banks with respect to supervisors also led to their mutual development.

System of Banking

There has been rapid development in the banking institutions in various countries in the past few decades. With the development of banking institutions, various systems of banks have come into existence. Banks can be classified on the basis of volume of operations, business pattern, and area of operation.

The following are the common systems of banking:

(a) Branch banking.
(b) Unit banking.
(c) Group banking.
(d) Chain banking.
(e) Correspondent banking.
(f) Investment banking.
(g) Mixed banking.
(h) Deposit banking.
(i) Virtual banking.
(j) Universal banking.
(k) Local area banking.

Branch Banking

Branch banking is a system where the banking business is carried on by a single bank with a network of branches throughout the length and breadth of the country. The bank will have its head office in one town and branches in different parts of the country. The affairs of the branch are directed by the branch manager in accordance with the regulations and policies of the head office. Each bank is a single entity owned by a group of shareholders and centralised by a group of directors.

England offers an example of branch banking system. There are only five banks popularly known as the "big five" maintaining large branch network within the country. Apart from Britain, branch banking is also found in Canada, Germany, France, Australia, South Africa, India, etc.

Advantages of Branch Banking

Economies of Large-Scale Operation

The branch banking system possesses advantages of large-scale operations such as division of labour and specialisation. The entire working of the banks might be divided into different sections such as foreign exchange section, agricultural section, etc. For each section specialised staff can be appointed. With greater resources and better training facilities they can appoint skilled people to cater to the needs of the banking services. Thus, the branch banking system makes higher quality of management possible.

Economy of Reserve

Branch banking ensures economy of cash reserve, each bank is dependent not only on its own reserve but also on the total of all branches and hence in times of need, one branch can draw upon the resources of the other bank. In other words, each branch can manage its affairs with low cash reserves.

Remittance Facilities

Remittance of funds from one place to another can be provided at a cheaper rate under the branch banking system. This is possible because inter-branch indebtedness can be more easily adjusted than inter-bank indebtedness.

Greater Stability

The branches command great financial resources. They can meet the financial needs of a large number of customers. Besides, they can withstand depression and meet an emergency.

Reducing Interest Rate Disparities

The branch banks increase the mobility of funds between various regions and bring about uniformity in the rate of interest over a wide area. Funds are transferred from the region where they are in plenty and demand for it is low to the regions where it is scarce and the demand is high. In both the areas money supply is brought to equilibrium and so the interest rate tends to be uniform.

Quick Expansion of Branches

Under the unit banking system, starting a new bank requires much time and resources. But a branch bank can organise its new branches more quickly and economically.

Spreading of Risks

In the branch banking system, each bank has a group of branches scattered far and wide and each branch has its own deposits and assets. This diversification of assets is the most important advantage of this system. By diversifying resources they invest in different kinds of assets in different industries in several places. So, in times of crisis in a place, the other branches are not affected much and the profits of one branch can neutralise the loss of the other branch.

Clearing of Cheques Made Easy

Clearing of cheques is comparatively easy. Cheques deposited at a branch can be sent to the office in the city where there is a clearing house and cleared in a customary way. Clearing of cheques involves greater complication and expenses in the unit banking system.

Enhance Profitability

The lending limit of a branch bank is greater. People in an area may demand in excess of the deposit of the branch. The excess demand could be met by transferring money from other branches. The free movement of funds which is possible through branch banking will add to the profitability of banking operations.

Effective Central Bank Control

The central bank of a country can have effective control over the branch banks. It is easy for the central bank to regulate the functions of a limited number of banks having a number of branches. With little difficulty, the central bank can issue directions and supervise the branch banks.

Disadvantages of Branch Banking

Lack of Personal Knowledge

The branch managers lack close contact and personal knowledge of the financial position and characters of their customers. The frequent transfers make them unfamiliar with local conditions that is essential for the success of the business.

Lack of Effective Control

There is an optimum limit for the expansion of any business enterprise and banks are no exception to this rule. Once the optimum limit is exceeded, proper supervision and control become impossible. Thus, an unwieldy branch banking is brought with the danger of mismanagement or incompetent management.

Branches located at long distances may not be effectively controlled by the head office because of poor transport and communication links. Cases of irregularities and embezzlement could be detected too late to be rectified.

Delay and Red-tapism

The branch managers have to refer each loan application to the head office. They have no freedom of action and they have to seek the advice and guidance of the head office on several matters. So delay and red-tapism are but natural.

Neglect of Particular Locality

The funds of a particular locality received by the branch bank as deposits are sent to big financial centres for investment and so are not devoted to local economic development.

Creates Monopoly Power

A serious argument against branch banking is that it is monopolistic and it tends to develop monopoly power. The entire credit facilities of a country would be placed in the hands of a few powerful bankers and so the future of economic development of the country would depend upon a handful of bankers. They also have strong influence in government and no effective banking legislation is enacted to exercise an effective check on anti-social monopolistic activities.

Effect of Banks, Failure on the Economy

In case of the branch banking system, a weak branch may be permitted to continue for a long time with possible deleterious effects on the bank as a whole. Moreover, in case of a bank failure, the economy may be affected to a greater extent because of the liquidation of so many branches spread all over the country.

Unit Banking

In the unit banking system, the banking operations are carried through a single office and confined to a particular area. The banks maintain no branches. In some exceptional cases the banks are allowed to have branches within a limited area. The size of the bank is usually small and capital is limited. The unit banking system is predominant in the United States of America. Approximately two-thirds of the American banking offices are unit banks. The unique feature of the unit banking system is the correspondent banking system. This is an arrangement with which banks carry accounts with banks in the neighbouring cities and these banks in turn have accounts with the larger cities like 'New York banks' in New York having correspondent bank relations with many branches throughout the country.

The major service of the correspondent bank is clearing of cheques for the transfer of funds from one place to another. Another valuable service rendered by the banks is strengthening of the financial resource and helping in various banking operations. According to Sayers, "a comparison between branch banking and unit banking is essentially a comparison between a large-scale operation and a small-scale operation. Branch banks enjoy all the advantages of large-scale operation and unit banks get the advantage of small-scale operations".

Advantages of Unit Banking

Quick Decisions

The manager of a bank can take quick decisions regarding sanctions of loans and helps to curb delay and red-tapism.

Economy of Small-Scale Operation

In the unit banking system, banks get all the advantages of small-scale operations. Being small makes the bank's supervision easier and efficient management becomes a reality. Chances of fraud or irregularities are minimised.

Personal contact

A manager of a unit bank can have first-hand knowledge of the locality and can establish personal contact with the people of that area. So he is able to evaluate the credit worthiness of the borrowers and meet their specific requirements.

Disadvantages of Unit Banking

Personal Contact a Risk

Because of the personal relationship with local people, the manager of the bank cannot deny loan facilities to some influential persons although they are not worthy of credit. If the banker lends, there is a risk of non-payment and if he denies, he may become unpopular in the area. But a branch bank can evade by referring to the head office and escape from the awkward situation.

Limited Financial Resources

The financial resources of the unit banks are limited since they operate in a small area. With the limited resources they are unable to provide finance to large-scale business and also serve all people. Further, the banks may not be able to employ skilled people and so the management may not be efficient.

Economic Changes and its Impact

The ebb and flow of the economy has its immediate impact on the unit banks. They prosper when the economy is healthy. A business depression causes immediate failure of the unit banks. During the depression period 1930–1933, nearly 9000 banks went in liquidation. In 1993 alone, 4000 banks suspended their activities because of financial difficulties.

Due to the above disadvantages, USA is changing its trend and turning towards branch banking. Eighteen states in USA have permitted state-wide branch banking. To cite an example, the Bank of America has 800 branches throughout the state of California.

Group Banking

The group banking system aims at increasing the efficiency in banking operations with a decrease in operational cost. The term 'group banking' refers to bringing two or more banks under single control and management. To be more precise, group banking refers to two or more individually incorporated banks operating under the control of a holding company. It is important to note that the holding company need not necessarily be a banking company. A typical banking group consists of a certain number of individual banks whose interest and stocks are vested in the hands of an independently incorporated non-bank corporation. The banks might be either unit banks or branch banks; the ownership and operations controlled by the holding company. Group banking enjoys economies of scale, extensive customer services, greater mobility, efficient management, training programmes, etc. The member banks of the group need not maintain larger cash resources. The member banks are able to pool large resources to finance large borrowers.

The group banking system faces the risk of the holding company locking the bank funds for its own interests. The group banking system also faces supervisory problem, risk of speculation and manipulation, restriction on healthy competition, etc.

Chain Banking

The chain banking system is basically a development over the group banking system. Unlike group banking the powers are not vested in a holding company, but vested in a single person, by the same group of persons although the ownership of stock, through common membership of board of directors or otherwise. The managing directors of three or four banks can have a memorandum of understanding. Their internal group shall control the member banks. These banks coming under the group are called chain banks. The chain banking system has more or less the same advantages and disadvantages which are inherent in the group banking system.

Correspondent Banking

Correspondent banking refers to linking banks through deposits. In simple terms, the regional banks or small banks operating in smaller localities will deposit their cash reserves in bigger banks or nearby city banks. The city banks shall hold deposits in efficient banks in metropolitan cities. These banks will also hold deposits in city banks and city banks in turn in smaller banks. The smaller bank is called the respondent bank, whereas the major bank who holds the deposit for the smaller one is called correspondent bank. Hence, the system of banking results in connecting all the unit banks all over the country. The link is very difficult to distinguish as the respondent banks may have deposits in various major banks at the same time and vice versa. The correspondent banks perform two important services – clearing outstation cheques and loan participation for their respondent banks – while they benefit from the deposit funds of their respondent banks.

Deposit Banking

The major activity of commercial banks is to accept deposits from the public which is repayable on demand and to provide loans and advances through available resources. This system of attracting deposits to mobilise resources for the purpose of short-term lending can be termed as deposit banking. This system gives importance to the fact that commercial banks accept deposits repayable on demand. They act as trustees for the hard-earned money of a large number of depositors. They should never forget the fact that these deposits can be demanded any day, at any time, and for any amount.

Deposit banking is justified only when the following conditions are present:

(a) Banks can confine themselves to deposit banking only when there is financial machinery to meet the fixed capital requirement. There should be major financial institutions or corporations who should be catering to long-term loans and advances of the industry. If these institutions are not sufficient, banks can restrict themselves only to deposit banking.

(b) The nature of banks is a major criterion for deciding deposit banking, as the watch-word for banks are safety and liquidity, the banks which have lesser capital and reserves cannot acquire long-term asset or speculative or risky or non-negotiable securities which cannot be easily converted into cash in an emergency.

(c) When the economy is prosperous enough to have industry through owned capital rather than borrowed capital (i.e. through public subscription of shares and debentures, reinvestment of profit, etc). The need for bank finance for investment in industries does not arise at all.

Mixed Banking or Universal Banking

The essence of mixed banking consists in attracting deposits from the general public and in providing short-term, medium-term, and long-term capital to industries. Under the mixed banking system, banks play a major role in the industrial development of the nation. This banking system is basically comprised of deposit banks but in addition to it undertake the risk of meeting heavy capital requirements of the industry. In India, mixed banking is very popular.

The mixed banking system was recommended by the Central Banking Enquiry Committee (1931), the Shroff Committee (1954). Since then Indian banks have been financing industry through direct participation by lending long-term loans and through indirect participation by pending shares and debentures of Food Corporation of India and various state financial corporations. The RBI has also provided refinance facilities for banks entering into industrial finance. The deposit habits of people are also increasing and hence commercial banks have huge resources at their disposal for participating in underwriting shares and debentures, financing the financial institutions, and promoting industrial development in the country.

Investment Banking

Investment banks are those financing institutes which provide long-term finance to business corporations and government organisations. They invest in shares, stocks, and bonds of different companies. These banks, unlike commercial banks, act primarily as intermediaries between companies and customers. Generally they purchase the entire issue of new shares and bonds of business corporates or government bodies and resell them to the public. More often, they act as agents on commission basis. Investment banks are classified into originators, underwriters, and retailers. As originators, they bring out new issues of securities. As underwriters, they underwrite the issue of shares and debentures. As retailers, they retail the securities to individual and institutional investors.

The operational technique of the investment bankers are as follows. As originators, they enter into preliminary negotiations with the issuing corporations. They seek detailed reports regarding the history of the corporation including its corporate powers, nature and type of products produced, conditions of plant machinery and other assets, its capital structure as the object of the new issue. They ask for the opinion of the expert technicians and professional accountants with an attorney's report regarding the majority of the issue. If the details are found to be satisfactory, the originator enters into an agreement with the issuing corporation undertaking to sell the new issue. If the issue is very large, investment bankers form an underwriting syndicate. The next step is to invite small retailers to join the syndicate and finally the securities are offered for public subscription.

An investment banker thus performs a highly useful service to the corporate world by supplying long-term capital. He has been described as "entrepreneur of entrepreneurs". They render a useful service to the small investors by providing necessary guidance for investment. In our country UTI, LIC and GIC are considered as investment institutions. There are mutual funds started by public sector banks and financial institutions, and private mutual funds which mobilise funds and invest in shares and bonds of a variety of companies so as to minimise risk. Similarly, LIC and GIC invest the premiums collected on insurance policies in shares and bonds of companies.

Virtual Banking

The practice of banking has undergone significant transformation in the nineties. While banks are striving to strengthen customer relationship and move towards "relationship banking", customers are increasingly moving away from the traditional branch banking and are seeking the convenience of remote electronic banking services. Virtual banking in the field of banking is prominent these days.

Virtual banking denotes the provision of banking and related services through extensive use of information technology without direct recourse to the bank by the customer. The origin of virtual banking in the developed countries can be traced back to the seventies with the installation of Automated Teller Machines (ATMs). Subsequently, driven by the competitive market environment as well as various technological and customer pressures, other types of virtual banking services have grown in prominence throughout the world.

The virtual banking services include Automated Teller Machines (ATMs), shared ATM networks, Electronic Fund Transfer at Point Of Sales (EFTPOS), smart cards, stored value cards, phone banking, and more recently, internet and intranet banking. The salient features of these services are the overwhelming reliance and information technology and the absence of physical bank branches to deliver these services to the customers.

Three evolutionary phases of virtual banking services, which represent the impact that the particular application has allowed within the industry. These include: (a) the inceptive phase where the technology behind the application is in its infancy and a substantial amount of investment is required so as to make the application widely available commercially (b) the growth phase, where the application is increasingly available to the customers and the technology behind the application is widely available, and (c) the maturity phase, wherein the application is in widespread use and institutions not offering such applications are likely to be at a competitive disadvantage.

The financial benefits of virtual banking services are many, such as: (1) Virtual banking has the advantage of having a lower cost of handling a transaction (via) the virtual resources compared to the cost of handling the transaction (via) the branch. (2) The increased speed of response to customer requirements under virtual banking vis-à-vis branch banking can enhance customer satisfaction and lead to higher profits (via) handling a number of customer accounts. It also implies the possibility of access to a greater number of potential customers for the bank without the costs of physically opening the branches. (3) The lower cost of operating branch network along with reduced staff costs leads to cost efficiency under virtual banking. (4) Virtual banking allows the possibility of improved quality and an enlarged range of services being available to the customer more rapidly and accurately and at his convenience.

Virtual banking has made some beginning in the Indian banking system. ATMs have been installed by almost all the major banks in major metropolitan cities, the Shared Payment Network Systems (SPNS), the Electronic Fund Transfer (EFT), and the very small aperture terminal (VSAT) is expected to provide a significant thrust to the development of Indian Financial Network (INFINET) which will further facilitate connectivity within the financial sector. The popularity which virtual banking services have won among customers, owing to the speed, convenience and round-the-clock access they offer, is likely to increase in the future (RBI Report on Trend and Progress of Banking in India, 1989–1990).

Universal Banking

Universal banking refers to providing all financial services under one roof. These include long-term loans to industries, venture capital, underwriting, brokerage, corporate advisory services, insurance, and so on. Indian banks are already moving towards universal banking.

Local Area Banks

With a view to providing an institutional mechanism for promoting rural and semi-urban savings as well as provision for credit for viable economic activities in local areas, local area banks (LABs) are established in the private sector. The related guidelines were announced by the RBI in 1996. The RBI has given its principle approval for setting up seven local area banks in the private sector.

2

Functions of Modern Commercial Banks

Introduction

Banks play an important role in the economic development of a country by acting as catalysts in commercial and industrial activities. One cannot imagine the cessation of banking activities even for a day. An economic crisis may emerge in the country if the banks stop functioning for some days.

A bank is an institution which deals with money and credit. It accepts deposits from the public, makes funds available to those who need them, and helps in the remittance of money from one place to another. In fact, a modern bank performs such a variety of functions that it is difficult to give a precise and general definition to it. According to Crowther, a bank "collects money from those who have it to spare or who are saving it out of their income, and it lends this money to those who require it". In the words of Kinley, "A bank is an establishment which makes to individuals such advances of money as may be required and safely made, and to which individuals entrust money when not required by them for use". According to John Paget, nobody can be a banker and not (i) take deposit accounts (ii) take current accounts (iii) issue and pay cheques, and lastly, (iv) collect cheques – crossed and uncrossed – for its customers. Professor Sayers defines the term bank and banking distinctly. He defines bank as "an institution whose debts (bank deposits) are widely accepted in settlement of other people's debts to each other". Again, according to Sayers, "Ordinary banking business consists of changing cash for bank deposits and bank deposits for cash; transferring bank deposits from one person or corporation to another; giving bank deposits in exchange for bills of exchange, government bonds, the secured promises of businessmen to repay and so forth". According to the Indian Banking Companies Act, 1949, "banking means the accepting, for the purpose of lending or investment, of deposits of money from the public, repayable on demand or otherwise, and withdrawable by cheque, draft or otherwise".

Features of a Modern Bank

The features of a modern bank are:

(a) It accepts deposits and advances loans.
(b) It also deals with credit, has the ability to create credit, that is, the ability to expand its liabilities as a multiple of its reserves.

(c) It is a commercial institution; it aims at earning profit.
(d) It is a unique financial position that creates demand deposits which serves as a medium of exchange and as a result, the banks manage the payment system of the country.

Functions of Modern Commercial Banks

In the modern world, banks perform such a variety of functions that it is not possible to make an all-inclusive list of their functions and services. However, some basic functions performed by the banks are discussed below.

Accepting Deposits

The first important function of a bank is to accept deposits from those who can save but cannot profitably utilise the savings themselves. People consider it more rational to deposit their savings in a bank as they earn interest and avoid the danger of theft. To attract savings from all sorts of individuals, the banks maintain different types of accounts.

(a) *Fixed Deposit Accounts:* Fixed deposits are deposits made by the customers for a specified time period, ranging from seven days to 5 years or more with a fixed rate of interest. The rate of interest depends on the maturity period. It is higher in case of a longer period. The depositors are assured of the safety of funds, apart from higher returns. The depositor as per the terms, agrees not to withdraw the amount before the specified period. In acknowledgement of the fixed deposit, the customer is given a receipt called 'Fixed Deposit Receipt' popularly known as FDR which has its rules printed on the reverse side. At the end of the term, the customer may either withdraw the amount along with interest or renew the deposits for a further period at his convenience. Since the customer would withdraw the fund at the end of the specified period, the banker can lend the money confidently without keeping any reserve to meet the withdrawals. In case the customer needs money prior to the due date, although he may not be able to withdraw from the fixed deposit, he can obtain a loan from the bank, on the strength of the fixed deposit receipt. The banker charges interest for this loan. Fixed deposit account is ideal with high disposable income and can deposit a lumpsum towards a safe investment, yielding high returns. Some banks provide Auto Renewal Plan facility, which enables automatic renewal of deposit after maturity.

(b) *Current Account:* A current account is primarily meant for businessmen, firms, companies, etc., which has numerous daily banking transactions with a minimum balance of INR 1000. It is a non-interest bearing account. A banker should be doubly cautious to get an introductory letter from the customer at the time of opening such an account. He should also see that such introductory letters are verified, due to the following reasons:

(a) The RBI has given a direction that the prospective customer should produce an introductory letter at the time of opening the account.
(b) The banker has to ascertain the bonafide nature of the customer.
(c) Since third-party cheques are collected through the account, there is a chance for fraud by unscrupulous elements.
(d) Since overdraft and cash credit facilities are available, the banker should not be exploited by any unscrupulous customer.

In a current account a customer can deposit and withdraw any amount of money any number of times, as long as he has funds to his credit. However, if the customer overdraws the account, he has to pay interest to the banker. Overdraft is granted for a temporary period depending on the requirement of the customer.

Bankers allow certain special facilities such as cash credit facility, free collection of outstation cheques, and issue of demand drafts and mail transfers without any extra charges.

(c) *Savings Bank Accounts:* This type of account is suited to those who want to deposit their small savings in a bank, which they can withdraw when required. The interest allowed on saving bank deposits is certainly lower than that allowed on fixed deposit accounts and is calculated on the lowest balance kept during the month. The prevailing rates allowed by banks in India on saving bank deposits are less than 5 per cent on the balance maintained from tenth day to the last day of the month, subject to not more than fifty debits in six months. Deposits received on these accounts form a large part of the total deposits of the banks. The main aim of these deposits is to promote thrift among lower-income, middle-income and salaried people. The balance of a savings bank account is not allowed to cross a certain limit. Its main advantage is its high liquidity and safety. It can be opened by any person or on behalf of any minor relative or on behalf of any minor of whom the person is the guardian, etc. Almost all the banks allow the facilities of cheques to their savings bank depositors. But a certain minimum balance must be maintained in the account before a depositor can avail of this facility.

When a person wants to open a savings bank account, he is supplied with a copy of rules and a printed form to be duly filled. The depositor also submits his specimen signature to the bank. The amount deposited at the opening of the account is then entered into a passbook which is handed over to the depositor. When the depositor wants to withdraw money, he or his agent must present the passbook together with a duly filled-in withdrawal form or cheque. The passbook need not be presented to the bank at the time of drawing a cheque. Nowadays, a banker facilitates the collection of cheques drawn in the name of the customer through the savings bank account. However, the bank does not collect third-party cheques which are drawn in the name of a person other than the customer. Nomination facility is also available in this account.

(d) *Recurring Deposits:* This is a combination of both savings as well as fixed deposit account. In this account, a specific amount is invested on a monthly basis for a fixed rate of return. The deposit has a fixed tenure ranging from 6 months to 120 months. This account is preferred by salaried persons or individuals with regular income. It provides an element of compulsion to save for a pre-determined time period. Compound rate of interest is provided by the banker.

(e) *Home Savings Safe Account:* Home savings safe account is another scheme aiming at promoting savings habits among people. Under this scheme a safe is supplied to the depositor to keep it at home and to put his small savings in it. Periodically, the safe is taken to the bank where the amount in the safe is credited to his account.

Loan Advances

Banks usually lend money in the form of loans and advances, overdrafts, cash credit, and discounting of bills of exchange. This function of the bank is the largest contributor to the bank's profit. Advances made by a bank may be either clean advances against personal credit with a second signature on the pronote, or against tangible or marketable securities, lodged or pledged with the bank. Advances are generally taken in the form of cash credit, overdraft, and loans.

(a) *Cash Credits:* A cash credit is a short-term cash loan to a company. It is an arrangement by which a banker allows his customer to borrow money up to a specified amount against either a bond of credit by one or more sureties or against securities. This is the most common mode of borrowing by large commercial and industrial houses in India because the company or business that receives the loan can continuously draw from the bank up to a specified amount. The customer may deposit the surplus amount as may be with him for the time being. The banker, while granting cash credit and overdraft facilities, has to estimate the amount of the customer's requirement. If the actual drawings better his estimate, he may lose interest on the funds that remain unused. In order to minimise such losses, a banker in cash credit agreements generally provides a-half or a-quarter of the amount of cash credit allowed to him, even when he does not use that amount. Interest rates on cash credit range from 13.5 per cent to 17 per cent.

(b) *Overdraft:* An overdraft is provided when businesses make payments from their business current account exceeding the available cash balance. It enables to obtain short-term fund which is repayable with interest on demand by the bank. The essential difference between a cash credit and overdraft is that the latter is a form of bank credit to be made use of occasionally, while the former is used for long tenure by commercial and industrial concerns doing regular business. Banks charge 18 per cent interest on overdraft.

(c) *Loans:* A loan is a contractual promise between the bank and the customer where the bank agrees to provide a sum of money to the customer, who promises to return the money either in a lump sum or in instalments over a fixed period of time. The bank charges interest on the entire loan amount. The banks have also started advancing medium-term and long-term loans. The maturity period of such loans is more than one year.

(d) *Discounting of Bills of Exchange:* This is another popular type of lending by the modern banks. Through this method, a holder of bill of exchange can get it discounted by the bank.

In a bill of exchange, the debtor accepts the bills drawn upon him by the creditor (i.e., holder of the bill) and agrees to pay the amount mentioned on maturity. After making some marginal deductions (in the form of commission, the banker pays the value of the bill to the holder. Where the bill of exchange matures, banks receive payment from the party which had accepted the bill. Thus, such a loan is self-liquidating. The bill of exchange discounted with a bank may be clean or documentary. The personal security of the drawer and acceptor is the only security in the case of clean bill. If the bill happens to be a documentary one, it is followed either by a railway receipt, bill of lading, or a wharfinger's certificate, etc., which means that the security of the drawer and the acceptor is further strengthened by the goods which are lying with the railway, shop, or wharfinger's. This type of advance by bankers is becoming increasingly popular.

The reasons for such popularity are:

(a) Deduction of discount from advance.
(b) Continuity of payment on the due date.
(c) Continuous supply of funds through planned arrangement.
(d) A fixed and unalterable amount irrespective of any fall in the value of securities.
(e) Re-discounting facilities by the central bank at bank rate.

Creating Credit

It is always an objective of bankers to minimise their cash holdings to the lowest extent possible. Creating credit is the process whereby commercial banks make it possible for more deposits to be made through loan and this process of creating credit is called creation of money or money creation. It does not mean that they increase legal tender currency, which they cannot do.

When a banker lends money it is given in the form of deposits in the account of the borrower who gets a right to draw cheques against it. Thus, the borrower acquires a claim against the bank, just as a sum of money deposited by him with the banker creates a claim against the bank. When the borrower draws cheques in favour of the parties, they produce these cheques to their banks for collection and deposit in their accounts and with this their deposits go up. This proves the correctness of Martley Withers saying "Every loan creates a deposit". Thus, commercial banks increase the volume of money in circulation by increasing the purchasing power of the people through the deposit money created by them.

Illustration

Let us take the case of a small community where there is only one bank and all transactions are settled by means of cheques. Further, let us assume that the total amount of money in circulation is INR 1,00,000 and the banker knows by experience that 10 per cent of its deposits as reserve is sufficient to meet the demands from customers. As the banker is required to maintain a cash reserve of only 10 per cent of its total deposits to meet the demands of customers and can safely lend the balance of INR 90,000 to persons who want to borrow from the bank. The banker will lend INR 90,000 to the borrower and will place the sum to the credit of borrowers account, thereby giving them the right to operate their accounts with cheques. The total deposits of the banks would consequently go up to INR 1,90,000.

These deposits are now credit balances in the account of borrowers and can be considered as good as money. They can draw cheques in favour of their creditors, who in turn will deposit these cheques to the bank for collection. It is merely a transfer of credit balance of borrowers to the credit of the account of the payees of their cheques. Now the banker has brought into effective circulation an additional amount of INR 90,000, thereby raising the total supply of money from INR 1,00,000 to INR 1,90,000. The banker should maintain a cash deposit ratio of only 10 per cent and additional amount of INR 9,000 over and above the amount of INR 10,000 previously maintained. Even after this, a balance of INR 81,000 can be advanced by the bank without any risk. Now the total deposits of the bank is INR 2,71,000 (INR 1,00,000+INR 90,000+INR 81,000=INR 2,71,000). The total cash reserve is (INR 10,000+INR 9,000)=INR 19,000). In this way, the banker can go on increasing the credit. But there is a limit up to which the bank can create credit.

The power of a bank to create credit is limited by the cash reserves that they are required to keep against their total demand and time liabilities and the total amount of legal tender currency issued by the central bank (RBI). Every bank has to keep a reserve of liquid cash to meet the demands of customers to pay cash as and when demanded. In societies where banking habits of people are not well developed, a higher cash reserve is needed and in societies where the banking habits of the people are well developed a lower amount of cash reserve may be sufficient. But a working reserve of liquid cash, according to the needs of the society is always necessary, and this acts as a limit on the power of bank to create credit. In most of the countries the law prescribes a minimum cash reserve ratio (CRR) to be maintained by every bank. Thus, a banker's power to create credit is limited by two factors, viz; the minimum Cash Reserve Ratio (CRR) and the total amount of currency in the country.

Promoting Cheque System

Banks also render a very useful medium of exchange in the form of cheques. Through a cheque, the depositor directs the bankers to make payment to the payee. Cheques are the most developed credit instruments in the money market. In the modern business transaction, cheques have become a much more convenient method of settling debts than the use of cash.

Functions of the Bank as an Agency

The functions of the bank as an agency are:

(a) Collection and payment of cheques, bills, promissory notes.

(b) Execution of standing orders: A customer may leave standing instructions with his banker for the payment of sums to various persons or institutions against his account. Such orders are usually given in respect of payment of insurance premiums, subscriptions to clubs and societies, and similar payment of a regularly recurring nature. The bankers may charge a small fee for rendering such services.

(c) Collection of dividend and interest: The customer may instruct the issuer of securities that he should pay the interest or dividend that may be declared on them to his own bank. He will thus avoid the trouble of endorsing and paying in such dividend warrants. The banker usually levies a very small charge for the collection of dividend and interest on behalf of his customers.

(d) Purchase and sale of securities: Although it is not the usual practice of the banker to advise his customer regarding investments, he does furnish herewith such information as he has obtained from stock exchanges. He also undertakes to purchase or sell stocks or shares on behalf of his customers.

(e) Remittances of funds: The big commercial banks have a network of branches throughout the country. With this facility banks can conveniently provide the service of transfer of funds from one place to another. Remittance of funds by banks are simple, convenient, safe and inexpensive. Some of the important methods of transfer of funds are:

(i) Mail transfers
(ii) Telegraphic transfers
(iii) Bank drafts
(iv) Traveller's cheque.

(i) Mail transfers

A mail transfer is a form of remittance in which the amount remitted by a customer or a non-customer is directly credited to the account of the beneficiary with another branch. For this purpose the sender shall have to furnish details such as the name of the beneficiary, his/her account number, the amount to be transferred, and the name of the branch where the account is maintained.

(ii) Telegraphic transfers

A telegraphic transfer is a form of remittance which is advised by telegram, telex or fax by payment of a nominal charge as per the bank. But this facility is available at select branches only. In case of both telegraphic transfer and mail transfer, money can also be made payable to a beneficiary on identification. For this purpose, the beneficiary's address is also given.

(iii) Bank draft

Banks issue bank drafts or demand drafts in their branch at the place of destination for remitting money from one place to another. A bank draft is an order from one branch to another branch of the same bank to pay a specified sum of money to a person therein or to his order. A draft is always payable on demand. According to Section 85A of Negotiable Instruments Act, a bank draft is "an order to pay money, drawn by one office of the bank upon another office of the same bank for a sum of money payable to order or demand".

(iv) Traveller's Cheque

A traveller's cheque is a pre-printed fixed amount cheque. A banker may issue traveller's cheques at the request of the customer after obtaining the customer's signature. When he travels either within the country or out of the country, he may pay by traveller's cheques. The traveller's cheques are accepted in banks, restaurants, hotels, and in certain other places. Before receiving the traveller's cheques, the customer is expected to sign the traveller's cheque which is to be countersigned by the banker. At the time of payment, the customer is expected to sign in the presence of the person who accepts the traveller's cheques. The signature should tally with the signature already affixed at the time of issue.

General Utility Services

Safe Custody Deposits

The commercial banks provide safe custody facilities. Under this facility, the valuables may be handed over to the banker as per regulations. The banker verifies the value of items deposited with him and keeps them in his locker. He gives an acknowledgement for the valuable he has received from the customer stating the descriptions of the items and value. The bank charges the customer depending on the period for which the valuables are kept with the bank and the value of the items kept under safe custody.

Safe Deposit Locker Facilities

This is a unique method by which a customer can make use of the locker kept by the banker in the safe room. The locker can be operated only with two keys, one with the banker and the other with the customer. The locker can be opened only if both keys are used. The customer is allowed to keep any kind of valuables in the locker. The customer needs to pay rent periodically. Normally his bank account would be debited towards rent. The customer can use the locker at any time during the banking hours. The banker does not have any lien on the item kept in the locker except for the outstanding rent from the locker. In case of loss of items, the banker is not directly responsible as the relationship between the banker and customer is that of a lessor and a lessee. The services have gained much importance now that some of the banks have branches exclusively for providing this service.

Merchant Banking

Some commercial banks have also started merchant banking divisions in order to offer financial services and advise to industries on better use of their money. The banks assist the promoters to obtain technical details relating to feasibility, market demand, and other relevant information. Banks also underwrite shares and debentures of companies.

Automated Teller Machines (ATM)

In the last few years, the ATMs have revolutionised the banking system in the country. An ATM is a computerised telecommunication device with access to financial transactions. Many banks have introduced Automated Teller Machines (ATMs) to facilitate their customers to withdraw and deposit cheques without wasting time. An ATM machine dispenses cash as well as credit card cash advances. The customers could have considerable waiting time while depositing and withdrawing cash.

Acting as Referees

A bank acts as a referee when any seller wants to verify the financial status of an unknown buyer to sell his goods, particularly when the buyer makes an urgent query to seek the goods. The bank may respond to such an enquiry only with the customer's consent.

Teller System

It is often felt that the waiting time of the customers should be reduced. In order to minimise the waiting time of customers, the teller system has been introduced. Under this system, the teller examines the cheques presented to him and pays cheques to the holder on identification. In case of doubt, he may refer to the records. Some banks allot codes on cheque forms based on the credit worthiness of the account holder. In case of doubt about the balance in the customers' account, the teller may direct the presenter to the accounts counter where the cheque will be dealt with.

Gift Cheques

The gift cheques are issued by the commercial banks in different denominations to facilitate their customers to make payments to their relatives and friends on important occasions like marriages, birthdays, religious, and other festival days, etc.

Debit Card

Debit card differs from the conventional credit card in the sense that the debit cardholder's account gets instantaneously debited unlike in the case of credit cards, where the cardholders are given credit for a fixed period.

Credit Cards

Many commercial banks in India, particularly the foreign banks, have introduced credit cards among their customers and non-customers The credit cardholders need not carry cash. They may purchase goods from authorised dealers using their credit cards. The credit cards can also be used to settle accounts with restaurants, hotels, petrol bunks, etc. For cash advances too, the cardholders can draw cash from ATMs maintained by bank at important cities throughout the country. The customers have to pay service charges to the bank, apart from paying interest on the outstanding balances while using this card.

Electronic Fund Transfer System (EFT)

EFT is an application developed to facilitate customers to transfer funds from one bank account to another within the country. Its objective is to facilitate an efficient, secure, economical, reliable, and expedient system of fund transfer between banks.

E-banking

With the introduction of computers in Indian banks and with arrangements of shared payment network system, services are provided across the banks. Customers need not visit the banks to complete banking transactions when their banker provides them with electronic banking, tele-banking, or remote banking facilities.

Tele Banking

Tele-banking carries the concept of 24-hour banking to the customers' home or business place. Tele-banking services function based on the voice processing facility available with the bank computers. The customer will be able to call the bank anytime and enquire balances or transactions leisurely, transfer funds between accounts, between branches, request for draft, cheque books, information on new schemes, maturity of deposits, details of interest rates, and give instructions to stop payment.

Anywhere Banking

With the introduction of tele-banking and networking of all branches through communication network, customers become the customers of entire bank rather than a branch as all the branches are connected by satellite. Inter-station connectivity of ATMs has facilitated withdrawal from other stations. Financial details can be accessed from remote a locations and basic transactions can be effected from outside the bank.

Banking through Internet

Many Indian banks have set their own websites with interactive features, for example, account-opening forms can be printed from the sites and used for opening accounts under different schemes. Banks like ICICI use their websites for public views by making the application forms and details of the customer available over the net. Customers can connect to the bank website over the internet, log in to the internet banking service, and access their account, view statement of account, correct financial transactions, etc.

Corporate Banking

Corporate banking has become very popular among corporate customers especially big industrial houses which are already automated. Corporate banking is to provide financial products/services of a wide range for large, medium, and small customers, both domestic and international. More and more banks are providing customer terminals right in the customer's office, which facilitates the customers to operate the account without physically coming to the bank.

At present, by utilising corporate banking facility, corporate customers are able to get the following services:

(a) Ordering cheque books.
(b) Instructing to stop payment of cheques.
(c) Ordering intra-bank and inter-bank fund transfers.
(d) Getting their account balance or getting their statements of accounts for any predefined period.
(e) International remittances.
(f) Opening letters of credit.

Foreign Exchange

Banks also deal with the foreign exchange transaction. The commercial community receives facilities for its dealing with foreign materials – a fact which is also a profitable business for a banker. In assisting foreign trade by discounting foreign bills of exchange, a bank has to arrange for the transport, insurance and warehousing of goods. In India, however, there is a group of specialised institutes known as exchange banks which handle the business in foreign exchange. In most foreign countries, the business in foreign exchange is handled by ordinary commercial banks.

Letters of Credit

A banker issues personal as well as commercial letters of credit. Money can be promptly paid out to customers or his agent, and bills drawn by his creditor can be accepted by the bank or any of its branches, agencies, or correspondents.

Other Miscellaneous Services Offered by Banks

The bank offers various other miscellaneous services such as:

(a) Factoring.
(b) Mortgage loans.
(c) Non-life insurance services.

(d) Travel and entertainment cards..
(e) Technical consultancy.
(f) Travel-related services.
(g) Maintaining clients' accounts of securities.
(h) Safe-keeping of securities.
(i) Personal tax and financial planning.
(j) Securities dealing and undertaking.
(k) Property and real estate management/brokerage.
(l) Pension and Trust management.
(m) Pre-deals/services related to insurance and banking.
(n) Merchant banking-related services.

Investment Policy of Commercial Banks

A prudent banker is cautious in investing his funds so as to bring maximum benefits to the shareholders without affecting the depositors. The guiding principles of investment policy are *Safety*, *Liquidity*, and *Profitability*. The major portion of a bank's funds is employed by way of loans and advances, which is the most profitable employment of its funds. A major part of a bank's income is earned from interest and discount on the funds so lent. Largely, depending on the borrower's funds, a banker can afford to take undue risk in lending. While lending his funds, a banker therefore follows a very cautious policy and conducts his business on the basis of the well-known principles of sound lending in order to minimise the risks.

Nationalised banks in India, like others, too follow the above-mentioned principles in the employment of their funds. Under Section 8 of Banking companies (Acquisition and Transfer of Undertaking) Act 1970, banks are guided by the directions given by the Central Government regarding matters of policies involving public interest as one of their functions. The Central Government and RBI have issued a number of directions in this regard, highlighting the social purpose to be subserved. The traditional principles of bank lending have, therefore been followed with certain modifications. The concept of security has undergone a radical change and profitability has been subordinated to social purpose with respect to certain types of lending.

Safety

The term safety is interrelated with securities. Since a banker deals with people's money, the banker should ensure the safety of such funds as security of such deposits. If the banker is reckless in his investment policy, the safety of such investment is sacrificed at the cost of the depositors who lose their security. In case a banker is not able to get back his investment, he cannot manage to meet his commitment and consequently loses the confidence of

Table 2.1: Functions of nationalised and private, commerical banks in India

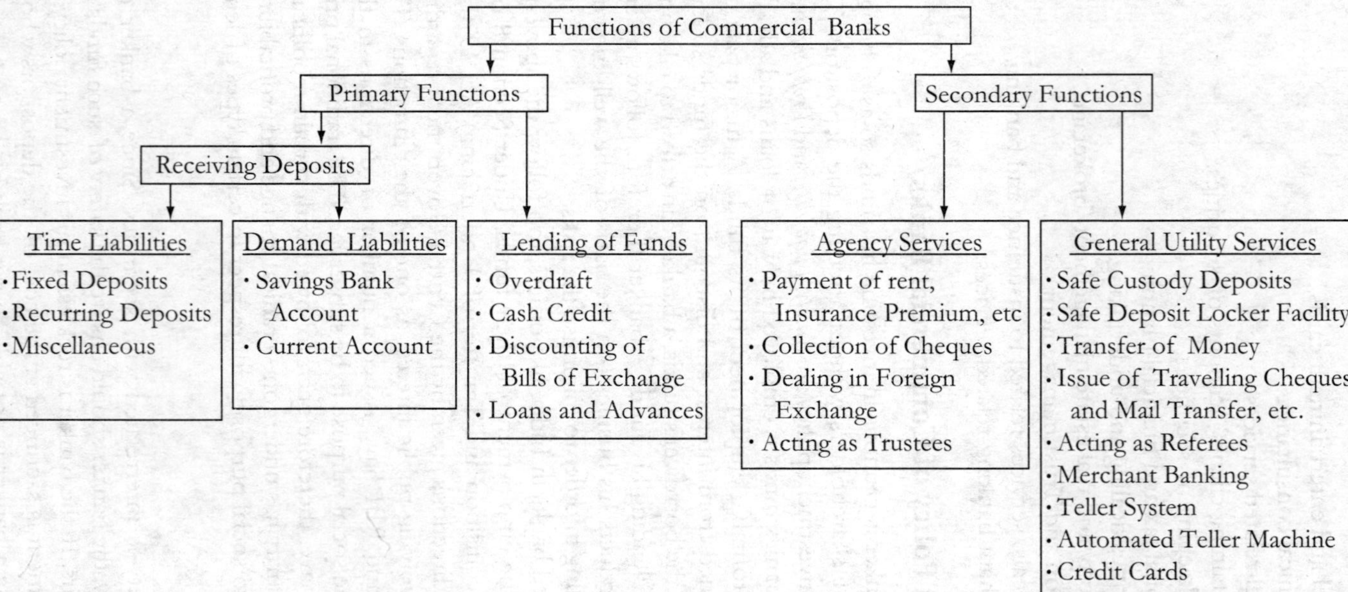

the depositors. Consequently, the business of the bank suffers. The traditional banker emphasises on the safety of funds insisting upon security on the following guidelines:

(a) The banker can exercise some degree of control over his customer's behaviour.
(b) Failure to collect loans may lead to insufficient funds in the bank leading to serious consequences.
(c) The customer understands that the need of security to the bank is for him to take genuine interest in repaying of the loan which, otherwise, could be taken for granted.
(d) The bank can sell the security in order to meet the depositor's claims, if the borrower fails to pay his debts in spite of the bank's efforts to recover it.

Regarding securities, the value, in some cases, deteriorates in course of time. The banker tries his best to realise his money even under adverse conditions. If the security becomes inadequate, he asks his customer to provide more security or asks the customer to arrange for the repayment of a portion of the loan. However, if the banker seriously insists on security, those who cannot afford to give any security may avoid any bank loan at all.

Liquidity

Banks are essentially intermediaries for short-term funds. Therefore, they lend funds for short periods and mainly for working capital purposes. The loans are, therefore, largely payable on demand. The banker must ensure that the borrower is able to repay the loan on demand or within the short period. This depends upon the rate of interest owned by the borrower and pledged to the banker. For example, goods and commodities are easily marketable while fixed assets like land and buildings and specialised types of plants and equipments can be liquidiated after a time of interval. Thus, the banker regards liquidity as important as safety of the funds and grants loans on the security of assets that are easily marketable without much loss.

Profitability

Commercial banks are profit-earning institutions. The nationalised banks are no exception to this. They must employ their funds profitably so as to earn sufficient income to pay interest to the depositors, salaries to the staff and to meet various other establishment expenses and distribute dividends to the shareholders (the government in the case of nationalised banks). The rates of interest charged by the banker were in the past primarily dependent on the directives issued by the RBI. Now banks are free to determine their own rates of interest on advances of above INR 2 lakhs. The variations in the rate of interest change from different customers depending upon the degree of risk involved in lending to them. A customer with high reputation is charged a lower rate of interest as compared to an ordinary customer. The sound principle of lending is not to sacrifice safety or liquidity for the sake of higher profitability, which means that the banks should not grant advances to unsecured parties with doubtful repaying capacities, even if they are ready to pay a very high rate of interest. Such advances ultimately prove to be irrecoverable and detrimental to the interests of the bank and its deposits.

The Purpose of the Loan

Another important point to be studied by a banker before lending is the purpose for which the loan is required and the resources from which the borrower is expected to repay. Loans may be required for productive purposes, trading purposes, agriculture, transport, self-employment. If a loan is required for a non-productive or speculative purpose, the banker should be very cautious in entering such a proposition. Even in cases of good business propositions, which cater to national interest or to priorities of the five-year plans, the application for loans may be turned down. The banker should advance loans only for a worthwhile purpose as determined justified as by the RBI and the government. Nowadays, there is a certain amount of official control on bank advances, and a bank has to keep within the limits of such control. For example, Section 21 of the Banking Companies Act, 1949 empowers the RBI, inter alia, to determine the policy to be followed by a banker and to give directions as to the purpose for which advances may or may not be made. These powers are used by the RBI through selective credit control measures. A good proposal would facilitate continuous recycling of funds in preference to looking up of funds.

Borrower—His Character, Capacity, Capital (3 Cs)

The Character, Capacity, and Capital of the borrower have to be ascertained carefully. The banker has to use his judgement and take a firm decision whether the borrower will be able to repay as agreed upon. Character does not simply refer to the moral character of the individual. It refers to his honest financial dealing with others. It is virtually impossible to assess one's character after one meeting. Some customers may have money but they may not have the willingness to repay the loan whereas some others may take every effort to repay their dues despite any difficulty they may face. Such characters have to be identified by the banker through proper inquiries. A more reliable method of ascertaining the credit worthiness of the borrower is to examine whether he has honoured his other financial commitments in time.

Capacity of the borrower may refer to his technical qualification and the know-how in the line of business for which the loan is sought. It refers to the resourcefulness of an individual. Capacity also refers to the ability to repay the loans in time. The banker has to ascertain whether his borrower has a regular flow of income. Apart from this, the bank may also see whether the customer has enough capital in the form of assets – movable or immovable – in his name. Capital refers to his stake in the business. A customer may have landed property which do not give him any returns due to some reason or other. Such securities are of little value.

Diversification of Risks

This is also a cardinal principle of sound lending. A prudent banker tries to select the borrower very carefully and takes tangible assets as securities to safeguard his interests. Tangible assets are no doubt valuable and the banker feels safe while granting advances on the security of such assets, and yet some risk is always involved therein. An industry or trade may face depressionary conditions and the price of the goods and commodities may sharply fall. Natural calamities like floods, earthquakes, and political disturbances in a certain part of the country may spoil even a prosperous business. To safeguard his interest against such unforeseen contingencies, the banker follows the principle of diversification of risks based on the famous maxim "do not keep all the eggs in one basket". It means that the banker should not grant advances to a few big firms only or to concentrate them in a few industries, or in a few cities or in one region of the country only. The advances on the other hand, should be spread over a reasonably wide area, distributed amongst a good number of customers belonging to different trades and industries. The banker thus diversifies the risk involved in lending. If a big customer meets with misfortune, or certain trades or industries are affected adversely, the overall position of the bank will not be jeopardised.

Nature and Location of Business

A business may be subdivided into different categories, for example, manufacturing, trading, import and export, wholesale and retail, a business having monopoly of the market or a business having a keen competition in the market, a business having tremendous scope for increase in demand or a business having not much scope for increase in demand in the future. It may be seen here that there may be innumberable types of business and the repaying capacity of a borrower depends, to a great extent, on the nature of the business he is engaged in. The location of business largely influences the type of security that can be offered in a bank advance. In big industrial cities like Mumbai, Delhi, Kolkata, Chennai, Kanpur, Ahmedabad, Bengaleru, Hyderabad, etc., the banker would naturally be offered a large quantity of shipping documents, or other documents of title to goods as security for advances. In the countryside or interiors, the security may be the produce of an agricultural area which has to be financed for the purpose of being taken to various centres of consumption. Title deeds of property for the purpose of raising temporary loans are also handled in almost every locality, whether it is in a commercial town or the countryside. In industrial areas, ready goods as well as raw materials would be offered as security against advances. A bank which has a large number of branches is undoubtedly in a favourable position because the securities on which its money is advanced are well spread out.

Safe Margin

When a security is offered to cover a bank advance, the banker has to consider two aspects. The first is economic, consisting of an estimate of the probable market value of the security at the time of its realisation, and the second is the legal aspect, that is, the validity of the security offered and the difficulties that may arise in its enforcement. The principle generally followed in these cases, with a view to arriving at the maximum amount which could be safely advanced, is to take the market value of the security offered and leave a sufficiently safe margin, both for fluctuation in value and interest accumulation. The banker should ensure not only the accuracy of its valuation but also that in the case of securities of a speculative nature which are subject to heavy fluctuations, the margin of safety is maintained in the form of much higher percentage than it is in other cases. Moreover, if there is a subsequent fall in the market prices of the securities deposited with the banker, it would be necessary to call for more margin.

National Policy Objectives

In a developing country like India, banks are also required to fulfill some social responsibilities. After the nationalisation of banks in 1969, a major thrust in policies of banks has been to provide credit facilities to the so-far-neglected sections of the economy. Banks are now playing an active role in serving the development needs of the economy in conformity with the National Policy and Objectives. With the changing perspective, the attitude of banks in following the principles of security in lending to the weaker sections of society has changed. Securities for the advances is not demanded exclusively in the tangible assets of the borrower, but banks also rely on the technical competence, managerial ability, honesty, and integrity of the borrower. In recent years, banks have been providing finance on a large scale to agriculturalists, small industrialists, professionals, personal transporters, self-employees, etc.

Under 'Priority Sector' and "20-Point Programme", some advances to weaker and under-privileged sections are given at concessional rate of interest. The Deposit Insurance and Credit Guarantee Corporation guarantees such loans. But it may be noted, that despite changes in the lending policies, the banks follow the basic principles of sound lending which are fundamental. However, the methods of lending are from time to time modified to suit the present needs of the society.

Analysis of Balance Sheet of a Bank

A balance sheet represents the financial status of a business entity and is often titled as a "statement of financial position" or "statement of sources and uses of funds". The balance sheet of a bank is a statement of its liabilities, and assets at a particular time. The business of the bank is reflected in the balance sheet. The financial position of the bank is made known through the balance sheet. It indicates whether the bank is sound and solvent or not. The balance sheet of the bank is of a greater importance than that of a trading concern because a bank deals in others' money and as such the entire community interest rests in it.

Banks in India have to prepare their profit and loss account, and balance sheet in forms set out in Third Schedule of the Banking Regulation Act, 1949. RBI has given guidelines for computing the balance sheet of Form A which is given on pg. 38.

Liabilities of a Commercial Bank

Every commercial bank gets its funds mainly from share capital, reserve fund, and deposits from the general public. Share capital is the contribution made by the shareholders of the bank. Reserve fund is the amount accumulated over the years out of undistributed profits which actually belongs to the shareholders. Share capital and reserve fund are liabilities of the bank, as they have to be paid to shareholders.

The deposits from the public constitute the biggest proportion of the bank's working funds. These funds are the liabilities of the bank as they have to be returned to their owners (deposit holders). But at the same time these funds are also assets to the bank since the latter can make use of them to get certain interest-yielding assets. The proper functioning of the bank is reflected in the distribution of its funds in various assets. A good banker is one who follows a wise investment policy – a policy which will bring in maximum profit for the shareholders and provide maximum security to the deposit holders.

FORM-A

BALANCE SHEET OF … BANK AS ON 31st March.

PARTICULARS	SCHEDULE	CURRENT YEAR(Yrs) AMOUNT (Rs)	PREVIOUS YEARS(Yrs) AMOUNT (Rs)
Capital and Liabilities			
Capital	01	*********	*********
Reserve & Surplus	02	*********	*********
Deposits	03	*********	*********
Borrowings	04	*********	*********
Other Liabilities & Provisions	05	*********	*********
Total			
Assets			
Cash and balances with RBI	06	*********	*********
Balances with bank and Money at call and short notice	07	*********	*********
Investment	08	*********	*********
Advances	09	*********	*********
Fixed Assets	10	*********	*********
Other Assets	11	*********	*********
Total			
Contingent Liabilities, Bills	12	*********	*********
Bills for collection, Acceptance, Endorsements/ Guarantees		*********	*********
Total		*********	*********

SCHEDULES

Sl. No.	Schedule-1 Capital	Amount (Rs)	Sl. No.	Schedule-2 Reserves as Surplus	Amount (Rs)
i	For Nationalised Banks	********	i	Statutory Reserve	***
				(op. bal + Add – deduct)	***
ii	For banks incorporated outside India	********	ii	Capital Reserve	***

(*Continued*)

(*Continued*)

iii	Authorised / issued / subscriber called up / + forfeited – un	********	iii	Share previsions	***
			iv	Reserve & other Reserves	***
			v	Balance in P&L A/c	***
	Total	********		Total	***

Sl. No.	Schedule-3 Deposits	Amount (Rs)	Sl. No.	Schedule-4 Borrowings	Amount (Rs)
i	Demand Deposits	********	i	Borrowings in India (I) RBI (II) other Banks	******
ii	Savings Bank Deposit	********	ii	Borrowings outside India	******
iii	Term Deposit	********	iii		
	Total			Total	******

Sl. No.	Schedule-5 Other Liabilities & Provision	Amount (Rs)	Sl. No.	Schedule-6 Cash and Balances with RBI	Amount (Rs)
i	Bills Payable	********	i	Cash in Hand	******
ii	Inter office Adjustments	********	ii	Balance with RBI	******
iii	Interest accrued	********			
	Total	********		Total	******

Sl. No.	Schedule-7 Balances with banks and money at call and short notice	Amount (Rs)	Sl. No.	Schedule-8 Investments	Amount (Rs)
i	In India	********	i	Investments in India Govt Securities Approved Securities Shares Securities Debentures and Bonds	******
ii	Outside India	********	ii	Investments outside india	******
	Total	********		Total	******

(*Continued*)

(*Continued*)

Sl. No.	Schedule-9 Advances	Amount (Rs)	Sl. No.	Schedule-10 Fixed Assets	Amount (Rs)
i	Bills Purchased & Discounted	*******	i	Premises (Opening + Add – deductions)	******
ii	Loans, Cash Credits and Over debts	*******	ii	Other fixed Assets	******
iii	Terms Loans	*******		Total	******

Sl. No.	Schedule-11 Other Assests	Amount (Rs)
i	Inter office Adjustments	********
ii	Interest Accrued	********
iii	Tax deducted at source (TDS)/Tax paid in Advance	********
iv	Stationary & Stamps	********
v	Non Banking Assets acquired	********

Sl. No.	Schedule-12 Contingent Liabilities	Amount (Rs)
i	Claims against the bank not acknowledged as debt	********
ii	Liability for partly paid investments	********
iii	Liability on account of outstanding forward exchange contracts	********
iv	Guarantees given and endorsement of constituents	********
v	Acceptances, endorsements and other obligations	********
vi	Other items for which the balance is contingently liable.	********
	Total	********

Capital

A bank secures capital by issuing shares to the public.

(a) *Authorised Capital:* The authorised capital is the maximum amount up to which the bank can issue shares to public. Only a part of the authorised capital is issued in the form of shares to public subscription. The other part is kept in reserve to be issued later in times of business expansion.

(b) *Issued Capital:* The part of the authorised capital which is offered to the public for subscription is known as issued capital.

(c) *Subscribed Capital:* It is the part of the issued capital which is actually subscribed by the public.

According to Banking Regulation Act, the subscribed capital of a bank shall not be less than 50 per cent of the authorised capital and the paid-up capital shall not be less than 50 per cent of the subscribed capital.

Reserve and Surplus

A bank generally transfers a portion of its profits to "Reserve Fund" every year. The fund is built up to meet unforeseen and unexpected contingencies. It is a source of strength for the bank as it can withstand heavy losses. It also operates an additional security to the customers. The amount in the reserve fund is invested in first-class securities.

Deposits

Deposits are the largest amount on the liabilities side of the balance sheet. A bank accepts various types of deposits such as:

(a) Saving Deposits.
(b) Annual Deposits.
(c) Fixed deposits.
(d) Recurring Deposits or Cumulative Deposits.

These funds are liabilities of the bank because they are to be repaid to the depositors. At the same time these funds are assets to the bank, since the bank can invest them in income yielding assets.

Section 194A of the Income Tax Act provides for deduction of tax at source from interest on time deposits, payable by a bank or cooperative society, where it exceeds INR 5000 in a financial year. Deduction of tax will not be made in case of depositors who furnish an affidavit or statement that their income is below taxable limit or that the tax on their estimated income would be nil. Tax is to be deducted at source at the prescribed rates.

The banker may also grant a loan to the depositor on the security of the fixed deposit receipt. The Reserve Bank of India had advised the banks to give loans to depositors against FDR maintained with them, up to 75 per cent of the total of actual deposit or the interest accrued on them up to the time the loans are advanced. The fixed deposit receipts are marked "Not Transferable" and cannot be transferred by endorsement.

An important feature of Indian banking is that deposits of the public with the banks are insured up to the limit of INR 1 lakh in each account. The Deposit Insurance Corporation of India was established by an Act of the Parliament to insure the deposits in the banks and the scheme of deposit insurance was introduced with effect from 1 January 1962. The corporation was renamed as 'Deposit Insurance and Credit Guarantee Corporation' with effect from 15 August 1978.

Banks have introduced various attractive savings schemes like Re-Investment Plan (RIP), Cash Certificates, Pension Plan, Annuity Deposit, Education Plan, Super Saving Package, etc. Different schemes are introduced as per the needs of the public.

Borrowing from Banks

Under this, the bank shows the loans which it has received from other banks. The bank takes loans from other banks, especially from the central bank (RBI) in times of necessity.

Other Liabilities and Provisions

This includes Drafts, Traveller's Cheques, Banker Cheques, Telegraphic Cheques, Mail transfers payable, Interest accrued and Interest adjusted, etc. These items will be shown on the liabilities side of balance sheet under Schedule 5.

Asset Structure of a Commercial Bank

Cash Balances

The first asset in the portfolio of a commercial bank's assets is cash – cash with the bank and cash reserves kept with the central bank of the country. Some part of the cash is kept in the bank's premises, some part with other commercial banks for the purpose of inter-bank adjustments, and a certain part is kept as a reserve with the central bank of the country. Deposits of a bank with other commercial banks or with the central bank (RBI) of the country is always regarded as cash by a commercial bank. In India, commercial banks are obliged, by law, to keep a certain proportion of the total deposits in the form of cash reserves with the RBI.

Cash is called the primary reserve of a bank, but it is an idle asset as it does not yield any revenue to the bank. The bank knows from its experience, the minimum cash reserve it should keep to meet the depositors' demand. Generally, 10 per cent of the total deposits is kept as cash reserves. The success of a bank depends on the maintenance of sufficient cash reserves, to honour the cheques presented by the clients. But only a small percentage of depositors may withdraw their deposits through cheques and other instruments at any particular time. At the same time, if some depositors withdraw, others may deposit. A commercial bank has, therefore, to manage its business in such a way that the amount of cash inflow and outflow should be in equilibrium, keeping a margin of surplus cash from the point of safety. High cash reserve reduces the profit-earning capability of the bank and low reserve affects the credibility of the bank.

Money at Call and Short Notice

Cash, being a barren asset, should not be kept idle beyond a minimum period. But a banker may anticipate that there might be a heavy pressure on its cash reserves due to seasonal changes in depositors' and borrowers' requirements. To meet the pressure, the bank may be inclined to stock large cash reserves although this may not be necessary. A better alternative for the bank is to keep some highly liquid securities like government bonds but earning assets which can be converted into cash quickly without any loss.

Such highly liquid assets consists of call and short notice loans to the brokers in the stock market, dealers in the discount market, and to other banks. These loans are often for short periods of a few days. These assets can be quickly converted into cash without any loss, as and when the bank needs additional cash; hence, they are known as money at call and money at short notice. Banks regard such assets as secondary reserves, even though these assets bring in some revenue income to the banks, as different from cash which is their primary reserve.

Short-Term Bills

A bill of exchange is a written promise by a merchant who has ordered certain goods to pay a specified sum of money on a specified date. This bill may additionally be guaranteed by a bank. Bill of exchange are discounted (sold) with commercial banks. The latter may keep them till the date of maturity (normally 90 days) when they will be paid up by the drawee of the bills. The banks can also re-sell the bills in the market (i.e. re-discount) them. Every commercial bank prefers these short-dated bills because of their high marketability, their easy discountability with RBI, and their interest income. These are regarded as ideal bank assets because they fulfill the two principles of investment policy, that is, liquidity and profit. Besides commercial bills, there are short-dated treasury bills through which the government borrows for short periods. Commercial bills, treasury bills, money at call and short notice are together known as money market assets.

Investments

Investments are for longer periods. Bank investments are generally in government bonds or in fixed interest yielding debentures or bonds of well-established commercial enterprises. These investments are preferred by banks for two reasons – they are highly shiftable to the central bank (RBI) or to other bank institutions and they have good income-yielding capacity. They can be sold easily without loss, but there is a risk element in selling them in times of need, if their market price is lower than the price at which the bank originally purchased them. However, if a commercial bank has a certain amount of funds which can be left undistributed for a number of years, investment for a long-term is ideal. Securities provide a convenient medium of investment during slack season.

Loans and Advances

Loans of non-productive and speculative purposes cannot be granted. Although the earning on non-productive business may be higher, banks cannot resort to non-productive loans being contrary to the national interest.

According to the Section 5(a) of the Banking Regulation Act, 1949, a secured loan or advance means "a loan or the advance made on the security of the assets, the market value of which is not any time less than the amount of such loans or advances". The Banking Regulation Act, 1949, prohibits unsecured as well as secured advances to directors of the Banking Company. An unsecured loan or advance means a loan or advance without any security. A partly covered loan or advance is partly covered by the security of assets, the market value of such securities being less than the amount that has been lent or outstanding at any time.

The RBI does not permit other banks to give clean advance in excess of 15 per cent of their total outstanding advances including 20 per cent of unsecured guarantees.

Usually advances are made by way of Overdraft, Cash Credit, Discounting Bills or Loans and Advances. As loans and advances carry high rate of interests, they are good assets from the point of profitability. But these assets are low on liquidity and are not shiftable. This is the fourth line of defence of the bank.

Fixed Assets

The total volume of movable and immovable properties of the bank are divided under fixed assets. This is often referred to as "Dead Stocks". They cannot be realised without much loss of value.

Other Assets

This includes non-banking assets as acquired in satisfaction to claim, taxes paid in advance, interest accrued, etc.

Sources of Bank Funds

The funds of a banking institutions, like any other business entrepreneur, fall into two categories. They are owned funds consisting of paid-up capital, reserves and surplus, that is, internal funds, borrowings, deposits, etc.

Credit Creation

The creation of credit is one of the most important functions of commercial banks. In the ordinary course of business, a bank accepts deposits from the public and lends money to its customers. When a bank advances a loan, it does not pay the amount in cash. But it opens an account in the customer's name and allows him to withdraw the required amount by cheque. In this way, a bank creates credit or deposit which is regarded as money which can be used for the purchase of goods and services and also for the payment of debt just like currency notes.

Bank deposits can be created in two ways. These are:

(a) People can deposit their cash with the banking system, that is, they convert their cash into bank deposits. Here, cash with public has been changed into another form of money, that is, bank money. The initiative for creating deposits is taken by the customers themselves. Such deposits are known as primary deposits. Primary deposits bring cash to the banking system.

(b) Using the cash received from the depositors, the banking system buys assets from the market (bills, bonds, debentures, etc.) or it lends to businessmen and industrialists. Whenever a bank buys assets from the market or lends to certain parties, it does not provide cash to them directly but creates demand deposits in their name or in the alternative's. When a bank buys an asset, it pays through a cheque which is deposited in the account of the seller of the asset. These deposits are secondary since they are based on or derived from the primary deposits, also known as derivative deposits. The initiative for creating these secondary or derivative deposits comes from the banking system. In a modern economy, the second form of deposits has become quite significant.

Edwin Cannan, Walter, and Leaf do not agree with the view that banks can create money. Banks can only lend from what they have in cash. So they cannot and do not create money. The above view is based on the argument relating to a single bank. So it cannot be considered correct. Professor. Samuelson says, "The banking system as a whole can do what each small bank cannot do. It can expand its loans and investments many times the reserves of cash created for it, even though each small bank is lending out only a fraction of its deposits".

By experience banks know that all depositors do not withdraw their money simultaneously. Some withdraw while some others deposit on the same day. So by keeping a small cash reserve for day to day transactions, the bank is able to grant loans on the basis of excess reserves. The amount lent may come back again to the same bank or some other bank as deposit.

The bank having increased deposits will lend more. This process will continue till the total deposits have increased by a number of times of the original deposit of cash.

Bank Loans Create Bank Deposits

Money at Call and Short Notice is an extremely short period loan made by a bank to speculators and brokers in the money market and the capital market (i.e. stock exchange). Against their promises to return the loan as and when required, a commercial bank credits the deposit accounts of speculators and dealers. The latter would use these deposits to pay off their creditors. The creditors who received cheques or drafts credit them to their bank accounts. Thus, as a result of loans made by a bank, to speculators and others for short periods, deposits equal to the value of the loans have been created.

Bills Discounted

This refers to the commercial bills and financial bills which are short term (generally for 90 days), which a bank acquires from the bill market. When a bank buys (or discounts) a bill of exchange from the party, it credits the account of the latter (if the party keeps an account with the bank) or it pays the party through a cheque on itself. The party getting the bill deposits the cheque in its bank account. In both cases, bank deposits increase the amount of the bill discounted by the bank.

Investments

A commercial bank also creates a deposit by making investment in securities like government bonds, shares, debentures, etc., which have longer life. The bank pays for the bonds through a cheque on itself to the central bank. If it buys bonds or debentures from stock exchange, it credits the amount in the account of the seller. In any case a deposit is created, either in this bank or in some other bank.

Loans and Advances

Banks provide credit facilities to businessmen, firms, companies, etc., by way of loans and advances, overdraft, and cash credit. When a loan is granted or overdraft is sanctioned, the amount of loan or overdraft is deposited in the account of the customer and he is allowed to draw cheques up to the amount agreed upon. Thus, the bank creates a deposit in the name of the borrower. Banks can create more credit in a similar way.

By giving loans and buying assets from the market, which is collectively called bank credit, a commercial bank is creating money. Every asset acquired by a bank creates an equivalent bank deposit. Banks take initiative to give loans and advances and acquire other earning assets. By doing so, they control the total volume of deposits in the banking system. In simple terms, more bank credit means more bank deposits, and more bank deposits means more money in the country.

Commercial banks monetise the debt of others. Banks give assurance of payment against the assurance of others. Thus, banks create money. Commercial banks have absolute control over the volume of bank deposits, subject to the conditions that:

(a) The supply of cash will be with the banking system.
(b) The public demands for cash.
(c) The cash reserve ratio is to be maintained by the banking system. The central bank can assist in increasing or decreasing of earning assets and bank deposits by increasing or decreasing the monetary power of commercial banks.

The Techniques of Credit Creation: Deposit Multiplies

Demand deposits or cash deposits are money and used as such, for every depositor who has a current account in a commercial bank can meet his obligations through cheques drawn on his account. Expansion or contraction of demand deposits, therefore, means expansion and contraction of money in the country.

Banks have the power to expand or contract demand deposits and they exercise the power through granting loans and advances and acquiring other assets. Now this power of commercial banks to expand deposits through expanding their loans and advances is known as credit creation.

Bank credit refers to bank loans and advances and credit creation means multiplication of loans and advances. As every bank loan creates an equivalent deposit, credit creation by banks also implies multiplication of bank deposits. The word "creation" implies that banks are unique institutions and they can create bank deposits or create bank money (by giving loans and purchasing bills and bonds) out of nothing or with a small amount of cash, they are in a position to acquire a large amount of assets.

A bank cannot lend more than what it has got. But, what is lent out by a bank comes back to it by way of new deposits, which may again be lent out, and so on. Commercial banks are, therefore, able to multiply loans and investments and this multiply deposits. A small volume of cash is the basis for multiplication of deposits through multiplication of loans and advances ("loans create deposits"). It is in this sense that banks create credit. Credit creation can be defined as the expansion of bank deposits through the process of more loans and advances and investments.

Illustration of Credit Creation

The technique of credit creation can be explained by the following illustration. Let us assume:

(a) the existence of a number of banks, A, B, C, D etc., each with different sets of depositors.
(b) every bank has to keep 20 per cent of cash reserves, according to law.
(c) a new deposit of INR 10,000 has been made by a depositor with bank A to start with.

After the new deposit of INR 10,000 has been made in Bank A, the balance sheet of Bank A(taking only new transaction) is as follows.

Liabilities	INR	Assets	INR
New Deposit	10,000	New Cash	10,000
Total	10,000	Total	10,000

Under the double-entry system, the amount of INR 10,000 deposited by a person is shown on both sides. The new deposit of INR 10,000 is a liability for Bank A since it is obliged to return the amount to the depositor whenever he demands it. At the same time, the amount is an asset (cash) to the bank and it appears on the asset side of the balance sheet.

Bank A has to keep only 20 per cent cash reserve, that is, INR 2,000 against its new deposit. It has a surplus of INR 8,000 which it can employ profitably. We know that banks do not keep idle cash with them. They would like to lend out their idle cash or would like to buy securities from which they can earn some interest income. Bank A gives a loan of INR 8,000 to Mr X who uses the amount to pay off his creditors.
After the loan has been made and the amount withdrawn by Mr X to pay off his creditors, the balance sheet of Bank A will be as follows.

Balance Sheet of Bank A

Liabilities	INR	Assets	INR
Deposit	10,000	Cash	2,000
		Loan to Mr X	8,000
Net	10,000		10,000

Now the creditors of Mr X who got INR 8,000 from him, may be assured to deposit the amount with their bank, that is, Bank B (this assumption is necessary, for creditors of Mr X may be banking with Bank B and depositing

INR 8,000 with Bank B itself). The balance sheet of Bank B will be as follows:

Balance Sheet of Bank B

Liabilities	INR	Assets	INR
New Deposit	8,000	New Cash	8,000
Total	8,000	Total	8,000

After keeping a cash reserve of INR 1,600, that is, 20 per cent of INR 8,000, Bank B is free to lend the balance of INR 6,400 to any one. Suppose Bank B pays for discounting bill of exchange worth INR 6,400 from the market. The balance sheet of Bank B will be as follows:

Balance Sheet of Bank B

Liabilities	INR	Assets	INR
Deposit	8,000	Cash	1,600
		Bills of Exchange	6,400
Total	8,000	Total	8,000

We can assume that the sellers of bills to Bank B, who received INR 6,400 from Bank B would be depositing the amount in their bank, that is, Bank C. Bank C's balance sheet will be as follows:

Balance Sheet of Bank C

Liabilities	INR	Assets	INR
New Deposit	6,400	New Cash	6,400
Total	6,400	Total	6,400

Bank C finds that it has surplus cash reserves of INR 5,120 (under 20 per cent cash reserve, it will have to keep a cash reserve of INR 1,280 only against a deposit of INR 6,400). Suppose Bank C buys long-term government bonds from Mr Y worth INR 5,120, then the balance sheet of Bank C will be as follows:

Balance Sheet of Bank C

Liabilities	INR	Assets	INR
Deposit	6,400	Cash	1,280
		Government Bonds	5,120
Total	6,400	Total	6,400

Now Mr Y, who sold the bonds to Bank C for INR 5,120 may be expected to deposit the amount with his bank, that is, Bank D which, in turn, will keep 20 per cent as cash reserve and lend the rest.

This process of deposit which becomes a loan or investment and again a new deposit goes on until the original deposit of INR 10,000 becomes additional deposits of INR 8000, 6400, 5120, and so on. The total of these deposits amount to INR 49,999 or INR 50,000.

We can understand from the above illustration that:

(a) Bank credit is expanded by banks lending more amount and buying more assets

(b) Bank credit eventually comes back to the banking system in the form of new deposits to become the basis for new bank credit.

Credit creation and deposit multiplication are the two processes taking place in the banking system simultaneously. Credit creation is the cause and deposit multiplication is the effect.

It is assumed, so far, that credit creation takes place only when many banks are available, but it is not so. Only one bank is sufficient for the same process of credit creation to take place. This can happen in one bank in an isolated town in the banking system as whole in a region or country. Whenever the bank has surplus cash reserves, it lends or invests the same. This amount comes back to the bank in the form of a new deposit (new cash) which becomes the basis for yet another loan, and so on. The money which goes out from the bank in the form of loans, etc. and the money which comes back in the form of new deposits are the same.

The Formula of Credit Creation: Deposit Multiplication

As deposit multiplication depends upon the ratio of cash reserves to deposits, the deposit multiplier is:

$K = 1/r$, in which
K = Deposit multiplier
r = ratio of cash reserves to deposits

If cash reserve ratio is 20 per cent or 0.2, the deposit multiplier is:

$K = 1/r = 1/0.2 = 5$

If the cash reserve ratio is 10 per cent or 0.1, the deposit multiplier is 10 and so on. The higher the cash reserve ratio, the lower the deposit multiplier. The additional deposit creation (D) is the additional cash $\Delta M \times K$.

Suppose the commercial bank gets fresh cash of INR 10 crores as a result of Government Spending. They can multiply deposits through loans and investments to the extent of INR 50 crores (assuming a cash reserve of 20 per cent) or deposit multiplier of 5, that is:

$$D = \Delta M \times K = \text{INR } 10 \text{ crores} \times 5 = \text{INR } 50 \text{ crores}$$

The Techniques of Credit Contraction

Commercial banks are able to multiply credit when deposits are made with them. If cash is withdrawn from the bank, it results in multiple contraction of credit. The process of multiple credit contraction can be explained by making certain assumptions. These are:

(a) There is one bank with a cash reserve of INR 1,000 investment INR 9,000 and deposits INR 10,000.
(b) The bank is required to keep 20 per cent cash against the deposit.

The balance sheet of the bank would appear as follows:

Balance Sheet

Liabilities	INR	Assets	INR
Deposit	10,000	Cash	1,000
		Investments	9,000
Total	10,000	Total	10,000

Suppose INR 100 is withdrawn from the bank, the balance sheet of the bank would appear as follows:

Balance sheet

Liabilities	INR	Assets	INR
Deposits	9,900	Cash	900
		Investments	9,000
Total	9,900	Total	9,900

Against a deposit of INR 9,900 the bank has got a cash reserve of INR 900 only. But it should have cash reserve of INR 1,980. To fill in the cash reserve of INR 1080 the bank may either realise the loan or dispose off its investments. As getting back the loan at once is difficult, the bank will make up the deficit by disposing the investment worth INR 1080.

Assume that the bank sells the security to A who issues a cheque against his bank for payment. After the amount is collected, the balance sheet of the bank would be as follows:

Balance Sheet

Liabilities	INR	Assets	INR
Deposits	9,900	Cash	1,980
		Investments	7,920
Total	9,900	Total	9,900

Similarly, other banks may have to dispose of their securities to fill in the deficit in the cash reserve. The initial withdrawal of INR 100 leads to a reduction of deposits to the extent of INR 500.

Limitations of Credit Creation

The following are the limitations on the power of commercial banks to create credit.

Adequate Cash Reserve

The first factor that limits the capacity of banks to expand credit is the necessity to keep adequate cash reserves. By creating deposits, banks create their own liability and are prepared to honour customers' cheque up to an agreed sum. The success of the bank depends upon the ability to meet the demand of its depositors and failure to do so would result in loss of confidence of the customers. A part of primary deposit received from the public is kept for this purpose. If the banks maintain more cash, they would create less credit, less cash would enable them to multiply more credit.

Quantity of Money in Circulation

Another limiting factor is the total quantity of money in circulation. The central bank of a country has the monopoly power to issue currency notes. The quantity of circulation of money increases with the issue of more currency and declines with the decrease in it. Increased circulation improves the cash position of banks with which they create more credit. A decrease in circulation depletes the cash reserve which restricts the capacity to expand deposit.

Availabililty of Securities

The power of banks to create credit is curtailed by the availability of adequate securities in the market and possession of the same by the borrowers. Banks do not create anything out of thin air. They acquire wealth such as shares, debentures, bonds, etc., and exchange policy wealth in the form of I.O.U. which functions like money. Banks can create credit when the borrowers produce such security.

To quote Professor Sayers, "the banks put this newly created money into the hands of not of every body at once", but those individuals who can offer attractive assets to the bank. The possession of such security by borrowers ultimately depends upon the availability in the market.

Policy of the Central Bank (RBI)

The policy of the central bank influences the capacity of the banks to multiply credit. Every commercial bank is required to keep certain percentage of cash against its deposit liabilities with the central bank. For instance, if the central bank directs the banks to keep 20 per cent cash against deposit liabilities, the banks could expand the amount in deposits to 5 times. If banks are required to keep more, say 25 per cent, they could expand to 4 times only. Thus, higher the percentage of cash reserve ratio, smaller will be the volume of credit and vice versa.

Attitude of People

The desire of the people to hold cash has its impact on the power of banks to multiply credit. If the public decides to hold more cash due to uncertainity about economic conditions, they would draw a large part of deposits. As a result, banks are left with depleted cash reserve which restricts the capacity to create credit. On the other hand, if people deposit more with the banks, it adds to the cash position and that would multiply the credit to a greater extent.

Nature of Business Condition

The volume of credit creation depends on the nature of business conditions. During the period of business prosperity, due to the prevalence of optimism among the public, demand for loans and advances will be large and so banks could expand more deposits. During the period of recession, economic activities are at a low ebb. Recession leads to more cautious attitude by bankers, causing them to hold larger reserve balances. The loan demand will be less and banks could credit to a limited extent.

Behaviour of Banks

The power of credit creation is limited by the behaviour of other banks. If some banks do not grant loans to the extent required of the banking system, the credit expansion will be restricted.

Use of Cheques

When the use of cheque is popular among public, they pay one another by cheque and the cash position of the banks is unaffected. When this use is scant, people will withdraw cash for every transaction and banks ought to keep more cash and this restricts the power to create credit. In developing countries like India, the use of cheques is not so popular as in developed countries.

Leakages

The actual expansion of deposit is usually below the maximum possible limit because of several types of leakages. First, the banks may not be able to expand credit according to its surplus funds. Second, the loans extended by the banks may return by way of new deposit, but only a part of it, credit creation is limited to that extent.

Loans and Advances

Lending always involves much risk because there is no certainty of repayment. But a banker earns a bulk of his income only through lending. A banker should be very cautious in lending, because he is not lending money out of his own capital. A major portion of the money lent comes from the deposits received from the public. These deposits are mostly repayable on demand. Hence, while lending money, a banker should follow a very cautious policy and must take into account the following general principles of sound lending.

General Principles of Sound Lending

The banks have to follow the following principles for sound lending.

Safety

"Safety-first" should be the guiding principle to be followed in granting loans and advances. Since banks deal with their customer's money, they have to ensure the safety of these funds. Safety means that the borrowers should be in a position to repay the loans borrowed with interest on due date. The repayment by borrowers depends upon: (a) their capacity to repay, (b) their willingness to repay, and (c) the collateral security offered. The capacity of a borrower depends upon the success of his venture and willingness upon his honesty and integrity. Hence, before lending money, the banker should ascertain the character and integrity of the borrower and whether the security offered is adequate and easily realisable.

Liquidity

Liquidity in banking terminology means the ability to convert the assets into cash without any loss of time and value. The traditional banker usually supports his loans with tangible security which offers a cushion for safety. Whenever there is a withdrawal, the banker should honour his customer's demand without any delay. In case the banker delays repayment due to insufficiency of funds, the news might spread like wildfire, leading to spread of false rumours about the solvency of the bank. If all the customers withdraw their deposits at the same time, bank will have inadequate cash to pay back their depositors although the bank may be solvent at that point of time. Therefore, a bank should be careful in the use of its funds without giving any opportunity at any time to lose faith in the banking system. Fixed assets like land and buildings, as securities, may pose problems of sale at times of emergencies.

Profitability

Commercial banks exist for earning profit too. A banker cannot run the banking business without profit. Profit is essential to meet the day-to-day expenses, to pay interest on deposits, to meet the salaries of staff, etc. Profitability demands that a banker should deploy all funds to earn maximum profit. But liquidity demands that the banker should maintain a large cash reserve to meet the demands of the customers. Thus, these two principles are opposing to each other. In fact, an experienced banker knows that these two opposing factors must meet with each other at a point called safety. Hence, safety and liquidity should not be sacrificed for profitability.

Security

When compared with the purpose and viability of the scheme, security is relegated to the secondary position. A security is valued at purchase price or market price or controlled price, whichever is the lowest. A charge is created on the tangible assets acquired with the borrower funds and collateral security need not be necessarily insisted. Such advances without security are called unsecured advances. Till the nationalisation of banks in 1969, the commercial banks used to insist on security to decide on the credit proposals. In the post-nationalisation scenario, there has been a shift from security orientation to need-based orientation. Based on the turnover, level of inventory, book debts, other sources of finance, and own equity disclosed in the sales-tax returns or income-tax return of the borrower, the quantum of advance is decided.

Purpose of the Loan

The purpose of the advance is of prime consideration. The purpose for which loans are desired has to be ascertained clearly. The borrower should not use borrowed funds for any purpose other than the ones mentioned at the time of taking loan. The banker should not advance any loan for speculative or unproductive purposes such as social functions. Consumption loans for small amounts constitute an exception for this general rule.

Diversification of Risks

The banker should not concentrate on only one or two sectors while lending. He should not keep all his eggs in one basket. In other words, he has to spread his risk over different sectors and industries spread widely over different geographical regions. This ensures that the bank credit is made available to a much wider section of hitherto neglected sectors and backward regions in the country. The rate of interest charged is based on exposure to a particular sector and experience of the banker in the given sector.

Assured Repayment

A banker should come forward to lend only when repayment is assured. When there is default in repayment, a banker's ability to create further credit is affected. Hence, while advancing money, he should check the source of repayment. For example, loans against an FDR which is going to mature shortly. A life insurance policy which is going to mature soon, a debenture which is to be reduced shortly, etc., are considered as sound loans. Thus, a sound credit is one where, timely repayment is assured.

Debt Service Coverage Ratio

Debt service coverage ratio is a total that guides to determine the period of repayment of loan. It is calculated as follows. Cash accruals include net profit after taxes with depreciation provision added to it. An average of 1.5:1 is considered as satisfactory for debt service coverage ratio.

The Law of Limitations Act

A lending banker should also bear in mind the Law of Limitations Act. According to this Act, a debt will become a bad debt after the expiry of three years from the sanction or disbursal of loan. It is applicable to loans and advances granted by banks. Hence, each and every banker should be very careful in reviewing the loan, year after year. Otherwise these loans would become bad subsequently.

Margins and Advances

Margin refers to the extra amount which the banker keeps for the interest of the bank. In other words, the higher the margin, the more is the safety and security for the bank. The percentage of margin on a security is determined based on its nature. The margins may differ from bank to bank. The amount of finance provided by the bank after deducting the margin is called permissible limit. The suggested margin for stock is 20 to 25 per cent, for equipment and other immovable property the margin is 30 to 50 per cent, for book debts the margin is 40 to 50 per cent, and on letter of credit the margin is around 10 per cent.

Social Objectives

While making advances, the banker should give the highest priority to the national interest. Today banks have a strong social objective and social conscience. It is the responsibility of each and every bank to ensure that the bank credit flows smoothly to the neglected sectors of the economy and to the under-privileged sections of the society. Banks have given up their "security-oriented lending" and have taken up "need based loans" or "productivity of the loan". The viability of the profit is given more weight than the security behind a loan under the compulsive pressure of social banking; banks were required to lend 40 per cent of their advances to priority sector. A banker should follow the RBI guidelines relating to the lending of funds.

Recycling of Loan

A good proposal would facilitate continuous recycling of funds in preference to locking up of funds.

Re-finance

The bank may look for re-financing facilities from RBI, IDBI, or NABARD. Between two proposals, weightage should be given to the proposal which carries re-finance facilities.

Loans and Advances

A credit refers to the loan advanced by the banker for a specific purpose. The advances made by the banker are traditionally grouped under two broad categories.

(a) Demand loans, cash credits, overdrafts, and term loans.
(b) Purchase and discount of bills.
(c) Demand loans, cash credits, overdrafts, and term loans constitute 80 per cent of the total outstanding bank credit. Discounting of bills is a very popular means of bank credit abroad.

The loans and advances granted by the banker can also be classified into the following segments:

(i) Priority sector advances covering mainly the sectors of agriculture, small scale industry, and so on
(ii) Personal loans for consumption purpose such as gold loan, marriage loan, education loan, and so on
(iii) Commercial and institutional loan for trading, service and manufacturing purposes.

Demand Loan

Demand loan is one-time advance for a fixed amount granted against the personal liability of the borrower. Demand loans are sanctioned against a security. Gold ornaments, bank's own term deposit receipts, stocks, Kisan

Vikas Patras, or national saving certificates can be offered as security to raise demand loans from a bank.

Cash Credits

Cash credit accounts for the majority of total bank credit. Under cash credit facility, the banker sanctions a limit called cash credit limit for each customer up to which the customer is permitted to borrow against the security of tangible assets such as stocks, book debts, etc. The customer can withdraw from cash credit amount whenever he wants. If he has surplus cash with him, he can also deposit into the account on any day. Thus, cash credit account is an active and running account. The borrower has to pay interest only on the actual amount used by him and to the period of actual utilisation on the daily outstanding balances. The banker will fix a limit for cash credit facility after carefully analysing the particulars relating to the production, sales, inventory levels, utilisation of such cash credit facility in the past, and so on. The cash credit advances are repayable on demand. There is no specific time frame for repayment.

Overdrafts

Overdraft is an arrangement whereby a customer is allowed to overdraw his current account up to a specified limit. It is purely a temporary one and it is also granted against securities. Overdraft is not granted on a regular basis, as in the case of cash credit. Withdrawals and deposits can be made frequently. Interest is charged on the amount actually utilised. However, there is a minimum interest clause which will apply in case the overdraft is not made use of. This type of advance is very popular among business people.

Bills Discounted and Purchased

Banks grant advances to customers by discounting a bill of exchange or promissory note. The amount after deducting the interest from the amount of the instruments, is credited in the account of the customer. In this form of lending, the interest is received by the banker in advance. Discounting of bills constitute a clean advance and banks rely on the credit worthiness of the parties to the bill. Bank sometimes purchase the bills instead of discounting them. Bills which are accompanied by documents of title to goods such as bills of lading or railway receipt are purchased by the bankers. In such cases, the banker grants loan in the form of overdraft or cash credit against the security of the bank. The term "bills purchased" seems to imply that the bank becomes the purchaser/owner of such bills. But in almost all cases, the bank holds the bill only as a security for the advance.

Hire-Purchase Advances

Hire purchase advances are very popular in western countries. It is gaining popularity in India too. Under this system, banks provide finance to business concerns engaged in hire purchase business. They do not give finance to ultimate buyers directly. If they do so, it comes under the category of "personal loans". The business houses engaged in hire purchase selling obtain loan facilities on the security of hypothecation of goods sold out on hire purchase basis. Hire purchase business is very popular in the case of durable goods like TV sets, refrigerators, motor vehicles, etc. Hence, this type of advances are particularly popular in transport operations.

Working Capital Credit

Working capital constitutes the blood and life of every business organisation. To finance the purchase of a raw material, work-in-progress, finished goods, sundry debtors, and other business-related expenses such as wages, salaries, and insurance, working capital is essential. There are cases where the business units collapse for reasons of non-availability of working capital. Bankers provide working capital loans and these are called working capital credit. Working capital credit has three components cash – credit, letter of credit and bank guarantee. "Letter of credit" is an undertaking issued by a bank on behalf of the buyer to the seller, to pay for goods and services. "Bank guarantee" is the customer's financial worth, credit worthiness, and his capacity to take up financial risk.

When the banker provides cash credit, there is flow of funds from the banker to the borrower, and hence it is called fund-based service. For issue of letter of credit and bank guarantee, the banker levies charges and hence these services are called fees-based services.

Lending Policies Guidelines from Reserve Bank of India

The RBI issues guidelines from time to time to maintain the risk to a level which can be manageable and to prevent an asset – liability mismatch position. Adherence to these guidelines bring discipline in banks in delivery of credit without losing national priorities and objectives. These guidelines are:

(a) Each lending bank may decide on the limit up to which it can provide credit facilities within the overall limit. The ceiling is linked to the capital funds of the lending bank. Capital funds is the sum total of Tier I and Tier II capital recognised for the purpose of computation of capital adequacy. Tier I capital comprises paid-up capital, statutory reserves, disclosed free reserves, and capital reserves arising out of sale of assets. Tier II capital consists of undisclosed reserves, revaluation reserves, general provisions.

(b) In case of a single borrower, the exposure ceiling is 15 per cent of capital funds and in the case of a borrower group, it is 40 per cent with effect from 1 April 2002.
(c) If the credit is to all infrastructure projects, exposure to borrowers, belonging to a group may exceed the exposure norm of 40 per cent of the bank's capital funds by the additional 10 per cent (i.e. up to 50 per cent).

As per the directions of the RBI, every commercial bank should have an in-house policy document outlining the following:

- maximum limit for the loan
- the standards of appraisal
- the documentation standards
- the decision-making powers at each level
- the premises on which credit officers base their lending decision.

Lending Decision

In the light of the above guidelines by RBI, every bank is free to formulate its own lending policies. Every branch manager has to observe certain basic and well-known principles of lending so that he can minimise the risks and the bank's income accrues from interest on loans and advances. The banker has to follow a cautious policy and conduct his lending business. Lending policies may vary from bank to bank as they are based on the risk perception of each bank and the profile of banker and customer.

Priority sector lending has been adopted by RBI since 1967. Targets have been fixed for both Indian banks and foreign banks at 40 per cent and 32 per cent, respectively. Since foreign banks do not have rural network, to facilitate them to achieve this target of 32 per cent, the delimitation of priority sector was amended to include export finance in the target for advances to priority sectors. The banker has to necessarily take care of the detailed aspects of priority sector lending and has to ensure that he will achieve the given targets every year.

Priority sector advances include advances to:

(a) Agriculture (18 per cent of advances)
(b) Small-scale industries (40 per cent of advances to the small-scale industries should be granted to cottage industries, khadi and village industries, artisans, tiny industries or other SSI units)
(c) Retail trade (advances not exceeding INR 5 lakhs)
(d) Road transport operators (up to 10 vehicles)
(e) Lending to agro-processing units

(f) Housing in rural and semi-urban areas (up to INR 5 lakhs)
(g) Banks lending to Non-Banking Financial Companies (NBFCs) for providing finance to agriculture
(h) Professional and self-employed (total borrowing should not exceed INR 5 lakhs of which working capital not to exceed INR 1 lakh)
(i) Advances by foreign banks to the SSI sector and export credit should not be less than 10 per cent each in the net bank credit. If there is any shortfall in achieving the sub-target in respect of advances to the SSI sector, such difference should be deposited with Small Industries Development Bank of India (SIDBI).

Recent Trends in the Lending Rates

(i) **Prime Lending rates:** Today each bank prescribes its own interest rates in the form of a spread over its prime lending rate (PLR). The interest rates for loans of long-term and short-term period are governed by PLR, which may vary from sector to sector.

(ii) **Interest on reducing balance method:** Earlier, banks used to apply interest on loan accounts once every quarter. Today the practice is not so any more. The commercial banks apply interest on a monthly basis and the practice is called application of interest on reducing balance method, the practice which is followed all over the world.

(iii) **Floating rate of interest:** Ever since the globalisation of Indian economy, the rates of interest in banks have been on the decline. To give benefits of such decline in interest rates, the banks have the scheme of floating rates of interest on the outstanding loan. The customer also can opt for fixed interest rate schemes, if he chooses.

(iv) **Deregulated interest rates:** With deregulation of interest rates, individual banks have operational freedom to decide their own interest rate to be charged. The individual branches have to take decisions for themselves whether to sanction credit or not, based on the merits of the case. In the present conditions of competition where foreign banks also have been making their strong presence in every sector in India, Indian banks have been striving hard to maintain their market share and sustain hold on customer base. Deregulation of interest rates implies that the RBI does not control the interest rates any more but leaves them to market forces of demand and supply. In case of priority sector lending (loans below INR 2 lakhs) and differential rate of interest lending, the RBI still prescribes the interest rates, except for those, in all other cases, the interest rates are deregulated.

Credit Appraisal

Credit appraisal is a technique by which a banker estimates the soundness of a credit proposal by careful analysis. Credit appraisal leads to finding out the quantum of credit required for a borrower and the safety of such credit. In recent years, the banks and financial institutions have developed certain sophisticated techniques for ascertaining credit limits and to decide whether it would be worthwhile to accept such proposals.

Traditionally, commercial banks lend short-term credit needs, meeting the working capital gap. There is a close relationship between the success of the proposal and safety of the bank. Therefore, the banker takes adequate care in selecting the right proposal and looks for various particulars like sales, cost of sales, expected profit, general and administrative expenses, tax factor, indirect income, etc. The banker may also ask for current assets and current liabilities. The banker may ascertain the maximum permissible bank finance for the working capital as per the Tandan Committee Report, towards fluctuating demand credit, fixed loan, discounting bills, etc. Appraisal of the loan application is the starting point for fixing credit limit for the borrower.

Assessment of credit requirements for enterprises working at a small scale is often difficult because of a lack of data relating to operations of the unit. The RBI has therefore suggested that lending banks may not insist on submission of audited financial statements up to credit requirements of INR 25 lakhs from prospective borrowers. Beyond this level, lending bankers usually compute the credit requirements after undertaking structured analysis of the financial statements.

Till about 1990, bank credit was considered as scarce of commodity and therefore, there was a strong focus on the need to optimally use this resource towards the creation of primary assets, which are known as primary security charged in favour of a lending bank. With gradual liberalisation, commercial banks are providing credit.

Nature of Business Conditions

The volume of credit creation depends on the nature of business conditions. During the period of business prosperity, due to the prevalence of optimism, demand for loans and advances will be large and so banks could expand more deposits. Due to liberalisation, commercial banks began providing credit to other sectors also and even for those commodities which are not in the manufacturing sectors. In the Monetary Policy of 1997–1998, RBI declared the Maximum Permissible Bank Finance (MPBF) method as optional and suggested that commercial banks may evolve their own rational methods for financing. RBI suggested cash budget method as an alternative option. Under cash budget, no tangible security can be created or charged in favour of the bank. Due to non-performing assets, credit appraisal methods are increasingly focusing on the assessment of repayment capacity of the borrower, which in turn depends on cash generating ability.

Sea changes were made by the government in the year 2002 and 2003 by providing with a very strong recovery weapon by means by 'SARFAESIA' (Securitisation and Reconstruction of Financial Assets and Enforcement of Security Interest Act).

The banker evaluates the proposal taking into account the following:

Approval

The banker evaluates whether the proposal project submitted has been approved by the respective bodies.

In the case of a company, there should be provision for such a project in the Memorandum of Association and Articles of Association. In addition to this, the Directors approval is necessary. The banker may satisfy himself as to whether the project has the legal sanction in terms of the required licenses, approvals, and clearances from the appropriate authorities or government.

Technical Feasibility

A new project submitted with the banker for consideration of financial assistance requires a thorough scrutiny. One of the most important considerations affecting the feasibility of the project is the type of technology proposed to be employed by the borrower. The banker ascertains, if necessary, with the help of the experts in the field, as to whether the technology is the latest or outdated, capital intensive or labour intensive, etc. He also examines the borrower's capability in case of changes in the product or shift in consumer preference. The experts may also give their approval after considering the availability of raw materials, labour, fuel, power, water, transport, market technology, etc. Location of the project is another important factor for the success of the project. In case of a manufacturing unit, proper location may be related to adequate supply of raw materials, availability of power, water, labour, and other infrastructural facilities.

Financial Feasibility

The nationalisation of commercial banks in 1969 had a tremendous impact on the lending policies of the commercial banks. The security-oriented approach has been relegated to the background. Instead, the thrust is more on purpose and performance. Due to these changes in the policies, the bankers assess the project on the above lines by examining the financial statements and analysing the balance sheets. The bankers evaluate the project by using certain important techniques of financial evaluation for lending decisions, viz., Ratio Analysis, Break-even Analysis, Cash flow and Funds flow Analysis, Return on Investment, Commercial Feasibility, Managerial Competence and Socio-Economic Viability. These have been dealt with below.

(a) *Ratio Analysis:* Ratio refers to the numerical or quantitative relationship between two items/variables. Although there are many ratios for evaluation of a firm, a banker may use only a few ratios related to his needs. The banker is to judge not only the profitability of the firm but also cash flow in the firm as the repaying capacity of a borrowing concern is not influenced by profit alone. Some of the ratios widely used by the bank at the time of project appraisal are as follows:

(a) $$\text{Current Ratio} = \frac{\text{Current Assets}}{\text{Current Liabilities}} \times 100$$

Current ratio states the relationship between current assets and current liabilities. It is an index of the firm's financial stability. Current assets are cash and other assets which could be converted into cash in the near future. Current assets are cash, short-term investments, bills receivable, book debts, etc. Similarly, current liabilities are those which are to be assets in the near future, viz., creditors, bills payable, income tax, overdraft, etc.

An ideal current ratio is said to be 2:1. A high current ratio is an assurance that the firm will have adequate funds to meet current obligations. However, one of the limitations is that current ratio fails to indicate the rate of liquidity of individual components. For example, a large inventory does not mean cash. In credit analysis, a banker will not be satisfied with the mathematically good current ratio, which is required more in the qualitative aspect of the composition of the current assets.

(b) $$\text{Liquid Ratio} = \frac{\text{Liquid Assets}}{\text{Liquid Liabilities}} \times 100$$

The Liquid ratio of a firm examines the relationship between the liquid assets and liquid liabilities. This can be worked out only if the current assets are classified into liquid assets and deferred assets. Similarly, the current liabilities may be classified as liquid liabilities and deferred payments. This classification can be effected by establishing a single rule that assets and liabilities are liquid if they are expected to be realised or paid within a month. The components of liquid assets are cash, bank, debtors, bills receivable, marketable securities, etc.

(c) $$\text{Net Profit ratio} = \frac{\text{Net Profit}}{\text{Sales}} \times 100$$

Net profit is the relationship between net profit and sales. It indicates the profitability of the business.

(d) $$\text{Debt-Equity Ratio} = \frac{\text{Long Term Debt}}{\text{Shareholders Equity}} \times 100$$

This ratio shows the relationship between borrowed funds and owner's capital. This ratio is used for measuring the long-term financial solvency of a firm. The debt refers to the long-term debt alone and equity may include both ordinary and preference capital but excludes past accumulated losses. It is the ratio of the account invested by with that of the amount contributed by. Since the preference shareholders do not have the voting risks, a doubt has often been expressed as to whether preference capital should be taken into account while computing shareholders' equity. The exact treatment may depend on the purpose for which the ratio is used. If the banker intends to calculate the financial solvency of the firm, preference capital should be included. On the other hand, if the debt-equity ratio is calculated for contribution of earning per share, it need not be taken into account.

(e) $$\text{Capital/Asset ratio} = \frac{\text{Fixed Assets}}{\text{Capital Funds}} \times 100$$

This ratio states the relationship between the fixed assets and paid-up capital + reserves. Fixed assets are taken at its depreciated book value. This ratio may indicate as to whether the long-term funds have been effectively utilised. It may also indicate whether short-term funds have been invested in long-term assets. If any firm has done so, it may land itself sooner or later into financial constraints to meet its immediate obligations. The current ratio in such concerns may not be satisfactory.

(f) $$\text{Cash Flow Ratio} = \frac{\text{Operating profit} + \text{Depreciation}}{\text{Net Sales}} \times 100$$

This ratio enables a banker to assess the cash generating capacity of the firm as well as the extent to which the funds are derived. Some firms may have a good net profit rates. But their cash flow ratio may be poor.

(b) *Break-even Analysis:* Break-even analysis is an analytical technique for studying the relationship between cost, volume, and profit. It is used to determine the efficiency of the profit planning. As the banker is interested in getting back his money, he wants to make sure when the surplus is likely to be received by his unit. He may like to fix the break-even point of sales volume at which the total revenue is equal to the total costs. The break-even point is calculated as follows:

$$\text{Break-even Point} = \frac{\text{Fixed Cost}}{\text{Contribution Per Unit}}$$

Contribution = Selling price – Variable cost (per unit)

The break-even point is one where the firm does not make either profit or loss when it manufactures/sells a particular number of units. It is a point of recovering just the amount that it has spent initially in the manufacturing of the products. This analysis is very important for the banker as the repayment of the term loans is generally scheduled to begin after the break-even point.

Apart from the analysis of data, the facts given in the project proposal are carefully examined and verified. The banker also checks the calculations shown the project report and examines the feasibility report given by the technical experts. The experts may give their comments after considering the availability of raw material, labour, fuel, water, transport, market, technology, etc.

(c) *Cash Flow and Fund Flow Analysis:* Cash flow and funds flow analysis are important analytical tools for a banker for evaluating the employment of funds. Cash flow may be of two types – actual cash flows and notional cash flows. Actual cash flows refer to the actual movement of cash in or out of the business whereas notional cash flow refers to the increase or decrease in the current assets. The cash flow estimates are prepared to indicate the yearly inflow and outflow of funds of the firm covering the entire period of term advance. These estimates would help the banker to schedule the repayment of loan over a period of time, making provisions for certain allowances favouring the borrower. Cash flow and funds flow techniques help the banker to find out from where the funds would come and how such funds would be applied. Once the funds flow and cash flow statements are favourable, it enables the banker to decide the case easily to the advantage of the borrower.

(d) *Return on Investment:* The very first information that a banker seeks in a project report is the returns on the investment. He may compare this with the cost of capital. He may think of further appraisal of the project only if the return on investment is more than the cost of capital. There are four methods to evaluate the return on cost of capital. These are:

(i) Payback period method
(ii) Average rate of return
(iii) Net present value method
(iv) Internal rate of return.

(i) *Payback Period Method*

Payback Period Method is a technique by which the banker finds out the number of years required to recover the original cash outlay invested in a project. The following formula can be adopted for its calculation.

$$\text{Payback Period} = \frac{\text{Cash Outlay}}{\text{Annual Cash Inflow}}$$

One of the limitations of this method is that it does not consider the flow of funds after the payback period. However, it is an usual technique for a banker who lends funds to the borrower.

(ii) *Average Rate of Return* (*ARR*)

Average Rate of Return is a method to determine the average annual profit during the lifetime of the project. It is normally expressed in percentage. The following formula is adopted for its calculation.

$$\text{ARR} = \frac{\text{Annual Average Profit}}{\text{Initial Investment}} \times 100$$

(iii) *Net Present Value Method* (*NPV*)

Net Present Value Method is the most classic method of evaluating the investment proposals. It is one of the discounted cash flow techniques, recognising the time value of money. Under this method, the future costs and revenue are discounted by a required rate of return in order to compare the present value of future benefits with the present value of investments. If the present value of future benefits exceeds the present value of investment, the banker will accept the project, otherwise he may outrightly regret it.

(iv) *Internal Rate of Return* (*IRR*)

Internal Rate of Return is a technique by which the banker matches the present value of future benefits with the present value of the project and finds out the IRR. He may compare the Internal Rate of Return with the expected rate. If the IRR is satisfactory, he may proceed further in evaluating the project.

(e) *Commercial Feasibility:* Commercial feasibility involves the study of the product relating to its current and future demands, market share, fluctuations in demand for the product due to changes in customer preferences or technology, etc. Normally, increase in production may lead to reduction in the cost per unit. But after exceeding a particular limit, it need not be true. The products manufactured by the firm should be sold in the market to enable the producer to move along the operating cycle as the inventory is not cash. The capacity to repay the loans is dependent on the sales revenue of the project.

(f) *Managerial Competence:* The banker also examines the organisational and managerial capabilities of the applicant. Managerial ability is the most essential factor considered by both commercial banks and developed banks in sanctioning the application. Sometimes the profit may be technically sound, commercially viable and financially profitable, but if it cannot be managed properly, it cannot be considered as a worthwhile project. Hence, the banker gives more weightage for the managerial competence of the applicant.

The banker takes into account the controllable and non-controllable factors. The controllable factors are the inputs, viz., money, materials, machines, methods, etc. They are to be scientifically designed and combined. It is very difficult to predict the non-controllable factors like changes in government policy, competitor's behaviour, legal restrictions, political changes, etc. All these factors are carefully visualised in advance before granting loans.

(g) *Socio-economic Viability:* The banker and the financial institutions evaluate the project on the basis of their socio-economic viability. It is an assessment to analyse whether such project, as a whole, brings any social benefit to the nation to fulfill the national objectives. Some of the socio-economic benefits to the nation are employment generation, removal of regional imbalances, minimisation of inequalities in the distribution of income and wealth, development of import substitution, export orientation, development of agriculture and other priority sectors, upliftment of weaker sections of the society, etc. The banker may consider a lower rate of interest, low margin, lower repayment schedule, etc., for certain types of projects. For instance, 4 per cent per annum is charged towards the Deferential Interest Rate (DIR) loans.

In the case of long-term loans, the banker should not undertake any risk and block his capital. The bank normally expects the borrower to prove adequate stake in the cost of the project to ensure this continued interest and care of the project. The owner's contribution should be in the form of risk capital and the balance is provided by the bank.

Reserve Bank Guidelines for follow-up of Bank Credit (Based on the Reports of Tandon and Chore Study Groups)

Apart from performing the traditional function of credit control, the Reserve Bank of India has also played a significant promotional role in bringing about desirable reforms in the system of bank lending. After the nationalisation of major banks (1969, 1980) there has been a sense of direction in bank lending and consequently advances to priority sector have stepped up. The objective of the

RBI has been to establish a system of credit planning in the country. The task of credit planning becomes difficult due to imbalance in the demand and supply of funds for which the banks extend credit under the cash credit system of lending. There are two main defects in the system: (a) the level of advances in a bank is determined not by how much a banker can lend at a particular point of time but by the borrower's decision to borrow at that time (b) cash credit advances are repayable on demand only in name. Realising the drawbacks in the cash credit system, the RBI appointed in July 1974, a study group under the chairmanship of Shri P L Tandon, to frame guidelines to the follow-up of bank credit.

The important terms of reference for the study group were as follows:

- To suggest criteria regarding satisfactory capital structure and sound financial basis in relation to borrowings
- To make recommendations for obtaining from borrowers' periodical forecast of business production plans, and credit needs
- To make recommendations regarding the source of financing the minimum working capital requirements
- To make suggestions for presenting inventories for different industries both in private and public sectors and indicate the broad criteria for deviating from these norms
- To make recommendations as to whether the existing pattern of financing working capital requirements by way of cash credit/overdraft system, etc., requires to be modified. If so, suggest suitable modifications.

Reserve Bank of India Guidelines Based on Tandon Committee Report

The study group submitted its final report in August 1975. It suggested norms for 15 major industries. These norms suggested by the study group and accepted by the RBI have been given below:

(a) These norms are to be applied in respect of both the existing and new borrowers with immediate effect. All fresh proposals (including those from the existing borrowers seeking enhanced credit facilities) may be regulated by these norms

(b) In the case of all existing borrowers, if their levels of inventories and receivables are excessive on the basis of suggested norms, the matter should be discussed with them and a programme for a phased reduction worked out therein

(c) The new policy is applicable to all industrial borrowers including small-scale industries obtaining credit facilities exceeding INR 10 lakhs are covered too. The RBI has issued directions to all commercial banks with deposits of INR 50 crores and above for implementing the new inventory norms

(d) The industries may have to pay a higher rate of interest if these happen to continue to hold excess inventories. Even in the case of such industries not covered by the present norms, the banks will have general supervision. The banks exercise control with due flexibility and understanding of the circumstances, which sometimes mean deviation from the norms for a temporary period.

Approach to Lending_

The Study Group was of the opinion that:

(a) the borrower should be expected to hold only a reasonable level of current assets in relation to his production requirements. The working capital gap has been defined as total current assets minus current liabilities other than bank borrowings. The working capital group of the borrower could be bridged partly from his own funds and long-term borrowings and partly through bank borrowings.

(b) the banks should supplement the borrower's resources to enable the latter to carry on acceptable level of current assets. In the light of the above approach, the group suggested these methods for working out in maximum permissible bank borrowings to meet the working capital gap. It is to be noted that each successive method is intended to increase progressively by the involvement of long-term funds comprising the borrower's owned funds and as term borrowings to support the current assets. The three methods are as follows:

   (i) The bank can workout the working capital gap, that is, total current assets, minus current liabilities other than bank borrowings and finance a maximum of 75 per cent of the gap. The balance is to be met by owned funds and term loans. This will be a minimum current ratio of 1:1.

   (ii) The borrower is to provide a minimum of 25 per cent of total current assets out of long-term funds (i.e., owned funds plus borrowings). Total amount liabilities inclusive of bank borrowings will not exceed 75 per cent of current assets. The current ratio is of at least 3:1.

   (iii) The borrower will have to contribute a minimum of entire core current assets and minimum of 25 per cent of the balance current assets. The core current assets should be financed out of long-term funds.

Style of Credit

(a) The Study Group also suggested the need to change the style of extending bank credit. As recommended by the group, instead of making available the entire credit limit as cash credit, banks may bifurcate the accommodation into loan comprising the minimum level of borrowing which the borrower expects to use throughout the year and into demand cash credit to meet the fluctuating requirements. Both of these limits are to be reviewed annually and within the overall availability. Bill limits may also be allowed.

(b) The group has also suggested that priority should be given to bill finance against seller's receivables over cash credit against book debts. The proposed system of lending may be extended to all borrowers with credit limits in excess of INR 10 lakhs from the banking system on them extended progressively to others.

(c) With a view to bring about a discipline in the use of bank credit, the study group also suggested a slightly higher rate of interest for demand cash credit component. Accepting this recommendation, the RBI asked banks to charge differential rates of interest to implement the Study Group's credit norms.

(d) RBI has directed the banks that the interest rate on demand cash credit should be higher by one per cent than the rate on the loan component that on term loan representing surplus borrowing to be depreciated higher by half a per cent than cash credit.

(e) Banks were required to start charging differential rates from the time the borrower's accounts were bifurcated as described above or at the time of considering additional credit limits in case of borrowers seeking enhancement.

(f) The directives are based on the assumption that the lower rate of interest on the loan component will give the borrower an incentive for more effective planning of his credit requirements.

(g) The Study Group also devised an information system to be introduced by the banks. The group has recommended for submission of an operating statement and funds flow statement for the whole year and also a projected balance sheet as at the end of the year by the borrower.

(h) In future while financing new projects, the term-lending institutions may proceed for margins on the basis of the recommended proposals and the bank which finance the working capital as margin requirements.

(i) Stock statement will continue to be submitted, but they need to be improved on the basis of valuation of stock statements and the balance sheet should be uniform.

(j) The proposed system of lending and the style of credit may be extended to all borrowers having credit limit in excess of INR 10 lakhs from the banking system.

(k) Management competence is an important factor in the efficiency operation reflected in profitability and working capital and financial management.

(l) The recommendations regarding inventory/receivables, norms and mechanics of lending are to be viewed as a package. It is an integrated scheme and the borrower is expected to subject himself to the entire discipline envisaged.

(m) For the purpose of better control, there should be a system of borrower classification in each bank. The only feasible manner in which the banker can satisfy himself with regard to end use of funds would be to ensure, by calling for appropriate operational data and figures relating to financial position at periodical intervals.

(n) While financing trade, banks should keep in view inter alia the extent of owned funds of the borrower in relation to the credit limits granted, the annual turnover.

(o) In the case of consortium advances or where a borrower is financed by more than one bank, the concerned banks should evolve a procedure to ensure a uniform handling of the account in confirming with the inventory and receivable norms on the financial discipline suggested.

(p) The Indian Bankers' Association has an important role to play in a study of the environment and particularly the impact of regulations and enactments on working of banks.

(q) Inventory receivable norms should be given effect to immediately, while action should be initiated to implement the new approach to lending within the time-bound schedule.

(r) Banks should conduct training sessions for their operating officials.

(s) Seminars may be convened in the Bankers' Training College where operating officials can find solutions to any operational problems.

(t) Steps should be taken simultaneously to introduce suggested information system for all industrial borrowers with limits aggregating INR 1 crore.

(u) Special courses should be organised by the National Institute of Bank Management and the Bankers' Training College for training the bank's operating officials.

(v) To facilitate inter-firm and industry-wise comparisons for assessing efficiencies, companies in the same industry could be grouped under three or four categories, say, according to size and the group-wise financial ratio compiled by RBI for furnishing to banks.

(w) Besides examining financial and operational ratio, certain productivity ratios may also be examined to determine labour efficiency, capital efficiency, and fixed assets efficiency.

(x) For the purpose of better control, there should be a system of borrower classification in each bank. This will facilitate easy identification of the borrowers whose affairs require to be watched with more than ordinary care and will also provide a rational base for the purpose of fixing rates of interest for the respective borrowers.

Chore Committee Report on Cash Credit System

In 1979, the RBI set up a working group to review the cash credit system under the chairmanship of Shri K B Chore, Chief Officer in the Department of Banking Operations and Development. The working group made a number of recommendations which were accepted by the RBI with certain modifications. The salient features of the guidelines issued by the RBI in December 1980 are as follows:

(a) The Chore Committee examined various forms of lending – overdraft, cash credit, discounting bills of exchange and loans and advances. After analysing the merits and demerits of each system, it was found that no system is superior to the other. It was also found that there was a credit gap. However, the committee could not find any evidence to show that the gap was misused. It was pointed out that the unused gap in the public sector units was much more than in the private sector.

(b) It was clearly pointed out that it would be difficult to replace the cash credit system totally by any other system. Therefore, the periodical review of credit limits and streamlining the system were recommended. An annual review of all borrowers' accounts exceeding INR 10 lakhs as working capital was suggested. Borrowers having working capital limits of INR 50 lakhs and over from the banking system are required to submit quarterly statements.

(c) Bifurcation of cash credit limit into a demand loan position and a fluctuating cash credit component has not found acceptance either on the parts of the bank or the borrower. Such bifurcation may not serve the purpose of better credit planning by narrowing the gap between sanctioned limits and the extension of utilisation thereof.

(d) The advantages of the existing system of extending credit by a combination of three types of lending, namely cash credit, loan and overdraft should be retained. At the same time it is necessary to give some directional changes to ensure that wherever possible the use of cash credit would be supplemented by loans and bills.

(e) Banks are required to fix credit limit for the normal peak level and non-peak level credit needs of the borrowers, wherever feasible. These separate limits are to be fixed on the basis of utilisation of such limits in the past. The period during which they have to be utilised is also to be specified. Separate limits needs to be fixed in case of all agriculture-based industries and consumer goods industries having seasonal demands. For others, only one limit is to be fixed.

(f) Each borrower shall have to submit two quarterly statements to his bank as given below:

(i) Statement giving estimates of production, sales, stock position, and current liabilities (to be submitted in the week preceeding the beginning of a quarter).

(ii) Statements showing actual performance in the quarter (to be submitted within six weeks from the end of the quarter). On the basis of these statements, the banks are required to prepare the quarterly review of accounts.

(g) Banks should carefully consider requests for adhoc/temporary limits in excess of the sanctioned limits to meet unforeseen contingencies. Such limits should be allowed for pre-determined short duration and may be in the form of a separate demand loan or 'non-operable' cash credit account, bearing an additional interest of 2 per cent over the normal rate. If the borrower in such a case is unable to provide corresponding additional contribution, the bank may ignore the same.

(h) Banks should advise their own checklists in the light of the instructions issued by the RBI for the scrutiny of data at the operational level.

(i) Banks should give particular attention to monitor the key branches and critical accounts.

(j) Banks should review the system of financing book debts through cash credit and insist on the conversion of such cash credit limits into bill limits.

(k) In case of a large borrower, who is already enjoying credit limits with another bank/banks, no bank shall grant any credit facility without the consent of the existing banker. Thus, concurrence of the main bank and/or the banks which have already sanctioned inventory limit is essential for opening new accounts or for sanctioning post-sales limits to a borrower.

(l) To encourage bill system of financing and to facilitate call money operations, autonomous financial institutions on the lines of the discount houses in the USA may be set up.

(m) Banks are permitted to grant additional credit limits to the borrowers, if such higher limits become necessary due to increased production. But they must insist on the incremental current ratio of 1.33:1, and no increase in the working capital term loan (WCTL) component.

(n) The communication channels, systems, and procedures within the banking system should be toned up so as to ensure that minimum time is taken for collection of instruments.

(o) The borrower would be required to submit his budgeted requirements in triplicate and copy of each would be sent immediately by the branch to the controlling office and head office for record.

(p) Under the existing guidelines, export units having export activities need not bring in any contribution from their long-term sources towards financing that portion of current assets as if represented by export receivables.

(q) Under the revised guidelines, banks must obtain from all borrowers enjoying aggregate fund-based working capital credit limit of INR 1 crore and more from the banking system, the statements prescribed under the quarterly information system/monthly cash budget system(the cut-off rate was INR 50 lakhs earlier).

(r) Banks would continue to invariably charge penal interest of at least 1 per cent per annum for a period of one quarter on the outstandings under various capital limits sanctioned to a borrower who fails to submit any of the above referred statements.

(s) Credit control measures to be effective will have to be immediately communicated to the operational level and followed up. The central officers of the banks should take a second look at the credit budget as soon as changes in credit policy are announced by the RBI and revise their plan of action in the light of the new policy and correct the connective measures to the operational levels as quickly as possible.

(t) No conclusive data are available to establish the degree of correlation between production and quantum of credit at the reducing level. As this issue is obviously of great concern to the monetary authorities, the RBI may undertake a detailed scientific study in this regard.

Nayak Committee Recommendations

In 1992, the committee examined the adequacy of institutional credit to the small-scale industries sector and related aspects under the chairmanship of Shri P R Nayak, submitted its report to RBI. The committee has made major recommendations regarding sanctioning and following of credit to the SSI (Small-Scale Industry) sector. As per the committee report:

(a) The SSI sector has received a level of working capital which was only 0.1 per cent of its output. The village industries and the smaller tiny industries among the sector got working capital finance to the extent of only about 2.7 per cent of their output.

(b) The banks may satisfy themselves about the reasonables of the projected annual turnover on the basis of annual statements and other related documents to ensure the realistic growth density of the year. The SSI units should also bring in 5 per cent of their annual turnover as margin money.

(c) At present, norms for inventory and receivable are applicable to all units enjoying aggregate fund-based working capital credit limit of INR 10 lakhs and above from the banking system. As per the new norms, the first method of lending (under lending norms) will not apply to all those industries under this sector which are enjoying aggregate fund-based working capital credit limits ranging from INR 10 lakhs to INR 50 lakhs. Instead, such amounts may be provided to working capital limits computed on the basis of minimum of 20 per cent of their projected annual turnover for new as well as existing units.

(d) In case where output exceeds projections, where the initial assessment of working capital is found inadequate, suitable enhancement in the working capital limits should be considered by the competent authority as and when this is deemed necessary.

(e) SSI units having aggregate fund-based working capital limits of above INR 50 lakhs would continue to be governed by the existing guidelines on lending norms, method of lending, etc.

(f) As a part of the rehabilitation package, the interest on the Working Capital Term Loan (WCTL) has been modified as under. The rate of interest applicable may be 1.5 to 3 per cent points below the prevailing fixed rate/minimum lending rate, whenever applicable, but not more than the lowest lending rate for tiny decentralised sector units and not more than 5 per cent points below the minimum lending rate in the case of advances of over INR 2 lakhs, that is, the highest lending rate for the other SSI units.

In October 1993, RBI slightly relaxed the method of calculation of Maximum Permissible Bank Finance (MPBF). Since October 1993, one-third of instalments are to be treated as current liability, unless the loan has been re-scheduled by the financial institutions/banks. The entire amount of term loan due within twelve months will continue to be current liability for the purpose of computing the current ratio. This will enhance the maximum permissible bank finance.

In April 1997, RBI withdrew the instructions relating to maximum permissible bank finance and permitted the banks to evolve their own method of assessing the working capital requests of borrowers within the prudential guidelines and exposure norms. RBI has suggested the following alternatives:

- The turnover method for small borrowers may be continued as a tool of assessment for this sector
- Banks may follow cash budget system for assessment of working capital finance of large borrowers

- Banks may retain the present Maximum Permissible Bank Finance (MPBF) system with necessary modifications
- The loan policy in respect of each broad category of reduction shall be laid down by every bank with the approval of its board.

Cash Budget System

The current loan policies of most of the banks state for assessing the working capital needs of a borrower who enjoy or require fund based limits in excess of INR 10 crores to use the cash budget system.

A cash budget is a statement of cash receipts and cash payments. It is distinct from cash flow statement, as the latter deals both with cash and non-cash funds, while the cash budget deals with cash transactions only. Cash budget is a substitute for the operating cycle method for assessment of working capital requirements. A cash budget is usually prepared for short periods, that is, a week/fortnight/month/quarter.

Cash budget has got following steps in sequence when preparing for a quarter.

(a) Actual receipts and payments during 1st, 2nd, and 3rd months.
(b) The position of cash surplus/deficit is then computed at monthly intervals. A surplus is generated if receipts exceed payment and a cash deficit occurs if payment is more than receipt during the month.
(c) The opening cash balance for the 1st month is adjusted with the cash surplus/deficit generated during the month. The adjusted figure is the closing balance at the end of 1st month, this becomes the opening balance for the next month viz., 2nd month.
(d) A cash surplus generated during a month results in a higher closing cash balance vis-à-vis the opening balance of the month. Conversely, a cash deficit during the month would cause a lower level of closing cash balance compared to the opening balance.
(e) If the enterprise has a net position of borrowed funds (i.e. the company maintains a cash credit/overdraft account), a cash surplus generated during a month brings down the level of the borrowed funds at the end of the month.

A cash budget is, therefore, a projection into the future as against a cash flow statement that is usually historical in nature. Cash budgets are essential for:

(a) Opening letters of credit.
(b) Ad hoc working capital.
(c) Bill financing.
(d) Financing construction activities.
(e) Financing seasonal industries.

(f) Tea growing.
(g) Sugar manufacturing.
(h) Software development activities.
(i) Coffee/rubber/cardamom agriculture/rice milling, etc.

Advantages

Short-term lending on the basis of cash budget offers a viable alternative in the existing security-oriented pattern of credit allocation by banks. The main advantages of the cash budget system are:

(a) The customer plans his cash requirement in advance and in case his balance is unable to layout additional funds, the customer can seek alternative sources well in advance.
(b) The banker is in close touch with his customers. He would, therefore, be able to spot danger signals quickly and initiate corrective action on time.
(c) The banker can plan his resources to meet expected credit demands. Credit planning would, thus, become a meaningful exercise.

Credit Management

Credit management is the management of credit portfolio of bankers and financial institutions. The expression "credit" refers to short-term loans and advances as well as to medium/long-term and off balance sheet transactions. Management includes within its purview pre-sanction, appraisal sanction, documentation, disbursement and disbursal and post-lending supervision and control.

Credit management is no longer a "Rule of Thumb" game. In a highly competitive and deregulated environment, banks and financial institutions have to evolve better system and procedures to manage the credit needs of highly demanding customer, particularly in the corporate and retail sectors. The development of the past decade have totally changed the prospective of management of credit. Credit management now includes:

(a) Capital adequacy norms
(b) Exposure norms
(c) Risk management including Asset Liability Management(ALM)
(d) Risk pricing policy and credit risk rating
(e) Asset classification, income recognition, and provisioning norms
(f) Appraisal, credit decision-making, and loan review mechanism.

Capital adequacy of banks is essential as per Bassel Agreement. Now all banks are required to have 10 per cent of paid up capital and reserves to meet risk weightage of credit provided to borrowers w.e.f. 31 March 2004. The capital fund is the sum total of Tier I and Tier II capital recognised for the purpose of computation of capital adequacy.

From 1 April 2002, the exposure ceiling is 15 per cent of capital funds in case of single borrower and 40 per cent in the case of a group of borrowers. Exposure to borrowers belonging to a group may exceed the exposure norms of 40 per cent of the bank's capital funds by an additional 10 per cent of total up to 50 per cent provided the additional exposure is on account of extension of credit to all infrastructure projects.

Several risks affect credit decisions. The main risks are credit risk, marked risk, (mainly liability risk/interest rate risk), and operational risk. Credit risk is defined as the possibility of losses associated with diminution in the credit quality of borrowers or counter parties. Such risks are:

(a) Principal/interest amount may not be paid.
(b) Funds may not be forthcoming from clients upon invocation of letters of credit, guarantees.
(c) Payments or series of payments due from the counter parties may not be coming in case of treasury operations.
(d) Funds/securities settlement may not be affected in securities trading.
(e) Availability and free transfer of foreign currency funds may either cease or restrictions may be imposed by the sovereign.

RBI defined market risk as one possibility of loss to bank caused by changes in market variable which are: (a) liquidity risk (b) interest rate risk (c) foreign exchange rate risk (d) commodity price risk (e) equity price risk.

Assets and liability management committee functions as the top operational unit for the bank. Banks also face another risk known as operational risk. The operational risk arises from human or technical error or acts of omission and commission such as ineffectiveness or breakdown of the internal control and internal audit systems. The risk can lead to losses through fraud, error or failure in performance in a timely manner. Operational risk includes legal risk but excludes strategic and reputational risk.

Advances portfolio of banks has been classified under four categories. These are:

(a) Standard asset – performing assets
(b) Sub-standard – non-performing up to two years
(c) Non-performing – non-performing three years to over five years
(d) Loss making – negligible realisable value with salvage value of 1 per cent of total outstanding.

The provision required under first three categories are as given below.

(a) Standard assets @ 0.25 per cent
(b) Sub-standard @ 10 per cent
(c) Doubtful @ between 20 per cent to 50 per cent of the secured and 100 per cent for unsecured position.

The impact of the appraisal record at the time of fresh sanction or extensions should be reflected in the credit risk rating as per the risk pricing policy of the bank. The position should be periodically reviewed with the concerned borrowers and remedial measures recorded and implemented without loss of time.

Notices for renewal or reviews of loan accounts must be sent to borrowers well in advance. Although renewal for working capital advance are done annually, for loan accounts showing signs of deteriorating credit risk, quarterly short reviews should be conducted. Close monitoring of loan accounts with high or deteriorating credit risk by branches and controlling officers and/or head office will ensure that the overall risk exposure of the bank is controlled.

Credit Monitoring

To ensure that the funds are utilised for the sanctioned purposes/employing with terms and conditions/to avoid time lag and cost overruns/to detect easily warning signals and systems of sickness for initiating timely action for recovery or rehabilitation.

In October 1988, the RBI introduced the post-sanction scrutiny of large borrower limits, working capital limits of INR 10 crores and term loan limits of INR 5 crores sanctioned by banks. RBI subjects such proposals sanctioned by the banks to close scrutiny and if they consider the limits sanctioned as unjustified they may reduce the limits.

Under Credit Monitoring Management (CMA), RBI gives various directions to banks and borrowers with a view to ensure credit discipline. Some of such important provisions are as follows:

(a) Borrowers should maintain reasonable estimates of current assets, current liabilities and working capital.
(b) Should maintain classification of current assets and current liabilities as per bank guidelines.
(c) Should maintain minimum current ration of 25 per cent except for export industry and for new units.
(d) Quarterly Information System (QIS) should be submitted in time.
(e) Should submit annual audited accounts in time and banks should review them annually.
(f) Ad hoc limits may be sanctioned for periods not exceeding three months, subject to report to RBI.
(g) Bill financing should be for atleast 75 per cent of credit sales.
(h) Bank should forward a copy of board memo sanctioning the credit limit to RBI along with the balance sheet of the company and Credit Monitoring Arrangement (CMA) data within 15 days of sanction.

(i) From December 1997 the above system has been discontinued and now RBI needs to be reported on monthly basis in the Form I/V/VI.

Credit Monitoring by Kannan Committee (1997)

The mercantile community were complaining to RBI that the method of assessment for inventory and receivable and insisting for 1.33 current ratio by the Tandon Committee were not providing them enough credit. Shri K Kannan, Chairman and Managing Director of Bank of Baroda was appointed to look into the above problem.

The suggestions given by Shri K. Kannan are:

(a) New method of lending based on cash flow or the borrower called cash budget bifurcating into monthly or quarterly.
(b) Deficit about determining the limits/assessment of working capital/margin to be kept/holding levels of stocks/book debts/QIS forms and regulation are all left at the discretion of banks.
(c) Deficit in cash budget would be financed by banks.

The committee has suggested that monitoring through periodical statements of stocks/bank debts/coupled with physical verification of securities business site of the borrower to be the basic credit monitoring tool of the banks. The borrower should also give data relating to production, sales and other information and which working capital assessment is made by the financing bank. Annual verification of current assets including compliance of pollution control requirement (where applicable) by borrower's auditor in respect of borrowers with working capital limits over INR 5 crores) should be insisted. Alternatively, the company may also engage Chartered Accountant/Chartered Engineer, Architect, as may deem fit for the purpose.

Laxminarayan Committee (1973) Consortium Arrangements for Working Capital Lending

The object was to evolve guidelines which would ensure better coordination and cooperation among banks with respect to multiple banks.

Suggestion

RBI's advise to banks in 1978 and 1979 were as given below:

(a) Consortium arrangements is obligatory where the aggregate credit limits to a single party amounts to INR 5 crores or more.
(b) Share of each member bank should not be less than 10 per cent of total requirements. Maximum members of a consortium should not normally exceed five except, where the limits are very large, say above INR 50 crores.

(c) Consortium committee consisting of lead bank and one or to two other banks should be entrusted with appraisal.
(d) Banks were advised that ancilliary business of borrowers, for example, guarantees, letter of credit, etc., should as far as possible be shared by a number of banks.

Vaz Committee (1993)

The committee recommended the turnover method of assessment as recommended by Nayak Committee to all categories of borrowers up to INR 1 crore. RBI subsequently raised this turnover method of assessment to INR 2 crores for all categories of borrowers.

Shetty Committee for Consortium Advances

The Shetty committee submitted its report in August 1994 and recognised the need to shift to market driven banking from the current system. The main features of recommendations are:

(a) Banks are free to leave a consortium after a minimum benefit of two years.
(b) Documentation under single-window concept is to be adopted.
(c) Minimum share by a single bank should at least be 5 per cent of the credit limit or INR 1 crore whichever is higher.
(d) Consortium finance was obligatory if the fund-based working capital limits to a single borrower exceeded INR 5 crores, now enhanced to INR 50 crores.
(e) Alternative route to adopt from sole/multiple banking/consortium arrangement, banks are free to adopt syndication route.
(f) Individual bank's exposure to a single borrower should not exceed 25 per cent of net worth of the bank, income of borrowers' group should not exceed 50 per cent.
(g) Size of consortium should not exceed five members except for higher credit limits it may go up to ten members. Now this limit ceiling is removed.
(h) Maximum time frame prescribed for disposal of proposals are, sanction/fresh/enhanced credit limits – 60 days; renewals of existing limits – 45 days; sanction of ad hoc liabilities – 30 days.

Non-Performing Assets

A loan is classified as non-performing when the interest and/or instalment of principal remain overdue for a period of more than 90 days w.e.f. 31 March 2004. A loan/advance shall be NPA where:

(a) Interest and/or instalment of principal remains overdue for a period of more than 90 days in respect of a term loan.
(b) The bill remains overdue for a period of more than 90 days in the case of bills purchased and discounted.
(c) The accounts remains out of order for a period of more than 90 days, in respect of the overdraft/cash credit/hypothecation in case of bills purchased and discounted.
(d) Any amount to be received remains overdue for a period of more than 90 days in respect of other accounts.
(e) If one facility of a borrower is classified as NPA, then all the facilities are to the classified as NPA.
(f) Staff loans which are problematic cases to be treated as NPA.
(g) The outstanding in the account based on drawing power calculated from stock statements older than three months.
(h) Non-renewal of regular/ad hoc limits within 180 days from the due date will be treated as NPA.
(i) Advances granted against National Savings Certificates (NSC), Indira Vikas Patra (IVP), Life Insurance Corporation (LIC) policies, Kisan Vikas Patra (KVP) if outstanding beyond the realisable value/ surrender value are treated as NPA.
(j) Project financing/Agricultural plantations, etc., where moratorium for payment of interest/instalment is granted, the accounts need not be treated as NPA till the period is over.
(k) Interest and/or instalment of principal remains overdue for two harvest seasons but for a period not exceeding two-and-a-half years in the case of an advance granted for agricultural purposes.
(l) Advance granted to unit which are placed under rehabilitation package approved by BIFR (Board of Industrial Financial Reconstruction); Term Lending Institutes (TLIs) are treated as NPA and provisions are required to be made. However, for additional credit facilities sanctions to units under rehabilitation package approved by BIFR/TLI provision need not be made for a period of one year from the date of disbursement.

3

Nationalisation of Banks in India

Soon after independence, the demand for the nationalisation of banks in India was raised by some of those members of the Congress party who had pronounced leaning towards the Left, and by some of the members of the socialist and communist parties. They had been thinking about some means which would hasten the slow pace of the economic development of the country, and felt that the nationalisation of banks would be a valuable means of achieving this.

The nationalisation of the RBI in 1949 was the first step in this direction. Another was passing of the Banking Companies Act in 1949. The Act gave extensive controlling powers to the RBI and the government over the joint-stock banks. The Imperial Bank of India was nationalised in 1955 and renamed as the "State Bank of India".

Nationalisation of banks was considered to be one of the measures to achieve the objective of growth with distributive justice. In order to stimulate economic growth and promote all sectors of the economy, it was considered essential to nationalise the banks.

The Government of India, therefore, nationalised fourteen major banks with deposits of INR 50 crores or more on 19 July 1969 and another six banks in 1980. Their takeover was intended "to serve better the needs of development of the economy in conformity with national priorities and objectives".

The nationalised banks were:

(a) The Central Bank of India
(b) The Bank of India
(c) The Punjab National Bank
(d) The Bank of Baroda
(e) The United Commercial Bank
(f) The Canara Bank
(g) The United Bank of India
(h) The Dena Bank
(i) The Syndicate Bank
(j) The Union Bank of India
(k) The Allahabad Bank
(l) The Indian Bank
(m) The Bank of Maharashtra and
(n) The Indian Overseas Bank.

On 15 April 1980, six more banks in the private sector were nationalised. These banks were:

(a) The Andhra Bank Limited
(b) Corporation Bank Limited
(c) The New Bank of India Limited
(d) The Oriental Bank of Commerce Limited
(e) The Punjab and Sind Bank Limited
(f) The Vijaya Bank Limited.

The objective of this nationalisation was to enhance the ability of the banking system, to meet more effectively the needs of the development of the economy and to promote the welfare of the people adequately. The amount to be paid in respect of the transfer of undertakings of the six banks was INR 18.50 crores. The demand and time liabilities of these banks on 14 March 1980 were about INR 200 crores. With the nationalisation of 20 banks, the number of public sector banks increased to 28 (comprising the State Bank of India and its 7 subsidiaries and 20 nationalised banks) exclusive of regional rural banks. These banks accounted for 91 per cent of the total deposits and credit of commercial banks in April 1980.

The Indian banking industry is very traditional in practice and outlook, and is not particularly well endowed with managerial competence, particularly of the innovative kind required to break new ground and make credit a more purposeful instrument of social policy. This requires an altogether different kind of expertise and experience at various levels, which is in short supply. The National Institute of Bank Management, Mumbai and many more banker's training colleges have been opened to conduct research and train bank officials for this purpose.

The nationalised banks play a new and pioneering role in helping the public sector stand on its feet. Current notions of public accountability have made severe in-roads into the autonomy of public undertakings, while close association with the secretariat in terms of officials, protocol, procedures and personnel has resulted in a certain bureaucratisation in their outlook. Public undertakings would turn to the banks for financial assistance which would only be advanced on the basis of techno-economic feasibility and commercial viability of any given proposal or project. Banks would probably be in a better position to evaluate the working of a project than the secretariat and would not have to answer questions on the manner of management in parliament every other day.

In order that it may become an effective instrument for the mobilisation of savings and the distribution of credit along socially desirable lines, bank nationalisation must be related to a larger policy framework from which a series of mutually compatible programmes derive. It may not be correct to assume that nationalisation would necessarily make the economy more socialist. Everything will depend on how the nationalised banks are managed, the type of supporting policies adopted, and how vigorously they are implemented. In their actual working, it is even possible for the nationalised banks to build up and support interests in agriculture and industry which are very different from those that the advocates of nationalisation had in mind. If effectively implemented and followed up, nationalisation would prove an extremely important step in the management of credit. On the other hand, if banks do not function effectively, nationalisation may promote serious dislocations and distortions in the economy, and transfer of deposits may take place from the nationalised banks to the smaller banks (private sector).

The broad objectives of the government's decision to nationalise the fourteen major banks in 1969 were summed up by the then Prime Minister Mrs Indira Gandhi in the Parliament on 21 July 1969 as follows:

"While the nation is committed to establish a socialist pattern of society, the Government felt that the public ownership and control of the commanding heights of the national economy and its strategic sector were essential and important aspects of the new social order which we are trying to build. All the financial institutions are amongst the most important levers for the achievement of its social objectives, the nationalisation of major banks was felt a significant step in the process of public ownership over the principal institution for the mobilisation of people's savings and canalising them towards productive purposes. The Government felt that the public ownership of the major banks will help in the most effective mobilisation and development of national resources so that our objectives can be realised with a great degree of assurance".

Arguments for Nationalisation of Banks

Economists offer some arguments for nationalisation of banks:

(a) It was alleged that private banks had facilitated the concentration of economic power in a few hands and in the creation of industrial or business monopolies. The commercial banks were owned and controlled by a very small number of shareholders who were able to decide the pattern of allocation and investments of bank finance according to their whims and fancies. The large business houses became virtually monopolistic powers. The directive principles of the Indian constitution are against the excessive concentration of economic power and wealth in a few hands and hence the need for nationalisation.

(b) Even though agriculture was the basic industry in the country and occupied a prominent position in the economy, the private commercial banks were indifferent to the credit needs of the agricultural sector. Commercial banks had failed to contribute to the development of the vital primary sector in the economy viz., agriculture and small-scale industries.

(c) A charge was also levelled against commercial banks that their resources were being misused for the benefit of directors and their concerns. The manipulation of bank advances helped in building up inventories and hoarding as well as speculative activities and creation of artificial scarcity as a result of which continued price spirals took place in our economy. Nationalisation of banks would help in stabilising the price by eliminating/levelling artificial scarcity of essential goods and encouraging the exploitation of bank credit for productive purposes.

(d) The All-India Bank Employees' Association (AIBEA) contended that state monopoly in banking would check the incidence of tax evasion and black money.

(e) It was also hoped that nationalisation would bring down the excessive emoluments of the top executives of some private banks, who were receiving unduly high salaries than their counterparts in the public sector. Further, wide disparities in the salaries in different commercial banks would be removed when banks were under state control.

(f) The banks in India were catering to the requirements of large business houses and they were not accessible to small businesses. These small firms had to raise funds from the unorganised money market at exorbitant rates of interest depending mostly on friends and relatives. It was felt that nationalisation will create confidence in the minds of young entrepreneurs and nationalised banks will be more accessible to the small and dynamic entrepreneurs and hence the need for nationalisation of private banks.

(g) In developing economies, commercial banks act as trustees in promoting national interest and institutions for catering to the financial needs of the common people. They thus acquire the status of a public utility. Hence, like other public utilities, the banking sector was also the most legitimate field of public ownership and control.

(h) For the all-round progress of the Indian economy, and in the general interest of the country, for the welfare of the people and for the purpose of mobilisation of potential resources of the community for development, control of production system was regarded as an important factor. Further, the policy of Indian economic planning was towards assigning an increased role to the public sector. Thus, state ownership of the banking system could be regarded as an essential condition for successful planning in the country. The Government of India can make use of the resources of the bank for financing the plans with greater vigour and government may be successful in realising the plan objectives.

(i) It was contended that nationalisation of banks would safeguard and promote the interest of depositors, as the board of directors of the joint-stock banks were resorting to many malpractices. Nationalisation would promote the confidence of the public in the banks, thereby bringing about a rapid and very large increase in deposits and prevent bank failures and strengthen the banking system.

(j) The leftists argued that since the banking sector commanded an enormous economic power, it was desirable that in the interest of the community and furtherance of socialism, commercial banks should be nationalised soon.

(k) The sole objective of the private commercial banks was profit motive and the commercial banks failed to open branches in small towns and villages. As a result, they had failed to mobilise the savings of the community, especially the rural sector and the lower income groups. Nationalisation of banks would replace the profit motive by service motive in the functioning of the banks, thereby helping greatly in achieving the goal of socialism.

(l) If all the commercial banks are nationalised, the RBI would be in a position to implement its monetary policy more effectively. It would also facilitate a perfect harmony of monetary and fiscal policies. A central bank (RBI) can have effective control and financial authority only when the entire system is integrated which is possible only under state monopoly of banking sector.

(m) Distribution of credit by the nationalised banks would be much more efficient as it would flow into productive and socially desirable channels, and its credit would be relatively less costly. It would also evolve service consciousness among the bank employees and bring about a much greater efficiency of operation and management. Nationalisation would also secure standardisation of banking services in the country. The employees will have confidence in their employment, will work with a sense of purpose, with great amount of motivation, and will work fearlessly for the good of the organisation and in the interest of the general public.

(n) It is possible to help the young entrepreneurs, small businessmen, small farmers, and weaker sections of the society by providing loans at a lower rate of interest on priority basis only when banks are nationalised. Banks in the private sector may have profit as the only goal and they may not bother to help the young entrepreneurs. For rapid development of the economy and for bridging the gap between the poor and rich and for backing up young and educated persons with ideas but without finance, nationalisation was necessary.

Arguments Against Nationalisation of Banks

While some economists favour nationalisation of banks, others give arguments against it.

(a) It was incorrect to say that commercial banks were responsible for creating monopolies and concentration of economic power in a few hands, in fact, it was the operation of government policies of industrial import and other licensing and of plan priorities that had encouraged some big concerns to come into existence and flourish. Bank finances were made available to these concerns only because they have been assigned a vital and commanding role in the economic set-up, planned and assigned by the government. If these firms were denied bank credit, it would not have been possible for them to run their business, and their failure would have meant a wastage of community's resources. Thus, what the private banks did was in the general interest of the nation. Moreover, large credits were not granted only by banks in the private sector. Most of the state owned corporations and many of the big industrial companies in the private sector borrowed from the SBI and its subsidiaries. Further, although representation of big concerns were with bank managements, they did not have the freedom to lend in any associated way they liked. The lending operations of bank management were conditioned and governed by the requirements of planned economic development and RBI's credit policy.

(b) Banks function on "confidence". If the banks fail to gain the confidence of the customers they simply collapse. Nationalisation cannot be a substitute for confidence. The government could build proper checks and balances in an appropriate manner and see that the depositors are not disillusioned with the banks. The RBI and Deposit Insurance and Credit Corporation can function effectively in safe-guarding the interests of the customers of the bank.

(c) Those who vehemently opposed nationalisation of banks pointed towards the existing government run institutions and the way they were functioning over the world. They feared that nationalisation would lead to delayed decisions, political interference in policy making at all levels, and the banks would ultimately suffer from gross inefficiency.

(d) Leaders of opposition parties expressed the fear that complete nationalisation of banking would give vast powers to the ruling party, which would jeopardise the healthy growth of democracy in the country.

(e) Banks were not at all responsible for the evasion of taxes or for the creation of black money. It was the product of an irrational tax structure, high deficit financing, and a corrupt public administration in the country. It was totally unconvincing to say that bank nationalisation would in any way help in checking tax evasion or in curbing the evil of black money.

(f) Even in a comprehensive policy of socialisation, bank nationalisation should follow and not precede nationalisation of all major trades and industries of the country. Furthermore, where Indian private banks were becoming increasingly progressive in their approach and outlook and were reforming their methods of work and policies and adopting themselves to the changed needs of the country's growing economy, there seemed to be hardly any sound economic reason for taking the bold step of nationalisation.

(g) It was also feared that if banks were nationalised, the state authorities might discriminate in granting of credit and the whole banking system would come under political pressure in banking policies. The whims of politicians rather than economic considerations would gain an upper hand.

(h) Nationalisation of banks would involve huge compensation package for the shareholders of the private sector banks and the burden would fall on the people of the country. People of developing country such as India, cannot afford to bear the brunt of heavy compensation package.

(i) It was strongly believed that nationalisation of banks would, in the long term, result in irresponsibility, lack of accountability, rigidity, bureaucracy and red tapism, corruption and political interference. Banks ultimately having become state monopolies may be completely insensitive to the very mission of banking.

(j) Nationalisation of banks appeared to be a politically motivated step rather than an economically correct measure. Late Mrs Indira Gandhi, the then Prime Minister of India, in 1969, hardly required the support of the members of the left parties in parliament and hence the measures such as nationalisation, abolition of privy purses, and introduction of Monopolies Restrictive Trade Practices Act (MRTP) were taken up to woo the leftist parties and it was part of a political strategy to woo the general public.

(k) When the existing inflationary price spirals in the country were the product of unsound monetary and fiscal policies of the government, how could one assume that nationalised banks would be in a position to pursue genuinely correct policies and bring about price stabilisation? Price instability in our country was the result of budgetary impact which cannot be checked by mere nationalisation. It was unfortunate for the country that the ruling party equated socialism with nationalisation.

(l) It was illogical to argue that just because some nations like the East European countries, Indonesia, Burma, United Arab Republic (UAR), Tanzania and Libya resolved to nationalisation and benefited to some extent, India too should adopt the same step. Objective conditions and circumstances in these countries have altogether been different from those existing in India. Their banking structure was also not sound as it was in our country.

(m) It was too much to expect that joint-stock banks, when nationalised, would receive better cooperation from their employees. The experience of the RBI, the SBI, the LIC, and other undertakings in the public sector in this regard had been disappointing. It was well known that relations between their managements and employees have not been cordial and that the former had numerous complaints to make regarding the uncooperative attitude of the latter. With regard to the efficiency of the services rendered to the customers, it could not be said that SBI was doing better than the joint-stock banks.

(n) If banks were functioning as monopoly organisations, the remedy lies in diffusing the concentration of economic power and wealth by curbing monopolistic tendencies, and nationalisation is not the solution. Social control and regulation would be a better remedy. If banks were neglecting agricultural sector and small scale sector, the government could direct banks to provide assistance to these priority sections taking into consideration the risk factors. Penal action could be levied against the erring banks. With the vast powers acquired by RBI through Banking Regulation Act 1949, they had complete statutory control of banking system. Banking system and money market had recognised the undisputed leadership of RBI and was willing to abide by its suggestions even though they were outside the statutory powers.

Social Control of Commercial Banks

Even though the Indian banking structure has grown since independence in strength and stability, thanks to the effective control of RBI, the banking system as well as the structure was suffering from certain inadequacies. The network of bank branches covered only a limited segment of the population, that too in big cities. The rural areas and small towns more or less were completely neglected. Certain sectors such as agriculture and small-scale industries, education, retail trade and so on, were neglected and in some sections of the population such as unemployed graduates, rural artisans, retail traders, and small business did not enjoy institutional credit and most of them were neither aware of the bank credit nor were the banks accessible to them. Leading business houses controlled the major banks.

To cure such ills, it was felt that radical changes in the structure and functioning of commercial banks were absolutely necessary. The policies and practices of the banking system must serve the basic social and economic objectives. In this respect, a new banking policy was initiated by the Congress Government in 1967, described as the "social control" of banks.

The concept of "social control" was introduced by the All India Congress Committee (AICC) resolution on the eve of the fourth general elections. "Social control" of banks was deemed to be a via media between complete social ownership, that is, nationalisation and maintenance of the statuesque. According to the AICC resolution, social control means greater participation of banks under the effective guidance of the state in the mobilisation of deposits and allocation of credits to the socially desirable sectors of the economy, which would ensure enlarged material benefits to the nation at large. The term "social control" of banks thus connotes a sort of stiff regulation of banking activities through appropriate policy measures and legislation.

The scheme of social control of banks was introduced by the government on 14 December 1967 when the Finance Minister Mr Morarji Desai made a statement in the Lok Sabha while explaining its objectives, main features and the mode of functioning. In his statement, Mr Desai categorically stated that there was no need for nationalising banks at that time, and social control measures alone would effectively serve the purpose.

The main objectives of the scheme were:

(a) To achieve a wider spread of bank credit.
(b) To prevent misuse of credit.
(c) To ensure large volume of credit flow to priority sectors.
(d) To make the scheme of social control a more effective instrument of development for facilitating rapid economic growth and achieving the ideas of socialist pattern of society.

(e) To meet the challenges of the current economic problems such as inflation, etc., through an effective integration of monetary policy with fiscal measures.

(f) To strengthen the banking system by preventing bank failures and thus sustain public confidence in banking to promote the growth of banking on sound lines.

(g) To produce an all-round development of the banking structure by appropriate expansion, coordination and integration of all allied banking institutions.

(h) To stress the need for extending banking services to the rural sector and to check concentration of economic power through equitable distribution of credit.

Steps Towards Social Control

A scheme was attempted to eliminate the control of business houses over banks without disturbing the private ownership of bank. The elements of social control were: (a) Organisational Changes (b) National Credit Council (c) Agricultural Finance Corporation Ltd (AFCL).

The first step under the scheme of social control was the introduction of organisational changes by way of reconstitution of the board of directors of banks and introducing experts/experienced persons in the field of agriculture and rural economy, small-scale industries, cooperation banking and so on, and replacing industrialist chairman by a person who is an expert in banking, finance and economics, and so on. The legislative measure for social control of banks was introduced by enacting the Banking Laws (Amendment) Act, 1968, which came into effect from 1 February 1969. Under the social control scheme, the board of directors of banks were to be reconstituted. The RBI was empowered to appoint, remove or terminate the services of the chairman, any director, the chief executive of any bank, or any other officer or employee of bank under specific circumstances. The new act also specified that all foreign banks were to set up an advisory board consisting of Indians and conduct their lending policies and activities under the guidance of such an advisory board. Above all, the new act also empowered the government to take over (nationalise) any bank in the country, without resorting to legislation, in the interest of depositors and better provision of credit. Under this scheme, advances and guarantees to directors and their concerns were prohibited in order to eliminate favouritism.

The National Credit Council (NCC) was established at an all india level in December 1967 as an instrument of credit planning. It consisted of representatives from large, medium, and small-scale industries, agriculture, cooperative sector, trade, and bankers and professional accountants. The finance minister was its chairman and the governor of RBI its vice-chairman. The NCC began to function from February 1968. The main functions of the NCC were:

(a) The NCC would assess the demand for bank credit from various sectors of the economy.
(b) It would determine the priorities for the grant of loans and advances, or for investment, depending on the availability of resources and the needs of the priority sectors such as agriculture and small industry.
(c) It would coordinate the lending and investing policies of the commercial banks, cooperative banks and specialised agencies to ensure optimum utilisation of resources.
(d) The banks were supposed to adhere strictly to the execution of credit policies, plans and directions specified by the NCC.
(e) The RBI introduced changes in its branch expansion policy as guided by the NCC for extending banking facilities to wider areas, to tackle other related issues as may be referred to it by the chairman or the vice-chairman of the council.

Agricultural Finance Corporation Ltd. (AFCL)

AFCL was established as a joint venture by leading banks for financing priority agriculture projects and also to help the banks to participate actively in developing the agricultural sector. Several committees such as "Gadgil Committee" for organisational framework for implementation of social control objectives, and "Dehejia Committee" to study the extent to which the credit needs of industry and trade are likely to be inflated, and how such trends can be checked were appointed to examine the effectiveness of the scheme of social control.

Pre-Nationalisation Developments

Within eighteen years of planning from the first plan in 1950–1951 till the beginning of the fourth plan in 1969, substantial changes took place in the Indian banking system in all its major aspects – structural, geographical, and functional. During this period, Indian banks endeavoured to adopt themselves (though at a slow pace) to the changing economic, political and psychological outlook and atmosphere under planned development of the country. Basically, the working of commercial banks in India is governed by the provisions of the Banking Companies (Regulation) Act, 1949. The act has, however, been amended from time to time to bring about the improvements in their functioning and better control over their activities.

In India, the commercial banking system is largely of the branch banking type. However, the most striking feature of the changing banking scene has been a drastic cut in the number of banks and an enormous rise in the number of branches during 1949–1969. In fact, the process of weeding out substandard non-viable banking units had begun with the recommendations of the Travancore-Cochin Banking Inquiry Commission in 1956 and subsequent efforts relating to the merger of small banks with big banks to make them viable units. The process of amalgamation accelerated after the amendment of the Banking Regulation Act in 1960 in this regard.

A notable feature of the growth in bank offices is the extension of banking facilities to the rural or backward areas, especially on account of the SBI's efforts in this direction. It is also interesting to note that within the scheduled banking sector, a few big banks acquired the bulk of the banking business. Although there has been considerable expansion of bank offices in rural and semi-urban areas, banking has remained more or less urban in character.

In the field of commercial banking, the seeds of nationalisation were sown in 1955 when the government nationalised the Imperial Bank of India, following the recommendations of the All India Rural Credit Survey Committee. Subsequently in 1960, seven state-associated banks were taken over as subsidiaries of the State Bank of India. The SBI group made considerable progress in achieving its goals of branch expansion in rural areas and catering to the credit needs of small scale industries and agriculturists. In 1962, the Deposit Insurance Corporation (DIC) was established by the RBI to implement a system of deposit insurance with a view to develop banking habits among the people by providing an assured safety of their deposits.

Another important feature of Indian Banking has been that a major part of it was under the control of a handful of business magnates so that commerce and industry claim a lion's share of bank credit. In November 1965, a scheme called Credit Authorisation Scheme (CAS) was introduced by the RBI in order to impose financial discipline on the big borrowers. Banks were also getting conscious of their social responsibilities, so they had adopted a changed outlook and had been giving up their traditional views on lending. But the people at large and the government were dissatisfied with the progress of banking. Thus, in 1967, the move for the social control of banks was started. Banks have whole heartedly taken certain measures to achieve the objectives of social control. The government felt that public ownership was inevitable to reach socialism. Hence, fourteen major Indian scheduled commercial banks were nationalised on 19 July 1969 by Government of India.

Bank Nationalisation Event

Saturday 19 July 1969 was a historical day for Indian Banking. The government issued an ordinance, promulgated by the then acting president, for the takeover of fourteen major scheduled commercial banks with more than INR 50 crores of deposits. The Nationalisation Bill was subsequently passed by parliament as the Banking Companies (acquisition and transfer of undertaking) Act, 1969 which received president's assent on 9 August 1969. The ordinance was however challenged by a few, and a stay order of Supreme Court was obtained. On the ground of violation of Article 14 (discrimination) and Article 31 (compensation on compulsory acquisition of property) of the Indian constitution, the Banking Companies (Acquisition and Transfer of Undertakings) Act, 1969 was declared invalid by the Supreme Court on 10 February 1970. It was observed that fourteen banks had been discriminated against in favour of other small banks and foreign commercial banks, also the method of compensating the companies for the acquisition of their shares did not accord with the constitutional determination of compensation for acquisition of undertakings. On 14 February 1970 the President of India promulgated the Banking Companies (Acquisition and Transfer of Undertaking) Ordinance, 1970, which nationalised fourteen banks, removing the loopholes in the earlier ordinance struck off by the Supreme Court. According to the new ordinance, these companies were permitted to re-enter the banking business under some statutory confinement, and provision was made for payment of compensation at a higher rate in cash or in government securities maturing at the end of ten or thirty years, or partly in cash and partly in government securities as might be opted for by the companies concerned. Subsequently, the Banking Companies (Acquisition and Transfer of Undertaking) Act was passed on 31 March 1970 with retrospective effect, keeping the original nationalisation (of July 1969) intact.

The aggregate compensation payable to these nationalised banks amounted to INR 87.4 crores. Altogether 85 per cent of aggregate deposits, 80 per cent of the number of offices and 84 per cent credit, therefore came into public sector banking by July 1969.

As Professor Sinha rightly observed in his article ("The Banking Revolution in India", *Southern Economist*, 15 February 1973), the nationalisation of July 1969 was a unique phenomenon, different from that of nationalisation of the RBI in 1949 or the nationalisation of the Imperial Bank of India in 1955, as these were very modest and tame affairs, having little socio-economic impact, compared to the present one which, though untimely, caused a massive and radical socio-economic change in the country. However, most Indian economists are of the view that under the then existing situation, the 1969 nationalisation was purely a politically motivated step, without economic need behind it. As a matter of fact, even the RBI was not in favour of nationalisation. But now, after nationlisation, its achievements and future developments are more significant.

Nationalisation of Banks—Aims and Objectives

Irrespective of the criticism against nationalisation of banks, the Government of India, through an ordinance, nationalised fourteen banks. The broad aim of nationalisation was to control the heights of the economy and to meet progressively and serve better the needs of development of the economy in conformity with national policy and objectives (Preamble to the Banking Companies Act, 1970). The broad aims and objectives of nationalisation were as follows:

(a) To take the economy to commanding heights.
(b) To serve in a better way the requirements of the development of the economy in conformity with the state policy and objectives.
(c) To ensure that the needs of the productive efforts of diverse kinds are met.
(d) To provide credit based on equity and justice and not based on size and social status of the borrowers.
(e) To provide credit on priority basis to hitherto neglected sections such as small farmers, small business, self-employed professional groups, and so on.
(f) To re-orient the concept of security for loans.
(g) To prevent the use of credit for speculative purposes.
(h) To reduce the regional imbalances by creating fresh opportunities for backward areas in different parts of the country.
(i) To see that the large borrowers do not take undue advantage and prevent misuse of credit by them.
(j) To expand branches in rural areas and small towns and mobilise savings of the population.
(k) To expand deposit mobilisation all over the country and from all sections of the population.

Undoubtedly, a banking revolution took place in the country as a result of the impact of the 1969 bank nationalisation. The nationalisation of banks opened new vistas before the banking system as a whole and gave new dimensions to the growth of the economy. Banks ceased to be mere money-dealing institutions. They assumed a pivotal role on the development front. The new banking system took upon the role of a catalyst and development agent of the country's economy.

Achievements of Commercial Banks after Nationalisation

The progress of commercial banks in India was rapid since nationalisation and the rise was very quick in areas such as expansion of banks in rural areas, lending in the priority sector, mobilisation of deposits, expansion of credit, and so on. The orientation and approach was towards development and the philosophy was of more social banking rather than traditional conservative commercial banking. The achievements of commercial banks after nationalisation were as follows:

(a) Before nationalisation, the banks focused their attention on large business houses and other industries for financing. In fact, several commercial banks were under the control of large business houses. Petty farmers, small industrialists and businessmen, transport operators, self-employed people, students looking for education loans, general population looking for a home loan were completely neglected by the bank as bank finance was not accessible to them. After nationalisation, these neglected sectors were given top priority and they were given the status of "priority sector". To encourage exports, concessional rate of finance have been provided. One of the important reasons for nationalisation of banks was to provide finances at concessional rate to the priority sector. In 1969, the total credit to the priority sector was INR 441 crores but by 2000, the priority sector lending from nationalised banks has increased to INR 1,27,478 crores. The advances to the priority sector lending from nationalised banks from 15 per cent in 1969 to 45 per cent in 2000. During 1999–2000, advances to the priority sector by Indian private banks was 39 per cent and that of foreign banks was 34.5 per cent of their total bank credit.

(b) Following nationalisation of major commercial banks, there was a sharp increase in the rural and semi-urban branches which could successfully mitigate the sufferings of rural masses from the hands of moneylenders. The Government of India cared more for reach of the banks in remote areas than the commercial viability. As against 22.4 per cent branches located in rural areas in June 1969, there were 49.5 per cent branches by March 2001.

(c) The advances in 1969 were around INR 3600 crores. By 2002, the advances have gone up to INR 6,00,000 crores. The main reasons for such a massive expansion of bank credit are increase in commercial activity, increase in deposits, agriculture and food procurement financing, larger increase in consumer credit through credit cards, personal loans, housing loans, and so on, larger export credit, financing public sector requirements, especially during the 1970s and the 1980s.

(d) With increase in number of branches all over the country, the banks could reach large number of customers of different profile such as institutions, industrialists and so on. In 1950–1951, the bank deposits crossed INR 820 crores. By 1969, they increased to INR 4,640 crores. By 1990–1991, they rose phenomenally to INR 1,92,540 crores. By the end of 2001, the deposits approximately totalled INR 10,00,000 crores. Today the figure may reach to more than INR 15,00,000 crores. The bank deposits increased phenomenally after nationalisation due to the following factors:
- massive expansion of branches
- government policy in respect of deficit financing. Deficit financing refers to the practice of financing the government's expenditure through borrowing. It becomes necessary when its normal revenue receipts from tax and tax sources are not adequate enough to finance its expenditure needs.
- increase in loans and increase in deposits. Deficit financing policy of the Government of India led to increase in money supply which further increased cash reserved with the banks. The banks in turn used these funds for creation of credit and thus led ultimately for massive expansion of deposits.
- increase in money supply
- increase in cash reserves with the banks
- favourable business climate
- attractive interest rates at least till the late 1990s
- aggressive policies of banks for mobilisation of deposits.

(e) Initially, the banks were very conservative and the goal was profitability, and hence they opened their branches mainly in metropolitan cities and in other cities where business was assured. But after nationalisation, the banks have expanded their branches tremendously. In the year 1969, the total number of branches were 8,260 and the population per branch/bank office was 63,800. But by 1991, the total number of branches increased to 60,650 and the population per branch/bank office was 14,150. The percentage of rural branches out of the total branches increased from 22 per cent in 1969 to 54 per cent in 1991. Today there are over 67,000 branches in the country and about 50 per cent of the branches are in rural areas and the population per branch/bank office is 15,000. From this it is clear that there has been rapid increase in the expansion of branches since 1969, and the phenomenon is stated to be unparalleled anywhere else in the world. Nationalisation of banks could successfully integrate rural and urban India. It promoted savings habits even among households with meagre incomes. Only after nationalisation could banks become accessible to common man in such a wide manner. After nationalisation, attempts were made by the government to concentrate on backward states and on backward regions of the developed states in order to rectify the imbalances in the banking facilities. The expansion of branches of nationalised banks was faster in backward states such as Assam, Bihar, and Orissa.

(f) There is a clear shift from traditional banking of receiving deposits and making advances to merchant banking and underwriting, mutual funds, housing loans, venture capital funds, factor services, leasing, and so on. Several specialised subsidiaries were set up to look after some of these functions by most of the nationalised banks.

(g) When banks restricted their customer base to the well-to-do segment, the have-nots were not aware of what good the banks could do them. They never ventured to enter banks to save their money – leave alone seeking loans. Due to nationalisation of banks, the growth in the number of branches has made banking as an integral part of everybody's life including that of common man. Seeking credit from banks has become an order of the day, social banking and priority sector lending attracted the weaker sections towards the banks and developed banking habits. The number of account holders increased phenomenally. Earlier the banks used to have the patronage of less number of rich customers. Today banking has turned from class banking to mass banking characterised by a large number of small size account holders.

(h) Earlier banks preferred to finance traditional industries such as jute, cotton, sugar, steel, and so on. Nationalisation of banks created awareness and their involvement in social development increased. For every district in the country, a lead bank was identified and entrusted the task of opening bank branches in all important localities, providing maximum credit facilities for development in the district by mobilising the savings of the people in the given district. The contribution of the lead bank for the economic development was significant in terms of employment generated and number of projects supported/nurtured from trade and big industry orientation. The banks moved towards development orientation by concentrating more on both industry and agricultural sectors. The banks did not confine to short-term finance only. They started proving medium and long-term finances to both agriculture and industry, irrespective of their size.

(i) The Government of India could successfully use bank funds to finance various social sector schemes for employment generation and poverty alleviation. The central government introduced the scheme of Differential Interest Rates (DIR) from 1972 to cater to the requirements of the weaker sections of the society, and loans with no security were provided to them at abnormally lower interest of four per cent per annum, and this scheme became a tremendous success with phenomenal increase in the number of accounts. Other schemes launched to promote social banking include Integrated Rural Development Programme (IRDP) which is to correct the imbalances in the rural economy and contribute to the economic improvement of the rural households. Prime Minister Rozgar Yojana for educated unemployed youth (PMRY), Scheme for Urban Micro Enterprises (SUME), Prime Minister's Integrated Urban Poverty Eradication Programme, National Employment schemes, and many others.

4
Money Market

Introduction

The main function of a financial system is to provide funds for financing operations relating to agricultural, industrial, and service sectors and act as a catalyst for rapid economic growth and development. The essential components of financial systems are money market and capital market that constitute the lifeline of the economy. If these markets are organised, the economic development of the country will be more rapid. Both borrowers and lenders find it convenient to carry out their operations in an organised money market.

According to Crowther, money market is a collective name given to the various firms and institutions that deal with various grades of near money. The RBI defines money market as "the centre for dealing mainly of a short-term character, in money assets; it meets the short-term requirements of borrowers and provides liquidity or cash to the lenders".

Objectives of Money Market

The primary objective of money markets are:

(a) To equalise the short-term surpluses and deficiency.
(b) To maintain liquidity in the economy.
(c) To provide appropriate instruments to ensure access to the users of short-term funds at minimum cost and delay.
(d) The funds involved in the money market are huge in volume, that is, a whole-sale market for short-term funds. There is a large room for creative and innovative dealings in this market as the degree of regulations is still in the nascent stage.
(e) In the money market, funds are borrowed for periods varying from a day, a week, three to six months and against different types of instruments such as bills of exchange, short-term securities, bank's acceptances, and so on. These are called "near money".
(f) It is considered very significant in view of its liquidity and its capacity for providing liquid funds to any part of the country within a few hours' notice. It is a supplementary to the commercial banking system.

In different countries, different money markets play significant roles in providing short-term funds and credit. For example, New York money market,

London money market, Mumbai money market are very well known throughout the world.

Features of a Developed Money Market

A developed money market is characterised by the following requisites. The absence of one or more of these will make a particular money market an underdeveloped one.

(a) Developed Banking System

A developed money market requires a highly developed banking system which can cater to the requirements of short-term credit needs of the economy. A well-developed and integrated commercial banking system is the nerve centre of a well-developed money market.

(b) Presence of a Central Bank

A money market cannot function properly without a central bank. A strong central bank is an essential pre-requisite for economical employment of cash as it permits banks to maintain stable or lower cash ratios. When the banking business is subjected to seasonal market fluctuations, banks can, against the lodgement of security with the central bank, meet the demand for loans or cash on those occasions. The central bank also rediscounts eligible securities of banks, converting near money assets into cash in times of crisis. It also undertakes open market operations wherein it absorbs surplus cash during off seasons and provides liquidity in terms of financial stringency. Thus, in a developed money market, the central bank intervenes from time to time and controls the operations of commercial banks.

(c) Availability of Proper Credit Instruments

A continuous availability of readily acceptable negotiable securities such as bills of exchange, treasury bills, etc., in the market is necessary for its existence. There should be a number of dealers in the money market to transact in these securities. Availability of negotiable securities and the presence of dealers and brokers in large number to transact in these securities are needed for the existence of a developed money market. There is absence of adequate and proper credit instruments as well as dealers to deal in these instruments in an underdeveloped money market.

(d) Existence of Well-Organised Sub-markets

A developed money market constitutes several specialised sub-markets such as bill market, acceptance market, call money market, collateral loan market, foreign exchange market, etc. The extent of development of money a market is directly related to the number and size of these sub-markets. All these sub-markets provide greater liquidity to the money market ensuring free flow of funds among them. A properly integrated sub-market system enhances the efficiency of the money market.

(e) Perfect Mobility of Funds

Perfect mobility of funds is a fundamental requirement of a developed money market. Free movement of money and monetary assets from surplus points to places of demand tends towards equality of rates for similar types of business at widely separated points in the economy. A developed money market mobilises funds not only from the country, but from all over the world.

(f) Well-Developed Secondary Market

Secondary market enables trading of instruments of money market. The money market influences the liquidity of the secondary market and above all gets influenced in the process. The money market and capital market are interlinked as far as liquidity is concerned.

(g) Existence of an Integrated Structure of Markets and Institutions

It is considered to be the most essential characteristic of developed money market. All other characteristics emerge out of an appropriate degree of integration. A favourable balance of payments, large quantum of international trade, stable political conditions, price stabilisation, organised stock exchange markets, responsible banks, and financial institutions are the characteristics of a well-developed money market similar to that in New York or London.

(h) International Attraction

The developed money markets attract funds from foreign countries too. The dealers, borrowers, and lenders of foreign countries participate in the activities of the money market. There must be availability of sufficient funds to finance transactions in the sub-markets. These funds may come from within the country and also from foreign countries. The London, New York, and Paris money markets attract funds from all over the world. The underdeveloped money markets are starved of funds.

(i) Efficient Legal Infrastructure

Commercial disputes can be settled effectively and efficiently only when there are sound legal enactments and instructions. Such a legal system will create confidence in the minds of the players in the market and there will be greater credibility of the instruments dealt in the market.

(j) Remittance Facilities

A developed money market provides easy, quick, and cost-effective remittance facilities for transferring funds from one market to another. For example, the New York money market provides remittance facilities efficiently and effectively throughout the world.

(k) Integrated Internal Rates

The interest rates prevailing in the sub-markets in a developed money market are closely integrated to one another. The variations in the interest rates are likely to be marginal in the sub-markets. When the bank rate is varied, the corresponding interest rates also undergo a change.

(l) Primary and Satellite Dealers

There should also be adequate number of primary dealers in the money market dealing in credit instruments offering their specialised services in a professional way. Satellite dealers supplement the efforts of primary dealers for organised dealing and distribution arrangements in the money market instruments.

In the words of Professor Sengupta, "the central bank, to be a skillful driver in the money market, should keep an effective control over the steering wheel to keep the car on the middle of the road and prevent it from dangerous swings". Such a condition would exist only if the money market is adequately knit, widely expensive and closely coordinated. An underdeveloped money market is a great hindrance to the smooth monitoring management by the central bank.

Structure of the Indian Money Market

The structure of the money market in India has the following characteristics:

(a) Broadly speaking, the money market in India comprises two sectors.
   - organised sector
   - unorganised sector

(b) The organised sector consists of the RBI, the SBI with its seven subsidiaries, nationalised commercial banks, other scheduled and non-scheduled commercial banks, foreign banks and regional rural banks. It is called organised because it is systematically coordinated by the RBI.

(c) Non-bank financial institutions such as the LIC, the General Insurance Corporation (GIC) and subsidiaries, the UTI and other money mutual funds also operate in the market, but only indirectly through banks.

(d) Quasi government bodies and large companies also make their short-term surplus funds available to the organised market through banks.

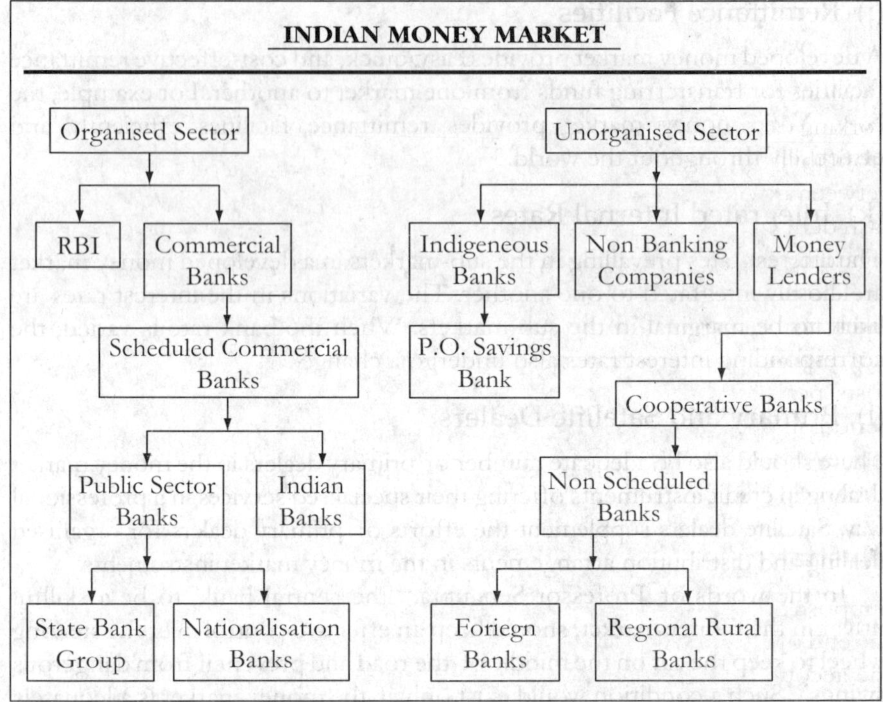

The development banks such as IDBI, IFCI, SFCs, ICICI Bank, EXIM Bank also provide funds for short-term purposes to the money market.

(e) Cooperative credit institutions occupy the intermediary position between organised and unorganised sectors of the Indian money market. These institutions have a three-tier structure. At the top, there are state cooperative banks. At the local level, there are primary credit societies and urban cooperative banks. Considering the size, methods of operations, and dealings with the RBI and commercial banks, only state and central cooperative banks should be included in the organised sector. The cooperative societies at the local level are only loosely linked with it.

(f) The unorganised sector consists of indigenous banks and money lenders. It is unorganised because activities of its parts are not systematically coordinated by the RBI.

(g) The money lenders operate throughout the country, but without any link among themselves.

(h) Indigenous banks are better organised because they enjoy rediscount facilities from the commercial banks which, in turn, are linked with the RBI. But this type of organisation represents only a loose link with the RBI.

Money markets become increasingly relevant to address the problems of working capital management. It is absolutely essential to balance liquidity and profitability in managing working capital. The money market provides a link between organisations having surplus cash and organisations suffering from cash deficit. Both such organisations can transact and reach an understanding regarding the cost of funds, namely interest rates.

The funds transacted in money market are of high volume, low risk, and short term in nature. Transaction costs in the money market are relatively very high compared to the interest earned. In order to reduce the transaction costs per rupee, the volume of funds transacted is very high. Short-term period, in general, refers to any period less than one year. In the contexts of money markets, short term may imply any period such as overnight, a day, one week, one month, 90 days or 364 days.

Illustration

Suppose Syndicate Bank needs to pay SBI INR 10 crores balancing figure at the end of the day. This transaction takes place by requesting RBI to increase the account balance of SBI by INR 10 crores and corresponding decrease in the account balance of Syndicate Bank. With this, the balance or total money with Syndicate Bank gets reduced. But it might be requiring that amount for transactions with its other customers. This means one party, here, Syndicate Bank wants to borrow money now. There may be another party, say, Indian Bank having surplus funds for the next 20 days (it does not require those funds in the next 20 days), Syndicate Bank may require funds, more or less, for the same period. Thus we now have Indian Bank lending funds to Syndicate Bank of INR 10 crores for 20 days at an agreed rate of interest. This is the way transaction takes place in the money market.

Constituents of the Money Market

The money market is composed of several sub-markets each dealing in different types of short-term credit.

(a) Call Money Market

Call Money Market is for short-term loans lent for a period not exceeding 14 days. Sometimes, money is lent overnight. These loans are called call money or call loans or overnight money since the banks recall loans at a very short notice. Commercial banks and a few financial institutions who have been permitted by the RBI are the only players in call money market. Individual investors are not allowed to buy or sell the call money. However, the commercial banks provide loans to bill brokers, dealers in stock exchanges, whose financial requirements may be for a very short period only.

There may also be inter-bank call money market where banks can borrow from those having surplus reserve balance in order to maintain their reserve positions according to stability requirements. The business is transacted over the telephone and the concerned parties generally do not meet to structure the deals. Call money receipt is one of the major instruments used in the Indian money market. It is a document issued by the banks while receiving deposit and it is not transferable.

(b) Acceptance Market

It is a market for bankers' acceptances involved in trade transactions. A bankers' acceptance is a draft drawn by an individual or firm upon a bank ordering it to pay to the order of a designated party or to the bearer a certain sum of money at particular future date and the draft is accepted by the bank. Unlike cheques, bankers' acceptances are used mainly in financing the movement of goods in international trade. Bankers' acceptances can be easily sold or discounted in the money market called the acceptance market.

(c) Collateral Loan Market

Collateral loan market deals with collateral loans, that is, loans backed by security. In the Indian collateral loan market, the commercial banks provided short-term loans against government securities, shares and debentures of the government, etc.

(d) Treasury Bill Market

The treasury bill market deals in treasury bills that constitute debt obligations of the government that mature in one year or less. Ninety-one days' treasury bills has been the oldest bill introduced by the Government of India. They were issued to meet temporary needs of funds of the government. This treasury bill continued to be the only instrument in the treasury bill market for a long time to raise funds by Government of India for a short period.

The 182-day Treasury bill, introduced in 1986, emerged as a widely accepted money market instrument. The cut-off yields to investors from 182-day treasury bill has been as high as an interest rate of 9.86 per cent per annum and this was more than double the yield from 91 day treasury bill (these offered a fixed discount rate of 4.6 per cent per annum). The 182-day treasury bill was further converted into 364-day treasury bill. The auction of 182-day treasury bill on a fortnightly basis was reintroduced in 1998. Treasury bills of 364-day, 28-day, and 14-day were also introduced. While 364-day treasury bills are being issued on a fortnightly basis, all others are issued on a weekly basis. The treasury bills of various maturities are being issued on auction basis.

All treasury bills are sold by the RBI on behalf of the Government of India. Bills are bought and sold on discount basis. It means that the amount of interest due on the bills is paid in the form of discount. Thus, the price of the bill is lower than its face (par) value by the amount of interest due on the bill. The rate of discount is the treasury bill rate. When the RBI buys back the bill, it rediscounts them, namely, it discounts the bill all over again for its remaining life. For the central bank of a country, the treasury bills are the chief instruments of open market operations. In India, open market operations of the RBI are found to be ineffective because of the underdeveloped nature of the bill market.

The treasury bills are being used by the government as a cheap source of long-term funds even though they are supposed to be used only for temporary needs of the government. The artificial pegging of the interest rate at a very low level is the cause for its disinterest towards banks and other institutions. Perhaps, as a corrective measure the RBI introduced 182-day treasury bills and the first auction for these new bills was held in November 1986. The response from banks was good. The amount was bid at a high discount rate of 84 per cent. The auction system will introduce some kind of flexibility in the fixation of interest rates.

Treasury bills have become very popular, both in India and abroad, for the following reasons:

(a) The income earned on treasury bills is exempt from income tax.
(b) They are considered to be risk free, that is, essentially free from default risk.
(c) Bills are sold in maximum denominations making them appropriate for the needs of both large and small investors.
(d) They are highly liquid because there is a very large and efficient secondary market that enables investors to convert bills easily into cash.

(e) Commercial Bill Market

Commercial bills comprise bills of exchange and promissory notes. Like treasury bills, commercial bills have a market of their own. The indigenous bills are called *Hundis*. A bill of exchange is drawn by the creditor on the debtor, duly accepted by the debtor for a certain sum, for a certain period, generally not exceeding three months or ninety days. In the case of promissory notes, the debtor (generally the buyer of goods), makes an unconditional promise to pay a certain sum at a future date to the seller of goods.

The commercial bills are a very important sources of short-term finance to trade and industry. They have a fixed term to maturity called usance. The usance is reasonably short for banks to invest their funds in them (the holders of bills can discount them with bank) and reasonably long for the buyers of goods (draw's/acceptance of bills) to recover cost of goods from their resale of processing of raw materials into finished goods and sale. The bills are marketable instruments as they are negotiable by nature. They carry competitive rates of interest. Hence, banks have a preference for such bills for their investment. Discount and Finance House of India (DFHI) has been set up on the lines of acceptance houses or discount houses in the United Kingdom. The bill market in India is not as much developed as that of the United Kingdom and the United States of America.

The banks borrow from call market frequently for two reasons. Banks may have a surplus or shortage of funds while they close their accounts on a daily basis. In such a case, the main function of the market is to redistribute the pool of day to day surplus funds of banks among other banks in temporary deficit of cash. The banking business is such that the cash position of the banks fluctuates from hour to hour and their closing cash position at the end of the day may be different from their opening cash position. Some banks may end the day with surplus and some others with deficit. Call money market provides an institutional arrangement to channelise the surplus cash holdings, towards those banks with cash shortage. Another reason why banks face the shortfall of cash is to meet the Cash Reserve Ratio (CRR).

The participants in the money market include all scheduled commercial banks, (private sector, public sector, and cooperative banks) financial institutions (term lending institution, insurance companies) and mutual funds. The participants are classified into two categories: those who can both borrow and lend in the market (only banks can do both) and those who can lend but not borrow. Recently, the RBI has permitted non-banking financial entities to lend in the call money markets up to 85 per cent of their average lending. Consequently, the percentage share of lending of financial institutions such as the Unit Trust of India (UTI), Life Insurance Corporation (LIC), and Industrial Development Bank of India (IDBI) has come down.

The RBI regulates the call money market and as a regulator, it intervenes in the market when call money rates fluctuate violently. It intervenes through two markets interactions – the Securities Trading Corporation of India (STCI) and Discount and Finance House of India (DFHI). It is to be clearly noted that the RBI can neither lend nor borrow funds in the call money market. Its role is confined to that of a regulator.

The call money market helps banks economise their cash and improve their liquidity by providing them the facility of borrowing on call basis. The call market is a highly competitive and sensitive market. It acts as a key indicator of the liquidity position of the money market. By its very nature, the call money rate is highly volatile. The market experiences some regular seasonal changes. It is normally tight during the busy season (October to April). Call money market is very active in Mumbai, Kolkata, and Chennai. Mumbai call money market is a very important one.

Participation Certificates (PCs)

Participation Certificates were very popular during the 1970s. They were initially intended to serve as a short-term money market instrument. But unfortunately they were used by the financial institutions for parking their funds for long maturities and participation certificates (PCs) were not developed to even out inter liquidity between banks/and financial institutions. From 1979 onwards, the RBI has taken up certain measures to phase out PCs as they were not being used for the purpose for which they were originally introduced.

Participatory Notes

Participatory Notes (p-notes) is a unique Indian aberration that enables foreign investor gain from India's growth without disclosures. SEBI must push its plan to ensure that they wind up. P-notes are instruments issued by Foreign Institutional Investors (FIIS) to enable foreign investors trade in stocks without disclosing their identity. Allowed by SEBI since February 2000 to enable foreign companies and high net-worth investors invest in the Indian market. P-notes account for US $88 bn of the total US $176 bn FIIs inflow (50 per cent).

Risk Factors

The funds are often highly leveraged, may be used in prop-up shares and could be from terror networks.

Hot Money

It may not necessarily be "Hot Money" but huge investments in derivatives can trigger "herd trading" aggravating a cash.

The Rising Tide

P-notes have grown from INR 31,875 crores in 2004 to INR 3,53,484 crores in August 2007.

What SEBI wants:

> Allow P-notes in equity and debt but wind them in derivatives in 18 months, limit issuance of P-notes to 40 per cent and of FII's assets under custody. (*India Today*, 5 November 2007).

Indian Money Market

Before 1987, the situation in Indian market lacked vitality and was almost stagnant without any progress due to certain reasons.

(a) The entry into the money market was very much restricted.
(b) The number of participants in the market were limited to banks and all India financial institutions such as IDBI (Industrial Development Bank of India). Participation certificates which were popular in the market during late 1970s became non-existent while treasury bill transactions were confined only to banks and the RBI.
(c) The market was polarised with a few large lenders and a large number of borrowers.
(d) The rates of interest in the unorganised money market were more governed by market forces of demand and supply and they were markedly higher than in the organised sector.
(e) The number of instruments in practice was limited to money at call and short notice, inter bank deposits/loans and bill rediscounting. In other words, there was paucity of instruments.
(f) There were strict regulations on the rates of interest in the market. These rates were controlled either by RBI directly or by voluntary agreement between the participants through the intermediation of Indian Bank Association (IBA). This is predominantly one reason why an unorganised money market emerged on the scene.
(g) The participants did not alternate between the borrowing and lending activity, which is a primary requirement for a vibrant money market. In other words, the lenders continued to be lenders and borrowers continued to be the borrowers.

Deficiencies of the Indian Money Market

The money market in India is not only underdeveloped but it also has a heterogeneous entity. As such, it has a number of drawbacks, some of which are as follows:

(a) Dichotomy between Organised and Unorganised Sectors

The most important defect of the Indian money market is its division into two sectors – the organised sector and – unorganised sector. There is little contact, coordination, and cooperation between these two sectors. In such conditions, it is difficult for the RBI to ensure uniform and effective implementation of its monetary policy in both the sectors.

(b) Inadequate Banking Facilities

Banking facilities are either entirely non-existent or inadequate in the villages of India. Commercial banks are largely urban oriented in our country. Although there has been rapid expansion of bank branches in recent years, as compared to the size and population of the country, the banking institutions are not enough.

(c) Divergence of Lending Rates and Policies

Due to lack of homogeneity in the composition of the Indian market, there is wide divergence not only in the structure of interest rates, but also in the lending policies of the different financial institutions. Money lenders especially charge exorbitant rates of interest and lend mainly for unproductive purpose.

(d) Absence of Bill Market

The existence of a well-organised bill market is essential for the proper and efficient working of money market. Unfortunately, in spite of serious efforts made by the RBI, the bill market in India has not yet been fully developed. The short-term bills form a much small proportion of the bank finance in India as compared to that in the advanced countries. Indian traders resort to hundies, rather than draw bill of exchange. Further, there is lack of standardisation in drawing bills and hundies in India. Again the banking habit is not much developed in our country, and so cash transactions are more popular than credit transactions. As a consequence of all these conditions, no adequate supply of bill can take place. Heavy stamp duty discourages the use of exchange bills. The practice of advancing loans by the sellers also limit the use of bills. Cash credit is the main form of borrowing from the banks. Cash credit is given by the banks against the security of commodities. No bills are involved in this type of credit. In their desire to ensure greater liquidity and public confidence, the Indian banks prefer to invest their funds in first class government securities than in exchange bills. The RBI also prefers to extend rediscounting facilities to the commercial banks against approved securities.

(e) Seasonal Shortage of Funds

A major drawback of the Indian money market is the seasonal stringency of credit and higher interest rates during a part of the year. Such shortage invariably appears during the busy months of November to June, when there is excess demand for credit for carrying on the harvesting and marketing operations in agriculture. As a result, the interest rates rise in this period. On the contrary, during the slack season from July to October, the demand for credit and the rate of interest decline sharply. Disparities in the interest rates adversely affect the smooth and effective functioning of the money market.

(f) Inadequate Control of Unorganised Money Market

The RBI has no adequate control over the policies and functioning of the unorganised sector of the money market, which is quite large in size and which plays a significant role in rural finance. The money market is sometimes in a stable and at other times in an unstable situation which is a hindrance to the rapid economic development of the country.

(g) Isolation from Foreign Market

The Indian money market is isolated from foreign money markets. There is hardly any movement of funds between the Indian money market and the foreign markets. This is partly due to the exchange control restrictions on capital movement. Another reason is delay in execution, preservation from localisation, etc.

(h) Blending of Lending and Trading Activities

In the organised sector, the financial agencies do not resort to money dealings only. They usually carry on retail trade agriculture and other business activities along with lending operations.

(i) Call Money Receipts

The major instruments used in the Indian money market are call money, treasury bills, Certificate of Deposit (CD), Commercial Paper (CP), and commercial bills. The call money receipts are the major instruments which resembles any other receipt issued by the banks while accepting deposits. The receipts are not transferable. Hence, the secondary market is generally absent.

(j) Wasteful Competition

Wasteful competition exists not only between the organised and unorganised sectors, but also among members of the two sectors. The relations between various segments of the money market are not cordial. They are loosely connected with each other, and follow separatist tendencies. Even today SBI and other commercial banks look at each other as rivals. Similarly, competition exists between the Indian commercial banks and foreign banks.

Measures to Improve the Indian Money Market

In view of the various defects in the Indian money market, the following suggestions have been made for its proper developments.

(a) Link between Indigenous Banks and Commercial Banks

Steps were taken to establish relationship between indigenous banks and commercial banks. Those indigenous banks who are on the approved list of joint-stock banks and the SBI are entitled to receive cash credit from those banks against demand promissory notes signed by two of their bankers.

(b) Control Over Money Lenders

In 1918, the Government of India passed a law to check usury under the "Usurious Loan Act 1918". Similarly, laws were enacted to compel many lenders to maintain proper registers and accounts of their lending business. Money lenders were also required to obtain licenses for carrying on their lending business.

(c) Credit Guarantee Scheme

The credit guarantee scheme of the RBI was extended to cooperative banks to enhance public confidence in cooperative banking.

(d) Development of Cooperative Banking

As an alternative to moneylenders in rural finance, the development of cooperative credit societies has been encouraged by the government since independence. Cooperative banking is regarded as the only practical solution to usury. This has a significant role to play in the present structure of the Indian financial system. To place cooperative banking on more scientific lines and to regulate it properly, the Banking Laws (Application to Cooperative Societies) Act was passed in 1964.

(e) Control and Regulation of Nidhis and Chit Funds

The facilities of post office savings are spread over the country. Nidhi and chit funds which are recognised by law are required to be registered under the Indian Companies Act. However, to effectively control them, the central government has proposed to introduce a special legislation called the Nidhis and Chit Fund Act, with a view to controlling and regulating their activities. The banking commission has also suggested one uniform chit fund legislation for the entire country.

(f) Credit Facilities to Agriculturists

To meet the credit need of the agriculturists more comprehensively, the Agriculture Refinance Corporation was established in 1963, which refinances long-term loans furnished by loan mortgage banks (now land development banks) and other credit institutions. It was replaced by the National Bank for Agriculture and Rural Development (NABARD) in 1982.

(g) Priority Sector Financing

Commercial banks in India were originally in the private sector. These banks neglected agriculture and other priority sectors. Therefore, the Government of India took the bold decision to nationalise a number of commercial banks in 1969. Nationalised banks have made considerable progress in the rural areas in financing the priority sectors.

(h) In 1970, a scheme to finance primary agricultural credit societies by the commercial banks was introduced. Thus, a link between cooperative and joint-stock banks was created. The banking commission has suggested for constituting a rural bank for replacing the weak primary credit societies. Accordingly, in 1975, regional rural banks were established through commercial banks.

(i) To develop the bill market, the RBI introduced two schemes – the bill market scheme in 1952 and the new bill market scheme in 1970, but not with much progress.

(j) In December 1969, the RBI introduced Lead Bank Scheme to eliminate banking deficiencies in rural areas. The Lead Bank Scheme helps the area approach for development. The scheme entrusted to the individual banks the responsibility to locate growth centres, assess deposit potential and identify credit gaps and evolve a coordinated programme to each district.

Reserve Bank of India and Working Groups

In order to develop the money market, the RBI appointed a committee to review the working of the monetary system in 1985 under the chairmanship of Professor S Chakravarty. The committee recommended an indepth study of the issues relating to the development of the money market. The working group on the money market (1987) was set up under the chairmanship of M H Vaghul by the RBI. The working group submitted the report in January 1987. The recommendations were:

(a) By April 1987, a treasury bill refinance facility should be introduced. The refinance rate should at least be 1.5 percentage points higher than the prevailing treasury bill rate.

(b) The finance house of India as an autonomous public limited company should be established to deal in short-term money market instruments. It should be jointly formed by the RBI, the public sector banks and the financial institutions.

(c) The feasibility of introducing CDs may be considered at an appropriate time.

(d) Inter bank participation certificates should be reintroduced in a modified form.

(e) Stamp duty on bill should be abolished and commercial paper should be exempt from stamp duty.

(f) Banks and private non-bank institutions should be encouraged to provide factoring service.

(g) Commercial Papers (CPs) should be introduced to start with, on a limited scale, confining its access to only "A" rate companies. The interest rate on commercial paper should be freely determined by market considerations.

(h) A genuine bill culture is to be developed by taking a number of positive measures pertaining to interest rates and legislative amendment.

(i) It should be ensured that the number of participants to bid regularly in the auction should be as large as possible to ensure active secondary market in 182-day treasury bill. A portfolio of varying maturities should be built up. Suitable steps should be taken to ensure that the treasury bill rates remain flexible. The periodicity of auctions should be increased. A treasury bill refinance facility should be introduced.

(j) Suitable legislative measures should be undertaken to give effect to various recommendations.

Keeping with the recommendations of Vaghul Working Group, a series of reforms have been introduced continuously. The developments in the money market as a result of these reforms can be categorised into the following groups:

- New money market instruments
- New institutions such as Discount and Finance House of India (DFHI) and Money Market Mutual Funds (MMMFs)
- Supporting structure through primary dealers and satellite dealers in secondary market.

Indigenous Bankers and Moneylenders

Indigenous bankers constitute the ancient banking system of India. They have been carrying on their age-old banking operations in different parts of the country under different names. In Chennai these bankers are called *Chettys*, in Northern India *Sahukars*, *Mahajanas*, and *Khatris*, in Mumbai *Shroffs* and *Marwaris*, and in Bengal *Seths* and *Banias*. According to the Indian Central Banking Enquiry Committee, an indigenous banker or bank is defined as an individual or private firm which receives deposits, deals in *hundis* or engages itself in lending money. The Report of the Agricultural Finance Sub-committee 1945 observes that the distinguishing features of an indigenous banker lies in accepting deposits but in discounting *hundis*. Until the middle of the nineteenth century, the indigenous banker constituted the bulk of the Indian financial system. The Banking Commission (1972) grouped them under four categories.

(a) Gujarati *Shroff* (active in the industrial and trading centres of Gujarat, Mumbai).
(b) Shikarpuri or Multani *Shroff* (active in the metropolitan areas of Mumbai and Chennai).
(c) *Chettiars* of the South (active in Chennai and southern parts of India).
(d) Marwari *Kayas* (active in the gardens of Assam, *Rastogi* bankers numbering about 500 are also an important group of bankers) serving craftsmen and traders in the Oudh area of Uttar Pradesh. The commission has rated that, if they are linked with the RBI, the entire financial system in the country will get strengthened.

Characteristics of Indigenous Bankers

A few characteristics of indigenous bankers are:

(a) Indigenous bankers accept deposits and deal in hundis. Modern bankers do not deal in *hundis* but in bills of exchange.
(b) Operations of indigenous bankers are free from formalities and delays. Their business hours are flexible.
(c) Indigenous bankers provide finance to the traders, artisans as well as small industrialists, but they do not give direct loans to agriculturists.
(d) In comparison with a modern banker, indigenous banking establishments are small and economical. As against modern joint-stock commercial banks, the business of indigenous bankers is carried on as a family concern with their own working capital.
(e) They do not have any formal banking education. They conduct business on the basis of their experience.
(f) They have a thorough knowledge about the family history of their customers and all details regarding their business and financial standing.
(g) Indigenous bankers keep a close watch over the activities of the borrowers.
(h) Indigenous bankers maintain simple accounts in the vernacular. They have a high sense of responsibility and are keen on maintaining their business reputation. They generally lend on the mortgage of land, houses, etc. They also draw and discount *hundis.* The discounting rate charged by them is called the *bazaar* rate.
(i) A majority of indigenous bankers combine banking business with trading and speculative activity based on common capital fund employed by them.

Functions of Indigenous Bankers

The functions of indigenous bankers are:

(a) They accept deposits on current and fixed accounts.

(b) They give loans to artisans and small urban traders against collateral security or personal security.
(c) They accept valuables of their clients for safe custody.
(d) They buy and sell *hundis* for remitting funds.
(e) They finance (retail/wholesale) including the movement of agricultural commodities like cotton, sugar, oil seeds, etc. But they do not give direct loans to farmers.
(f) A part of the credit will be in the form of clean advances with small borrowers badly needed.
(g) They provide prompt, flexible and personalised services to their customers devoid of delays and formalities of complex nature.
(h) Their establishment overheads are also lower. Their recovery rate is very high. Their turnover of operations is relatively high and cost effective.
(i) They may charge differential rates of interest to their personal advantage based on the emergency and profile of the borrower.

Defects of Indigenous Bankers

The problems of indigenous bankers are:

(a) The indigenous bankers generally combine banking and non-banking business. This is against the principles of sound banking.
(b) They are unorganised.
(c) The main business of the indigenous bankers is to give loans and deal in *hundis*. Their deposit business is very small. They do not mobilise savings of the general public.
(d) They maintain informal business relations.
(e) The indigenous bankers largely depend upon their own capital or that of their family members or relatives. The financial resources of these bankers, therefore, are insufficient to meet the demand of the borrowers.
(f) They adopt a traditional accounting system in vernacular.
(g) They have no regular contact with the commercial banks.
(h) The indigenous bankers charge much higher interest rates from their borrowers than those charged by the commercial banks.
(i) The indigenous banking business is unregulated. The RBI has no control over these bankers and cannot regulate their activities. They are creating a great hurdle for organised markets in the country.
(j) The indigenous bankers also stand in the way of developing a proper bill market in the country.
(k) The indigenous bankers do not pay attention to the purpose for which the loan is used. They lend for unproductive and speculative business, for paying interest or for paying off old debts.
(l) The indigenous bankers indulge in all types of malpractices and exploit their customers by making unauthorised deductions from the loans,

overstate the amount of loans in the discount and they do not give receipt against payments received. Majority of them are conservative in approach and attitude.

Suggestions for Reforms

Given below are some suggestions for reforms for indigenous bankers.

(a) The indigenous bankers should be directly linked with the RBI.
(b) They should separate non-banking business from banking business.
(c) Licensing should be introduced.
(d) Their activities should be linked with commercial banking.
(e) They should be members of an association.
(f) They should adopt modern methods of book keeping, audited regularly by authorised auditors and allow their records to be inspected by the RBI.
(g) The commercial banks should be encouraged to cooperate with and provide help to indigenous bankers.
(h) They should develop bill broking business like bill brokers in the London Money Market.

Indigenous Bankers and the Reserve Bank of India

The indigenous bankers choose to be away from the domain of organised banking sector in spite of their valid contribution to economic advancement of the rural masses. The Central Banking Enquiry Committee (1931) underlined the need to integrate the unorganised money market with the organised sector of the money market. The following are some of the suggestions from the RBI during the 1930s to bring indigenous bankers into organised sector.

(a) They should have a minimum working capital of INR 1 lakh, which should be increased to INR 6 lakhs within five years.
(b) The leading indigenous bankers should play the role of the discount houses as in London to buy and sell bill of exchange.
(c) They should switch over to the western system of accounting.
(d) They should submit to RBI periodical statement of affairs.
(e) The indigenous bankers should give up their trading and commission business and concentrate only on banking business as defined by the Indian Companies Act.

These suggestions did not enthuse the indigenous bankers who were obsessed with their age-old independent practices. Thus, the efforts of RBI to bring the indigenous bankers into organised banking activity could not take off.

The Banking Commission (1972) observed that the indigenous bankers played purposeful role by providing the required credit available to small-scale business units and retail trade. Even though these units were productive, they were not in a position to get loans and risk involved, commercial banks were reluctant to come forward to lend to these units. Indigenous bankers, on the other hand, were prepared to bear these costs and risk and make loans available to these units.

The Commission made the following observations:

(a) Their method of operation are expeditive and flexible.
(b) The indigenous bankers create *hundis* and the commercial banks would discount these hundies. Thus these *hundis* provide liquidity in the money market.
(c) The Commission wanted RBI to regulate the indigenous banking system.

However, these recommendations of the Commission were ignored.

Future of Indigenous Bankers

In spite of rapid banking development in the country, both in urban and rural areas, and also with electronic banking, the indigenous bankers were prepared to take risk, which could not be undertaken by the commercial banks in the organised banking sector. They were prepared to lend even without security, which is not possible with organised credit institutions. When one does not have enough fixed assets to offer as security, the only alternative is to seek loan from indigenous bankers. For this reason, the indigenous bankers all over the rural and urban areas have promising future.

Therefore, the Banking Commission felt that the indigenous bankers would have to grow in size from small to bigger, conduct their operations in a professional manner and link themselves with the organised financial system. There is a lot of scope for them to emerge as non-banking financial intermediaries.

Moneylenders

Moneylenders are heterogenous groups whose main activity is moneylending. They may be classified into: (a) Professional Money Lenders and Non-Professional Money Lenders (b) Rural Money Lenders and Urban Money Lenders.

Banias, Mahajans, Sahukars, etc., are the professional moneylenders and moneylending is their main activity by profession. Non-professional money lenders do not conduct moneylending as their main business activity. They are engaged in other types of activities such as trading, farming, etc. They include landlords, merchants, gold smiths, large farmers, jobbers, and material and labour contractors in urban areas.

Moneylenders operating in villages are called rural moneylenders and those operating in urban and metropolitan areas are urban moneylenders. Rural moneylenders provide credit to the farmers and village artisans. Urban moneylenders provide credit to poor labourers, factory workers, and employees of government and quasi-government organisations. The moneylender's funds are mostly owned funds. Generally they do not borrow. They may receive small amounts of temporary deposits from clients, relatives, and friends.

Distinction between Moneylenders and Indigenous Bankers

The following are the distinctions between moneylenders and indigenous bankers:

(a) The primary business of the moneylenders is moneylending. The primary business of indigenous banking is banking.

(b) Moneylenders usually finance consumption loans, indigenous bankers finance productive loans.

(c) The moneylenders lend money but normally do not undertake any banking business such as accepting of deposits or dealing in *hundis*, whereas, indigenous bankers are basically concerned with receiving deposits and dealing in *hundis*.

(d) Usually the transactions of moneylenders are conducted in cash or at the most in terms of promissory notes. Indigenous bankers, on the other hand, conduct their transactions on the basis of short-term credit investments like *hundis*.

(e) Accounts of moneylenders are not subject to audit and scrutiny. Indigenous bankers accounts are subject to audit and scrutiny.

(f) Moneylenders function individually and they compete among themselves. Indigenous bankers, however, function in an organised way, in harmony, they are more concerned with the development of their profession.

(g) Moneylenders operate in a limited area, so the scope of their business is limited. Indigenous bankers have a wider area of operations and a large scale of financial operations.

(h) Moneylenders do not bother much about the purpose or end-use of loans given by them to the borrowers. Indigenous bankers are, however, more careful regarding the objects/purpose loan.

Operations of Moneylenders

The following are the main operations of money lenders in India:

(a) Moneylenders obtain reliable information about the character and creditworthiness of the borrowers so that the recovery risk is minimised.

(b) They maintain personal/social contacts with the clients.
(c) They maintain flexible lending policies and procedures. They are not bound by any regulations. They are free to lend or refuse and they are free to charge a high rate of interest with or without demanding security.
(d) They give their customers loans against personal security for personal consumption. They are not keen to know about the purpose of the loan, whether the loans are used for productive or unproductive purposes.
(e) They exercise social control over the borrowers in the recovery of loans. The social control may take the form of caste disapproval, pressure of *panchayats*, loss of social prestige, and so on, that will minimise the chances of repayment defaults.
(f) They adopt strong-arm methods such as using muscle power to recover loans both in rural and urban areas. They do not depend upon the legal system. They do not approach courts for recovery of loans. Their economic, social, and political power helps the moneylender to recover their loans speedily.
(g) Moneylenders also resort to certain undesirable and repressive practices such as:
    - charging a high rate of interest
    - demanding interest in advance
    - demanding gifts and donations
    - granting loans in installments and collecting repayment of loans in kind, namely livestock
    - manipulating accounts.

Importance of Moneylenders in Rural Finance

In the absence of an organised money market in the countryside, money lenders play a significant role in catering to the money needs of the rural population in India. To eliminate or minimise the exploitative nature of operations of money lenders, the following legislative measures have been taken up in the past.

These are:

(a) restrictions in the alienation of land.
(b) control of the rate of interest charged.
(c) to give to borrowers regular statement of accounts.
(d) the requirement of license to maintain proper books of accounts.
(e) restrictions on the maximum amount of interest of loan so that the total does not exceed double the initial amount of loan.

But these measures are not useful to the rural borrower to get out of the clutches of the moneylender.

The Government of India took up measures to provide credit from cooperative societies and regional rural banks to provide the rural and urban borrowers an alternative source of borrowing. During the eighties and nineties, due to the rapid expansion of institutional sources of rural credit, the importance of moneylenders has declined greatly, although moneylenders still play a dominant role in the rural lending.

New Money Market Instruments

The following are new instruments introduced in the money market on the recommendations of the Vaghul Working Group.

(a) Inter Bank Participation (IBP) Certificates

These are modified forms of participation certificates that were very popular during the 1970s. IBP are designed to even out short-term liquidity within the banking system.

There are two types of IBP – risk sharing basis and without sharing risk. IBP with sharing risk can be issued for 91–180 days in respect of advances. The issuing bank and the participating bank are free to decide the rate of interest on such IBPs. IBPs without risk-sharing would be treated, subject to reserve requirement, as part of Net Demand and Time Liabilities (NDTL) of the borrowing bank.

(b) Treasury Bills of Different Maturity Periods

From 1996–1997, the 14-day treasury bill was introduced without any collateral security. Deposit receipt is issued to the lender who on recalling the funds, discharges the receipt and gives it back to the borrower upon which the borrower will repay the amount together with interest. The participants in this market are commercial banks, foreign central banks, financial institutions and cooperative banks who can borrow and lend funds. Mutual funds and all-India financial institutions approved by RBI can participate in this market as lenders only.

Treasury bills are popular in the secondary market due to their short span of life and liquidity. They are also approved liquid assets for the purpose of banks Statutory Liquid Ratio (SLR). They can be acquired by any investor (other than state government) and provident funds. These instruments have the potentialty of providing a link between various segments of the financial markets through shift of funds from cash to treasury bills and vice versa.

The interest of 182-day treasury bills is variable. These are sold in auctions once in a fortnight. They enjoyed high degree of liquidity as the yield was found to be very attractive. These were replaced by 364-day treasury bills but again introduced in 1999–2000. The 182-day treasury bills are eligible for

SLR purposes as also for borrowing under stand-by refinance facility. It can be purchased by any person resident in India including individuals, firms, companies, corporate bodies, and institutions.

364-day treasury bills were introduced in the year 1992 to widen and stabilise the money market. They were sold in auction on a monthly basis. The RBI does not provide rediscounting facility for these bills. They are known for their higher yield and safety and hence the response for these bills was satisfactory.

(c) Commercial Paper (CP)

In 1989, Commercial Paper (CP) was introduced by the RBI. CP is a short-term negotiable money instrument. These are unsecured promissory notes issued by well-rated corporate bodies to raise short-term working capital requirements directly from the market instead of borrowing from banks. Both listed and unlisted companies can raise commercial papers. It shall be issued at a discount and redeemed at a premium. They are transferable by endorsement and delivery as per the guidelines of the RBI in April 1990. CP is allowed to be issued by a non-banking companies for a period of 3 months. CP is also known as direct paper. The working capital (fund-based) limit of the company should not, be less than INR 5 crores and net worth of the company should not be less than INR 5 crores. The issue should be a minimum amount of INR 25 lakhs to a single investor with the denomination of INR 5 lakhs and multiples thereof. A company can issue CPs up to 75 per cent of its working capital (fund based) limit and after issue of the CPs, company's working capital limit with the bank is correspondingly reduced.

The issuing company has to obtain in advance the specified minimum credit for issuing of commercial paper from credit rating agencies such as Credit Rating Institution Services of India Limited (CRISIL). Investment information and Credit Agency of India Ltd. (ICRA) or any other credit rating agency identified by RBI from time to time. NRIs can invest in CP only on non-repatriable and non-tangible basis. Discount and Finance House of India (DFHI) is permitted to acquire the CP in the primary market and also to provide in secondary market for the different issues of CP by bidding for purchases and offering sales prices. The effective rate of interest on CP issued ranges between 12 per cent and 14 per cent.

(d) Certificate of Deposits (CDs)

A novel scheme of Certificate Deposits (CDs) has been introduced by the RBI in June 1989. It provides an opportunity for investment at better rates in the banking sector. Under the scheme the scheduled commercial banks are permitted to issue CDs without any regulation on interest rates. The minimum amount of certificate of deposit has to be INR 1 crore and in multiples of INR 25 lakhs thereafter. RBI, however, presented a limit to each bank for funds raised under the CDs scheme. CDs are subject to stamp duty applicable to usance notes.

A bank can issue CDs to the extent of seven per cent of its average fortnightly aggregate deposits from 1989–1990. Being a negotiable instrument, it can be transfered by endorsement and delivery but only after the expiry of 45 days from the date of delivery of issue to the primary investor.

The RBI introduced Certificate of Deposits (CDs) with twofold objective – to widen the range of money market instruments, and to provide greater flexibility to the investors in the deployment of their short-term supply funds.

A certificate of deposit shows that a deposit is made with a bank for a fixed period of time and it will be repaid with interest at the end of the maturity period. When one institution accepts a deposit, it is said to issue a CD, where it makes a deposit or buys a certificate in the secondary market, it is said to hold a CD. From the institution point of view, therefore, issued CDs are habituates and CDs held are assets. CDs are instruments for short-term, wholesale lending and borrowing. They can be issued for varying periods of maturity.

As per the directons of RBI, CDs could be issued initially only by scheduled commercial banks. Later on, even financial institutions were permitted to do so. From 1997, the minimum size was reduced to INR 5 lakhs and in multiples of INR 1 lakh with a view to make it popular and widen the money market. In order to bring CDs on part with similar instruments like commercial paper, the minimum maturity period was reduced to fifteen days from April 2000 which was earlier for three months.

To give a wider choice to both investor and issuers and to make the price of CDs more flexible, banks and financial institutions are allowed to issue CDs on floating rate basis. Floating rate means charging a variable interest rate instead of a fixed rate of interest. Floating rates are charged to minimise interest expenses. CDs were converted to demat from 1982. CDs outstanding amount increased from INR 43,568 crores at the end of March 2006 to July 2007 to INR 57,256 crores.

(e) Commercial Bills

Bills of exchange are drawn by the seller (drawer) on the buyer (drawee) for the value of goods delivered to him. Such bills are called trade bills. Where trade bills are accepted by commercial banks, they are called commercial bills. The main objective of having and accepting the bill of exchange is to raise the primary funds and to multiply his turnover. If the seller wishes to give some period for payment, the bill would be payable at a future date (usance bill). During the currency of the bill, if the seller is in need of funds, he may approach his bank for discounting the bill. One of the methods of providing credit to customers by banks is by discounting commercial bills at a negotiated discount rate. The bank will receive the maturity proceeds (face value) of discounted bill from the drawer. In the meanwhile if the bank is in need of funds, it can rediscount the bills already discounted by it in the commercial bill rediscount market at the market related discount rate. Besides the Discount and Finance House of India (DFHI), scheduled commercial banks, all-India financial institutions, mutual funds and select scheduled state cooperative banks and scheduled urban cooperative banks are approved participants in the market. The eligibility criteria prescribed by the RBI for rediscounting commercial bills are that the bills should arise out of genuine commercial trade transaction evidencing sale of goods and the maturity date of the bill should not be more than 90 days from the date of rediscounting.

(f) Repos and Reverse Repos

Repo deal is a contract to buy securities and then to sell them back at a particular price and date. It is essentially an opportunity for short-term investment of surplus funds. Reverse Repos involves a contract to sell securities and then to repurchase it at a stated future date for a slightly higher price. Repos provide liquidity and depth to the underlying securities market. Repos have been effectively used in every developed country such as USA, Germany, Canada by their respective central banks to maintain liquidity in the economy.

New Institutions

Discount and Finance House of India (DFHI)

The working group on money market, in its report submitted in 1987, recommended, among other things, that a finance house should be set up to deal in short-term money market instruments. As a follow-up on the recommendation of the working group, the RBI, in collaboration with public sector banks and financial institutions, set up the DFHI in April 1988. DFHI is the apex body in the Indian money market and its establishment is a major step towards developing a secondary market for money instruments. DFHI which commenced its operations from 25 April 1988, deals in short-term money market instruments.

DFHI has an authorised share capital of INR 100 crores subscribed by the RBI (INR 51 crores), public sector banks (INR 33 crores) and all-India Financial institutions (INR 16 crores). The initial paid-up capital of INR 100 crores was increased to INR 150 crores in 1989–1990 and further to INR 200 crores during 1991–1992. This was done with a view to broad base its activities and further enhance its role in the development of money market. In September 1994, the RBI started the process of divestment of part of its shareholding in DFHI in favour of other shareholding institutions.

Objectives of setting up DFHI:

(a) To provide greater liquidity to money market instruments.
(b) To even out the liquidity imbalances in the banking system that is to balance the demand with the supply for short-term finance in the money market.
(c) To provide rate and risk-free short-term investment opportunities to institutions.
(d) To provide money market transactions for small-and medium-sized institutions who are not regular participants in the market.
(e) To provide secondary market in short-term money market instruments. That is to be an active trader in money market instruments rather than a mere repository, and thereby impart improved liquidity to short-term money market instruments.

The activities of DFHI are:

(a) In the initial years DFHI confined itself mainly to call notice, term money markets, treasury bills, and commercial bills.
(b) With the introduction of new money market instruments such as certificate of deposits and commercial paper, it started dealing in these instruments too.
(c) With effect from 1992–1993, it was authorised to deal in dated government securities.
(d) It essentially caters to the requirement of the small and medium-sized institutions operating at these centres. It integrates the markets at these regional centres with main money market at Mumbai.
(e) It was accredited as a primary dealer in February 1996. Since then, its operations increased greatly more so in treasury bill and dated government securities. During these years DFHI opened its branches at Ahmedabad, Bangalore, Kolkata, Chennai, New Delhi, and Hyderabad.

The introductions of variety of money market instruments, the series of reform measures introduced in the money and securities market lane enlarged the role and responsibilities of DFHI as one of the leading market players in the country.

Money Market Mutual Funds (MMMFs)

Money Market Mutual Funds (MMMFs) are investment pooling arrangement, which allow retail participation in money markets through size intermediation. Securities Exchange Board of India (SEBI), Mutual Funds Regulations, 1996 defines MMMFs as "a scheme of a mutual fund which has been set up with the objective of investing exclusively in money market instruments". Further money market instruments "include commercial papers (CP), commercial bills, treasury bills (T-Bills), government securities (G-Securities) being an unexpired maturity up to one year, call or notice money, certificate of deposit (CD), usance bills and any other instruments as specified by the RBI from time to time". Retail inventions do not have ready access to either T-Bills or call lending. MMMFs make it possible for retail inventions to earn relatively higher yields offered by money markets.

MMMFs offer diversification of short-term assets in terms of issues, maturity, and size, thereby spreading the risk for the investors. Through MMMFs even high net-worth investors can diversify their money market portfolio and enjoy high liquidity. Investors with monthly income/accrual, like the salaried class, provident funds, etc., also have the advantage of parking their funds in MMMFs till a long-term investment avenue of their choice, emerges. The units of MMMFs are negotiable instruments and are transferable by endorsement and delivery.

Similar to other Mutual Funds (MFs), less MMMFs are also exempt from income tax under Section (23D) of IT Act, 1961. Further income from MMMFs enjoys tax benefits, subject to certain conditions, which effectively enhance the post tax returns for the investors. The Indian mutual fund industry has grown chiefly due to tax incentives granted to it from time to time.

It is evident from the development of money market that it was largely a corporate affair. MMMFs, therefore emerged in the US and UK in 1970 as vehicle for retail investors to arbitrage between the low bank deposits rates and the higher money market rates.

MMMFs, introduced in the US in 1971, opened a new short-term asset class to retail investors. Price decline in the equity markets during the decade combined with rising interest rates made MMMFs, a very popular investment. In India, the RBI outlined the broad framework for selling up MMMFs in its credit policy in April 1991.

The objective was, "providing an additional short-term avenue to investors and to bring money market instruments within the reach of individuals". RBI appointed a task force to work out the detailed operative guidelines and documentation for MMMFs with D Basu (Dy Managing Director of SBI) as the chairman. Based on the task force recommendations, the RBI announced a detailed scheme for MMMFs in April 1992. The Basu Committee had recommended a lock-in-period for investment in MMMFs at 46 days, coinciding with the minimum maturity period of fixed deposits in 1991. The maximum term of CP was increased to twelve months from three months by the RBI in October 1993. Mutual funds set up by banks or financial institutions had access to call markets. Mutual funds set up by private sector were allowed to lend in the call notice money markets and bill rediscounting by RBI only from June 1995. Mutual funds have been allowed to participate in repo market from March 2003 to provide an alternative to lending in call markets.

The RBI is the most important constituent of the money market. The primary aim of RBI's operation in the money market is to ensure that the liquidity and short-term interest rates are maintained at levels consistent with the monetary policy objectives of maintaining price stability, ensuring adequate flow of credit to productive sectors of the economy and bringing about orderly conditions in the foreign exchange markets.

Private sector mutual funds and mutual funds already set up by public sector banks and financial institutions came under the regulatory oversight of SEBI. RBI guidelines for MMMFs issued in April 1992 allowed only banks, financial institutions and their subsidiaries to set up MMMFs. Corporate and others were allowed to invest in MMMFs only from April 1996. All MMMFs came under the regulatory oversight of SEBI and were governed by the SEBI (Mutual Fund) Regulations, 1996. However, banks and financial institutions setting up mutual funds have to still seek clearance from RBI. At present, RBI no longer regulates MMMFs.

The poor impact of mutual funds at the macro level can be attributed to their task of retail. Penetration by innovative modes, establishing point of contact with retail investors through branch networks could be the key factor. Market funds floated by banks will have to fully support the branch network of their parent banks. Other mutual funds may explore tie-ups with post office branches for establishing point of contact with retail investors.

Bill Market Scheme

Bill market refers to the market for short-term bills generally of three months' maturity. A bill is a promise to pay a specified amount by the borrower (Drawer) to the creditor (Drawee).

Bills are of three types: (a) Bill of Exchange or commercial bills used to finance trade (b) Finance bills or promissory notes and (c) Treasury bills used to meet temporary financial needs of the Government. These bills may be bought and sold in the discount market which consists of commercial banks, discount houses and other institutions.

The bill market plays an important role in the banking and monetary system of the country because of the following reasons:

(a) It helps to meet the short-term financial requirements of individuals, companies and the Government.
(b) The commercial banks which have surplus funds can invest them profitably in these bills.
(c) The commercial banks can dispose of these bills easily or can get them discounted by the RBI whenever they require cash.

Old Bills Market Scheme

The Bill Market Scheme was introduced by the RBI in January 1952. Under this scheme, the RBI undertook to advance loans to commercial banks against their demand promissory notes supported by the security of usance bill of their constituents or customers. According to the Bill Market Scheme, a bank can grant loans to its customers against their promissory notes and can further use the same promissory notes to borrow from the RBI.

Initially the Bill Market Scheme was introduced on an experimental basis. It was restricted to the scheduled banks with deposits of INR 10 crores and above. It was for the loans with the minimum limit of INR 10 lakhs and against the individual bills. The minimum value of each should be INR 1 lakh.

The Dehajia Committee Report brought out the abuses of cash credit system and suggested the use of bill financing for the supervision of the funds lent by the commercial banks.

Dissatisfied with old bill market scheme, the RBI in February 1970, constituted a study group under the chairmanship of Shri Narasimham to go into question of enlarging the use of bill of exchange as an instrument of credit and creation of genuine bill market in India. On the recommendations of the report of the study group, the RBI introduced the New Bill Market Scheme in November 1970 under Section 17(2) of RBI Act.

Features of the New Bill Market Scheme

The features of the New Bill Market Scheme are:

(a) The bills should have maximum usance of 90 days.
(b) The bills should bear at least two good signatures.
(c) The bills covered under the scheme must be genuine trade bills relating to the sale or dispatch of goods.
(d) All licensed scheduled commercial banks including the public sector banks will be eligible to offer bills of exchange to the RBI for rediscounting.
(e) The bill should be drawn on and accepted by the purchaser's banks. If the purchaser's bank is not a licensed scheduled bank, the bill

should, in addition, bear the signatures of a licensed scheduled banks.

(f) According to the modifications of the scheme in 1971, the bills of exchange relating to the sale of goods to government departments and quasi-government bodies as well as to statutory corporations have also been covered by the scheme.

(g) With effect from April 1972, the bill of exchange drawn and accepted by the Industrial Credit and Investment Corporation of India (ICICI) were also made eligible for discount under this scheme.

Advantages of a Developed Bill Market

A developed bill market is useful to the borrowers, creditors and to financial and monetary system as a whole. The following are the advantages of a developed bill market.

(a) Bills provide greater liquidity to their holders because they can be shifted to others in the market in case of need for cash.

(b) Bill finance is better than cash credit. Bills are self-liquidating and the date of repayment of a bank's loans through discounting or rediscounting is certain.

(c) A developed bill market is also useful to the banks in case of emergency. In the absence of such a market, the banks in need of cash have to depend either on call money market or on the RBI's loan window.

(d) The commercial bill rate is much higher than the treasury bill rate. There the commercial banks and other financial institutions with short-term surplus funds, find in bills an attractive source of both liquidity and profitability.

(e) A developed bill market is also useful for the borrowers. The bills are the additional security in the form of acceptor's signature. Therefore, for the borrowers, the cost of bill finance is lower than that of cash credit.

Disadvantages of Bill Market Scheme

Despite the above advantages, the Bill Market Scheme has its share of disadvantages too. These are:

(a) The bill market scheme has not been successful in developing a genuine bill market. The main reason is that the borrowers as well as the banks still have preference for cash credit and dislike for bill finance.

(b) The scheme is restricted to banks and some selected financial institutions. It has not been able to cover the indigenous banks and other constituents of unorganised sector of the Indian money market.

(c) The scheme has mainly concentrated in the fields of industry, trade and commerce. It has not been extended to the agriculture sector.

(d) The scheme has been, generally, used by the banks and their borrowers to offset the credit control measures of the RBI. Whenever the RBI tried to control the bank credit without restricting the bill rediscounting facility, the banks increasingly utilised this facility. This made the RBI's tight money policy ineffective.

With a view to enlarge the scope of bills rediscounting market, a few more financial institutions, namely Exim Banks, LIC Mutual Fund, Small Industries Development Banks of India (SIDBI), etc., were permitted to participate in the bills rediscounting market during 1989–1990. The DFHI has been rediscounting bills on a large scale since its inception in 1988. The DFHI operates the bill financing scheme with a greater flexibility for providing greater liquidity to commercial bills.

Development of the bill market make the monetary control measures as adopted by RBI in a more effective way. The Narasimham Study Group pointed out that "the evolution of the bill market will also make the bank rate variation by RBI as a more effective weapon of monetary control as the impact of such change could be transmitted through its sensitive market to the rest of the banking system".

Supporting Infrastructure

Primary Dealers (PDs)

A system of Primary Dealers (PDs) was introduced in 1995 primarily to strengthen the infrastructure in the government securities market including money market in order to make it vibrant, liquid and broad-based. PDs are the market players for government securities market operating and are regulated by RBI. Even subsidiaries of commercial banks and financial institutions dedicated predominantly to the securities. Business may act as primary dealers. DFHI, ICICI Securities Limited, SBI Gilts Limited are some of the major primary dealers. PDs with the support of satellite dealers ensure wider distribution of government securities.

Satellite Dealers (SDs)

In order to strengthen the supporting infrastructure, a system of Satellite Dealers (SDs) was introduced to widen the scope for organised dealing and distributor arrangements in the government securities/money market institutions. SDs play an active role in both primary and secondary segments of the government securities market/money market. They supplement the efforts of primary dealers in the direction.

One of the objectives of setting up of DFHI is to provide a depth to secondary market for money market instruments. The role of primary dealers is very significant in the development of secondary market particularly in the dealings on treasury bills, repo facilities and soon. The measures such as abolition of stamp duty also strengthened the functioning of secondary market.

Various steps taken by the RBI in view of the recommendations of the working group to introduce reforms in the money market have changed the face of the money market in the country. With so many reforms that have been introduced in the money market, today's Indian money market is more or less comparable to money markets in advanced countries. The Indian money market can no more be categorised as underdeveloped money market.

5
Capital Market

Capital Market is a growing component of the financial system in India. The capital market differs from the money market in terms of maturity, structure, and liquidity. The money market comprises financial instruments having a maturity period of one year or less. It involves short-term transactions.

Capital market contains financial instruments of maturity period exceeding one year. It involves long-term transactions. Capital market instruments are relatively less liquid in comparison to the money market instruments. Capital market in a broad sense encompasses all kinds of arrangements and financial institutions involved in long-term funding. Capital market is, however, commonly referred to as the stock market in the country. From the stock market point of view, capital market comprises both primary and secondary market. The primary market deals with new issues made by the companies. The secondary market relates to the trading in the existing securities. An investor can buy securities in secondary market.

Capital market forms the nerve centre of the industrial development of any economy. If they are transparent and vibrant, investors come forward to invest their surplus funds which can be channelised for the economic and industrial development of the country.

The efficiency of capital market is indicated by the number of new companies promoted, the amount of funds raised (in terms of shares, debentures or bonds) and the frequency with which the securities are being traded. Capital markets are also called markets for corporate securities.

Structure/Composition of Capital Market

The Indian capital market is well diversified in terms of ownership pattern and industry structure. There are companies with a market capitalisation of more than one billion in industries as diverse as software, oil refining, consumer goods, telecom, petrochemicals, pharmaceuticals, banking, and entertainment.

Capital market in India consists of:

- Primary Markets and Secondary Markets – Stock exchanges provide liquidity and the current market price of the corporate securities.

- Development Financial Institutions which provide long-term debt capital to the corporate sector. For example, IDBI, IFCI and APSFC.
- Investment financial institution which provides long-term finance. For example, Life Insurance Corporation of India (LIC), Unit Trust of India (UTI).
- Insurance Sector – Insurance Regulatory and Development Authority (IRDA), issued licenses for several private sector insurance companies both in the life and non-life sectors.
- Commercial Banks which provide long-term finance. For example, State Bank of India, Andhra Bank, Corporation Bank, Canara Bank, Punjab National Bank, Oriental Bank of Commerce, Syndicate Bank, etc.
- Mutual Funds – mutual fund industry is no more the domain of public sector banks and financial institutions. After 1990, private sector mutual funds were also permitted. Mutual Funds, over the last 10 years have become a significant mechanism for financial intermediation in the economy. The mutual fund industry now offers more than 450 products to consumers and managed INR 1,50,000 crores by October 2002. It can be observed that private mutual funds, despite their recent entry, account for over 55 per cent of mutual fund assets. The stock of assets managed by mutual funds work out to only 10 per cent of the assets of the banking industry. Mutual funds today can invest in rated securities in countries with fully convertible currencies and this enables them to deliver better risk/turn trade off through international diversification.
- Foreign Institutional Investors (FIIs) – FIIs are the institutions such as mutual funds, pension funds, banks and insurance companies. They are allowed to buy and sell shares in the stock exchange and replicate the proceeds freely to their home countries (as on 31 March 2000). FIIs had in the aggregate invested US $11.23 billion repressuring about 5 per cent of the market capitalisation.
- Venture Capital Funds–venture capital is the seed capital required by the start-up companies. Venture capital companies provide funds for the existing small companies, with high risk, suffering from shortage of capital. Emerging growth companies that have high profit potential especially in the various fields of high technology are selected for venture capital funding. Most of the nationalised banks provide venture finance. Securities Exchange Board of India (SEBI) has recently liberalised the regulation for venture capital funds and has also permitted foreign venture capital funds to operate in India. They will have the freedom to invest in unlisted companies with the full freedom to repatriate sale proceeds.

The above institutions may be classified as: (a) Financial institutions such as IDBI, IFCI, LIC, UTI, commercial banks and State level financial institutions, etc. (b) The Government securities market (Gilt-edged market), and (c) Corporate securities market.

Features of Indian Capital Market

The features of the Indian capital market are:

(a) Fast growth of mutual funds
(b) Growth of the merchant banking
(c) Issue of debentures
(d) Growing debt instrument
(e) Banks subsidiaries for financial services into the capital market
(f) Floatation of mega issues
(g) Liberalisation policy of the Government
(h) Avoidance of underwriting
(i) Increased transparency through SEBI's regulations
(j) Emerging new financial instruments such as zero coupon bonds, discount bonds, warrants, convertible bonds, foreign currency rates, etc.

Government Securities/Gilt-edged Market

Government securities/gilt-edged market is a market which deals in Government securities or such securities guaranteed by the government both for payment of principal and interest. These are considered to be risk free or gilt edged (i.e. of the best quality) as the government cannot default on its commitment for payment.

The following are the features of the Government securities:

(a) There is a guarantee for payment of both principal and interest with a defined yield, at a given point of time.
(b) Government securities market can be categorised into new issues and secondary market. Only RBI is authorised to deal with government securities.
(c) Government securities are the most liquid debt instruments and each transaction in the Government securities market is so large that the amount will be in several crores.
(d) The investors are mostly financial institutes like LIC, banks, provident funds which have a statutory obligation to invest a certain part of funds in Government securities.

Growth in Government Securities Market

Primary market borrowings of the central government were:
in 1980–1981 — INR 2,871 crores
in 1990–1991 — INR 8,990 crores
in 2000–2001 — INR 1,15,183 crores

The primary market borrowings of state governments were:
in 1980–1981 — INR 333 crores
in 1990–1991 — INR 2,569 crores
in 2000–2001 — INR 13,300 crores

The secondary market transactions in Government securities started in September 1994. This market witnessed a sharp growth from INR 50,570 in 1994–1995 to INR 2,25,675 in 1998–1999 and INR 6,99,146 crores in 2000–2001. The common investor has been looking for some sort of security in terms of liquidity and safety of his funds.

Corporate Securities Market

Corporate securities market is a market where shares, debentures and bonds of joint-stock companies (whether new companies or existing companies) are traded. The new issue market is called the primary market. It deals with securities of new companies and also that of the Government. When a company wants to raise capital for the first time, it goes to the primary market. A company may raise capital through primary market in any of the following ways:

(a) Through issue of shares and debentures or bonds by prospectus or public issue. Public companies go for public issue where in long-term securities are issued to a large number of investors through prospectus.
(b) Through private placement, the shares are offered only to a small group of investors from a close circle of contact.
(c) When a company wants to raise further capital, it may prefer to issue shares or securities to the close shareholders or debenture holders on priority basis.

The primary market in India has grown substantially since 1991 when the restrictions on investments were removed. During 1991–1992, INR 62.15 billion was raised in the primary market. In 1994–1995, INR 27.6 billion investment was raised through public issues and rights issues. Since then, there has been a constant decline in the number of public issues due to the overall downfall in the market and lighter entry barriers introduced by SEBI to protect the interest of small investors.

During 2000–2001, an amount of INR 61.08 billion was mobilised through 124 public and 27 right issues, much lesser than the amount of INR 7817 billion mobilised through 65 public issues and 28 right issues during 1999–2000. Resources mobilised during April to December 2001 announced to be INR 37.77 billion through 12 public issues and nine right issues, and was INR 42.4 billion through 109 public issues and 15 right issues during the corresponding period in the year 2000.

Public offerings can be classified into:

(a) Initial Public Offerings (IPO), where a company goes public for the first time.
(b) Rights issues, where a company sells additional shares to existing sharesholders.
(c) Seasoned Equity Offerings (SEOs), where a listed company sells shares to the public.

India enjoyed a major boom in the primary market in respect of new issues (IPOs), in the mid-1990s. In 1995–1996, there was a fall in the stock market and downturn in the economy. The stock market scam and the consequent debacle in the stock market completely shattered the confidence of the investors. Several investors who subscribed during the boom period suffered heavy losses. The primary market has not yet recovered from this shock. The primary markets could not recover precisely for two reasons:

(a) The old economy companies (such as Iron, Steel, Jute, Textile and cotton industries) were not able to withstand the global competition and their share prices started tumbling in the process. They did not have any new proposals to enter the primary market.
(b) The new economy companies were making huge profits and their stock prices were skyrocketing. They were already flush with funds. They did not find any need to enter the primary market for funds. Debt instruments are sought more in comparison to equity shares during 2001–2002 and 2002–2003.

The secondary market is an organised market for trading existing corporate securities. In a secondary market existing securities of companies are bought and sold with regard to corporate securities.

Stock exchanges are the secondary markets. Stock exchanges can buy or sell the securities of listed companies, whose securities are permitted to be traded in stock exchange through a broker, because one cannot buy or sell shares on stock exchange directory. A broker is an authorised member of the stock exchange. The barometer of a secondary market is the number of listed companies and the amount of market capitalisation. Market capitalisation is the total value of a company's issued capital as per its current share price on the stock exchange. A transparent and vibrant equity market constitutes the lifeline of any economy. As on 31 March 2000, the Indian stock market had a market capitalisation of over INR 10 trillion (US $230 billion) representing 58 per cent of Gross Domestic Product (GDP). As on 30 April 2006 the market capitalisation was INR 62,45,765 crores. The annual trading volume in all the exchanges put together was approximately thrice the market capitalisation. The average daily trading volume was about US $3 billion. In the last few years, however, new economy stocks such as software and entertainment have shown rapid increase in their market capitalisation and turnover. Market capitalisation is the market's valuation of the company. It can be calculated as follows.

Number of Shares × Market Price

Developments in the Indian Capital Market

The capital market in India is one of the oldest in the world and is considered to be the fastest growing and the best among all the markets of the emerging economies. The history of Indian capital market dates back 200 years towards the end of eighteenth century when India was ruled by the East India Company. The development of the capital market in India concentrated around Mumbai where no less than 200 to 250 security brokers were active during the second half of the nineteenth century.

The financial market in India today is more developed than many other sectors because it was organised as early as the nineteenth century, with the establishment of securities exchange of Mumbai, Ahmedabad, and Kolkata. By the early 1960s, the total number of securities exchanges in India rose to eight, with the inclusion of exchanges in Chennai, Kanpur, Delhi, Bangalore, Pune, and Hyderabad, apart from exchanges in Mumbai, Ahmedabad, and Kolkata. Today there are 21 regional securities exchanges in India in addition to the centralised NSC (National Stock Exchange) and OTCEI (Over The Counter Exchange of India).

However, the stock markets in India remained stagnant due to stringent control on the market economy that allowed only a handful of monopolies to dominate their respective sectors. The corporate sector was not allowed into many industry segments, which were dominated by the state controlled public sector resulting in stagnation of the economy right up to the early 1990s. Thereafter, when the Indian economy began "liberalising" and the control began to be dismantled or eased out, the securities markets witnessed a flurry of IPOs that were launched. This resulted in many new companies across different industry segments to come up with the newer products and services.

A remarkable feature of the growth of the Indian economy in the recent years has been the role played by its securities markets in assisting and fuelling that growth with money raised within the economy. This was in marked contrast to the initial phase of growth in many of the fast-growing economies of East Asia that witnessed huge doses of FDI (Foreign Direct Investment) decontrol. During this phase in India, much of the organised sector had been affected by high growth as the financial markets played an all-inclusive role in sustaining financial resource mobilisation. Many Public Sector Undertakings (PSUs) that decided to offload part of their equity were also helped by the well-organised securities market in India.

The launch of the NSE and the OTCEI during the mid-1990s by the Government of India was meant to usher in an easier and more transparent form of trading in securities. The NSE was conceived as the market for trading in the securities of companies from the large-scale sector and the OTCEI for those from the small scale sector. While the NSC has not just done well to show any sign of growth and development, the integration of "Information Technology" into the capital market infrastructure, has been particularly smooth in India due to the country's world class IT industry. This has pushed up the operational efficiency of the Indian stock market to global standards and as a result, the country has been able to capitalise on its high growth and attract foreign capital like never before.

SEBI, came into prominence in 1992 after the capital markets experienced some turbulence. It had to take drastic measures to plug many loopholes that were exploited by certain market forces to advance their vested interests. After this initial phase of struggle, SEBI has grown in strength as the regulator of India's capital markets and as one of the country's most important institutions.

Since independence, India opted for a socialist society and public sector played a dominant role in the planning and development of the Indian economy. Banks and insurance companies were nationalised and several development financial institutions were established. The promotion and growth of joint-stock companies in several sectors of economy depended on the financial assistance, provided by the state-sponsored financial institutions. As a result of increasing role of state in promotion, regulation and control of the industry and the financial sector, the role of stock markets was marginalised. From the 1960s to the early 1980s, there was no significant improvement in stock markets which was considered as the life-blood of capital markets.

1984 to 1992 was considered as the Golden Period for Indian capital markets. The markets responded enthusiastically to the first phase of reforms in the mid-1980s and to the major reform initiative of 1991. The stock market was at its peak during this period. From October 1984 to September 1992, the stock market index went up more than 10 times representing an annual compound return of over 30 per cent.

As a consequence of securities scam of 1992, the confidence level of the investors, especially the small investors reached a new low and it also adversely affected the reform process. During the scam period, funds to the line were over and one-billion dollars were siphoned off from the banks into the stock markets. The scam exposed the weaknesses in the internal control system of Indian and foreign banks operating in India and provided an opportunity to plug the loopholes and strengthen the institutional framework.

The present capital market in India is completely different from what it was twenty years ago. Today's capital market is characterised by adequate number of checks and balances to protect the interest of the investor. There is greater degree of transparency in transactions. The emergence of the new economy and the decay of the old economy in the context of globalisation paved the way for structural changes in the economy with the systematic reforms. The stock markets became safer, more transparent, and investor-friendly. The absorption of Capital Issues (control) Act 1947 was a major change, and free pricing of equity issues was introduced in 1992. SEBI was made the apex regulator of the Indian capital markets. SEBI brought in several regulations on a number of issues relating to capital market. The measures introduced in the primary market were:

(a) Improvement in disclosure norms
(b) Tightening of entry norms for capital issues
(c) Laying down code of conduct for merchant bankers, mutual funds, bankers and underwriters to the issue.

Stock Exchanges

The Securities Contracts (Regulation) Act of 1956 defines a "Stock Exchange" as a "body of individuals, whether incorporated or not, constituted before corporatisation and Demutualisation under 4A and 4B, for the purpose of assisting, regulating or controlling the business of buying, selling or dealing in securities". In simple words, a stock exchange is an organised market for the purchase and sale of second-hand, listed industrial and financial securities. The stock exchange is otherwise known as secondary market. The securities dealt within the stock exchange include shares and debentures of public companies already issued by them, government securities and bonds and debentures issued by municipal bodies or port trusts.

The stock exchanges should provide a well-developed, efficiently administered and properly regulated market system for the efficient mobilisation of resources for the corporate sector and to provide liquidity on investments, by providing a fair and orderly market. The stock exchange has a wide responsibility towards investors, corporate sector, the government, and society at large.

Role and Functions of Stock Exchanges

A well-organised stock exchange performs a number of useful functions in an economy.

(a) Stock exchange helps in determining the prices of securities.
(b) Stock exchange provides a ready market for trading in securities and in this way capital is made more mobile.

(c) Stock exchange enables the business firms to raise large volumes of funds from the market.
(d) An organised stock exchange operating under the well-defined rule and regulations minimises the dangers of speculative dealings and price manipulations.
(e) A competitive and efficient stock exchange acts as a barometer of business conditions in the country.
(f) Stock exchange increases the credit worthiness of the business enterprises. A company whose shares are listed in a stock exchange is considered to be a sound company.
(g) Stock exchange helps the investors to utilise their surplus funds gainfully and helps them to shift from one business to another.
(h) Stock exchanges lessens the risks of the investors by providing a continuous market, high negotiability of securities, correct evaluation, facility to liquidate investment and to know the worth of securities.

In order to protect the interest of the investors, it is obligatory that all securities which are to be traded in the stock exchange be listed.

Listing of Securities

Listing means inclusion of the securities of a company in the official list of a stock exchange. Section 73(1) of the Companies Act, 1956 insists that every company intending to offer shares or debentures to the public for subscription should make an application for listing to one or more recognised stock exchanges. Every stock exchange which is recognised has the power to make by-laws for the listing of securities on the stock exchange, the inclusion of any security for the purpose of dealings, and the suspension or withdrawal of any such securities. The power to make by-laws is subject to the previous approval of the Central Government. Further, the Central Government has the power to make or amend by-laws of recognised stock exchanges.

Requirements

Rule 19 of the Securities Contracts (Regulation) Rules, 1957 provides for requirements with respect to the listing of securities on recognised stock exchanges. This rule is very exhaustive and comprehensive.

Rule 19(1) maintains that a public company as defined under the Companies Act, 1956, desirous of getting its securities listed on a recognised stock exchange, shall apply for the purpose to the stock exchange and forward along with its application the following documents and particulars.

(a) Memorandum and articles of association and in the case of a debenture issue, a copy of the trust deed.

(b) Copies of all prospectuses or statements in view of prospectuses issued by the company at any time.

(c) Copies of offers for sale and circulars or advertisements offering any securities for subscription of sale during the last five years.

(d) Copies of balance sheets and audited accounts for the last five years or in the case of new companies, for such shorter period for which accounts have been made up.

(e) A statement showing:
- dividends and cash bonuses, if any, paid during the last ten years (or such shorter period as the company has in existence, whether as private or public company)
- dividends or interest in arrears, if any.

(f) Certified copies of agreements or other documents relating to arrangements with or between:
- vendors and/or promoters
- underwriters and sub-underwriters
- brokers and sub-brokers.

(g) Certified copies of agreements with:
- managing agents, secretaries, and treasurers
- selling agents
- managing directors and technical directors
- general manager, sales manager, manager, or secretary

(h) Certified copy of every letter, report, balance sheet, valuation contract, court order, or other document, part of which is reproduced or referred to in any prospectus, offer for sale circular or advertisement offering securities for subscription or sale during the last five years.

(i) A statement containing particulars of the dates of, and parties to all material contracts, agreements (including agreements for technical advice and collaboration), concessions and similar other documents (except for those entered into in the ordinary course of business carried on or intended to be carried on by the company) together with a brief description of the terms, subject matter, and general nature of the documents.

(j) A brief history since its incorporation giving details of its activities including any reorganisation, reconstruction, or amalgamation, changes in its capital structure (authorised, issued, and subscribed) and debenture borrowings, if any.

(k) Particulars of shares and debentures issued:
- for consideration other than case, whether in whole or part
- at a premium or discount or
- in pursuance of an option.

(l) A statement containing particulars of any commission, brokerage, discount, or other special terms including an option for the issue of any kind of the securities granted to any person.

(m) Certified copies of:
- letters of consent of the "controller of capital issues"
- agreements if any, with the Industrial Finance Corporation Industrial Credit and Investment Corporation and similar bodies.

(n) Particulars of shares forfeited.

(o) A list of highest ten holders of each class or kind of securities of the company as on the date of application along with particulars as to the member of shares or debentures held by and the address of each such holder.

(p) Particulars of shares or debentures for which permission to deal is applied for.

Obligations Under a Listing Agreement

Rule 19(2) maintains that an applicant company shall satisfy the stock exchange that:

(a) Its articles of association provide for the following among others:
- that the company shall use a common form of transfer
- that the fully paid shares will be free from all lien, while in the case of partly paid shares, the company's lien, if any, will be restricted to moneys called or payable at a fixed time in respect of such shares
- that any amount paid up in advance of calls on any share may carry interest but shall not entitle the holder of the share to participate in respect thereof, in a dividend subsequently declared
- there will be no forfeiture of unclaimed dividends before the claim becomes barred by law
- that option or right to call of shares shall not be given to any person except with the sanction of the company in general meeting.

(b) At least 10 per cent of each class or kind of securities issued by a company should be offered to the public for subscription through advertisement in newspapers for a period not less than two days.

Rule 19(3) maintains that a company applying for listing shall, as a condition precedent, undertake *inter alia*:

(a)
- That letters of right will be issued simultaneously
- That letters of allotment, acceptance or rights will be serially numbered, printed on good-quality paper, examined and signed by a responsible officer of the company

- that letters of allotment and renunciable letters of right will contain a provision for splitting
- that letters of allotment and letters of right will state how the next payment of interest or dividend on the securities will be calculated.

(b) To issue, when so required, receipts for all securities deposited with it whether for registration, subdivision, exchange or for other purposes. To issue, when so required, consolidation and renewal certificates in denominations of the market unit of trading to split certificates, letters of allotment, letters of right, and transfer, renewal, consolidation and split receipts into smaller units, to split call notices, issue duplicates thereof and not require any discharge on call receipts, and to accept the discharge of members of the stock exchange on split, consolidation and renewal receipts as good and sufficient without insisting on the discharge of the registered holders.

(c) When documents are lodged for sub-division or consolidation or renewal through the clearing house of the exchange:

- to accept the discharge of an official of the stock exchange clearing house on the company's split receipts and consolidation receipts and renewal receipts as good and sufficient discharge without insisting on the discharge of the registered holders and
- to verify when the company is unable to issue certificates or split receipt or consolidation receipt or renewal receipt immediately on lodgment whether the discharge of the registered holders, on the documents lodged for subdivision or consolidation or renewal and then signatures on the relative transfers are in order.

(d) On production of the necessary documents by shareholders or by members of the exchange, to make on transfers an endorsement to the effect that the power of attorney or letters of administration or death certificate or certificate of the Controller of the Estate Duty or similar other document has been duly exhibited to and registered by the company.

(e) To advise the stock exchange of the date of the board meeting at which the declaration or recommendation of dividend or the issue of right or bonus share will be considered.

(f) To recommend or declare all dividend and/or cash bonuses at least five days before the commencement of the closure of its transfer books.

(g) To notify the stock exchange of any material change in the general character or nature of the company's business.

(h) To issue certificates in respect of shares or debentures lodged for transfer within a period of one month of the date of lodgment of transfer and issue balance certificates within the same period where the transfer is accompanied by larger certificates.

(i) To forward to the stock exchange copies of statutory and annual reports and audited accounts as soon as issued, including Directors' Report.

(j) To notify the stock exchange of any change:
- in the company's directorate by deaths, resignation, removal, or otherwise
- of managing director, managing agent or secretaries and treasurers
- of auditors appointed to audit the books and accounts of the company.

(k) To notify the stock exchange in the event of reissue of any forfeited securities or the issue of securities hold in reserve for future issue.

(l) To notify the stock exchange of any other alteration of capital including calls.

(m) To forward to the stock exchange an annual return immediately after each annual general meeting.

(n) To grant to shareholders the right of renunciation in all cases of issue of rights, privileges, and benefits.

(o) To close the transfer books only for the purpose of declaration of dividend or issue of right or bonus shares or for such other purposes as stock exchange may agree and to give notice to the stock exchange.

(p) To notify the stock exchange prior to intimating the shareholders of any new issue of securities whether by way of right, privilege bonus or otherwise and the manner in which it is proposed to offer or allot the same.

(q) To forward to the stock exchange as soon as they are issued, copies of all other notices and circulars sent to the shareholders including proceedings of ordinary and extraordinary general meetings of the company and to fill with the stock exchange certified copies of resolutions of the company as soon as such resolutions become effective.

(r) To promptly notify the stock exchange:
- of any action which will result in the redemption, cancellation, or re-tirement in whole or in part of any securities listed on the exchange
- of the intention to make a drawing of such securities, intimating at the same time the date of the drawing and the period of the closing of the transfer books (or the date of the striking of the balance) for the drawing
- of the amount of securities outstanding after any drawing has been made.

(s) That, in the event of the application of listing being granted, such listing shall be subject to the rules and by-laws of the exchange in force from time to time and that the company will comply within a reasonable time, with such further listing requirements as may be promulgated by the exchange as a general condition for new listings.

(t) To intimate the stock exchange any other information necessary to enable the shareholders to appraise the position of the company and to avoid the establishment of a false market in the shares of the company.

Rule 19(4) maintains that a fresh application for listing will be necessary in respect of all new issues desired to be dealt in, provided that, where such new securities are identical in all respects with those already listed, admission to dealings will be granted on the company intimating to the stock exchange particulars of such new issues.

Rule 19(5) maintains that a recognised stock exchange may suspend or withdraw admission to dealings in the securities of a company or body corporate either for a breach of or non-compliance with any of the conditions of admission to dealings or for any other reason to be recorded in writing, which in the opinion of the stock exchange justifies such action.

Rule 19(6) maintains that a recognised stock exchange may, either at its own discretion or shall in accordance with the orders of the Central Government under sub-rule (5) restore or re-admit to dealings in any securities suspended or withdrawn from the list.

Rule 19(7) maintains that the Central Government may, at its own discretion or on the recommendation of a recognised stock exchange, waive or relax the strict enforcement of any or all of the requirements with respect to listing prescribed by these rules.

Operators at Stock Exchanges

(a) Jobbers

Jobbers are security merchants dealing in shares, debentures as independent operators. They deal with securities on their own behalf and earn through price changes. They cannot deal on behalf of the public. Generally, two prices are quoted by the jobbers, one at which they want to sell, and the other at which they want to purchase the security. The difference between the prices is the jobber's profit which is known as jobber's turn. For example, a jobber may quote equity shares of "A" company at INR 78–80. This indicates that a jobber is prepared to purchase these shares at INR 78 each and sell at INR 80 each. The difference between these two prices is his turn.

(b) Brokers

They act as intermediaries between buyers and sellers of securities. The main job is to bring the buyers and sellers together and help them in making a deal. They charge commission from both the parties and therefore they are known as commission agents.

Types of Speculators

(a) Bull

A bull or *tejiwala* is an operator who expects a rise in the prices of the securities in the near future. He purchases the securities with the intention of selling them at a higher price in the future. He, as a speculator, deals only with difference of prices, and does not take the delivery of the securities. He is called a bull because a bull throws his victim up in the air. Similarly, a bull speculator, by placing huge orders, tries to raise the prices of the securities.

(b) Bear

A bear or *mandiwala* is a speculator who anticipates the prices to fall in the near future and sells securities at present to purchase them at the lowest price in the future. He will earn profits out of these transactions if the prices move down as per the expectation of the bear. He is called a bear because a bear presses its victims down to the ground. Similarly, a bear speculator tends to force down the prices of different securities. A bear takes the difference if price falls down but does not take delivery of securities. In case if there is a rise in prices then, he will have to pay the difference between the prevailing prices and the price at which he purchased the security. A market is said to be bearish when there is a strong expectation of fall in prices. In case there is no fall in prices of the securities then these speculators shall start spreading rumours to pressurise price downwards.

(c) Stag

A stag is a speculator who applies for shares in new companies to sell them at a premium, if the shares are allotted to him. He selects those companies whose shares are more in demand and are likely to be issued at a premium. A stag applies for shares in large numbers so that he gets some allotment even if there is over subscription.

Procedure for Dealing at Stock Exchange

Selection of a Broker

(a) Selection of a broker through the investor or seller's bank for purchase or sale to be made.

(b) The bankers approach their brokers at exchange for dealings on behalf of their customers.

(c) The broker on the recommendation of the bank opens the client's account.

(d) Assurance given by the broker about the financial condition of the client.

Placing an Order

(a) The client places the order for purchase and sale of securities after the selection of the broker.
(b) The broker guides the client regarding the purchase and sale of securities, the favourable time for purchase and sale, etc.
(c) The client then informs the broker regarding the purchase of shares, number of shares to be purchased, the prices to be paid, etc.
(d) The broker then tries to purchase the securities as far as possible to the nearest price offered by the client.
(e) The broker is given the choice for bargaining for the purchase and sale of securities.

Making the Contract

(a) There are different trading posts for different types of securities in the trading floor of the stock exchange.
(b) The clerk of the broker goes to the concerned post and expresses his intention to buy or sell the security.
(c) A deal is struck where the other party also agrees for the same price
(d) The parties note the bargain in their note books.
(e) The slip giving details of the bargain is put in a box for making announcement in the official price list publicly.

Contract Note

(a) The brokers (buying and selling) prepares notes after their mutual consent next day.
(b) The buyer is sent a buying note and the seller is sent a selling note.
(c) The entire details of securities traded are given mentioning their price, number, etc.

Settlement

The selling broker after receiving the price hands over the transfer form and share certificates to the buying broker. Different procedures are adopted for settlement of ready delivery and forward contracts.

(a) Settlement of ready delivery contracts: if the settlement is done by giving actual delivery of securities after receiving the price is called liquidation in full.
(b) Settlement of forward delivery contracts: These contracts are done for speculative purposes. Only active market securities are traded in forward contracts. The settlement of these contracts can be done in any of the following ways.

- Liquidation in full: After crossing all intermediate purchases and sales the payment is received and the securities are delivered
- Liquidation by payment of differences: The purchase and sale of securities are finalised at the ruling price by paying or receiving the difference amount. Here the securities are not delivered but only current prices and the differences of prices contracted are paid or received as the case may be
- Carry over to the next settlement: If the contract is not settled but carried over to a future date by the buyer, this is called carryover. For this concession the buyer has to pay a certain amount to the seller, which is known as *Badla* or 'Contango' charge.

Changes Introduced in the Secondary Market

Certain major changes were introduced by SEBI in the secondary market to promote the capital market and protect investor interests particularly in the areas of: (a) structure and functioning of stock exchanges, (b) automation of trading and post-trade systems, (c) introduction of surveillance and monitoring systems. The following are the changes introduced:

- Enforcement of margin system
- Improvement in the governance of stock exchanges
- Dematerialisation of stocks
- Capital adequacy and prudential regulation were made applicable to brokers, sub-brokers, and other intermediates
- Introduction of derivatives market
- Revamping of regulatory framework for takeovers
- Formulating and implementing a comprehensive code of corporate governance
- Online trading in all stock exchanges for better transparency in transacting
- Framing of regulations for insider trading
- Reduction in settlement period through rolling settlement system from T + 3 to T + 2 from 1 April 2003.

With the result, there has been significant development in the functioning of stock exchanges.

(a) All stock exchanges today have computerised online trading systems. They have set up clearing houses or settlement guarantee funds. With the result, the trading systems have been much more transparent and quicker than in the past. The stock exchanges are permitted to expand their trading to locations outside their jurisdiction through computer terminals.

(b) Till the introduction of reforms, stock exchanges were characterised by paper-based settlement systems, open outcry, unregulated intermediaries such as brokers, etc. There was no single regulatory agency to control the market operations. The management of stock exchanges was more dominated by the brokers. Neither insider trading nor fraudulent and unfair trade practices were under check. With online trading and SEBI Act enactment, the scenario has tremendously changed.

(c) Scripless trading system is operated. Depository has become operational and all certificates of securities have to be handed over to the selected depositors for the purpose of "dematerialisation". The account of such owners with dematerialised securities are maintained with the depository and trading process is simplified and made faster. The conventional process of handing over delivery of the scrip or getting it transferred in the name of buyer is done away with.

(d) There is a strong presence of foreign institutional investors in the Indian capital markets. The National Stock Exchange in India occupies third position among the stock exchanges in the world, and Bombay Stock Exchange, the oldest stock exchange in Asia, occupies the sixth position in the world in terms of number of transactions per year. This shows the vibrancy and dynamism of Indian stock markets. Even the Indian companies are allowed to raise resources abroad through Global Depository Receipts (GDRs) and Foreign Currency and Convertible Bonds (FCCBs). This way Indian capital markets have been truly globalised since 1991.

(e) The major strengths of today's capital market in India are vibrant financial press, dynamic financial analysts, and a large number of capital market intermediaries.

Derivatives

A derivative is a financial contract, between two or more parties, which is derived for future value of an underlying asset.

In amended Section (2) of the Securities Contract (Regulation) Act, 1956 as amended by Securities Laws (Amendment) Act, 1999, derivatives include:

(a) A security derived from a debt instrument, share, loan whether secured or unsecured, risk instrument or contract for differences or any other form of security.

(b) A contract which derives its value from the prices, or index of the prices, of underlying securities. There are four main types of derivatives traded, and they are:

- Forward contracts
- Future contracts
- Option contracts
- Swap contracts.

A forward contract is a transaction in which the buyer and seller agree upon the delivery of a specified quality and quantity of asset (usually a commodity) at a specified future date. A price may be agreed on in advance or at the time of delivery.

A future contract is a firm contractual agreement between a buyer and seller for a specified asset on a fixed date in future. The contract price will vary according to the market place but it is fixed when the trade is made. The contract also has a standard specification, so both parties know exactly what is being traded.

An opinion contract confers the right, but not the obligation, to buy (call) or sell (put) a specific underlying instrument or asset at a specific price. The exercise price on a specific future date – the expiry date. The price paid by the buyer to the seller is a premium.

A swap contract is the simultaneous buying and selling of a similar underlying asset or obligation of equivalent capital amount where the exchange of financial arrangement provides both the parties to the transaction with more favourable condition that they would otherwise expect.

Shares are traditionally held in physical or paper form. This method has its own inherent weakness like loss, theft of certificates, forged, fake certificates, cumbersome, and time-consuming procedure. A new system called Depository System has been introduced, to eliminate these weaknesses in transfer of shares, etc.

A depository is a system which holds the shares in the form of electronic accounts in the same way as the bank holds money in a savings account.

The advantages of depository system are:

(a) There is no risk of bad delivery.
(b) The shares cannot be lost, stolen or mutilated.
(c) There is no need to doubt the genuineness of the shares.
(d) Transaction costs are usually lower than on the physical segment.
(e) Shares transaction like transfer, transmission etc., can be effected easily.
(f) Bonus, right shares allotted will be immediately credited.
(g) The statement of accounts of the transactions, holdings can be received periodically.

When the shares are in electronic form, one should approach a Depository Participant (DP) who is an agent of the depository to open an account. The share certificates should be surrendered in the physical form, and the

DP will arrange to get them sent to and verified by the company and on confirmation credit the account with an equivalent number of shares. This process is know as dematerialisation. One can always reverse this process if desired and get the shares reconverted into paper format. This format is known as rematerialisation.

Share transactions (like sale or purchase and transfer/transmission, etc.,) in the electronic form can be effected in a much simpler and faster way. What needs to be done is that after confirmation of sales, purchase transaction by the broker, one should approach the DP with the request to Debit/Credit the account for the transaction. The depository will immediately arrange to complete the transaction by updating the account. There is no need for separate communication to the company to register the transfer.

The process of selling mortgages (mortgages are loans backed by real estate as collateral security) is called securitisation, because the mortgages are effectively charged into securities that can be bought and sold in the resale market. Banks normally lend against the mortgage of a fixed asset. Over a period of time, if the bank wants to encash such mortgages, securitised loans come very handy. Mortgage loans can be sold by the banks. The buyers of such mortgages get a security for their investments in the form of claims on the mortgages. Securitisation of loans enables the bank to pass on the interest rate risk to the buyer of the security.

Since its inception, SEBI has been working by targeting the securities and is attending to the fulfillment of its objectives with commendable zeal and dexterity. The improvements in the securities market like capitalisation requirements, margining, establishment of clearing corporations, etc., reduced the risk of credit and also reduced the market.

SEBI has introduced the comprehensive regulatory measures, prescribed registration norms, the eligibility criteria, the code of obligations, and the code of conduct for different intermediaries like bankers, merchant bankers, brokers and sub-brokers, registrars, portfolio managers, credit rating agencies, underwriters, and others. It has framed by-laws, risk identification and risk management systems for clearing houses of stock exchanges, surveillance system, etc., which has made dealing in securities both safe and transparent to the end investor.

Another significant event is the approval of trading in stock indices (like SXP, CNX, Nifty and SENSEX) in 2000. A market index is a convenient and effective product because of the following reasons:

(a) It acts as a barometer for market behaviours.
(b) It is used to benchmark portfolio performance.

(c) It is used in derivative instruments like index futures and index options.
(d) It can be used for passive fund management as in case of index funds.

Two broad approaches of SEBI is to integrate the securities market at the national level, and also to diversify the trading products, so that there is an increase in number of traders including banks, financial institutions, insurance companies, mutual funds, primary dealers, etc., to transact through the exchanges. In this context, the introduction of derivatives trading through Indian stock exchanges permitted by SEBI in the year 2000 is a real landmark.

SEBI appointed the L C Gupta Committee in 1998 to recommend the regulatory framework for derivatives trading and suggest by-laws for regulation and control of trading and settlement of derivative contracts. The Boards of SEBI in its meeting held on 11 May 1998 accepted recommendations of the committee and approved the phased introduction of derivatives trading in India beginning with Stock Index Futures. The Board also approved the suggestive by-laws as recommended by Dr L C Gupta Committee for regulation and control of trading and settlement of derivative contracts.

SEBI then appointed the J R Verma Committee to recommend Risk Containment Measures (RCM) in the Indian Stock Index Future Market. The report was submitted in November 1998. However, the Securities Contract (Regulation) Act 1956 (SCRA) required amendment to include derivatives in the definition of securities to enable SEBI to introduce trading in derivatives. The necessary amendment was then carried out by the government in 1999. The Securities Laws (Amendment) Bill, 1999 was introduced in December 1999, the new framework was approved. Derivatives have been accorded the status of securities. The ban imposed on trading in derivatives in 1969 under a notification issued by the Central Government was revoked. Thereafter, SEBI formulated the necessary regulations, by-laws and intimated the stock exchanges in the year 2000. The derivatives trading started in India at National Stock Exchange (NSE) in 2000 and at Bombay Stock Exchange (BSE) in the year 2001.

The important institutions in capital markets include National Stock Exchange of India Limited (NSE), National Association of Securities Dealers Automated Quotation (NASDAQ), Over the Counter Exchange of India (OTCEI), Stock Holding Corporation of India Ltd. (SHCIL), and Credit Rating Agencies. The detailed information about the above institutions are discussed here in brief.

National Stock Exchange of India Limited (NSE)

The National Stock Exchange of India (NSE) was incorporated in 1992 with an equity capital of INR 25 crores. It commenced its operations in 1994. It aims at promoting professionalism in the capital market by providing computerised debt and stock trading facilities to the investors across the nation. The main objectives of NSE are:

(a) To achieve international standards in the operation of securities market.
(b) To provide a fair, efficient and transparent securities market using electronic trading systems.
(c) To enable shorter settlement cycles and book entry settlement systems.

The NSC classifies its listed shares as Group A, B_1, or B_2 shares. The classification of these shares are made on the basis of the following attributes. The attributes are guiding factors and their totality is taken into account. No simple factor is considered in isolation. The NSE continuously reviews the scrips for reclassification. Therefore, the number of stocks in each group is subject to change.

A Group Shares

- Scrips having very high liquidity
- Company having large equity base and large public holding
- Company having consistently good performance over the years.

Group A scrips are eligible for *Badla* transaction.

B_1 Group Shares

- Scrips having high liquidity
- Company having an equity of above INR 30 million
- Company having fundamentals and financial parameters in line with the industry.

B_2 Group Shares

- Scrips trading below par value at the NSE
- Company having an equity below INR 30 million
- Company's shares being not widely held
- Company having surveillance measure initiated against it by the NSE for suspected price manipulation.

National Association of Securities Dealers Automated Quotation (NASDAQ)

NASDAQ started in USA in 1971, is a computerised communication network. An OTC member can get up-to-date "bid and ask prices" on OTC securities from a small console that is electronically connected to the NASDAQ computer. These provide automated quotations for all OTC members. They can then contact dealers offering the best prices and negotiate deal. This rapid centralisation of "bid asked codes" replaced a long archaic system of "shopping around by brokers". NASDAQ is a dealer market which stands ready to buy and sell the securities in the system.

Over the Counter Exchange of India (OTCEI)

OTCEI is a company incorporated in 1990 and commenced its operations in 1992. It is a recognised stock exchange. Its objective is twofold – to help companies raise finance from the capital market and a cost-efficient avenue of investment in capital market for investors at large. It entered into a memorandum of understanding with the NASDAQ in 1994 for better cooperation between the two stock exchanges in the areas of market technology, regulations, and business developments. OTCEI world support NASDAQ in their efforts to encourage international listing of Indian issues. The NASDAQ would support OTCEI in its efforts to establish market of international standards in India.

Stock Holding Corporation of India Limited (SHCIL)

Stock Holding Corporation of India Limited (SHCIL) was sponsored by seven all India Financial institutions such as the Industrial Development Bank of India (IDBI), Industrial Finance Corporation of India (IFCI), Industrial Credit and Investment Corporation of India (ICICI), Unit Trust of India (UTI), Life Insurance Corporation of India (LIC), General Insurance Corporation of India (GIC), and Industrial Reconstruction Bank of India (IRBI). The main objective is to introduce a book entry system for the transfer of shares and other types of securities in place of existing system which is cumbersome as it involves a lot of paperwork. It will provide electronic clearing settlement and depository services of UTI, LIC Mutual Fund, LIC, GIC, and so on. SHCIL, by directive from the Government of India, covers all public sector banks, all subsidies and mutual funds set up by public financial institution and public sector banks.

Credit Rating Agencies

As and when business firms issue securities, credit rating agencies express opinions about the credit quality of the issue of the securities with reference to a particular instrument. Credit rating agencies rate each company based on its credentials and such rating will help the common investor to take appropriate decisions for investment.

At present, we have four credit rating agencies in India, namely – The Credit Rating Information Services India limited (CRISIL), Credit Rating Agency of India Ltd. (ICRA), Credit Analysis and Research Limited (CARE) and DuFF and Phelps (India) Private Limited. Credit rating has been made mandatory particularly when large number of financial institutions including banks have been approaching the capital market through debt instruments.

Challenges to Indian Capital Markets

The following have been the major challenges the capital markets face today:

(a) Market infrastructure can be improved by ensuring efficient flow of information and effective corporate governance.
(b) Adherence to international Accounting Standards and the internationally accepted accounting practices is the need of the hour. Otherwise, the corporate financial irregularities will continue to take investors for a ride.
(c) The legal system should be strengthened so that the interests and rights of small shareholders are protected and they can monitor corporate performance.
(d) The National Capital Market has to be integrated through consolidation of stock exchanges. A country like India may not require all the stock exchanges that we have today. They can be merged or consolidated based on the merits of each stock exchange. This may be helpful to develop a uniform settlement cycle and common clearing system. The speculation based on price differences between different stock exchanges can be brought to an end.
(e) Markets cannot be efficient unless there is constant and continuous flow of informations to all the parties concerned. Though this problem is taken care of through on-line trading systems and procedures, still the "insider trading" calls for more monitoring from the regulatory agencies such as SEBI are needed.
(f) By linking the banking and securities industries, the payment system can be improved. EFT has been the superior method to conduct

financial transactions to the conventional method of "Cheque System". EFT is used all over the world to make direct payments of dividends through bank accounts, eliminate counterparty risk and augment foreign institutional investments. Although most of the companies in India today have shifted to EFT, there is a still a long way to go.

(g) The development of capital market is directly dependent on factors such as level of interest rates, fiscal deficit, efficiency of the banking system, and so on. For the development of efficient capital market, it is necessary to liberalise the interest rates, reduce the fiscal deficit, and make the banking system more competitive. The government has to play a crucial role in this direction.

The economic growth of our country is heavily dependent on our security market. It is, therefore, necessary to ensure that our security market is efficient, transparent, and safe. In this direction SEBI has been working since its inception and would continue to work continuously to improve market design to bring in further efficiency and transparency to market and make available newer and newer products to meet the varying needs of market participants, while protecting investors in securities. The aim is to make Indian securities market a model for other jurisdictions to follow and make SEBI the most dynamic and respected regulator globally. Some of the initiatives on which SEBI is working are:

(a) Introducing exchange traded interest rate derivatives
(b) Facilitating dematerialisation of stock exchanges
(c) Rationalising margins trading, securities lending and short selling
(d) Promoting secondary market for corporate debt securities
(e) Setting up of a central listing authority to dynamise listing requirements
(f) Promoting an Index to comprehensively reflect the level of corporate governance
(g) Constructing a central registry of securities market participants and professions through training and certification
(h) Reviewing all regulation of SEBI and code of conduct for intermediaries
(i) Implementing market-wide Straight Through Processing (STP) from trade initiation to settlement
(j) Proceeding a legal framework for central counter party in consolidation of exchanges and other market participants
(k) Bench marking Indian securities market best in the world.

Reforms in Indian Capital Market/Stock Market

Some of the important reforms introduced in Indian capital market/stock market since 1992 are as follows:

(a) SEBI is delegated the power to regulate the functioning of stock exchanges.
(b) Primary market and secondary market intermediaries have been brought into the financial system and the regulatory framework of SEBI.
(c) Public issues are governed by a code of advertisement of SEBI to ensure faith and truthful disclosures.
(d) The companies are free to fix price and premium on their own issue of the securities. The office of the Controller of Capital Issues is abolished with the repealment of Capital Issues (Control) Act, 1947. The companies have just to file prospectus with the SEBI and go for public issue.
(e) Primary market reforms, as enforced by SEBI, include improved disclosure standards, introduction of prudential norms, and simplification of issue procedures. It is mandatory that the companies have to disclose all mutual facts and specific risk factors associated with the investments in their projects at the time of public issue.
(f) Listed companies have to furnish annual statement to the concerned stock exchange showing variations of funds in the offer document and actual figures. This may help the shareholders to compare the performance against the promise.
(g) The National Stock Exchange (NSE) was established with nationalised electronic trading network.
(h) Capital adequacy norms have been introduced for broker accounts.
(i) Over The Counter Exchange of India (OTCEI) has been formed.
(j) National Securities Clearing Corporation Limited (NSCCL) was set up by NSE.
(k) SEBI regulations for venture capital funds have become operational.
(l) Improved disclosures norms through cash flow statements.
(m) New issue-procedures have been introduced to reduce the cost of issue.
(n) Foreign direct investment is allowed in stock broking, asset management companies, merchant banking, and other Non-Banking Finance Companies (NBFCs).
(o) Through Euro issue, Indian companies are permitted to access international capital markets.

(p) The governing boards of stock exchanges have been reconstituted under the provisions of SEBI Act.

(q) Substantial acquisition of shares and takeover are governed by SEBI regulations, revised and strengthened in 1996.

(r) Mutual funds are permitted in the private sector. They can also participate on the public issue and seek firm allotment. This measure is initiated to reduce the issue costs.

(s) Mutual fund regulations have been revised in 1996 offering more flexibility to the fund managers. Better degree of transparency, disclosure, and acceptability have been other objects of these 1996 regulations.

(t) With the enactment of the Depositors Act, the electronic transfer of securities through depositors is facilitated.

(u) Foreign institutional investors must have registration with SEBI to access to Indian capital markets. They can invest in enlisted securities, corporate and Government debt securities.

(v) Screen-based trading was first introduced by BSE (Bombay Stock Exchange). Today 17 to 18 exchanges conduct their trading operations on-line. BSE is permitted to expand its trading network to other centres.

(w) The surveillance mechanisms are strengthened and SEBI directs each stock exchange to set up separate surveillance department.

6
Development Banking

Concept of Development Banking

In the field of industrial finance, the concept of "Development Bank" is a recent origin. In a country like India, the emergence of development banking is a post-independence phenomenon.

In the western countries, however, development banking has a long period of evolution. The origin of development banking may be traced to the establishment of "Société Générale pour favoriser I'Industrie Nationale" in Belgium in 1822. But the famous institution was the "Credit Mobilier" of France, established in 1852, which acted as an industrial financier.

In 1920, Japan established the "Industrial Bank of Japan" to cater to the financial needs of their industrial development. In the post-war era, the "Industrial Development Bank of Canada" (1944), the "Finance Corporation for Industry Ltd." (FCI), and the "Industrial and Commercial Finance Corporation Ltd.," (ICFC) of England (1945) etc., were established as modern development banks to provide term loans to industry. In 1966, the Government of UK set up "the Industrial Reorganisation Corporation (IRC)". In India, the first development bank called the "Industrial Finance Corporation of India" was established in 1948.

Definition of Development Bank

William Diamond and Shirley Bosky consider industrial finance and development corporations as "development banks". Fundamentally, it is a term-lending institution. A development bank may be defined as a financial institution concerned with providing all types of financial assistance (medium as well as long-term) to business units, in the form of loans, underwriting, investment, and guarantee operations, and promotional activities – economic development in general, and industrial development in particular. In short, a development bank is a development-oriented bank.

The concept of development banking is universal, the main objective being rapid economic development of the country. Even a developed country like Germany and a fast developing country like China established Development Financial Institutions (DFIs). Even Russia has decided to establish a development bank to finance its restructuring and investment needs.

Features of Development Banks

(a) It is a multi-purpose institution that shares entire financial risk unlike commercial banks, it does not accept deposits from the public.
(b) It provides medium and long-term finance to business units.
(c) It encourages new industrial projects and strikes to bring rapid economic growth with balanced regional development.
(d) It provides financial assistance not only to the private sector but also to public sector undertakings.
(e) It helps industrial units through discovery of investment projects and preparation of project reports.
(f) It reduces technical advice and management consultancy services to assist the management of industrial units.
(g) It aims at promoting the saving and investment habit in the community.
(h) Its motive is to serve public interest rather than to make profits. It works in the general interest of the nation.

Functions of Development Banks

(a) To provide funds to manufacturing activity that produces goods which are perfect substitution for existing imports and also for export purposes i.e., for export promotion.
(b) To provide funds for industrial sector for the growth of traditional commodity sectors such as textiles, sugar, jute, cement, steel, etc.
(c) To promote entrepreneur development, energy construction, pollution control, generation of direct and indirect employment opportunities as well as institution building.

The DFIs are the source of funding for the growth of industrial and infrastructure sectors in India in the coming years. The emergence of new financial instruments such as derivatives and futures widened the scope and depth of the debt market. DFIs have played a pivotal role in this process.

The main objective of setting up of DFIs has been to get certain government policies implemented to accomplish the long-term goals of the country. But in the process, the government reached a stage where further pumping of funds into DFIs was an uphill task. Several committees have suggested that every development financial institution should set up its own bank to meet the financial requirements. The DFIs, world over, have never been completely market driven.

The government support in the form of ensuring adequate level of capitalisation legal reforms, access to long-term resources like pension and insurance funds, improvement in overall business sentiment, efficient and effective trade, and industrial policies will go a long way in strengthening the viability of development financial institutions.

Development Banks in India

During the post-independence period, India was well served by a network of development banks at the national as well as state levels. The Industrial Finance Corporation of India (IFCI), the first development bank of the country, was established in 1948. Gradually many other financial institutions were set up. Development banks in India may be classified into three groups. These are:

- Industrial Development Banks
- Agricultural Development Banks
- Export-Import Development Banks.

Industrial development banks may further be divided into two groups.

- All India Institutions
- State level Institutions.

At present the All-India Industrial Development Banks are:

- The Industrial Finance Corporation of India (IFCI)
- The Industrial Development Bank of India (IDBI)
- The Industrial Reconstruction Bank of India (IRBI)
- The National Small Industries Corporation (NSIC)
- The Industrial Credit and Investment Corporation of India (ICICI).

The first four institutions are owned by the state, while the fifth one is a private sector institution. All these institutions, except for the NSIC, cater to the financial and development needs of the large industries, while the NSIC deals with the small-scale industries. The state-level industrial development banks include:

- State Financial Corporation (SFCs)
- The State Industrial Development Corporation (SIDCs)
- State Industrial Investment Corporation (SIICs).

Agricultural development banks are classified into: (a) All-India level (b) State level, and (c) Local level Institutions. At present there is only one All-India level agricultural development bank called National Bank of Agriculture and Rural Development (NABARD). Originally there was the Agricultural Refinance and Development Corporation (ARDC) established in 1963 to provide medium-and long-term finance for the development of agriculture. It was replaced by NABARD in 1982.

At the state level, there are the State Land Development Banks (SLDBs), formally known as Central Land Mortgage Banks, for supplying medium- and long-term credit to agriculture. Further at the local level, there are primary land development banks and the branches of SLDBs.

For promoting and developing exports and imports, an all-India level institution called Export-Import Bank of India (Exim Bank) was established in 1982 (see figure 6.1).

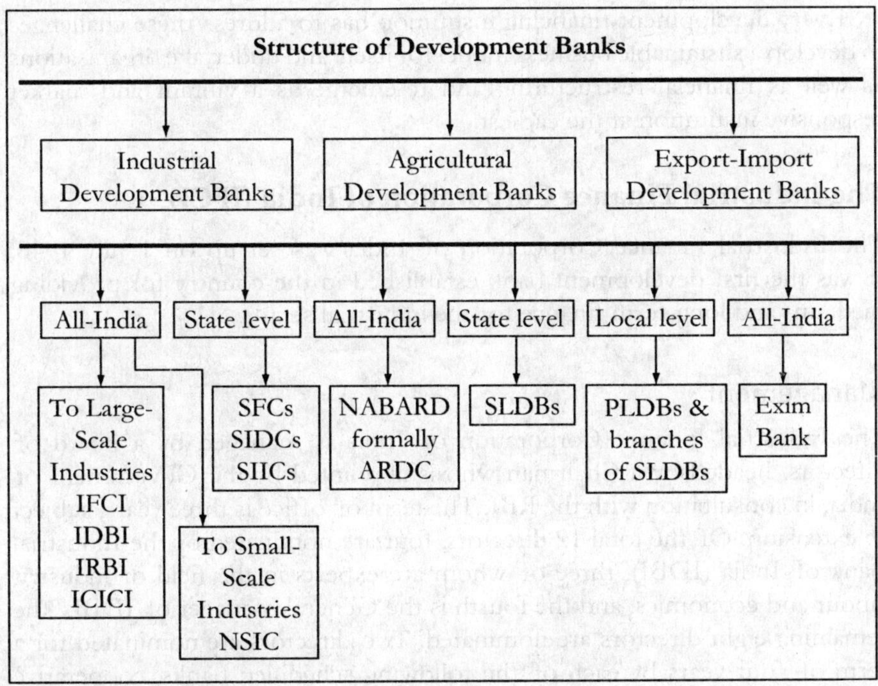

Figure 6.1

The term financing institutions are development banks like IDBI, IFCI, ICICI, IRCI, SFCs, SIDCs, SIICs plus the Life Insurance Corporation of India (LIC), the General Insurance Corporation of India (GIC) and its subsidiaries, the Unit Trust of India (UTI). The LIC, GIC and UTI are specialised forms of financial institutions in the capital market of India.

Many institutions in developing economies across Asia have been facing certain challenges and conflicts during the last fifteen years. These challenges have compelled them to redefine their role, reinvest their business models, revamp their organisational set-up and initiate steps for financial restructuring.

(a) Changes in the operational environment for development banks in India are due to:
- Increased competition
- Consolidation within the financial sector
- Revolutions in the field of communication and information technology
- Globalisation, liberalisation, and integration of financial markets.

(b) Problems of corporate governance and moral hazards.

(c) Developmental financing with a commercial outlook.

Every development financing institution has to address these challenges to develop a sustainable business model for itself and undertake organisations as well as financial restructuring and re-emerge as a vibrant and market responsive institution at the earliest.

The Industrial Finance Corporation of India (IFCI)

The Industrial Finance Corporation of India was set up on 1 July 1948. It was the first development bank established in the country for providing medium- and long-term finance for the industrial sector.

Management

The Industrial Finance Corporation of India is managed by a board of directors, headed by a Chairman who is appointed by the Government of India, in consultation with the RBI. The term of office is three years, subject to extension. Of the total 12 directors, four are nominated by the Industrial Bank of India (IDBI), three of whom are experts in the field of industry, labour and economics, and the fourth is the General Manager of IDBI. The remaining eight directors are nominated. Two directors are nominated for a term of four years by each of the following scheduled banks, cooperative banks, insurance companies and investment companies.

The board is assisted by a central committee and various advisory committees in discharging its multiple funding. The headquarters of the IFCI is in Delhi and branch offices at different places in India. The board meets once a month regarding the operations of IFCI. The supreme authority lies with the Government of India.

The authorised share capital of the corporation was INR 10 crores as per the IFC Act, 1948. This has been however raised to INR 20 crores by the IFC (amendment) Act, 1972. The corporations's 50 per cent of the share capital is held by the IDBI and the remaining 50 per cent is held by commercial and cooperative banks.

The objectives of IFCI are integrated with the objective of the five year plans and the broad national policies formed by the government from time to time.

The sectors that have benefited from IFCI disbursements include:

(a) The consumer goods industry (textiles, paper and sugar).
(b) The service industry (hotels and hospitals).
(c) Basic industries (iron & steel, fertilisers, basic chemicals, and cement).
(d) Capital and intermediate goods industries (electronic, synthetic fibres, synthetic plastics and miscellaneous chemicals).
(e) Infrastructure (power generation and telecom services).

The corporate philosophy of Industrial Finance Corporation of India has been to:

(a) Be a dominant player in the financial sector, providing a range of financial services, with core strength in project finance.
(b) Create and sustain long-term relationship with credit-worthy clients.
(c) Expand fee-based business to capitalise on emerging opportunities in infrastructure, corporate restructuring, and investment banking.
(d) Develop a new paradigm as a corporate specialist, with increased focus on small- and medium-sized enterprises.
(e) Empower on skilled and professional employees to function proactively.
(f) Enhancing shareholder's value through new strategic initiatives.

The economic contribution of IFCI can be assessed from the following:

(a) Huge amounts of sanctions and disbursements.
(b) IFCI has been instrumental in generating both direct and indirect employment through its assistance to industrial and infrastructure sectors.
(c) IFCI has been the nodal agency for the development of cooperatives in sugar and textile sectors. IFCI extended assistance to nearly 400 cooperative societies of these two sectors.
(d) 50 per cent of IFCI's assistance has been extended for financing more than 2300 units located in backward areas and catalysed investment of approximately INR 1,22,000 crores.
(e) To provide necessary technical consultancy services to the promoters, primarily in lesser developed states, of small and medium industries, IFCI promoted Technical Consultancy Organisations (TCOs) in collaboration with other institutions/agencies and banks.
(f) IFCI provides subsidies to self-employed youth and women entrepreneurs under a Benevolent Reserve Fund (BRF) and an Interest Differential Fund (IDF).
(g) IFCI has also been offering a number of schemes to low-cost quality consultancy services to tiny and small-scale sector entrepreneurs.

IFCI has the credit of promoting institutions such as:

(a) ICRA for credit rating.
(b) Management Development Institute (MDI) for management training and development.
(c) Tourism Finance Corporation of India (TFCI) for the promotion of hotel and tourism industry.
(d) Institute of Labour Development (ILD) for rehabilitation and training of displaced and retrenched labour force.
(e) Rashtriya Gramni Vikas Nidhi (RGVN), an important voluntary agency, to promote, support, and develop voluntary agencies engaged in socioeconomic upliftment of rural and urban poor in the east and northeastern parts of India.

IFCI has also promoted the following organisations that play a key role in the Indian capital market today.

(a) Discount and Finance House of India (DFHI).
(b) National Stock Exchange (NSE).
(c) Stock Holding Corporation of India Ltd (SHCIL).
(d) Over the Counter Exchange of India (OTCEI).
(e) Securities Trading Corporation of India Ltd (STCI).
(f) LIC Housing Finance Ltd.
(g) GIC Griha Vittha Ltd.
(h) IFCI has sponsored the Risk Capital Foundation (RCF) which provides interest-free personal loans to new entrepreneurs to enable them to provide a part of the equity capital as promoters' contribution.

The main functions of IFCI are:

- direct financing
- promotional activities
- incidental activities

Direct Financing

IFCI grants assistance for setting up of new industrial projects, expansion of units or diversification, and renovation and modernisation of units. Under the IFCI Act of 1948 the following concerns are eligible for direct financial assistance.

(a) Limited Companies (private, public, joint sector) incorporated in India.
(b) Cooperative societies registered in India carrying out at present or proposing to carry out in the future the following:

  - production, preservation, or processing of goods
  - shipping, mining, hotel industry

- development of land as an industrial estate
- generation and distribution of any kind of power
- provision of specialised knowledge or services promoting industrial growth and research for development
- transport of passengers or goods by road, water, air, ropeway, or lift
- maintenance, repair, testing of machinery, vehicles, motor boats, trailors, tractors, etc.

While financing new projects, IFCI attaches importance to the following considerations apart from their industrial priority.

- export-oriented projects
- projects which benefit rural areas and those which aim at conservation of energy
- projects which are to make use of indigenously available technology, know-how, raw materials
- projects to be located in backward areas
- projects which are employment oriented and labour intensive in nature.

Promotional Activities

The schemes for promotional activities of IFCI are:

(a) There is 50 per cent reduction in case of rupee loans in IFCIs normal charges, such as legal and commitment charges to projects in less developed areas.
(b) More liberal debt equity ratio.
(c) Greater equity, reserve capital participation.
(d) There is 50 per cent reduction in underwriting commission.
(e) Concessional interest rate for rupee loans and foreign currency sub-loans.
(f) A 25 per cent reduction in rate of commission on deferred payment guarantees.
(g) IFCI provides concessional finance for renewable energy systems like:

- bio-gas plants and engines
- equipment utilising ocean waves and geo-ocean thermal energy
- agricultural and municipal waste conversion devices
- solar pumps, power generation systems, solar cooker, water heater, crop drivers, refrigerators, cold storages and air-conditioning systems, wind mills, electric generators and pumps.

IFCI has negotiated various loans – credit allocations in US dollar, loans from US Aid, French Francs Credit (FFCE) from Paris and Pound Sterling allocated under UK/India capital loans and grants. Soft loan schemes was introduced in 1976–1977 for modernisation assistance. It was operated by the IDBI in participation with IFCI and ICICI for providing modernisation assistance to five selected industries, namely, cement, sugar, engineering, jute, and cotton mills. The period between 1980–1981 saw the extension of the facility of modernisation assistance to all industries by the IFCI criteria and procedure adopted by IFCI for providing financial assistance.

The IFCIs approach is project oriented. Hence, the technical, financial, economic, and managerial aspects of a project are carefully appraised. The views of experts having specialised knowledge of the particular industry are obtained. Based on the recommendations of the advisory committee of experts, the directors of the IFCI take a decision.

After sanction of assistance, a letter of intent is issued to the applicant indicating the main terms and conditions. The borrower is required to execute a loan agreement. Disbursement starts after the completion of legal and other formalities. The corporation is required to stipulate a condition for option to convert a portion of the loan into equity in all cases where the aggregate assistance exceeds INR 1 crore. The IFCI is also required to nominate its representatives on the board of all assisted concerns where substantial assistance has been sanctioned.

Loans are repayable in semi-annual installments over a number of years (10 to 12 years) with an initial grace period of two to three years. Repayment and moratorium period are determined by profitability and cash flow of the concern. IFCI obtains periodical reports from borrowers and undertakes periodic inspections to enquire proper utilisation of loans, adherence to schedules, improvement on the quality of products, etc.

Incidential Activities

To advise the corporate clients, IFCI offers the following:

(a) FDI (Foreign Direct Investment) advisory services which include facilitating foreign business entities.
(b) Corporate restructuring advisory services (includes buy/sell, mergers, joint ventures, alliances, privatisation, etc).
(c) Infrastructure advisory services which include facilitation of credit documentation, due diligence, agreements and documentation review/advice, and so on.
(d) Corporate finance and investment banking advisory services which include placement of debt and equity, mergers and amalgamations strategy, arrangements of ECBs, public sector units disinvestments, etc.
(e) Ancillary services which include advising regulating agencies, industry research and information services, legal advisory services, etc.

Performance and Progress

IFCI had started lending during the last year and sanctioned and disbursed INR 4,105 crores and INR 3,351 crores during the financial year 2008–2009. IFCI also raised resources of around INR 2000 crores by 30 September 2009 to create fresh assets.

Net Non-Performing Assets (NPA) stands at almost nil as on 30 September 2009. The profit after tax was INR 657 crores as on 31 March 2009. The total assets after depreciation as on 31 March 2009 was INR 881 crores and reserve and surplus amounted to INR 2,633 crores for the same period.

IFCI suffered a significant loss during the year 2001–2002. The deterioration in performance has been primarily due to the efforts to clean up the balance sheet by making it more transparent, meet higher provisioning requirements and consolidation of business activities. The loan portfolio is heavily weighed towards traditional sectors, especially iron and steel and textile industries which were exposed to demand recession and excess capacity during the last few years, impairing borrower's debt servicing capability. Huge amounts of disbursed funds were also locked up in projects under implementation that faced financial crunch on account of the dampened business climate and depressed capital market. All these factors affected IFCI's cash flow in a significant manner. Premature retirement of high-cost funds during the last couple of years further led to the liquidity crisis. IFCI could not raise fresh resources from the market due to gradual downgrading of its credit rating. This resulted in curtailment of disbursements and new business, leading to decline in earnings.

The basic challenges IFCI has been facing today can be attributed to a mismatch in asset-liquidity position leading to acute liquidity crunch, accumulation of non-performing assets and a non-sustainable business model. To overcome these challenges, IFCI has taken the following steps.

(a) To improve liquidity through securitisation and sale of assets.
(b) To restructure the liabilities, especially by seeking rollover of investment, reduction in interest rates, and extension of maturity profile.
(c) To reduce exposure to project finance and diversify into short-term products and advisory services.
(d) To provide corporate advisory services through its full-fledged department created at the head office.
(e) To enter into aggressive negotiated settlements, to restructure impaired assets in a timely manner and to obtain recovery certificates for disposal of mortgaged assets.
(f) To conduct credit audit of all large standard assets so that early warning signals are identified and measures for preventing their slippage are recommended.

With the promulgation of the securitisation and reconstruction of financial assets and enforcement of Security Interest Ordinance, 2002, the formation of securitisation/asset reconstruction companies got facilitated. The ordinance provides more powers to the secured lenders in realising their securities and recovering their dues faster.

Industrial Development Bank of India (IDBI)

The rapid pace of industrialisation under India's five year plans underlined the need for a new institution with wider functions and much larger resources at its command than the existing ones. The Industrial Development Bank of India (IDBI) was accordingly established in 1964 to meet this requirement. The bank started functioning on 1 July 1964. The central role of IDBI in the industrial finance system in the country was defined by the then Finance Minister, Shri T T Krishnamachary, while introducing the bill in Parliament for setting up IDBI, in his words, "where a long-term view is necessary and a certain amount of risk has to be taken, the existing institutions tend, by reasons of their statutory obligations and traditions, to be conservative and cannot in any case, 'be' very helpful. We are envisaging the new industrial development bank as a central coordinating agency, which ultimately will be concerned, directly or indirectly with all problems or ambitions relating to take long- and medium-term financing of industry and will be in a position, if necessary to adopt and enforce a system of promoters, in promoting future industrial growth".

IDBI was initially set up as a wholly owned subsidiary of the RBI with a mandate of providing credit and other facilities for balanced industrial development. The Government of India enacted in 1975 legislation de-linking IDBI from RBI, thus making IDBI the principal financial institution for coordinating in conformity with national priorities, working of institutions engaged in financing, promoting or developing industry, for assisting the development of such institutions and for providing credit and other facilities for development of industry. Under this legislation, the ownership of IDBI was transferred from RBI to the Government of India and various responsibilities which RBI earlier had vis-à-vis industrial institutions financing in the country were vested in the reconstituted IDBI. The Act came into force on 16 February 1976.

Objectives:

The objectives of IDBI are:

(a) Coordinating the working of institutions engaged in financing, promoting and developing industry.
(b) Assisting in the development of such institutions.

The resources of IDBI are:

(a) Share capital and reserves.
(b) Market borrowings by way of bonds.
(c) Borrowings from the Government and RBI.
(d) Deposits and other borrowings.
(e) Foreign currency borrowings from World Bank, Asian Development Bank and International Markets (vis repayment of past assistance by borrowers).

Following amendment to IDBI Act in October 1994 to permit public ownership up to 49 per cent of its issued capital, IDBI went in for a public issue in July 1995. The shareholding of the Government of India in IDBI currently stands at 58.5 per cent.

IDBI is managed by a Board of Executive Directors. The responsibility of the day-to-day management of operations of the bank is vested with the Chairman and Managing Director. IDBI has its headquarters at Mumbai, operates through a network of five zonal offices at Chennai, Guwahati, Kolkata, Mumbai, and New Delhi, and 38 branch offices all over India.

IDBI became the first All India Financial Institution to obtain ISO 9002:1994 certification for its treasury operating in August 2000. Also it was the first organisation in the Indian financial sector to obtain ISO 9001:2000 certification for its forex services. Now it is moving towards universal banking.

Products and Services

IDBI provides finance for the establishment of new industrial projects as well as for expansion, diversification, and modernisation of existing industrial enterprises. IDBI undertakes/supports wide-ranging promotional activities. IDBI has made efforts to respond to the financial needs of the industry by constantly expanding its range of products and services. It developed the following financial institutions, capital market-related agencies and training institutions. The financial institutions are:

- EXIM Bank Ltd.
- Small Industries Bank of India
- IDBI – Principal Asset Management Company Ltd.
- North Eastern Development Finance Corporation Ltd.
- Securities Exchange Board of India (SEBI)
- National Stock Exchange of India Ltd. (NSE)
- Stock Holding Corporation of India Ltd. (SHCIL)
- Credit Analysis and Research Ltd. (CARE)
- National Security Depository Ltd. (NSDL)
- Clearing Corporation of India Ltd. (CCIL)
- IDBI Trustee Services Ltd. (ITSL)

IDBI has established two training institutions. These are: (a) Jawaharlal Nehru Institute of Development Banking (JNIDB) (b) Entrepreneurship Development Institute of India (EDII).

Functions

The main functions of IDBI may be stated as follows:

(a) Planning, promoting, and developing industries with a view to fill the gaps in the industrial structure by conceiving, preparing, and floating new projects.
(b) Providing technical and administrative assistance for promotion, management, and expansion of industry.
(c) Providing refinance facilities to the IFCI, SFCs, and other financial institutions approved by the government.
(d) Coordinating the activities of financial institutions for the promotion and development of industries.
(e) Purchasing or underwriting shares and debentures of industrial concerns.
(f) Guaranteeing deferred payments due from industrial concerns and for loans raised by them.
(g) Undertaking market and investment research, surveys, and technoeconomic studies helpful for the development of industries.

IDBI has played a pioneering role in fulfilling its mission of promoting industrial growth through financing of medium and long-term projects, in turn with national plans and priorities.

(a) IDBI provides financial assistance both in rupee and foreign currency for greenfield projects, expansion, modernisation, and diversification purpose.
(b) IDBI provides loans to corporates for meeting working capital requirements.
(c) IDBI provides facilities for direct discounting of bill of exchange and promissory notes which arise from the sale of machinery on deferred payment basis by a seller to a domestic purchaser.
(d) The bank offers a number of foreign related services on a commission basis, including opening of letters of credit and remittances of foreign currency on behalf of its assisted companies for import of goods and services.
(e) Venture capital finance is extended by IDBI for projects involving the development and use of indigenous technology and for the adoption and development of imported technology, as well as high-risk, high-return ventures.

(f) IDBI is providing merchant banking and a wide array of corporate advisory services as a part of its fee-based activities. These include professional advice and services for issue management, private placement of equity, debt investments, project evaluation, credit syndication, share valuation, corporate restructuring including mergers and acquisitions, and divestment of equity.

(g) As a project finance and capital market activities, IDBI underwrites public and rights issues and provides direct subscription support in respect of equity as well as debt instruments.

(h) IDBI is registered as a debenture trustee with SEBI and provides these services to holders of debentures issued by companies.

(i) IDBI grants re-finance facilities to State Financial Corporations, State Industrial Development Corporations and Banks against their loans to medium-sized industrial concerns throughout India. It also provides Letters of Credit to select SFCs and SIDCs by way of resource support.

(j) IDBI provides rupee and foreign currency loans to pollution control and prevention projects in highly polluting industrial sector.

(k) Bills of Exchange discounted by banks arising from the sale of indigenous machinery on deferred payment loans and rediscounted by IDBI.

(l) Under equipment finance, rupee and foreign currency loans are given to industrial units confirming to certain minimum financial criteria for the purpose of financing acquisition of specific clients of machinery and equipments. Such loans are secured by charge on specific assets and have a maturity of up to five years. Asset credit facility extends a line of credit to industrial units for financing of their normal capital expenditure over a period. Such credit is normally extended for a period of five to six years and is secure by a charge on the assets so required.

Performance and Progress

IDBI sanctioned a total assistance of INR 16,000 crores in 2001–2002. The disbursements during this period amounted to INR 11,150 crores. A glance of the sanctions and disbursements since 1998 reveals that this has been the lowest of all the years. The slackening pace of industrial activities compounded by depressed business sentiment and sluggish capital market is reflected in the performance of IDBI.

The following table 6.1 lists out the details of sanctions and disbursements of IDBI during 1998–2002.

Table 6.1 Sanctions and Disbursements (INR in Crore)

	Financial year ending (31 March 2002)				
	1998	1999	2000	2001	2002
Sanctions	20,632	20,842	23,712	25,418	16,034
Disbursements	15,369	14,473	17,063	17,474	11,158

The industry-wise trends during the year show a shift towards infrastructure and services sector as against commodity sector in the earlier years. Sector-wise sanction and disbursements during 2001–2002 (see table 6.2).

Table 6.2 Sector-wise Sanction and Disbursements during 2001–2002

Sector	**% of total sanction during 2001–2002**
Financial Sector	17.8
Electricity Generation	13.4
Electrical & Electronic equipment	11.1
Other Services	7.7
Telecom Services	4.8
Total	54.8

As on 30 June 2010, IDBI's total business (deposits and advances) stood at INR 292533 crores. The aggregate assets stood at INR 224657 crores. The net profit for the year 2009–2010 was INR 1031 crores. The Bank's Capital Adequacy Ratio (CAR) stood at 11.86 per cent as on 30 June 2010. IDBI Bank opened its first overseas branch at The Dubai International Centre (DIFC) in June 2010.

The above five industries together accounted for 54.8 per cent of the total sanctions. The IDBI has many milestones to its credit such as institution development offering distinct financial products, such as deep discount bonds, etc. It has pursued both short-term and long-term strategy to attain global standards in banking. The short-term strategies would help for business growth, quality and reduction in costs and improved risk management practices.

The bank will emphasise the following:

- Containing the volume of non-performing assets (NPA) through maximising the recovery of outstanding loans

- Enlarging the scope of its fee-based activities
- Reduction of average cost of funds through concerned efforts
- Optimising the combination of cost and maturity through fresh borrowings, retail funding through its fixed deposit scheme.

As a long-term strategy, IDBI has chosen universal banking as its bank business model to emerge as a global player.

Industrial Credit and Investment Corporation of India (ICICI)

Industrial Credit and Investment Corporation of India (ICICI) was incorporated on 5 January 1955 with its headquarters at Mumbai for the specific purpose of assisting the industrial enterprises within the private sector. It was sponsored by the World Bank with the sole purpose of promoting new industries and to assist the expansion and modernisation of existing industries.

The objectives of ICICI are:

(a) Assisting in the creation, expansion and modernisation of industrial enterprises within the private sector.
(b) Encouraging and promoting the participation of private capital both internal and external in such enterprises.
(c) Encouraging and promoting private ownership of industrial investments and the expansion of investment markets.

The initial resource of ICICI was INR 17.5 crores, that is, INR 12.5 crores in Rupees and US $10 million in foreign currencies, being loan from World Bank. By March 1985, the paid-up capital of the corporation amounted to INR 92 Crores, borrowings of the corporation aggregated to INR 1,617 crores.

The major institutional shareholders were Life Insurance Corporation (LIC) of India, General Insurance Corporation (GIC) of India and its subsidiaries, Unit Trust of India (UTI) and Banks, the World Bank, Industrial Development Bank of India (IDBI), Government of UK/KFW (an agency of Government of the Federal Republic of Germany), the development loan fund (now merged with the agency for international development), issue of bonds/debentures in India and commercial markets abroad has been another source of funds.

Till the early 1990s, it was just a development financial institution focusing more on sanctioning project finance. During the mid-1990s, it transformed its business to a diversified financial services group offering a wide variety of products and services, both directly and through a number of subsidiaries and affiliates like ICICI Bank. In 1999, ICICI became the first Indian company and the first bank or financial institution from non-Japan Asia to be listed on the New York Stock Exchange (NYSE).

Activities of ICICI

(a) The ICICI has so far assisted industries manufacturing paper, chemicals and pharmaceuticals, electrical equipment, textiles, sugar, metal ore, lime cement works, glass manufactures, etc. The assistance comprised of foreign currency loans, rupee loans, guarantees and subscription of shares and debentures.

(b) Since 1973, identification of promising projects and suitable entrepreneurs was done and the selection of projects was done to complete immediate and emergent gaps in the economy. New projects were also looked for assistance and was given to entrepreneurs for the selection, formulation, and achievement of the project maturing at a profitable stage.

(c) In 1975, ICICI commenced opening letters of credit to its clients for different foreign currency loans to reduce delays in acquiring them. ICICI's establishment of correspondent relationship with several banks abroad has enabled in rendering additional services to its clients.

(d) Merchant banking services to clients on raising finances, restructuring finances, on amalgamation proposals for submission to financial institutions and banks and advise for negotiations with them for loans and underwriting.

(e) Provision of foreign currency loans and advances to enable Indian industrial concerns to secure essential capital goods from foreign countries.

(f) ICICI has shown keen interest in the development of new industries in backward regions. ICICI is also participating in the soft loan schemes.

(g) ICICI commenced leasing operations in 1983. It provides leasing assistance for computerisation replacement, equipment of energy conservation, export orientation, pollution control, etc. The industries for which leasing assistance is provided are textiles, engineering, chemicals, fertilisers, cement, and sugar.

(h) Housing loans were provided by promoting HDFC (Housing Development Finance Corporation) for giving long-term finance in 1977, to individuals in middle-class and lower-income groups, cooperatives, etc., for the construction and purchase on ownership basis of residential houses all over the country.

(i) To provide advice on risk management-related issues.

(j) To provide loan syndication services.

(k) To evolve treasury-based financial solutions.

(l) To provide guarantee for credits given by Indian and foreign sources.

(m) Credit Rating Information Services of India Ltd (CRISIL) was set up by ICICI in association with Unit Trust of India (UTI) to provide credit-rating services to the corporate sector.

(n) ICICI helped establish the Programme for Advancement of Commercial Technology (PACT) to assist market-oriented research and development activity, jointly undertaken by Indian and US companies. ICICI launched Technology Development and Information Company of India Ltd (TDICI) to finance and upgradation of technology and provide technology information. ICICI launched its Programme for Acceleration of Commercial Energy Research (PACER) which was funded by US aid with a grant of US $20 million (US) to support selected research and technology development proposals in Indian energy sector (see figure 6.2).

Performance and Progress

During 2000–2001, ICICI continued the process of diversifying the assets base to mitigate the investment risks of operating on a single product portfolio. It could consolidate its position in wholesale banking. The trial assistance sanctioned and disbursed for the year 2000–2001 by ICICI was INR 56,092 crores and INR 31,946 crores, respectively, up to March 2001. The cumulative sanctions and disbursements from ICICI stood at INR 2,47,588 crores and INR 1,46,167 crores, respectively. ICICI was an important source of foreign currency loans to the private and joint sector enterprises in India. The paid-up capital of ICICI as on 31 March 2001 was INR 1134.9 crores.

In January 2002 ICICI merged with ICICI Bank. ICICI promoted ICICI Bank in 1994 as a wholly owned subsidiary, after consideration of various corporate structuring alternatives in the context of the emerging competitive scenario in the Indian banking industry, and the move towards universal banking. The management of ICICI and ICICI Bank formed the view that the merger of ICICI with ICICI Bank would be the optional strategic alternative to both entities, and would create the optional legal structure for the ICICI group's universal banking strategy. The merger would enhance the value for ICICI shareholders through the merged entity's access to low-cost deposits, greater opportunities for earning fee-based income and the ability to participate in the payments system and provide transition banking services.

In January 2002, the shareholders of ICICI and ICICI Bank approved the merger of ICICI and two of its wholly owned retail finance subsidiaries, ICICI Personal Financial Services Limited and ICICI Capital Services Limited, with ICICI Bank. Consequent to the merger, the ICICI group's financing and banking operations, both wholesale and retail have been integrated in a single entity.

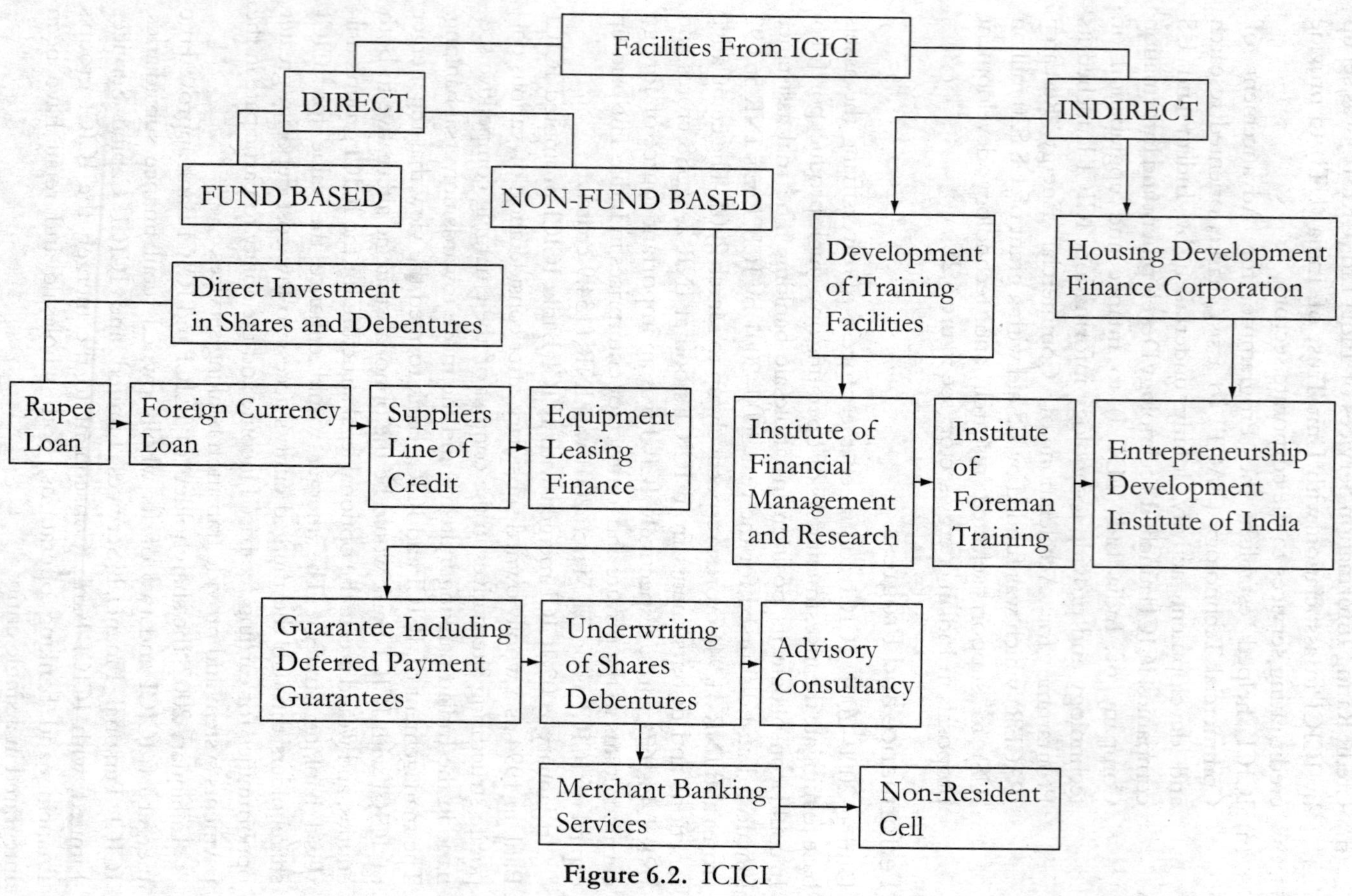

Figure 6.2. ICICI

The merger enhanced value for the entire ICICI group through:

- a large capital base and scale of operations
- entry into new business segments
- higher market share in various business segments, particularly fee-based services
- access to the vast talent pool of ICICI and its subsidiaries.

Financial position as on 31 March 2008:

Total reserves and surplus in (INR thousands)	– 453, 575, 309
Total deposits in (INR thousands)	– 2,444,310,502
Total assets in (INR thousands)	– 3,997,950,762
Total investments in (INR thousands)	– 1,114,543,415
Profit after Tax in (INR thousands)	– 24,363,159
Earnings per share (face value of INR 10)	– 39.15 (in INR)

Today ICICI bank is India's second-largest bank with total assets of about INR 1 trillion. It services a customer base of more than five million through a multi-channel access network. This includes more than 392 branches and extension counters, over 1000 ATMs, call centres, and internet banking. ICICI Bank offers a wide range of banking products and financial services to corporate and retail customers. One can access the various services, ICICI has to offer at any time, any where, and from any place.

ICICI has a variety of delivery channels and specialised subsidiaries and affiliates in the areas of investment banking, life and non-life insurance, venture capital, asset management, and information technology. ICICI Bank's equity shares are listed in India on stock exchanges at Delhi, Kolkata, Chennai, Vadodara, the Mumbai Stock Exchange, and the National Stock Exchange of India Limited. Its American Depository Reciepts (ADRs) are listed on the NYSE.

Non-banking Financial Companies (NBFCs)

In recent times, the Non-banking Financial Companies (NBFCs) have emerged as substantial contributors to the Indian economic growth by having access to certain deposit segments and catering to the specialised credit requirements of certain classes of borrowers. In the structure of Indian financial system, they play a key role in the direction of savings and investment. They help to bridge the credit gaps in several sectors which the traditional institutions like commercial banks are unable to fulfill. In the Indian economy today, the financial intermediation is being conducted by a wide range of financial institutions including the banks. The segment of institutions which consists of financial companies other than banks is called non-banking sector. The RBI has classified them in several categories to the purpose of exercising control over them. The companies that will come under NBFCs as per the definition of non-banking financial companies directions under Section 45 of RBI Act 1934, as amended in 1997 include:

(a) Hire-Purchase Finance Companies which undertake hire-purchase transactions or financing of such transactions.
(b) Equipment Leasing Companies which undertake equipment leasing or finance such activity.
(c) Loan Companies which provide finance by making loans or advances or otherwise to any activity other than its own.
(d) Investment Companies which undertake acquisition of securities like primary dealers who deal in underwriting government securities.
(e) Residuary Non-banking Company (RNBC) is one which is not covered by any of the above. RNBC may receive deposits under any scheme or arrangement.

The other non-banking financial companies regulated by RBI include:

- Mutual Benefit Financial Company (MBFCs) – *Nidhi* company
- Mutual Benefit Company (MBC) – potential *Nidhi* company
- Miscellaneous Non-Banking Company (MNBC) – Chit fund company.

The principal business of non-banking financial company is that of receiving deposits in any form or under any scheme and advance loans, invest in securities, provide hire-purchase finance or equipment leasing. These companies are just like banks since they perform the basic functions of attracting deposits from the public and making loans. But they cannot be regarded as banks as they need not follow cash reserve ratios, liquidity ratios, etc. A non-banking company may also undertake investment in securities, equipment leasing, and hire purchase.

Functions of Non-banking Companies

The functions of non-banking companies are:

(a) They attract deposits of large accounts by offering attractive rates of interest and other incentives. Half of the deposits are below two years' time period.
(b) They provide loans to wholesale and retail merchants, small industries, self-employment schemes.
(c) They provide loans without security also. Hence, they are able to charge 24 to 36 per cent interest rate.
(d) They run chit funds, discount *hundis*, leasing finance, merchant banking, provide hire purchase, etc.
(e) These companies also invest their surplus money on various outlets. In the case of investment companies, their main function is to invest on principal securities and pass on the benefits to small investors.

By the end of March 2001, there were 1005 NBFCs which reported to RBI with total assets of INR 53,878 crores and the aggregate public deposits of INR 18,085 crores. Over the last three decades, there have been significant development in the functions of NBFCs. The development was substantial especially in the case of hire-purchase and leasing companies. The following are the important reasons for the rapid growth of NBFCs.

(a) The ability to attract household savings.
(b) Higher return offered by NBFCs to depositors when compared with banks.
(c) Less formalities with regard to sanction requirements.
(d) Funding the sectors, such as vendors in the unorganised sector that are ignored by the commercial banks.
(e) A high level of customer-orientation through customised and cost-effective services around the needs of legal clients.
(f) Relatively lower degree of regulation of NBFCs when compared with banks.

In view of the above, the NBFCs have become an accepted and integral part of the Indian financial systems. They have been complementary to the banking systems and at the same time competitive also. They have been competing with the nationalised banks in their business activities. At the same time, they have been complementary as they could successfully take care of the credit gaps left over by the commercial banks.

Commercial Banks Vs Non-banking Companies

Commercial banks and non-banking companies are both financial intermediaries receiving deposits from public and lending them or investing them as the case may be according to circumstances. Hence, NBFCs are called 'Para Banks'. Some others call commercial banks as a big brother, the small brother being NBFC. But there are certain differences between them:

(a) Cheques can be issued against bank deposits whereas no such facility is available in the case of NBFCs.
(b) Generally commercial banks offer less rate of interest and also charge lesser rate of interest than that of the NBFCs.
(c) Commercial banks are subject to strict supervision and control by the RBI whereas NBFCs are more or less completely free from the RBI's control.
(d) Commercial banks are able to enjoy certain facilities like rediscounting facilities, deposit insurance coverage facilities, refinancing facilities, etc. These facilities are not extended to NBFCs.

(e) The commercial banks can manufacture credit out of the raw material of deposits by creating clients against themselves. But NBFCs cannot create credit as commercial banks do. They can lend only out of the limited resources on hand.

Services Rendered by NBFCs

The services rendered by NBFCs are:

(a) Mobilisation of savings
(b) Provision of easy, simple and adequate credit
(c) Acting as a financial super market
(d) Encouraging thrift and developing savings habit
(e) Channelising funds to productive purposes
(f) Providing housing finance
(g) Rendering investment advice
(h) Increasing the standard of living of the people
(i) Promoting economic development.

NBFCs business have undergone a qualitative change in recent years. They enjoy growth in size and better edge over commercial banks due to the following reasons.

(a) They assume greater risk.
(b) They are relatively quick in taking decisions.
(c) Their flexible structure allow them to market the components on a competitive basis.
(d) They deliver credit to the unorganised sector and to small borrowers at the local level, customising their services and charges, more according to the needs of the clients.

With de-regulations as the main thrust of the Government of India, the distinction between banks and non-banks has been gradually getting reduced since both the segments of the financial system engage themselves in many similar types of activities. Today NBFCs have been highly innovative and creative in their marketing strategies and also in devising their products and services as per the specific requirements of their clients. The deposits they received in the recent years speak volumes of their efforts in this direction. By the end of March 2001, the volume of public deposits as reported by 981 companies amounted to INR 18,085 crores, equivalent to 1.7 per cent of aggregate deposits of scheduled commercial banks. No doubt they have grown faster but it also gave rise to many problems and irregularities which were diagnosed during the reform era.

During the second half of the 1990s many NBFCs defaulted on the payment of principal and interest in view of their faulty lending policies. It was also noticed that managements of several NBFCs were indulging in malpractice. This necessitated an amendment to RBI Act, 1997. The salient features of the amended Act are:

(a) Minimum entry norms.
(b) Maintenance of a portion of deposits in liquid assets.
(c) Creation of reserve fund and transfer of 20 per cent of profit after tax annually to the fund.
(d) The compulsory registration of NBFCs with the RBI for commencing non-banking finance business and for carrying on business operations.
(e) Empowerment of RBI to issue directions to companies and its auditors, to prohibit deposit acceptance, to prohibit alienation of assets by comparing and to effect winding up of companies.
(f) Direction by RBI to monitor financial solvency and reporting by NBFCs to adhere to prudential norms such as capital adequacy, income recognition, asset classification.
(g) Provision for bad and doubtful debts.
(h) Stipulation for keeping a minimum net owned funds of INR 2 crores by NBFCs which are commencing operations after 21 April 1999.
(i) Vesting powers with the company law board for directing the defaulting NBFCs to return deposits.

Despite these safeguards, a number of NBFCs were getting closed defaulting their commitments to the individual depositors. A task force was announced for working out an efficient and quick system for redressing such grievances. RBI has taken the following measures to protect the depositor's interests:

(a) Coordination with state government to curb unauthorised and fraudulent activities.
(b) Involving the state government for enacting legislation for protection of interests of depositor in financial establishments.
(c) Training programme for the civil and police personnel of the state governments to equip with the skills of identifying and apprehending unscrupulous elements in NBFCs.
(d) Publicity campaign for depositors' education and awareness through workshop, seminars involving trade and industry organisations, depositors associations, chartered accountants, etc.
(e) Special training programmes organised at the College of Agricultural Banking, Pune and also at some of the regional offices of RBI for personnel executives of NBFCs to orient them with the objectives and focus on RBI guidelines.

Regulatory and Supervisory Framework of NBFCs

To protect the interests of depositors and safeguard the financial stability, there is a need for increased regulatory attention and focused supervisory scrutiny in the activities of NBFCs. As a part of addressing this need, RBI Act, 1934 was amended in 1997 providing NBFCs a comprehensive regulatory framework.

Changed measures of the amended Act are:

(a) Deposit taking NBFCs are under close regulation and supervision than those not accepting public deposits.
(b) Similar prudential norms as applicable to banks.
(c) Off-site surveillance based on periodical returns.
(d) Supervision through – onsite inspection, offsite monitoring through returns, market intelligence, and exception reports by statutory auditors.
(e) Asset liabilities and risk management systems for NBFCs.
(f) Punitive measures such as the cancellation of certificate of registration, prohibition from acceptance of deposits and alienation of assets, filing criminal complaints, and winding up petitions in extreme cases, appointment of RBI observers in certain cases.

RBI's Control over NBFCs

In the interest of the economy as a whole and in order to pursue an effective monetary policy, it is desirable that the NBFCs should be brought under the control of RBI in the same way as the commercial banks are. It is so because whenever RBI increases its bank rate or changes the lending rates or deposit rates, they will have no impact on the rates charged by these non-banking financial intermediaries. Again, when the RBI follows a policy of "credit squeeze", the industrial houses can escape from the policy by resorting to the system of financing through public deposits. Besides, any person with any type of security can approach a NBFC at anytime and obtain a loan. The RBI has no say over it. Another drawback of these companies has been the conspicuous lack of transparency of operation and proper financial disclosures. Again, several residuary non-banking companies are found to be operating with meagre capital and some of them even with negative capital. Moreover, some of the NBFCs have been found to be issuing misleading advertisements for attracting deposits. In these circumstances, the RBI cannot function effectively and implement its fiscal and monetary policies unless the NBFCs are brought under its control. Hence, the RBI has been taking several steps in this direction. Some of them are as follows.

(a) The RBI has issued various directions from time to time to control the deposit acceptance activities of these companies. For instance, the non-banking financial companies are regulated by the RBI under the Non-banking Financial Companies (Reserve Bank) Directions, 1997. The miscellaneous companies are governed by the Miscellaneous Non-banking Companies (Reserve Bank) Directions, 1997. The residuary non-banking companies are regulated under the Residuary Non-banking Companies (Reserve Bank) Directions, 1987. The housing finance companies come under the Housing Finance Companies (National Housing Bank) Directions, 1989. The RBI regulates the activities of non-banking non-financial companies under the Companies (Acceptance of Deposits) Rules, 1975. The RBI exercises control over NBFCs by the issue of various directions as stated above.

(b) The RBI has also prescribed certain ceiling limits for the acceptance of deposits by these non-banking financial intermediates. The RBI has started regulating the period as well as the rate of interest of the deposits of these companies. The RBI has issued a circular stating that the companies should accept deposits for a minimum period of one year and the maximum being 10 years. The deposits are subject to a ceiling limit of 14 per cent interest per annum.

(c) The RBI has prescribed certain limits on the payment of brokerage. For deposits not exceeding one year, the rate of brokerage shall be one per cent of the deposit, for a period of one to two years it shall not exceed 1.5 per cent of such deposit, and for a period of above two years, it shall not exceed two per cent of such deposit.

(d) The RBI has stipulated that these companies must designate a commercial bank of their own.

(e) All the NBFCs are required to submit periodical returns to the RBI on various matters pertaining to their operations.

(f) NBFCs with net owned funds of INR 50 lakhs and above are required to register with RBI compulsorily.

(g) The RBI has issued directions insisting these companies to maintain 10 per cent of their deposits in liquid assets.

The following norms are to be observed by every NBFC whether it accepts/holds public deposits or not.

(a) Taking loans against own shares will not be allowed.

(b) Income recognitions on the non-performing assets is allowed on cash basis only.

(c) Accounting standards issued by Institute of Chartered Accountants of India should be strictly followed.

(d) The policies for demand and call loans relating to cut off date for recalling the loans, the rate of interest, periodicity of such interest, periodical reviews of such performance, and so on are to be clearly defined.

(e) Recognition of income on accrual basis before the asset becomes Non-Performing Asset (NPA) as under loans and advances up to six months and 30 days, respectively. Lease and hire-purchase finance – 2 months.

(f) Clear-cut guidelines for accounting in respect of investment such as – every NBFC to have a well-defined investment policy. Investments are to be categorised into long term and short terms or current investments. Current investments are to be valued at lower of cost or market value and so on.

A task force committee under the chairmanship of Shri C M Vasudev, Special Secretary (Banking) was set up in 1998 for receiving the regulatory framework for non-banking finance companies. The committee has two basic objectives: (a) to create an environment for healthy growth of sound NBFCs. (b) to safeguard the interests of the depositor in NBFCs.

The committee submitted its report with the following recommendations.

(a) Minimum Capital Reserve (MCR) to be raised from present level of INR 25 lakhs to INR 2 crores from 20 April 1999 for the new incorporated NBFCs.

(b) NBFCs which are in the transitional period should be inspected annually.

(c) Credit rating and enhanced capital-to-risk asset ratio. Companies which have obtained credit rating from their investments enjoy higher ceiling as stipulated by the RBI, for public deposits. The proposed ceiling limits are:
- NBFCs with Net Owned Fund (NOF) less than INR 25 lakhs
- equipment leasing/hire-purchase company higher with credit rating with Capital to Risk Weighted Asset Ratio (CRAR) of 15 per cent
- loans and investment companies (higher [CRAR] of 15 per cent) with investment grade credit rating or above.

The limit on public deposits are as following:

- no access to public deposits
- one-and-a-half times or INR 10 crores, whichever is lower
- four times of the NOF
- one-and-a-half times the NOFs.

(d) The RBI should prescribe maximum limit for both exposure to the real estate sector and also on investment in capital markets, especially on unquoted shares.

(e) The RBI should consider measures for easing the flow of credit from banks to NBFCs. Also it should consider prescribing a suitable ratio between secured and unsecured deposits for NBFCs.

(f) The RBI should stipulate that the NBFCs seeking deposits should disclose their credit rating or that the quantum of public deposits is less than one-and-a-half times NOF or INR 10 crores and as such they are exempted from obtaining a credit rating. The credit rating particulars should be prominently disclosed in the application form for public deposits and in all advertisements.

(g) The RBI should continue to take more intensive measures for a sustained depositors' awareness campaign through print and electronic media, seminars, conferences, and so on. It also should involve in the process of associations to NBFCs and various investors' forums such as Consumer Education Research Centre, Investors Grievances Forum, Depositor Association, etc.

(h) The committee recommended that the norms for exposure to connected companies need to be lightened to ensure prevention of deployment of public deposits in high-risk and speculative avenues.

(i) Extension of time for attaining minimum Net Owned Funds of INR 25 lakhs beyond February 2000 to be made conditional. The three year period for attaining minimum NOF of INR 25 lakhs would expire in January 2000. Extension can be granted by the RBI if the concerned NBFC shows evidence of having taken additional steps to:

- Increase NOF in the initial three-year period
- Make all satisfactory arrangements for attaining the minimum capital requirement as may be applicable at the point of time within the extended period.

(j) If there is any significant spurt in non-performing assets or any bunching of repayment of deposits, off-site surveillance mechanism should be initiated.

Non-Banking Financial Companies (NBFCs) are now called financial companies as per the Financial Companies Regulations (FCR) Act, 2000. This Act was enacted by the Government of India to protect the interests of the depositors and regulate the financial institutions more effectively. RBI Act has been modified and certain safeguards have been incorporated to monitor and regulate the activities of NBFCs more closely.

The salient features of Financial Companies Regulation (FCR) Act, 2000 are as follows:

(a) All the financial companies need to be registered with the RBI.

(b) With Deputy Governor, RBI as the chairperson and other members of council, an Advisory Council is constituted to advise and recommend on the matters referred to it by the RBI.

(c) The Act may regulate or prohibit a financial company from issuing advertisements.
(d) A financial company has to create reserve fund and 25 per cent of such fund has to be invested in specified unencumbered securities.
(e) If any substantial changes are planned in the management, location of registered office or its name, prior approval from RBI is required.
(f) The minimum net owned fund required for registration of a financial company receiving from public deposits has been raised from INR 2 crores to INR 10 crores. In case of a financial company not receiving public deposits, the minimum net owned fund required for registration has been raised from INR 25 lakhs to INR 2 crores.
(g) The financial companies receiving public deposits are prohibited from carrying on any other business other than the business of financial institution.
(h) All unincorporated bodies are prohibited from issuing advertisement in any manner to solicit public deposits.
(i) RBI is certified with powers to direct a financial company or a class of financial companies to seek prior approval for the appointment of statutory auditors in certain cases. The RBI may be empowered to appoint one or more special officers.
(j) The Board of Company Law Administration constituted under the Companies Act is vested with more power for redressal of depositors' grievances. The board is empowered to prohibit any alienation of assets by financial companies and attachment and sale of their assets for effecting repayment of the deposits.
(k) Some financial companies may default in repayment of public deposits. To safeguard the interests of deposits in such a case, the Act makes a provision for depositors to have first charge on certain assets of the financial companies and specified unencumbered securities created out of a part of reserve fund.
(l) Acceptance of public deposits without appropriate authorisation is viewed as a cognizable offence. Acceptance of public deposits by unincorporated bodies is also a cognizable offence.

Types of NBFCs

Equipment Leasing Company

Equipment leasing company means any company which is carrying on as its principal business the activity of leasing of equipment or the financing of such activity. The leasing business arises out of a contract between the lessor (the leasing companies) and the lessee (the borrower) whereby the lessee is permitted to use a special capital equipment, as a hire, against the payment of a monthly rental fee. Thus, the lessee does not make any outright purchase of the capital equipment, but he buys the right to use it. The consideration received in respect of a lease transaction is in the form of:

(a) Interest on the lessor's investment.
(b) Charges borne by the lessor-like repairs, insurance, maintainance, etc.
(c) Depreciation.
(d) Servicing charges.

Types of Leases

Operating Lease

Operating lease where the asset is not wholly amortised during the non-cancellable period, if any, of the lease and where the lessor does not rely for his profit on the rentals in the non-cancellable period. Under an operating lease, the lessor who bears the cost of machinery, insurance, maintainance, repair cost, etc., is unable to realise the full cost of equipment and other incidental charges during the initial lease period. The lessee uses the asset for a specified time. The lessor bears the risk of obsolescence and incidental risks. Either party to the lease may terminate the lease after giving due notice of the same, since the asset may be leased out to other willing lessees. Specialised services are provided by the lessor who has specialised knowledge in handling and operating the asset. This type of lease is usually preferred where the long-term suitability of the asset is uncertain, where the asset is needed to solve a temporary problem and the asset is subject to rapid obsolescence.

Financial Lease

In financial lease, the producer of capital equipment sells the equipment to a leasing company, who in turn leases it out to the ultimate user of the equipment. Thus, there are three parties in finance leasing, and the leasing company virtually acts as a middleman between the producer and the user.

A finance lease is also called a capital lease or a loan in disguise. According to T M Clark, "it is a contract involving payment over an obligatory period of specified sums sufficient in total to amortise the capital outlay of the lessor and give some profit".

Leases of assets of smaller value are generally referred to as small ticket leases and that of larger value are referred as big ticket leases. Leasing across national frontiers is referred to as cross-border leasing.

Merits of Leasing

(a) It is an alternative to obtain loan and other facilities from financial institutions.

(b) A leasing company can provide 100 per cent financing for the cost of equipment where as banks and other financial institutions may not provide for the same.
(c) Flexibility is the main advantage. The leasing company modifies the arrangements to suit the lessees requirements.
(d) The lessor bears the risk of obsolescence in the case of operating lease.
(e) Less documentation is involved in a lease agreement compared to term loans from banks or other financial institutions.
(f) The lessee can avail of tax benefits depending upon his tax status.

Demerits

(a) The cost of interest in lease financing is very high.
(b) Leasing does not prove very useful in the setting up of new projects as the rentals become payable soon after acquisition of the assets.
(c) The asset reverts back to the owner on the termination of the lease period and the lessee loses his claim on the residual value.
(d) The lessor generally leases out assets which are purchased by him with the help of bank credit. In the event of default made by the lessor in making the payment to the bank, the asset would be seized by the bank much to the disadvantage of the lessee.

The first leasing company of India promoted by the "Chidambaram Group" in 1973 in Madras (Chennai) was the first of its kind in India. Later, the Twentieth Century Leasing Company was established in Mumbai in 1980. In 1982, another four companies namely, Motor and General Finance, Sundaram Finance, Jayabharathi Credit and Finance, Shetley Investment and Finance were established. Equipment leasing was first introduced by ICICI which now provides leasing for computerisation, exports, expansion, etc.

Leasing plays an important role in the financing of machinery, plant, and equipment. Lease financing being helpful for the small and medium-sized units which face financial constraints has gained importance with the increasing number of enterprises. The new industrial policies, liberalisation, and other economic measures of the government, withdrawal of investment allowance have made leasing as a finance function.

Leasing companies may be an independent one like the Twentieth Century Leasing, subsidiaries of manufacturing companies like Tata Industries Ltd., departmental financial institution of state and central government, etc. The expansion of financial services at a very fast pace has left its impact on the financial services scenario in the country. SEBI is looking after the financial services sector in its coordinated efforts to reorganise and restructure the industry.

Hire-Purchase Finance Company

A hire-purchase finance company means any company which is carrying on, as its principal business, the hire-purchase transaction or the financing of such transactions. Hire-purchase finance companies help small transport operators, professionals and the middle-income group people to buy equipment on the basis of hire purchase. It is a less risky business since the goods purchased on hire-purchase basis themselves serve as securities till the last installments of the loan is paid. A major share of the hire-purchase finance goes to the automobile industry. The recovery problem does not arise in most cases, since the borrower is able to repay out of future earnings, viz., the regular inflow of funds out of the asset purchased. There are a large number of individuals and partners doing this business. Some of them are well-organised and some of them are very small and financially weak. With a view to organise them effectively, the banking commission has made the following suggestions:

(a) Licensing procedure should be extended to hire-purchase finance companies and all companies doing this business must be compelled to obtain a license from the controlling authority.
(b) The equity debt ratio and the liquidity ratio which are applicable to banking companies must be made applicable to hire-purchase finance companies also through a different rate.

Differences between hire-purchase and leasing companies are:

(a) In hire-purchase, ownership of asset is transferred to user on payment of the last installment. Ownership is never transferred to user in the case of leasing.
(b) In hire-purchase asset is capitalised in the books of users. Leased asset is capitalised in the books of lessor/leasing company/owner.
(c) Depreciation is claimed by the user in hire-purchase whereas in leasing depreciation is claimed by the lessor or leasing co-owner.
(d) In hire-purchase value of capital asset is low as compared to lease transactions. Value of assets is very high in leasing. e.g., aircrafts, ships, etc.
(e) Hire-purchase finance is subject to margin requirements whereas it is 100 per cent in lease.
(f) Seller claims tax benefits in respect of interest payable on acquiring asset in hire purchase. In the case of leasing, lessee claims benefit of tax on lease rental paid by him.

Housing Finance Company

Housing Finance Company means any company which is carrying on, as its principal business, the financing of the acquisitions or construction of house including the acquisition or development of plots of land in connection there with. Housing Finance Companies also accept deposits and lend money only for housing purposes. Although there is heavy demand for housing, these companies have not made much progress. ICICI and all nationalised banks have sponsored housing finance companies. At the national level, national housing bank was also established.

Investment Company

An investment company is a company which is carrying on, as its principal business, the acquisition of business. An investment company may also be called as an investment trust. The principal aim of an investment company is to protect the small investor by collecting their small savings and investing them on diversified securities so that the risk may be spread. In India, investment trust companies are popular. They channelise the savings of the people into productive ventures. Small investments are protected by providing the much needed diversification of investments. They render expert investment advice and manage the investment portfolio of their clients. Some of them undertake underwriting, promoting and holding company business besides financing. These investment trusts promote business stability in the economy by keeping the capital market active and busy. They have a healthy influence on the stock market by discouraging speculative dealings.

Loan Company

A Loan company is any company which is carrying on, its principal business, providing finance for any activity other than its own. It is also called "Finance Company or Finance Corporation".

Loan companies are popular in the states of Gujarat and Karnataka. Generally they have very little capital, but they depend on deposits as their main source of funds. Hence, they use it to attract deposits by offering a high rate of interest. Generally they make loans to wholesalers, retailers, small-scale industries and the self-employed. Most of their loans are unsecured and risky, and hence they charge high rates of interest. Although loans are given for short periods, they can be renewed and thus become long-term loans. The Banking Commission has made the following suggestions:

(a) Every loan company must obtain a license from the RBI without which it should not be allowed to function.
(b) There should be ceiling on the interest rates offered on deposits.
(c) A certain liquidity ratio and owned funds to deposits ratio must be prescribed, though at a lesser rate than that of a commercial bank. 20 per cent of the deposits of the non-banking sector comes from loan companies.

Residuary Non-Banking Company

It is a company which does not fall into any of the other categories. It receives deposits by different ways – in lump sum amount, in installments, by subscriptions, by sale of units or certificates, etc. It may be called by different names in different areas.

Mutual Benefit Financial Company

It is a company which is notified by the central government under Section 620A of the Companies Act, 1956. It is popularly known as "*Nidhi*". Generally it is registered with nominal shares of INR 1 only. It receives deposits from its members and lends only to members against tangible securities. Loans are given for marriages, redemption of old debts, for the construction and repairs of houses, etc., which do not come within the purview of commercial bank's lending. These companies have meagre resources and hence they are not able to meet the full requirements of their customers. However, they are linked with reasonable assurance of credit on reasonable terms. They do not follow any cumbersome procedures. The Banking Commission has made some recommendations such as licensing of *Nidhis* and prescription of certain liquidity and other ratios.

Miscellaneous Non-banking Company

A miscellaneous non-banking company means a company carrying on the business of managing, conducting, and supervising as a promoter, foreman or agent of any transaction or conducting any form of chit or *kuri*. A chit fund is a financing agency which collects subscription from a group of persons and distributes the same to each member of the fund. It may be a simple chit or business chit. In a simple chit subscriptions are paid regularly. Lots are drawn to select the person to whom the whole amount of the chit is payable. Everyone will ultimately get the amount. But the lot winner will get it earlier. There is no promoter or foreman.

In a prize chit, there is promoter or foreman who collects periodic subscriptions. A prize winner is picked up by lot periodically and he gets the chit amount. He need not pay the subscription thereafter. Those who could not get the prizes, will get their chit amount after the specified period is over. In a business chit, instead of picking out a person by lot, it is given to the highest bidder in an auction. The discount is distributed among the non-bidders.

Chit funds have may defects, in the sense, that the rate of interest involved in the chit fund is not uniform and it varies from person to person and it results in irrational distribution of gains and losses. The Banking Commission has made strong suggestions to pass a uniform chit fund legislation for the whole country.

Non-banking Non-financial Company

A non-banking non-financial company means an industrial concern as defined in the Industrial Development Bank of India Act or a company whose principal activity is agricultural operations or trading in goods and services or real estate and which is not classified as financial or miscellaneous or residency non-banking company. The Government of India regulates the activities of these companies under the Companies (Acceptances of deposits) rules. A positive role is being played by such companies in mobilising deposits from public. The RBI has appointed a working group to offer suitable suggestions to put NBFCs alongwith the main stream of the overall financial sector. A committee under the chairmanship of Professor Shaw has put the following suggestions.

(a) It has recommended dismantling of category-wise classification of NBFCs and application of a uniform regulation for all kinds of NBFCs.
(b) A separate supervisory board to be set up under the auspices of the RBI to deal with the NBFCs.
(c) It envisages the setting up of Self-Regulatory Organisations (SROs) to see that individual members observe the guidelines of the regulatory authorities and function on prudential lines.
(d) The minimum period of deposit must be reduced from 120 months to 84 months.
(e) It has recommended credit rating to be made compulsory for all registered companies at least after a period of five years from now.
(f) The regulatory authority should be empowered to suspend the registration of those companies and even more for winding up where it so deems necessary.

The RBI has accepted the recommendation and implemented them. It will create a heavily and orderly working of NBFCs and also ensuring the solvency and safety of the financial system. It will make the NBFs sector wither not only from the depositor's point of view, but also from the point of view of the economy as a whole.

Small Industries Development Bank of India (SIDBI)

The small-scale industries sector (SSIs) is a vibrant and dynamic sector of the Indian economy. The sector presently occupies an important place and its contribution in terms of generation of employment, output and exports is quite significant. The SSIs sector includs tiny units, comprises the domain of Small Industries Development Bank of India's business. Besides, the projects in the services sector with total cost up to INR 250 million are also taken within the area of SIDBI's operations. The bank also finances industrial infrastructure projects for the development of the SSI sector.

Small Industries Development Bank of India (SIDBI) was set up as a wholly owned subsidiary of IDBI in 1990 under the SIDBI Act, 1989 enacted by the parliament. It is the principal financial institution for:

- promotion
- financing
- development of industry in the small-scale sector
- coordinating the functions of other institutions engaged in similar activities.

Since its inception, SIDBI has been assisting the entire spectrum of SSI sector including the tiny village and cottage industries through suitable schemes tailored to meet the requirement of securing up of new projects, expansion, diversification modernisation, and rehabilitation of existing units. SIDBIs financial assistance to the small-scale sector have three major dimensions. These are:

- indirect assistance to primary lending institutions (PLIs)
- direct assistance to small units, and
- development and support services.

SIDBIs schemes of indirect assistance envisages credit to SSIs through a large network of 913 PLIs spread across the country with a branch network of over 65,000. The assistance is provided by way of refinance, bill discounting, and resource support in the form of short-term loans, line of credit (LOC) in view of refinance, etc. The bank extends development and support services in the form of loans and grants of different agencies working for the promotion and development of SSIs and tiny industries. Over the years, the initiatives of SIDBI under promotional and developmental activities have crystallised into the following important areas:

(a) Technology upgradation.
(b) Quality and environment management.
(c) Human resource development to suit the SSI sector needs.
(d) Enter prize promotion with emphasis on rural industrialisation.
(e) Marketing and Promotion, and
(f) Information dissemination.

The authorised capital of SIDBI is INR 250 crores which could be increased to INR 1000 crores. Consequent upon amendments to SIDBI Act, 51 per cent of the shareholding of IDBI in SIDBI has been transferred to State Bank of India (SBI), Life Insurance Corporation (LIC), public sector banks, General Insurance Corporation (GIC), and other financial institutions owned or controlled by Government of India. At present, the shareholders of SIDBI include 35 banks, insurance companies, investment, and financial institutions, in addition to IDBI (IDBI continues to hold 49 per cent shares in SIDBI).

Functions

(a) SIDBI provides seed capital/soft loan assistance under national equity fund and other schemes through specified financial institutions.
(b) SIDBI provides both direct and indirect assistance. Direct finance is provided through project financing, equipment financing, infrastructure financing, and bill discounting schemes. Indirect assistance is provided to regional rural banks, NGOs, cooperative banks, state financial corporations, etc., mainly through refinance and rediscounting.
(c) SIDBI finances projects relating to transport, health-care and tourism sectors and also to the professional and self-employed persons, setting up small-sized professional ventures.
(d) SIDBI co-promotes state-level venture funds in association with respective State Governments.
(e) SIDBI takes initiative for setting up of incubation centres (SIDBI set up two incubation centres in collaboration with Indian Institute of Technology, Kanpur and Birla Institute of Technology, Ranchi) under its National Programme on Innovation and Incubation for Small Industries with a view to harnessing the entrepreneurial talents.
(f) SIDBI provides support services such as finance, training, application/scanning of new technology and market information and advice to enhance the inherent strength of SSI units and employment generation, economic rehabilitation of the rural poor.
(g) SIDBI provides services such as leasing, factoring and so on to industrial units in the small-scale sector. It also renders financial support to National Small Industries Corporation for providing leasing, hire purchase, and marketing support to industrial units in the small-scale sector.

SIDBI plays a key role in the implementation of government policies and initiatives for the sector. It facilitates creation of an environment for self-sustaining and growing SSI units. Some of the institutions SIDBI has promoted include:

(a) SIDBI Venture Capital Ltd.
(b) Credit Guarantee Fund Trust for small industries.
(c) Technology Bureau for Small Enterprises.
(d) SIDBI Foundation for Micro Credit.

As a part of its operational strategy, SIDBI lays emphasis on:

(a) Improving the capabilities of SSIs at all levels with a focus on adoption of modern technology.
(b) Increase in flow of financial assistance to SSIs. SIDBI was ranked 25 in position, both in terms of capital and assets among all development banks in the world as per the assessment of "*The Banker*", London in May 2001.

It is one of the professionally managed organisations with considerable emphasis on corporate governance. SIDBIs assistance now covers equity, term loan (both in Indian and foreign currency), working capital for inventory, raw material through finance against bills receivables and for intangibles. SIDBI has been operating schemes like single window scheme and composite loan scheme to ensure that financial assistance is made available to a large number of micro-enterprises which require special nurturing.

SIDBIs policy is to identify the areas of gaps in credit delivery system and fill them through devising appropriate new schemes and implementing them.

The purpose for which SIDBI extends financial assistance include new projects, expansion, diversifications, technology upgradation, modernisation, quality improvement, environmental management, marketing (domestic and international) and rehabilitation of sick small scale industries.

Performance and Progress

Table 6.3 Sanctions and Disbursement of SIDBI

F. Year	**Sanction (S)**	**Disbursements (D)**	**Outstanding (O)**	**D/S**	**(Rs billion) % of**	**CAGR of S**	**CAGR of D**
1991	24.1	18.4	51.8	76.3			
1992	28.5	20.3	64.8	71.2	25.1		
1993	29.1	21.5	72.5	73.8	12.0		
1994	33.6	26.7	88.0	79.6	21.3		
1995	47.1	33.9	97.0	72.0	10.2	18.2	16.5
1996	60.7	48.0	108.7	79.1	12.1		
1997	64.9	45.9	121.9	70.7	5.6		
1998	74.8	52.4	128.6	70.0	10.5		
1999	88.8	62.9	142.1	70.8	6.9	14.1	9.7
2000	102.7	69.6	151.9	67.8	−4.1		
2001	108.2	64.4	145.7	59.5	−9.7		
2002	90.3	59.2	131.6	65.6	−3.3		
2003	109.0	67.9	127.3	62.3	−20.9	−8.7	−11.8
2004	82.5	44.1	100.6	53.5			
1991–2004	944.3	635.2		67.3			

Source: SIDBI

The trends in sanctions and disbursements of SIDBI as per the above table 6.3 shows a steady decline in such over the years. Infact, the Compounded Annual Growth Rate (CAGR) shows that for the period 2000–2004, both sanctions and disbursements have turned negative.

The various disbursal activities of SIDBI shows the decline in Disbursements and Sanctions Ratio (D/S Ratio) has been the maximum for refinance and also in project financing, both of which are of significance for the small-scale industries sector (SSI) (see table 6.4).

Table 6.4 Disbursements to Sanction Ratios for SIDBI for Various Activities (%)

FY	Refinance	Bill discree-tly	Resource supprt (percentages)	Project finan-cing	Equity assis-tance	Promotion development assistance
2000	65	87	52	75	90	43
2001	55	88	55	77	83	59
2002	65	91	92	43	66	55
2003	61	93	63	49	76	80
2004	40	92	77	41	88	103

Source: SIDBI

An interesting aspect relates to the fact that over the years, SIDBI has consciously reduced the direct assistance component, but for the year 2004, when there was an increase. Infact SIDBI has been following a cautious approach in considering fresh loans to existing borrowers over the years as a part of strategy to keep in check the prospect of non-performing assets loans. The reason for a cautious approach lies in the fact that its resources profile is characterised by long-term funds, with long-term borrowings from RBI, among others. However, the declining interest regime after the year 2000 has now made the same loans costly. The margins have also been squeezed for the same reason (see table 6.5).

Table 6.5 Financials of SIDBI (percentages)

	1996	1997	1998	1999	2000	2001	2002	2003	
Average	–	–	–	–	–	–	–	–	–
Return									
Of Funds	14.1	14.6	14.3	14.0	13.4	12.9	12.0	11.8	–
Average	–	–	–	–	–	–	–	–	–
cost									
Of Funds	10.2	10.4	10.2	10.5	10.4	10.5	10.3	9.4	–
Margin	3.9	4.2	4.1	3.5	3.0	2.4	1.7	2.4	–
CRAR	21	25	26	27	28	28	45	44	–

Source: IDBI Development banking reports.

However even then the CRAR of SIDBI has continued to be comfortable.

Table 6.6 Refinancing by SIDBI (Rs Billion)

Sanctions/ F. Year	Banks	SFC	SIDC	Total
2001	65,174	13,553	2,153	80,880
2002	51,995	10,993	762	63,750
2003	72,664	7,499	184	80,347
2004	37,254	5,188	62	42,504
	–	–	–	–
2001	33,124	9,482	1,509	44,116
2002	32,690	8,117	637	41,444
2003	42,756	5,802	5,188	53,745

Source: SIDBI

As for the refinancing facilities of SIDBI, as in the above table 6.6, SIDBI has reduced its exposure to SFCs and SIDCs. This is because most of the SFCs and SIDCs are financially weak with recurring losses, with high NPAs and negative capital adequacy.

Table 6.7 Purpose-wise Assistance by SIDBI (in percentage)

Purpose	1999	2003
New	38.0	34.9
Expansion	7.6	6.5
Modernisation	11.6	10.6
	3.4	2.0
Rehabilitation	0.1	0.9
Others	39.3	45.1

Source: SIDBI

As for the purpose-wise assistance by SIDBI, as per the above table 6.7 shows that there have been further decline in the already low shares in SIDBI assistance relating to modernisation, working capital requirements, and expansion.

SIDBI continues to work in close partnership with the Government of India and is the nodal agency for various schemes aimed at building competitive strength of the SSI sector, such as Technology Upgradation Fund Scheme (TUFS) for textile and jute industries, Tannery Modernisation Scheme (TMS), and so on.

In the area of micro-finance operating, the bank has a good working relationship with department for international development, Government of UK, which also have been providing SIDBI financial resources in its capacity building efforts for the sector. SIDBI has been raising resources through international and domestic markets. The bank has raised borrowings from Japan Bank for International Cooperation and KFW, Germany (a German development bank). It has emerged as a financial services group, providing a complete range of services to the small-scale sector.

The major challenges for SIDBI include:

- softer interest rate
- accelerated pace of deregulation of financial sector
- decline of refinancing by banks which until now were the major chunk of bank business.

The challenge can be met by SIDBI by gearing up direct financing infrastructure, marketing, technology upgradation, and service sector. SIDBI's future strategy should be exploring avenues for raising cost-effective resources, building quality long-term assets, containing non-performing assets and bringing greater value to the shareholders. Containment of NPAs and monitoring the health of state financial corporations are the major areas of attention. SIDBIs endeavour would be to remain a strong, viable, and vibrant financial institution in the years to come to serve the important small-scale sector.

State Financial Corporations (SFCs)

State Financial Corporations (SFCs) are set up under State Financial Corporation Act, 1951 with a principal objective of meeting the credit needs of medium and small-scale industries located in backward areas in different states. A few of them also cater to the needs of the adjoining states/union territories that do not have state financial corporations of their own. The main purpose of SFCs is to induce industrial activity in the entire country including backward regions. The industrial units located in backward regions are given special treatment in terms of concessional rate of interest, lower margins, reduced service charges, preferential sanction and disbursements of loans and so on. By the end of March 2002 there were 18 SFCs, out of which one Tamil Nadu Industrial Investment Corporation of India (promoted as a joint-stock company under Companies Act of 1956) which operates on the line of SFCs.

As per the provisions of SFC (amendment) Act 1985, the corporations can provide assistance to such small and medium industrial units whose paid-up capital and reserves do not exceed INR 3 crores or such higher limit up to INR 30 crores as may be specified by the central government. SFCs act as agents of respective state governments, IDBI, SIDBI or any financial institution notified by the state government concerned. It also operates special schemes for artisans and special target groups such as SC/ST, women, ex-servicemen and physically handicapped.

SFCs provide long-term finance to industrial units of both small and medium scale. The units may be cooperatives, partnerships, proprietary concerns, private companies or public companies. In case of partnership firms, the maximum limit for assistance per unit is INR 30 lakhs. In case of companies, and cooperative societies, the maximum limit of assistance is INR 60 lakhs. SFCs provide assistance to the industrial units mainly through:

(a) Underwriting of or directly subscribing to shares, bonds, and debentures.
(b) Granting of term loans repayable over a maximum period of 20 years.
(c) Guaranteeing of loans, repayable over a period of 20 years, raised in the market or from scheduled banks or cooperative banks by industrial concerns.
(d) Guaranteeing of deferred payments in connection with purchase of capital goods, such as machinery in India.
(e) Operating a number of schemes of refinance and equity type assistance on behalf of IDBI/SIDBI.

Capital

The capital resources of SFCs include:

(a) Share capital and resources.
(b) Bonds and debentures.
(c) Borrowing from the RBI, and state governments.
(d) Finance from Industrial Development Bank of India (IDBI).
(e) Deposits from public.

The share capital of SFCs is to be fixed by the concerned state government subject to the limits between INR 50 lakhs and INR 5 crores. The shares of the SFCs can be subscribed by the state governments, the RBI, commercial banks, cooperative banks, other financial institutions, and the public. The shares of the SFCs can be regarded as trustee securities under the Indian Trust Act, and as approved securities for purposes of the Banking Companies Act. The SFCs can also raise funds by issuing bonds and debentures. Bonds and debentures issued by the corporations are guaranteed by the respective state government and mostly subscribed by the commercial banks as other financial institutions.

Financial Assistance

At present, there are 18 SFCs in the country. Sanctions and disbursements of SFCs during the period 1996–2001 are outlined as under.

Table 6.8 Sanctions and disbursements of SFCs.

(INR Crores)

	1996–1997	1997–1998	1998–1999	1999–2000	2000–2001
Sanctioning	3,532	1,859	1,859	1,849	2,389
Disbursements	2,775	2,104	1,620	1,519	1,698

Source: SIBI

From the above table 6.8, it can be seen that the loans sanctioned from 1996–1997 to 2000–2001 indicates that the amount of loans sanctioned is gradually declining from year to year. The amount of loan disbursements have also declined year after year.

In terms of sanctions, the Top Five SFCs were those in Andhra Pradesh, Kerala, Gujarat, Karnataka and Tamil Nadu during 2000–2001. New projects accounted for 68 per cent of the total assistance sanctioned, followed by 23 per cent expansion and diversification during 2000–2001.

Critical Appraisal

(a) The financial resources of SFCs are inadequate, moreover, they face the difficulty of finding funds.
(b) The SFCs are not able to provide adequate financial assistance to meet the requirements of small and medium industries.
(c) The SFCs charge very high interest rates on all the loans other than the soft loans. Moreover, the terms and conditions of assistance are also hard.
(d) The SFCs also face the serious protection of increasing magnitude of overdues. The main reasons for overdues are delays in the implementation of projects and industrial sickness.
(e) The SFCs lack self-sufficient organisational set up along with adequate specialised and trained staff for ensuring their efficient factoring.

(f) There is also shortage of technical personnel for judging the soundness of the proposed schemes of the borrowing units.
(g) Many difficulties are faced by the SFCs while extending financial assistance to the small industrial units.

But without SFCs, the industrial economy of India would not have advanced as much as it has today. The RBI appointed a working group to assess the functioning and effective performance of the various SFCs which was far from satisfactory.

The Gupta Committee appointed by the Government of India to look into the functioning of SFCs, submitted its report in January 2001. In the wake of World Trade Organisation (WTO) provisions becoming effective, SSI sector would face new challenges. The need of the hour is, as the committee concluded, the financial institutions should assume a new role for specialising in and dedicated to financing and development of the SSI sector. Therefore, SFCs would continue to play a strategic role in financing the SSI sector in India.

Unit Trust of India (UTI)

The Unit Trust of India (UTI) is a public sector investment institution. It was established in 1964 under Unit Trust of India Act, 1963 with the initial capital of INR 5 crores. It was fully subscribed by RBI, LIC of India, the SBI and the other scheduled banks and other financial institutions. The management of affairs, business of the trust and the general supervision and direction is vested with the board of directors.

Objectives of UTI

The objectives of UTI are:

(a) To stimulate and bring in the savings of the middle- and low-income groups.
(b) To enable them to share the prosperity and benefits of the rapidly growing industrialisation in the country.

In order to achieve the above objectives, UTI has adopted the following approaches:

(a) To pay dividends to those who have brought the units of the Trust.
(b) To invest the sale proceeds of the units and also the initial capital in corporate and industrial securities.
(c) To sell the units of the Trust among as many investors as possible in different parts of the country.

Advantages of UTI Units

(a) The divided income of UTI enjoys various tax concessions.
(b) The units can be converted into cash very easily.
(c) The holders receive a steady and decent income from their investment.
(d) The investments in the units are safe because it is spread over a wide range of securities.

From its inception, the sale of units by the UTI was acclaimed as a landmark in the development of the Indian capital market. It leads to the mobilisation of the community's savings for investment in trade and industry. UTI has won the public confidence. An investment in the different schemes of UTI meets the principles of safety and liquidity. Small and medium groups are encouraged to invest in different schemes of UTI.

UTI invests in the corporate sector in the form of equity and preference shares, debentures, special deposits, etc. It accounts for 85 per cent of its total investment. The remaining funds are in the form of investments in government securities and deposits with banks.

UTI witnessed a serious jolt when US-64 came under serious trouble in September–October, 1998. The proportion of equity to debt instruments held by UTI was 64:36. An expert committee was appointed under the chairmanship of Deepak Parekh, to make comprehensive review of the functioning of UTI and make recommendations to restore investor confidence. The committee suggested to convert US-64 into net asset value drawn scheme over a period of three years, fiscal incentives to investors in US-64, revamping of distribution policy, portfolio restructuring process, etc.

The government had to interface in order to protect the interests of the investors. The government interfered only in the structural reforms of UTI. Now this scheme is linked with the daily Net Asset Value (NAV) and it has no link with administrative pricing. It has been realised that it should work under the regulation of SEBI. The Government of India has started its interference as under:

(a) The Government of India repurchased the shares of UTI invested in public sector enterprises in June 1999, which were higher in price than that of market price.
(b) The investors were allowed to sell the units to UTI at administered prices. In December 2001, the units of US-64 to be sold by investors was increased and to be paid more than NAV or INR 10 per unit. UTI was adversely affected by the share of mutual funds in the market. The failure of US-64 revealed the mismanagement and political interference in the working of financial institutions. Because of the failure to check

mismanagement of UTI by the Ministry of Finance, private investors have started to invest their saving in private sectors with the splitting of the mutual funds into two. The government will have a control on UTI-I whereas professionals will control UTI-II. UTI has completed 47 years of operations, inspite of facing various problems.

Life Insurance Corporation of India (LIC)

Life Insurance Corporation is the largest investment institution established on 1 September 1956, amalgamating a total of 245 companies (154 Indian insures, 16 non-Indian insures and 75 provident fund companies) with its beautiful emblem or insignia and the performed motto "Yoga Keshemam Vahamyaham". It has 2060 branches having been computerised with Interactive Voice Respond System (IVRS) in 60 cities, Metro Area NetWork (MAN) and Wide Area Network (WAN) in major countries. Being the second-largest information technology user in India, LIC has today reached gigantic proportion in size, strength, reach and efficient service, and consumer orientation. LIC's products which match to any need, any age group, are well appreciated and accepted.

The importance of Life Insurance is:

(a) Life Insurance encourages "Thrift". Long-term savings may be relatively painless because of easy installments facility. The premium can be paid monthly, quarterly, half-yearly or yearly. Salary Saving Scheme (SSS) provides a convenient method of paying premium each month by deduction from salary. The employer remits the deduction premium to LIC.

(b) Life Insurance guarantee full protection against risk of death, full sum assured is payable (with bonus wherever applicable), whereas in other savings only interest is payable.

(c) Loans can be raised on the sole security of a policy which has acquired loan value. Besides, a Life Insurance policy is also generally accepted as security for even a commercial loan.

(d) Life Insurance Corporation of India also offers loans to the non-resident indians. It offers housing loans to NRIs by providing finance to construct/purchase residential house/flats. Assistance is also provided for extension/renovation of residential unit.

(e) Tax relief in income tax and health tax is available for amount paid by way of premium for Life Insurance subject to income tax rates. Assessees can avail themselves of provision in the law for tax relief. In such cases the assured in effect pays a lower premium for insurance than he would have to pay otherwise.

(f) The corporation has been promoting social welfare through socially oriented investments. It also provides financial assistance to state electricity boards, power corporation for power generation projects by way of loans/subscription to their bonds.

(g) The corporation also make investments in the corporate sector in the form of long-, medium-, and short-term loans to companies/corporations. The total investment made by way of loans up to 31 March 2002 was INR 3,021 crores and by way of subscription to shares/debenture bonds as on 31 March 2002 was INR 46,476 crores.

7

Cooperative Banks in India

Introduction

The Indian Cooperative Banks (CB) have a unique position in the rural credit delivery system of India. This sector of the banking industry plays a crucial role in the dispensation of credit for agriculture and rural development. Over the years, they have remained the prime institutional agencies with their vast network, with wider coverage and outreach extending to remote parts of the country. Both the short-term and long-term cooperative credit institutions are basically farmers' organisations and are primarily meant to meet their credit-related requirements. Although commercial banks and regional rural banks have established a large network of rural branches to cater to the credit needs of the rural poor, the cooperative banks continue to enjoy a place of crucial importance in the rural credit scenario. The reasons for above are as under:

(a) These institutions are primarily owned by the farmers, rural artisans, etc.
(b) They have been set up with the objective of promoting thrift and mutual help.

It can be pointed out here that cooperative credit societies in India, at the grassroots level, are intended not only to cater to credit requirements of the members, but also to provide several other credit-linked services like input supply, storage, and marketing of produce, etc. The cooperative banks with extensive networks and wide reach in remote areas play a significant role in the Indian economy, especially in creating banking habits among the lower- and middle-income groups and in rural credit delivery.

Cooperative credit institutions in India comprise both rural and urban cooperative credit institutions. While rural cooperatives play a pivotal role in the rural credit delivery system, urban cooperatives aim at mobilisation of savings from urban population and also provide credit to the weaker section.

Under the Banking Regulation Act 1949 only Urban Cooperative Banks (UCBs), State Cooperative Banks (SCBs) and District Central Cooperative Banks (DCCBs) are qualified to be called as banks in the cooperative sector.

We discuss here issues relating to long-term structure of rural cooperatives credit. While many cooperative banks are healthy and conduct their business efficiently within the regulatory norms, some others are confronted with many constraints. Major concerns of the cooperative sector include high levels of loan non-recovery, erosion of capital base, paucity of funds for fresh deployment, high level of dependence on other agencies for funds, lack of professionalism in conduct and management, in adequate internal contests, governance structure and non-adherence to norms and regulations. Measures for improving the overall health and conduct of cooperative banking system became imperative. Cooperative banks are under the regulatory control of multiple authorities like state governments, RBI, NABARD, and in certain cases the central government too.

An important segment of the organised sector of the Indian banking system is the Cooperative bank. Cooperative banks originated in India with the enactment of Cooperative Credit Societies Act 1904. The increase in demand for cooperative credit resulted in a new act which was passed in 1912, paving the way for the establishment of Cooperative Central Bank. In 1914, the Maclagan Committee was appointed to examine the cooperative movement and make recommendations to improve it. The committee recommended for the establishment of state cooperative Apex Bank. Accordingly, Central Cooperative Apex Banks were established in Bombay and other provinces. The cooperative banking movement gained momentum only after the Second World War.

The Structure of Cooperative Banking System in India

The Cooperative Banking System in India is federal in structure. (See Figure 7.1). It has pyramid type of three-tier structure constituted by:

(a) Primary Credit Societies (PCSs).
(b) Central Cooperative Banks (CCBs).
(c) State Cooperative Banks (SCBs).

In each state, there is a State Cooperative Bank at the apex level. In each district, there is a Central Cooperative Bank and at the basic level there are Primary Credit Societies. These cooperatives provide short-term and medium-term credit. There are agriculture and non-agricultural credit societies. Primary agricultural credit societies function in villages whereas urban banks and non-agricultural credit societies function in towns and cities. In addition, there are farmers' service societies and grain banks. For providing long-term agricultural credit, there are Primary and Central Land Development Banks.

Agricultural sector in particular is the major beneficiary of the cooperative banking system. Cooperative banks were the only institutional service of rural credit for agriculture sector till the nationalisation of banks in 1969. After nationalisation, the government has adopted a multi-agency approach

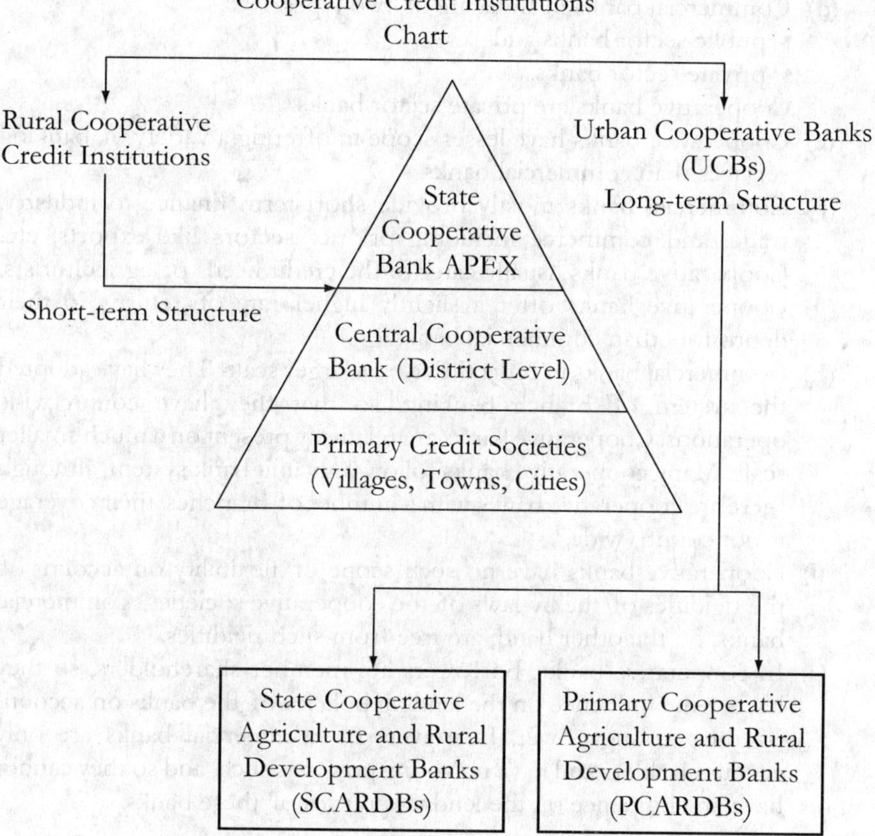

Fig. 7.1 Cooperative Credit Institutions Chart

wherein both cooperative banks and commercial banks supplemented by regional rural banks were encouraged to serve the rural sector.

Differences between Cooperative Banks and Commercial Banks

Cooperative banks and commercial banks can be distinguished on the following points.

(a) Commercial banks are joint-stock banks. Cooperative banks, on the other hand, are cooperative organisations.
(b) Commercial banks are governed by the Banking Regulation Act. Cooperative banks are governed by Cooperative Societies Act of 1904.
(c) Commercial banks are subject to the control of RBI directly. Cooperative banks are subject to the rules laid down by the Registrar of Cooperative Societies.

(d) Commercial banks in India are of two types.
- public sector banks and
- private sector banks.

Cooperative banks are private sector banks.

(e) Cooperative banks have lesser scope in offering a variety of banking services than commercial banks.

(f) Commercial banks mostly provide short-term finance to industry, trade, and commerce including priority sectors like exports, etc. Cooperative banks usually cater to the credit needs of agriculturists.

(g) Cooperative banks offer a slightly higher rate of returns to their depositors than commercial banks.

(h) Commercial banks in India thrive on a larger scale. They have adopted the system of branch banking, so that they have countrywide operations. Cooperative banks are relatively present on a much smaller scale. Many cooperative banks follow only unit bank system, although there are cooperative banks with a number of branches, their coverage is not countrywide.

(i) Cooperative banks have no such scope of flexibility on account of the rigidities of the by-laws of the cooperative societies. Commercial banks, on the other hand, are free from such rigidities.

(j) In cooperative banks, borrowers are member shareholders, so they have some influence on the lending policies of the banks on account of their voting power. Borrowers of commercial banks are only account holders and have no voting power as such, and so they cannot have any influence on the lending policies of these banks.

State Cooperative Banks

State Cooperative Banks (SCBs) constitute the apex of the three-tier cooperative structure. Every state in the country has one State Cooperative Bank, as cooperative is a state subject under the constitution. There are 29 State Cooperative Banks in India.

Functions of State Cooperative Banks

The following are the major functions of State Cooperative Banks.

(a) They give loans to the central cooperative banks in order to enable them to help in promoting the lending activities of the primary credit societies. The SCBs thus serve as the final link between the money market and the cooperative sector.

(b) In the absence of a district cooperative bank in a state, the SCB may give direct financial assistance to the primary credit societies.

(c) They act as a balancing centre by balancing excesses and deficiencies in the resources of central cooperative banks.
(d) They have no power to supervise or control the activities of the affiliated central cooperative banks.
(e) As a bank, a SCB is expected to mobilise and create deposits for the benefit of cooperative credit movement and provide the essential banking services.
(f) A SCB serves as a leader of the cooperative movement in a state.
(g) SCBs borrow from NABARD. It leads to cooperative societies as short-term loans for seasonal agricultural operations.
(h) They also provide medium-term loans to enable the CCBs and primary societies to facilitate easy payment.
(i) The SCBs also provide loans for various agricultural and non-agricultural purposes such as purchase of pumpsets and repairs of wells, etc.
(j) The SCBs finance, coordinate, and control the working of the central cooperative banks in every state.
(k) They serve as a link between the National Bank for Agriculture and Rural Development (NABARD), and money market on one hand, and the central cooperative banks and primary credit societies on the other.

Capital

Capital is raised largely from the members of cooperative societies, including CCBs and the rest from the state government concerned. The deposits are largely held by cooperative societies. They procure working capital from its capital resources, deposits from public, loans and advances from NABARD. The SCBs are subject to CRR and SLR requirements of the RBI at the minimum level, unlike in the case of commercial banks. As on 31 March 2001 – the capital of the SCBs amounted to INR 695 crores, deposits amounted to INR 32,600 crores and borrowing from RBI/NABARD amounted to INR 12,000 crores. The total loans disbursed in the year 2001 amounted to INR 30,000 crores. Out of 29 SCBs, 23 were in profits and remaining six were making losses.

Drawbacks

The following are the major defects of SCBs.

(a) They utilise their reserve funds as working capital.
(b) They have insufficient share capital.
(c) They mix up commercial banking activities with cooperative banking.

(d) Some SCBs are not pure federations as they permit individual membership along with affiliation to the CCBs.

As per the recommendations of the Committee on Agricultural Productivity, the following important measures have been brought under the programme of rehabilitation.

(a) Banks were advised to extend concessions such as rescheduling of installments of loan and waiver of penalty to borrowers of term loans affected by genuine hardships.
(b) The security norms for loans by cooperative banks were brought at par with those of connected banks for loans to avoid ambiguity.
(c) The registrar of cooperative societies in eastern India, that is, in Bihar, Orissa, eastern Uttar Pradesh, and West Bengal were advised to make necessary arrangements for introduction of cash credit system in lieu of short-term agricultural loans on trial basis in selected primary agricultural cooperatives.
(d) The existing stipulations of providing fresh finance by PACS to small/marginal farmers; defaulters whose defaults do not exceed 10 per cent of their eligibility under short agricultural loans, has been liberalised to 20 per cent for the next three years.

District Central Cooperative Banks (CCBs)

The district central cooperative banks are federations of primary credit societies belonging to a specific district. The Central Cooperative Banks (CCB) are of two types.

- pure
- mixed.

A pure CCB confines its membership to cooperative organisations only. It is called the banking union. A mixed CCB keeps its membership open to cooperatives as well as individuals. Mixed CCBs are found in the states of Assam, Andhra Pradesh, Tamil Nadu, Karnataka, etc. There are 367 district Central Cooperative Banks in India. The share capital of the CCBs is raised largely from affiliated cooperative societies and the balance from state governments. They also accept public deposits, loans from SCBs and other commercial banks. NABARD gives long-term loans to state governments to enable them to contribute to the share capital of CCBs. They provide loans and advances to the village primary cooperative societies to enable them to lend to their members. Apart from lending to the primary societies, the CCBs also take up normal commercial banking business.

Functions

The major functions of CCBs are:

(a) They accept deposits from public.
(b) They provide remittance facilities.
(c) They grant credit to their customers on the security of first-class gilt-edged securities, gold, etc.
(d) They finance the primary credit societies. CCBs serve as a link between these societies at the base level and the money market of the country.
(e) They act as balancing centres by shifting the surplus funds of primary societies to the deficit ones.
(f) They keep watch on the debtor primary societies working and on progress of recovery of loans.

Progress

In the year 2001, the capital of the CCBs amounted to INR 3,124 crores. Deposits amounted to INR 61,786 crores, borrowing from NABARD/SCBs amounted to INR 17,000 crores while the total amount of loans issued was INR 52,500 crores. During the year 2000–2001, income and expenditure of CCBs increased by 12.7 per cent and 10.8 per cent, respectively, over the previous year. The growth rate of operating expenditure of CCBs during 2001–2002 was received at 4.7 per cent. The number of CCBs was 367 during 2001–2002, out of which 245 made profits while 122 CCBs made losses.

Defects of CCBs

The following are the major defects of the CCBs.

(a) They violate the principle of cooperation by working on the line of commercial banks.
(b) They do not appoint experts to examine the credit worthiness of the primary societies. Hence, there has been problem of recovery and overdues.
(c) Many CCBs are financially and organisationally weak.
(d) The CCBs charge very high interest rates to meet their high administrative costs of small and uneconomic units.
(e) Mixed CCBs violate the very purpose of federation of the primary societies.
(f) Some CCBs have been utilising their reserve funds as working capital. This is not a very sound practice.
(g) They combine financing and supervising work together. As a result, supervising work has been a failure in many cases.

Primary Agriculture Credit Societies (PACS)

Primary Agriculture Credit Societies (PACS) are the grassroots level areas of the short-term cooperative credit structure. The PACS are organised at the level of village or group villages. The PACS directly deal with the rural (agriculture) borrowers by giving them loans and making recovery of the loans from the borrowers. They serve as the link between the ultimate borrowers and the higher financing agencies, namely the SCBs and the RBI/ NABARD. They also undertake distribution and marketing functions.

The PACS are generally organised on the RAIFFISEN (the renowned German Cooperator) model. Their members have unlimited liabilities. The members contribute to their share capital and elect members of the managing committee, all of whom work on an honorary basis. The PACS raise their funds by way of share capital, membership fees, deposits of members and non-members and loans from District Central Co-operative Bank and the government. They Deposit their reserve funds with the District Central Cooperative Banks (DCCBs). The PACS grant short-term and medium-term loans only to their members against the personal security. The rates of interest charged by them vary from state to state.

Grants

There were nearly one lakh PACS existing as on 31 March 2001 with a membership of approximately ten crores. Outstanding deposits and loans of PACS were INR 13,500 crores and INR 34,500 crores, respectively, on 31 March 2001. In fact, the fate of the cooperative movement depends greatly on the health and support of the PACS. In spite of government efforts and support, the working of PACS and their health is far from satisfactory.

Shortfalls and Remedial Measures

Although the PACS have made remarkable progress in the area of rural finance, their shortfall may be listed as under:

(a) A large number of them lacked potential viability.
(b) They have failed to adequately fulfill the credit needs of the small farmers and tenants. The banking commission (1972) observes that PACS neither provided credit for all productive activities of the farmer nor fulfilled their credit needs adequately.

Remedial measures such as financial support for compensation, steps towards better effective recovery performance, human resource development and so on have been undertaken to improve the financial health of the PACS.

NABARD has recently shared the need for a time-based programme for improving the centres of services rendered by the PACS. It has been suggested that PACS should:

(a) Provide diversified credit facilities to their members.
(b) Extend marketing facilities.
(c) Mobilise rural deposits.

Primary (Urban) Cooperative Banks (PCBs)

Cooperative credit societies established in the urban areas are referred to as Urban Cooperative Banks. Urban cooperative banks are confined to the municipal area of the town. They are:

(a) Unit banking.
(b) Branch banking.

Urban cooperative banks almost function like commercial banks in providing essential banking and non-banking agency and utility services. They are also known as Primary Cooperative Banks (PCBs).

PCBs commenced their operations from 1 March 1966. They are registered under Cooperative Societies Act, 1904 of their respective state governments before 1966. PCBs are exclusively under the purview of state governments. But from March 1966, certain provisions of the Banking Regulation Act, 1949 have been made applicable to these banks. Since then, the RBI has become the regulatory and supervisory authority of PCBs with respect to their banking-related operations. However, major aspects of PCBs continue to remain with the state governments governed by the provisions of the Cooperative Societies Act.

RBI sanctions credit limits to SCBs on behalf of PCBs for financing the small-scale industrial units and also conducts their statutory inspections. PCBs are required to channelise 60 per cent of total loans and advances towards priority sector within the private sector lending and 15 per cent to weaker sections. Fulfillment of priority sector lending targets by individual PCBs are taken into consideration by the RBI while granting permission for branch expansion, expansion of area of operation, etc. The RBI grants banking licenses to existing/new banks and branches. The urban bank department, established by the RBI in 1984, monitors and regulates the growth of PCBs.

The number of urban cooperative banks at the end of March 1995 was 1,431 including 91 salary earners' societies.

A scheme called Small Loans (cooperative banks) Guarantee Scheme 1984 has been introduced from 1 July 1984 to provide guarantee cover to primary (urban) cooperative banks to facilitate their lending to retail traders, small business and professionals, single transport operators, and self-employed persons, etc., where the eligible banks join the scheme by paying guarantee fees. The guarantee cover is automatically extended to it.

The standing advisory committee for urban cooperative banks, in its sixth meeting held in February 1987, recommended that UCBs be allowed to grant loans for purchase of consumer durable articles such as television sets, refrigerators, two-wheelers, etc., to individuals who are not their regular members by admitting such borrowers as nominal members. It has been suggested that the SCBs should devote more attention to create some development and healthy growth of urban cooperative banks.

The High Power Committee under the chairmanship of Shri K Madhava Rao (1999) recommended revision in the entry point norms for PCBs. In accordance with this recommendation, entry point norms for PCBs were revised, linking the minimum capital requirements to the population of place of incorporation and membership. Depending upon the parameters, the minimum start-up capital requirements for PCBs was fixed between INR 25 lakhs and INR 4 crores. The terms and conditions for licensing were also made stringent; granting license to PCBs now depends upon the fulfillment of specific experience/qualification by the board of directors and the chief executive officer. The RBI also has constituted an advisory screening committee consisting of eminent experts for examining the individual applications for licensing of PCBs. PCBs will be inspected every two years.

Progress and Performance

The number of PCBs has increased to 2,890 by the end of March 2002. Not all banks have been reporting their financial performance. The percentage of profitable PCBs among the 1,854 reporting banks, increased to 88 per cent during 2001–2002 from 84 per cent in the previous year.

Thc performance of scheduled PCBs which are included in the second schedule of RBI Act, 1934 was evaluated. A PCB becomes a scheduled PCB if its net demand and time liabilities are at least INR 100 crores and its overall functioning in terms of select parameters is satisfactory. There were 52 scheduled PCBs on 31 March 2002.

Evaluation

The degree of control of RBI over PCBs has been under fire with collapse of a series of PCBs such as Sravya Cooperative Urban Bank and Charminar Bank in Andhra Pradesh. Other states such as Gujarat and Maharashtra have also witnessed this. The hard-earned money of the small deposit holders such as pensioners, salaried class, small sector, etc., could not be protected despite the regulations by RBI, Registrar of cooperatives and state governments. As a consequence, the small investor completely lost confidence in the cooperative urban banks. The mismanagement, scams, and frauds in selected PCBs tarnished the image of the entire cooperative sector. In fact, the licensing policies have been made more stringent only after witnessing the high failure rate of PCBs.

Monitoring

It was observed in the past that, some PCBs developed serious financial problems immediately after they received licenses. Various measures such as close monitoring of submission of statutory returns by the banks, special scrutiny of their books of accounts in case of default in maintaining CRR/ SLR have been initiated to strengthen the supervisory efforts towards such banks. Chitale Committee (1995) recommended that the audit should be professional and there should be mandatory concealment audit for large banks. The committee further observed that there should be mandatory audit committee for all PCBs and statutory audit should be conducted by chartered accountants only, and not by government officials. The RBI has accepted these recommendations and advised the state governments to implement them. The RBI has also set up a task force headed by the executive director of RBI to review the supervisory framework of PCBs on a regular basis and to recommend suitable measures to strengthen the existing PCB system. The focus of supervision should be on prevention of irregularities rather than taking penal actions after their occurrence. Accordingly, some concrete steps have been taken up to formulate an interactive mechanism between the central office and the regional offices with RBI. This mechanism emphasises on improving market intelligence scenes, early warning signals, setting up of the code of responsibility on the auditors of PCBs, revising the guidelines for statutory audit, etc. The RBI has advised the state governments to appoint professional chartered accountants at the earliest for the statutory audit.

Primary Cooperative Agriculture and Rural Development Banks (PCARDBs)

Primary Cooperative Agriculture and Rural Development Banks(PCARDBs) were earlier called Land Development Banks (LDBs) or Land Mortgage Banks (LMBs).

Indian farmers need three types of credits viz., short term, medium term and long term. Their short-term and medium-term credit requirements are fulfilled by the cooperative banking institutions like PACs, CCBs, and SCBs. Sometimes farmers have to borrow for the long-term (for a period of five years to 20–25 years) for buying equipments like tractors, pumpsets, etc., and for other development purposes such as reclamation of land, fencing, digging of new wells, constructing of a tank or tube-well or for buying additional lands. Thus, a need for a special kind of institution to provide long-term finance to the Indian agriculturists was earnestly felt. Consequently, land development banks came into existence.

Initially the land development banks were instituted in the form of Cooperative Land Mortgage Banks. The first Cooperative Land Mortgage Bank was established at Jhind in Punjab in 1920. However, it did not function well. A real beginning was made by the establishment of the Central Land Mortgage Bank in Madras (now Chennai) in 1929. Later on, the movement spread to many other states. The Land Mortgage Banks grant long-term loans to the farmers against the conveyance of land as security. The Land Mortgage Banks were renamed as Land Development Banks in 1966–1967.

Organisation and Structure of Land Development Banks (PCARDBs)

The Land Development Banks and Primary Cooperative Agricultural and Rural Development Banks (LDBs/PCARDBs) are essentially cooperative institutions. All the LDBs are registered under the Cooperative Societies Act. In a strict sense, however, they are semi-cooperatives. In fact, they are limited liability association of agricultural borrowers, as their members have limited liability. Further, unlike other cooperatives, LDBs do not have personal involvement in their functioning.

The working capital of LDBs are raised from share capital, debentures, deposits, and borrowings from SBI, commercial banks, and the State Cooperative Banks. However, a large part of their funds is raised through long-term debentures. The debentures can be issued only by the Central Land Development Banks and not by the Primary Land Development Banks. The LDBs (PCARDBs) have no uniform pattern. In some states, they are unitary and in some others, they are federal in nature. Under the federal structure, the LDB/(PCARDB) consists of two-tier institutions.

(a) The Central Land Development Bank (CLDB) at the state level.
(b) The Primary Land Development Bank (PLDB) at the district level.

There is only one Central Land Development Bank in each state and one Primary Land Development Bank in each district level. Under the federal structure, the PLDB deals with farmers directly and the Central Land Development Bank deals with the Primary Land Development Banks. Under unitary structure, however, the state may have more than one CLDBs and they make direct deals with the farmers. In some cases, the CLDB has its branches spread over the state and they do direct business with the farmers. In some cases, CLDB serves as a department of State Cooperative Bank. In states such as Himachal Pradesh and West Bengal, there is a mixed type of LDB/PCARDB combining the features of both the unitary and federal structure.

Functioning of the LDB/PCARDB

The LDBs provide long-term loans to the agriculturists for permanent improvements of land. They usually charge nine per cent interest. They grant loans against the security of land or other agricultural property. Loans are usually given on the first mortgage and sometimes even on the second mortgage of land or agricultural property. Generally they give loans up to 50 per cent of the market value of the mortgaged property.

By the end of march 2002, deposits and borrowings of PCARDBs were INR 251 crores and INR 9,077 crores, respectively. Loans extended by them amounted to INR 8,090 crores. During 2000–2001, recovery performance of PCARDBs worked to 53 per cent from 58 per cent during the previous year. During 2000–2001, there were 284 profit-making and 448 loss-making PCARDBs, and in aggregate they registered a loss of INR 158 crores. The functioning of LDBs reveal the following defects:

(a) On account of red tapism, there are delays in granting loans even beyond a year.
(b) No second loan is given until the first loan is repaid.
(c) The overdues have been mounting up year by year.
(d) They adopt complicated procedure which compels the illiterate farmers to resort to moneylenders to meet their urgent financial requirements.
(e) There is acute shortage of trained personnel and this restricts the professionalism in the organisation.
(f) The LDBs charge very high rate of interest.
(g) These give loans only up to 50 per cent of the value of the land mortgaged. Thus, a very high margin is kept.
(h) Quite often, loans are granted to discharge prior debts rather than for land development.
(i) Issues such as valuation of property and verification of the ownership letter involves greater scrutiny and these may lead to more delays in processing loans.

The RBI had appointed a committee on Cooperative Land Development Banks under the chairmanship of Shri K M Das in 1973 to examine the working of Land Development Banks. The committee submitted its report in December 1974 and made a number of recommendations such as:

(a) There should be one integration of the short-term and long-term credit structures.
(b) Concrete efforts should be made to recover overdues.

(c) Lending operations of LDBs (PCARDBs) should be diversified by linking them with specific and other rural developmental programmes.
(d) There should be essential training imparted to the technical and managerial staff.

The total outstanding refinance by NABARD for SCBs, state governments and Regional Rural Banks (RRBs) stood at INR 7,075 crores at the end of June 2002, as against INR 6,857 crores at the end of June 2001. The outstanding refinance to SCB and RRBs stood at INR 53 crores and INR 1,234 crores respectively as in June 2002.

National Cooperative Development Corporation (NCDC)

The National Cooperative Development Corporation (NCDC) was established in March 1963. Its major functions involved the promotion of various economic programmes in the cooperative sector and the provision of financial assistance in the form of loans and subsidies to the cooperatives as per the pattern of assistance evolved for the default schemes.

Since its inception, the NCDC has been very active in planning and promotion of programmes through cooperative societies for the production, processing, marketing, storage, export and import of agricultural goods, food stuffs, etc. One has been progressively moving in this direction. Besides, the corporation has been designing various programmes in such a manner as to benefit the weaker sections of the society, particularly the Scheduled Castes and Scheduled Tribes. These programmes include poultry, fisheries, minor forest produce, handlooms, coir products, sericulture, dairy farming, etc., in the rural sector organised on a cooperative banks.

Recent Developments in Cooperative Banking

The cooperative banks have extensive networks with their reach in remote parts of the rural areas too. They play a significant role in the Indian economy. They have been successful in creating banking habits among the lower- and middle-income groups and in rural credit delivery. The cooperative banking sector is characterised by substantial heterogeneity in both financial position and performance within and across different strata. While many cooperative banks are healthy and conduct their business efficiently as per the regulatory norms, some other are confronted with many constraints.

The constraints are:

(a) Monthly overdues.
(b) Paucity of funds for fresh deployment.

(c) Erosion of capital base.
(d) High levels of dependence on other agencies for funds.
(e) Lack of professionalism in conduct and management.
(f) Government structure and non-adherence to norms and regulations.

It is the immediate necessity to take certain measures for improving the overall health and conduct of the cooperative banking system. Several committees have been constituted in the recent past to explore the possibilities for the rejuvenation of cooperative banks through appropriate initiatives and suitable reforms. Some policy measures have been recommended to recast the cooperative credit system and to place it on the viable and sustainable paths. They can be broadly categorised into the following.

(a) There have been many weak banks in this sector. Identify those banks having potential to grow, if additional funds are made available. Close down those which are considered unviable.
(b) It should be ensured that the cooperative banks adhere to prudential discipline and the given guidelines for institution and systematic viability.
(c) The cooperative banks have been under the regulatory control of multiple authorities such as state governments, the RBI and NABARD and in certain cases under the central government too. Such multiple controls may not facilitate coordinated regulation and supervision. The reforms in this sector should address such critical issues. In case immediate measures are not taken to remove duality of control, it will be difficult to make the supervisory system effective.

Policy Measures

Re-capitalisation Formula

So far, larger burden was on the state governments to find adequate capital base for the cooperative banks. It is proposed that the capital contribution ratio should change. The ratio between the central and state governments should be 60:40 along with the increase in the share capital of members. A total provision of INR 100 crores has been made for this by the Government of India.

Capital-to-Risk-weighted Asset Ratio (CRAR)

The greater the risk in the nature of advances, the more likely is the danger for the liquidation of the cooperative banks. To prevent this situation, capital should be in proportion to the risk-weighted assets. Capital-to-Risk-weighted Asset Ratio (CRAR) for Urban Cooperative Banks (UCBs) has been fixed. Statutory audit of UCBs should be conducted by chartered accountants rather than governmental officials. Entry Point Norms (EPN) have been recast for UCBs.

Minimum Capital Requirement

The minimum capital requirement as specified for cooperative banks by the Banking Regulation Act, 1949 is met by rural cooperative banks.

Statutory Liquid Ratio

UCBs are advised to increase the proportion of statutory liquid ratio holding in the form of government and other approved securities.

Other Restrictions

The exposure of cooperative banks to capital markets and inter-bank money markets has also been restricted. The norms for granting permission to a UCB to extend its area of state of incorporation have been restricted. Supervisory efforts have been strengthened.

More Operational Autonomy

The practice of fixing floor interest rates chargeable on loans and advances made by UCBs has been discontinued. UCBs now have to internally decide their own lending rates taking into account cost of funds, transaction costs, and so on with the approval of the managing committee. To maintain transparency, the cooperative banks have to publish the minimum and maximum lending rates and display such information in every branch.

Payment of Interest

The cooperative banks are encouraged not to pay any additional interest on the savings bank accounts over and above what is payable by commercial banks. In addition, cooperative banks are encouraged not to pay interest on current accounts.

Structural Reforms in Cooperative Banking

Efforts to develop the cooperatives were intensified following the recommendations of the All India Rural Credit Survey Committee (1969). A multi-agency approach to rural credit was adopted with the commercial banks supplementing the efforts of the cooperative banks. To further strengthen the rural credit system, a third channel to the Rural Financial Institutions (RFI) was added by instituting Regional Rural Banks (RRBs) in 1975. While these RFIs made impressive gains in terms of branch expansion, deposit mobilisation and credit disbursements, the agricultural sector still suffers from inadequate institutional credit. The problem has been intensified by the emergence of a wide range of high-tech and capital-intensive segments in some pockets of the rural economy. Thus, there is an imperative need for rejuvenating the rural credit system so that it can meet the credit requirements of higher order across all sections of the rural economy. The key to the success in revamping the rural credit delivery system lies in improving the effectiveness of the cooperative system.

Two major problems confronting the cooperative banking system are the high transaction costs and poor repayment performance. Organisational structure of the cooperative banking system in India is a contributory factor for high transaction costs. Thus, some restructuring of the organisational set up is considered as one option for improving the viability of the cooperative banking system.

Two alternatives in this regard can be:

(a) Merger of the long-term and short-term structure.
(b) Delaying of the short-term structure.

As regards the poor recovery performance, linking self-help groups to the banks for delivery of rural credit is an innovative strategy which is gaining momentum.

In 1975, RBI appointed the Agricultural Refinance Development Committee in 1976 under the chairmanship of Dr R K Hazari for studying the feasibility of granting the two wings of cooperative credit structure (short-term and long-term) in the country. Noticing certain imbalances in the growth of the two wings of the credit structure, the committee felt that the cooperative credit system can play its expected role completely if it is enabled to provide credit facilities in an integrated manner. Integration of the cooperative structure was also perceived to benefit the farmers providing them with one contact point. The committee included that integration would prove to be beneficial from the angle of credit institutions too, as this will help them to improve the scale of business, and consequently viability, which would in turn enable them to employ full-time paid secretaries and function effectively. Thus, the committee recommended that the two wings of the cooperative credit structure should be integrated at all levels, viz., the primary, the intermediate (District) and the apex (State).

Andhra Pradesh is the only state which has implemented the integration of short-term and long-term structure in 1986. A recent study examining the impact of such integration concluded that:

(a) The management costs showed decline during the post-integration process.
(b) Bad debts of casualties in absolute terms and as a proportion of working capital/loan outstanding showed declining trend.

(c) Short-term and long-term loans was higher during post integration than what would have been possible had there been no integration.

The results of the above study suggest that, integration of the short-term and long-term structure may have several beneficial impacts.

De-layering of the cooperative system is considered as another alternative restructuring option to bring down the transaction costs. The mounting overdues of the cooperative institutions have severely restricted their capability of recycling funds for promoting faster agricultural growth. High overdues also make these institutions ineligible for availing of refinance facility from NABARD. The Second Narasimhan Committee on Banking Reforms (1998) urged that consideration be given to delayering of the cooperative credit system with a view to reducing the intermediation costs and providing the benefit of cheaper NABARD credit to ultimate borrowers.

Linking Self-Help Groups (SHGs) and NGOs to banks in the rural credit delivery is considered to be another innovative mechanism, which may help in reducing the transaction costs and also ensure better repayment performance. NABARD has been actively encouraging the concept since the launching of a pilot project in 1992. Under this scheme, NABARD provides policy support and 100 per cent refinancing to banks for financing the SHGs. The field studies conducted by NABARD revealed that other encouraging features of this linkage programme and the shift in loan pattern from non-income-generating activities to production activities, gradual increase in income levels of members, social empowerment of members, the increase in savings level, etc.

The role of strong leadership in the success of cooperative system cannot be over emphasised. Thus, institution of democratically elected management and removal of excessive state control in the working of cooperatives can help in their effective functioning.

National Bank for Agriculture and Rural Development (NABARD)

With the increasing role of institutional credit in the integrated rural development of the country, a need was felt for a single broad-based organisation which would not only extend adequate credit to the financial institutions of the rural areas but also provide guidance in all matters relating to the formulations and implementation of rural development programmes. These functions have been performed by the RBI and the Agricultural Refinance and Development Corporation (ARDC). Refinance is made available by the corporation to eligible institutions for financing agricultural development projects. Refinance was administered through cooperative land development banks, Regional Rural Banks, State Cooperative Banks, and other institutions approved by the Reserve Bank of India.

At the instance of the Government of India, the RBI, set up the Sivaraman Committee in March 1979 to review the activities of the ARDC. The committee pointed out the deficiencies in the working of the ARDC in dispensing of rural credit, and it did not have the capacity to promote rural development aimed at uplifting weaker sections within a given time span. Moreover, there has been a slight change in the policy of extending rural credit not only for agricultural purposes but also for non-agricultural purposes in rural areas. Hence, there was a need for a separate agency for providing full attention for designing and administering the rural development programmes. The committee, therefore, in its report in 1979 recommended for a separate agency solely for giving prompt attention to rural credit and development with organisational links with RBI. Hence, NABARD was established by an Act of Parliament in July 1982, to provide credit to rural artisans, agriculturists, cottage and village industries, and other allied economic activities in the rural areas. Thus, NABARD has taken over the entire undertaking of ARDC as well as the refinancing functions from the RBI in relation to cooperative banks and Regional Rural Banks.

Organisational Set-up

NABARD is managed by a board of directors comprising of 15 members which include the chairman, managing director, two experts in rural economics, three experts from the cooperative and commercial banks, three sitting directors from the board of the RBI, three directors from the Government of India and two members representing the state governments. The board of directors can constitute an advisory control.

Capital

The paid-up share capital of NABARD is INR 100 crores, contributed equally by the RBI and the Government of India. The other sources of funding include:

(a) Borrowings from the Central Government, the RBI and the market.
(b) Its two national rural credit funds namely:
- National Rural Credit (long-term operations) Fund, and
- National Rural Credit (stabilisation) Fund.

NABARD depends upon the RBI, for short-term funds. It issues and sells bonds and debentures (guaranteed by the Government of India), makes borrowings from the Central Government and any other organisation approved by the Central Government.

(c) External borrowings through the Government of India from World Bank group, IFAD, other countries like UK, Germany, EEC, Switzerland, Netherlands, Canada. Section 20 of the NABARD Act states that these loans can be guaranteed by the Central Government in respect of repayment of principle together with interest and other incidental charges.

Objectives

The main objectives of the NABARD are as follows.

(a) It serves as a refinancing institution for providing long-term and short-term credit for the promotion of activities in rural areas.
(b) The bank has to play the role of an apex institution in respect of all matters relating to policy, planning, and operational aspects, relating to promotion of credit for agriculture, small-scale industries, cottage and village industries, handicrafts, and other allied economic activities in the rural areas.
(c) To support and promote agriculture and rural development.
(d) To support all matters connected with rural development.

Functions

(a) NABARD provides refinance to eligible institutions, normally state cooperative banks and Regional Rural Banks for conversion and rescheduling of loans under conditions of draught, famine or other natural calamities, military operations, enemy action, and so on.
(b) NABARD can provide short-term credit to State Cooperative Banks, (SCBs), Regional Rural Banks (RRBs) and other financial institutions approved by RBI for the following purposes.
  - agricultural operating or marketing of crops
  - bonafide commercial or trade transactions
  - marketing and distribution of inputs necessary for agriculture or rural development
  - production and marketing activities of artisans, small-scale industries, industries in tiny and decentralised sectors, village and cottage industries for those engaged in handicrafts and other rural crafts.

(c) NABARD provides medium-term credit to SCBs, LDBs, RRBs, and other financial institutions approved by the RBI. The medium-term loan is allowed for a period between eighteen months and seven years for any investment connected or associated with agriculture and rural sector requiring medium-term credit assistance.

(d) NABARD can provide long-term loans and advances by way of refinance through land development banks, Regional Rural Banks, state cooperative banks, scheduled banks and other financial institutions for promotion of agriculture and rural development not exeeding 25 years. Such refinance facilities for investment loans are also available for marketing loans and advances to artisans, small-scale industries, village and cottage industries, industries in tiny and decentralised sectors, those engaged in handicrafts, and other rural crafts.

(e) It has the responsibility of coordinating the activities of Central and state governments, the planning commission and other All India and state level institutions, engaged in the field of rural development.

(f) The bank maintains a research and development fund to promote research in agriculture and rural development, providing facilities for training and dissemination of information in the field of rural banking.

(g) NABARD is obliged to inspect Regional Rural Banks and primary cooperative banks and other cooperative banks.

(h) NABARD's activities include relevant banking operations and also related functions like inspection, monitoring and technical services, long-term planning, corporate policy programming, institutional development, research, advisory and other related functions. Its services are administration, accents, personal management, human resources development training, etc.

(i) NABARD has been playing a significant role in strengthening and reorganising the cooperative structure in the country. It has formulated a set of guidelines for planning the future development of reorganised cooperative societies in a phased manner. It is constantly reviewing the rehabilitation programme of central cooperative banks (CCBs) which have been identified as weak and which are being helped to rehabilitate themselves. It also helps in the rehabilitation of the state land development banks as well as the primary land development banks.

(j) NABARD finances agro-based processing industries like sugar mills, spinning mills, etc., even though they are located outside the rural areas as such activities are conducive to rural development.

(k) NABARD is making sincere attempts to bring awareness in the minds of rural borrowers about the development of credit under a new programme known as Vikas Volunteer Vahini (VVV).

(l) Developing and promoting Self-Help Groups (SHGs) and other micro-finance institutions continue to be a thrust area of work for NABARD.

(m) NABARD played a vital role in implementing the 20-point programme under which IRDP (Integrated Rural Development Programme) absorbed a major refinance. It widened the scope of refinance to solar pumpsets, windmill pumps, and other schemes formulated by the Government of India which are very useful in developing new irrigation projects.

(n) NABARD provides assistance to handloom weavers for acquisition, modernisation of looms as well as for the construction of worksheds adjoining cottages of weavers through scheduled commercial banks and registrar of cooperative societies.

(o) With a view to improve the quality of loans and supervision over the utilisation of credit, NABARD has prepared a pilot project for strengthening the credit delivery system. The major feature of this project is to provide adequate staff to the credit institutions in order to limit the number of borrowers to be supervised by each official to a manageable level. Timely supply of credit and use of credit is also monitored.

NABARD provides two types of refinance. The main type includes RRBs and apex institutions namely SCBs and state governments. The second type of refinance is extended to augment resources for ground level deployment of rural credit. The total outstanding refinance by NABARD to SCBs, state goverments and RRBs amounted to INR 7,075 crores as on the end of June 2002. It was higher than that of the amount (INR 6,857 crores) as on the end of June 2001. The outstanding refinance to SCBs and RRBs stood at INR 5,353 crores and INR 1,234 crores, respectively, at the end of June 2002. Outstanding refinance to state governments was at INR 488 crores as on the end of June 2001. The aggregate refinance by NABARD during 2001–2002 was INR 18,075 crores.

Micro-Financing

A micro-finance development fund was constituted in NABARD in 2000–2001 with a contribution of INR 45 crores from NABARD and INR 40 crores from RBI. A sum of INR 20 crores was contributed by eleven commercial banks. A sum of INR 5.84 crores was utilised for soft loan assistance. The balance fund available as on 31 March 2002 was INR 102 crores.

NABARD with SDC (Swiss Agency for Development and Cooperation) collaboration created credit and financial services fund in 1995 in terms of MOU (Memorandum of Understanding), signed between them supported many of the initiatives.

NABARD-GTZ protect for technical collaboration under the SHG bank linkage programme focuses on capacity building of the National Bank and partner agencies in micro-finance-related fields and for taking up other supportive initiatives including the conduct of special studies.

NGO's, banks, farmer's clubs, government organisations, and departments have been playing a major role as Self Help Promoting Institutions (SHPI). NABARD is providing grant support to NGO's for meeting other infrastructure support to SHGs, staff and mobility support, and sharing of administrative expenses incurred for formation and nurturing of SHGs. The various initiatives and support programmes are outlined below.

- supporting RRBs as SHPI
- supporting farmer's club as SHPI
- supporting individual volunteers to act as SHPI
- resolving fund assistance to NGOs
- supporting NGOs and SHPIs.

NABARD continues to provide financial and other requisite support for training of the bank's staff, NGOs, and government agencies to further enhance their effectiveness in promoting micro-finance.

8
Regional Rural Banks (RRBs)

After Independence, the major aim of rural credit policy in our country has been to expand institutional financing with a view to curtail the role of indigenous financial agencies like moneylenders. The All-India Rural Credit Survey Committee perceived that only multi-purpose cooperatives can be a viable solution to the problem of rural finance. The State Bank of India as well as the nationalised commercial banks (since 1969) made some efforts to improve their share in contributing to rural finance. However, to bridge the vast "credit gap" in the rural sector, it was essential for the government to adopt a "multi-operating approach" in developing rural credit institutions. The banking commission in its report in 1972 recommended the creation of "Rural Banks".

Until June 1975, the Government of India, however, did not pay any attention to the proposal for instituting a chain of "Rural Banks" in the country. The idea of "Rural Banks" once again cropped up when the then Prime Minister Mrs Indira Gandhi announced the governments' 20-Point Economic Programme on 1 July 1975.

The Government of India then appointed a working group on rural banks headed by Shri M Narasimham, to examine in detail the issues involved in the establishment of new rural banks as subsidiaries of the public sector banks to deal with the problem of rural finance. The working group submitted its report on 30 July 1975. The working group recommended the establishment of state sponsored regionally based and rural-oriented commercial banks called Regional Rural Banks (RRBs). Based on the recommendation and after due consideration of the scheme suggested by the Narasimham Committee Report, the Government of India instituted Regional Rural Banks in October 1975, under the Regional Rural Banks Ordinance 1975, promulgated by the President of India on 26 September 1975. Subsequently on 9 February 1976, the Government of India passed the Regional Rural Banks Act, 1976 which provides for the incorporation, regulation and winding up of RRBs. The RRBs are scheduled commercial banks which are in the second schedule of the RBI Act.

The following are the provisions of the Regional Rural Banks Act, 1976 (as amended by the Regional Rural Banks Amendment Act, 1988):

As per Section 2(f) of the Act, "Regional Rural Banks" means "Regional Rural Banks" established under Sub-section (1) of Section 3 of the "Regional Rural Banks" Act.

(a) The Central Government may, if requested to do so by the Sponsor Bank, by notification in the Official Gazette, establish in a State or Union Territory, one or more Regional Rural Banks with such name as may be specified in the notification and may, by the said or subsequent notification, specify the local limits within which each Regional Rural Bank shall operate.

(b) Every Regional Rural Bank shall be a body corporate with perpetual succession and a common seal with power, subject to the provisions of this Act, to acquire, hold and dispose of property and to contract and may sue and be sued in its name.

(c) It shall be the duty of the Sponsor Bank to aid and assist the Regional Rural Banks, sponsored by it by: (a) subscribing to the share capital of such Regional Rural Bank, (b) training personnel of such Regional Rural Banks; and (c) providing such managerial and financial assistance to such Regional Rural Bank during the first five years of its functioning, as may be mutually agreed upon between the Sponsor Bank and the Regional Rural Bank: provided that the Central Government may, either on its own motion or on the recommendation of the National Bank, extend the said period of five years by such further period, not exceeding five years at a time, subject to such conditions as it may deem fit to impose.

The main objective of the RRBs was to provide credit and other facilities particularly to the small and marginal farmers, agricultural labourers, artisans, and small entrepreneurs so as to develop agriculture, trade, commerce, industry, and other productive activities in the rural areas.

The RBI constituted a committee in June 1977 to evaluate the performance of the rural banks in the light of the objectives for which they were set up. The committee was to examine precise role of the rural banks in the rural credit structure and make recommendations with regard to the scope, method and procedure of their functioning. The committee submitted its report in February 1978. The committee concluded that with certain modifications in the operational structure, the RRBs could play a very useful role in providing rural credit in the rural areas. In compliance with recommendations of the committee, the RBI in 1978 formed a steering committee for policy making, periodical review, and identification of the districts for establishing the RRBs.

Capital

As per Section 5 of the Act, the authorised capital of each RRB shall be INR 5 crores. The issued/paid-up capital of minimum INR 25 lakhs and maximum of INR 100 lakhs is to be contributed in the ratio of 50:15:35 by the Central Government, State Government, and the sponsoring commercial bank, respectively.

At the end of March 2002, the Government of India raised the issued share capital of 196 RRBs to INR 75 lakhs each, while the same of 20 RRBs was raised to INR 100 lakhs. The paid-up capital of all the 196 RRBs stood at INR 195.66 crores by the end of March 2001.

The working and affairs of the RRB are directed and managed by a board of directors. The board of directors consists of a chairman, three directors to be nominated by the Central Government, not more than two directors to be nominated by the State Government concerned, and not more than three directors to be nominated by the sponsored bank. The chairman is appointed by the Central Government and his term of office does not exceed five years.

Regulation

The RBI is the regulatory authority for the RRBs in accordance with the provisions of the Banking Regulation Act, 1949. The Banking Regulation Act also empowers NABARD referred to in the Act as 'National Bank' to undertake the inspection of the RRBs. A Regional Rural Bank seeking the permission of the RBI for opening branches has to obtain the recommendation of NABARD. The returns and documents to be furnished under the Banking Regulation Act of the Reserve Bank are also to be forwarded to NABARD.

Differences between RRBs and Scheduled Commercial Banks

The Regional Rural Banks are also scheduled banks. The RRB, however, differ from a scheduled commercial bank in the following respects.

(a) The RRB is deemed to be a cooperative society for the purpose of Income Tax Act, 1961.
(b) The area of operations of the RRB is limited to a specified region relating to one or more districts in the concerned state.
(c) The RRB grants loans and advances only to the small and marginal farmers, agricultural labourers, rural artisans, and small entrepreneurs or small traders.
(d) The RRB charges interest rates as adopted by the cooperative societies in the state.
(e) The RRB is a sponsored bank. It is sponsored by a scheduled commercial bank.

(f) The interest paid by the RRB on its term deposits may be half a per cent more than that of paid by the commercial bank.
(g) If an RRB completes the limit of 100 branches, it has to seek the permission of RBI before growing beyond 100 branches.

Functions of RRBs

The functions of RRBs include:

(a) Providing short-term crop loans.
(b) Granting loans to cooperative societies for agricultural purposes or agricultural operations or for other purposes connected therewith.
(c) Extending term loans for agricultural activities for rural artisans, village and cottage industries, retail trade and self-employed, consumption loans, and so on.
(d) Implementation of differential rate of interest (DRI), schemes to extend loans to weaker sections, physically handicapped persons (for purchase of artificial limbs, wheelchair, etc).

Every RRB shall carry on and transact the business of banking as defined in Clause (b) of Section 5 of the Banking Regulation Act, 1949 and every RRB may, in particular, undertake the following types of business.

(a) The granting of loans and advances, particularly to small and marginal farmers and agricultural labourers, whether individually or in groups, and to cooperative societies, including agricultural marketing societies, agricultural processing societies, cooperative farming societies, primary agricultural credit societies, primary agricultural credit societies of farmer's service societies, for agricultural purposes or agricultural operations or for other purposes connected there with.
(b) Accepting deposits.

Progress of the Regional Rural Banks (RRBs)

In 1975, initially five RRBs were started at Moradabad, Gorakhpur, Bhiwani, and Malda under the sponsorship of the Syndicate Bank, State Bank of India, Punjab National Bank, United Commercial Bank, and United Bank of India, respectively.

On 30 March 1995, there were 196 RRBs with 14,536 branches covering 417 districts. These banks have an aggregate deposits of INR 10,938 crores and advances of INR 6,226 crores. Of this, agricultural advance claimed 47 per cent of the total amount. The RRBs obtained refinance amounting to INR 2,312 crores from the sponsor banks and other financial institutions.

They borrowed INR 1,839 crores, that is, nearly 80 per cent from NABARD. There were 196 RRBs functioning in 26 states (including newly created states) spread over 500 districts with a network of 14,313 branches as on 31 March 2001 excluding satellite branches and extension counters. RRBs have nearly 37 per cent of the total branch network of all scheduled commercial banks.

The number of profit making RRBs increased from 44 per cent in 1996–1997 to 170 in 2000–2001. However, there has been decline in the number of profit making RRBs to 167 during 2001–2002. The combined net profit of the RRBs for the year 2001 aggregated to INR 608 crores as against the combined net profit of INR 601 crores in the year 2000.

By the end of March 2002, the deposits of RRBs aggregated to INR 44,539 crores implying a growth of 16.26 per cent over the previous year, showing a growth in deposits. There was spectacular growth in loans issued by RRBs. The loans issued by RRBs aggregated INR 10,267 crores in 2001–2002. This was 16 per cent higher than the loans issued in 2000–2001.

During the year 2000–2001, an amount of INR 868 crores has been availed as refinance by the RRBs towards investment credit. The asset quality of RRBs has improved over the past few years as a result of improved recovery performance. In order to reduce the level of NPAs (Non-Performing Assets) and also to improve recovery of sick advances, one time settlement scheme for recovery of NPAs was introduced in RRBs, effective up to March 2002. As a result, there has been significant improvement in asset quality.

As on 31 March 2006:

Key performance indicators-

Number of RRBs - 133; number of branches - 14494

Number of districts covered - 525; Deposits - INR 71329 crores

Advances issued - INR 25427 crores

Number of RRBs in profit - 111

Investments - INR 41182

Owned funds - INR 6647

RRBs have been an important segment of the rural financial institutions in the country. They are at par with the scheduled commercial banks in respect of priority sector lending, investment schemes, credit discipline, and transparency. They have been actively associated with all the government programmes such as the 20-Point Programme, Integrated Rural Development Programme (IRDP), and other special programmes for Scheduled Tribes and other weaker sections. Despite their significant contribution in strengthening the rural economy of India, there were several problems that were noticed in the functioning of RRBs.

Problems Faced by RRBs

Difficulties in Deposit Mobilisation

The RRBs encountered a number of practical difficulties in deposit mobilisation. On account of their restructured lending policy which excludes richer sections of the village society, these potential depositors show least interest in depositing their money with these banks.

Mounting Loan Losses

Despite the impressive geographic coverage and intermediation activity, the RRBs suffered from poor financial health, especially because of mounting loan losses. While loan losses wiped on the equity and reserve of some banks, they were eating into the deposits of others. The overall loan quality of portfolio management, administration, and collection of dues remains a matter of grave concern. For instance, accumulated RRB losses on 31 March 2002 were reported at almost INR 2,694 crores.

Slow Progress in Lending Activity

The RRBs' pace of growth in loan business is slow. For this the following reasons may be given: (a) there maybe limited scope for direct lending by RRBs in their fields of operations. (b) it is always difficult to identify the potential small borrowers and the bank staff have been required to make special and sincere efforts in this regard (c) most of the small borrowers do not like the bank formalities and prefer to borrow from the informal/ indigenous sources of finance such as moneylenders (d) the anomalies in the Differential Interest Rates (DIR) scheme also posed a special problem to the RRBs. While the RRBs charge 14 per cent interest, the commercial banks charge only 4 per cent under the DIR scheme in rural areas. Thus, no borrower would go to RRBs or cooperative societies in the area when a loan from the commercial bank is available under DIR scheme (e) there is no effective link between the RRBs and PACS and the farmer's service societies (f) there is lack of coordination between officials of the District Credit Planning Committees and RRBs.

Mindset of Stakeholders

RRBs were set up in consequence to the recommendations of the Narasimham Committee in 1976, which stated that any losses incurred by RRBs would be a price worth paying, given the social benefits that would be attained. Most stakeholders deemed these losses incurred by the banks over the next two decades as normal and acceptable. There should be change in the mindset of the stakeholders. For proving better service to the clients, the RRBs must be in a position to make profits. This fact must be understood by the stakeholders, especially politicians and policy makers.

Haste and Lack of Coordination in Branch Expansion

Haste in branch expansion programme in many areas have resulted in lopsidedness due to lack of coordination. In several cases, it could not be ensured that the branches of the RRBs are opened at centres where no commercial or cooperative banking facilities were provided.

Unviable Business Policies

The rural banking policies as prescribed by RRB Act, made the business of RRBs very much unviable. For instance, the policy of maintaining high Statutory Liquidity Ratio (SLR) of 25 per cent reduced the availability of capital for business purposes. Also the yields on SLR were lower than the prevailing lending rates. This implicity taxed the RRBs. Further, norms for income recognition were not standardised and this made it difficult to accurately assess the financial performance of the banks. For example, the income in terms of interest on loans included both interest that was paid as well as interest that was due. When the duration of outstanding loan interest payments was not clear, most managers found it difficult to provide for non-performing assets. Other barriers to sustain profitability include the lack of norms to select the borrowers, define geographic markets, opening and closing branches, sanction and collecting of loans, contain administrative costs and selling interest rates. For example, without any collateral security, loans were sanctioned and disbursed to economically weaker sections of the rural population – households with land holdings less than 6.5 acres and incomes less than INR 10,000 – located in specific and restricted geographic areas.

Poor Governance

The boards of RRBs did not monitor their performance as they had no interest in the affairs of the banks. In a large number of cases, the appointments to board were made based on political consideration rather than banking expertise. Multiple ownership, control, little prospects for profits, and diluted accountability have weakened the vision of the RRBs.

Procedural Rigidities

The RRBs follow the procedures of the scheduled commercial banks in the matter of deposits and advancing loans which are highly complicated and time consuming from the villager's point of view. The rural borrowers always appreciate informal ways and simple procedures as have been followed by the moneylenders and the indigenous bankers.

Urban-Oriented Staff

A crucial practical difficulty experienced in their working by the RRBs is the urban orientation of their staff which is rarely inclined to serve in rural areas. There is no true local involvement of the bank staff in the villages where they serve.

Consumption Credit Ignored

RRBs were permitted to lend only predetermined amounts for specified lending terms. Loans were disbursed for production purposes only and consumption credit, namely marriage loans and so on. It was seldom considered for sanction.

No Freedom to make Commercial Improvements

Given the nature of policies and practices of RRBs, the owner's representatives on the board of directors, and the sponsor bank as well as the RRB managers had virtually no authority to make any strategic decision regarding the RRBs. As there was no freedom to make any commercial improvements to the system, most stakeholders, especially the sponsor banks, become apathetic towards the problems of RRBs.

Despite these problems, the RRBs have been trying their level best to achieve their social objectives. They are in fact development banks of the rural poor. They have been trying to fill regional and financial gaps in rural finance in our country. They have succeeded in projecting their image of a small man's bank.

Suggestions for Improvement

The RRBs have been under severe financial strain on account of higher transaction costs involved in handling a large number of small-sized loan accounts and lower income on account of concessional rates of interest on small sized loans. The need for securing a strong agricultural base necessitates that there should be an adequate flow of rural credit. This means massive expansion and diversification of rural credit delivery system which is an important segment of RRBs. A number of policy initiatives have been taken to improve the viability of RRBs.

Professor Charan Wadhva, Kamath Group and several other experts on rural credit made some suggestions for the improvement in the working of RRBs.

(a) A uniform interest rate structure should be devised for the rural financial agencies. The activities of the RRBs, primary agricultural societies and commercial banks regarding rural credit must be complimentary and not competitive. There should not be duplication and overlapping of services which would unnecessarily enhance the overall operational costs.

(b) The RRBs should function primarily as rural banks of the rural poor but they may also be permitted to lend up to 25 per cent of their total advances to the richer sections of the village society, so as to involve grater participation and seek greater cooperation from the village people including the richer sections, regarding deposit mobilisation. Participation of the local people in the equity share capital of the RRBs should be allowed and encouraged.

(c) Local staff may be appointed, as far as possible in the RRBs, and banking in rural areas should be further expanded by the RRBs, rather than by the commercial banks. The RRBs should be the core of banking operations in a district and it should help in promoting the all-round development of the rural areas in its own district.

(d) The RRBs must strengthen effective credit administration by way of credit appraisal, monitoring the progress of loans and their efficient recovery. The RRBs may also provide marketing guidance and consultancy services to the villages. They may relax procedures for lending and make them easy so that villagers can approach RRBs with confidence and borrow the amounts without inhibition for their timely needs. The RRBs should be permitted to provide full range of banking services, such as remittances and other utility/agency services which would help a lot in developing banking habits among the villagers.

(e) The reforms of RRBs should pay more attention to the institutional dimensions of the problems facing the banks. Adequate incentives must be given to the different stakeholders such as political leaders, policy makers, stockholders, bank staff and clients.

(f) The sections of beneficiaries should be decided by the concerned bank officials rather the local government officials. This ensures better recoveries.

(g) There is an urgent need for radical changes in the way RRBs conduct business. They should make use of technology and introduce new schemes which would facilitate long-term relationship with the customers.

(h) The need of the hour is to focus their attention on the attainment of sustainable viability, improved customer services, new and innovative loan products, and diversified business portfolio.

(i) The RRBs may initiate certain new insurable policies like deposit linked cattle and other animals insurance policy, crop insurance policy, or life insurance policy for the rural depositors.

(j) The image of RRBs should be improved. They should not be identified as second class banks or an extension of the urban-oriented commercial banks. They must develop their own identity.
(k) The RRBs should be linked with PACS and Farmer's Service Societies (FSS). They should also be linked with the sponsoring commercial banks and the RBI.
(l) Coordination between district-level development planning and district-level credit planning is also required in order to chart out the specific role of the RRBs as a development agency of the rural areas.
(m) The RRBs should be encouraged to form their separate associations at state and national levels. These associations may coordinate training and research activities of the member banks and publish newsletters and journals, etc.

Dantawala Committee Report on Regional Rural Banks (RRBs)

In June 1977, the RBI appointed a committee to review the working of RRBs. It was headed by Professor M L Dantawala. The following terms of reference were assigned to the committee.

(a) To spell out the precise role of the RRBs in the rural credit structure.
(b) To evaluate the performance of the RRBs in view of the objectives set out for them.
(c) To make recommendations on the scope, methods, and procedures of functioning of the RRBs and other related matters.

The committee submitted its report to the RBI in February 1978. The committee conducted a detailed study of the working of twelve selected RRBs of different states.

The Dantawala Committee observed that the performance of the selected RRBs was good in general in fulfilling the objectives set out for them. The following are the major findings and recommendations of the Dantawala Committee.

(a) The jurisdiction of a RRB should be confined to one district.
(b) Forms and procedures of the RRBs should be simplified further.
(c) The RRBs should adequately recruit technical staff.
(d) Sponsoring banks should provide training to the staff of the RRBs.
(e) The committee recommended the following scheme of composing the share capital of the RRBs. Sponsor bank – 40 per cent, RBI – 25 per cent, state government – 15 per cent, local participants – 20 per cent.
(f) The RRBs should function at the intermediate level. It should progressively fill the "credit gap" in the rural sector.

(g) The committee, however, did not favour the proposal of connecting selected PACS into rural banks. It suggested of providing rural credit in a more efficient manner.

(h) The RRBs with some modifications in their operations and functions can become a very useful component in the locality of the rural credit structure. The RRBs can make a substantial contribution to improve the quality and quantity of credit flows to the rural areas by becoming an integral part of the rural credit structure.

(i) The RBI should ensure uniformity in the interest rate policy at par with all rural financial agencies in the organised sector of the money market.

(j) The RRBs should be allowed to provide full banking facilities in the areas of their operation.

(k) The commercial banks should prefer to meet the credit requirements of the rural areas through the RRBs rather than through their own rural branches.

The James Raj Committee, 1978, on the funding of the public sector banks, also opines that the RRBs can play a significant role in the financing of the rural poor. The RRB should be the "core" of banking operations in a district and it should help in promoting the all round development of the rural areas in its own district. RRBs, along with cooperative and commercial banks constitute the multi-agency approach adopted in rural financing.

NABARD introduced several policy initiatives for improving the overall performance of the RRBs during the year 1998–1999. These are as follows:

(a) To hasten the process of turn around of RRBs and to further strengthen these, their sponsor banks have been advised to explore the possibility of the merger of RRBs coming under them and operating in adjoining areas.

(b) Kisan credit cards are being introduced in the RRBs to facilitate the provision of credit to farmers.

(c) RRBs have been encouraged to adopt self-help groups for channelling credit to the poor on a sustainable basis.

(d) The Government of India in consultation with NABARD has framed appointment and promotion rules (1998) for the staff of RRBs.

(e) In order to monitor the performance of RRBs especially the weak ones, sponsor banks have been advised to undertake quarterly/half-yearly reviews of the banks coming under their jurisdiction. NABARD, RBI, Government of India may selectively participate in the half-yearly review meeting.

(f) In order to evolve an early warning system as part of the supervisory function of the NABARD, an off-site surveillance system has been introduced to supplement on-site inspection, though NABARD had recommended adoption of "CAMELS" (Capital Adequacy, Asset Quality, Management, Earning Capacity, Liquidity, Systems and Controls) approach for a sharper focus of inspections. On-site examinations to be supplemented by additional instruments like system study, portfolio inspection, commissioning audit, and monitoring visits.

9
Exchange Banks

Exchange Banks are those banks which deal with foreign exchange and are specialised in financing foreign trade. These banks are also known as foreign banks and have their head offices located outside the country. Although the main business of these banks is financing of foreign trade, they also perform normal commercial banking functions, and thus compete with local commercial banks. Exchange banks/foreign banks have been doing business in India since 1870. They are multinationals, that is, having a widespread banking business in many countries of the world. Entry of foreign banks was banned in India in 1969 during nationalisation of banks. However, the ban was lifted in 1980. The Government of India with liberalisation and globalisation policies, extended a warm welcome to all foreign banks to set up their branches in India.

Meaning of Exchange Bank

Exchange banks are those banks which are of foreign origin with specialisation in foreign trade. According to a survey of RBI, 80 per cent of foreign trade was financed by exchange banks.

Functions of Exchange Banks

The functions of exchange banks are as follows:

Financing Foreign Trade

They primarily finance India's foreign trade. The functions are: (a) financing of imports and exports of India (b) financing of movement of goods from and to Indian ports/to or from the distributing or collecting centres in the interior parts of the country (c) they discount or purchase foreign bills.

Financing Inland Trade

They also finance trade in many up country centres, as they have opened a number of branches in the main ports and trading centres of the country.

Render Agency Services

Like other commercial banks, foreign exchange banks render several agency services to their customers.

Merchant Banking

Some exchange banks provide merchant banking services.

Banking Business

The exchange banks conduct all types of banking business. They accept deposits from the public, grant loans, discount trade bills, and provide remittance facilities competing with Indian Banks.

The Role of Exchange Banks in Financing Foreign Trade

Exports

In the case of exports, the Indian exporters draw up bill of exchange against credits opened by the foreign buyers with foreign banks. These bills are known as Documents Against Acceptance (D/A) bills. They are normally drawn for three months. These bills are sent by the exchange banks in India to foreign countries. After acceptance by the buyer or his bank, they are discounted in the foreign money market. Once the foreign buyer accepts the bills of exchange, he is given shipping documents and possessions of goods soon after their arrival. Thus, the foreign buyer of Indian goods is able to sell the goods and pay the amount on the bill at the time of maturity.

Imports

Imports to India are financed by means of Documents Against Payment (D/P), bills drawn on Indian imports. Exchange banks present these bills to the Indian importers. Once they are accepted by the importer, the exchange banks keep them with themselves and do not sell or discount as there is no market for these bills in India. The exchange banks deliver shipping documents to the Indian importers only after the full payment is made, or they may deliver these documents to the importers only on execution of a trust deed in favour of the exchange bank. The Indian importer will have to pay interest up to the period when the proceeds of the bill reach the exporter's place.

In this process, the exchange banks show undue favour to foreign exporters and importers by discriminating against their Indian counterparts. The documents accompanying the bills are handed over to the foreign importer when the bill is accepted by him so that he can obtain the possession of goods immediately. On the other hand, the documents are not handed over to the Indian importer except on payment.

Exchange banks enjoy monopoly in financing of foreign trade due to the following strong reasons.

(a) The former Imperial Bank of India was not authorised to transact foreign exchange business till the passing of the Imperial Bank of India Act, 1934.
(b) Commercial banks could not keep pace with exchange banks and as a result could not compete with them.

According to the Central Banking Enquiry Committee, the reasons for backwardness of the Indian banks in foreign exchange business were:

(a) Absence of Indian bank branches in foreign countries.
(b) The competition of big foreign banks having enormous goodwill and prestige with huge account of capital and resources.
(c) Lack of information and expertise regarding foreign exchange business.
(d) Higher returns which the Indian banks could get from employing their funds in internal finance. History reveals that some Indian banks such as Alliance Bank of Simla and Tata Industrial Bank took up some business proposals of financing foreign trade but very soon they failed. In recent years, however, the situation has changed because Indian Banks have started acquiring the necessary information and expertise to indulge in foreign trade and set up branches in foreign countries.

Defects in the Working of Exchange Banks

Despite going strong in the Indian markets for the past so many years, there are certain defects that plague the working of exchange Banks. These are:

(a) They were not subject to legal restrictions or statutory obligations.
(b) For many years in the past, Exchange banks did not maintain any adequate cash reserves.
(c) Their directors, governing bodies, and shareholders were foreigners.
(d) The exchange banks, due to their monopolistic position in the financing of foreign trade, had split the money market into European and Indian.
(e) They had entered into unfair competition with the Indian banks by attracting deposits in India by underquoting Indian banks.
(f) The exchange banks enjoyed, till recently, a substantial monopoly in financing foreign trade of the country. They exploited their monopoly power to their advantawge and earned high profits. They also forced the Indian importers and exporters to give business to the foreign

shipping companies and insurance companies for accommodating them. This has restricted the scope of growth of Indian enterprises in shipping and insurance business.

(g) They do not provide any guidance or information regarding foreign market, prices, etc., to the Indian exporters.

(h) By extending their business from financing of foreign trade to banking in the up country centres, they restrict the growth of Indian commercial banks.

(i) Till recently the exchange banks did not have any Indians on the higher posts. They were absorbed in the clerical posts.

(j) The managerial bodies of foreign banks do not have any close social contact with their customers. They rely mostly on the information supplied by the staff, brokers, etc. They give poor references about Indian firms and markets to enquiries abroad.

(k) The exchange banks follow different margin rates and interest rates based on the nationality of their clients. There was clear-cut discrimination in the treatment given to Indian firms and foreign firms.

Remedial Measures

In order to protect the Indian banks against unfair competition, the following remedial measures have been suggested by Central Banking Enquiry Committee.

(a) RBI should have a more effective control over exchange banks.

(b) The exchange banks should not be allowed to open branches in places other than the port towns so that they do not encroach upon the business of Indian banks in the home trade.

(c) The exchange banks should not be allowed to undertake trustee business in India.

(d) The exchange banks must register their share capital in Indian Rupees to enable Indians to acquire shares so as to increase their participation in these banks.

(e) An exclusive Indian "Foreign Exchange Bank" should be jointly set up by the Central Government and Indian joint-stock banks to transact the foreign trade business.

(f) The exchange banks should not have any direct or indirect controlling interest in any Indian bank. For this purpose, Indian joint-stock banks should maintain separate registers of their Indian and non-Indian shareholders and even transfer of shares between them should be carefully scrutinised.

(g) The exchange banks should not be allowed to form any business combinations, mergers, pools, trusts, rings, cartels, etc., without the permission of the RBI.

(h) While granting licenses to these banks, the RBI should put restrictions on the size of the deposits raised by them.

(i) In order to restrict the flight of capital abroad, the exchange banks should not be allowed to transfer their profits/capital to their head office abroad.

(j) Each branch of every exchange bank should appoint a local advisory board which will advise the bank regarding the grant of advances and cash credit. The board is supposed to maintain sympathetic contacts with their Indian clients. This will help in resolving the difficulties presently experienced by Indian customers.

With the enactment of Banking Companies Act, 1949 and the exercise of effective control through this act by the RBI, many defects in the functioning of foreign exchange banks have been eliminated. As now, without the approval of RBI, no exchange bank can open a branch in India, the interests of Indian banks have been adequately protected.

Section 22 of the Banking Regulation Act, 1949 laid down the provisions for granting licenses to the banks by RBI, which was also recommended by the Indian Central Banking Enquiry Committee. The main provisions of Section 22 are:

(a) No company shall carry on banking business in India unless it acquired license from the RBI, and a license maybe issued by the RBI only when it is satisfied with the compliance of the certain conditions.

(b) Every banking company shall apply in writing to the RBI for a license.

(c) Before granting license, the RBI may inspect the books of the banking company and be satisfied with the books and with certain other conditions.

Every exchange bank has to deposit with the RBI an amount not less than the minimum required by way of paid-up capital and reserves. The deposit may be in the form of either cash or unencumbered securities approved by the RBI or partly in cash and partly in such securities. As per the amendment of the Act, in 1962, the banking companies incorporated outside India (exchange banks) should deposit with RBI an amount of 20 per cent of the profit as per their profit and loss account every year in respect of all business transacted through the branches in India. The government of the country where the exchange bank is incorporated should assure the Government of India at the time of incorporation that its laws are not discriminatory against Indian banks. In case of failure of an exchange bank, the Indian depositors and creditors of that bank shall hold the first charge on the amount deposited with the RBI. This will protect the Indian depositors and creditor's interests. The Government of India introduced some social control measures in 1968 over foreign exchange banks like constitution of advisory boards for these banks, confirmation of account of exchange banks by registered Indian auditors.

The demand to nationalise the foreign exchange banks along with private banks in 1969 was refused by the government in view of the legal restrictions and international repercussions in the process.

The Central Banking Enquiry Committee and many other experts have suggested that well-established Indian joint-stock banks should actively participate in financing India's foreign trade by enlarging their foreign connections rather than establishing branches at foreign centres. In the pre-independence era, some Indian banks had started doing foreign exchange business with remarkable success. Indian banks have the capacity to do this business very well. In fact, their volume of deposits is far greater than that of exchange banks. Indian banks have their own branches in all important centres of the world. Indian banks can play a significant role by participating increasingly in financing the country's foreign trade. Major public sector banks including the SBI have the foreign exchange departments through which they can function in financing India's foreign trade (export and import) to a certain extent.

Exchange banks were permitted to carry on their business through a branch or representative office or agency arrangement with the Indian company/firm or individual. Capital funds equivalent to eight per cent of the risk weighted assets were required to be retained in India with effect from 1 April 1993. New foreign banks for conducting the business in India are considered only if they are financially sound and hold good domestic and international ratings. The important aspect is that the economic and political relations between the two countries should be sound and harmonious. The bank should be under consolidated supervision of the home country regulator, that is, in case of India, RBI.

The minimum capital requirement for a foreign bank should be US $25 million spread over three branches, namely US $10 million for the first branch, additional US $10 million for the second branch, and further US $5 million for the third branch. Additional branches are permitted after monitoring performance of the existing branches of the banks, their financial results, inspection findings, and so on. The number of licenses is fixed in conformity with India's commitment to world trade organisation, which is currently twelve licenses (both for new and expansion by existing banks) per year, excluding off-site ATMs, which also require licenses.

As on 30 September 2002, there were forty foreign banks operating in India with 203 branches. Four banks have 10 or more branches, 18 banks are operating with one branch each. The branches of foreign banks have also set up representative offices in India. As on 30 June 2002, 23 banks from twelve countries had representative offices in India, of which nineteen are in Mumbai, three in New Delhi and one in Chennai. Total 63 banks have presence in India, either through bank branches or representative offices.

Under the Foreign Exchange Regulation Act of 1973, apart from foreign banks, a number of specified public sector banks, including the SBI, have been authorised to deal in foreign exchanges and foreign currencies in India. These Indian banks have foreign departments at head offices and selected branches to conduct foreign exchange business. The foreign department of a bank may consist of export sectors, import sectors, foreign remittance sectors, and exchange sections. The export section has the following functions:

(a) advising and conformity of letters of credit.
(b) negotiating and collection of foreign bills.

The import section does the job of opening of letters of credit and arranging for the payment for imports against the letters of credit on behalf of its clients, collecting inward bills and executing deferred payment guarantees covering the import of capital goods by its importer clients.

The foreign remittance section provides the services of issuing traveller's cheques and drafts, encashment of foreign currency drafts and traveller's cheques.

The exchange section looks after the maintenance of accounts, exchange position and control, forward dealings, buying and selling of foreign currencies, operating in foreign exchange markets, and reconciliation of bank's foreign accounts.

Thus, the Indian banks are today well organised and well equipped to deal in the business of financing foreign trade of the country.

India's foreign trade as on 2002–2003 – Imports – INR 25,5737 crores: Exports – INR 29,7206 crores.

Export–Import Bank of India (Exim Bank)

The Export–Import Bank of India (Exim Bank) was set up on 1 January 1982, to take over the operations of international finance wing of IDBI. It provides financial assistance to exporters and importers and functions as the principal financial institution for coordinating the work of other institutions engaged in financing of exports and imports of goods and services. The Exim Bank provides refinance facilities to the commercial banks and other financial institutions against their export–import financing activities. The establishment of the Exim Bank meant a great relief to all Indian businessmen who were depending mostly on foreign exchange requirements.

Functions of Exim Bank

The Exim Bank performs several functions. These are:

(a) It provides direct financial assistance to Indian exporters.
(b) Financing of joint ventures in foreign countries.
(c) The bank provides to the authorised dealers in foreign exchange, 100 per cent of refinance of deferred payment loans for export of eligible Indian goods.
(d) Undertaking merchant banking functions.
(e) Financing of exports and imports of goods and services of not only of India but also of third-world countries.
(f) Financing of export and import of machinery and equipment on lease basis.
(g) Providing technical, administrative, and financial assistance in connection with export or import.
(h) The bank provides to the commercial banks authorisation to deal in foreign exchange, a facility to rediscount the short-term export bills for unexpired usance period not exceeding 90 days.
(i) Term loans/deferred payment guarantees are provided for project, cost financing of units, registered 100 per cent export oriented units, and units in free trade zones.
(j) Pre-shipment credit is extended to companies executing export contracts involving a period exceeding six months.

The Exim Bank is operating nine lending programmes under different categories.

Fund Assistance

(a) As loans to Indian Companies:
- direct finance to exporters
- technology and consultancy service
- pre-shipment credit in case of export contract for capital goods
- overseas investment financing for equity participation by an Indian company in joint venture abroad.

(b) Loans to foreign governments, companies, and financial institutions:
- overseas buyers credit scheme
- line of credit to foreign governments
- re-lending facility to banks overseas.

(c) Loans to commercial banks in India:
- export bills rediscounting scheme
- refinance of export credit.

Non-Fund Assistance

Non-Fund assistance is given by way of guarantee of various types.

Assistance for Export Bids

The Exim Bank provides funded and non-funded assistance for export bid and ongoing projects.

Finance for Deemed Exports

Deemed exports occur in case of specified transactions within India which result in foreign exchange earnings or foreign exchange savings. Exim Bank provides deferred credit at an internationally competitive rate for eligible deemed export through suppliers or directly to buyers. The bank also extends term finance for export-oriented units set up in free trade zones and units recognised by government as hundred per cent export-oriented units.

Capital and Resources

The authorised capital of the bank is INR 200 crores and the paid-up capital is INR 100 crores wholly subscribed by the Government of India. The bank can raise resources from:

(a) Borrowings from the Government of India.
(b) Borrowings from Reserve Bank of India.
(c) Issue of bonds and debentures.
(d) Borrowing foreign currency from other countries.

With effect from 1 July 1993, the target of priority sector lending was raised from 15 per cent to 32 per cent of their net bank credit to align the priority sector lending of exchange banks with that of Indian banks. The priority sector lending definition for exchange banks has been enlarged to include export credit. Under this overall target for priority sector lending, advances by foreign banks to the small-scale industries sector and export credit should each be not less than 10 per cent of net bank credit. Any shortfall in achieving the sub-target in respect of advances to the SSI sector would have to be made good by depositing with the Small Industries Development Bank (SIDBI), the amount equivalent to the shortfall. Such stipulation has shown good results.

With the target of 32 per cent priority sector lending for foreign banks, there is semblance of fair competition between Indian banks and foreign banks.

Exim Bank offers advisory services too.

(a) Advise on exchange control practises in other countries.
(b) Guiding Indian companies on contracts abroad.
(c) Exposing Indian exporting companies to Euro-financing.
(d) Advise and assign financial packages for export oriented industries in India.

Foreign Exchange and Exchange Control

Money is a medium of exchange for all transactions that take place inside and outside the country. In India, we have the Rupee currency for financing the internal trade and other obligations. But, no country is self-reliant in all fields and so it has to engage in multiple trade with other countries. The home currency has to be converted into currencies of other countries to meet the obligations that arise out of import of goods and services from other countries.

The Foreign Exchange Reserves were US $291,819 as on 26 September 2008.

Definition

According to Dr Paul Einzing, "Foreign Exchange is the system or process of converting one national currency into another, and of transferring money from one country to another". The Foreign Exchange Act, 1973, viewed in a broader sense includes:

(a) The rate at which such an exchange takes place.
(b) The method by which the exchange takes place between two countries.
(c) The method and means by which one country's currency is converted into another country's currency.

Foreign Exchange Market

Foreign exchange transactions arise mainly from trade transactions among residents of different countries. The foreign exchange market is the clearing house through which the purchase and sale of foreign exchange are offset against each other. The main link between the buyers and sellers of foreign exchange in the foreign exchange market is the bank.

Functions of Foreign Exchange Market

The functions of Foreign Exchange Market are:

(a) To provide adequate credit facilities which is very essential for the promotion of the foreign trade. The banks which play a dominant role in this market provide pre-shipment and post-shipment credit facilities. Documentary bills are also routed through banks.

(b) To make necessary arrangements to transfer purchasing power from one country to another. This is the most important function. Otherwise there would be no foreign trade or transfer of capital from one country to another.

(c) To cover the exchange risks, the market provides hedging facilities. It gives a chance for the exporters and importers to enter into future transactions in the forward market so as to guard against losses, which may occur due to fluctuations in exchange rates.

Methods of International Payments

Payments by one country to another country may be made in the following ways.

Telegraphic Transfer

Telegraphic transfer (TT) is a method of transferring money by telegram, telex, or fax issued by a bank from one centre to another in a foreign centre, it is the quickest method of transmitting funds. Transfers of large amounts of money between banks are generally done by TT.

Mail Transfer

A mail transfer (MT) is an order in writing sent by mail to pay cash to a third party. On receipt of an MT order, the receiving bank issues to the beneficiary its own cheque or makes payments to the beneficiary's account with itself or with another bank. An MT is similar to a cheque, but it is neither transferable nor negotiable. The purchaser of an MT pays cash in domestic currency immediately on its purchase. But the beneficiary receives the payment only after the arrival of the MT at the foreign centre.

Bills of Exchange

A bill of exchange is an unconditional order in writing addressed by one person to another, requiring the person to whom it is addressed to pay a certain sum on demand or within a determinable date.

Drafts and Cheques

A draft is a pay order issued by a bank on its own branch or some other bank abroad. It is payable on site. The purchaser of a draft pays to the issuing bank money in local currency. The funds in the foreign centres are available to him only after the presentation of the draft to the paying bank.

The rate of exchange is the price of one currency in terms of another currency. It may be defined as the number of units of one currency that will be exchanged for one unit or a given number of units of another currency. The external purchasing power of a currency is called its exchange rate. The rate of exchange is nothing but the price fixed for one currency in terms of another. The rate of exchange is not a constant factor and it depends upon the market conditions.

Kinds of Exchange Rates

The different kinds of exchange rates are as follows:

Spot Rate

The term spot exchange rate refers to the rate being quoted for international transactions which require the immediate delivery of currencies. However, in actual practice, the settlement takes place within two days in the spot market.

Fixed Rate

If the rate of exchange of a currency is fixed permanently in terms of gold or another currency, it is called a fixed rate.

Forward Rate

If the rate quoted requires the delivery of currencies at a future date as per the agreement, it is a case of forward rate. It takes place in a future market and it facilitates the exporters and importers to cover the risks arising out of exchange rate fluctuations. Again, this rate may be quoted at par with the spot rate or at a premium or discount over the spot rate.

Floating Rate

A floating rate is one which is fixed on the basis of demand and supply of currencies in the foreign exchange market. This rate is not a constant one and it fluctuates from time to time according to market conditions and therefore it is called a floating rate.

Flexible Rate

Under this system, the rate is *not fixed* permanently. A specified rate is fixed for a short period and, thereafter, it is subject to revision from time to time depending upon the need of the country.

Multiple Rate

Under the multiple exchange rate system, a country adopts different rates for different countries or different rates for exports and imports. One of the forms of multiple exchange rate is the two-tier exchange rate system under which different rates are charged for different kinds of transactions and a lower rate is charged for capital transfers. Each country adopts a rate of exchange according to its need.

RBI and the Foreign Exchange Control

The Foreign Exchange Regulation Act, 1973 (FERA) empowers the central government and the RBI to control and regulate all dealings involving foreign exchange transactions. Maintenance of the external value of rupee is an essential function of the RBI and the RBI achieves this objective only through exchange control mechanism.

In India, the exchange control regulations are clearly laid down in the FERA of 1947. This act was consolidated, amended, and replaced by the FERA of 1973 which came into force on 1 January 1974. Many provisions of this Act are in the nature of giving wide powers to the Central Government and the RBI so as to administer the exchange control mechanism properly. The policy of the government is to relax the act to a considerable extent with a view to encouraging foreign investments in India and promoting exports. The provisions of the act are:

(a) The RBI is authorised to issue license to those who are involved in buying and selling foreign exchange and all other transactions involving foreign exchange like import and export of gold, silver, currency rates, etc.
(b) RBI has appointed a number of authorised dealers who are alone permitted to carry out all transactions involving foreign exchange.
(c) The RBI issues directions, from time to time, to the authorised dealers, relating to imports and exports, foreign travel remittances, capital transfers, transfer of investment incomes and invisible items. The public are required to conduct their exchange transactions only through these authorised dealers.
(d) RBI fixes the exchange value of the home currency "rupee" in terms of other currencies. The rate fixed is known as official rate of exchange and all the authorised dealers and money changers are required to follow this rate strictly in all their foreign exchange transactions. The RBI announces its buying and selling rates from time to time and this must be strictly followed. As per the foreign exchange regulation (amendment) ordinance 1993, the RBI is permitted to express its exchange rate in terms of rupees per US dollar instead of US dollars per INR 100. Exchange rates are quoted in terms of rupees per unit of foreign currency.

(e) The FERA gives power to the RBI to regulate foreign travel. Foreign travel comes under invisible items. Residents of India are eligible to get release of foreign exchange up to a specified limit for undertaking travel abroad from the RBI against proper applications. However, permission is granted for foreign travel without any request for the release of foreign exchange in certain cases like going abroad as guests, as students on scholarships granted by foreign governments, etc. Proceeds obtained from foreign travel by non-residents must be surrendered to the RBI. The foreign currencies brought in must be declared at the entry point and they must be sold only to authorised dealers in foreign exchange.

(f) The RBI regulates imports into the country. Imports are permitted only against proper licenses and the necessary foreign exchange is released by the RBI. A few specified raw materials required by certain industries are allowed to be imported freely under Open General License (OGL). The items to be included for the purpose of OGL are being announced from time to time. All payments for imports have to be made only through authorised dealers. In the case of bilateral trade agreements, payments are to be made only in Indian rupees. In other cases, it can be made in the currency of the country of origin of the goods or in sterling. Similarly, RBI regulates the export trade also. The foreign exchange obtained from exports must be remitted to India and surrendered to the RBI. The export earnings must be disposed off in the manner prescribed by the RBI, and all the shipping documents connected with the export trade must be routed through the authorised dealers only. The RBI exercises control over export trade in collaboration with the customs authorities and the authorised dealers. Export of gold, jewellery, etc., are permitted only with special permission from the RBI.

(g) Non-residents can make investments in India only after obtaining the necessary permission from the Central Government or the RBI. The investments by non-residents are governed by the industrial policies of the Government of India being announced from time to time. In recent times such investments are more liberally allowed in order to give them wider investment opportunities. Money restrictions on the ceilings of investments have been relaxed considerably. The FERA has been relaxed considerably with a view to encouraging exports and foreign investments.

(h) The limits fixed for bringing gold or assets made of gold have been relaxed considerably in recent times. The RBI has been given wide powers to give general or special permission for the import and export of gold or silver or foreign currency notes. All imports must be declared in the relevant forms prescribed by the authorities.

(i) Authorised dealers can open non-resident accounts without prior permission from the RBI. This account can be opened by remittance from abroad in an approved manner. Accounts opened and maintained with authorised dealers in the names of persons resident outside India are called Non-Resident (External) Accounts (NRE Accounts). Many benefits like exemption from income tax, gift tax, wealth tax, etc. are available under NRE accounts. The operation of these accounts is subject to the rules framed by the RBI from time to time.

(j) All foreign exchange transactions made by authorised dealers must be reported to the RBI in prescribed returns and must be submitted once in two months. It enables the RBI to have a close watch on the foreign exchange dealings in India.

New Provisions of FERA

The main objective behind the new provisions of FERA is to remove many restrictions and to create a more liberalised environment for foreign investment.

The changes are:

(a) RBI's general permission is necessary to hold immovable property abroad.
(b) Joint ventures abroad are permitted freely without any restrictions.
(c) Resident Indians can possess foreign currencies up to US $500.
(d) A 51 per cent foreign equity has been permitted in a more range of industries.
(e) Foreign investment in real estates have been considerably liberated.
(f) Trading in gold and silver coins alone come under the purview of the Act.
(g) Exporters are permitted to take out goods as rental, lease or hire, or any other basis without any intention of disposing them.
(h) FERA companies are permitted to borrow or raise deposits or to take over any business by way of transfer from a resident in India without any restriction.

Foreign Exchange Management Act, 1999 (FEMA)

Introduction

The RBI, and the Central Government framed various rules, regulations, and issued directions and orders under FEMA for the actual implementation of the check on foreign exchange transactions.

The main objective of Foreign Exchange Regulation Act, 1973 (FERA) was to consolidate and amend the law, regulate certain payments, dealings in foreign exchange and securities, transactions, indirectly affecting foreign exchange, the import and export of currency, for the conservation of the foreign exchange resources of the country, and finally proper utilisation of this foreign exchange so as to promote economic development of the country. The FERA has been repealed.

The objective of enacting Foreign Exchange Management Act, 1999 (FEMA) is to consolidate and amend the law relating to foreign exchange with the objective of facilitating external trade and payments and for promoting the orderly development and maintenance of foreign exchange market in India. The provisions of FEMA extend to all over India and also apply to all branches, offices and agencies outside India owned or controlled by a person resident in India and also to any contravention committed outside India by any such person to whom this Act applies.

Meanings of Certain Important Terms Used in FEMA

(a) "Authorised Person" means any bank or other person including authorised money changer or dealer, authorised under FEMA to deal in foreign exchange or securities.

(b) "Capital Account Transaction" means a transaction by which there may be a change (either an increase or decrease) in the assets or liabilities outside India of persons resident in India, or in assets or liabilities in India of persons resident outside India.

(c) "Current Account Transaction" means a transaction other than Capital Account Transactions.

- payments due like interest on loans and as income from investments
- payments due with respect to foreign trade done in businesses, services, and short-term banking and credit facilities in the ordinary course of business
- remittances for living expenses of parent, spouses, and children residing abroad and
- expenses in connection with foreign travel, education, and medical care of parents, spouse, and children.

(d) Currency: currency is defined under the FEMA not only to include all currency notes but also postal notes, postal orders, moneyorders, cheques, drafts, traveller cheques, letters of credit, bills of exchange and promissory notes, credit cards, or such other similar instruments as may be notified by the RBI.

(e) Foreign currency is defined to mean any currency other than Indian currency.

(f) The term "foreign exchange" is much wider than the foreign currency. In addition to foreign currency, it includes the following:
- amounts payable in any foreign currency
- drafts, traveller cheque, letters of credit, or bills of exchange, express orders in Indian currency but payable in any Foreign currency
- drafts, traveller cheques, letters of credit, or bills of exchange drawn by banks, institutions or persons outside India, but payable in Indian currency.

Under the FEMA "security" is defined to include shares, stocks, bonds and debentures, government securities, savings certificates, deposit receipts and units of any mutual fund, etc. However, it does not include bills of exchange or promissory notes other than government promissory notes or any other instrument which may be notified by the RBI.

Under the FEMA, the term "foreign security" means any security as stated above.

Under the FEMA, a person is defined to include the following entities:
- an individual
- a Hindu undivided family
- a company
- a firm
- an association of persons or a body of individuals, whether incorporated or not
- every artificial juridical person and
- any agency, office or branch owned or controlled by such person.

"Person resident in India" means the following:

(a) A person residing in India for more than 182 days in the preceding financial year but does not include:
   (i) a person who has gone out of India or who stays outside India
   - for taking up employment outside of India or
   - for carrying on a business or vocation outside India, or
   - for any other purpose, in such circumstances as would indicate his intention to stay outside India for an uncertain period.

   (ii) a person who has come to India or stays in India, otherwise than,
   - for taking up employment in India or
   - for carrying on a business or vocation in India
   - for any other purpose, in such circumstances as would indicate his intention to stay in India for an uncertain period.

   (iii) any person or body corporate registered or incorporated in India

(iv) any office, branch, or agency in India owned or controlled by a person resident outside India
(v) any office, branch, or agency outside India owned or controlled by a person resident in India.

Accordingly, a "person resident outside India" means a person who is not a resident in India as above. "Repatriate to India" means bringing into India foreign exchange and selling it to authorised persons in India in exchange for Indian rupees.

Regulation and Management of Foreign Exchange

Any person who wants to carry out the following activities has to do so in accordance with the provisions of FEMA. At times, if FEMA prescribes approval of the RBI, it has to be obtained.

(a) Deal/transfer any foreign exchange or foreign security to any person other than an authorised person.
(b) Make any payment to any person resident outside India.
(c) Receive (other wise through an authorised person) any payment on behalf of any person resident outside India.
(d) Enter into any financial transaction in India in relation to a right to acquire any asset outside India by any person.

A person resident of India can hold, transfer or invest in foreign currency, foreign security or any immovable property situated outside India if it was acquired, held around by such person when he was resident outside India.

There is no bar on a person resident outside India to hold, own, transfer, or invest in foreign currency, foreign security, or any immovable property situated outside India.

Every exporter of goods and services has to furnish the necessary data by way of declarations to the RBI. Such export proceeds cannot be held in the foreign countries and has to be repatriated to India. Non-repatriation is a violation of the provisions of FEMA.

Powers of RBI with Respect to Authorised Persons

The powers of the RBI with respect to authorised persons are:

(a) The RBI appoints authorised persons to deal in foreign exchange. The person appointed shall work under the directions of RBI and shall have to comply with the rules and regulations framed or formulated by the RBI from time to time for this purpose.
(b) The RBI has the power to inspect the authorised persons so appointed to ensure that the said person complies with all the rules and regulations formulated by the RBI from time to time.

Contravention, Penalties, Adjudication and Appeals

Under the FEMA any violation of the provisions of the said Act will attract penal provisions resulting in arrest and detention. Penalty can be levied to thrice the sum involved in such contravention where such amount is quantifiable, or up to INR 2 lakhs, where the amount is not quantifiable, and where such contravention is a continuing one, further penalty which may extend to INR 5,000 for everyday after the first day during which the contravention continues.

Directorate of Enforcements

The Central Government established a directorate of enforcement with a director and other officers, called officers of enforcement.

Power of Search, Seizure, etc.

The Director of enforcement and other officers of enforcement not below the rank of an assistant director can investigate contraventions. The Central Government can also authorise any class of officers in the Central Government, state government or the RBI to investigate contraventions.

Empowering Other Officers

The Central Government can, subject to conditions and limitations, authorise any customs officer/central excise officer/any police officer/any other officer of the central government or state government to exercise the powers and discharge the duties of the Director of Enforcement or any other officer of Enforcement.

Like any other statutes there exists the right of appeal. The first of such appeals shall be with the Special Director (Appeals). Thereafter, if someone is aggrieved by the said appellate order they can prefer to appeal against the order before the appellate tribunals established for this purpose. Wherein questioning of law are involved and need to be interpreted, an appeal lies to the high court. Only questions of law are referred to the high court, and there after to the supreme court.

Appellate tribunal is a special judicial body established for dealing specific transactions for which it was established. Before appealing to the High Court, all the reference cases will be dealt with appellate authority, that is, tribunal. Tribunal judgement is generally followed. The aggrieved party can appeal to the High Court against the judgement of the tribunal. It is a statutory body under judicial supervision.

International Monetary Fund (IMF)

The origin of International Monetary Fund (IMF) can be traced back to the United Nations Monetary and Financial Conference held at Bretton Woods,

New Hampshire, USA, in 1944. This conference discussed the major international economic problems and the reconstruction of world economies shattered by the world war. The outcome of this conference is the establishment of the two popular international institutions namely:

(a) The International Monetary Fund to provide short-term capital to member countries to tide over their temporary balance of payments deficit, and
(b) The International Bank for Reconstruction and Development (IBRD or World bank) to provide long-term capital for the purpose of reconstruction and development of economies savaged by war.

The IMF came into existence in 1945 and it started its operations in March 1947.

Objectives

The objectives of the IMF are:

(a) To promote international monetary cooperation through a permanent institution which provides the machinery for consultation and collaboration on international monetary problems.
(b) To promote exchange stability, to maintain orderly exchange arrangements among member countries and to avoid competitive exchange depreciation.
(c) To facilitate the expansion and balanced growth of international trade and to contribute thereby to the promotion and maintenance of high levels of employment and real income of member countries.
(d) To give confidence to the members by helping the members with funds to correct their balance of payments deficits.
(e) To provide for multilateral convertibility of currencies and to remove all foreign exchange restrictions which hamper the growth of world trade.

To achieve the above objectives, the fund has laid down the following stipulations:

(a) The fund requests every member country to fix the par value of its currency. This par value cannot be changed except for the purposes of correcting a fundamental disequilibrium and that too up to 10 per cent only after notifying the fund.
(b) A member country can convert its own currency into foreign currencies up to 125 per cent of its gold quota subject to the condition that it should not exceed 25 per cent of its quota during any one year or till the purchasing country's currency with the fund becomes equal to 200 per cent of its quota.

The Structure and Management of IMF

The highest authority of the IMF is the Board of Governors consisting of one governor and an alternate governor for each member country. Generally, the finance minister or the governor of the central bank (RBI in the case of India) of the member country represents the country concerned in the Board of Governors. The Board of Governors has delegated most of its powers to the Board of Executive Directors which consists of six directors appointed by the largest quota-held member countries (USA, UK, Germany, France, Japan and Saudi Arabia) and the remaining sixteen are elected by the other member countries. The chairman of the executive board is the managing director of the fund and he is also the chief of the staff of the fund. His term of office is five years. The staff is organised into five departments area wise viz., for Africa, Asia, Europe, the Middle East, and Western Hemisphere.

The resources of the fund is gathered through two sources:

- subscriptions quota
- borrowings.

Every member country of the IMF has been assigned a subscription quota. This quota has been fixed on the basis of each member country's national income and its position in the global trade. These quotas are used to determine the voting rights of members, their subscription to the funds resources, and then eligibility to get finance from the fund. These quotas were expressed in terms of US dollars and from 1970 onwards quotas have been expressed in Special Drawings Rights (SDRs). Quotas of member countries are subject to periodical revision then and there depending upon the growth of the world economy and the need for additional international liquidity.

IMF is authorised to borrow in any currency and from any source. The IMF has entered into a General Agreement to Borrow (GAB) with 11 industrial countries to borrow in times of international liquidity crisis. IMF can supplement its resources through borrowings.

Functions of IMF

The functions of the IMF are:

(a) IMF has to act as a guardian of the code of economic behaviour set up by its articles, to maintain a stable system of exchange rates. It should get the cooperation of member countries.

(b) IMF lends from its financial resources to member countries who are suffering from balance of payments deficits, so that they may carry out programmes to tide over the crises without resorting to restrictive measures. This financial help is on temporary basis. Members have to repay within a stipulated period and thus resources are replenished.

(c) The fund also helps members to coordinate their national economic policies with that of the rest of the world so as to ensure a stable world financial system and sustainable economic growth.

(d) The fund advises its members and assists them in deriving appropriate corrective steps in time so that their balance of payments problems may not become a serious one. Each member country has to supply a wide range of easier and financial information to the fund and advises the member keeping in view the international liquidity positions.

Generally, member countries face many problems in fulfilling its commitments to the fund and hence the IMF has designed and introduced many schemes to help them solve their problems. The schemes are:

- Temporary facilities
- Supplementary financing facilities
- Permanent facilities like buffer stocks facilities and compensability financing
- Extended fund facilities
- Enlarged access facilities
- Standby arrangements
- Systematic transformation facility (STF)
- Tranche policies – credit tranche and reserve tranche.

The above facilities should enable the members to solve their temporary and structural disequilibrium in their balance of payments position.

IMF and India

The fund has been actively assisting developing countries like India in having a healthy balance of payments position and in maintaining monetary stability both at national and international level. At present, even developed countries look at the fund for financing their economic development, since they also do not have adequate foreign exchange reserves. The fund has been helping India in a very positive way extending finance whenever our country faces exchange crisis. India, being one of the founder members, has been one among the five largest subscribers till recently. The present subscription is SDINR 2200 millions of which SDINR 550 million consists of gold and silver.

India has been approaching the fund whenever it faces temporary exchange crisis and the fund has been responding to India's request with a positive gesture. The borrowings of India from the fund has been as follows:

In the year 1948–1949	US $100 million
In the year 1957	US $200 million
In the year 1961	US $250 million
In the year 1980–1981	SDR 5000 million
In the year 1991	$5 billion.

When India's balance of payments position became very critical in 1980–1981 and again in 1990–1991, the fund extended adequate credit under the extended fund facility scheme. SDR 5000 million sanctioned in 1980–81 was the single largest loan made by the fund to any member country. In January 1984, India on its own informed the IMF that the last tranche of SDR 1.1 billion was not needed. It clearly shows that the fund's programmes have been able to secure sustained improvements in the balance of payments position of India.

IMF has been rendering technical assistance to India on many matters relating to monetary, fiscal and exchange system. But for the existence of the fund, India would not have successfully overcome the exchange crisis that occurred in 1980s and in 1990s. When the balance of payments difficulties increased due to a hike in oil prices, the fund helped the developing countries like India by providing a special oil facility under which, members were permitted to borrow at lower rate of interest.

Due to fiscal and current account deficits of the late 1980s, faster growth of imports of oil, have had their worst impact on India's foreign exchange position. India was almost on the brink of international default of its debt obligations in June 1991. At this stage, the new government under the Prime Ministership of Shri P V Narasimha Rao, introduced many macroeonomic stabilisation measures such as 19 per cent devaluation of the rupee, bringing down the fiscal deficit from nine per cent to five per cent of Gross Domestic Product, abolishing the complex system of industrial licensing, strengthening of the competition between the private and public sectors, initiating steps to make the rupee fully convertible, liberalisation of foreign investment, renewal of quantitative restrictions on imports, etc. It was adequately supported by the financial sector reforms like reduction of Cash Reserve Ratio (CRR), Statutory Liquidity Ratio (SLR), and the interest rate subsidy to the priority sector.

With the help of IMF loan in 1991, India was able to achieve tremendous success in the balance of payments position. Foreign exchange reserves increased to US $10.2 billion in 1994 from the low level of US $1.147 billion at the end of August 1991. The inflation rate has been considerably brought down to below six per cent by time 1993. This was due to the timely assistance given by IMF, otherwise, it would not have overcome the scheme balance of payments cases in 1991. The fund has declared India as the sixth-largest economy in the world. The IMF has come out openly approving and praising India's macro economic reforms by devolving a separate section on India in its annual report. The IMF study declares that India's economy is more than three times as large as previously measured on the basis of the purchasing power parity conversion.

Achievements of the IMF

The achievements of the IMF are:

(a) The major achievement of the fund in the field of international liquidity is the creation of new world paper gold currency, commonly acceptable to all core times, namely SDRs.

(b) The membership and financial resources of the fund have registered a phenomenal growth over a period of 50 years of its existence. The fund started with only 29 members with a subscription quota of US $7000 million. But, today it has got more than 178 members with the quota aggregating more than SDRs 90 million.

(c) To enable the member countries to solve their temporary balance of payments difficulties, the fund has devised and introduced many new schemes so as to provide more financial help. The schemes are standby arrangements, extended fund facility, compensatory financing, etc.

(d) To pay special attention to the economic development of poor countries, where the per capital annual income is less than US $360, a special fund called Trust Fund has been created by IMF. This fund was financed by the sale of IMF gold and voluntary contributions by other developed member countries. More than 55 countries here so for been benefited by this fund.

(e) The fund has been helping the developing countries by providing them technical advice on various matters like monetary, fiscal, and exchange system. It has a fiscal affairs department which deputes its officers to member countries to advice them on matters of tax policy, tax system and administration, etc. The fund has been acting as a guide to many developing countries for their rapid economic development through adopting proper monetary and fiscal policies.

(f) The fund has also created special funds then and there to help the member countries whenever they are affected due to some unexpected developments like hike in oil prices. The fund created "special oil facility" to grant loans at lower rates of interest.

(g) IMF has entered into agreements with many of the international organisations like International Bank for Reconstruction and Development (IBRD) (World Bank), General Agreement on Trade and Tariff (GATT), World Trade Organisation (WTO), Asian Development Bank (ADB) for the promotion of international monetary cooperation. IMF has cooperated with these organisations and contributed significantly to the economic development of many countries so that the world economy as a whole may not be hampered due to unwanted restrictions on global trade.

Shortcomings of the IMF

The shortcomings of the IMF are:

(a) Even after 50 years of existence, the fund has not been successful in eliminating the exchange restriction imposed by its member countries, still a vast majority of chain adopt different exchange control measures.
(b) The IMF has failed to promote exchange stability through prescribing fixed exchange rates.
(c) The IMF has also failed to provide for convertibility of currencies. Even today many countries are adopting the system of multiple exchange rates which is quite contrary to the policies of the IMF.
(d) Another major limitation of the IMF is recovery of its loans. If the resources are affected, the fund cannot function effectively as a leader in monitoring the internal and liquidity.
(e) The developed countries as creditors exercise a dominant influence on the IMFs policies. The developing countries by virtue of their lesser allotment of quotas, limitation of economic position are always at the receiving end.
(f) The policies and programmes of the fund in the borrower member countries do not always exercise a strong influence on the fiscal and monetary policies, impose large social costs and many of them break down before completion.

In spite of these shortcomings, the IMF has been taking concrete steps to bring about stable exchange rates and to promote international monetary cooperative and the days are not for away for the fund to achieve its objectives set forth in its Articles of Agreement.

10
The Reserve Bank of India

Introduction

Banking in India is mainly governed by the Banking Regulation Act, 1949 and Reserve Bank of India Act, 1934. The Reserve Bank of India and the Government of India exercise control over banks from the opening of bank to their winding up by virtue of powers conferred under these statutory.

Banking is defined in Section 5(b) of the Banking Regulation Act as the acceptance of deposits of money from the public for the purpose of lending or reinvestment. Banks in India fall under one of the following categories:

(a) Body corporates constituted under special statutes.
(b) Company registered under the Companies Act of 1956 or foreign companies.
(c) Cooperative society registered under the Cooperative Society Act.

Reserve Bank of India Act, 1934

The RBI Act of 1934 was enacted to constitute the Reserve Bank of India: (a) to regulate the issue of bank notes (b) for keeping reserves for securing monetary stability in India and (c) to operate the currency and credit system of the country to its advantage. The Act came into force on 6 March 1934. The Act has been amended from time to time to meet the demands of changing times.

The last major amendment to the Act was effected by the RBI (amendment) Act 1997. A provision was inserted by the Information Technology Act of 2000 for enabling the RBI to make regulations for regulating payment systems of banks and financial institutions.

The Act deals with the constitution, powers, and functions of RBI. The Act does not directly deal with the regulation of the banking system except for Section 42 which provides for cash reserves of scheduled banks to be kept with the bank, with a view to regulating the credit system and ensuring monetary stability. Section 18 of the Act also provides for direct discount when special occasion arises making it necessary for the purpose of regulating credit in the interest of trade, industry, and agriculture.

The Act deals with:

(a) Incorporation, capital management and business of the banks.
(b) Management of foreign exchange and foreign reserves.
(c) Central banking functions like issue and management of bank notes, monetary control, cash reserves of scheduled banks, acting as banker to government and banks, lender of last resort, etc.
(d) Financial supervision of banks and financial institutions.
(e) Collection and furnishing of credit information.
(f) Acceptance of deposits by non-banking financial institutions.
(g) General provisions regarding reserve fund, credit funds, publication of bank rate, audit and accounts, etc.
(h) Penalties for violation of provisions of the Act or directions issued thereunder.

The Banking Regulation Act, 1949

The Banking Regulation Act, 1949 was enacted to consolidate and amend the law relating to banking and to provide for a suitable framework for regulating the banking companies. Initially the Act provided for a regulation of banking companies only, but in 1965, the Act was amended to cover cooperative banks as well, with certain modifications. The Act does not apply to primary agricultural credit societies and cooperative land development banks. The provisions of the Act are applicable to banking companies in addition to other laws which are applicable to such companies, unless otherwise specifically provided in the Act. Thus, Companies Act, 1956 which deals with the incorporation and working of companies is applicable to banking companies except where special provisions are made in the Banking Regulation Act.

The act deals with: (a) the regulation of business of banking companies (b) the control over the management of banking companies (c) suspension and winding up of banking business (d) penalties for violation of the provisions of the Act.

The RBI is a body corporate having perpetual succession and common seal and shall sue and be sued in its name. The whole capital of the bank is held by the Central Government. The bank has its central office in Mumbai and offices in Mumbai, Kolkata, Delhi, and Chennai and branches in most of the state capitals and some other cities.

The bank functions under the general superintendence and directions of the Central Board of Directors. The board has to abide by the directions given by the Central Government in public interest after consultation with the governor of the bank. The board shall consist of governor and not more than four deputy governors to be appointed by the Central Government and other directors nominated by the Central Government. Apart from the Central Board, the bank has also local boards situated at Mumbai, Kolkata, Delhi, and Chennai, which perform any duties delegated to it by the Central Board. The governor has the power of general superintendence and direction of the affairs of the bank and exercises all powers of the bank unless otherwise provided in the regulations made by the Central Board. The deputy governor, executive directors, and other officers in different grades assist the governor in the discharge of the bank's functions.

The bank is the sole authority of issue and management of currency in India under Section 22 of the RBI Act. The bank may issue notes of different denominations from two rupees to 10,000 rupees as the Central Government may decide on the recommendations of the central board. Such notes shall be legal tender at any place in India.

The bank is the banker of the central and state governments, under Section 20 of the Act, and accordingly it is obligatory to undertake banking business for the Central Government. In the case of state governments, their banking business is undertaken by the bank based on agreements as provided in Section 21A. The bank provides ways and means of advances to the central and state governments. These are temporary advances to meet immediate needs when there is interval between expenditure and flow of revenue. Reserve Bank also inspects banks and exercises supervisory powers and issues directions from time to time in public interest and the interest of the banking system in respect of interest rates, lending limits, investments, and various other matters.

The major powers of the bank in different roles as regulator and supervisor can be summed up as under:

- power to license
- power of appointment and removal of banking boards/personnel
- power to regulate the business of the banks
- power to give directions
- power to inspect and supervise banks
- power regarding audit of banks
- power to collect and furnish credit information
- power relating to moratorium, amalgamation and winding up, and
- power to impose penalties.

The need for a central bank in India was felt as early as 1773, when Warren Hastings, the Governor of Bengal recommended the establishment of a Central Bank of Bengal and Bihar. It was set up but could survive only for a brief period. Several other suggestions were also made but the proposal assumed a definite shape during the twenties of the Twentieth Century. In 1921, three Presidency Banks were amalgamated to form the

Imperial Bank of India. It was primarily a commercial bank but discharged certain central banking functions, especially as a banker to the government. The issue of notes continued to be the direct responsibility of the British Government.

In the year 1926, the RBI was set up on the basis of the recommendations of the Royal Commission on Indian Currency and Finance also known as the Hilton-Young Commission. In pursuance of its recommendations, a bill was introduced in the Indian Legislative Assembly in 1927 which was dropped on constitutional grounds. Again, the question assumed importance with the Central Banking Enquiry Committee recommending the immediate creation of a central bank. The White Paper on Indian Constitutional reforms, published in 1933 contained a provision that before the federal constitution's operation, a Reserve Bank free from political influences should be established. A fresh bill was introduced in the Indian legislative assembly on 18 September 1933 and the RBI Act was passed in September, 1934. The RBI started functioning from 1 April 1935.

The Reserve Bank was originally constituted as a shareholder's bank with a capital of INR 5 crores divided into 5 lakh fully paid shares of INR 100 each. The entire share capital was contributed by private shareholders. The government held shares of nominal value of INR 2.2 lakhs. After independence, the public opinion was strongly in favour of nationalisation of the RBI. The RBI was nationalised with effect from 1 January 1949 on the basis of the RBI (Transfer to Public Ownership) Act, 1948. All shares in the capital of the bank were transferred to the central government on payment of a compensation of INR 118.10 per share.

Organisation and Management of the Bank

The general superintendence and direction of the affairs and business of the bank was entrusted to the Central Board of Directors consisting of 20 directors including:

(a) A governor and four Deputy Governors, appointed as whole time officers of the bank by the Central Government for a term not exceeding five years.

(b) Four Directors nominated by the Central Government one from each of the local four boards constituted.

(c) Ten directors nominated by the Central Government for a term of four years. These directors are experts in business, industry finance, and cooperation.

(d) One official nominated by the Government of India (Secretary Finance Ministry, Government of India).

All the powers of the bank are exercised by the Central Board which must meet at least six times each year and at least once in each quarter.

The whole country has been divided into four areas – the western area, the eastern area, the northern area, and the southern area, having head quarters in Mumbai, Kolkata, Delhi, and Chennai, respectively. For each of these four areas, there is a Local Board consisting of five members appointed by the Central Government for a term of four years. The function of this Board is to advise the Central Board on local matters and to represent territorial and economic interests of local cooperative and indigeneous banks; to perform such other functions as delegated by Central Board from time to time.

The governor is the chairman and chief executive authority of the RBI. Policy decisions are taken by the Central Board. The Board has delegated some of its routine functions to the Committee of the Central Board. This committee meets frequently, generally once in a week. A sub-committee is also appointed, if necessary, by the Central Board to study certain specific problems. In order to function efficiently and economically, the organisation is classified into central office and local office. The central office is divided into various departments, which are as follows.

- Customer Service Department
- Department of Administration and Personnel Management
- Department of Banking Operations and Development
- Department of Banking Supervision
- Department of Communication
- Department of Currency Management
- Department of Economic Analysis and Policy
- Department of External Investments and Operations
- Department of Government and Bank Accounts
- Department of Information Technology
- Department of Non-Banking Supervision(DNBS)
- Department of Payment and Settlement System
- Department of Statistics and Information Management
- Financial Markets Department
- Foreign Exchange Department
- Human Resource Development Department
- Inspection Department
- Internal Debt Management Department
- Legal Department
- Monetary Policy Department
- Premises Department
- Rural Planning and Credit Department
- Secretary's Department
- Urban Banks Department.

The local offices are situated at seven important cities. Each office consists of the banking supervision and currency management department. Wherever the RBI does not have a branch, the SBI and its subsidiaries have been authorised to act on behalf of the RBI.

Objects and Functions of RBI

The Reserve Bank of India Act, 1934 sets out the objectives of the Reserve Bank as "to regulate the issue of Bank Notes and the keeping of reserves with a view to securing monetary stability in India and generally to operate the currency and credit system of the country to its advantage".

(a) Prior to the establishment of the Reserve Bank the Indian financial system was totally inadequate on account of inherent weakness of the dual control of currency by the Central Government and of credit by the Imperial Bank of India. The Hilton-Young Commission, therefore recommended that the dichotomy of functions and division of responsibility for control of currency and credit and the policies in this respect must be ended by setting up of a central bank – called the Reserve Bank of India – which would regulate the financial powers and develop banking facilities throughout the country. Hence, the RBI was established in cities primarily with the above objective in view.

(b) The RBI is to remain free from political influence and be successful in operations for maintaining financial stability and credit.

(c) The fundamental objective of the RBI is to discharge purely central banking functions in the Indian money market, that is, to act as the note issuing authority, bankers' bank and banker to government, and to provide growth of the economy within the framework of the general economic policy of the government, consistent with the need of maintaining price stability.

(d) RBI also assists the planned process of development of Indian economy, besides the traditional central banking functions. With the launching of five year plans in the country, the RBI has been moving ahead in performing a host of developmental and promotional functions, which are normally beyond the purview of a traditional central bank.

The first five year plan document has stated "central banking in a planned economy can hardly be confined to the regulation of the flow of the bank credit. It would have to take on a direct and active role, firstly, in creating or helping to create the machinery needed for financing developmental activities all over the country and secondly, ensuring that the finance available flows in the directions interested".

The RBI as such, aims at the promotion of monetisation and monetary integration of the economy, filling in the "credit gaps" and gaps in the financial infrastructure, catering to the financial needs of the economy with appropriate sectoral allocation, as well as supporting the planners in the efficient and productive deployment of investible funds with a view to attain the macro-economic goals of maximisation of growth with stability and social justice.

Functions of the RBI

The functions of the RBI may be divided under two categories.

(a) Central banking functions
(b) Other functions.

(a) Central Banking Functions

Issue of Bank Notes

Under Section 22(i) of the RBI Act, 1934, the bank was given the sole right to issue bank notes of all denominations in India from 1 April 1935. For this purpose, the bank maintains a separate department known as the issue department. Notes are issued on a basis of minimum currency reserve system. By the Reserve Bank Amendment Act, 1956, a provision was made for a minimum reserve of INR 400 crores in foreign securities and a minimum reserve of gold of the value of INR 115 crores resulting in a total of INR 515 crores. This minimum currency reserve has been fixed at INR 200 crores by the Reserve Bank Amendment Act, 1957. There must be a reserve of gold of the value of INR 115 crores and securities of the value of INR 85 crores.

As per the requirements of the RBI Act, the issue of notes and the general banking business of the bank are undertaken by the two separate departments of the bank. The issue department is responsible for the issue of new notes. The currency of our country consists of coins and one rupee notes issued by the Government of India and bank notes (two rupee to one thousand rupee notes) issued by the RBI. One rupee notes and coins issued by the Government of India are put into circulation through the RBI only. The notes issued by the RBI are unlimited legal tender.

For proper distribution of currency notes and coins, adequate arrangements have been made by the RBI. There are offices of the issue departments in ten big cities. To facilitate expression and circulation of the currency in the country, currency chests are maintained all over the country. Currency chests are boxes or containers in which stocks of new or reissuable notes are stored along with rupee coins. The total number of currency chests and repositories are run by the RBI, SBI and its subsidiaries, public sector banks and government treasuries and sub-treasuries. Thus, a stock of new currency notes is held in currency chests scattered over the entire country and maintained by the RBI or other public sector banks on behalf of the RBI. The important advantages of maintaining currency chests or treasuries to the bank are as follows:

(a) If payments, on a particular day, exceed the balance with bank, it can withdraw funds from the chest. Similarly, if there is surplus, due to less payments, the surplus funds may be deposited into the chest. This avoids the physical transfer of cash at frequent intervals from one place to another. It facilitates the treasuries and bank branches to work with relatively small balances.

(b) The currency chests facilitate the exchange of rupee coins to notes and supply of notes of lower denominations for those of higher denominations and vice versa and also the issue of new notes for old and soiled notes.

(c) The currency chests also serve as the basis for providing remittance facilities to banks and the public.

Banker to the Government

The RBI also acts as a banker to Central and State governments. As a banker, it is obliged to keep money on account for the Central and State governments to make payments up to the accounts standing to the credit of their accounts respectively, to carry out their exchange remittance and other banking operations and manage the public debt. It has to transact the business of the Central government without any remuneration. The bank also floats loans and treasury bills on behalf of the Central and State governments and advises the government on all financial matters. In the absence of RBI's office, the government accounts are maintained with SBI and its subsidiaries who are authorised agents of the RBI.

According to M H Dekock, "As the Government banker, the central bank conducts the banking accounts of government departments, boards and enterprises. It makes temporary advances to the government in anticipation of collection of taxes or raising loans from public and extraordinary advances during a depression, war or other emergencies, and it carries out the government transactions involving purchases and sales of foreign currencies. The central bank is also called upon to perform various services as the government financial aspect, and it acts generally as a financial advisor to the government".

The financial operations of the government may have tremendous influence over the money market, unless they are properly regulated and controlled. Therefore there must be a closer coordination and cooperation between the government and the RBI. The RBI is entrusted with the responsibility of maintaining the public debt. It raises loans on behalf of the Central and state governments. The RBI coordinates the borrowing of the Central and state governments to avoid any clash or unhealthy competition between them. The policy decisions are taken by the government and the RBI is to implement them. In order to take right decisions, the RBI feeds the government the necessary financial information and statistical data. The government also consults the RBI before formulating the monetary policy. The RBI advises the government on all monetary policies concerning allocations of funds, floatation of loans, banking legislatures, etc.

Banker's Bank and Lender of Last Resort

The RBI acts as the banker's bank. It is said about the central bank that, "The central bank acts as a conductor of the banking orchestra and leader of the banking world. It is the friend, philosopher and guide to the commercial bank". The RBI Act, 1934 and the Banking Regulation Act, 1949 have given extensive powers to the RBI to control and regulate the working of commercial banks. As per the Section 42 of the RBI Act, every scheduled bank should maintain the minimum cash reserve with the RBI. It should also maintain the Statutory Liquidity Ratio (SLR) as prescribed by the RBI. The Cash Reserve Ratio (CRR) will change from time to time and is fixed as a percentage of the time and demand liabilities.

The commercial banks should abide by the directives issued by the RBI. In return, they enjoy the benefits of deposit insurance schemes. The credit guarantee scheme and refinance facilities from development banks. They can rediscount approved commercial/trade bills with the RBI. In case of emergency, they may resort to RBI's help and the RBI will act as the lender of the last resort. If the commercial banks fail to adhere to the RBI directives, penalties may be levied according to the provisions specified in the Banking Regulation Act including the withdrawal of certain benefits. The RBI acts not only as a custodian of cash reserves but also as controller of all banks in India. The RBI arranges for the settlement of inter-bank indebtedness through its clearing house. The clearing system reduces the expense, delay and risk involved in collection and clearing of cheques.

Further, the bank has been given the following special powers to control banking companies under the Banking Companies Act, 1949.

(a) The power to issue licenses to banks operating in India.
(b) The power to have supervision and inspection of banks.
(c) The power to control the opening of new branches.
(d) The power to examine and sanction schemes of arrangement and amalgamation.
(e) The power to recommend the liquidation of weak banking companies.

(f) The power to receive and scrutinise prescribed returns, and to call for any other information relating to the banking business.
(g) The power to caution or prohibit banking companies generally or any banking company in particular from entering into any particular transaction or transactions.
(h) The power to control the lending policy of, and advances by, banking companies or any particular bank in the public interest and to give directions as to the purpose for which advances may or may not be made, the margins to be maintained in respect of secured advances and the interest to be charged on advances.

Foreign Exchange

The RBI is responsible for maintaining the external stability of the rupee. It enforces the regulations strictly in accordance with the FEMA – Foreign Exchange Management Act 1999 and the International Monetary Fund to maintain the parity value of the rupee. As the RBI is the custodian of foreign exchange reserves, the bank buys and sells foreign exchange at rates determined by the Central government from time to time. The RBI has a separate "Exchange Control Programme" to supervise and control the scarce foreign exchange.

Miscellaneous Central Banking Functions

Apart from the central banking functions, the Reserve Bank performs a number of subsidiary or ancillary functions incidental to its position as the apex bank of the country. These include:

(a) Supply of different forms of currency
(b) The extension of remittance facilities
(c) The management of clearing house
(d) Tendering advice on financial matters, collection, and dissemination of banking statistics, etc.

Controller of Credit

It has been provided in the Preamble to the RBI Act that one of the functions of the bank is to control currency and credit. The control that a central bank is able to exercise in the monetary system largely depends upon the control that it is able to exercise on the constituents of the purchasing power. In all countries, including India, token coins and currency notes form the bulk of the purchasing power, the latter being more important than the former, in countries, where banking has developed, the deposit currency also plays an important role in the creation of credit and purchasing power.

The methods of credit control are usually categorised into: a) General or Quantitative methods or b) Selective or Qualitative credit control methods. The bank rate policy, variable reserve requirements, statutory liquidity requirements, and open market operations policy fall in the category of general credit control methods. The various directions issued by the RBI restricting the quantum and other terms of granting credit against certain specified commodities constitute the selective control methods.

The main difference between the general and selective credit control methods is that the former influence the cost and overall volume of credit granted by banks. They affect credit granted to the whole economy where as the selective control affect the flow of credit to only a specified sector of the economy, wherein speculative tendency and rising trend of prices due to excessive bank credit is noticed. The general credit control measures affect the: (a) cost and (b) availability or (quantitative) of bank credit. The cost of credit is influenced by the bank rate at which the central bank provides refinance to the banks. During recent years, the RBI has relied upon its powers to regulate the interest rates on the bank advances and is directly regulating the interest rates of banks rather than through the instrument of bank rate.

The overall quantum of credit created by banks depends on their cash reserves, comprising cash in hand and balance with the RBI. The cash reserve increase through: (a) a rise in deposit resources of banks, (b) borrowings from the RBI, or (c) by sale of their investments. Regulation of credit by the RBI means regulations of quantum of cash resources of commercial banks. These control measures exert their influence on the assets pattern of commercial banks. When the RBI desires to control, it adopts various methods where by the quantum of refinance is restricted and the flow of bank resources to investments and statutory reserves with the RBI is enhanced, thereby curtailing the availability of loanable resources with the banks.

Control of Currency

The RBI has been given the monopoly of note issue to enable it to exercise control over the volume of bank notes. Ordinarily, the expansion or contraction of currency is effected under the Section 33(i) by increasing or decreasing the assets of the issue department, which are kept in the form of rupee coins, including rupee notes, gold coins and bullion, rupee securities, including treasury bills, and foreign securities. An expansion in currency can be effected by increasing any of these forms of assets and issuing notes of equal value from the issue department. A contraction in currency can be similarly effected by withdrawing notes from circulation and reducing any of the assets held by the RBI. Ordinarily when it wants to expand currency, the bank increases the assets of the issue department by transferring rupee or foreign securities or both from the banking department to the issue department or by cancelling *ad hoc* treasury bills held with the issue department. Sometimes, currency is expanded or contracted as a result of revaluation of securities held in the issue department.

Other Functions

The RBI is authorised to transact the following ordinary banking business:

(a) Acceptance of money on deposits without interest from the central and state governments, banks, local bodies, and any other person.
(b) The purchase, sale, and rediscount of bill of exchange and promissory notes drawn and payable in India and arising out of bonafide transactions, bearing two or more signatures one of which must be that of a scheduled bank, and maturing within 90 days from the date of purchase or rediscount.
(c) The purchase, sale and rediscount of bills drawn and payable in India for financing agricultural operations or marketing crops, and maturing within 15 months from the date of purchase or rediscount.
(d) The making of ways and means of advances to central and state governments.
(e) The purchase and sale of securities of the central and state governments.
(f) The making of loans and advances to states, local bodies, scheduled banks, and state cooperative banks.
(g) The issue of demand drafts made payable at its own offices or agencies and making issue and circulating bank post bills.
(h) The borrowing of money from a scheduled bank in India or from central banks or other countries.
(i) Transactions in precious metals.
(j) The purchase, sale, and rediscount of bills issued or drawn for holding or trading in securities of the central or state governments and maturing within 90 days.
(k) The opening of an account, or making of any agency agreement, with central banks in other countries and acting as their agent and investing funds in their shares.
(l) The RBI also plays an important role in the maintenance of exchange value of the rupee and acts as an agent of the government in respect of India's membership of International Monetary Fund.
(m) All such transactions as may be incidental to or consequential upon the exercise of its powers or the discharge of its duties under the Act.

Methods of Credit Control

The most important function of the Central Bank (RBI) is to control credit created by commercial banks. Money and credit represent a powerful force to good or evil in the economy. It is the duty of the central bank to ensure that money and credit is properly managed so that inflationary and deflationary pressures can be controlled in the economy. In modern times, bank credit has become the important source of money and commercial banks have unlimited power to expand or contract credit. A central bank has a number of weapons to control credit created by commercial banks.

Methods of credit control are broadly divided into two:

- quantitative credit control methods
- qualitative or selective credit control methods.

The quantitative methods aim to control the total quantity and cost of credit created by banks whereas the qualitative methods control the use and direction of credit. The quantitative methods are traditional and indirect. They include bank rate policy, open market operations, and variable reserve ratio. The qualitative controls are direct which consists of regulation of consumer credit, margin requirements, rationing of credit, direct action, moral suasion, and publicity.

Bank Rate Policy

Section 49 of the Reserve Bank of India Act, 1934, defines bank rate as "the standard rate at which it (the Reserve Bank) is prepared to buy or rediscount bills of exchange or other commercial paper eligible for purchase under this act". As the provision regarding rediscounting of bills by the RBI had remained in operative for a long time in the past, the rate charged by the RBI on its advances to banks has been treated as the bank rate.

Thus, the bank rate or discount rate is the rate at which the central bank is prepared to discount the first class bills of exchange and government securities held by the commercial banks. The Bank of England was the first to develop the bank rate as a weapon of credit control.

When the central bank feels that inflation in the country is on account of excessive creation of credit by the commercial banks, it raises the bank rate. Following this, the lending rates of commercial banks also go up. A rise in interest rate discourages fresh loans and puts pressure on borrowers to repay their past debts. As a result business activities are curtailed, fall in business activities leads to contraction of income and expenditure, reduction in demand for goods and services, and ultimately fall in prices. The rising of bank rate controls inflation. The opposite happens in times of deflation.

The central bank reduces the bank rate to expand credit. Following this the commercial banks reduce their lending rates. As the cost of loans is low, businessmen are encouraged to borrow more and make investments. Consequently production, employment and prices increase. The lowering of bank rate offsets the deflationary tendencies in the economy.

Theory of Bank Rate

The bank rate changes have great influence on the level of business activity. But how does a change in bank rate affect the level of business activity? The Hawtrey–Keynes controversy is quite well known in this regard.

Hawtrey's View

According to Hawtrey, changes in the bank rate leads to changes in the shortterm rates of interest. The willingness of dealers to hold more stock or less stock of goods depends on the cost of holding it, which varies with the short-term rates of interest.

When the bank rate is reduced, the short-term rate of interest falls and so the cost of holding stock is less. This encourages the dealers to hold more stocks. As a result the orders to manufacturers rise, output expands, employment increases, money income and inflationary spiral with rising prices, and production starts.

Conversely rise in short-term rates due to rise in the bank rate increases the cost of holding stocks. The dealers, therefore, try to reduce their stock of goods and place less orders to producers. In other words, producers secure less orders and curtail production. As a result, some of the factors of production become unemployed. Money income falls due to employment. This further reduces the sale of goods and dealers place less orders to producers who in turn curtail production. Besides, producers postpone expansion of the industries. So demand for capital goods falls. Ultimately there will be fall in prices, production, and employment and the deflationary spiral starts.

Keynes' View

In the opinion of Keynes, bank rate changes affect prices, investment and employment through the long-term interest. When the bank rate is raised, the short-term interest increases in the money market and the long-term interest rate remains unchanged. As a result, short-term securities become more attractive because they carry high rate of interest. The holders of long-term securities, therefore, sell their securities and invest in short-term securities. Consequently, long-term rates of interest rise. The volume of investment depends on the marginal efficiency of capital and rate of interest. If the rate of interest rises the volume of investment falls. The propensity of entrepreneurs to hold fixed capital is affected adversely. As a result, capital goods industries suffer and production and employment declines in these industries. Income falls and demand for consumer goods reduces, producers of consumer goods reduce their production. This leads to further fall in income and demand for goods. The opposite happens when the bank rate is lowered.

From time to time, the bank rate has been changed by the RBI. During the planning era, on 14 November 1951 the bank rate was raised for the first time, from 3 per cent to 3.5 per cent with a view to checking an undue expansion of bank credit. The bank rate was further raised to 4 per cent on 16 May 1957 but this restrictive effect of the higher bank rate did not prove to be very significant in checking the inflationary forces induced by the typical methods of financing adopted by the government during the second plan period.

As an anti-inflationary device of the controlled expansion programme of the monetary policy in October 1960, the RBI introduced a system of slabs in interest rates. The borrowings of member banks from the RBI was regulated by means of a three-tier structure of rates. Up to a specified quota for each quarter, equal to the half of the average amount of the statutory reserve which a member bank was required to maintain with the RBI during the previous quarter, the bank could borrow from the RBI at 4 per cent bank rate. The excess of borrowings up to 200 per cent of the quota was to be charged 5 per cent interest. The system was further revised in July 1962, by changing it from three-tier to a four-tier structure of rates. As such, in the third slab, between 200 and 400 per cent, the quota was charged at 6 per cent and the excess of borrowings charged at 6.5 per cent.

In September 1964, the rate was further raised to 5 per cent and the system (of quota cum slab) was replaced by a new system. The rate charged by the RBI on the bank's borrowing varies with the net liquidity position which is defined as a ratio of net liquid assets to aggregate demand and time liabilities. In February 1965, the bank rate was further raised to 6 per cent. In March 1968, however, it was reduced to 5 per cent with a view to stimulating recovery from the industrial recession of 1967. In January 1971, the bank rate was however, raised to 6 per cent as an anti-inflationary device.

Along with bank rate policy, the RBI had also introduced the liquidity ratio system since 1964. Under this system, the rates charged by the RBI on its lending to scheduled banks varied with the net liquidity position of each borrowing bank. Under the scheme, the net liquid assets were defined as the total of cash in the till, and balances with the RBI, current account balances with the other banks, and investments in government and other eligible securities minus borrowings from the RBI, the SBI, and the IDBI. Thus, the RBI agreed to grant credit to a bank at the prevailing bank rate, if it maintained the Net Liquidity Ratio (NLR) below 28 per cent, the rate on the entire borrowings amount was to be raised by 0.5 per cent. The objective of introducing the NLR scheme was to control, more directly, the cost of credit so as to make it reflect more appropriately the relative shortage of capital in the country. In 1971, the minimum net liquidity ratio was increased to 34 per cent and a penal rate of 15 per cent was imposed on all excess borrowings of a bank having an NLR at 26 per cent. By 1972, the minimum NLR was raised to 36 per cent and again to 37 per cent in March 1973, which was again raised to 40 per cent in September 1973.

Since 1973, the RBI has adopted a strictly clear money policy and resorted to a credit squeeze in order to reduce the inflationary pressure on the economy. In fact under the credit squeeze policy the RBI has employed a series of monetary measures with the following objectives.

(a) To curb overall loanable resources of banks.
(b) To enhance the cost of credit to borrowers from banks.
(c) To improve interest rates on deposits and raise the cost of money lent to commercial banks.
(d) To increase the cost and reduce the availability of refinance from the RBI.

The structure of interest payable by banks to depositors on savings account and fixed deposit accounts have been revised by raising it. For instance, the saving deposit interest rate was increased to 5 per cent. The clear money policy was made more pronounced in May 1973, by raising the bank rate at 7 per cent and further raising to 9 per cent in June 1974. A credit squeeze policy was initiated by the RBI to check the severe inflation experienced by the country during 1973–1974 when the wholesale prices had risen by about 30 per cent in single year. Therefore, two objectives of such well-defined money policy are:

(a) High cost of bank credit was intended to reduce its demand from businessmen and traders and to act as disincentive to be improved.
(b) High rate of interest on bank deposits was intended to induce the people to save more and to reduce their consumption expenditure.

The bank rate was further raised to 10 per cent on July 1981, together with certain other measures to contain the inflationary pressure in the economy. Although the bank remained at this level during the next decade, different rate of interest were charged by the RBI on the refinance provided by it against different types of credit granted by banks. The interest rate on deposits and advances of commercial banks were also prescribed by the RBI without varying the bank rate itself. The bank rate in India thus ceased to be an effective rate influencing other rates in the banking system and was of limited significance.

After retaining the bank rate at 10 per cent for a decade (1981–1991), the RBI hiked the bank rate to 11 per cent from 4 July 1991. The RBI also hiked the lending and deposit interest rates of the banks. These steps were preceded by the devaluation of Indian rupee in two installments on 1 and 3 July 1991. The overall objective is to curb the imports and to reduce aggregate demand in the economy. Bank rate was further raised to 12 per cent on 10 October 1991. The two percentage points increase in the bank rate within a period of three months indicated the commencement of clear money policy by the RBI. At the same time, the RBI withdrew all refinancing facilities to the banks (except refinance facilities on export finance) and increased bank deposits and lending rates also.

In April 1997, the RBI felt the necessity of making the bank rate an effective signal rate as well as a reference rate. Bank rate changes from time to time. It is a signal or benchmark for commercial banks. Accordingly, the bank rate was reduced by one percentage point to 11 per cent per annum. The objective was that changes in the world bank rate reflect the stance of monetary policy. The RBI also revised penal rate on shortfalls in rescue requirements that are linked with the bank rate. Interest rate on other categories of accommodation from the central bank, which were not linked with the bank rate, are now linked with it. Ceiling on deposit rates up to one year was also linked with the bank rate. The role of bank rate as an effective signal rate was restored.

The RBI further reduced the bank rate of 10 per cent with effect from 26 June 1997. All rates linked with the bank rate were consequently reduced by one percentage point. With effect from 22 October 1997, the bank rate was further reduced by one percentage point to 9 per cent. But on 16 January 1998, bank rate was hiked by two percentage points to 11 per cent because of the significant pressure on the external value of the rupee. On 18 March 1998, bank rate was reduced to 10 per cent and further to 9 per cent on 29 April 1998. With the variation in bank rate, all other rates linked with the bank rate also vary in the same direction. During 1999–2001, bank rate has moved in both the directions. It was reduced from 9 per cent to 8 per cent on 2 March 1999, and further to 7 per cent with effect from 1 April 2000. Consistently low prevailing inflation rate led the RBI to curtail the bank rate. Another objective has been to cut the cost of bank credit. But shortly thereafter the bank rate was raised to 8 per cent on 21 July 2000 mainly to stabilise the value of the rupee vis-á-vis US dollar. During the first quarter of 2001, the RBI reduced the bank rate twice from 8 to 7.5 per cent on 16 February and further to 7 per cent on 1 March 2001. It has been reduced by 0.25 percentage point from 6.5 per cent with effect from 29 October 2002.

Highlights of RBI's Mid Term Review, October 31 2006.

- Repo rate increased to 7.25 per cent from 7 per cent
- Reverse Repo rate unchanged at 6 per cent
- Bank rate and cash reserve ratio stable at 6 per cent and 5 per cent
- Gross domestic product (GDP) forecast at around 8 per cent during 2006–2007
- Inflation to be contained within 5–5.5 per cent in 2006–2007
- Monetary and credit growth likely higher than projected
- When issued trading for fresh issues of central securities
- Resident individual free to remit up to US $50,000 a fiscal
- Banks with overseas presence to meet Basel-II by March 2008
- Other banks to migrate to Basel-II norms by 31 March 2009
- Non-banking financial companies can issue co-branded credit cards with banks
- ECB eligible borrowers can avail additional US $250 million
- Prepayment of ECB up to US $300 million without RBI approval
- Foreign institutional investments in government securities enhanced to US $3.2 billion
- Overseas investment ceiling on mutual funds increases to US $3 billion.
- Opening small accounts with banks simplified.

As anticipated the RBI hiked the "repo rate", the rate at which it lends to banks, by 0.25 per cent to 7.25 per cent while keeping reverse repo, the rate at which it borrows from banks unchanged at 6 per cent, in the monetary policy review. But the silver lining is that bankers said there will be no impact on home and auto loans due to the 0.25 per cent hike is one of the key short-term rates by RBI, but lenders having liquidity problems may hike loan rates for personal, real estate, consumer goods, and equity market.

Bankers should, however, be very glad that all key rates like CRR, bank rate and SLR (Statutory Liquidity Ratio) have been left unchanged and only repo rate has marginally increased by 25 basis points reflecting the market realities that cost of money is heading up as demand for money outstrips the growth in deposits in the banking sector.

Repo rate hike signals that productive sectors should get sufficient credit while non-productive sectors should pay a little more. The banks having less liquidity will have two options before them, to mobilise resources from the public through deposits or borrow from the RBI. Repo rate hike is a caution about credit growth, especially to banks that are aggressive towards market.

Those banks borrowing from the RBI to meet liquidity demand may jack up interest rates. There is a movement for full capital account convertibility. RBI's decision to give banks greater headway in raising resources overseas, especially in tier-I where the limit has been increased from 25 to 50 per cent. Deposit accretion would become a major source of raising resources of banks. Banks must ensure that credit is channelled towards productive segments like manufacturing. There may not be any immediate upwards bias on inflation. The policy is prudentially productive and supports the push towards fuller Capital Account Conversion (CAC).

In a bid to move towards full float of rupee, the RBI announced a slew of measures such as doubling of resident individual remittances to US $50,000 per year. The RBI maintained that resident individuals are free to remit up to US $50,000 per year for any current of capital account transaction or a combination of both, from earlier limit of US $25,000.

Clearly the credit policy display continues optimism towards full capital account convertibility in a phased manner. If the signals given out by the RBI are to be interpreted in the right senses, there are reasons to be vigilant on this front, as inflationary expectations have remained firm because of elevated levels of international commodity prices and demand pressures visible in the expansion of money supply and reserve money.

The RBI governor announces review of Annual policy for 2007–2008. These are:

- Hike in CRR by 50 basis points (bps) or 0.5 per cent to 7.5 per cent to suck out excess liquidity. (CRR increased from 7 per cent to 7.5 per cent implies an increase of 50 basis points)
- Bank rate same as 6 per cent
- Repo rate 7.75 per cent, reverse repo rate at 6 per cent. CRR is the amount of cash every bank needs to compulsorily park with the RBI for which it does not get any interest. It is essentially a liquidity controlling measure and the current hike is expected to suck out INR 13,000 to INR 14,000 crores from the system thereby attempting to control the excess liquidity which leads to more funds in the system and there by increase inflation
- The RBI has so far between December 2006 and July 2007 raised the CRR by 2 per cent to 7 per cent and has sucked out estimated amount of INR 60,000 crores from the Indian financial system
- Apart from liquidity, other issues like escalating real estate prices are a matter of concern. These issues can have long-term implication to monetary management of the nation
- Inflation has to be contained close to 5 per cent during 2007–2008 while resolving to contain to 4 to 4.5 per cent with a medium-term objective of inflation at around 3 per cent.

- President of the Associated Chamber of Commerce and Industry of India, (ASSOCHAM) said, banks now find it difficult to reduce the interest rates and CRR hike may also further hurt the credit off late which is crucial to small-scale and medium-scale industries
- FICCI the leading trade body has also expressed concern on pressures of bank lending due to the CRR hike. While RBI has maintained the bank rate and repo rate at the earlier levels, the increase in CRR by 50 basis points will impact liquidity thus reducing lendable resources of the banks
- No significant measures had been taken to reduce the cost of credit to the SME export sector in view of the fact that the appreciating rupee had severely impacted export growth.

Limitations of Bank Rate Policy

Some of the limitations of Bank Rate Policy are:

(a) The commercial banks must be in the habit of rediscounting or borrowing from the central bank. In underdeveloped money market, the banks do not approach the central bank for borrowing. In the absence of such a practice, the bank rate becomes ineffective.

(b) The bank rate will not succeed if banks have excess cash reserve. The bank may secure large funds due to deficit financing by the government. The creation of money by the government to finance development schemes finds its way to commercial banks and they are in the position to lend more without resorting to rediscounting or borrowing from the commercial bank. Thus, the commercial banks are not completely dependent on the central bank and consequently the bank rate is not successful.

(c) The success of the bank rate policy depends upon the extent to which the other market rates move in line with the bank rate. If the market rates do not change along with the bank rate, the change in the bank rate becomes ineffective. Such a relationship is possible only when the money market is fully developed and the banking system of the country is well organised. In countries like UK and USA, the bank rate policy has been successful but in underdeveloped countries it has not succeeded to that extent.

(d) The effectiveness of the bank rate policy depends upon the existence of eligible bill of exchange. Nowadays the use of bills of exchange as an instrument of financing trade and commerce has reduced considerably. The cash credit and overdraft are the most convenient methods of borrowing for businessmen. The absence of rediscounting makes the bank rate policy ineffective instrument of credit control.

(e) The success of bank rate policy depends on the effect it produces on entrepreneurial activities. In practice the entrepreneurial activities are not adversely affected by the changes in the market rate of interest but by the margin of profit. If they expect higher return, they will borrow and invest in spite of the increase in the rate of interest. Besides, the investments in public sector are not governed by the changes in the rate of interest. Therefore, it is difficult to establish a relationship between the rate of interest and investment.

(f) The economic system of the country must be elastic for the success of the bank rate policy, that is, the cost of production, wages and bank rates, etc., should respond to the changes in the bank rate. Nowadays the economic system has become rigid in all the countries. The government control over wages, prices and businesses, etc., has been responsible for the rigidity of the economic system. As a result of this, the bank rate policy has become ineffective.

Net Liquidity Ratio System (NLR)

The RBI advances to commercial banks are regulated not only by the bank rate but also by the Net Liquidity Ratio (NLR). The net liquidity ratio is the relationship between its net liquid assets and its total demand and time liabilities. The net liquid assets of a borrowing bank comprises of cash in hand, cash with RBI, balances with other banks, investment in the government and other approved securities, minus its borrowings from the RBI, SBI, and IDBI.

Every commercial bank is expected to maintain the NLR as prescribed by the RBI from time to time. In recent years, the NLR and the bank rate are going up to check the commercial banks from borrowing heavily from the RBI.

Open Market Operations

Open market operations refers to the deliberate and direct buying and selling of securities and bills in the money market by the central bank. Purchase and sale of securities may lead to expansion and contraction of money supply in the money market. The RBI has employed this weapon mainly to assist the government in their borrowing operations. Section 17(8) of the RBI Act 1949, empowers the RBI to buy and sell government securities. Immediately after the Second World War, the commercial banks experienced heavy withdrawals of deposits by the depositors due to political and other uncertainties and they were forced to sell their securities to meet their customers' demand. At this stage, the RBI was compelled to enter into the money market and bought the securities on a large-scale to maintain stability in the securities prices. The purchase and sale of these securities are made through approved brokers in Chennai, Mumbai, and Kolkata. Major part of the transactions are made in Mumbai only. Although open market operations can be effectively used for maintaining price stability as in other commodities, the RBI has not used it to its full advantage. In the recent years, there has been large-scale government borrowings for development purposes which are responsible for increase in the volume and variety of securities. The RBI can handle these securities effectively.

Conditions for the Success of Open Market Operations

The success or failure of open market operations depends upon a number of factors. These are:

(a) The central bank should have adequate stock of securities with it. Moreover, those securities should cover a wide maturity range. This helps the central bank in reaching all potential buyers.

(b) There should be a developed and well-organised securities market. In the absence of well-developed market, the central bank will not be able to buy and sell securities on a large-scale and thereby influence the reserves of commercial banks.

(c) The commercial banks may maintain a stable CRR. It influences when the central bank sells or buys the securities, the reserves of banks decrease or increase accordingly to maintain fixed ratio.

(d) The ideal conditions for the success of open market operations are:
   - the existence of broad and active market
   - the existence of fixed CRR by the banks
   - the absence of rediscounting and borrowing from the central bank.

(e) The commercial banks should not have access to the central bank for financial accommodation. If there is direct access, the reduction in the cash reserves through the sale of securities will be neutralised through borrowing from the central bank.

Open Market Operations and Bank Rate

The open market operations are supposed to be superior to the bank rate policy as an instrument of credit control. The bank rate influences the cost and supply of commercial bank credit. The success of bank rate depends upon the willing cooperation extended by commercial banks and its constituents of money markets. On the other hand, open market operations influence the cash reserves directly and immediately, and thereby affect the credit creating power of banks. In case of the open market operations, the initiative is in the hands of the monetary authority whereas the effectiveness of bank rate depends on the response of commercial banks and their customers to the changes in the bank rate.

Open market operations can be used for correcting temporary and permanent maladjustments in the money market whereas the bank rate should be used only to correct permanent maladjustments in the economy.

Open market operations are flexible with respect to the timing and magnitude as compared with the bank rate policy. They are carried on continuously and do not have a destabilising effect on the economy that accompany changes in the bank rate.

Financially, open market operations are used to support the bank rate policy and make it effective. In a period of depression, the bank rate is reduced to bring about the cheap money power. To supplement this, the central bank buys these securities in the market to increase the cash reserves of banks and to expand more credit. These open market operations are used to create conditions necessary for the success of bank rate policy.

Limitations of Open Market Operations

The limitations of Open Market Operations are:

(a) In a number of countries, the cash reserve of commercial banks do not increase or decrease in accordance with the sale or purchase of securities. When the banks maintain higher cash reserves than they are required to or if they maintain other type of secret reserves, the policy will not be successful.

(b) In many countries, especially in underdeveloped countries, the money market is not well organised and developed. They do not have broad and active security market and also bill market. So open market operations are not successful.

(c) The open market operations can be successful only when commercial banks do not approach the central bank for accommodation. If the banks have direct access to the central bank, the reduction in cash reserve will be neutralised by the banks through borrowing from the central bank. Similarly, commercial banks may repay the loans to the central bank when the cash reserve is increased instead of granting more credit.

(d) During the boom periods, the central bank absorbs the surplus funds in the market by selling the securities and thereby forces the banks to restrict their loans and advances. But during depression, the business prospects are not bright so the entrepreneurs are not encouraged to borrow funds from banks even if they are available liberally. Hence, open market operations are more successful in controlling the expansion of credit rather than stimulating expansion of credit.

Despite these limitations, open market operations are recognised as more effective than other instruments of credit control.

Variable Reserve Ratio (VRR) or Cash Reserve Ratio (CRR)

Variable Reserve Ratio as a method of credit control was suggested by Keynes in 1930. This method was introduced by the Federal Reserve System of USA in 1935. Now in almost all countries of the world, the central bank adopts this instrument as an effective credit control.

Every commercial bank is required by law to maintain certain percentage of its deposit with the central bank which is called the reserve ratio. The central bank has the power to change the percentage of cash reserves to be kept with it. By changing the reserve requirement, the central bank is able to effect the amount of cash with the commercial banks and force them to curtail or expand credit.

When the central bank (RBI) raises the reserve ratio, the commercial banks have to keep more cash with it. Consequently, the amount of money available with the banks declines. Hence, they are compelled to reduce their lending activities. Suppose, the central bank raises the CRR from 3 per cent to 10 per cent. A bank with INR 100 crores of deposits has to keep INR 7 crores as additional cash with the central bank. Now the bank is compelled to reduce its loans and advances. On the other hand, if the central bank wants to expand credit, it lowers the reserve ratio. Suppose the reserve ratio is reduced from 10 per cent to 5 per cent a bank with INR 100 crores of deposits has to keep INR 5 crores instead of INR 10 crores. That means the bank has INR 5 crores more cash to lend. Thus, by varying the reserve ratio of commercial banks the central bank influences the power of credit creation and thereby controls credit in the economy.

Superiority of Cash Reserve Ratio

Variation of cash reserve is regarded as superior to open market operations because of the following reasons:

(a) A central bank can change the reserve requirements by mere stroke of a pen and control credit effectively.

(b) The success of open market operations depends upon the existence of active stock market and availability of large stock of securities. The CRR can be used effectively even in those countries where the above conditions do not exist.

(c) This method is suitable in those countries where there is underdeveloped money market and bank rate and open market operations are not successful for various reasons.

(d) It is an effective device because it acts directly and it has no direct impact on the prices of government securities or on the rate of interest.

Limitations

The Variable Reserve Ratio is subject to a number of limitations.

(a) This method affects different banks differently. Banks having large reserves do not suffer much compared to banks having little or no reserves. This policy is also discriminatory in the sense that non-banking financial intermediaries like cooperative societies, development banks, etc., are not affected by variation in reserve requirements.

(b) The commercial banks usually possess large excessive cash reserves. When the central bank raises the ratio, they transfer a part of the excess reserve. They stick to the legal requirement of cash to deposit and continue to create credit.

(c) The policy is inflexible in the sense that the reserve ratio is applicable to all regions of the country without regard to local situation. More credit may be required in one region and it may be superfluous in the other region. Raising the reserve ratio is not justified in the former case where as it is appropriate in the latter case.

(d) Variable Reserve Ratio restricts the freedom of commercial banks. Even if sufficient funds are available, the banks may expand credit on account of fear that the ratio may be raised after sometime.

(e) It introduces an element of uncertainty in the working of banks. Banks do not know when the reserve ratio will be changed. So Keynes suggested that the reserve ratio should be changed after giving reasonable notice and by a small percentage.

(f) The employment of this weapon may have depressive effect on the securities market. When the central bank suddenly raises the reserve ratio, the banks may be forced to sell the securities to maintain the requirement. The widespread selling of securities may bring down the prices of securities and collapse the security market.

(g) Finally the success of this system depends on the willingness of the businessmen to borrow and invest. During period of inflation, the banks may not reduce credit even though the reserve ratio is raised. Similarly, during period of depression, banks may not be able to expand credit if the businessmen are pessimistic about the future.

In spite of the above limitations, this method is a powerful instrument in controlling the credit.

Qualitative Credit Control or Selective Credit Control

The quantitative credit control affects all sections of the economy without any discrimination. It fails to influence the purpose for which the advances are made and does not effect credit in a particular direction. It also fails to check undesirable expansion of credit in specific channels. But the qualitative credit controls are used to check the credit extended to non-essential purposes or uses with a view to control inflation in the country.

As per the Banking Regulation Act, 1949, the RBI has been empowered to control all advances made by the commercial banks. The RBI has the right to make the necessary instructions to the commercial banks in relation to the quantum of credit, the purpose of advances, margin to be maintained, the rate of interest, etc. The RBI has identified certain essential commodities like food grains or seeds, oil, sugar, cotton and textiles, etc., so that it could arrest such loans for speculative or hoarding purposes. Higher margin may also be prescribed if loans are obtained on these items.

The RBI introduced prior authorisation scheme in 1965 under which the commercial banks have to obtain prior permission from the RBI before granting any loans exceeding INR 1 crore to a single party. This includes a public sector undertaking also where the ceiling is fixed at Rs 3 crores. The prior authorisation scheme restricts the flow of funds to a group of industries/persons. As per the scheme, the commercial banks must collect and furnish information about borrowing concerns to the RBI. Inter-corporate lending, over-stocking, improper working capital management, etc. are being scrutinised. This enables the commercial banks to grant loans on the basis of credit appraisal and actual need of the borrowers.

The commercial banks have been following the directions of the RBI in this regard and have reduced the pressure of demand rising from bank credit. The RBI encourages the commercial banks in financing export-oriented industries with an objective of restoring favourable balance of payments. The following are the different methods of selective credit controls.

(a) Rationing of credit.
(b) Prescribing margin requirements.
(c) Consumer credit regulations.
(d) Control of balance advances.
(e) Publicity.
(f) Moral suasion.
(g) Direct action.

Rationing of Credit

This is the oldest method of credit control. It aims to control and regulate the purposes for which the credit is granted by commercial banks. Credit rationing is generally of two types. The first is Variable Portfolio Ceiling. According to this, the central bank fixes a ceiling on the amount of loans and advances for each bank and the bank cannot advance loans beyond this limit. The second method is known as Variable Capital Asset Ratio. This is the ratio which the central bank fixes in relation to the capital of a bank to its total assets. In Soviet Russia, this method was used effectively. It is an important tool in a planned economy and is used to divert the available funds into the channels fixed by the authorities. In a mixed economy, the central bank does not use this technique except under extreme inflationary situations and emergencies.

Prescribing Margin Requirements

This method was first adopted in USA in 1934 to control speculative activities in securities. Under this method, the central bank prescribes the margin to be kept for loans against stock exchange securities. For example, the central bank fixes 10 per cent margin on the value of the security. A borrower approaches a bank for a loan against a security worth INR 1,000. The bank keeps a margin of 10 per cent and lends only INR 900. If the central bank raises the margin to 30 per cent the bank can lend INR 700 against the security. A higher margin reduces the amount of loan given by the banks. When the central bank wants to curb speculative activities it raises the margin requirements. On the other hand, the central bank reduces the margin to expand the credit.

This method has certain merits. These are:

(a) It applies equally to borrowers and lenders. It limits both the supply and demand for credit
(b) Higher margin helps to divert funds for more productive uses
(c) It controls the expansion of credit in those sections of the economy which breeds inflation. So it is very effective instrument of credit control.

Consumer Credit Regulations

With the introduction of installment trading, the trading in non-essential consumer products like motor vehicles, electrical, and electronic goods have gone up to an unpredicted level. The RBI may restrict consumer expenses on non-essential items by directing the commercial bank to fix the minimum percentage of down payment, length of period over which installment payment may be spread, etc. They may also prescribe the exemption limit for installment purchase. By lowering the exemption cost, the installment buying is discouraged. Similarly, the commercial banks restricted to allocate lesser amounts in their budget for consumer credit.

Control of Bank Advances

The RBI has been granted powers in the state to exercise a general control over the lending policies of commercial banks, mainly to prevent the flow of credit into undesirable channels and to direct into useful channels. Immediately after the nationalisation of the commercial banks, the RBI gave directions to the commercial banks to lend 40 per cent of their loans to priority sector. Through such directives, there has been a tremendous transformation in the concept of bank advances. This act also authorises the RBI to caution or prohibit banks generally or any bank in particular against entering into any particular transaction or class of transactions. The RBI may raise the discounting rate in respect of bill financing import trade during the periods of unfavourable balance of trade. The RBI has been adopting this technique since 1956.

Publicity

Quite a number of central banks use publicity as an instrument of credit control. They regularly publish statements of assets and liabilities of commercial banks for information to the public. They also publish reports of general money market and banking conditions. This is a way of exerting moral pressure on the commercial banks and also making the public aware of the policies being adopted by banks and the central bank in the light of the prevailing economic conditions in the country. This method is useful to highly industrialised countries. It has been quite extensively used in USA.

Moral Suasian (Persuasian)

Moral suasion, unlike other credit control methods is not a statutory obligation. It is merely a persuasion or request to commercial banks not to apply for further accommodation from the RBI and also not use the accommodation already obtained for financing speculative activities. As there is no element of compulsion, the effectiveness of this method depends on the prestige enjoyed by the central bank. In USA, it is found that this method is not successful. In 1931, the Federal Reserve Bank observed, "it is impracticable to the moral suasion as an effective part of a programme designed generally to restrict or control expansion in or use of federal reserve credit. It is not possible for the Federal Reserve Bank by moral suasion to prevent credit from being used for speculative purposes". Looking back, it is seen that the RBI has sent requests to commercial banks on various occasions for restricting on bank advances. By and large, the commercial banks, responded favourably.

With the nationalisation of the commercial banks, this method has gained much importance.

Direct Action

Direct action refers to the directions and controls which the central bank may enforce on all banks or a particular bank concerning their lending and investments. The commercial bank may issue directives from time to time to the banks to follow a particular policy regarding loans and advances. The direct action also includes coercive measures taken by the central bank against the offending bank in three ways, namely,

(a) It may refuse to sanction further accommodation to a bank.

(b) The central bank may reject altogether any application for grant of discounting facilities to the bank.

(c) It may change penal rate interest on loans taken by a bank beyond the prescribed limit.

This method has been most extensively used by the central banks to implement their credit policy. But it has certain limitations.

(a) The banks cannot control the ultimate use of credit.

(b) It is to easy to make a distinction between productive and non-productive use of credit. So the banks cannot invest bank credit from less productive to more productive uses.

(c) The banks at time, may manipulate their accounts for advancing loans to their clients under different names for various uses which have been prohibited.

The above reasons have made direct action quite ineffective.

Limitations of Selective Credit Control

(a) The commercial banks, for the purpose of earning large profits may advance loans for purposes other than laid down by the central bank.

(b) It is very difficult to ensure that the borrowers use the amount for that purpose for which it is borrowed.

(c) Even if banks ensure, that loan amount is properly used, they have no control over the use of additional income created by the original investment.

(d) It may be difficult for the central bank to distinguish between essential and non-essential sector for the purpose of enforcing selective credit control.

(e) Selective credit controls are applicable only to the commercial banks. The other sources of financing such as issue of shares and debentures, ploughing back of profits and borrowing from non-banking financial institutions are not covered by the selective credit controls.

Monetary Policy

Monetary policy in India has to be designed and pursued in the context of "planning in the mixed economy" where the main objective is to accelerate the process of economic growth with stability and social justice. Monetary policy is a arm of economic policy and in that sense, the objectives of monetary policy are no different from the overall objectives of economic policy.

The monetary policy stances during the course of planning of India (1951–1987) may be stated as follows.

(a) During the first five year plan period (1951–1956), the role of monetary policy was confined to the allocation of resources in conformity with the plan objectives, initially in 1951, to contain inflationary pressures. The RBI raised the bank rate from 3 per cent to 3.5 per cent in November 1951.

(b) During the second plan period (1956–1961), the policy was more or less anti-inflationary. The bank rate was raised further to 4 per cent in May 1957 and the selective credit control scheme was introduced in May 1956.

(c) During the period of third plan (1961–1966) and annual plans (1966–1969), the RBI adopted a credit policy of restraint. It raised the bank rate further to 4.5 per cent in January 1963 to 5 per cent in October 1964 and again to 6 per cent in March 1965. The credit authorisation scheme was introduced in 1964; a system of differential interest rates (DIR) was also introduced. The SLR (Statutory Liquid Ratio) was raised from 20 per cent to 25 per cent.

    In 1969, the Government of India nationalised the major commercial banks, thereby bringing nearly 85 per cent of the banking activity in the hands of the public sector.

(d) During the fourth plan period (1969–1974), the restrictive credit control measures were adopted very sharply. The Net Liquidity Ratio (NLR) was stipulated from 31 per cent to 34 per cent between April 1970 and January 1971. The SLR was enhanced to 30 per cent and NLR further to 37 per cent by March 1973. The bank rate was raised to 7 per cent and CRR to 5 per cent in May 1973. In September 1973, CRR(Cash Reserve Ratio) was raised further to 7 per cent.

(e) During the fifth plan period (1974–1979), the policy had remained basically as anti-inflationary.

(f) During the sixth plan period (1980–1985), efforts have been continuously directed towards containing the inflationary pressures. In 1981–1982, the SLR was raised from 34 per cent to 35 per cent. It was further raised to 36 per cent in September 1984 and again to 37 per cent in July 1985. The selective credit controls were rationalised and simplified.

During the above plan period, the RBI has tried its level best to manage money and evolve a sound monetary system but with not much appreciable success in realising the social objectives of the monetary policy of the country.

Chakravarthy Report on the Working of the Indian Monetary System

In December 1982, Dr Manmohan Singh, the then Governor of RBI, appointed a committee under the chairmanship of Sukmoy Chakravarthy to review the functioning of the monetary system in India. The committee was assigned major terms of reference as follows.

(a) To critically review the structure and operations of the monetary system in the context of the basic objectives of planned development.
(b) To assess the interaction between monetary policy and public debt management in so far as they have bearing on the effectiveness of the monetary policy.
(c) To evaluate the various instruments of monetary and credit policy in terms of their impact on the credit system and on the economy. In this context, links among the banking sector, the non-banking financial institutions, and the unorganised sector could be assessed.
(d) To recommend measures for improvement in the formulation and operation of monetary and credit policies and to suggest specific areas where the various policy instruments need strengthening.
(e) To make such other recommendations as the committee may deem relevant to the effective operation of monetary and credit policy.

The Findings of the Committee

For the efficiency of the system, there should be no mismatch between the responsibility of the RBI to supervise and control the monetary system and its authority in this regard. The committee has thus, hinted at the undue interference of the government in the monetary management of the RBI. The committee observes that till now the Indian monetary system has not succeeded in attaining its major social objectives satisfactorily for the following reasons.

(a) Excessive fiscal deficits.
(b) Unduly large credit of the banking sector to the government.
(c) The RBI's main concentration on supporting public borrowings at cheaper rates rather than taking relevant action for the effective monetary management; monetary tools like the statutory liquidity requirements (SLR) and policy being used to facilitate a large public debt from the banking sector.

The committee has made the following noteworthy observations.

(a) The growth of money supply (M3) has greatly exceeded the growth of output during the period 1971–1984. The money supply (M3) has increased on an average at the rate of 17.2 per cent per annum, while the output (Net National Product – NNP at a factor cost) has increased just at the rate of 3.7 per cent, the wholesale price index has registered a 9.8 per cent rise per annum.
(b) The government's report to RBI credit has increased excessively; this has caused a phenomenal expansion in reserve money adversely affecting the conduct of monetary policy since 1970.
(c) The government borrows at a much lower rate than the prevailing market rates by resolving to the RBI and the captive market of the banks.
(d) The system of administered interest rates is typical of the Indian monetary system.
(e) Concessional rates of interest seems to have permitted the rise of economically non-viable projects.
(f) The currency deposit ratio has steadily declined from 1.53 in March 1951 to 0.3 in March 1984.
(g) Yields on treasury bills at 4.6 per cent discount rates are very low.

Recommendations of the Committee

The following recommendations of the committee are noteworthy and need the immediate attention of the monetary authorities (Reserve Bank as well as the government).

(a) Reduction in the growth of reserve money during the seventh plan period and the years to follow.
(b) The Reserve Bank should adopt monetary planning by assuming money supply growth rate targets year by year along with the operation

of the country's five-year plans. It should also prepare a credit budget for this growth and allocation of credit.

(c) Ceiling on all call-rates should be removed.

(d) Long-term deposits and loans must yield a minimum of 3 per cent real rate of returns.

(e) There is need for an upward revision of the administered interest rates. Yields on treasury bills and the government securities must be enhanced corresponding to the prevailing market rates of interest on other financial assets.

(f) Money supply growth target should be determined in view of the expected growth rate in Gross National Product (GNP), the real income elasticity of demand for money, and a permissible price rise of say 4 per cent per annum.

(g) Relative price stability is to be maintained by not allowing the annual price rise to go beyond 4 per cent. It would be desirable, in the Indian context, to assign to the monetary authority a major role in promoting price stability, and also to accord price stability a dominant position in the spectrum of objectives pursued by the monetary authority.

(h) There should be only two concessional lending rates applicable to bank credit provided to the specified priority sector borrowers, one of which should be equivalent to the bank (minimum) lending rate and the other somewhat lower than it. Banks should have freedom to fix their other lending rates.

(i) Banks should be assisted by the RBI by extending larger refinance and bills discounting facilities.

(j) Bill markets should be strengthened by removing impediments like payment of stamp duty, difficulty in obtaining supplies of stamp paper and administrative rigidities, etc.

(k) It is a misconception to assign to the trade sector a low priority for bank finance in comparison to the industrial sector in the present stage of development in Indian economy. Hence, the trade sector must be given due recognition and should not be made to be starved of bank credit.

The Chakravarthy Committee's report is comprehensive, analytical, and lucidly written. It has favoured a monetary system with some free air as against the present rigid and administered structure of the monetary system in India.

During the last 59 years of its existence, the RBI has been sincerely performing its various functions. It has brought many new dimensions, to the role of central banking in a developing country like India. There are, however, certain plus and minus points in its working. Along with its glorious success in some spheres, it has also miserable failures in some others.

The need is an effective check on the undue expansion of money supply. Inspite of the RBI's desire to follow independent and pragmatic policies, it cannot do so because of the pressure brought to bear on it by the Ministry of Finance, Government of India as the former cannot function as an equal but as a subordinate of the later. It is absolutely essential to accord perfect autonomy, not only in principle but in practice as well, to the RBI. The relation between the treasury and the RBI should be of equal status. There is, therefore, an urgent need to bring some radical reforms in the present system.

Prof P R Brahmananda, National Research Fellow of the ICSSR, University of Bombay made a number of observations in reforming the RBI and the banking system in his talk delivered on 30 May 1988 sponsored by the "Forum of Free Enterprise", Bombay, which are

(a) The Governor of the RBI should be independent of political ties. He should be of a high calibre, bold personality, and independent view. He has to think, exercise value judgement and come to a definite conclusion in the economic interest of the nation as a whole, rather than in the political interest of the party in power.
(b) The second suggestion of Dr P R Brahmananda was to revert to the proportional reserve systems of note issue which was followed by RBI from 1935–1956. Under the system, it has to maintain at least 40 per cent of assets in its issue department in the form of gold coin and bullion. The present system is creating easy expansion of money supply in the country.
(c) As there has been a long-term fiscal policy on the fiscal front, on the banking side there is need for a pragmatic long-term monetary policy.
(d) There should be a perfect understanding between makers of fiscal policy and monetary policy with an accord on terms of fiscal monetary mix.
(e) For the Indian economy, there is a need to have a 8 per cent annual growth rate of money supply. It is difficult to contain inflation potential of the economy. The growth rate of money supply (M1) may be fixed as per the recommendations of the Chakravarthy report. Assuming the demand for money (D) to be unitary elastic, the real growth of national income (Y) at 5 per cent and inflation at 3 per cent (P), the monetary target (T) is

$TM1 = DY + P = 5 + 3 = 8$. The annual growth may be 8 per cent.

Narasimham Committee Report (1991) on Financial Sector Reforms

In August 1991, the central government constituted a high-powered committee under the Chairmanship of M. Narasimham, former Governor of RBI. The task of this committee was to examine all aspects relating to the structure, organisation functions and procedures of the financial system. The committee submitted its recommendations on 16 November 1991. The committee highlighted the measures for improving the financial health of public sector banks and development financial institutions to make them viable and vibrant. The following is the summary of committee recommendations with regard to banking reforms.

Reduction of Statutory Liquid Ratio (SLR)

All the banks have to maintain liquid assets in the form of gold, cash, and unencumbered approved securities equal to not less than 25 per cent of their total demand and time liabilities. Such a ratio is called Statutory Liquid Ratio (SLR). Higher-liquidity requirement compels the scheduled banks to maintain larger proportion of their resources in liquid form and thus reduce their capacity to provide loans and advances to business and industry. It also diverts funds of the banks from loans and advances from industry and trade to investment in low interest bearing government securities and bonds of public sector financial institutions. On reduction of SLR, the banks will be left with more funds for lending. The committee recommended that SLR should be reduced from the statutory maximum of 38.5 per cent to 25 per cent of the net demand and time liabilities over the next five years. Instead of depending upon resources from banks at lower rate of interest for financing its activities the government should raise from the market at prevailing rates of interest.

Reduction of Cash Reserve Rate (CRR)

The minimum cash reserves to be kept by every scheduled bank with the RBI is known as cash reserve ratio. CRR and SLR are the weapons in the hands of the RBI to control inflation. RBI should resort to open market operations rather than depending on CRR. The committee felt that the present CRR at 15 per cent was abnormally high. It recommended that CRR should be progressively reduced to between 3 and 5 per cent. Such a reduction of CRR will enable banks to have more funds which can be used to expand their credit operations.

Policies on Interest Rates

The committee was for the removal of the control and regulations of the interest rates on lending and deposit rates of banks and financial institutions. The market forces should determine the interest rates in the country and they should not be fixed arbitrarily by the government. The committee recommended that concessional rates of interest to the priority sector lending should be gradually phased out. The committee also proposed that the RBI should be the sole authority to simplify the structure of interest rates. The bank rate should be the anchor rate and all other interest rates should be closely linked to it.

Changes in the Priority Sector Credit Policies

The committee proposed radical changes in priority sector lending. It suggested that the social purpose of bank credit should not jeopardise sound banking principles, and social banking need not come into conflict with sound banking. The committee proposed that the priority sector lending should be phased out gradually. Priority sector should be redefined and lending should be restricted for some time to small and marginal farmers, the tiny sector, small business and transport operators, village and cottage industries, rural artisans, and other weaker sections. The committee stated that such lending should be fixed at 10 per cent of the aggregate bank credit. The system should be revived after a period of three years and there should be reassessment of the need to continue or terminate the programme. The objective of priority sector lending is to see that the productivity in agriculture and small industry increases but such objective should not be at the cost of productivity and profitability in banking.

Restructuring the Banking System

The committee proposed mergers and acquisitions among the public sector banks to reduce the number of public sector banks so that they can reap economies of scale and become more efficient. The committee also suggested that the public sector banks should be focused in their operations. The broad pattern should be as follows.

(a) Three or four large banks including SBI should become international in character.

(b) Eight to 10 banks should become national banks with a wide network of branches throughout the country engaged in universal banking.

(c) Local banks whose operations are confined severally to a specific region.

(d) Rural banks (including regional rural bank) whose operations are confined to the rural areas mainly financing agriculture and allied activities.

Allowing Foreign Players

Foreign Banks should be allowed to open offices in India either as branches or as subsidiaries. This would lead to upgradation of technology and provide healthy competitive environment. Only when there is healthy competition, the customer will get the benefit of low-cost and high-quality service.

Encouraging Joint Structure

The committee suggested that foreign banks and Indian banks should be allowed and encouraged to set up joint ventures with regard to merchant banking, investment banking, leasing, and other innovative forms of financial services.

Encouraging Competition in the Banking Sector

With nationalisation of banks, there was virtually no competition among the banks which is not a healthy sign. The committee recommended that the competition should be encouraged among the banks. The RBI should permit setting up of new banks in the private sector provided they comply with the necessary legal provisions and other requirements such as start-up capital, maintenance of prudential norms, with regard to auditing, and provisioning. The government should not discriminate between the public sector banks and private sector banks. The committee also suggested that there should not be further nationalisation of banks.

Discretion to Banks to Open Branches

Branch licensing system should be abolished and opening or closing of the branch should be left to the discretion of the concerned bank which may decide on economic viability.

Overhauling of Organisational Methods and Procedures

The committee observed that the existing organisational methods and procedures were old and updated. These have to be overhauled for better commercial orientation. The following are the major suggestions made in this regard.

The guidelines of the Government of India and RBI should not unduly affect freedom and autonomy of the banks. Banks should be given freehand to determine the rates of interest to borrow and also to lend.

Technology is to be viewed as a means of reducing transaction costs and better customer service. The banking operations have to be computerised. Better control systems should be instituted for strengthening the banking operations. Improved work culture – greater reliance on internal audit and internal inspection. The banks have been in dual control of both RBI and Ministry of Finance, Government of India. This practice should end immediately. RBI should be allowed to function as real apex bank in controlling the banking system. The appointments of Chief Executive Officer (CEO)/ Chairman and Managing Director (CMD) and the directors to the board should be done strictly on professional competence and integrity rather than political considerations. Banks should achieve a capital adequacy ratio of 4 per cent by March, 1993. Further banks which have an additional international presence shall achieve a capital adequacy ratio of 8 per cent by March 1996.

Uniform accounting practices, particularly with regard to income recognition and provisioning for loan losses should be implemented. Sound practices with regard to valuation of investments should be adopted. No income should be recognised on non-performing assets.

A three-year period should be allowed for achieving income recognition norms and a four year period to achieve provisioning norms. Provisions made by banks should be allowed as deductions for income tax purposes. Special tribunals should be established to speed up the process of recoveries. An asset reconstruction fund should be established to take over the bad and doubtful debts of banks at a discount.

Narasimham Committee Report (1998) on Banking Sector Reforms

The Government of India appointed one committee on banking sector reforms under the Chairmanship of Mr M Narasimham to review the progress of banking sector reforms to date and chart a programme of financial sector reforms necessary to strengthen India's financial system and make it internationally competitive. The report of the committee submitted in 1998, covered the entire gamut of the issues ranging from capital adequacy, bank mergers, setting up off global-sized banks, recasting bank boards, and revamping bank legislation. The following are the major observations and recommendations of the Narasimham Committee (1998) on banking sector reforms.

(a) The capital adequacy ratio determines the interest strength of banks and their risk absorption capacity. The committee suggested for raising capital adequacy norms for banks. To enhance the risk absorption capacity of the banks Capital to Risk Weighted Asset Ratio (CRAR) of 9 per cent was prescribed with effect from March 31 2000.

(b) The committee recommended to enhance the shareholder value, a greater autonomy to the boards. Regulation of banks by the RBI should be confined to laying down prudential and disclosure norms and sound procedure and also ensure adherence of banks to these norms and procedures. Now there are clearly defined norms for income recognition asset classification and provisioning. These norms are designed to be more prudent, objective, transparent, and uniform. These norms make the inter-bank comparison more meaningful.

(c) At present, convertibility is allowed only on current account but not on capital account. Convertibility on capital account involves large inflows and outflows of capital with ramifications on exchange rate management and domestic liquidity. The committee recommended for (a) merger of strong banks and (b) three or four large banks (including SBI) must be of international character.

(d) Apart from advocating for three or four banks with international character and the setting up of eight to ten large national banks, the committee also suggested the setting up of small, local banks to serve local trade, small industry, and agriculture within a given state or cluster of districts. These local banks should be ensured of having compatible links with the larger national and international banks. To provide healthy competitive environment, the private sector banks were allowed to function in the private sector. Such a healthy competitive environment is intended to improve the efficiency and quality of service in the public sector banks.

(e) The volume of accumulated non-performing assets has been a concern for the bankers and the policy makers equally. The way to rehabilitate weak public sector banks having a high percentage of non-performing assets (in some cases as high as 20 per cent of the total assets) has been to adopt narrow banking concept. The concept of narrow banking refers to how the weak banks place their funds only in short-term and subtle free assets so that they can match their demand deposits by safe liquid assets. If the government cannot consider such a strategy for weak banks for rehabilitation, it should consider how best they can be closed. Banks now have to disclose certain key parameters such as CRAR, percentage of non-performing assets (NPA), provision for NPAs, net value of investment, return on assets, profit per employee, and interest income as a percentage to working funds. Such disclosure will help to accurately assess and evaluate the performance of the banks in terms of efficiency, productivity, and profitability.

(f) The Narasimham Committee (1998) suggested that there was an urgent need to review and amend the provisions of RBI Act, Banking Regulation Act 1949, State Bank of India Act 1955, and Bank Nationalisation Act 1969, so as to bring them in line with the current needs of the banking industry.

(g) To overcome the mounting over dues to the banks, Debt Recovery Tribunals (DRTs) were set up to facilitate the expeditious adjudication and recovery of debts due to banks. The recovery of debts due to Banks and Financial Institutions Act, 1993 has been amended to make the provisions for adjudication, enforcement, and recovery more effective. To see that the RBI does not interfere in the day-to-day management of banks, the board for financial supervision was set up under the RBI, in 1994, bifurcating the regulatory and supervision functions of RBI.

(h) To strengthen the capital base of banks improve profitability and enhance value to all stakeholders, the following steps were taken, (a) minimum prescribed government equity was brought down to 51 per cent (b) banks boards have been vested with more powers in operational matters such as rationalisation of branches, credit delivery, and recruitment of staff.

(i) The main aim of promulgation of securitisation ordinance is to enable banks and financial institutions to recover the NPAs by taking possession of securities without the intervention of the court. This was enacted in June 2002. It is expected that this act will create necessary fear among the defaulters and make them more responsible and accountable with regard to payment of the dues.

(j) The prudential norms, accounting, and disclosure upgraded to global standards. The financial soundness and supervision practices followed at present for effective banking supervision have made our banking system resilient to global shocks.

(k) The payment media has undergone a sea change. The traditional media for payment of funds were confined to cheques and drafts. Modern payment systems include smart/credit cards, electronic fund transfer, debit/credit clearing, and electronic banking. The RBI is likely to introduce Real Time Gross Settlement Systems (RTGS) to facilitate efficient funds management and mitigating settlement risks.

(l) The need for further refinements in our regulatory and supervision practices have been recognised. For the purpose, steps are being taken by the RBI to ensure growth oriented financial system in a planned manner without destabilising the systems. The banks should come out with appropriate initiatives such as, imaginative corporate planning, combines with operational and financial restructuring for achieving greater efficiency.

(m) To improve the transmission mechanism of monitory policy and develop further the money and debt markets, it has been decided to develop the repos market with appropriate regulatory safeguards. Further institutions, like UTI, LIC, IDBI, and other non-bank participants are allowed to access short term liquidity through repos. Money market Mutual Funds (MMF) have been allowed to offer "cheque writing facility" to their investors. To facilitate hedging of interest rate risks and ensuring orderly development of the derivative market, guidelines for interest rate swaps and Forward Rate Agreements (FRAs) are being issued by RBI. Recognition of bank-wise, as against industry-wise, uniform approach to HRD, technology etc., to keep phase with the economic reform process in other sectors of economy. RBI has already initiated steps to implement a number of measures on the committee recommendations.

RBI Macro-Economic and Monetary Developments in 2007–08 Approved on 29 April 2008 by Dr Y V Reddy, Governor of RBI

Rising inflation has clearly become a cause of concern not only for the government but also for the RBI. Going by its annual credit policy for 2008–2009, the RBI is concerned about the sliding growth using the Cash Reserve Ratio (CRR) as a preferred tool. The RBI raised the ratio by another 25 basis points (bps) in less than 15 days. It kept the other signal rates, the bank rate at 6 per cent, repo and reserve repo rates at 7.75 per cent and 6 per cent, respectively, unchanged.

With effect from 24 May 2008, scheduled banks will now be required to maintain a CRR at 8.25 per cent with the RBI. The rise in CRR will suck out nearly INR 9,000 crores from the system. The policy will help price stability, inflation expectations and orderly conditions in the financial markets. The logic used is, this hike may compel banks to increase interest rates and longer demand of loans, which in turn could help ease inflation. The Governor said that 2008–2009 inflation would be brought down to around 5.5 per cent with a preference for bringing it close to 5 per cent at the earliest, with a resolve to condition the policy and perception for inflation to be in the range of 4 to 4.5 per cent so that an inflation of around 3 per cent becomes a medium-term objective. The GDP growth projection for the current fiscal will be in the range of 8 to 8.5 percent.

The highlights of the policy are:

- GDP growth rate projected in the range of 8 to 8.5 per cent
- Inflation to be brought down to around 5.5 per cent from the present 8 per cent

- Deposits projected to increase by around 17 per cent
- RBI to disseminate details of various charges levied by banks
- All transactions of INR 1 crore and above made mandatory to be routed through electronic payment mechanism
- The limit of bank loans to individuals for housing having lower risk weight of 50 per cent enhanced from INR 20 lakhs to INR 30 lakhs.

11
The State Bank of India

The State Bank of India is the biggest commercial bank of the country and holds a special position in the modern commercial banking system in India. The State Bank of India was constituted on 1 July 1955, with the passing of the State Bank of India Act 1955, by taking over the assets and liabilities of the Imperial Bank of India.

The Imperial Bank of India which was established in 1921 through the amalgamation of three Presidency Banks of Madras, Bombay, and Bengal, was the biggest bank between 1921 and 1935. It performed both the commercial banking and central banking functions. The establishment of the RBI in 1935 brought about a change in the status and working of the Imperial Bank. It ceased to function as the central bank and was appointed as the agent of the RBI. It was authorised to transact government's banking business, that is, to pay, receive, collect, and remit money on behalf of the RBI, where the latter had no office of its own. Thus, it maintained a special position in the banking sector.

The Imperial Bank was in the hands of the non-Indians who discriminated against Indians in appointments, emoluments and loan facilities. Hence, nominating the Imperial Bank as the agent of the RBI was met with opposition from the other banks in India. There was a clamour for nationalisation of the Imperial Bank for better service to the nation. The All-India Rural Credit Survey Committee recommended the creation of State Bank of India by amalgamating certain state owned banks with Imperial Bank. Accordingly, the State Bank of India Act was passed on 8 May 1955 and the State Bank of India came into existence on 1 July 1955.

Organisation

The organisation of the State Bank of India can be studied under the following heads:

Capital

The State Bank of India has an authorised capital of INR 20 crores which has been divided into 20 lakhs shares of INR 100 each. The issued capital of the

State Bank is INR 5.6 crores. The shares of State Bank of India are held by the RBI, insurance companies and the general public. During 1990–1991, the authorised capital of the bank was raised to INR 1000 crores and issued, subscribed and paid-up capital was increased from INR 150 crores to INR 200 crores.

Management

The management of State Bank of India vests in a Central Board of Directors which consists of 20 members. These members are:

(a) A chairman and a vice-chairman appointed by the government in consultation with the RBI.
(b) Two managing directors appointed by the board with the prior approval of the Central Government.
(c) Six directors elected by the shareholders other than the RBI.
(d) One director nominated by the Central Government.
(e) One director nominated by the RBI.
(f) Six directors are nominated by the Central Government in consultation with the RBI. They are representatives of economic and territorial interest and have a special working knowledge and experience in various fields like finance, banking industry and commerce. At least two of them have a specific knowledge of rural economy and cooperation.
(g) Two directors are from officers and staff of the SBI.

The chairman and vice-chairman are appointed for an initial term of five years, and upon extension, for another five years. The directors elected by the shareholders and nominated by the government hold office for a period stipulated by the nominating authority. Apart from the central board, there are local boards working in Mumbai, Kolkata, Ahmedabad, Hyderabad, New Delhi, Chennai, Lucknow, Kanpur, Bhopal, Patna, Chandigarh, Guwahati, Bhubaneshwar, and Bangalore for the management of the branches of the State Bank in their areas. The central office of the State Bank of India is at Mumbai.

Through the SBI (subsidiary banks) Act 1956, major state-associated banks were converted into subsidiary banks of SBI. At present, there are seven subsidiary banks, now called associate banks, of the SBI. These are: (a) State Bank of Bikaner and Jaipur (b) State Bank of Hyderabad (c) State Bank of Mysore (d) State Bank of Patiala (e) State Bank of Saurashtra (f) State Bank of Travancore, and (g) State Bank of Indore. The SBI holds not less than 55 per cent of the issued capital of each subsidiary bank.

Objectives of the State Bank of India

The SBI has been established to operate on the normal commercial principles, with the only difference that, unlike other commercial banks in the country, it takes into consideration and responds progressively on small-scale industries, particularly in the rural areas of the country. The main objectives of the bank are:

(a) To encourage and mobilise savings by opening branches in rural and semi-urban areas and to promote rural credit.
(b) To act in accordance with the broad economic policies of the government.
(c) To establish government partnership in the provision of cooperative credit.
(d) To provide remittance facilities to the banking institutions.
(e) To provide financial help to the small-scale and cottage industries.
(f) To extend financial help for the establishment of licensed warehouses and cooperative marketing societies.

Functions of the State Bank of India

The functions of the SBI are:

(a) The State Bank of India acts as an agent of the Reserve Bank of India in all those places where the latter does not have its branches.
(b) The bank performs the general commercial bank functions such as accepting deposits, giving loans, providing remittances, issuing letters of credit, etc.
(c) It transacts in gold and silver.
(d) It acts as an agent of the registered cooperative banks.
(e) It acts as the government's bank, collects money, and makes payment on behalf of the government and manages public debt.
(f) It acts as the clearing house for commercial banks, rediscounts the bills of exchange of the commercial banks.
(g) It underwrites the issue of stocks, shares, and other securities.
(h) It undertakes mutual fund business.
(i) It is authorised to act as an agent to the Central Government, any state government or to any corporation for the purpose of working schemes.
(j) It invests its surplus funds in government securities, railway securities and securities of corporation and treasury bills.
(k) It is authorised to grant financial assistance to companies dealing in granting advances on hire-purchase basis against the security of book debts.

(l) It acts as an executor or trustee for the administration of estate on behalf of customers.
(m) It buys bills of exchange payable out of India with the approval of the RBI. It subscribes, buys, acquires, holds, and sells shares in the capital of banking companies.

The State Bank of India has been prohibited from doing certain business under the State Bank of India Act:

(a) The State Bank of India cannot grant loans against stocks and shares for a period more than six months.
(b) It can purchase no immovable property other than its own offices.
(c) It can neither discount bills nor grant credit to individuals of firms above the sanctioned limit, and also cannot offer loans against security of exchange bills whose maturity period exceeds six months.

Achievements

The SBI has made a tremendous progress since its inception in 1955. It is the largest bank in the country. The bank had 10186 domestic branches and 84 foreign branches as on March 2008. The total deposits of the bank amounted to INR 5,37,404 crores and the aggregate advances amounted to INR 4,16,768 crores as on March 2008. The associate banks of the SBI had a deposit of INR 2,34,168 crores and advances of INR 1,78,376 crores as on March 2008. The total number of the offices in India stood at 4,546 at the end of March 2003. The group has sponsored 44 RRBs with a network of 3,159 offices covering 102 backward districts.

The State Bank of India and Agricultural Finance

The SBI grants both direct and indirect advances to farmers for all agricultural operations. Under the "Village Adoption Scheme" the bank assisted all viable and potentially viable farmers in the adopted centres. The agricultural development branches were set up at the central office of the bank to coordinate the activities of the banks engaged in agricultural finance and provide guidance and assistance to RRBs. The bank's direct finance to agriculture stood at INR 15,870 crores at the end of March 2003. The bank provides investment credit for minor irrigation to increase irrigation facilities. SBI provided financial assistance for modernisation of farm practices, dry-land farming, and for increasing fish production. The SBI has introduced agricultural credit card known as SBI Green Card under "Kisan Credit Card Scheme" which was introduced in 1988–1989.

State Bank of India and Small-Scale Industries

The bank formulated a pilot scheme in 1956 for financing small-scale industries which was successfully implemented in selected centres. Term loans were granted for establishment, expansion and modernisation of small units. The amount of loans granted to small-scale industries during 2002–2003 was INR 12,392 crores. The bank introduced "Entrepreneur Scheme" in 1968 under which technically qualified and skilled persons who have viable projects but no capital are assisted to the full extent of their requirements. The bank introduced an equity fund scheme in 1978 under which equity support to small-scale units is provided by way of interest-free loans payable over a period of five to seven years. The bank organised Entrepreneurial Development Programmes (EDP) in its lead districts and in backward districts to motivate entrepreneurs to set up ventures. The bank provides advances to small business people like traders, transport operators, professional, and other employed persons.

The State Bank of India and Industrial Finance

The State Bank of India is in perceived position in industrial finance. Credit expansion was the highest for the basic industries which determine the overall industrial growth. Project finance focuses on core and infrastructure sectors like power, telecommunications, oil and gas, roads, bridges, ports, etc. The bank extends borrowing assistance to sick units under the aegis of Board of Industrial and Financial Reconstruction (BIFR). The bank's advances to priority sector stood at 41.53 per cent of net bank credit at the end of March 2002.

Assistance to Weaker Sectors of the Society

Integrated Rural Development Programme (IRDP)

The bank is actively associated with the government to alleviate poverty in rural areas. Under the government-sponsored Integrated Rural Development Programme (IRDP), the bank assists the rural poor in acquiring income generating assets.

Under Differential Interest Rate (DIR), the bank has been providing financial assistance at a concessional rate of four per cent to persons belonging to the weaker sections of society who are engaged in productive activities. Under the scheme for providing self-employment to educated unemployed youth, the bank has provided finance to educated unemployed youth to set up ventures. The assistance was provided to weaker sections including SC/STs, small farmers and marginal farmers, landless labourers and beneficiaries under the Swarnajayanti Grameen Swarozgar Yojana and financing the poor through Self-Help Groups (SHG). SBI has sanctioned to the extent of INR 7,200 crores at end of March 2002. The bank participated in all development schemes sponsored by the government like, Prime Minister Rozgar Yojana and Scheme for Liberation and Rehabilitation of Scavengers.

State Bank of India and the Cooperative Sector

The SBI provides the following assistance to cooperative and allied institutions:

(a) The bank has been assisting the development of land development banks by:
   - granting advances on the security of such securities
   - subscription to debentures issued by the central cooperative banks and land development banks
   - providing interim financial accommodation to cooperative central land development banks.

(b) The bank encourages the development of warehouses by increasing grant in direct loans against the security of warehouse receipts. It has subscribed to the share capital of the central warehousing corporation.

(c) The cooperative banks are given free remittance facilities thrice a week. The banks are granted short-term credit facilities against government securities at half-a-per cent less than the rates for other customers.

(d) The bank provides direct finance to marketing and processing cooperatives in areas where there are no cooperative finance agencies.

The bank (SBI alone) has sponsored 30 RRBs spread over 102 districts in 16 states. The bank contributes to the foreign trade through concessional financial assistance and development and promotional support to exporters. The bank administrates the gold and silver jewellery export promotion schemes as a canalising agency on behalf of the government. It maintains an information service for its customers on export possibilities in various commodities. The bank is actively associated with the efforts of NGOs which made significant contribution to poverty alleviation through micro credit, a new approach which has been successful in many Southeast Asian, African, and Latin American countries.

Capital Markets

The merchant banking division of the SBI was set up in 1972 to cater to the needs of the corporate sector. It gives financial advice to new projects and helps in making technical feasibility studies. The investment management advisory services by the SBICAP are in growing demand among individual investors including NRIs and institutions. SBICAP is providing new services like leasing and creation of secondary market for public sector bonds during the shut period of its existence.

SBI Cards and Payment Services Ltd. (SBICPSL) commenced operation in 1998–1999 with the launch of the credit card known as the SBI card. SBI Housing Finance Ltd. was set up in 1997–1998. SBI Life Insurance Company was incorporated to undertake life insurance and pension business. SBI Gilts Ltd. (SBGL) is the primary subsidiary dealer of SBI which deals in government security market.

The bank has three wholly covered subsidiaries and four joint ventures abroad. The subsidiaries are SBI Canada, SBI California, SBI International (Mauritius) Ltd. The joint ventures are Nepal SBI Bank, Bank of Bhutan, SBI Life Insurance Company Limited, and Indo-Nigerian Merchant Bank Ltd. (Lagos).

On 30 January 2001, SBI, HDFC, Dun and Bradsheet Information Services India Pvt. Ltd. and Trans Union International Inc., signed an agreement to establish a Credit Information Bureau(India) Ltd. The role of Credit Information Bureau (India) Ltd. (CIBIL) is to: (a) gather credit-related information regarding individual and corporate/commercial credit users (b) maintain a database of this information and sell this information in the form of credit regents for a price. The potential users of CIBIL are banks, financial institutions, non-banking financial companies, housing finance, and credit card companies. SBI has 40 per cent shareholding in this company.

Non-banking subsidiaries in India are:

- SBI Capital Market Ltd
- SBI Funds Management Ltd
- SBI Factors and Commercial Services Private Ltd
- SBI Discount and Finance House of India.

12
Financial Services

The financial system in India has been undergoing rapid transformation due to economic reforms introduced in the early nineties. The efficiency of the financial system is determined by the quality and range of financial services offered. The financial service sector emerged as a natural supplement of sophisticated and matured financial systems all over the world. Although financial markets are still at their infancy as far as Indian markets are concerned, the financial services sector holds tremendous future in view of the dramatic changes in the economy taking place both at the domestic and global front.

Financial Services

Earlier, banks were not providing non-banking financial services such as leasing, hire purchase, house finance, and so on. Banking Regulation Act of 1949 was amended in 1983 to permit banks to provide these services, either through their own departments or divisions or through their subsidiaries exclusively set up for this purpose.

Financial services can be broadly divided into two groups. These are:

(a) Fee based/advisory services.
(b) Fund/asset-based financial services.

(a) Fee-based financial service offering companies provide world-class financial services by charging a certain fee for their services. For instance, underwriting services, wherein the bank undertakes a commitment to get a portion of share capital subscribed by the general public. The bank charges fee for such service. This service does not involve much risk.

(b) Fund/asset-based financial service offers companies finance according to the specific requirements of their clientele. Here the required infrastructure, in the form of required assets or finance is provided for rent or interest, respectively. Such companies earn their income from interest spread, namely the difference between the interest paid and interest earned.

Today, virtually, every bank has created subsidiaries to specialise into each potential area of financial services. For example, Andhra Bank Financial

Services Ltd., Andhra Bank Housing Finance Ltd., State Bank of India Capital Markets, SBI Fund Management Limited, etc.

Activities of fee-based non-banking financial companies include: (a) Issue management (b) Underwriting (c) Portfolio management (d) Corporate counselling (e) Stockbroking (f) Syndicated credit (g) Arranging foreign collaboration services (h) Mergers and acquisition (i) Debenture trusteeship (j) Capital restructuring.

1. Corporate counselling – financial advise about debt capital and equity capital, needs for working capital as fixed capital.
2. For debenture holders the company assets are mortgaged as collateral security. These service organisations help the company debenture holders as trustees' assets of the company which are mortgaged or pledged to debenture holders.
3. Foreign collaboration services for starting ventures, targeting technical know-how, and foreign capital. Asset/fund based services include: (a) Leasing (b) Hire purchasing (c) Bill discounting (d) Venture capital (e) Housing finance (f) Finance for mutual benefit (g) Residual non-banking services (h) Factoring (i) Forfeiting.

Forfeiting is the conversion of foreign credit bills into cash by discounting them at a fixed rate. It applies to international trade only. The discount rate is decided based on the risks of the debtor country, currency risk, marine risk, and so on. Forfeiting service is provided through the Exim Bank or in collaboration with foreign forfeiting agency. Forfeiting may be either with recourse or without recourse in which case the forfeiting agency has to bear the risk. Forfeiting provides alternative source of finance mainly for exporters, particularly where there is delay in receiving payments from importers, forfeiting is a boon for exporters.

Financial intermediation is a process by which savings are mobilised from large numbers of people and made available to both corporate and non-corporate clients. Financial intermediaries are those who provide financial services in a specialised and focused manner.

Financial intermediaries include: (a) Primary and satellite dealers (b) Merchant banker (c) Registrars to issue and share transfer agents (d) Underwriter (e) Stockbrokers and sub-brokers (f) Depositories like National Securities Depository Limited (NSDL), Stockholders Corporation of India Limited (SHCIL) and Central Depository Services (India) Limited (CSDL) (g) Depository Participants (DP) (h) Debenture trustees (i) Bankers to issue (j) Portfolio management (k)Custodial services (l) Credit rating agencies (m) Housing finance companies (n) Mutual funds (o) Leasing companies (p) Venture capital companies (q) Insurance companies.

- Issue management – It is adopting a systematic process in issue of shares to public by companies, through prospectus, application. Procedure to be followed is prescribed by the Indian Companies Act of 1956. It is carried out by several intermediaries such as merchant bankers, lead managers, underwriters, bankers to issue, brokers to issue, registrars to issue, debenture trustees, portfolio managers, and so on
- Underwriting – It is an agreement to subscribe securities of a body corporate in the event of the investors not subscribing to the offered securities
- Portfolio – It refers to the list of securities held by a person at a given point of time. Portfolio management involves a balancing of risk and return associated with a particular portfolio
- Stockbroking is the process of transacting the selected securities is called stock broking and the person who does this function is called stockbroker
- Syndicated credit refers to an agreement between two or more lending institutions to provide a borrower with a credit facility, using common loan documentation. Syndicated loans are arranged by a syndicator who brings the lenders together
- Arranging foreign collaboration for getting technical know toward technology import
- Merger – it is a combination of two or more firms in which only one firm would survive and the other would cease to exist, its assets/liabilities being taken over by the surviving firm, by paying purchase as compensation in shares, debentures, and cash allotments
- Acquisition implies taking over the controlling interest in a company by another company
- Capital restructuring – refers to restructuring a company's loan commitments to generate cash surplus
- Leasing – it is a contract for granting or letting the possession of a fixed asset such as land and buildings, machinery, etc. for a specified period for a stated consideration. Providing the asset on long-term rental basis is called leasing. The person who takes the asset on leasing is called lessee and the person who provides the asset leasing is called lessor. The agreement between lessor and lessee is called lease agreement. Lease finance may be operating lease or capital lease
- Hire purchase – in hire purchase, in case the buyer fails to pay even one installment, the seller has the right to take back the possession of the asset and treat the installments paid earlier as hire charges for use of the asset
- Bill discounting – discounting of inland and foreign bills, import and export bills

- Venture capital funding is available for risky, but profitable projects
- Housing finance – providing loans for construction or purchase of houses
- Finance for mutual benefit – includes public deposits which is helpful for the both parties
- Residual non-banking services – are miscelleneous services and transactions
- Factoring is an arrangement to purchase the book debts of a firm or company
- Forfeiting is the conversion of foreign credit bill into cash by discounting them at a fixed rate

(a) Primary and satellite dealers.

(b) Merchant bankers are also called as managers to the issue as they are the specialised agency to manage capital issue.

(c) Registrar to issue and share transfer agents for undertaking transfer of shares and debentures.

(d) Underwriter – is a person who undertakes to purchase the company shares.

(e) Stockbroker and sub-brokers – Stockbrokers are members of recognised stock exchanges and primarily engaged in buying-selling and dealing in securities. Sub-brokers are appointed by a stock broker.

(f) Depositories – A depository is a place where something is deposited for safe custody. Depository in the capital market refers to an agency that holds securities on deposit in electronic form to facilitate surplus trading.

(g) Depository-participants – They are the business partners of depositories.

(h) Debenture trustees – They are the persons or agencies appointed to take care of mortgaged assets under charge.

(i) Bankers to issue – It facilitates rising of required money through banking channels.

(j) Portfolio management.

(k) Custodial services – It simplifies and expedites the process of transfer of securities.

(l) Credit rating – It indicates the current opinions of the rating agency as to whether the issuer of a financial instrument (say bond) is capable of meeting the debt service obligations as and when they arise.

(m) Housing finance companies – provide loans for individuals to construct or purchase houses.

(n) Mutual funds – They are investment companies that issue and sell redeemable securities that represent an undivided interest in the asset held by the fund.

(o) Insurance companies.

(p) Bancassurance means moving towards offering a holistic financial services package comprising banking, insurance, lending, and investment products to their existing customers and banks can maximise distribution of products and services to the customer base.

Venture Capital

Definition

Venture capital is funding invested, or available for investment in an enterprise that offers the probability of profit along with the possibility of loss. Indeed, venture capital was also known also as risk capital, but the term has fallen out of usage. Probably because investors do not like to see the words "risk" and "capital" in close conjunction. Venture capitalists often don't tend to think that their investments involve an element of risk, but are assured of a successful return by virtue of the investor's knowledge and business sense. "Data Merge", a financial information provider, says that venture capital investments in an enterprise are usually between US $500,000 and US $5 million, and that the investor is likely to expect an annual return of 20 per cent to 50 per cent.

Venture capitalists were instrumental in the enormous increase in the number of dot-com start-ups of recent years. As the internet was a new and untried business venture with enormous potential, many analysts feel that standard business rules were too frequently suspended in what was a very optimistic market. Internet-based enterprises were expected to enjoy unprecedented success; many venture capitalists were said to have encouraged dot-coms to focus on scaling upward rather than on realising early profits. According to Venture Wire, US venture capital funding for 2000 was US $105 billion which was more than the total funding available in all the 15 years before 2000. However, in April 2000, severe market corrections brought about a radical change in the financial climate, and since then online business has been failing at rates similar to the rates of startups in the early days of the dot-com boom. Venture capitalist, a term coined in the volatile financial environment of the 1980s, has been revived to refer to the venture capitalists that have recently begun to buy up failing dot-com enterprises at rock-bottom prices.

Venture capital is the second or third stage of a traditional start-up financing sequence, which starts with the entrepreneurs putting their own available funding into a shoestring operation. Next, an angel investor may be convinced to contribute funding. Generally an angel investor is someone with spare funds and some personal or industry-related interest. Angels are sometimes said to invest, "emotional money", while venture capitalists are said to invest "logical money" that is, willing to help give the new enterprise a more solid footing. First round of venture capital funding involves a significant cash outlay and managerial assistance, second round of venture capital involves a significant cash outlay and instructions to a stock or initial public offering (IPO) underwriter, who will sell stock in exchange for a percentage of what is sold. Finally, in the Initial Public Offer (IPO) stage, an investment bank, will take initiative to provide venture capital.

The term "venture capital" is normally considered as a synonym of high-risk capital. It is an early stage financing of a new and young enterprise seeking to grow rapidly. It is a combination of capital management expertise provided by the venture capitalists for the initial risk of a new and emerging company which has a good growth prospect in terms of products, technologies, business concerns, or services with the objectives of retrieving the investment with a handsome reward at a future date. In broad terms, venture capital is the investment of long-term equity finance, where the venture capitalist earns his return in the form of capital gains. The venture capitalist focuses on growth.

Features of Venture Capital

The salient features of venture capital financing are as follows:

(a) Investment is usually made in small- and medium-scale enterprises.
(b) Investment is made only in high-risk but high-growth-potential projects.
(c) Venture capital is usually in the form of equity participation. It may also take the form of convertible debt or long-term loan.
(d) Venture capitalists join the entrepreneur as a co-promoter in projects and share the risks and rewards of the enterprise.
(e) There is continuous involvement in business after making an investment by the investor.
(f) Venture capital is available only for commercialisation of new ideas or new technologies and not for enterprises which are engaged in trading, broking, financial services, agency, liaison work, or research and development.
(g) Venture capital is not just injuction of money but also an input needed to set up the firm, design its marketing strategy, and organise and manage it.
(h) Once the venture has reached the full potential, the venture capitalist disinvests its holding either to the promoters or in the market.

Venture Capital Process

All new projects become eligible for venture capital financing when they have the following benefits:

(a) A novel idea or new invention or improved technology.
(b) Capability of commercial exploitation and application.
(c) Large sales potential for the product or services.
(d) The project attained a pre-production stage.

As financing a new venture involves high risk, the investor always goes through the draft plan carefully and thoroughly to understand the prospects of the new business and assess the risk involved. This enables the venture capitalist to eliminate the chances of wrong selection of projects.

A careful study of the past performance of the entrepreneur, his expertise, competence in managing money and matters also helps in deciding the acceptance of the new proposal. After careful analysis, a structured deal would be entered between the venture capitalist and the entrepreneur. The deal contains matters relating to the method of financing, total outlay of funds, nature of business, payment of loyalty on the sales effected. Payment of changes for value added services, option for further financing, exit conditions, appointment of the board of directors, restriction on use, sale or transfer of technology, control on operations of the company, etc., method of valuation of shares in case of management buyouts are also dealt within agreement signed by the venture capitalist and the entrepreneur.

Stages of Financing

Early-Stage Financing or Seed Capital

It is the initial stage of finance given to the entrepreneur to enable him to demonstrate the worth or usefulness of the new inventions, that is, for pilot production of the product.

Research and Development Financing

At this stage, financing enables the entrepreneur to develop the product with a view to commercialise it for practical application. At this stage, the finance enjoys tax benefits.

Start-up Capital

This is the take-off stage where the product is fully developed and is launched for commercial use. Market penetration of new technology is enhanced.

Harvesting the Investments

Just like the farmers, the venture capitalists seed, tend, and feed portfolio companies in the hope of reaping a beneficial harvest. The strategies of harvesting are:

(a) Outright sale of the company.
(b) Initial Public Offerings (IPOs) to the public.
(c) Management buyouts.

(d) Mergers/acquisitions or control transfer.
(e) Liquidation of the company.

After assessing the liability of projects, the investors decide at what stage they should provide venture capital so that it leads to greater capital appreciation.

Venture capital is provided for seed capital or meeting the preliminary expenses, startup or second round financing. In other words, venture capital is available for new projects, projects relating to expansion, modernisation, diversification, buyouts or turn arounds. According to NASSCOM Strategic Review 2003, there were ten leading venture capital private equity firms in India with a total investment of US $1956 million.

Portfolio Management

Portfolio refers to the list of securities held by a person at a given point of time. Managing portfolio is a strategic task as it is concerned with maximising the return or yield while minimising the risk involved. In other words, it involves a balancing of risk and return.

Portfolio management refers to the process of managing an individual investor's portfolio by professionally qualified persons. Individual investors normally find it difficult to keep track of developments and decide whether to buy or sell a selected scrip or share. For this purpose, the individual investors take the professional advice from portfolio managers. Portfolio manager advises, directs or decides for the clients about the mix of securities at a given point of time. Generally, the portfolio managers and the investors enter into an agreement/contract. The objectives of portfolio management could be varied such as maximum return, balancing risk and return, capital appreciation, safety, liability, or tax planning.

The SBI's personal banking centres and Vysya Bank's investors' clubs are two such good examples. There are also a few private investment advisors who guide and help individual investors and manage their portfolios.

Mutual Funds

Mutual funds play a crucial role in the Indian economy, which is under transition on account of the ongoing structural adjustment programmes under liberalisation.

Definition

A mutual fund is a company that pools money from many investors and invests the money in stocks, bonds, short-term money market instruments, other securities or assets, or some combination of these investments. The combined holdings of the mutual fund owned are known as its portfolio. Each share represents an investor's proportionate ownership of the fund's holdings and the income those holdings generate. It is a common mode of community investment mobilisation. Mutual funds earn income by interest or dividend or both from the securities it holds. It deducts fees, operating expenses, and a management income and then passes the remainder to wealth holders through dividends on the mutual fund share. The dividend fluctuates with the income on mutual fund investments.

Role of Mutual Funds in Indian Economy

Mutual funds in India are playing a major role in bringing stability to the financial system and efficiency of resource allocation. Mutual funds have opened new vistas for the investors and imparted much needed liquidity to the system. It has emerged as a critical institutional linkage among various financial segments such as savings, capital market and corporate sector. The private sector in India is a deficit sector and the gap between demand and supply of financial resources is met by funds raised through loans and advances in issuance of securities. However, the buoyancies in the capital market has increased the reliance of the corporate sector on security financing. Direct financing by mutual funds to the corporate sector has substantially increased after SEBI guidelines allowed the corporate sector to reserve 20 per cent of public issues for mutual funds. Mutual funds have also widened the private placement market for corporate securities. It has enabled the corporate sector to raise capital at reduced cost and has opened an avenue for alternative source of capital. Unit Trust of India (UTI) is the first mutual fund company established in the year 1964.

Many banks now sell mutual funds, some of which carry the bank's name with it. But mutual funds sold in banks, including money market funds, are not bank deposits. As a result, they are not federally insured.

Different Types of Funds

When it comes to investing in mutual funds, investors have literally thousands of choices. The first step to successful investing is figuring only your financial goals and risk tolerance. Mutual funds can be open ended or closed ended and income funds, growth funds or balanced funds. Each type has different features and different risks and rewards. The higher the potential return, the higher the risk or loss.

Open-ended Schemes

Open-ended schemes are available for all the year round excluding the period of book closing. These may or may not have a specified redemption period. The sale and repurchase price are fixed by the mutual fund concerned from time to time. Repurchases are generally allowed at specified rates.

Closed-ended Schemes

These are open for subscription only during a specific period. Generally the redemption is also specified. This means that they terminate on certain specified dates when the investors can redeem their units. The duration of the scheme normally varies from five to seven years.

Income Fund

Income fund is established to maximise the current income (i.e. interest and dividend of investors). There are two aspects of income funds, viz., low investment risk-generating constant income and high investment risk-generating maximum income. Investment is made in various combinations of high-yielding common stocks and bonds with a view to extract income on a regular basis with safety of the principal amount of investment.

Growth Funds

Focus on stocks that may not pay a regular dividend but have the potential for large capital gains over a period of time. The investment is made in equity stock that have above average growth potential.

Balanced Funds

Where assets are a judicious mixture of industrial stocks and bonds with a view to embrace modest risk of investment and secure reasonable rate of return, the funds are employed in high grade common stocks, with 25 per cent to 40 per cent investment in conservative fixed income securities like debentures, bonds, and preference shares.

Sector Funds

This may specialise in a particular industry segment, such as technology or consumer products stocks.

Advantages and Disadvantages

Every investment has advantages and disadvantages. Whether any particular feature is an advantage for the investor depends on his unique circumstances. For some investors, mutual funds provide an attractive investment choice because they generally offer the following features.

Professional Management

Professional money managers research, select and monitor the performance of securities which the fund purchases. They also study changes in the economy and this takes care of macro-level uncertainties.

Diversification

Diversification is an investing strategy that can be neatly summed up as "don't put all your eggs in one basket". Spreading your investments across a wide range of companies and industry sectors can help lower risk, if a company or sector fails (micro-level – uncertainties company related or unsystematic risks).

Security

Adequate protection from SEBI is available.

Liquidity

Mutual fund investors can readily sell unlisted open-ended schemes back to mutual funds at the current Net Assessed Value (NAV) plus any fees and charges assessed on redemption. At any time, listed schemes of mutual funds can be sold in the stock markets.

Affordability

It offers economy of search and verification due to size and scale of operation. Also mutual fund investors get income tax benefit that increase the net yield of investments.

Ease of Investment

Automatic reinvestment of dividends and capital gains (revolving type of investment), no responsibility of keeping records like share certificates of various companies, tax rules, etc. A small amount can also be invested.

Some features that investors might view as Disadvantages are:

Cost Despite Negative Returns

Investors must pay sales charges, annual fees, and other expenses regardless of how the fund performs, and depending on the timing of their investment, investors may also have to pay taxes on any capital gains distribution they receive, even if the fund went on to perform poorly after they bought shares.

Lack of Control

Investors typically cannot ascertain the exact make-up of a fund's portfolio at any given time, nor can they directly influence which securities the fund manager buys and sells or the timings of those trades.

Price Uncertainty

With an individual stock, you can obtain real-time (or close to real-time) pricing information with relative ease by checking financial websites or calling the broker. We can monitor how a stock's price changes from hour to hour or even minute to minute. In contrast, with a mutual fund, the price at which you purchase or redeem shares will typically depend on the fund's NAV, which the fund might not calculate until many hours after you have placed your order.

Money Market Funds

Money market funds have relatively low risks compared to most other investments. By law, they can invest initially in only certain high-quality, short-term investments, issued by the government. Money market funds pay dividends that generally reflect short-term interest rates. The returns for money market funds are generally lower than returns for either bond or stock funds. Inflation risk can be a potential to earn for investment in money market funds. Money market funds are used in short-term liquid amounts like Certificate of Deposit (CD) or Commercial Papers (CPs). For them, capital is raised by selling shares to the investing public at a price equal to the asset value of the existing shares outstanding plus a loading fee or service charge.

Future of Mutual Funds

The market for mutual funds is determined by the growth rates in GDP, savings and household assets. The domestic market estimates, the savings market in India with inclusion of mutual fund investments would be around INR 2,00,000 crores. The asset allocation of mutual funds for December 2000 ending position is as follows in table 12.1:

Table 12.1 The Asset Allocation of Mutual Funds for December 2000

	UTI	Other Mutual Funds	Total (INR in crores)
Equity Shares	36,21,382	54,151	36,75,533
Preference Shares	26,903	270	27,173
Bonds and Debentures	24,77,285	32,159	25,09,446
Central/State Securities	5,05,284	10,449	5,15,733
Money Market Instruments	1,63,526	2,591	1,66,117
Units of other funds		1	1
Total	67,94,380	99,621	68,94,001

Hedging

Hedging is a process of protecting mutual fund assets from foreign currency fluctuations.

Net Asset Value (NAV)

Net Asset Value is the value of a fund's assets minus liabilities. Securities Exchange Commission (SEC) rules require funds to calculate the NAV at least once a day. To calculate the NAV per share, simply subtract the fund's liabilities from its assets and then divide the result by the number of shares outstanding.

Assets of world wide mutual funds as on 31 March 2002 was US $11.2 trillion. On 31 October 2003 in India there were 31 funds with 386 schemes which managed assets of INR 1,26,726 crores.

Resource Mobilisation by Mutual Funds:
2005–2006 – Private sector : Net Mobilisation – INR 42,977 crores.
Net assets – INR 1,81,515 crores.
Public sector : Net Mobilisation – INR 9,802 crores.
Net assets – INR 50,348 crores.
2006–2007 – Private sector : Net Mobilisation – INR 79,038 crores.
Net assets – INR 2,62,079 crores.
Public sector : Net Mobilisation – INR 14,947 crores.
Net assets – INR 64,213 crores.

Source: SEBI

Factoring

Factoring is a continuing legal relationship between a financial institution (the factor) and a business concern (the client) selling goods or providing services to trade customers (the customers) on open account basis whereby the factor purchases the client's book debts (accounts receivable), either with or without recourse to the client and in relation thereto, continues the credit extended to customers and administers the sales ledger.

Factoring is thus an asset based method of financing as well as a specialised service being the purchase of book debts of a company by the factor, thus releasing the capital tied up in accounts receivables and providing financial accommodation to the company. The book debts are assigned to the factor who collects them when due to which he charges an amount as discount or rebate deducted from the bills. Thus, the factor is an intermediary between the supplier and customers who performs financing and debt collection services.

During recent times in India, the growth of industrialisation and increase in the production and sales has led to the growing importance of timely collection of receivables and management of the same in a buyers' market.

Delay in collection of debts results in problems of working capital as a result of which the small suppliers with a limited finance-raising capacity ultimately suffer. Delay or non-realisation of dues have been responsible for the sick units in the small-scale sector. Collection of book debts is not undertaken by banks, though they provide collection services in respect of bills purchased/ discounted by them. The dishonoured bills must be reimbursed by the client and the latter enjoys no protection against default by the buyers. In addition to the working capital problem faced by the seller, no interest is realised for the period for which the payments are delayed beyond the estimated time. Manufacturers refrain from insisting on the payment of overdue interest, due to severe competition in the market, which ultimately results in the decrease in profits and deficits in working capital.

Hence, there is a need for efficient system of receivable management and collection machinery which will enable the manufacturers to concentrate on other important matters.

Factoring Services

The conventional services that a factor offers are as under:

(a) Financing Receivables

This is a key feature of factoring. The factor purchases the book debts of a client at a price. The debts are assigned in its favour. The factoring could be with or without recourse to the client. Being a purchase, and not an advance, a distinct advantage to the supplier is that his balance sheet shows an improved current ratio.

(b) Collection of Receivables

The factor takes over the responsibility of collecting receivables resulting in some benefits to the clients, which are as follows:

- elimination or reduction in cost of collecting in terms of saving of manpower, time, and energy
- increased focus on improvement and expansion of his business.

Here questions may arise whether the intervention of the factor would not adversely affect the client's relationship with customers and how the factor would be more effective than the supplier in receiving the collections. The factor does not adopt stringent or cohesive measures. It is equipped with trained and exclusive manpower. It has infrastructural aids such as access to communication network possibly dedicated. In other words, the follow-up of collections will be religiously systematic. As against this, very few organisations, even among larger ones, have separate or well-organised credit management departments exclusively devoted to collection matters. Units in the small-scale industrial sector can ill-afford separate staff or infrastructural back-up.

(c) Credit Control and Sales Ledger Administration

After concluding the factoring contract, the factor steps in through offer of his professional services, to control the credit extended and to be extended by the client. The factor is able to provide quality service in this area as it builds up extensive information files on the financial standing and credit rating of individual customers and their track record for payments. Often a customer or a potential customer is also the customer of other clients. Based on the information files, a factor is able to advise the clients on whether to extend credit to a buyer, the amount of credit to be extended and for what period. Further, the factor establishes credit limits for individual customers and indicates the extent to which it is prepared to accept the client's receivable on such customers. The factor is in a position to advise its clients about the customers who could be extended more liberal credit listing or with whom it may not be desirable to do business. Thus, this specialised service of the factor enables the client to handle for a greater volume of business with confidence than would otherwise have been possible.

The client sends to the factor copies of all invoices dispatched to the customers. The factor maintains the individual sales ledgers in respect of the customers, on behalf of the client. The client is furnished by the factor with periodical reports of the status of the receivables, together with age analysis and other useful information.

(d) Credit Protection

Factor provides insurance to the client against default of payment by a customer. Wherever finance facility is provided, the credit protection is available only under a "without recourse" arrangement. There could be cases where credit insurance is available, without resort to the finance facility as in the case of cash-rich companies. The insurance covers only the debt defaults arising out of the buyer's insolvency or financial inability to pay. Defaults occurring on account of commercial disputes such as those related to quality standards, faulting or delayed deliveries and other lapses in adhering to the terms of the sales contract are not covered.

(e) Advisory Services

A factor is in a position to render certain advisory services due to specialised knowledge and experience of industries, the data bank, and the information base it possesses. The skilled and technical personnel in its employment can extend financial and other industrial counselling services. It also provides to the client information on prospective buyers to facilitate market thrust.

Factoring services are not quite suitable for certain categories of business, for example, those undertaking job for works, those where work-in progress payments are involved and those prone to frequent disputes between sellers and buyers.

Types of Factoring

(a) Non-recourse Factoring

It is also known as "old line factoring". It is an arrangement whereby the factor has no recourse to the client when the bill remains unpaid by the customer. Thus, the rise of bad debt is absorbed by the factor.

(b) Recourse Factoring

The credit risk remains with the client although the debt is assigned to the factor, that is, the factor can have recourse to the client in the event of non-payment by the customer.

(c) Maturity Factoring

Under this method, the factor may agree to pay an amount to the client for bill purchased by him either immediately or on maturity. The latter refers to a date agreed upon, on which the factor pays the client.

(d) Advance Factoring

Immediate payment by the factor is called advance factoring. Under this type of factoring, the factor provides financial accommodation apart from non-financial services rendered by him.

(e) Confidential and Undisclosed Factoring

The arrangement between the factor and the client are left unnotified to the customers and the client collects the bills from the customers without intimating them of the factoring arrangements.

(f) Bank Participation Factoring

The bank takes a floating charge on the client's equity, that is, the amount payable by the factor to the client in respect of his receivables on this bank is lent by the bank to its client and enables him to have double financing.

(g) Supplier Guarantee Factoring

This is also referred to as drop shipment factoring. This happens when the client is a mediator between supplier and customer, that is, a distributor; the factor guarantees to the supplier against the invoices raised by the supplier upon the client and the goods may be delivered to the customers. The client thereafter raises bills on the customers and assign them to the factor. The factor thus enables the client to make a gross profit with no financial involvement at all. The steps involved in factoring are listed below, (see figure 12.1):

Step 1: The customer places an order with the seller (the client).
Step 2: The factor and the seller enter into a factoring agreement about the various terms of factoring.
Step 3: Sale contract entered into with the buyer and the goods are delivered. The invoice with the notice to pay the factor is sent along.
Step 4: The copy of invoice covering the above sale is sent to the factor, who maintains the sales ledger.
Step 5: The factor prepays 80 per cent of the invoice price.
Step 6: Monthly statements are sent by the factor to the buyer.
Step 7: If there are any unpaid invoices, follow-up action is initiated.
Step 8: The buyer settles the invoices on expiry of credit period allowed.
Step 9: The balance 20 per cent less the cost of factoring is paid by the factor to the client.

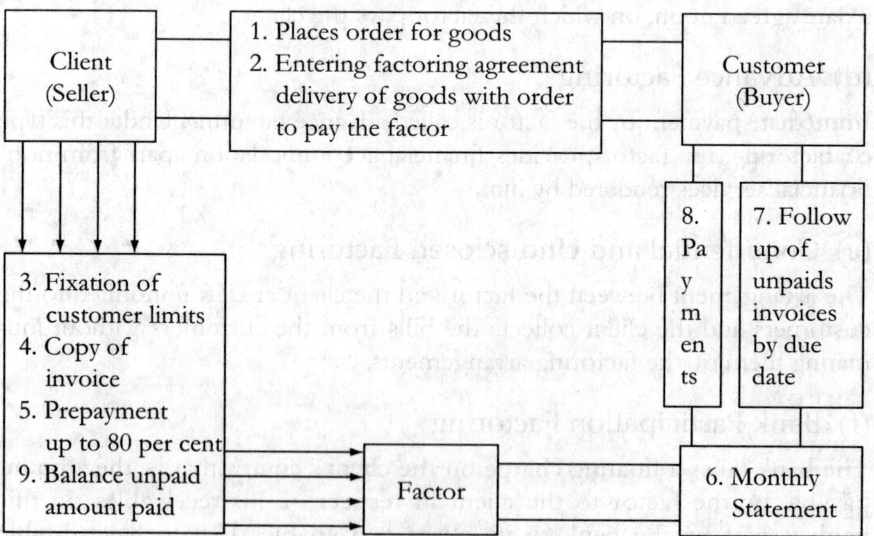

Figure 12.1 Mechanics of factoring

Financial services can be obtained by the suppliers from the banks and factoring organisations. Thus, a proper linkage between the two assumes importance. Banks and factors must furnish information to each other about those parties who approach more than one agency. The debt may be assigned to the factors by the suppliers and the factor may borrow from the banks. The supplier may, as an alternative, borrow from the banks and avail of all other services from a factor. Linkage between banks and the factors are to the advantage of the factors and suppliers who would avail of factoring services. Both the agencies would be able to bring about timely action and thus prevents the sellers and buyers' units from becoming sick.

Pricing of Various Services

The pricing of various services rendered by the factor depends upon the credit worthiness of the customers, his track record, turnover, etc., but the cost of funds and other costs to be borne by the factor influence the pricing. The price of financial services is suggested to be around 16 per cent per annum and for other services on the aggregate not to exceed 2.5 per cent to 3 per cent of the serviced debts.

Advantages of Factoring

Prompt Payment and Reduction in Debt

Capital locked up in the form of outstanding sundry debtors is available for use with the bankers as all sales become cash sales.

Improves Current Ratio

Improvement in the current ratio is an indication of improved liquidity which enables better working capital management. This enables the unit to offer better credit terms to its customers and increase orders.

Lesser Risk

The present risk in bill financing like finance against accommodation bills can be reduced to a minimum.

Improves Credit Rating

It improves the credit rating of an industrial unit.

Speeds Turnover

Turnover of stock into cash is speeded up and this results in larger turnover on the same investment.

Specialised Expertise

The factor with its own specialised expertise is in a position to provide information regarding product design and product mix, prices, market conditions, and economic prospects to the clients.

Collection of Dues

The client need not undertake any responsibility of collecting the dues from the buyers of the goods.

Limitations of Factoring

The limitations of factoring are as follows:

(a) Factoring is a high-risk-prone area and it may result in overdependence on factoring, mismanagement, overtrading, or even dishonesty on behalf of the clients.

(b) In a developing country like India, where factoring is in its infant stage, one may face problems, arising from lack of professional competence, undeveloped expertise, non-acceptance of change, etc.

(c) All companies may not be suitable for enterprising into factoring contracts. It is uneconomical for small companies with less turnover.

(d) It is not suitable for companies selling large number of small products to various types of people or companies having large number of debtors for small amounts.

(e) It is not suitable for speculative business companies, inefficient management companies, companies landing high bad debt expenses, companies selling, and manufacturing specialised items.

International Factoring

It is an efficient alternative to more traditional trade tools and helps the exporters to take advantage of the new markets abroad. Although their products are sold in the open market abroad, they are covered for credit risk as the collections made through export factoring.

Factoring in India

The various services provided by the factors could benefit the large number of suppliers in India. The need for factoring in India arises due to the limitations of the banking industry in the provision of finance, credit protection, or collection services. Moreover, an efficient system of receivables management for the manufacturers is the need of the hour. Many sellers in India, more so from small-scale industries are in need of advice on various aspects of credit extension, recovery of dues, receivable management, etc., which could be provided only by those who possess specialised knowledge of the same. This is more feasible by the factors who have a better knowledge of the affairs of the seller.

The RBI has accepted the recommendations of the "Kalyana Sundaram Committee". The factoring services in the initial stages is to be introduced only for domestic trade and commerce. Four or five zonal organisations are set up as subsidiaries of SBI and other nationalised banks. The nationalised banks for this purpose have already been shortlisted and SBI has already floated its subsidiary to look after factoring in the southern region. Private sectors are currently kept out of the factoring service. The RBI has also approached Central Government for exempting factors from stamp duty.

Although factoring is not by itself a complete answer for delays and doubts in payment, their professional approach in matters of credit is expected to improve the culture of payments. Much more has to be done in this sphere. There is good prospect for factoring in India.

Export Factoring

In the case of export factoring, four parties are involved. They are the seller (exporter), the buyer (importer), the export factor (exporting country), and the import factor (importing country).

(a) An exporter contacts the export factor in connection with his export of products. The export factor appoints an import factor in the importing country. The exporter submits a list of buyers in the importing country.

(b) The import factor evaluates the credit worthiness of the buyer and reports back to the exporter indicating the credit limits of the buyer/buyers.

(c) Once the credit limit is approved, the exporter enters into an export factoring agreement with the export factor. All export receivables are assigned to the export factor which in turn assigns them in favour of the import factor.

(d) The exporter ships the merchandise to the approved importer. All invoices bear the notification that all amount due in the invoices have been assigned and must be paid to the appointed import factor. A copy of such notification is sent to the import factor who will handle the collection. The import factor is responsible for all invoices and also for all aspects of the factoring operations.

(e) Once the authorised sales take place, the import factor is responsible for remitting the funds collected in the fastest possible way. If the importer fails to pay the amount due on the invoice on the due date, the import factor arranges to make the collection in accordance with the local practice. In case of any dispute between the exporter and importer, the import factor also resolves the issue.

(f) The import factor settles the account with the export factor as soon as it receives payment from the buyer. It should be noted that the import factor is responsible for all invoices factored, up to the approved limit.

(g) In case the approved buyer fails to pay or delays the payment, the import factor pays the receivables to the export factor at least about 100 days after the due date.

Advantages of Export Factoring

(a) Upon maturity, the exporter will recover the full value of the invoices as the payment period is guaranteed.

(b) Since the export factor undertakes the responsibility of collection, it will bear the credit risk in case of failure to effect payment by the importer.

(c) Exporter can entrust the responsibility of collection with the import factor in the respective buyers counters. Since the import factors have closer contact with the buyers, they closely monitor the sales ledgers and collect the dues as they bear the credit risk.

(d) The import factor evaluates the credit worthiness of the buyer. Since export of goods is only done after this, the exporters can expect a healthy relationship with such buyers.

(e) On presentation of the relevant invoice and support documents, the exporters can obtain 80 per cent of the invoice value as per the advance factoring arrangement. The subsequent invoices can also fetch such advances which is a flexible form of financing.

(f) Since the export factor provides a multicurrency sales ledgering system, the local exporter is able to understand the sales without any difficulty. This system makes the local exporter to concentrate on production, planning, and marketing without any worry of collection of funds.

(g) The value of currency is fluctuating from time to time. The export factor can make the necessary arrangements for appropriate forward exchange covers to protect exporters against such fluctuations.

(h) Being specialists in the field of international business, the export factor advises the exporters as to how they may have to proceed in the export trade with the help of the import factor and buyers with good reputation are identified. The sellers are able to take advantage of the situation and export quality products without any hesitation.

The buyers in the importing country can also expect quality products and prompt delivery if they make use of import factors.

Promotion of "SBI" Factors and Commercial Services Private Limited

SBI Factors and Commercial Services Private limited was set up by SBI in collaboration with Small Industries Development Bank of India (SIDBI), Union Bank of India, and State Bank of Saurashtra in February 1991, to serve the Indian industries and commercial concerns. Since the establishment of this company, the sellers of the industrial products, particularly the manufacturers have improved their cash flows through prepayment facilities, leading to increased sales, continuity of supplies and reduction in the cost of maintenance.

Underwriting

Underwriting is an assurance for the sale of shares and debentures issued by a company. It means undertaking a responsibility or giving a guarantee that the shares or debentures offered to the public will be subscribed for. The party who gives the guarantee for sale of the securities is known as the "underwriter". The dictionary meaning for the word underwriting is, "to engage in buying all the newly issued stocks of a company, not bought by the public".

Section 11 of the Companies Act of 1956 has defined "underwriting" that a person agrees to take up shares specified in the underwriting agreement if the public or other persons fail to subscribe for them. Consideration for this form of contract takes the form of payment of commission whether or not the underwriters are called upon to take up the shares.

The promoters or board of directors of a company may enter into a contract with the underwriters to take up the risk for payment of a certain commission either in the form of rupees or shares as agreed upon. In case the company's shares or debentures are not sold in the market, the underwriters themselves would take up the unsold shares.

According to Indian Companies Act of 1956, if a company fails to raise the minimum capital within 120 days from the date of issue of prospectus, the directors should return the money to the subscribers without any deduction. Moreover the promoters may not be mentally free till the time the minimum capital is raised. Section 77 of the Indian Companies Act of 1956 restricts a company from buying its own shares. Therefore, the best way for them would be to entrust the responsibility with the underwriters at a small cost known as "underwriting commission". They may entrust this work to any individual, firm, or a company. However in view of the magnitude of such an obligation, issue of shares/debentures are rarely undertaken by one person.

It would be prudent to entrust this underwriting responsibility with companies specialising in underwriting business.

Types of Underwriting

The following types of underwriting agreements are in vogue. They are

(a) Firm underwriting.
(b) Standby underwriting.
(c) Contingent underwriting.

Firm Underwriting

This signifies a definite commitment to take up a specific number of shares irrespective of number of shares subscribed by the public. In such a case, unless it has been otherwise agreed, the underwriters liability is determined without taking into account the number of shares taken up "firmly" by him. The underwriter has to apply to the firm for the number of shares he is obliged to take up, on the basis of the underwriting agreement.

Standby Underwriting

Whenever a company reserves a part of public issue for its employees or for the shareholders of promoting company, the issues go for standby underwriting. This will help the issue to add the unsubscribed portion of the reserved securities to the public issuer and the standby underwriter will take up the unsubscribed portion.

Contingent Undertaking

It is provided in the case of reserved categories only. Underwriting is generally undertaken by the following:

- public financial institutions
- banks
- investment companies or trusts of experience.

Members of the recognised stock exchange are prohibited from entering into underwriting or placing arrangements in connection with any floatation of new issues unless the permission of the stock exchange of which they are members is obtained. Such permission is granted subject to certain conditions. Members are not allowed to undertake underwriting commitment of more than 5 per cent of the public issue.

The procedure for underwriting is as follows: the underwriters issue application forms for shares or debentures to members of the public and such application forms are stamped with their name. These are known as "marked applications". If there is a sole underwriter who has underwritten the whole issue, his stamp is not required. The company can thus find out as to how many shares have been applied for, through that particular underwriter.

SEBI has issued guidelines for issue of capital by companies. The guidelines relating to underwriting are enumerated as follows:

(a) Underwriting is mandatory for the full issue, and minimum requirement of 90 per cent subscription is also mandatory for each issue of capital to public. The number of underwriters would be decided by the issuers.
(b) If the company does not receive 90 per cent of issued amount from public subscription plus accepted development of underwriters within 120 days from the date of opening of the issue, the company shall refund the amount of subscription. In the case of disputed development, the company should refund the subscription if the above conditions are not met.
(c) The lead manager(s) must satisfy themselves about the net worth of the underwriters and the outstanding commitments and disclose the same to SEBI.
(d) The underwriting agreement may be filed with the stock exchanges.

Underwriting should be only for issue to the public which will exclude reserved or preferential allotment to reserved categories. In other words, underwriting is mandatory only to the extent of net offer to the public. Minimum subscription clause is applicable for both the public and rights issue with a right remuneration. The lead manager should satisfy himself about the ability of the underwriters to discharge their underwriting obligations. A statement may be incorporated in the prospectus of issue that in the opinion of lead manager, the underwriters assets are adequate to meet their obligations.

Government has issued guidelines relating to the underwriting of capital issues to be followed by the stock exchanges, merchant bankers, and other agencies associated with the management of the public issues of capital. These should be followed along with SEBI guidelines.

(a) No member should be allowed to undertake an underwriting commitment of more than 5 per cent of the public issue.
(b) The underwriting of the public issues should be distributed among the members of the stock exchanges as widely as possible.
(c) The stock exchanges will satisfy themselves that the company's securities which are being underwritten would be officially qualified on a recognised stock exchange.
(d) The members of the stock exchange desiring to underwrite will satisfy themselves that the company has duly coupled with the listing regulations.

(e) The governing bodies of recognised stock exchange shall have the discretion to refuse permission or impose such conditions in respect of the underwriting of securities by members of stock exchanges as they deem necessary in the special circumstances of any given case.

(f) The stock exchanges should prescribe procedures for advance action to be taken up by the companies, merchant bankers, etc., for making underwriting arrangement so as to ensure that all the relevant information is furnished in the draft prospectus which is submitted to the stock exchange for approval.

Rights of Underwriters

The rights of underwriters are:

(a) Right to have full information about the company and the issue.
(b) Right to have sufficient number of applications and the offer documents.
(c) Right to sub-underwrite.
(d) Right to receive their remuneration or underwriting commission as per the agreement.

Underwriting Agreement

It is an agreement entered into, between the company and the underwriters agreeing to underwrite the proposed issue of the company. The agreement should provide the amount of issue agreed to be underwritten by the underwriters in case of under subscription and the commission payable for such undertaking. It should also stipulate that in the event of under subscription, the underwriters or their nominees would take up the shares for which they are liable or at least that quantity of issue which would make up the minimum subscription, within three or four weeks of the closing of subscription list. The agreement should provide that the underwriters would be discharged of their underwriting obligations to the extent of applications bearing their stamps.

Provisions of the Companies Act Affecting Underwriting

(a) According to clause (ii) of Section 11 of the Indian Companies Act, it is essential to mention the names of underwriters in the prospectus. The directors also should express their opinion that the resources of the underwriters are sufficient to discharge their obligations.

(b) The company should disclose in the statutory report a brief description of each underwriting contract and the particulars of any commission paid or payable to any director, manager, or association of underwriters.

(c) If the whole of issue has been underwritten by one person, he is responsible to subscribe for all the shares or debentures that have not been subscribed by the public. In such a case, it is not necessary to know the number of applications which had originated through the underwriter and those which had flowed directly to the company. In case, part of the issue has been underwritten or where there are a number of underwriters, a certain amount of difficulty may arise in determining the liability of each underwriter, such a difficulty may arise in deciding the basis on which the unmarked applications, that is, the applications which have directly flowed to the company should be allocated among the different underwriters.

This can be done in two following ways:

(a) The unmarked applications are allotted in the proportion of gross amount of capital underwritten as reduced by value of the marked applications.
(b) Marked application which is a common method.

Future of Underwriting Business in India

With the introduction of free pricing of securities, underwriting business is undergoing tremendous changes. There are reports of under-subscription of quite a few public issues and consequent development on underwriting. Capital adequately assumes significance for fulfilling underwriting obligations in the event of development, which is enough only with financial institutes and commercial banks. Merchant bankers' foremost test is to enhance their capital base. With mega issues coming in large number, it becomes essential to go on for syndicate approach. There is already a forceful demand from underwriters associations for upload increase in underwriting commission. In the free financing scenario, a liberal free market driven fee structure is likely to emerge. Brokers are also demanding for bank finance to be made available to carry on the business of underwriting.

Merchant bankers and underwriters will also have to develop a large investor base and network throughout India since they would be required to approach the investor directly and would also have to provide efficient secondary market services. The merchant bankers and underwriters will have to be selective in new floatations. The fundamental strength of the companies, will, therefore come under sharper focus and there will be increasing demand for more and more financial information and disclosures about the performance of the companies. The underwriters will have to develop their own assessment network for critical appraisal of projects. The market-driven forces will, therefore, help the capital market to attain greater depth and maturity in the coming years.

At present, the underwriters can play an effective role in promoting joint-stock companies as the Government of India's policy is in favour of privatisation. A number of private companies are likely to be promoted with good prospects awaiting for underwriters.

Merchant Banking

Introduction

The term "merchant banking" came from the early years of banking when only merchants required the facilities of finance. The term has been retained because it reflects the nature of those banks which provide financial services to the business community. When a promoter of a joint-stock company wishes to raise capital or borrow from the capital market, the first person or institution that can be of immense help is the merchant banker. Merchant bankers constitute the backbone of the public issue and they do whatever is required to make the public issue a grand success.

According to Rule 2(e) of SEBI (merchant bankers) Rules 1992, the definition of "merchant banker" is, "A merchant banker is any person who is engaged in the business of issue management either by making arrangements regarding selling, buying or subscribing to securities or acting as manager, consultant, advisor or rendering corporate advisory service in relation to such issue management".

Merchant banking is a process of consultation leasing, portfolio services, asset management, euro credit, loan syndication, and other allied services. It is a strategy activity concerned with mobilising savings of people and channelising the same towards a productive purpose.

In the 1980s, merchant banking which was, earlier, a corporate service emerged as a financial service. Grindlays Bank set up its merchant banking division in 1969 to undertake public issue management and financial consultancy, which was followed by other foreign banks. SBI started its merchant banking division in 1973 followed by ICICI, the first development financial institution to start merchant banking service in 1974. Most of the public sector banks promoted subsidiaries exclusively to look after merchant banking activity. Even non-banking financial companies, corporates, stockbrokers promoted merchant banking organisations.

In 1992, SEBI had brought out a series of guidelines, norms, and regulations to mould merchant banking as a professional service in the country. For instance, it is mandatory for a merchant banker to register with SEBI to undertake activities related to (a) capital issue (b) mergers and acquisitions (c) portfolio management.

In today's scenario the merchant banker and management consultant undertake advisory services to the corporate sector. The merchant banker advises corporations and firms relating to opening of issues, receiving loans etc., which the management consultant do too. The management consultant has a wide area operations like production, marketing, personnel relations, finance, etc. But they take statutory recognition to undertake capital market-related activities only which has enabled the merchant banker to cater to the needs of the corporate sector.

A merchant banker's main function is acceptance of bill of exchange drawn on other parties. Many of todays leading merchant banks have their origin in trading activities. As large and trusted merchants in the business, they found that as an additional source of income they could lend then "Good name" at a suitable commission, to the bill of exchange of lesser known traders. As a result of such banking, the bill could be discounted in the market at a finer rate of interest than would have been possible. The business proved profitable for many of the merchants that they concentrated on their bill accepting role rather than on business. Thus, merchant banks got the name "accepting house". The merchant banking provide a number of specialized services like lending money on short or medium-terms or advising companies on the best method of raising long-term loans. Merchant banking may also run something akin to a "marriage bureau" – matching companies wishing to expand by amalgamation or help fight against a takeover bid. They provide fund management services and advices on the best methods of using these funds profitably. Many merchant banks also run their own unit trusts and also manage pension funds for their clients.

In the United Kingdom, merchant bankers lend, borrow, underwrite, deal on securities and provide other banking services. Merchant banks in India do not take up banking business. They manage and underwrite new issues. In fact, it is not an exaggeration to say that there is no capital market, particularly primary market, without merchant bankers. They can underwrite the whole or a part of public issue. At the time of registration and also throughout, the merchant banker has to satisfy the SEBI norms of capital adequacy requirement of INR five crores. A non-banking finance company cannot act as a merchant banker. The guidelines of SEBI stipulate that merchant bankers conduct their business with a sense of integrity and fairness to all concerned.

Functions of Merchant Bankers

Merchant bankers offer a range of services such as determining the type of securities to be issued, drafting prospectus and application forms, compliance with the SEBI guidelines, appointment of registration to deal with the share issue-related activities such as receiving applications and effecting transfers, arrangement of underwriting, sub-underwriting, placing of issues, selection of brokers, bankers to issue, publicity and advertising agents, printers, and so on.

Management of Issues of Securities

The merchant bankers are also called the managers to issue as they undertake the following activities in the primary market.

- Drafting of prospectus and application forms
- Compliance with procedural formalities
- Providing advice on issues related to capital structure of a company
- Decide different types of instruments offered and the terms and conditions associated with each instrument to the issue
- Advice on how to price the issue particularly in today's context of free pricing. This service is very strategic in nature
- Evaluation and appraisal of project report
- Finalising the appointment of bankers, underwriters, brokers, registrar, advertising agents to issue, etc
- Coordinating and holding press, brokers', and investors' meetings
- Ensuring and obtaining subscription to the issue
- Getting the basis of allotment approved from stock exchange
- Finalising publicity strategy and advertising material, printing matter, and so on
- Getting shares listed on selected stock exchanges.

Loan Syndication

Sometimes merchant bankers might be approached for loans by its clients. In such cases, the merchant banker surveys the market and acquires loans from rich organisations and also sometimes from foreign organisations to be invested in the country. It helps its clients and at the same time increases the foreign currency reserve of the country.

Off-shore Banking

Merchant bankers are now allowed to get loans from other countries and invest it in safe and profitable ventures. Here the merchant banker receives loans from a foreign country which can be invested in the home country but the service cannot be done vice versa.

Corporate Advisory Services

Merchant bankers act as advisors to the corporate bodies on strategic issues relating to arrangement of financial collaboration, disinvestment, restricting and sale of unity, identification of joint venture passers and strategic investors, etc.

Project Counselling Services

Merchant bankers provide services such as preparation of project reports, analysing the financial viability of the profits, estimation of financial requirements, planning the financial structure, getting the project evaluated with funding organisations, documentation, etc.

Provide Venture Capital

Merchant bankers provide venture capital for risky, yet profitable technology oriented projects. Venture capital is provided to new entrepreneurs, commercialisation of new technologies, and support to small- and medium-scale business units in the manufacturing and the service sectors, for research and development projects, projects relating to expansion, modernisation, diversification, etc.

Portfolio Management Services

Portfolio management is the process of balancing the risk and return of a set of securities held by the investor at a given point of time. Merchant bankers make an exhaustive study of the market and economy on issues relating to monetary and fiscal policies of the government and their impact on different sectors of the economy and industry. Merchant bankers advise their clients how best they can balance the three basic properties of investment, namely, liquidity, solvency, and profitability. They also suggest which sector of the economy can be relied upon for better returns with least or moderate degree of risk. They carefully analyse the financial statements of the shortlisted companies which offer liable scope for both short-term and long-term investment.

Marketing and Underwriting of Public Issue

Marketing of public issue involves several key functions such as launching of publicity campaign through print and electronic media. Investors' conference are also organised for addressing the specific questioning of the investing public. Since the issue management is a time-bound programme, merchant bankers race against time to make the public issue a grand success. Merchant bankers underwrite, for a fee, the whole or part of public issue, as an assurance delivery mechanism, to the promoters of the issue, that is, the merchant banker agrees to subscribe the unsubscribed portion of the public issue. A well-marketed public issue minimises such risk for the merchant banker. As per the SEBI regulations, every public issue needs to be underwritten. The details of underwriting agreement have to be stated in the prospectus.

Debenture Trusteeship

Merchant bankers act as debenture trustee for the assets against which a charge is created. The fixed assets of the company are mortgaged in favour of trustees. They are expected to project the interests of the debenture holders in the event of default of the company. A trust deed is executed between the company and the trustee. The details of the asset under the charge, particulars of the debentures, and the obligations of the trustees are mentioned clearly in the trust deed.

Processor of Mergers and Acquisitions

Merchant bankers facilitate a smooth process of mergers and acquisitions which otherwise is a very complex and long procedure. Merger is a combination of two or more firms in which only one firm would survive and the other would cease to exist, its assets and liabilities being taken over by the surviving firm. Acquisition implies taking over the controlling interest in a company by another company. With the economic reforms, the number of mergers and acquisitions is on the rise in the name of consideration.

Arrangement of SWAP

SWAP is another trading instrument. "SWAP" is a derivative in which two counterparties agree to exchange one stream of cash flow against another stream, these streams are called the legs of the SWAPS. It can be used to hedge certain risks such as interest rate risk, or to speculate changes in the expected direction of underlying prices. It is a combination of forward by two counterparts. It is arranged to reap the benefits arising from the fluctuations either in the currency market or interest market or any other market. By arranging SWAPS, merchant bankers can earn additional income in the form of brokerage.

Promotion of Mutual Funds and Stock Option Schemes

Merchant banker also promotes mutual funds and stock option schemes which is employees' participation scheme to invest in new issues of the company, as part-owners of the organisation.

SEBI prescribed a legal framework for the operation of merchant bankers in the primary market. This framework consists of a series of guidelines for the strict compliance by merchant bankers. Their activities are supervised and regulated by SEBI which monitors issues relating to issue of corporate securities. If the merchant banks are the subsidiaries of commercial banks, then these also come under the purview of RBI. If the merchant banks want to raise public deposits, they have to conduct themselves as per the RBI guidelines.

According to the Narasimham Committee, merchant banks have large degree of potential to emerge financially strong and act independently in the deregulated Indian economy. SEBI has issued clear guidelines to merchant bankers in respect of capital adequacy norms, responsibility towards investors about pricing, fixation of premium for issues, disclosure norms, and so on.

The following are the salient features of SEBI's legal framework on the operation of merchant bankers.

(a) The registration with SEBI is compulsory for the merchant banker to carry out his activities. Based on the activities undertaken, the merchant bankers can be classified into four categories. A category I merchant banker can act as advisor, consultant, manager, underwriter, and portfolio manager. Only category I merchant bankers can act as lead manager to a security issue. Registration is mandatory only for category I merchant bankers. The merchant banker has to obtain separate certificates of registration from SEBI to carry out the activities of underwriters and portfolio managers.

(b) SEBI grants certificate of registration only after considering all pertinent matters such as professional qualifications, infrastructural facilities, number of employees, past experience, market regulation, and ability to organise the transactions relating to issue effectively and efficiently.

(c) Every merchant banker has to pay the prescribed fee at the time of registration and also to get his registration renewed from year to year.

(d) SEBI prescribed a minimum net worth requirement for each category of merchant banker and registration is permitted only subject to the condition that net worth requirement will be maintained all through. Every merchant banker has to file half-yearly unaudited financial results with SEBI to facilitate time to time monitoring. The minimum net worth for category I merchant banker is INR one crore, category II is INR 50 lakhs, category III is INR 20 lakhs, and for category IV, it is nil.

Obligations and Responsibilities

The following are the obligations and responsibilities of every merchant banker.

- He has to render at all times, high standards of service with diligence and proper care
- He has to maintain high standards of integrity and fairness in all his dealings
- He should not make any exaggerated statements about his qualifications or his capabilities
- He should not misguide his clients
- He has to exercise independent professional judgement
- He should not conceal with his clients the possible sources of conflict of duties and interest while providing services
- He has to endeavour to render the best possible service to the clients
- He should not take part in manipulating such as rigging, sharing price sensitive information with others

- He should abide by the provisions of SEBI guidelines, rules, and regulations as applicable to merchant bankers
- Category II merchant bankers can act as an advisor, consultant, co-manager, underwriter, and portfolio manager
- Category III merchant bankers can act as an advisor, underwriter, and consultant to all
- Category IV is not eligible.

Merchant Bankers as Lead Managers

The size of the public issue decides the number of lead managers. For instance, two lead managers are appointed, for an issue of size less than INR 50 crores. If the size is in the range of INR 50 crores to INR 100 crores, there can be three lead managers.

Duties and responsibilities of lead manager

There should be specific agreement between every lead manager and the client, or the issuing companies, setting out mutual rights, liabilities, obligations relating to such issues and in particular to disclosures, allotment, and refund. These details must be furnished to SEBI at least one month before the opening of the issue for subscription.

The lead manager is responsible for the accuracy and exactness of contents in the prospectus. A diligence certificate must be filed with the SEBI by the lead manager at least two weeks before the opening of the issue for subscription specifying that:

- all the legal requirements underlying the issue are fully complied with
- the contents of the prospectus are in conformity with the available documents
- the disclosure is true and fair and adequate to enable the investors to make a well-informed decision as to the investment in the proposed issue.

A merchant banker has to disclose to the SEBI all the details about his professional activities such as information relating to its activities as manager, underwriter etc. SEBI can take up inspection of the books of accounts, records, and documents of a merchant banker to ensure that the rules and regulations are properly complied with. In case these rules and regulations are not complied with, the registration may be suspended or even cancelled. The SEBI may even impose penalties for non-compliance of conditions for registration and contravention of the regulations. Thus, the merchant banker is made more responsible and accountable.

13
Banking Technology

Liberalisation throughout India has affected all sectors of the economy, and the centre of all these activities is the Indian banking industry. In such changing environment, to meet emerging needs, the operations in banks needed immediate automation to provide services comparable to best international standards and to match technological changes taking place in other countries.

Indian banks undertook very little efforts for modernisation in respect of Work Technologies. Work technology is inducting technology in bank working activities particularly in the areas of introduction of computers and communication networks till the early 1980s. The concept of bank computerisation practically started after 1980–1981 and more precisely gained the pace of computerisation in the year 1983–1984 after setting up a committee under the chairmanship of the then Deputy Governor of RBI, Dr C Ranga Rajan in 1983. The committee was set up to study the possibilities and stages involved in bank computerisation and to prepare guidelines for the same. The report which was submitted by the committee in 1984 is known as First Ranga Rajan Committee Report on Bank Mechanisation. Another committee was constituted in 1988, again under the chairmanship of Dr C Ranga Rajan, the then Deputy Governor of RBI to draw up a perspective plan on computerisation of banks for a five year period from 1990–1994.

The four objectives of computerisation in banking are to improve: (a) customer service (b) housekeeping (c) decision making, and (d) productivity and profitability. The main objective of computerisation at the branch level is to improve customer service, quality of housekeeping, and generation of data for better management control. At the regional and head office levels, the purpose of computerisation is to store, analyse and retrieve data received from branches so as to generate information speedily for strengthening internal control over branches for policy formulation.

Stand-Alone Computer System

The single-user computer system is a small system, which as its name implies, can be used by only one person at a time. Stand-alone systems are best suited for decision-making processes which involve processing and analysis of data. Today's stand-alone systems are also capable of handling multimedia, high-quality graphics, fax messages, etc. The stand-alone computers installed in the front office of the Indian banks are also called Advanced Ledger Posting Machines (ALPMs).

Multi-user Computer Networking

In this system, computers are based on centralised processing concept. All the information is kept and processed at main machine and various terminals are attached to the main computer. The main computer can store a huge amount of information at high processing speed. Large number of users can be connected to the main computer. Each user is given a terminal system like "UNIX" which is used as the operating system. Most of the banking systems are developed using centralised computing concepts. Most of the RDBMSs (Related Data Based Management Systems) and other DBMSs (Data base Management Systems) use "UNIX" platform. In most of the computerised information systems, the data is processed at one EDP (Entrepreneurial Development Programme) department. The EDP department has to process large volume of data everyday for which considerable amount of infrastructure and maintenance is required. Availability of corporate-level information at one location is possible.

The computerisation of the branch level can be used to:

(a) Provide better and speedy customer service.
(b) Improve house-keeping services.
(c) Analyse the branch-level data for decision making.
(d) To generate various types of reports.

The terminals or PCs can be connected together with one powerful PC acting as server. Various productivity tools can be used to analyse the branch level data to make branch-level policy decisions. Security measures play an important role in branch-level computerisation because of online banking applications. Most of the security features are in-built in the operating system and in the hardware, such as use of password protection at different levels, various access rights to system and data locking facilities, etc.

With total branch computerisation, the customers' business transactions are done with the help of computers. This is a real-time online banking. Electronic Fund Transfer (EFT) can be used to facilitate the automated transaction and processing of messages and funds from one branch/bank to another branch/bank.

Computerisation at regional/zonal office act in between branches and head office. They exercise effective control over the functioning of the branches and collection of data from them and transmit them to head office after amalgamation. The most common jobs performed by the regional office/zonal office are: (a) branch profile (b) inter-branch reconciliation (c) credit monitoring (d) personnel data management, etc.

The head office of a bank is responsible for bank-level planning and controlling functions and land policy decisions. The head office activities are divided into various functional areas like (a) operations (b) planning (c) personnel (d) international business (e) services, etc. Most of the banking business is carried out at the branches. The connecting authorities at head office, control and support the branch activities. To do this, the proper flow of management information is needed from branches to head office. This information may be provided by the branches by sending various reports at regular intervals. The purpose of the computerised credit information system is to provide comprehensive credit information that could be used for credit planning and monitoring. Banks invest substantial share of their assets in approved securities to meet the liquidity and current liabilities. The average yields from such investments are always lower than the other investments like commercial lending and personal loans. Various analytical tools can be used to analyse the investments. The target is to increase the yield on any investment. Various software packages are available that help to build mathematical and analytical models to solve the problems and can be used to select and manage the investment portfolio and maximise return on investment. The inflow of funds comes to bank from deposits, interest on loans and advances, return from approved securities, etc., as outflow constitutes interest on deposits. To increase their profits, the banks should limit their balances with RBI and investments in government securities to the minimum stipulated in the regulations. The fund management task is very complicated due to day-to-day variations in withdrawals and deposits. The communication network connecting such branches to head office computer may play a very important role to provide online information about the business position of such branches. This helps to do better fund management.

Lans and Wans

Local Area Network (LAN)

A computer network is basically a data communication network mainly used to share data, hardware and software resources and to improve the flow of information within an organisation or beyond. The computer network that links computers and peripherals within a localised area, for example, within a building is known as LAN. Computers and related equipments can be connected through nodes placed anywhere in the network. Generally LAN does not extend beyond 100 metres. However, it can be up to a maximum speed of one km and the number of devices supported may also vary from two to as many as 1000.

The way in which the devices are interconnected is known as Topology (layout). There are two forms of local area network design used in information transmission, centralised control, and distributed control in a bank. The popular centralised control networks are Star, Tree, and Loop topologies, while that of distributed controls are Ring and Bus topologies. Each topology has its advantages as well as disadvantages. When any two pieces of equipment are connected, effective communication will take place only when they talk and understand the same language. There should be a standard communication protocol. Protocols define message formats and the rules for message exchange. The networking software can run over any standard network. Generally, the network operating system falls into two categories. Those that use DOS as the file system on the server and those that use UNIX as the file system. The concept of LAN is becoming popular to branch computerisation in banks, especially where front office computerisation is concerned.

The advantages of using LAN in banks are that:

(a) The information stored on the host computer is available to all users of the system. Therefore, there is no necessity of duplication of database.
(b) The expensive resources such as computer hardware and software can be shared by several users. This brings down the overall cost of computerisation.
(c) Since all the terminals are intelligent terminals, the processing load is shared between the various machines and there is no overloading on any single machine.

There are also a few shortcomings of LAN, such as:

(a) Maintenance cost of such system is high since it has to be done frequently.
(b) Security risks are higher, since each user accesses the host computer independently.
(c) Complicated software has to be installed for data management.

Wide Area Network (WAN)

Wide Area Network (WAN) can be defined as a large-scale computer network spread over a span of sizeable geographic area, normally using the telecommunication network. In the banking sector, the WANs are generally used to interconnect branches with the regional offices, and regional/zonal offices to head offices, etc.

As the Wide Area Networks (WAN) are formed based on the telecommunication network and hence the type of network will differ on the method of telecommunication used. Computers can be linked by using ordinary telephone lines which is called dial-up network. The connectivity can also be established by using satellite links or microwave links. There could also be a combination of these methods in single network set-up. Microwave systems are capable of broadband transmission. The signals in a microwave system are transmitted directly from a dish antenna to a receiving dish antenna at the next microwave station located in a direct line of sight, not more than about 25 miles away. Each relay station can catch and boost the data signals, passing them on to other receiving stations.

Satellite communications network is an alternative to wire telecommunications. Text, data, voice, and video information are converted to radio waves at earth station and are beamed up over a broadband transmission channel to a satellite. The satellite relays the data back to the earth station or an antenna on top of a tall building at the receiving location across the country or around the world. Such transmission takes only fraction of a second. Each computer connected in a Wide Area Network, requires connectivity to the telecommunication line, a modem, and a communication software that will take care of the transmission and reception of data. The branch computers can also be linked with regional office/zonal office computers through WAN for faster transfer of data and various reports to them, which may help at greater extent in the quality of decision making and effective monitoring. Use of local area network, client server computing, RDBMS packages like "ORACLE", "Sybase", etc., and front-end tools like "Power Builder", "Developer 2000". Visual tools may provide better performance with considerable price. The use of various methods helps to analyse the regional office level or zonal office level data for manpower planning, credit monitoring, etc. The data, reports, or proposals can also be directly sent to respective departments of the head office by regional office/zonal office for quick decision and response. This may reduce the higher computerisation expenditure. The head office can also take decision for investments or can submit returns to regulating authorities in time. In the current technological environment the transfer of information at appropriate time and place is an important part of day-to-day business.

Uninterruptible Power System (UPS)

A UPS provides clean, reliable, AC power to computer system protecting them from power blackouts, brownouts, swells, sags, surges, and interface. In case of power failure, UPS attached with the file server automatically starts power supply to the file server or to the main computer to reduce the chances of data loss. The workstations and other terminals are also attached with the UPS. The general feature of a UPS is an inverter and battery charger with automatic change over of power supply from battery or load. The UPS are of two types: (a) online UPS (b) offline UPS. In banks' computerisation, online UPS are used. In online UPS, the main 230V input current is converted into 48V DC and from battery charger-cum-rectifier is then converted to a 230V AC; even in case of main supply available the power is supplied to the computer systems. In case of power failures, the batteries supply the 48V DC. It comes back automatically to the normal state when the main supply recovers.

Core Banking

It is a centralised branch computerisation model in which branches are connected to a central host. It incorporates branch automation modules and online multiple delivery channels like ATM, ABB, debit card, tele-banking, internet banking etc., under one roof. In core banking, there is a central database for the bank and transactions are done centrally and online. It offers integrated products and services to customers round-the-clock. There is scope for induction of modern banking services and one single software for all the branches and is operated on the bank's WAN infrastructure.

Business Components

The business components of core banking are the following:

- To have retail customer banking modules
- Deposits, loans, bills, remittances, lockers, clearings, etc
- Trade finance/FOREX modules, government business modules
- To have corporate finance and service branch modules
- To have enhanced MIS modules
- To have modules for business intelligence
- To integrate with the existing ATMs, tele-banking, debit card, kiosks, and other delivery channels
- To have any branch banking, internet banking, and call centre
- To interface with existing corporate systems like treasury, IBR, centralised accepting system, HRMS, ALM, credit appraisal and management, credit monitoring and NPA management, etc.

Benefits

The benefits of core banking are the following:

- Enables establishment of reliable centralised data repository to the bank
- Standardisation of branch automation software using a single version
- Enables centralised management information, decision support, and executive information systems
- Efficient and effective MIS, ALM, risk management, etc., using control data pool
- Facilitates Business Process Reengineering (BPR) to streamline the existing processes

- Cost of implementation for further branches and delivery channels relatively cheaper
- Servers are not mandatory at branch locations
- Attracts higher interest in the beginning
- Quick adoption of software changes and changes done only at the central site.

Essential Requirements

The essential requirements of core banking are the following:

Creation of Primary Data Centre

- For housing the central server for online transactions
- The central database will be used for all customer-centric delivery channel services integrated with the Core Banking Services (CBS) and for the bank's various corporate business requirements
- To be managed round the clock to offer 24x7 service to customers
- Skilled activities such as database administration, back-ups, network monitoring, on-call support, troubleshooting, parameterisation, customisation, support of delivery channels are performed at the data centre.

Business Process Re-engineering (BPR)

- To help the bank in re-aligning existing business processes in line with the benefits provided by the new technology platform
- To keep the bank in taking advantage of the best business practices available in the technology platform to provide more efficient services
- To align processes with the technology platform in order to provide the bank with the capability to deliver enhanced value to their customer and also gain from these changed processes.

Disaster Recovery Site (DRS)

- To avoid disruption in the business activities of CBS branches due to central system or network failures
- To ensure non-stop functioning of branches and online delivery channels integrated with CBS
- To act as a back-up for providing a reliable and continuous processing environment.

Specialised Consultancy

- CBS being a critical project with complexities of multilevel delivery systems involving higher investment and manpower requirement, a specialised consultancy services was suggested for centralised banking.

- Consultant to have expertise/experience in implementing CBS in other banks
- To assist in designing, crystallising requirements, and formulation of implementing strategies
- To advice the bank on all aspects of centralised banking requirements
- To proceed further, after getting expert recommendations/suggestions of the specific consultants.

Infrastructure

Software

The software to comprise:

- Branch functional modules
- Delivery channel requirements like ATMs, tele-banking, internet banking, and information kiosks.
- Interfaces to integrate systems like NDS, SFMS, RTGS, CFMS, etc
- Tools for business intelligence and management information.

Hardware

- The Hardware at the data centre and DRS is "sized" based on the transaction volume of the proposed branches.

Networking

- Leased lines of WAN is to be used as primary communication channel for CBS
- Adequate redundancies are built-in, to address network failures
- ISDN link is used as back-up.

Electronic Banking

With the introduction and implementation of recent technology in banking, electronic devices are making the payments of cash and non-cash payments easy and efficient. The introduction of Automated Teller Machines (ATMs) and the plastic cards has given the banking customers the facility of round-the-clock (24 hours) banking.

The concept of Electronic Banking is becoming popular with individuals as well as corporations in India with the introduction of computers in Indian banks.

- Any Time Banking (ATM)
- Anywhere Banking
- Home Banking (Corporate and Personal).

Electronic Payment Systems

The major routine processing in day-to-day banking operations starts at the cash counter or teller counters in the banks. The idea behind the electronic payment system is that one or few activities related to the payment should be done with the help of a computer.

ATMs

The growth of technology has changed the payment system across the world during the past decades. The introduction of Automated Teller Machines (ATMs) has given facility to the customers for banking beyond the banking hours.

An ATM is a device located on or off the bank's premises to receive and dispense cash round-the-clock. Customers can also use ATMs for depositing cash, cheques, obtaining balance, obtaining statement of last few transactions in his account, requesting cheque books, payment of card bills, and for transferring funds from one account to another.

A customer who wishes to utilise the service of ATMs will have access to it only with an ATM card. The ATM card consists of a Personal Identification Number (PIN) which is known only to the customer. A customer who wishes to transact through the ATM will have to place the ATM card in the slot before starting his operation and he will be able to transact his business through interactive visual display unit and the keyboard.

There are two types of ATMs – exterior ATMs and interior ATMs. Exterior ATMs are located in various places like shopping centres, airports, railway stations with or without drive-in facility, while the interior ATMs are located within the bank premises. ATMs which are directly interactive with the bank's computers are known as "online ATMs" and the others are known as offline ATMs. Online ATMs require the support of effective telecommunication facility. In some foreign banks' ATMs, the conversion of currency is also possible. Interactive and Voice recogniser ATMs are also installed to facilitate the customers to interface in multi-language.

Security Aids

There are various security aids provided in ATMs. There are access locks which covers the key pads, monitors, etc., and opens only with the ATM card. There are also video surveillance and recording system as a precaution against ATM crimes.

Advantages of ATMs

To the Customers

- ATMs provide services for 24 hours, 7 days a week, and 365 days a year
- Service is quick and efficient

- Privacy in transaction
- Free from errors
- On networking, cardholder can access a service at any location regardless of where he maintains account
- Wider flexibility in withdrawals
- Fund transfer across the branches/banks anywhere.

To Banks

- Alternative to extended banking hours
- Crowding at bank counter considerably reduced
- Service is cheaper, if there are large number of transactions
- Alternative to new branches and reduction in operating expenses
- Cash transportation and cash handling is avoided
- Can be installed in any form as wall unit, window unit or lobby unit
- Relieves bank employees to focus on more analytical and innovative work
- Increased market penetration.

Personal Identification Number (PIN)

Every bank customer is given an ATM card connected to his account. A magnetic strip is fixed on the back of these cards. The strip holds certain information about the customer such as his account number, personal identification number (PIN), etc. After the card is inserted into the appropriate slot, the ATM or POS (Personal Operating System) device reads the account number with the number embossed on the card itself and checks the number with the information stored into the database available to it through an attached computer. Once the card is found valid, the ATM/POS terminal prompts the cardholder to enter his/her PIN, that is, personal identification number. Once this PIN is entered by the cardholder, the ATM/POS terminal checks whether it is correct or not. Once the PIN matches with the one stored in the computer, the cardholder is allowed to proceed with his transaction on the ATM/POS terminal. A PIN is similar to the password that a user of a computer has to give when he/she wants to use it. Banks which issue cards to use ATMs/POS terminals etc., also give a PIN along with the card. The PIN is randomly generated sequence of digits which is printed on paper and is automatically folded and sealed before it even reaches the bank's own officials. The seal is to be opened only by the cardholder and has to be kept secure.

Electromagnetic Cards

In the modern day commerce, cards have acquired a fairly prominent and pervasive role with the increasing use of credit cards. The society is moving towards cashless transactions. In India however, the use of credit cards is restricted to small value and mostly personal transactions. The two international credit card giants, viz, Visa International and Master Card International are already present in India and are poised to make deeper inroads in the untapped Indian market.

There are different types of cards, some of which are discussed below.

- Charge Card
- Debit Card
- Credit Card
- Smart Card or Chip Card
- Restricted Card/Member Card

Credit Cards

Generally a bank enters into an agreement with its customer and issues the customer a credit card. A credit card is a small plastic card around 8.5 cm by 5.5 cm. It has the name and the account number of its holder embossed on it. In addition, the date up to which the card is valid is also embossed and a specimen signature panel is on the reverse. The card issuer should normally get the cardholder to sign on the specimen signature panel in his presence before parting with the credit card. The limit up to which the cardholder can make purchases in a month is also informed to the cardholder. This limit is called the card limit. Many card issuers being banks, also allow withdrawals of cash for emergency purposes and levy a service fee to such withdrawals. Many banks also have credit cards which double up as ATM cards.

A credit card is similar to charge card where the transactions are charged to the account with the total value of transactions debited to the cardholder's account once in a month. The difference between the credit and charge card is that in case of charge card, the account becomes payable immediately on debit to the account. In case of credit cards, the cardholder has the option to pay the entire account as soon as the account is debited or he may choose to pay only certain percentage of the amount debited and he gets the credit for the rest, that is, he can pay in monthly installments later. However, a service fee is charged on the rest of the deferred payment.

Charge Card

In these cards, transactions are accumulated over a period of time, generally a month, and the total amount charged, that is, debited to the account. The credit cardholder is given about 25 to 50 days time to credit his account, in case there are insufficient funds in his account at the time of debit. Since the transactions are only accumulated it is only charged, that is, not debited to the account immediately, such cards are called charged cards.

Debit Card

The only difference between a debit and a credit card is that the account of the cardholder is debited as soon as the transaction is notified to the issuer. If the balance is insufficient to cover the debit, the difference becomes payable immediately or else a service fee is levied. If the amount payable is overdue for a long period, the card may be cancelled.

Smart Card

A Smart card looks exactly like any other plastic card or an ATM card with an Integrated Circuit (IC chip) installed. The IC contains memory, may contain a processor, and communicates with the external world through contacts on the surface of the card. The size, position and utility of the contacts are specified by an international standard (ISO 7816), so that cards can interact with a variety of equipment. The future of the smart card in the banking and financial sector is very bright and it is evident that leading players in electronic funds transfer have already realised this. Earlier in 1993, Natwest Bank of the UK announced its Mandex System based on smart cards. Visa and Master card have also joined hands with Europe's largest ATM network "Europay", to set standards for smart card based electronic fund transfer systems. In India smart card was introduced in the year 2001. One of the most primary features of the smart card is security to prevent card related crimes and frauds. Chips for smart cards are not publicly available. There may be unique personal identification number (PIN) for each pockets as the smart card has different pockets for storage of cash for different type of transactions. A smart card will have a PIN.

Member Card

This is used exclusively by a member of a club or chain of hotels. For example, the Taj card is a card issued by the management of Taj Group of Hotels to be used by patrons of their hotels. The cards are used in their hotels only.

The advantages of a card system (all types of cards) are as under:

- It is convenient to the cardholder to carry a credit card in his wallet and make trouble free travel or purchase. It allows him to draw cash at his convenience too
- It inculcates a sense of financial discipline in the cardholder
- It provides a proof of purchase through banking channels to strengthen the cardholder's position in case of disputes with sellers, etc
- It extends additional facilities like insurance cover/discount, etc., to the cardholder

- To the business community credit card helps to maintain systematic accounting since sale receipts are routed through banking channels
- Credit cards help the merchants through advertising and promotional support on a national scale. Credit cards avoid all the cost and safety problems involved in handling cash
- Helps in establishing banking relationship with new customers
- Provides additional customer service to the existing clients
- Scope and potential for better profitability out of share earned from the trader's turnover to banks
- Savings of expenses on cash holding/stationery printing and man power to handle clearing transactions for banks.

The acceptance of the card is of two types:

(a) In manual mode, merchants have to verify the genuinity of the card from the warning bulletins which is supplied regularly. Manual acceptance is recommended at merchants with low ticket size except for jewellery, electronic goods, handicraft, hotels, and air tickets, where chances of fraudulent transactions are high.

(b) Electronic Card is accepted through Electronic Data Capture (EDC) machines where validity of the card and credit limit is verified online by the merchant.

Other security features are:

- Dynamic signature verification
- Finger print verification
- Voice recognition system
- Hand geometry – verification of individual hands by scanning them
- Visual recognition – picture of the person

"Electronic purses" to store amount to different types of accounts and can even be used at least for 50 transactions.

The advantages of smart card are:

- Electronic purse presents no risk of bad payments for the bank. The cash on electronic purse cannot be spent if the purse is reported stolen or lost. A new electronic purse can be issued after loss, theft or destruction with the original balance restored. It is single card which can conveniently pay all small to medium purchases
- Bank card service provider "European International" is embarking on a programme to update its European Payment Systems Network (EPS). "Europay" is a private network which carries transactions information on personal payment cards such as "Eurocard" and "Master Card". Europay provides a full range of services including travellers cheques,

cheque guarantee, ATM, electronic point of sale, credit and charge card services. It needs to update EPS, net due to demands for increased security and to keep pace with new card technology

- Smart Card can be used during Electronic Fund Transfer at Point-of Sales (EFTPOS). The transaction record is stored in the card
- Funds can be loaded into a card for use as cash. The electronic cash can then be used for making purchases
- Magnetic strip cards are often used at public telephone, parking meters and vending machines
- Smart cash can act as security to major account holders to view their accounts and transfer money automatically between accounts through the bank's mainframe computers.

Corporate Banking

Remote Banking has become very popular among corporate customers, especially big business/industrial houses which are already automated. More and more banks are providing customer terminals right in the customer's office which will facilitate the customers to operate the account without physically coming to the bank. For getting this type of service from the banks which have this facility, the customer requires a computer, a telephone connection, and a modem.

At present by utilising remote banking facility, corporate customers are able to get the following services.

- getting their current balance or getting their statement of account for any pre-defined period
- ordering cheque books
- ordering intra-bank and inter-bank fund transfers
- instructing "stop payments" of cheques
- international remittances
- opening letter of credit.

By obtaining a special SWIFT (Society for Worldwide Inter-bank Financial Telecommunications) authentication facility in arrangement with their bankers, customers are able to directly prepare messages in the SWIFT format by sitting in their office and transfer the particulars in the respective templates to their bankers. The bankers directly authenticate the transaction thereby completing the entire transaction across the globe within minutes.

Personal Banking

By using telephone facility, a customer can dial up the branch's designated telephone number, which is connected to the computer and he, by dialling his identification number will be able to get the connectivity to the branch's designated computer. A customer can have access to his balance, and also place order for statement of accounts, cheque books, and a few selected services through this tele (phone) banking.

Tele-banking

Tele-banking services function based on the voice processing facility available with the bank computers. The caller, generally a customer of the bank is able to call the bank any time and enquire balances of transaction history, and transfer funds between accounts. In this system, the computer at the back end is connected to a telephone link with modes. Apart from tele-banking, another system, simple and for limited services, known as voice mail facility is also available. There are several foreign banks now offering very advanced touch leave telephone answering services which route the customer's call directly to the department concerned. It allows the customer to leave a message for the concerned desk or department if the person is not available.

Update Facilities

These are Online updates and Batch updates.

Online Updates

Online updates may be defined as the direct linking of an operator or equipment to a computer system so that any stimulus provided by that operator or equipment is immediately accepted by the computer system. When a transaction is entered by the user, the computer acknowledges it and updates the related files which are affected by the particular transaction. So that, before the next transaction is produced, the files in the computer already contain the updated data. The first application of online updation in banks is in the front office mechanisation. Following are the few cases in which online updation is required.

Foreign Exchange Transaction

When the bank enters into a contract to buy or sell foreign exchange on behalf of its clients, the transaction is immediately entered into the computer of that authorised foreign exchange dealing branch which is transmitted to a central computer at the bank's head office. There the requisite files are updated immediately. This online updation is absolutely necessary as the bank must know its outstanding short or long position in each currency at any given time. This information is used by the banks to determine the action to be taken to safeguard its position by entering into currency swaps which they deem necessary.

Automated Teller Machine

Some of the ATMs function on the principle of online updation. These types of ATMs are linked to a central computer which contains the database of the customer accounts. The database is constantly updated with data from ATMs linked to it.

Batch Updates

Everyday at the end of the banking hours, the computer operators start entering the data of the day's transactions into the computer. One operator takes up the entry of all the cheques debited in customer accounts and cleared that day. The other operator is given the data in the scroll book to total up the cash deposits. A third operator takes up the work of entering the cheques which have been credited that day in the customer accounts and so on. After all the data are entered, it is processed by the computer. The branch officials can then access the computer for information relating to the following:

- Total cash deposits and withdrawals made during the day
- Reconciliation of cash receipts and withdrawals with that day's opening balance to arrive at the next day's opening balance, which should tally with the physical cash in hand
- Check whether the balances of the bank in the customers' accounts are reconciled after taking into account of all the debits and credits posted in the day
- Take the printout of the general ledger of the branch
- Generate statistical returns required by the regional/zonal or the head office
- Check whether the advances and fixed deposits are being maintained at the level required by the head office
- List of transactions entered would be taken which would be checked with the relative vouchers.

The input data is collected in a batch and then entered into the computer for processing. Next day again, same process is followed.

Internet Banking

Many banks have their own websites. Some of them offer banking facilities on the net such as account enquiry, request for statement and cheque books. The launch of Security First Network Bank (SFNB) on 18 October 1995 in the USA as the first virtual bank marks a turning point in the development of internet banking. Such banks exist only on the internet but have the same protections and regulatory approvals of a brick-and-mortar bank. The customers are able to open current/saving accounts. Further, the banks provide customers with an ATM card, a visa cheque and electronic bill payment facilities, etc.

Mobile Banking

Mobile banking comes with features like 128-bit encryption, open internet technology, that is, it is not dependent on any specific service provider and the handset company. The service is free of charge. The mobile banking facility is available in major cities of India. With this facility, customer, on his/her mobile screens can check the bank balance, or order a demand draft, stop cheque payment, request for a cheque book, look at the interest rates, or even the last three to five transactions round-the-clock.

Electronic Commerce (E-Commerce)

E-Commerce is digital parlance. If you think that e-commerce, per se, is limited to niche segment of Business to Business (B2B) transactions, think twice, no doubt, the bulk of the business done on the net would be in the Business-to-Business category, but this bulk will be generated by business-to-business transactions.

E-commerce translates your otherwise intangible benefits. Other exciting development arising from e-commerce includes a higher degree of personalisation, round-the-clock advantage, fast and flexible execution, immediate customer reaction, and reduction in operating cost.

E-commerce poses new challenges for all market participants. Banks face competition from non-banks and near banks, which because of low barrier to market entry can play much more easily in the electronic payment services market than in the markets for traditional bank services.

For better communication facility for e-commerce, Government of India has planned that all the state capitals and twelve major cities in the country will be provided exclusive optical fibre links.

Online Banking

Online banking may be defined as the direct linking of an operation or equipped to a computer system so that any stimulus provided by that operation or equipment is immediately accessed by the computer system. This means that when a transaction is entered by the user, the computer acknowledges it and updates the related files, which are affected by payments to facilitate fast payment to the beneficiaries. Clearing house debits the account of the bank effecting payment and credits to the accounts of the banks where the beneficiaries of the transaction maintains their accounts.

Signature Storage and Retrieval System

The computer which contains the signatures is kept with the passing office or the customer branch office. Each signature card is scanned using a device called a scanner, which takes an image of the specimen signature card and converts it to a digital form which is then stored on the hard disk of the computer. Along with the signatures, other details like account number, name, operating instructions are input to the computer. Once all the details of the signature and related details of the account are captured on the system, the data have to be verified, validated, and authenticated. Once they are authenticated, no changes can be made without proper authorisation. Once a cheque is received by the passing officer, he can recall the signature in seconds on the monitor by specifying the account number. Mostly fully computerised branches generally have a signature storage and retrieval as an integral part of the software.

Cheque Truncation

Cheque truncation means, a cheque which is truncated during the course of a clearing cycle either by the clearing house or by the bank whether paying or receiving payment, immediately on generation of an electronic image for transmission, substituting the further physical movement of the cheque in writing.

Cheque truncation truncates or stops the flow of cheques through the banking system. At some point after a cheque enters the banking system, information from the cheque is converted to a medium for electronic processing. The cheque itself is then stored (or truncated). Further processing of the cheque is done with the electronic information rather than paper (in the cheque itself).

Truncation of a cheque can be done using either the MICR data or image processing software. MICR cheques have the cheque number, city, bank and branch numbers, transaction code pre-coded, whereas image processing involves scanning of both sides of the cheque and storing the image in a digital form.

Note and Coin Counting Machines

To reduce the need of manual counting, note counting machines are available which counts a bundle of notes placed on it. Loose notes are inserted into the machine. The machine counts the notes at a high speed, while simultaneously indicating the number counted on a digital display. Every time the number reaches 100, the machine stops, subject to it being fixed at 100 and allows for the bundle to be taken out and stapled. However, one limitation of this machine is that the notes have to be in fairly good condition for the machine to be able to count properly. Similarly, coin counting machines are also available. These machines act like a sieve, separating the various denominations of coins into separate slots and also counting in the process.

Benefits of E-Banking

(a) Wherever the customer is in the world, he can transact business through e-banking. Banking customers can make some of the permitted transactions from his office or from his house or while travelling via mobile phone which generates greater customer satisfaction by offering unlimited access to bank, not limited by the walls of the branch.

(b) Scope and potential of better profitability increases.

(c) Online banking is an effective medium of parting of various schemes of the bank and acts as a marketing tool.

(d) Bring down "cost of banking" to the customer over a period of time.

(e) By connecting all the branches through Wide Area Network (WAN), any branch banking can be provided to the customer.

(f) Convenience acts as a tremendous psychological benefit all the time. It makes utility payments easier.

(g) It inculcates a financial discipline by recording each and every transaction.

(h) Online purchase of goods and services including online payments for the same benefits to the bank.

(i) E-banking reduces customer visits to the branches, thereby reducing intervention and the establishment costs for the bank.

(j) Inter-branch reconciliation becomes easy thereby reducing the chances of fraud and misappropriation.

(k) E-banking provides unlimited network to the bank and is not limited to the number of branches. Any computer connected to a modem and a telephone having internet connection can provide banking facility to the customer.

(l) Any time banking, managing funds in real time, and importantly e-banking provides 24 hours a day, 365 days a year services to the customers of the bank.

(m) E-banking expands the domain of access to the banking services, lowers the risk, and generates higher security to the customers as they can avoid travelling with cash. Cash can be withdrawn from any branch/ATM.

(n) Establishing centralised database can considerably reduce load on branches. Integrated customer data pave the way for individualised and customised services.

(o) By connecting ATMs and point of all terminals online, risk of overdraw can be eliminated in case of ATM, credit and debit cards. ATM can be better monitored and planned by establishing a centralised data warehouse and using latest data-managing tools.

Bottlenecks in Development of E-Banking

(a) The level of acceptance of e-banking channels by average customers remain low due to certain psychological facts and fear of technology.
(b) Lack of preparedness on the part of banks and general unawareness of changes in banking is also one of the bottlenecks.
(c) The cost of acquiring a computer, internet connection and other equipments is also a limiting factor in the development of e-banking facility.
(d) Banks need to address the security threats to reduce the risk of introducing new and advanced technology. Enactment of proper cyber laws is also required to take care of cyber enemies in the area of e-banking.

Electronic Commerce

In the past people exchanged commodities depending upon their requirements and called it commerce. E-commerce uses sophisticated computer technology to conduct business transaction. Electronic commerce or e-commerce refers to the paperless exchange of business information between operating systems and individuals and extends to any form of buying and selling by consumers and companies over a computer network. It is a market place where business uses information technology and network computing to securely transform their business relationship, sell and buy goods and services and exchange information and data. E-commerce encompasses all forms of commercial transactions, including both organisations and individuals that require the processing and transmission of digital data, including text, mechanism involving inter-bank funds settlement. At the national level it has come up only recently as an affiliate to the recommendations of the Saraf Committee on technology issues in payment and settlement system constituted by the RBI in 1994. The basic infrastructure at various branches/ offices for payment, however, is not capable of supporting such system, which is dependent upon sophisticated communication systems integrated with computers. Due to these factors, the EFT system introduced by RBI is largely built around the existing infrastructure for cheque clearing. The Saraf Committee has suggested a hybrid system, both paper and electronic media for message transmission. It had suggested that high value institutional funds transfer should be batched every hour. The batch system has since been implemented in 1996. The RBI acts as the service provider as well as the system regulator.

System of Message Transmission

The retail funds transfer instructions received from the customer on the prescribed format, are consolidated at the respective branch of the participating banks, the messages are converted into electronic format and are transmitted over network or to the NCC (National Credit Council) by a cut-off time. The messages are sent in encrypted form and checksum are generated at the record level to ensure data integrity.

Processing of the Messages

The NCC of the RBI operate at late evening hours to process the transfer messages received from participating banks. The messages are classified and consolidated according to the bank wise destination centres. The NCC sends the bankwise reports to the DAD (Deposit Accounts Department) of RBI at the originating centre for settlement. After DAD confirms the settlement, the files are sent to the NCC of RBI over the network after encryption on the same day. At the destination, NCC files are processed and necessary reports are sent to the banks next morning.

Real Time Gross Settlement (RTGS) System

RTGS is an electronic payment environment where payment instructions processed on a continuous or real-time basis and settled on a gross or individual basis without meeting the debits against credits payments so effected are 'final' and 'irrevocable settlement' is done in the books of RBI, the ultimate liquidity depository of the country. RTGS uses the Indian Financial Network (INFINET) and Satellite Financial Management System (SFMS). Each bank will be having a single gateway interface called Participant Interface (PI) for the RTGS system. The payment message/enquiry/clearing settlement originates from the participant's host system (Branch/Treasury). Transactions between RBI and commercial banks happens through RTGS system.

- The message is passed on by the participant and clearing system interface (PI) to the Inter-Bank Fund Transfer Processor (IFTP), which acts as a broker. Communication between PI and RTGS system will be through IFTP only and not directly
- IFTP stores the message and in case of payment, messages construct settlement message containing a core subset of the information required for settlement (settlement message) and is routed to the RTGS system at RBI
- On receipt of the subset, RBI checks whether the sending bank has sufficient covering funds in its account and informs the IFTP of the status of transfer, queued, or settled

- The settlement message is processed and the fate is advised to IFTP
- Based on response, IFTP enriches the message received from RTGS system by adding back corporate details and sends settlement advise to both the originating and beneficiary participant in case of successful settlement or failure advice to the originating participant in case of failed settlement
- Thus, the business information which is exchanged between the sending and receiving bank is not known by settlement agreement. Thus, the RBI acts only as a settlement agent.

RTGS Business Day

The RTGS business day is divided into four phases.

- RTGS Open Phase: All normal transactions are accepted and processed
- IDL Shut Phase: All transactions are processed as the RTGS open phase but no new IDL will be requested
- IDL Close Phase: Restriction on fresh IDL continues and no transaction which debits a member with an outstanding IDL will be settled
- RTGS Close Phase: Transactions reversing outstanding IDL will only be permitted. Outstanding Multilateral Net Settlement Batch (MNSB), Transactions for settlement (Provided member is designated as clearing entity) and MNSB return transactions are also permitted
- The existing clearing system will also continue.

The phase change notifications will be sent by the RBI to the members having the Participant Interface (PI). Any changes in timings in these phases will also be broadcast to all the members.

Digital Signature

Digital signature is the new concept brought under the ambit of legislation in India with the enactment of Information Technology Act 2000, which comprehensively addresses the legal issues concerning the electronic messaging and electronic payment system. The role of digital signature is going to be important for e-commerce, because e-commerce heavily relies on electronic transmission of message carrying digital signature. It is common belief that a digital signature is just a digital image of a signature (hand drawn). In fact, digital signature is not the replica of the manual signature captured through a scanner or otherwise. Digital signature is the key and must be applied in a manner to satisfy the following critical features of any digitally signed electronic message.

Authenticity

The validity of the source of the electronic message should be ascertained through digital signature by verifying the source or the originator of the message.

Integrity

Integrity of a message transmitted electronically is of paramount importance. The message has to be received intact and should not have been altered in any way during transmission.

Non-Repudiation

From a banker's point of view, non-repudiation is very important to act upon a fund transfer message. There should not be an opportunity for a sender of the message to deny that he has sent the message at all and in the form in which it has been received.

The digital signature is unique to each message and any change to the message changes digital signature. The most common manner of signing electronically is with the help of public key cryptography as contemplated by the Information Technology Act 2000. Cryptography is usually based on the use of algorithmic functions to generate two different but mathematically related keys (i.e. large numbers produced using a series of mathematical formulae applied to prime numbers). There are two parts to the keys.

- Public Key
- Private Key

Both keys are issued to the user by designated authorities of the government. Before a sender can digitally sign an electronic message, sender must first get public-private key pair. The private key is kept confidential and is used only by signer to create the digital signature. The public key is used by a relying party to verify the digital signature.

One such key is used for creating a digital signature or transforming data into a seemingly unintelligible form, and the other one for verifying a digital signature or converting the message to its original form. Encryption does not necessarily imply making any information confidential, the encrypted digital signature may be merely appended to a non-encrypted message. The process to sign an electronic message is as follows:

- The sender first delimits precisely the borders of what is to be signed
- A hash function in the signers software should compute a hash result which for all practical purposes is unique to the message

- The signer's software should then transform the hash result into a digital signature using signer's private key
- The resulting digital signature is thus unique to both the message and the private key used to create it.

Banking Ombudsman

A Scheme was introduced in the year 2002 to resolve complaints relating to certain services rendered by banks and to facilitate the satisfaction or settlement of such complaints. The scheme extends to the whole of India. It is applicable to all the banks in India. The RBI decides the appointment of banking ombudsman, his term of office, his secretariat, his powers, his territorial jurisdiction, etc. The RBI has the authority to suspend the operation of the scheme fully or partly for such period as may be specified in the order. Such suspension may be general or in relation to any specified bank. The period of suspension can be extended if deemed fit by the RBI.

Definitions

(a) "Banking Ombudsman" means "any person appointed under the scheme".

(b) "Award" means "an award passed by the banking ombudsman in accordance with this scheme".

(c) "Authorised Representative" means "a person duly appointed and authorised by a complainant to act on his behalf and represent" before a banking ombudsman him in the proceedings.

(d) "Bank" means:
- a banking company
- a corresponding new bank
- a regional rural bank
- SBI and its subsidiary bank as defined in Part 1, Section 5 of the Banking Regulation Act, 1949
- primary cooperative bank.

(e) "Complaint" means "a representation in writing" containing a grievance alleging deficiency in banking service or through electronic means.

(f) "Review Authority" is "the deputy governor in charge of rural planning and credit department of the RBI who shall review the award of banking ombudsman and shall also be responsible for implementing such award as per the scheme".

(g) "Settlement" means "an agreement reached by the parties either by a conciliation or mediation by the Banking Ombudsman".

Appointment and Tenure

(a) The RBI may, on the recommendation of a selection committee of four persons, constituted by its Governor, appoint one or more persons to be known as "banking ombudsman" to carry out the functions entrusted to them under the scheme. The maximum age of the person to be so appointed is 65 years. The appointment may be made for a period not exceeding three years but the same is extendable for two years, subject to an overall age limit of 65 years. The selection committee consists of three deputy governors of RBI and the additional secretary (Finance), Department of Economic affairs as a special invitee.

(b) The RBI may permit the banking ombudsman to undertake such part-time honorary work, as is not likely to interfere with his duties under the scheme.

(c) The Governor of RBI may remove any banking ombudsman from his office in the public interest or for the reason of incapacity of the banking ombudsman for reasons to be recorded in writing and by giving him three months' notice or by paying three months' emoluments in lieu of the notice period.

Territorial Jurisdiction and Location Office

(a) The RBI shall specify the territorial limit, to which the authority of each of the Banking Ombudsman shall extend.

(b) The office of the Banking Ombudsman will be located at such places as may be specified by the RBI.

(c) The banking ombudsman may hold sittings at such places within his area of jurisdiction as may be considered necessary and proper by him in respect of a complaint or reference before him.

Qualifications and Remuneration

(a) The Banking Ombudsman shall be a person of repute having experience in the legal, banking financial services, public administration, or management sectors. If such a person is a civil servant, he should be in the rank of joint secretary or above in the Government of India and in case of such a person being from the banking sector, he should have had the experience of working as a whole time director in a public sector or an equivalent position.

(b) The remuneration and other perquisites payable to a Banking Ombudsman will be determined by the RBI from time to time and shall be borne by the banks in such proportion and in such manner as may be determined by the RBI.

Secretarial Staff

(a) The Banking Ombudsman shall be provided with a Secretariat drawn from banks, RBI, etc.
(b) The cost of the Secretariat will be shared by banks in such proportion and in such manner as may be determined by RBI.

General Powers of Banking Ombudsman

The Banking Ombudsman shall have the following powers and duties.

(a) To receive complaints relating to banking services
(b) To consider such complaints and facilitate their satisfaction or settlement by agreement through conciliation and mediation between the bank and the aggrieved parties or by passing an award in accordance with the scheme, and
(c) To resolve by way of arbitration disputes between banks or between a bank and its constituents as may be agreed upon by the contesting parties in accordance with the provisions of the Scheme and the Arbitration and Conciliation Act, 1996.

Customer Relations – Grievances – Redressal

The following procedure is to be adopted to file a complaint and to deal with it. The aspects on which a complaint can be filed are extractive and covers all the services a bank offers to its customers. For effectively dealing with the complaint, the Banking Ombudsman has powers to call for information from the parties concerned. The complaint needs to be in writing and supported by documents and declarations as given in the scheme. The limitation period for filing a complaint is one year.

Grounds of Complaint

A complaint on any of the following grounds alleging deficiency in banking or other services may be filed with the Banking Ombudsman having the jurisdiction:

(a) Non-payment/inordinate delay in the payment or collection of cheques, drafts, bills etc.
(b) Non-acceptance, without sufficient cause, of small denomination notes tendered for any purpose, and for charging of commission in respect thereof
(d) Non-adherence to prescribed working hours
(e) Failure to honour guarantee/letter of credit commitments
(f) Refusal to open deposit account without any valid reason for refusal

(g) Complaints, from exporters in India, such as delays in receipt of export proceeds, improper handling of export bills, collection of bills, etc., provided such complaints pertain to the bank's operation in India.
(h) Delays, non-credit of proceeds to respective accounts, non-payment of deposit or non-observance of the RBI directives if any, applicable to rate of interest on deposits in any savings, current or any other account maintained with a bank.
(i) Claiming in respect of unauthorised or fraudulent withdrawals, from deposit accounts, of fraudulent encashment of a cheque or an bank draft, etc.
(j) Complaints from non-resident Indians having accounts in India in relation to their remittances from abroad, deposits and other bank related matters.
(k) Any other matter relating to the violation of the directives issued by the RBI in relation to banking or other services.

Complaints concerning loans and advances may also be filed only if so far as they relate to the following:

(a) Delays in sanction, disbursement, or non-observance of prescribed time schedule for disposal of loan applications.
(b) Non-observance of RBI directives on interest rates.
(c) Non-observance of any other directing or instructions of the RBI, as may be specified by it from time to time.
(d) Non-acceptance of applications for loans without furnishing valid reasons to the applicant.

The banking ombudsman may also deal with such any other matter as may be specified by the RBI from time to time in this behalf.

Procedure for Filing Complaint

Any person who has grievance against a bank relating to the banking services for reasons as detailed above may, himself or through his authorised representative make a complaint to the Banking Ombudsman. The complaint in writing shall be duly signed by the complainant or his authorised respresentative (other than an advocate) in the form specified in Annexture, 'A' of the scheme, stating clearly:

(a) The name and address of the complainant.
(b) The name and address of the branch or office of the bank against which the complaint is made.

(c) The facts giving rise to the complaint.
(d) Documents, if any, that are desired to be related upon by the complainant.
(e) The nature and extent of the loss caused to the complainant.
(f) The relief sought from the Banking Ombudsman.
(g) A declaration about the compliance of the conditions referred to the clause mentioned herein below.

No complaint to the Banking Ombudsman shall be considered unless:

(a) The complainant had before making a complaint to the banking ombudsman made a written representation to the bank and either the bank had reflected upon the complaint or the complainant had not received any reply within a period of one month after the bank concerned received his representation or the complainant is not satisfied with the reply given by the bank.
(b) The complaint is made not later than one year after the cause of action arisen as per clause (a) above.
(c) The complaint is not in respect of the same subject matter, for which any proceedings before any court, tribunal, or arbitrator or any other forum is pending or a decree or award or a final order has already been passed by any such competent court, or a final order has already been passed by any such competent court, tribunal, arbitrator, or forum.
(d) The complaint is not frivolous or vexatious in nature.

It would be open to the Banking Ombudsman to entertain a complaint under the scheme provided the Banking Ombudsman is satisfied with the documentary evidence produced before him that:

(a) The interest of the complainant have suffered adversely on account of lapse or in action on the part of the bank or due to connivance on the part of an employee of the bank facilitating the unauthorised or fraudulent withdrawal from the bank account of the complainant.
(b) No interim injunction or stay order or any other direction, either restraining the bank from making payment of the amount of claim as made by the complainant is pending adjudication.

Power to Call for Information

The Banking Ombudsman may require the bank named with the complaint or any other related bank to provide any information or furnish certified copies of any document relating to the subject matter of the complaint that is or alleged to be in possession of such bank. In the event of the failure of a bank to comply with the requisition without any sufficient cause, the Banking Ombudsman may draw the inference that the information, if provided or copies if furnished, would be unfavourable to such bank.

The Banking Ombudsman shall not disclose any information or document to any person except with the consent of the person furnishing such information or document. However, the Banking Ombudsman may disclose information or document furnished by one party in complaint to the opposite party of the complaint, to the extent considered by him to be reasonably required to comply with the principles of natural justice and fair play in the proceedings.

Settlement of Complaint by Agreement

The Banking Ombudsman has to serve a notice of the receipt of complaint along with a copy of the complaint to the branch or office of the bank named in the complaint. He has to attempt for a settlement of the complaint by agreement between the complainant and the bank through conciliation or mediation. For the purpose of promoting a settlement of the complaint, the Banking Ombudsman may follow such procedures as he may consider appropriate and he shall not be bound by any legal rule of evidence. The proceedings before the Banking Ombudsman shall be summary in nature.

Award by the Banking Ombudsman

(a) If a complaint is not settled by agreement within a period of one month from the date of receipt of the complaint or such further period as the Banking Ombudsman may allow the parties, he may, after affording the parties a reasonable opportunity to present their case, pass an award or reject the complaint.

(b) The Banking Ombudsman shall take into account the evidence placed before him by the parties, the principles of banking law and practice, directions, instructions, and guidelines used by the RBI from time to time and such other factors which in his opinion are relevant to the complaint.

(c) The award passed under the sub-clause above shall state the directions, if any, to the bank for specific performance of its obligations in addition to the amount to be paid by the bank to the complainant by way of compensation for the loss suffered by him along with the summary of the reasons for passing the award.

(d) The Banking Ombudsman may, while passing an award in respect of a complaint may direct the complaint to furnish an indemnity for refund of the amount received under the award along with interest in any competent judicial court deciding that there was no cause of action that has been covered under the award.

(e) In the event of the complainant refusing to honour the indemnity given by him in favour of the bank, it shall be open to the bank to approach a court of law for invoking its claim based on the indemnity against the complainant.

(f) The bank shall within one month from the date of receipt of the award on the acceptance in writing of the award by the complainant comply with the award and intimate the compliance to the Banking Ombudsman.

(g) If in the opinion of the bank the award passed against it is based on wrong appreciation of facts, or the award is likely to create a bad precedent for the bank or banking system in general, the bank may file a review application as per provisions of the scheme. The bank shall in relation to such award intimate to the Banking Ombudsman within one month from the date of receipt of a copy of the award its decision to file the review petition.

(h) The Banking Ombudsman shall report to the RBI which is a review authority about the non-compliance by any bank or an award, on receipt of such report the review authority shall pass necessary orders. In the event of the bank failing to comply with the award within the prescribed time limit, the complainant will, if he so desires, approach the review authority with a prayer to pass an appropriate direction to the bank for immediate compliance of the award.

Proceedings before the Review Authority

(a) A bank not agreeing to accept the award posed under the scheme may file a review application before the review authority within one month from the date of receiving copy of the award. The bank's application has to be approved by the bank's chairman or, in his absence, the managing director or the chief executive officer or any other officer of equal rank.

(b) The review authority shall not recover any additional or new material from any party, which was not produced before the Banking Ombudsman.

(c) The review authority on receiving such application shall serve a copy of the review application to the other party, requiring his reply in the review application within a period of two weeks.

The review authority may call for the comments of the banking ombudsman in the review application filed before him.

Directions Issued by the Review Authority

The review authority on complaints of the review application and being satisfied that the award requires review by the banking ombudsman shall reward the matter to the banking ombudsman for reviewing the award in the light of observation made by the review authority.

The reward of the matter by the review authority shall be made within a period of six weeks from the date of submission of the review application or within such reasonable time as the review authority may consider necessary.

If on consideration of the review application filed by the bank, the review authority is satisfied that time is no ground for review of the award it shall issue an appropriate direction to the bank for the implementation of the award, within six weeks from the date of submission of the review application.

Rejection of the Complaint

The banking ombudsman may reject the complaint at any stage if it appears to him that the complaint made is:

(a) Frivolous, vexatious, malafide.
(b) Without any sufficient cause.
(c) That it is not pursued by the complainant with reasonable diligence.
(d) Prima facie, there is no loss or damage or inconvenience caused to the complainant.

The banking ombudsman may reject a complaint at any stage, if after consideration of the complaint and evidence produced before him, the banking ombudsman is of the opinion that the complicated nature of the complaint requires consideration of elaborate documentary and oral evidence and the proceedings before the Banking Ombudsman are not appropriate for adjudiction of such complaint. The decision of the banking ombudsman in this regard shall be final.

Banks to Display Salient Features of the Scheme for Common Knowledge of the Public

(a) The banks covered by the scheme shall ensure that the purpose of this scheme and the name and address of the banking ombudsman to whom the complaints are to be made by the aggrieved party are displayed in all the branch/office premises.

(b) The banks covered by the scheme are required to ensure that a copy of the scheme is made available with the designated officer of the bank of perusal in the office premises of the bank. There should be a notice displayed at each office of the bank about the availability of the copy of the scheme with such designated officers.

Special Services Rendered by Banks to Customers

Securitisation

Securitisation is the process of acquisition of large Non-Performing Asset (NPA) loan or Portfolio of loans such as housing by 'Securitisation or Reconstruciton Company' from a bank or financial institution on mutually agreed terms and conditions, that is, the sale or transfer price with or without recourses transfer sale, etc.

The Securitisation or Reconstrution Company transfers the acquired loans to a Special Purpose Vehicle (SPV) set up by it that manages the assets for the purpose of realisation or holds them as investments till maturity. The SPV issues the consideration of transfer price to the originator bank in the form of cash or debentures/bonds as mutually agreed. To provide banks and financial institutions a summary procedure for recovery of their secured dues which have been classified as Non-Performing Asset (NPA) on their banks, and also for setting up of Securitisation or Reconstruction Company for taking over the defaulted loans of banks and financial institutions and recover thereof.

Securitisation and Reconstruction of Finanical Assets (SRFA) and Enforcement of Security Interest Act (ESI) – 2002

Till now banks/financial instituations had to enforce their security through courts which was a very slow and time-consuming process. There was also no provision in any of the present law in respect of hypothecation, although hypothecation is one of the major security interest taken by the bank/financial institution. Keeping in mind the above factors among many others, the Securitisation and Reconstructions of Financial Assets (SRFA) and Enforcement of Security Interest Act (ESI) was enacted with effect from 21 June 2002.

The Act deals with three aspects:

(a) Enforcement of security interest by secured creditor (bank/financial institutions).

(b) Transfer of Non-Performing Assets to Securitisation Company or Reconstruction Company (SCRC), which will then dispose of those assets and realise the proceeds.

(c) To provide a legal framework for securitisation of assets.

SCRC can either finance the acquisition from their own resources or raise resources from Qualified Institutional Buyers (QIB) by securitisation of the financial assets and issuing them security receipt as per mutually agreed terms and on assessment of risk involved. The guidelines for such acquisition have been prescribed by RBI.

The provisions of the Act shall not apply to the following:

(a) Any security interest created in agricultural land.
(b) A pledge of movables within the meaning of Section 172 of the Indian Contract Act.
(c) A lien on any good, money or security given by or under the Indian Contract Act 1872, or Sale of Good Act 1930, or any other law for the time being in inforce.
(d) Any properties not liable to attachment or sale under first provisions to Section 60(1) of Code of Civil Procedure.
(e) Any security interest for securing requirement of any financial asset not exceeding INR 1 lakh and in secured dues, INR 10 lakhs.
(f) Any rights of unpaid seller under Section 47 of Sale of Goods Act 1930.
(g) Creation of any security interest on any aircraft as defined under Section 2(1) of Aircraft Act.
(h) Any conditional sale, hire purchase, or lease or any other contract on which no security interest has been created.
(i) Creation of any security interest in any vessel as defined under Section 3(5) of Merchant Shipping Act.
(j) In case, interest, which the amount due less than 20 per cent of the principal amount and interest thereon, that is, where borrower has repaid more than 80 per cent of principal amount and interest.

Measures of Asset Reconstruction

An SCRC may, for the purpose of asset reconstruction, with regard to the guidelines formed by RBI, provide for any one or more of the following measures.

(a) Settlement of dues payable by the borrower.
(b) The sale or lease of a part or whole of the business of the borrower.
(c) Rescheduling of payment debits payable by the borrower.
(d) Enforcement of security interest in accordance with the provisions of this Act.
(e) Proper management of the business of borrower by changes, interest or takeover of, the business of the borrower.

(f) Taking possession of secured assets in accordance with the provisions of this Act.

RBI has laid down guidelines to be followed by banks or financial institutions for sale of financial assets. These guidelines are as follows.

(a) Setting up a system for sale, valuation, and pricing.
(b) Any non-performing asset, including a non-performing bond or debenture, can be sold.
(c) Setting of prudential norms for provisioning or valuation capital adequacy, exposure, and disclosure requirements.
(d) Bonds or debentures offered by SCRC should ensure as follows:
    - securitites must not have a term interest excess of six years
    - it should be secured by an appropriate charge on the assets transferred
    - interest on securities should not be less than 1.5 per cent above the bank rate (6 per cent at present)
    - notices of transfer of security should be issued to the SCRC
    - commitment to reduce securities must be unconditional
    - full or part payment to be given in the event of SCRC sells the assets before maturity.

Enforcement of Security Interest

A secured creditor means any bank or financial institution or any consortium or groups of banks or financial institutions and includes:

(a) Debenture Trustee appointed by bank or financial institution.
(b) Securities and Reconstruction Company.
(c) Any other trustee, holding securities interest, in whose favour security interest is created for the repayment by any borrower of any financial institution.

Any security interest can be enforced by a secured creditor without interevention of a court or tribunal in accordance with the provisions of the Act. Such action can be taken by the company on any borrower who is under liablility to a secured creditor under a security agreement, makes any default in repayment of secured debt or any installment thereof and the account is classified as NPA (Non-Performing Asset) by the secured creditor. No action can be taken if the debt is time barred under the Limitation Act.

Notwithstanding the rules contained in Section 69 or Section 69A of the Transfer of Property Act 1882, any security interest created in favour of any secured creditor may be enforced, without the intervention of the court or tribunal, by such creditor in accordance with Section 13 of Securitisation and Reconstruction of Financial Assets and Enforcement of Securities Interest Act 2002.

Banks and financial institutions may require expeditious recovery of their secured dues which may not have classified as non-performing assets in their books. Such cases may be those where the borrower is in financial distress or his intentions are malafide and he does not in terms repay the secured loan. In such cases, the bank or financial institution would have to move quickly to intimate recovery proceeding for recovery of dues before the borrower misappropriates the security or some other creditor seizes the security.

Bancassurance

Objectives

Banking and insurance have more commonality in the basic nature of their business. Banking and insurance rely on pooling of resources to protect financial security or to protect against adverse events(insurance). Banking and insurance are often complimentary, as in the case of mortgages that require both finance and property insurance.

In insurance the initial expenses, because of distribution costs are high and regulatory disclosure requirements are putting additional pressure on the insurance to reduce the costs. Distribution expenses being a major part of initial expenses, insurers are forced to think on alternate channels of distribution and banks have a host of common practices to integrate to achieve economies of sale.

Definition

Bancassurance in its simplest form is the distribution of insurance products through a banks distribution channel. In concrete term, Bancassurance which is also known as ALLFINANZ constitutes a package of financial services that can fulfill both banking and insurance needs at the same time.

The motives behind bancassurance also vary. For banks, it is a means of product diversification and a source of additional fee income, while insurance companies see it as a tool for increasing their market penetration and premium turnover. While for the customer, Bancassurance is a bonanza is terms of reduced price and high-quality product and delivery at single point or doorstep.

Benefits for a Bank/Insurance Companies

(a) Increased return on assets. The best way to increase return on assets is through fee income, by which operating expenses could be covered for better profitable operating expense ratio.

(b) Lower cost per head sales, which is made possible by banks sizeable and loyal customer base.
(c) Face to face interaction that is important in insurance is possible through large network of branches.
(d) Most large retail banks engender a great deal of trust in loans and advances, which they can protect by selling the personal life insurance polices.
(e) Marketing and processing capabilities are available extensively in marketing to both existing clients and non-clients. Banks also have access to various communication channels such as statement inserts, e-mail, ATMs, phone banking/telebanking, etc. Bank proficiency has resulted in improvements of customer services.
(f) Bulk of bank customers who are middle-income groups get little attention from insurance agents. Banks with nearly 65 branches all over the country can open market with a speed to insurance business expansion.

Challenges for Banks under Bancassurance

(a) Under Insurance Regulatory Development Authority (IRDA) regulations, selling insurance policies, agents are required to undergo four weeks of training and thereafter pass an examination before qualifying as licensed agents. In bank's branches at least twice the number of 65,000 branches employees would be required to be trained, which is a very big task in terms of time, expenses and other resources.
(b) The second challenge is, development of technology for insurance marketing. Most of 65,000 branches are not computerised and most of rural and semi urban branches are manually operated. Therefore, substantial information technology orientation is required.
(c) For making insurance sales, branches would be receiving commissions but it could not be passed on to employee due to human resource development/human resource management problems of other employees who are not associated with insurance selling.

For public sector banks with rigid reward systems, it could be a major challenge to install and make agreement to motivate employees to take higher and higher levels of selling specific product on behalf of outside insurance companies. The performance reorganisations and reward systems in most banks today do not give credit to employee's performance in terms of product selling. There is urgent need to revamp the system so as to make employees take stock of their specific contribution in terms of enhancing the fee-based income of the branch. There may also be a need for a system of rewarding the entire branch staff through incentives by the insurance company for performance levels beyond any stated benchmarks.

Success of Bancassurance

(a) Banks have target client base, and cross selling surely provides with an opportunity for optimum utilisation of their existing customer relationship, thus effectively creating a win-win situation for all, that is, bank, insurance company, or the customer.

(b) The operational difficulties at ground level have to be managed and one of the suggested ways is to restructure the bank compensation structure of the law of insurance companies.

(c) Banking and insurance have strong similarities that might have contributed to their re-approachment. LIC and other insurance companies have developed a range of products that have direct conflict with traditional bank offerings or products.

(d) Regulation of both IRDA and RBI should jointly formulate a policy and process route to avoid conflict of interest.

14
Negotiable Instruments

Negotiable instruments are playing a vital role in the business world. The instruments which are transferable by delivery or by endorsement may be called Negotiable instruments, for example, promissory notes, cheques, bills of exchange, etc. In India the law relating to negotiable instruments is contained in the Negotiable Instruments Act, 1881. The Act came into force on March 1 1882. The Act was amended in 1988 in certain respects. The Act does not define a negotiable instrument. But Section 13 merely states that a negotiable instrument means a promissory note, bill of exchange, or cheque payable either to order or to the bearer. The Act deals with only three instruments – promissory notes, bills of exchange, and cheques. Besides these, there are other instruments which satisfy the character of negotiability.

A negotiable instrument, thus, plays a key role in the modern business as a document which can be transferable with ease. Justice Wills defines, it as "one in which the property is acquired by anyone who takes it bonafide or for a value, notwithstanding any defect of title in the person from whom he took it".

The other instruments which satisfy the characteristics of negotiability should be freely transferable by delivery or by endorsement and delivery, by the custom of trade and the person, who obtains in good faith and for value, gets in free from all defects and the holder of the instrument may sue upon it in his own name. Documents such as dividend warrants, port trust bonds, railway bonds payable to bearer or railway receipts are regarded negotiable instruments either by trade, usage or custom or by other enactments. But money orders and postal orders, deposit receipts, share certificates, bill of lading, dock warrants, and so on, are not negotiable instruments. Although the instruments may be transferred by delivery and endorsements, they are not able to give a better title to the bonafide transferee for value than what the transferor has. Title of transferee in these cases, does not become free from the defects of the title of the transferor.

A negotiable instrument may be made payable to one or more payees jointly, or it may be made payable to one or some of several payees. But where it is payable to a specified person, the instrument loses its negotiability.

Essential Features of Negotiable Instruments

The features of negotiable instruments are as follows:

Transferability

The value in negotiable instruments is easily transferable from person to person. The ownership of property in the instrument may be passed on mere delivery in the case of bearer instruments, or by endorsements and delivery in the case of other instruments. Thus, the two ways of negotiating the negotiable instruments, therefore are: (a) delivery (b) endorsement and delivery. The transfer of ownership of a property is complete only when it is delivered to the transferee. Mere intention to transfer does not amount to transfer of the instrument. It must be actually delivered to the other party. By delivery, we mean voluntary transfer of property.

Contract to Pay Money

A negotiable instrument contains a contract to pay money only.

Title

A negotiable instrument confers absolute and good title on the transferee who takes in good faith, for value and without notice of defective title of the transferor. This is the most important characteristic of negotiable instrument. For instance, a person who takes negotiable instrument from another person who has stolen from somebody else will have undisputable title, provided he takes it in good faith and for value. He shall not have any knowledge of the defective title of the transferor. There is a difference between transferability and negotiability. In the case of commodities which are transferable from person to person, the general rule is the transferor cannot transfer better title than what he has. But a negotiable instrument stands on different footing. Suppose a person takes a cheque from another person without knowledge of the latter's defective title to the cheque. Still he will have good title thereto and will not be responsible to the true owner.

Evidence

It is capable of easy proof and has got special rules of evidence, for example, a presumption that consideration has been paid in it.

Instrument in Writing

The law requires that a cheque, bill or promissory note must be an instrument in writing. The amount to be paid on instrument must be certain and specified both in figures and in words.

Unconditional Order or Promise

A cheque or a bill of exchange contains an order to the drawee to pay money without attaching any condition. A promissory note contains a promise to pay money to the creditor unconditionally.

Payable to Order Bearer

They are to be normally payable to order. They are payable to order if it is expressed to be so payable or if the last endorsement is a blank endorsement.

Recovery of Money

The holder in due course is not in a way affected by the defective title of the transferor or any of the previous parties, if any. The term holder in due course means a holder who has taken the negotiable instrument for value, in good faith, and before maturity. Such a holder in due course has a right to sue upon the instruments in his own name. He can thus recover the amount from the party liable to pay on the instrument.

Presumptions to Negotiable Instruments

Section 118 and 119 of the Negotiable Instruments Act enumerate the presumptions as to negotiable instruments. According to Section 118, until the contrary is proved, the following presumptions shall be made.

(a) Every negotiable instrument bearing a date was made or drawn on such date.

(b) Every negotiable instrument was made or drawn for consideration, and that every such instrument, when it has been accepted, endorsed, negotiated or transferred, was accepted, endorsed, negotiated, or transferred for consideration.

(c) Every accepted bill of exchange was accepted within a reasonable time after its date and before its maturity.

(d) Every transfer of a negotiable instrument was made before its maturity.

(e) A lost promissory note, bill of exchange or cheque was duly stamped.

(f) The endorsements appearing upon a negotiable instrument were made in the order in which they appear thereon.

(g) The holder of a negotiable instrument is presumed to be a holder in due course.

Type of Negotiable Instruments

The negotiable instruments can be broadly classified into two a viz., Instrument Negotiable by custom or usage or trade. In India, we recognise only three instruments as negotiable and they are (a) Promissory Notes (b) Bills of Exchange, and (c) Cheques.

Promissory Note

According to Section 4 of the Negotiable Instruments Act, "a promissory note is an instrument in writing containing an unconditional undertaking signed by the maker, to pay a certain sum of money only to, or to the order of, a certain person, or to the bearer of the instrument". A promissory note is drawn and signed by the debtor. He promises to pay the creditor specified sum of money on demand or after the expiry of a specified period.

Specimen of Promissory Note

A specimen form of demand promissory note is given below.

(a) When promise is made to pay money on demand.

Hyderabad
Rs 5,000/- 4 May 2008

On demand, I promise to pay Shri K Shankar or order the sum of Rupees Five Thousand for value received with interest at 6 per cent per annum.

To
Shri K Shankar
H.No. 10 – 15,
Himayatnagar,
Hyderabad.

STAMP
Signed
Sreenivas

(b) Where promise is to pay money after the expiry of a fixed time.

Hyderabad
Rs 5,000/- 4 May 2008

Three months after date, I promise to pay Shri K Shankar or order the sum of Rupees Five Thousand for value received.

To
Shri K Shankar
H.No. 10–15,
Himayatnagar,
Hyderabad.

STAMP
Sreenivas

Essential Features of a Promissory Note

A promissory note has the following essential features:

(a) It is an instrument in writing.
(b) It should be signed by the maker.

(c) The maker must be certain.
(d) The payee must be certain.
(e) It is an unconditional promise and must be expressed in writing to pay money.
(f) Amount should be certain.
(g) The promise should be to pay money and money only.
(h) The other features like the place, date of execution, consideration are to be mentioned.

Bill of Exchange

Unlike a promissory note, the bill of exchange contains an order from the creditor to the debtor to pay a certain sum, to a certain person after a certain period. Section 5 of the Negotiable Instruments Act, 1881 defines a bill of exchange as follows.

"An instrument in writing containing an unconditional order, signed by the maker, directing a certain person to pay a certain sum of money only to, or to the order of, a certain person or the bearer of the instrument".

Specimen of a Bill of Exchange

Rs 10,000/-

Vijayawada
4 May 2008

Three months after pay to me or my order the sum of Rs 10,000 (Rupees Ten Thousand only) for value received.

To
K Shankar
Shankar Book House,
Beach Road,
Visakhapatnam.

STAMP
Krishna
for Krishna Enterprises

There are three parties to the bill of exchange, namely drawer, drawee and payee. The person who makes the bill is called 'drawer'. The person who is directed to pay money is called "drawee". The person to whom the payment is to be made is called "payee". The drawer and payee may be the same person. If it is kept till due date, it is transferred by endorsement, the holder in due course becomes the payee.

Essential Feature of Bill of Exchange

(a) It must be in writing.
(b) It must contain an express order to pay.

(c) It must be signed by the drawer.
(d) The order should be unconditional.
(e) The sum payable must be specified.
(f) The parties to the bill, drawer, drawee and payee must be certain.
(g) It should be properly stamped.

Difference between a Promissory Note and a Bill of Exchange

The following are the differences between a bill of exchange and a promissory note.

Promise and Order

A promissory note contains an unconditional promise to pay money by the debtor to the creditor. The maker makes the promise. A bill on the other hand contains an order to pay a certain sum of money.

Number of Parties

In the case of promissory note, there are only two parties, maker and payee. There are three parties in the case of a bill of exchange, drawer, drawee and payee. At times the drawer and payee may be the same person.

Acceptance

A bill of exchange requires acceptance by the drawee to become a legal instrument. But a promissory note does not require acceptance because the maker himself is the promiser undertaking to pay.

Conditional Acceptance

A bill may be accepted conditionally. But a promissory note cannot attach any conditions.

Nature of Liability

The liability of the maker of promissory note is primary and absolute. But the liability of the drawer of the bill is secondary and conditional. The drawee is primarily liable.

Presentment for Payment

Both bill and promissory notes are to be presented for payment. A promissory note may be dishonoured by non-payment. A bill of exchange is to be accepted before it is presented for payment. It may be dishonoured by non-acceptance or non-payment. Notice of dishonour must be given to all parties by the holder.

Maker's Position

In a promissory note, the maker stands in immediate pecuniary relationship with the payee. In the case of bill of exchange, the maker (i.e. drawer) stands in immediate relationship with the acceptor and not the payee. The maker of a promissory note cannot attach any conditions. The acceptor of a bill of exchange can accept the bill conditionally.

Formalities in Case of Dishonour

In the case of dishonour of a bill of exchange either by non-acceptance or non-payment, notice of dishonour must be given by the holder to all prior parties. In the case of dishonour of a promissory note for payment, no such notice is necessary.

Classification of Negotiable Instruments

Bearer v. Order Instruments

As per Section 11 of the Negotiable Instruments Act, a negotiable instrument is a bearer instrument when

(a) It is expressed to be payable to the bearer.
(b) The only/last endorsement or it is an endorsement in blank, for example, a bill is payable to Mr P or bearer. As per Section 13(i) of the Negotiable Instruments Act, a negotiable instrument is an order instrument, when
    - it is payable to the order of a certain person, and
    - does not restrict its transfer, e.g., a bill if payable to Mr P or order.

Demand v. Future Time Instrument

A negotiable instrument is payable on demand when

(a) It is expressed to be payable on demand or at sight or on presentment, or
(b) No time is fixed for its payment, for example, deemed bills and cheques are payable on demand only. An instrument is payable at a future time, when it is payable at a fixed period after its date or sight or an event which is certain to happen. Supposing the event is not certain to happen, the instrument becomes invalid.

Trade v. Accommodation Bill

A trade bill originates from a genuine trade transaction. An accommodation bill, on the other hand, is drawn and accepted without any consideration with a view to help each other. A draws a bill on B who accepts it without any consideration.

A, then, discounts it and obtains money on the due date. A gives the necessary funds to B to meet the bill. It is also called "cross firing" or "Kites".

Clean v. Documentary Instruments

If the bill or promissory notes are accompanied by certain documents like invoice, bill of lading, insurance, etc., they are called documentary instruments. They are used in foreign trade. They may be D/P bills (documents against payment). In the case of D/P bill, the documents will be handed over only after the payment is made by the importer. If no such documents are accompanied by, the instrument is said to be a clean instrument.

Inland v. Foreign Instruments

A negotiable instrument is deemed to be an inland one, when

(a) It is drawn and payable in India.
(b) It is drawn upon any person resident in India, irrespective of his place of origin, for example,
   - a bill of exchange drawn in Tirupathi on a merchant in Mumbai payable at New York
   - a bill of exchange drawn on Karimnagar merchant by an American merchant, and payable at Karimnagar.

As per Section 12 of the Negotiable Instrument Act, an instrument which is not an inland one is deemed to be a foreign instrument. The term usance, is generally employed in a foreign bill. Usance refers to the time fixed for payment of a bill. Foreign bills are usually drawn in sets. They are drawn in sets to ensure quick delivery and to avoid the possibility of loss in transit, since, they have to be sent over long distances.

Clean v. Ambiguous Instrument

Instruments which can be clearly identified as bill or promissory note or cheque are called clear instruments. But instruments which can be interpreted either as a bill or promissory note are called ambiguous instruments. It arises mainly because of faulty drafting of the instrument, for example, Augustine draws a bill on Gopal, a non-existent person. The bill is payable to the order of Augustine himself. Then, he endorses it to Janakiram. As Gopal is a non-existent person, Augustine becomes primarily liable, and hence, it cannot be treated as a promissory note also, in spite of the fact, that it has been worded as a bill. In this case, the holder has the option to treat it either way. But, once the option is exercised, it is final.

Complete v. Inchoate Instruments

When a negotiable instrument is complete in all its particulars, it is called a complete instrument. When it is an incomplete one, duly signed and stamped, which the holder can complete up to the value mentioned, or up to the value covered by the stamp affixed on it, it is called inchoate instrument. Any person who signs such an instrument is liable to the holder in due course, to the extent of such an account (completed) introduced by the holder. Others can get back the intended amount only, for example, X signs a promissory note and gives to his agent P, and instructs him to complete it with the amount of the purchase money. P buys goods for INR 1,000 from M and introduces INR 1,300 in the amount column. M cannot get INR 1,300 since he is not holder in due course.

Fictitious v. Escrow Bill

When the bill is drawn on fictitious persons, it is said to be a fictitious bill. When the drawer is a fictitious person, but the acceptor is genuine, the holder in due course can enforce the payment of such a bill. But, the first endorsement and the signature of the drawer must be in the same handwriting. A bill delivered conditionally or for a special purpose is called escrow. The liability in such a bill does not arise till the conditions are fulfilled or the special purpose is satisfied. Hence, again the right of a holder in due course is not affected. He can enforce the payment notwithstanding the fact, whether the condition is fulfilled or not.

Cheque

Section 6 of the Negotiable Instruments Act defines "a cheque is a bill of exchange drawn on a specified banker and not expressed to be payable otherwise than on demand".

Dr Hart in his "Law of Banking" defines a cheque as an unconditional order in writing, drawn on a banker, signed by the drawer, requiring the banker to pay on demand a sum certain in money to or to the order of a specified person or bearer, and which does not order any act to be done in addition to the payment of money.

A cheque is also a bill of exchange with two additional features. They are as follows:

(a) It is always drawn on a specified banker.
(b) It is always payable on demand.

Essential Features of a Cheque

(a) A cheque is an instrument in writing – Oral orders do not come under the definition of cheque. The writing may be done by means of a pen, pencil, typewriter or it may be printed characters. However, banks should discourage writing with lead pencil, as it is very easy to make unauthorised alterations which are difficult to detect.

(b) It is an unconditional order – The cheque must contain an unconditional order. There should not be any conditions attached to payment. The word "order" need not be used for the purpose of conveying the order. The order relating to payment may be conveyed by the word "pay" or words "please pay". The order to pay should be unconditional. In Section 5, the term "unconditional" has been explained to some extent. An order is not unconditional if the order to pay is with the condition that payment should be made on the happening of a specified event which is bound to happen. For instance, if it is stated that the payment shall be made on A attaining majority or his grandfather's death. It is not an unconditional order on the other hand, if the payment is to be made on X marrying Miss Y it is a conditional order, because X may or may not marry Miss Y. An order to pay from a particular fund is not an unconditional order. But an indication that the cheque should be debited to a particular account is unconditional, where the customer is maintaining more than one account. It does not become a conditional order merely because it specifies the particular account to which the amount of the cheque is to be debited. If it is stated that the amount of the cheque should be paid on the payee giving a receipt for the amount, it is a conditional order. But if it is not a part of the order, an instruction given to the payee at the foot of the cheque, it is not deemed a conditional order, in as much as it is addressed to the payee, but not to the banker.

(c) It should be drawn on a specified banker – A cheque is always drawn on a particular banker only. Usually the name and address of the banker is clearly printed on the cheque leaf itself. It is advisable that the full name of the banker is mentioned in the cheque. For example instead of "I.B" it must be written as "Indian Bank". A cheque drawn on a particular branch of a particular bank cannot be encashed at another branch of the same bank, unless there is an agreement between the parties.

(d) The payee must be certain – The person to whom the payment is to be made must be certain. A cheque may be made payable to certain person, or order or bearer. The term "person" refers to "person" in the legal sense of the term, and a cheque can be made payable to a firm, company, associations, etc. The payee is certain, notwithstanding the fact that it is made in favour of a particular office such as the secretary of an association or principal of a college. A cheque can also be made payable to two or more persons.

(e) It is always payable on demand – A cheque is always payable only on demand. It is not necessary to use the word "on demand" as in the case of a demand bill. As per Section 19 of the Negotiable Instruments Act, unless a time factor is specified by the drawer, the cheque is always payable on demand.

(f) A cheque must be an order to pay a certain sum of money – The order must be for the payment of a certain sum of money. In other words, it must not relate to the payment of a certain quantity of articles. Further the amount to be paid must be certain. In the case of promissory notes, the sum is certain although it includes a certain amount plus interest at a certain per cent for the period of the promissory note. Similarly if a cheque is drawn in foreign currency, the amount may be calculated at the ruling rate of exchange on that account if it does not cease to be certain sum of money.

(g) To be signed by the drawer – The cheque must be signed by the drawer, that is, the customer. The drawer normally puts his signature at the bottom right hand corner of the cheque. The signature must be that of the person in whose name the account is kept or his authorised agent. When the signature differs from the specimen or it is slightly different, the banker need not honour the cheque.

Form of the Cheque

A cheque can take the form of an order written on an ordinary piece of paper, but bankers usually insist upon the use of printed cheque forms supplied by them to their customer. A cheque is not invalid simply because it is made on an ordinary slip of paper, but usually the rules for opening an account specify that the customers should make use of printed cheque forms only. It is by virtue of such a rule that the banker would be justified in dishonouring cheques not drawn on the printed forms supplied to the customers. The use of printed cheque forms is desirable for the following reasons:

(a) The printed form ensures that all the legal requirements of a cheque are met. The customer is saved from the trouble of drafting each cheque in conformity with the requirements of law.

(b) It makes forgery difficult because the forger will first have to obtain the cheque book of the customer before he can think of forging his signature.

(c) The alterations are easier to detect when printed forms are used than when ordinary slips of paper are used.

(d) Where the drawer's signature is not legible, the banker can know the name of the drawer by referring to cheque book records.

(e) The customer can countermand a cheque by simply intimating the number of the cheque to the banker.

(f) The counterfoils of the cheque book serve as a record of the various payments made by the customer by means of such cheques.

Sometimes bankers supply special cheque forms to their customers. Magnetic Ink Character (MICR) of cheques, drafts technology has been introduced by the RBI to speed up the cheque clearing process. The process involves the following steps:

(a) Standardisation of quality, size, printing of cheques or drafts with suitable space for encoding information at the bottom.
(b) Encoding the magnetic ink, specific details on the cheque itself to facilitate mechanical sorting. The code line contains information in the following manner.
   - first six numbers indicate cheque number
   - next three numbers indicate city code
   - next three numbers indicate bank code and the next three numbers indicate branch code. The magnetic portion (right hand side), when put under MICR equipment allows instant readability and identification.

Specimen of MICR cheque.

Date:- __________
Pay ________________________ or bearer __________
Rupees ____________________________________
Account No. ____________
State Bank of Hyderabad
Nampally Branch Rs. __________
Hyderabad – 1.
005610005002100

Material Alteration

If there is any material alteration, namely, alterations of the date of the instrument or place of payment or the sum payable or the party to whom the money is payable, all such material alterations should generally be evidenced by the full signature of the drawer.

Mutilated Cheque

A cheque is said to be mutilated when it has been torn to two or more pieces but pasted afterwards, whether such a cheque should be paid or not will depend upon the available evidence and the surrounding circumstances and the extent of legality of material facts. In case a cheque is accidentally torn in the hands of payee, the banker can pay the sum after obtaining confirmation from the drawer or getting the guarantee from the collecting banker. If no confirmation is available, the banker must return it with the remark "Mutilated Cheque".

Bank Draft

Bank drafts are bills drawn either on demand or otherwise by one banker on another in favour of a third party or by one branch of a bank on another branch of the same bank. A demand draft is a bill of exchange drawn by a bank on another bank and is a negotiable instrument.

Cheque v. Bill of Exchange

The difference between a cheque and a bill of exchange are given here under.

(a) A cheque is always drawn on a printed form. A bill need not be drawn on a printed form.
(b) The drawer (banker) need not accept the cheque. Accordingly, there is no printing of contract between the payee and the banker. Acceptance by the drawee is essential in the case of bill of exchange.
(c) A cheque is always supposed to be drawn against the funds in the hands of the banker. There is no such supposition in the case of a bill.
(d) A cheque is an instrument for immediate payment. Bill is drawn for a specified period and so it is intended for circulation. Therefore, it is entitled to days of grace.
(e) In the case of cheque, the liability of the drawer continues for six months. Unreasonable delay in the presentation will discharge the bill of exchange.
(f) A cheque is free from stamp duty, where as a bill is subject to advalorum duty.
(g) Cheque is not drawn in sets. Foreign bills are always drawn in sets.
(h) Cheque can be crossed to ensure safety. The bill cannot be crossed.
(i) A cheque may be countermanded. Countermanding of a bill is not permissible.
(j) Cheque is not protested or noted on dishonour. Bill is usually protested and noted for dishonour.
(k) In case of dishonour, notice of dishonour to the drawer is not essential in the case of cheque. Notice of dishonour must be sent to hold the party liable for a bill.
(l) Statutory protection as given under Section 85 and Section 131 of the Negotiable Instruments Act applies only to cheque. Statutory protection is not available in the case of a bill.

Other Requisites of a Cheque

Issue of Cheque

A cheque is said to be issued when the drawer parts with it to another person. The intention is that the proceeds of the cheque shall be paid to that person or to his order or to bearer. The issue of the cheque is very important question in fixing the liability of the drawer because the drawer is not liable on a cheque until he has issued it. Sometimes the drawer may be induced by fraud to issue a cheque. Even then, it is taken to be duly issued.

Dating of Cheque

A cheque is not invalid simply for the reason that it is not dated. But bankers do not honour an undated cheque because they have no means of determining whether it is a late cheque or not. If the cheque is not dated by the drawer, any person in possession of the cheque can fill in the cheque, but this right of filling in the date must be exercised within in a reasonable time. The drawer of a cheque can put the date earlier than or later than, the date on which he draws it. A cheque is not invalid merely because it is ante-dated or bears the date of a Sunday. The banker cannot refuse payment of a cheque simply because it is ante-dated subject to the condition that it is not a stale cheque, that is, that six months have not elapsed from the date of issue. The banker cannot refuse payment of a post-dated cheque if other conditions are satisfied, it is presented after the date of issue.

Payee

If the payee's name is not written by the drawer of the cheque, any holder can insert the payee's name and the banker would be entitled to make payment to the payce as indicated in the cheque or to his order. If a cheque without the payee's name is presented to the banker for payment he should dishonour it, because it is doubtful whether it is a cheque at all. The payee has the duty of presenting the cheque for payment within a reasonable time after receiving it. If he fails to present the cheque for payment within a reasonable time, and if the drawer suffers a loss on account of his delay, he will lose his right against the drawer to the extent of such loss.

Amount of the Cheque

The amount to be paid to the payee must be clearly stated both in words, and figures. No blank space should be left before and after the amount stated in words and figures.

Signature

The cheque must be signed by the drawer himself or by the person authorised by him. If the drawer happens to be illiterate, cheques can be drawn by means of thumb impression of the drawer duly witnessed by a person known to the banker, preferably in the presence of the banker himself. The signature on the cheque must correspond to the specimen signature of the customer obtained at the time of opening the account. Where the customer authorises another person to sign on his behalf, a letter containing the authorisation must be sent to the banker and also the specimen signature of the person so authorised.

Delivery

Unless the cheque is properly delivered, the drawer does not become liable thereon. Section 46 says, the making, acceptance or endorsement of a promissory note, bill of exchange or cheque is completed by delivery actual or constructive. If a cheque is lost in transit, who should bear the loss that may arise? If the drawer sends the cheque through post without a specific request from the payee to do so, the drawer should bear the loss. Open cheques should not be sent by ordinary post. They should be crossed if sent by ordinary post. To avoid any confusion, cheques sent by unregistered post are crossed specially.

Banker's Cheques

A banker's cheque is drawn by a banker upon himself. The concept of banker's cheque was introduced by the SBI in 1976, on the recommendations of the working group on customer service in banks. Banker's cheques are issued on behalf of customers and non-customers for facilitating local payments only, since drafts cannot be issued for local payment, banker's cheques have become popular. They are payable at the issuing branch only and they are specifically marked "not transferable" and payable at par locally.

Crossing of Cheques

When two parallel lines are drawn on the cheque, it is called crossing and such a cheque is called a Crossed Cheque. A crossed cheque can be paid only to the bank. A person who receives the crossed cheque, can deposit into his account in the bank and the amount will be credited to his account on clearance but it can seldom be paid across the counter. Crossing provides protection to the owner of the cheque. If the owner of the cheque loses a crossed cheque, or if someone steals a crossed cheque, the possessor of the lost cheque cannot encash the cheque across the counter. Crossing is of two types namely, general crossing and special crossing.

General Crossing

Section 123 of Negotiable Instruments Act, 1881 defines general crossing as follows:

"Where a cheque bears across its face, an addition of the words, 'and company' or any abbreviation thereof, between two parallel transverse lines simply either with or without the words 'not negotiable', that addition shall be deemed a 'crossing' and the cheque shall be deemed to be crossed generally".

Essentials of General Crossing

Essentials of general crossing are:

(a) Two lines are of paramount importance in crossing.
(b) The lines must be drawn parallel and transverse. Transverse means, that, they should be arranged in a crossing direction. They should not be straight lines. Mathematical signs for plus and multiplication do not constitute crossing, because, they are not parallel and do not run transverse.
(c) The lines are generally drawn on the left-hand side so as not to alter the printed number of the cheque.
(d) The words "and company" or its abbreviation may be written in between the lines. They do not constitute crossing without two parallel transverse lines.
(e) The words "not negotiable" may be added to a crossing.

Forms of General Crossing

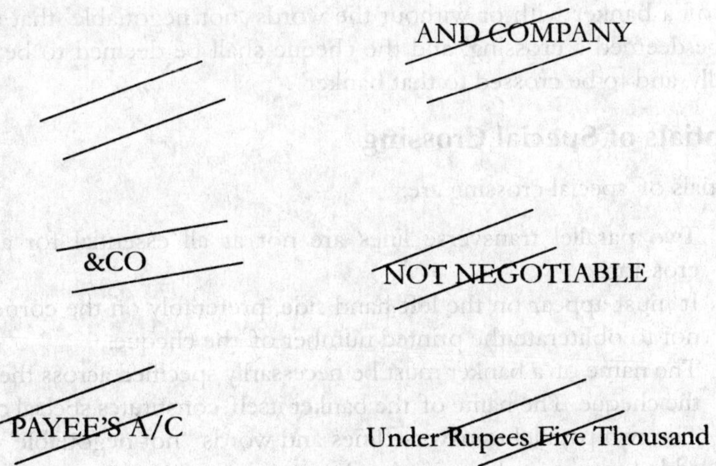

Significance of General Crossing

(a) The effect of general crossing is that it gives a direction to the paying banker. The direction is that, the paying banker should not pay the cheque at the counter. It should be paid only to a fellow banker. In other words, payment is made through an account and not at the counter. Section 126 of the Act clearly lays down that "where a cheque is crossed generally, the banker on whom it is drawn, shall not pay it otherwise than to a banker".

(b) The main intention of crossing a cheque is to give protection to it. When a cheque is crossed generally, a person who is not entitled to receive its payment, is prevented from getting that cheque cashed at the counter of the paying banker.

(c) If a crossed cheque is paid at the counter in contravention of the crossing, the payment does not amount to payment in due course, so the paying banker will lose his statutory protection. He has no right to debit his customer's account, since it will constitute a breach of his customer's mandate. He will be liable to the drawer for any loss which he may suffer. He will be liable to the true owner of the cheque who may be a third party, irrespective of the fact there is no contract between the banker and the third party. As a general rule, a banker is answerable only to his customer and thus liability to a third party here is an exception.

Special Crossing

Section 124 of the Negotiable Instruments Act of 1881 defines a special crossing as follows. "Where a cheque bears across its face, an addition of the name of a banker with or without the words 'not negotiable' that addition shall be deemed a crossing, and the cheque shall be deemed to be crossed specially, and to be crossed to that banker".

Essentials of Special Crossing

Essentials of special crossing are:

(a) Two parallel transverse lines are not at all essential for a special crossing.

(b) It must appear on the left-hand side, preferably on the corner, so as not to obliterate the printed number of the cheque.

(c) The name of a banker must be necessarily specified across the face of the cheque. The name of the banker itself constitutes special crossing.

(d) The two parallel transverse lines and words "not negotiable" may be added to a special crossing.

Forms of Special Crossing

SYNDICATE BANK

INDIAN BANK
NOT NEGOTIABLE

STATE BANK OF INDIA
PAYEES' A/C

Significance of Special Crossing

(a) It is also a direction to the paying banker. The direction is that, the paying banker should pay the cheque only to the banker, whose name appears in the crossing or to his agent. Section 126 of the Act clearly lays down that "where a cheque is crossed specially, the banker on whom it is drawn, shall not pay it, otherwise than to the banker to whom it is crossed or his agent for collection".

(b) A special crossing gives more protection to the cheque than a general crossing. It makes a cheque still safer because, a person, who does not have a real claim for it, would find it difficult to obtain payment. In special crossing, the cheque is specially crossed to the payee's banker. Hence, the banker, in whose favour the cheque has been crossed, knows the payee and his specimen signature well. So, he will not collect it for any person other than the payee. If there is any forgery, it can easily be detected by the banker. But we cannot say that, it gives full protection in the service, that, an unscrupulous person, who has an account in the same bank but at different branch, can encash it by forging the signature of the payee. It can also be detected. However, there is some danger in special crossing also. To overcome this danger "not negotiable" and "a/c payee" crossing have been introduced.

Not-Negotiable Crossing

Section 123, 124 of Negotiable Instruments Act permit the use of the words "not negotiable" in the crossing.

Forms of Not-Negotiable Crossing

NOT NEGOTIABLE
& Co.

NOT NEGOTIABLE
SYNDICATE BANK

NOT NEGOTIABLE

Significance of Not-Negotiable Crossing

A cheque crossed "not negotiable" can be transformed like any other cheque. But the transferee cannot obtain a better title than that of the transferor. Section 130 of the Negotiable Instruments Act provides that "A person taking a cheque crossed generally or specially in either case bearing the words "not negotiable" shall not have and shall not be capable of giving a better title to the cheque than that, which the person from whom he took it had".

The words "not negotiable" do not impose any additional duty on either the collecting banker or the paying banker. But it is a warning to the person, who takes this document, that he should be very careful in receiving it. Sir John Paget rightly says that the words "not negotiable" have no special meaning as far as a banker is concerned, and so, he can justifiably ignore it. The object of this type of crossing is to give protection to the true owner of the cheque by presenting his right against any subsequent holder. This type of a crossed cheques can safely be sent through post.

Account Payee Crossing

There is no provision in law regarding this type of crossing. But it has been developed in practice. If the words "a/c payee" are added to a crossing it becomes an a/c payee crossing.

A/C PAYEE

SYNDICATE BANK
GOPAL ACCOUNT

& CO A/C PAYEE

SALES TAX
OFFICER

Significance of A/c Payee Crossing

Account payee crossing does not restrict the transferability of cheques. In *British Bank of Middle East v. Abomal Brothers*, the drawer of a cheque (Abomal Brothers) pleaded that, since the cheque had been marked "a/c payee only" the negotiation on it was null and void. But it was held that "a/c payee" crossed cheque can be negotiated. But if the words 'or order' which appear immediately after the payee's name, are struck through and if the cheque is crossed a/c payee, the cheque will be considered to be not transferable. This type of crossing gives further protection to a cheque. This crossing gives a direction to the collecting banker. The direction is that, the collecting banker should not collect it for any person other than the payee. In other words, a collecting banker should ensure that the cheque is credited only to the account of the payee. Hence, practically such cheques cannot be negotiated further. If a collecting banker collects such a crossed cheque for any person other than the payee, it will constitute negligence on the part of the collecting banker and so, he will lose the statutory protection given under Section 131 of the Act.

In India, the a/c payee cheque directions were misused during the multi-crore securities scam period. The a/c payee cheque crossed to banker, on RBI instead of being credited to the payee banker, were credited directly to the broker's account. Hence RBI has issued the following strict orders with regard to an a/c payee crossing. "Crediting the process of a/c payee cheques to parties other than that clearly delivered in the instructions of the issuer of the cheques is unauthorised and should not be done under any circumstances". Thus in actual practice, a/c payee crossed cheques cannot be collected to the account of any person other than the payee himself. The safest form of crossing will be a combination of "not negotiable" and "a/c payee" crossing which gives the fullest protection to the cheque.

Double Crossing

Section 125 of the Act provides that where a cheque is crossed specially the banker to whom it is crossed, may again cross it specially to another banker, his agent for collection.

Section 127 of the Act lays down that "where a cheque is crossed specially to more than one banker, except when crossed to an agent for the purpose of collection, the banker on whom it is drawn, shall refuse payment thereof". Thus, if a cheque is crossed to two or more banks, the paying banker is put in a confused position as to whom he should pay. Such ambiguity renders the cheque invalid. But a banker in whose favour a cheque is crossed, can cross it again in favour of another banker for the purpose of collection. It does not render the cheque invalid.

Who can Cross a Cheque

(a) The drawer of a cheque can cross it at the time of issuing it.
(b) Any holder can cross an uncrossed cheque. He can convert general crossing into special crossing and he can even add the words "not negotiable" or "a/c payee" to a crossing.

(c) The banker in whose favour a cheque has been crossed, can again cross it in favour of another banker, for the purpose of collection as an agent.

Opening of Crossing

The cancellation of crossing is usually termed as "Opening of crossing". Law does not make any provision for the cancellation of crossing. But it has been evolved out of custom. When a drawer wants to cancel the crossing, he writes the words, "pay cash" upon the cheques, followed by his full signature. The drawer alone has a right to cancel the crossing. But once a crossed cheque has been issued, even the drawer's right ceases. In the words of Sir John Paget, "When the drawer has once parted with the cheque, he cannot retract or neutralise his mandate to the prejudice of any one who has taken the cheque on the faith of it".

Endorsement

In India and England, cheque does not operate as an assignment of debt. Hence, the payee of a cheque cannot have any claim against the paying banker. But in Scotland, it operates as an assignment of a debt and therefore, once a cheque comes into the hands of the payee, for all practical purposes, he is placed in the position of a drawer and he has a direct claim against the banker. The payee acquires all the rights that are available to the drawer.

In India, the payee has a claim against the banker only when,

(a) The banker marks a cheque and has taken up the liability to the payee.
(b) He makes payment in violation of the crossing.
(c) He is negligent in his duty of payment and collection of cheques.

Transfer of Cheque

However, a cheque can be transferred both in India and England in settlement of debt. It means that, the value represented by the instrument can be transferred from person to person. This transfer of cheque can be effected depending upon the nature of the instrument. A cheque may be either a bearer cheque or an order cheque. A bearer cheque can be transferred by mere delivery, where as an order cheque requires endorsement before delivery.

Endorsement is nothing but the process of signing one's name or affixing an accepted rubber stamp impression on a cheque, for the purpose of transfer. Thus, it is both a contract and a transfer. The delivery of the instrument is necessary to complete its endorsement.

The word "endorsement" can also be spelt as "indorsement". It is derived from the latin word "Indorsum" which means "upon the back" ('in' means "upon" and "dorsum" means "back"). The usual place for an endorsement is upon the back of the instrument. But there is no legal prohibition against the validity of the endorsement in the face of the instrument.

Possession of a bearer cheque is a conclusive evidence of the bearer's ownership. A bearer cheque in a strict legal sense, does not require endorsement. However, in practice, bankers request the holder of a bearer cheque to endorse it, before obtaining payment. This is only for identifying him, as the person receiving cash and moreover, it serves as a voucher for having paid the same. If the holder refuses to endorse, the banker may demand a stamped receipt from the customer, if the payment exceeds INR 500. There is no justification in compelling a holder of a bearer cheque to endorse it compulsory before encashing it.

Definition of Endorsement

Section 15 defines endorsement as follows:

"when the maker or holder of a negotiable instrument signs the same, otherwise than as such maker, for the purpose of negotiation, on the back or face thereof or on a slip of paper annexed thereto or so signs for the same purpose a stamped paper intended to be completed as a negotiable instrument, he is said to have endorsed the same and is called endorser. The person to whom the instrument is endorsed or transformed is called the endorsee".

Allonge

If the space available on the back has been completely covered, a piece of paper may safely be attached to the instrument and subsequent endorsement may be made on that paper. The paper so attached is known as allonge.

Significance of Endorsement

An endorsement consists of two contracts namely (a) Contract of transfer of property in the instrument, and (b) Contract of contingent assumption of liability on the part of the endorser. The endorser of a negotiable instrument, by his act of endorsing signifies the following to his endorsee and to any subsequent holder, that when the instrument left his hands,

- He had a good title to it
- It was genuine in all its particulars at the time of his endorsement

- All the previous endorsement were genuine. Thus, Section 122 of the Negotiable Instrument Act provides that, "no endorser of a negotiable instrument shall, in a suit thereon by a subsequent holder, be permitted to deny signature or capacity to contract of any prior party to instrument"
- Further the endorser, by his act of endorsing, promises to indemnify the endorsee or any subsequent holder for any loss suffered by him on the dishonour of the instrument, provided, the procedure necessary on dishonour has been duly followed
- In addition to the above, an endorsement carries with it a right of further negotiation to the endorsee, along with the right of ownership.

Thus, the significance of a simple signature, that constitutes an endorsement, is more than the purpose it serves namely "the transfer" of the instrument.

Assignment v. Endorsement

(a) An assignment means that transfer of legal title to a property. Endorsement not only means that transfer of legal title, but also it includes the assumption of liability of the assignor ceases, whereas the liability of the endorser continues till the instrument is finally discharged.

(b) In the case of assignment, the assignee's title is subject to the title of the assignor. But in the case of endorsement, good title can be passed on to the endorsee, even when there is defective title, that is, endorsement to a holder in due course cuts off defenses to the instrument.

Kinds of Endorsements

Blank Endorsement

In the case of blank endorsement, the endorser puts his signature on the back of the instrument without mentioning the name of any specified person in whose favour the endorsement is made. In this type of instrument, the instrument is payable to bearer, and consequently it can be negotiated by mere delivery.

Example

A cheque is payable to K Krishna or order. It is simply signed by Krishna on the back, it constitutes a blank endorsement.

Special Endorsement or Full Endorsement

In the case of special or full endorsement, the endorser mentions the name of a specified person or to the order of that person.

Example

Pay to Krishna Kumar or order.
Sd/- Ramesh Kumar.

An instrument with blank endorsement can be converted into a special endorsement by any holder by specifying the name of an endorsee and putting his signature. A cheque, originally a bearer cheque, can be converted in to an order cheque, by means of a full endorsement.

The endorsement in the following forms must be regarded as special, when the cheque is endorsed by A in favour of B.

- pay to the order of B – A
- A in favour of B
- B or order A
- please exchange B or A.

However, in practice, if a bearer cheque is endorsed in full and the banker has some doubts in his mind, he should find out the bonafide title of the holder before making payment, even though law does not require him to do so.

Restrictive Endorsement

In the case of restrictive endorsement, the endorser restricts the further negotiation of the instrument.

Example

To pay Ram Prasad only.
Sd/- K Ram Mohan.

Or the endorser restricts the endorsee to deal with the bill as directed by the former.

Example

Pay to Gopal Krishna or order for collection.
Sd/- Krishna Kishore.

Section 50 of the Negotiable Instruments Act of 1881 says, a restrictive endorsement is one which limits the further negotiation of an instrument. The endorsee in such cases cannot further endorse it. Generally the word "only" is added after the endorsee's name.

Partial Endorsement

If only a part of the amount of the instrument is endorsed, it is a case of partial endorsement. According to Section 56 of the Negotiable Instruments Act,

"No writing on a negotiable instrument is valid for the purpose of negotiability. If such a writing purports to transfer only a part of the amount appearing to be due on the instrument". Law recognises only an endorsement of the entire amount of the instrument. Hence, partial endorsement is not valid.

Example

A cheque of Rs 1000/- is endorsed by Nayeem as follows:

Pay to Ramam Rs 500/- only.
Nayeem.

Supposing the same cheque is endorsed as follows:

Pay to Ramam Rs 500/- only and pay to Laxman Rs 500/- only.

The validity of this endorsement is doubtful. Even though the entire amount has been endorsed, the endorsement in their favour is partial and invalid. But, where a bill of exchange has been paid in part, it may be endorsed for the balance.

Per Pro Endorsement

It is an endorsement made by an authorised agent. Prior information about the delegation of authority to the agent must have been given to the banker. Otherwise, a banker is not legally bound to accept this type of endorsement.

Conditional Endorsement

In the case of a conditional endorsement, the transfer of property in the instrument is made to depend on the fulfillment of a specified condition.

Example

Pay to Vijaya Kumar on arrival of ship *Krishna*.
Sd/- Sampath Kumar.

Pay to Y, if he marries X within one month.
- Sudhkar.

Pay to Sadanand on completion of house building.
- Abraham.

According to English law, the condition may be disregarded by the payer and the payment to the endorsee is valid, whether the condition has been fulfilled or not. In India, however if the drawer accepts a bill after it was conditionally endorsed, he should respect the conditions. Since a cheque must be an unconditional order, a conditional banker can simply return the cheque.

Hence, the banker should see the fulfillment of the condition before making payment, just to satisfy his customers. It is advisable to get the approval of the customer before making payment. The banker should yield to such requests only when the customer is ready to identify the banker for any loss, which he may suffer in such cases. Then the position of the paying banker is not certain as far as conditional endorsement is concerned.

Facultative Endorsement

In the case of facultative endorsement, the endorser waives some of his rights.

Example

Pay to Satyanarayana, Notice of dishonour waived,
Sd/- P Chidambaram.

In such endorsement, the endorsee need not give him notice of dishonour.

Sans Frais Endorsement

"Sans Frais" means "without expense". Here the endorser does not want any expense to be included on his account on the instrument. That is the endorser accepts with ability for the account of the instrument. But he does not want any additional expenses, like noting and protesting charges to be borne by him.

Example

K K Rao endorses the cheque as follows:

Pay to Ram Murthy or order without expense to me
- K K Rao.

Sans Recourse Endorsement

In the case of a "Sans Recourse" endorsement, the endorser removes himself for his liability to the endorsee by making it clean that the endorsee, or any subsequent holder, should not look to him for payment in case the bill is dishonoured.

Example

Pay to D V Ramana without recourse to me.
Sd/- S V Prasad.

In the above case, if S V Prasad endorses the bill "without recourse" to D V Ramana and D V Ramana agrees to take it with such endorsement, he takes it with the understanding that in case, he fails to recover the money from the acceptor or any of the previous endorsees, to S V Prasad (D V Ramana) cannot sue S V Prasad on the instrument.

Endorser's Liability

(a) As per Section 35 of the Negotiable Instrument Act, every endorser is liable to every subsequent holder, in case, the instrument is dishonoured.
(b) The endorser is liable only if he is served with a notice of dishonour.
(c) When there are two or more endorsements on an instrument, the liability of the endorser will be fixed in the order in which, their signatures appear on the instrument.
(d) This liability of the endorser can be excluded by a separate contract to the contrary.
(e) The endorser can get rid of his liability by making such endorsement like "sans recourse".
(f) When the instrument is paid in due course, the endorser is relieved from his liability.
(g) The liability of the endorser continues even after death till the instrument is paid. The endorsee can sue even after the death of the endorser supposing the endorsee dies, the right to sue the endorser is available to his legal representative. (Karupiah Palukki (Died) and others v. Periasami AIR 1968 Madras 260.)

Regularity of Endorsement

Complimentary and Courtesy Title

An endorsement should be in the form of an ordinary signature of the payee or endorsee. Complimentary prefixes and suffixes and other courtesy title should not form a part of the endorsement. According to Sheldon, endorsement that includes a courtesy, though legally valid, is not usually accepted in England. The same practice prevails in India also. Hence courtesy title like Mr, Mrs, Miss, Lala, Babjee, Captain, Bachelor, Esquire, Dr Padmasri, etc., should not precede or follow the names of the endorsees in the endorsement. But, if the courtesy title appearing in the endorsement is merely descriptive, then it is accepted.

Example

A cheque payable to Dr M Natarajan may be endorsed as:

Dr M Natarajan, M.D.

Endorsement by Illiterate Persons

Cheque payable to illiterate persons should be endorsed with their left thumb impression, which should be witnessed by an individual well known to both the parties. The witness should give his/her signature and the complete address.

A cheque is payable to Narayana, an illiterate person. The proper endorsement is thumb impression of Narayana attested by witness.

by
A Janakiram,
Advocate,
5, Express Road, Banglore.

Endorsement by the Deceased Persons

A cheque in the name of a deceased person must be endorsed by his legal representative.

Example

A cheque is payable to Mr Rama Swamy (now dead).
It is endorsed as follows:

Pay to Mr Venkata Swamy or order.
Raman Ramaswamy
s/o Late Rama Swamy.

Endorsement by Women

In the case of spinster, the correct endorsement consists of her first name and surname. That is her endorsement in her maiden name followed by her father's name.

If a cheque is endorsed as Miss Vyas, it is an incomplete name for a girl. So, the correct form of endorsement is Anita Vyas (Miss). Even the word "Miss" need not be used. If it is not used, it can be presumed to have the meaning of Anita, daughter of Vyas. In the case of married women, she should endorse it by her name plus the name of her husband. When a cheque is payable to a married women, in her maiden name, then the correct form of endorsement is her name followed by her husband's surname with the words "nee" (meaning born as or) and her maiden name.

Example

A cheque is payable to Miss Anitha Vyas. But now she is married to Arun Kumar. Here, the correct form of endorsement is:

Anitha Arun Kumar nee Vyas.

Correct and Incorrect Spelling

If the name of the payee or endorsee is spelt incorrectly on a cheque, then the endorsement must correspond with that of misspelt name.

Example

A cheque payable to Mr Ayyangar or order as whereas, the correct spelling of the payee's name is Iyyengar. Here the proper endorsement would be Ayyangar. If the payee wants, he can add his correct spelling in brackets.

Endorsement by Firms

Endorsement in the case of firms can be either in the name of the firm itself, or, it may be by an authorised agent, or by a legally authorised person on behalf of the firm, the name of the firm must be mentioned in full.

In *Arab Bank Ltd. v. Ross* 1952 Q.B 216, 218 (1952) All E.R 709, 716, it was held that the omission of the word 'company' in the endorsement amounts to an irregular endorsement.

Example

A cheque payable to 'Anand Trading Company' might be endorsed as follows:

(a) Anand Trading Company

It is a regular one, but in practice, most of the bankers do not accept this.

(b) Pay to 'Srirama Furniture Company'
For Anand Trading Company
Anand
(partner)

(c) Pay to 'Tirumala Traders'
Per Pro Anand Trading Company
Anand

It is usual practice to prefix 'Per Pro' to the name of the principal and not to that of the agent.

Endorsement by Companies

Section 47 of the Companies Act provides, "a bill of exchange, *hundi* or promissory note shall be deemed to have been made, drawn, accepted or endorsed on behalf of a company, if made, drawn, accepted or endorsed in the name of or by or on behalf or on account of the company, by any person under its authority expressed or implied". Hence, the endorsement in the case of companies consists of the signature of the authorised person, followed by the rubber stamp impression of his designation and also the company.

Example

A cheque payable to 'Narimam Co. Ltd.' is endorsed as follows:

'For Narimam Co. Limited'
XYZ (Managing Director or Director)

In the case of companies liquidation, the correct endorsement would be:

Pay to APEX Company Limited
For Narimam Company Limited
(In Liquidation)
ABC (Liquidators)

Endorsement by Public Authorities

A cheque payable to a public authority may be endorsed by the office-in-charge for and on behalf of the respective body.

Example
A cheque is payable to Vijayawada Municipal Corporation. The proper endorsement is:

For Vijayawada Municipal Corporation
Shiv Kumar,
(Commissioner)

Endorsement by Clubs and Other Non-trading Association

The proper endorsement in such case consists of the signature of the authorised persons followed by his designation and the seal of the association.

Example
A cheque is payable to Juniors Cricket Club. It is endorsed as follows:

Pay to Youth Association Club
For Juniors Cricket Club
Ranga Rao
(Secretary and Treasurer)

If a cheque is received in the personal name of the Secretary, but, the account is for the institution, then mere signature will constitute a regular endorsement.

Endorsement by Executors and Trustees

A cheque payable to executors and administration may be endorsed by all of them or any one of them acting for all.

Example
A cheque payable to the executors of late D Sanath Kumar. The endorsement might read:

Pay to the Income Tax Officer
M Murali,
V Anand (Executors of D Sanath Kumar)

In the case of trustees, the endorsement must be made by all of them.

Endorsement by Joint Payees

A cheque payable to two or more payees must be endorsed by each one of them. However, if any activity has been given to any of them, he can make a valid endorsement. If any one of the joint payees died and their banker has knowledge of it, he can permit the other payees to endorse the instrument.

Endorsement by Impersonal Payees

Where a cheque is payable to impersonal payees, it requires the endorsement of the authority in relation to the impersonal payees.

Example
A cheque payable to the "Income Tax" might be endorsed as follows:

V Nagarajan
(Income Tax Officer)
Nagpur

A cheque payable to cash or bearer may require the endorsement of the bearer.

Other Regularities

(a) All endorsements should be made in ink only even though, law does not object to an endorsement being made in pencil. But endorsements in pencil are liable to alterations and obliteration. So they are discouraged.
(b) An endorsement in block letters, is not a regular endorsement. Example "SYAMAL PRASAD".
(c) An endorsement in the form of fascimile of the payee's signature is also legally valid. But Sir John Paget discouraged this practice.
(d) A rubber stamp endorsement is as valid as a written endorsement. But, it is not for the safety of a banker and customer, if it is not accompanied by the handwritten signature of an authorised officer.
(e) A typewritten endorsement is valid under the act. Even, endorsement in printed character can be accepted. But in practice bankers do not normally permit it, as it can be duplicated very easily.
(f) Where the endorsement happens to be in a language which the banker is not expected to know, then the paying banker can refuse the payment for its confirmation. But he should give valid reasons for the same.

Endorser's Liability

(a) As per Section 35 of the Negotiable Instruments Act, every endorser is liable to every sub segment holder in case, the instrument is dishonoured.

(b) The endorser is liable, only if he is served with a notice of dishonour.

(c) The liability of the endorser can be excluded in a separate contract to the contrary.

(d) The endorser can get rid of his liability by making such endorsement like "Sans Recourse".

(e) When the instrument is paid in due course, the endorser is relieved from his liability.

(f) The liability of the endorser continues even after death till the instrument is paid. The endorsee can sue even after the death of the endorser. If the endorsee dies, the right to save the endorser in available to his legal representatives.

Marking of Cheques

"Marking" or certification of a cheque is the act, whereby, a drawer bank obligates itself to pay a cheque according to its terms. This is generally done by a paying bank, stamping across the face of a cheque the word "good for payment" or "certified" or "accepted" followed by the name of the bank and the signature of the authorised officer of the bank.

Marking v. Acceptance

(a) Marking of a cheque is not statutorily recognised in India, whereas acceptance of a bill is a legal one. In other words, a cheque is straight away processed for payment, where as a bill is first processed for acceptance and then for payment. Hence, acceptance is a must for a bill, whereas, it is not essential in the case of a cheque.

(b) The acceptor of a bill takes up his liability only by accepting the same. On the other hand, marking or acceptance of a cheque by the banker is superfluous because the banker is already under a contractual liability to pay it. Hence, marking of a cheque is not its acceptance.

(c) The drawee banker is under no legal obligations to mark a cheque, where as the drawer of a bill must accept it, when processed for acceptance. Hence, a cheque, though a bill of exchange, is of a special type, and marking on it cannot have the same effect of acceptance on a bill.

Significance of Marking

The significance of marking, therefore greatly depends on the usage and custom, of the places. If such marking, by custom amounts to the acceptance by the banker to honour a cheque, it adds the credit of the banker, to that of the drawer and hence, the banker should see to its payment at any cost. In India, there has been a custom to mark cheques for clearance purposes, and "marking for clearance purpose" has been recognised. If customer does not recognise marking, it simply indicates that at the time of marking, the paying banker has in his hands sufficient available funds of the drawer, and that, the signature of the drawer is genuine. It simply gives an additional currency to that cheque.

The position in America is quiet different, marking has been statutorily recognised in America. Certification of a cheque in America amounts to that,

(a) The drawer's signature is genuine.
(b) The cheque will be duly honoured when processed for payment.
(c) The cheque is drawn when sufficient funds are in the hands of the drawer.

The legal significance of marking depends upon, whether it is same at the request of the drawer, at the request of the payee, or of another banker.

Marking at the Request of the Drawer

A customer of a bank in order to satisfy the payee, may request his bankers to mark his cheque as good for payment. Once a banker marks such a cheque, he cannot defeat in liability thereon. In such cases, the banker takes up his liability to the payee, which is an absolute one. The certifying banker must keep in mind the following points.

(a) This certification, at the request of the drawer, amounts to a constructive payment of that cheque. However, the acceptance of this certified cheque by the payee does not discharge the drawer immediately.
(b) The banker is liable to the bonafide holder of a cheque marked by him regardless of the state of the drawer's account. The death, insolvency and insecurity of the customer should not stand in the way of payment of that marked cheque. It should be paid at any cost.
(c) Once the banker marks a cheque at the request of the customer, he is justified in regarding that cheque as "constructively paid".
(d) The banker can earmark sufficient funds to meet the marked cheque, and if necessary, he may even dishonour own cheque that might be

subsequently processed so that sufficient amount may be available to honour the marked cheque.

(e) Even a garnishee order cannot attach the customer account to the extent of the amount of the marked cheque. The funds, to the amount of the marked cheque, are regarded as having been appropriated to meet it.

(f) The drawer has no right to counter mark the payment of the cheque marked at his report. However, he can counter mark its payment, if the cheque has not yet left his possession.

(g) Certification of a cheque at the request of the drawer amounts to a guarantee of its payment, the certifying banker should deduct the amount of the cheque from the drawer's account and transfer it to the "marked cheques account" which will be cancelled at the time of payment of that marked cheque. Some bankers open a "suspense account", instead of marked cheques account.

Marking at the Request of the Payee or Any Holder

The practice of marking cheques at the request of the payee or any holder has been statutorily recognised in North America. Certification of cheque at the request of the holder discharges the drawer from his liability on the instrument in America. But in India, the practice has not been recognised. Hence, if a banker marks a cheque at the request of the holder, and if the customer countermands its payment before their cheque is presented for payment, the banker cannot pay the cheque. If he pays that cheque, he will have to bear the loss himself. Moreover, the death or unsoundness of the drawer does stand in the way of honouring such marked cheques. Due to the above reasons, bankers in India refuse to mark cheques at the request of the holder.

Marking at the Request of Another Banker

There is a custom among bankers to mark cheques as good for payment for the purpose of clearance. If cheques are received too late for clearing, the collecting banker may request the paying banker to mark the cheque, in order to ascertain the fate of the cheque. The cheques, so marked, are processed as usual on the next day and are paid. This marking of cheques, for clearance purpose, has been legally recognised in many countries including India. The banker, who has marked the cheque, should appropriate sufficient money to meet the marked cheque.

Forged Signature of the Drawer

By marking a cheque, the banker guarantees the genuineness of the signature of the drawer. Hence, even if the drawer's signature is forged, the certifying banker must honour it.

Forged Signature of the Payee or Endorsee

The certifying banker does not guarantee the genuineness of the signature of the payee or endorsee, if any, appearing on the instrument. Therefore, he is made liable for any forgery of their signatures.

No obligation to Mark a Cheque

There is no obligation on the part of a drawer bank to certify a cheque as good for payment. The banker's refusal to mark a cheque does not amount to the dishonour of that cheque.

Cancellation of Marking

The certifying banker can cancel the marking of a cheque, at anytime, before the cheque has been delivered by the drawer to the payee.

Marking of a Post-dated Cheque

It was held in the case between *Punjab National Bank Ltd. v. the Bank of Baroda Ltd.* (1939) that marking of a post-dated cheque is not valid.

The question, how a cheque can be marked if certification is not equivalent to acceptance is still open? However, Indian bankers look down upon the practice of marking, because, marking has been recognised only for clearance purposes. To quote Sir John Paget, "the intimation if any, conveyed by the marking of a cheque, is far too vague and indeterminate to operate as such admission". In view of its uncertainity, bankers do not encourage the practice of marking in India. Indian bankers have almost given up the practice of marking of cheques.

Holder

According to Section 8 of Negotiable Instruments Act, the holder of promissory note, bill of exchange or cheque means any person entitled in his own name to the possession thereof and to receive or recover the amount due thereon from the parties thereto.

Section 8 further states that where the note, bill of exchange or cheque is lost or destroyed, its holder is the person so entitled at the time of such loss or destruction. In other words, a holder is a person who is legally entitled to recover the amount from the parties of the instrument and who is in possession of the instrument. A person who has obtained possession of an instrument by theft or by any other unlawful method is not a holder.

Holder in Due Course

Section 9 of Negotiable Instruments Act, defines a holder in due course as any person who for consideration became the possessor of a promissory note, bill of exchange, or cheque if payable to bearer, or the payee or indorse thereof if [payable to order] before the amount mentioned in it became payable, and without having sufficient cause to believe that any defect existed in the title of the person from whom he derived his title. Thus, a holder in due course is one who

(a) Is in possession of the instrument in accordance with Section 8 of the Negotiable Instruments Act.
(b) Obtains possession of the instruments before maturity.
(c) Is a holder, without having sufficient cause to believe that any defect existed in the title of the person from whom he received his title.
(d) Obtains possession of the instrument for valuable consideration (in the case of a negotiable instrument valuable consideration is always presumed until the contrary is proved).

When a negotiable instrument is lost, the person who was the holder of it may apply to the drawer to give him another bill of the same tenor, giving security to the drawer to indemnify him against loss. As per Section 45A, if the drawer on request as aforesaid refuses to give a duplicate bill, he may be compelled to do so. He can also recover the instrument from the finder because the finder does not get title to the instrument, the instrument is discharged but the holder can claim damages from the finder. To be on safe side, the holder should at once give notice of loss of the instrument to all the prior parties.

Privileges of a Holder in Due Course

The holder in due course enjoys the following privileges.

Better Title than that of the Transferor

One who is a holder only gets no better title than that of his transferor, but a holder in due course is in privileged position in the sense that he gets a better title than that of the transferor. The defences on the part of a person liable that the instrument has been lost, or has been obtained from the holder thereof by means of an offence or fraud or for an unlawful consideration cannot be pleaded against a holder in due course (Section 59). A person who takes a negotiable instrument in good faith and for value obtains a valid title even if he takes the instrument from a thief (who has no title).

Once an instrument passes through the hands of a holder in due course, it is purged of all defects. But a forged instrument, even if it passes through the hands of a holder in due course cannot be cured of its defect because there is no defect of title but there is complete absence of title.

Liability of Prior Parties

All prior parties to a negotiable instrument (i.e. its maker or drawer, acceptor and intervening indorses) continue to remain liable to a holder in due course both jointly and severally (i.e. he can hold any or all prior parties liable) until the instrument is duly satisfied (Section 36) where as, only preceding party is liable to a succeeding party, if the succeeding party is only a holder.

Better Title Despite Incorrect Stamped Instruments

In case of incomplete stamped instrument, if the holder or original payee fills more amount than that was authorised, he cannot enforce the instrument for the whole amount (only actual authorised amount can be recovered). If such an instrument is transferred to holder in due course, he can claim the whole of the amount so entered, provided that the amount is covered by the stamp affixed thereon. Thus, the defence that the amount filled by the holder was in excess of the authority given cannot be taken against a holder in due course (Section 20).

Privileges in Case of Fictitious Bills (Section 42)

When a bill of exchange is drawn in a fictitious name and is made payable to the drawer's order (i.e. where both drawer and payee of a bill are fictitious persons) the bill is said to be fictitious bill. Such a bill is not a good bill and cannot be enforced at law. But the acceptor of such a bill is liable to a holder in due course provided the latter can show that the first endorsement on the bill and the signature of the supposed drawer are in the same handwriting.

Estoppel Against Denying Original Validity of Instrument

The plea of original invalidity of the instrument e.g., that no consideration actually passed between the maker and the payee of a promissory note, cannot be put forth against the holder in the due course by the drawer of a bill of exchange or cheque, or by the maker of a promissory note or by an acceptor of a bill for the honour of the drawer (Section 120).

Privilege when an Instrument Delivered Conditionally is Negotiated

When a negotiable instrument is endorsed or delivered conditionally or for a special purpose only, for example, as collateral security or for safe custody and not with the idea of transferring absolutely property therein, the property in the instrument does not pass to the indorsee, and he is merely a bailee with limited title and power of negotiating it. This however, does not affect the rights of a holder in due course, namely, if such instrument is negotiated to a holder in due course, the parties liable on the instrument cannot escape liability (Section 46 and 47).

Estoppel Against Denying Capacity of Payee to Endorse

No maker of a note and no acceptor of a bill payable to order small, in a suit there on by a holder in due course, be permitted to deny the payee's capacity, at the date of the note or the bill to indorse the same (Section 121).

Estoppel Against Denying Signature or Capacity of Prior Party

No indorser of a negotiable instrument shall, in a suit thereon by a subsequent holder, be permitted to deny the signature or capacity to contract of any prior party to the instrument (Section 122).

Holder for Value

The Negotiable Instruments Act does not define the term "holder for value". In England, according to Bill of Exchange Act 1882, where value of a bill has at any time been given, its holder is deemed to be a holder for a value as regards the acceptor and all parties to the bill who became parties prior to such time. The person who claims himself as the holder for value, need not himself give value. It may be given by prior party.

Example

A bill is drawn payable to X, who transfers it to Y for value. Y transfers it to Z without consideration. Z is called holder for value. He can sue X on the bill, if it is dishonoured.

Payment in Due Course

Any person liable to make payment of the amount due under a negotiable instrument must make the payment in due course in order to obtain a complete and valid discharge against the holder. He shall not be discharged from liability under a negotiable instrument in spite of the payment of the money due except when it amounts to "payment in due course".

"Payment in due course" means payment, in accordance with the apparent tenor of the instrument in good faith and without negligence, to any person in possession thereof, under circumstances which do not afford a reasonable ground for believing that he is not entitled to receive payment of the amount mentioned therein (Section 10).

The conditions for payment in due course are:

Payment must be in Accordance with the Apparent Tenor of the Instrument

Payment is said to be in accordance with the apparent tenor if it is made according to what appears on the face of the instrument to be the intention of the parties. Payment must be made by or on behalf of the drawer or acceptor in money and money alone, unless otherwise, agreed upon between the parties. Payment made before the due date, that is, date of maturity, or to a person not entitled to receive it or of a less or more amount or in terms of something other than money, will not be a payment in due course.

Payment in Order to be Payment in due course must be in All Good Faith i.e., Bonafide

Person making payment should not be in the knowledge of the defect in the title of the person demanding the payment. He should have made the payment under the belief that the person demanding the payment is legally entitled to it.

The Drawer must not be Guilty of any Negligence in Making the Payment

Payment negligently made to a "wrong person" will not be a payment in due course. Drawer shall not be discharged from his liability to the holder of the instrument. For example, in case of a Shajog Hundi Payment made without inquiring as to the respectability of person processed it for payment, is not a payment in due course.

Payment in due course must be made to Person Who has the Actual Possession of the Instrument

Person making the payment must insist on seeing the instrument before payment and obtain its delivery to himself on payment.

Payment Should not be made under Circumstances which Afford Reasonable Ground for Believing that the Person was not Entitled to Receive the Amount Mentioned in the Instrument

Payment of a bill by the acceptor after the drawer has countermanded payment or of a bill in the hands of a person whose possession appears to be suspicious will not be a payment in due course. Payment of an instrument bearing forged endorsement has been treated as not a payment in due course except in the case of cheques but even in the case of cheques bank will not be protected if the drawer's signature have been forged.

15
Banker and Customer

It is necessary to explain the legal meaning of the terms "Banker" and "Customer", before examining the relationship between the two. The definition of "Banker" is evolutionary and there is no universally acceptable definition.

Banker

Section 3 of the Negotiable Instruments Act, 1881 (as amended by Negotiable Instruments Amendment Act, 2002) states that the term "banker" includes any person acting as a banker and any post office savings bank.

According to Section 2 of the Bill of Exchange Act, 1882 the word "banker includes a body of persons, whether incorporated or not, who carry on the business of banking".

The Banking Companies Act of 1949 (Section 5) defines the term "Banking company" as: "A Banking company means any company which transacts the business of banking in India". "Banking means the accepting, for the purpose of lending or investment, of deposits of money from the public, repayable on demand or otherwise, and withdrawable by cheque, draft or otherwise".

According to Dr H L Hart, "A banker or bank is a person or company carrying on the business or receiving money, and collecting drafts for customers subject to the obligation of honouring cheques drawn upon them from time to time by the customers to the extent of the amounts available on their current accounts".

But a banker performs many more functions. He accepts not only deposits on current accounts but also on fixed deposit accounts.

While giving judgement in a classic case, Lord Denning mentions two essential characteristics of a banker: (a) a banker accepts money from and collects cheques for its customers and places them to their credit (b) the banker honours cheques or orders drawn on him by his customers and presents for payment and debits his customers accordingly.

According to Sir John Paget, an authority on banking, "a bank or banker is a corporation or a person (or group of persons) who accepts money on current accounts, pays cheques drawn upon such account, on demand and collects cheques for customers, that if such minimum services are afforded to all and sundry without restriction of any kind, the business is a banking business whether or not, other businesses, undertaken at the same time".

The modern banker performs several other functions like underwriting, lease financing, factoring, and so on, apart from traditional functions. He also provides several services other than banking services. But the primary functions of the banker are those stated by the Banking Regulation Act, 1949.

Definition of Customer

The term "customer" of a bank has not been defined either in English law or Indian law. According to Sir John Paget, "to constitute a customer, there must be some recognisable course or habit of dealing in the nature of regular banking business".

This definition points out two basic requirements for being a customer of a bank:

(a) To be a customer, the person should have some sort of an account with the bank.
(b) He should also have had a few transactions with the bank (the number of such transactions, that is, deposits/withdrawals, were not clearly stated by Sir John Paget).

This definition intends that the purchaser of a bank draft does not become a customer of the bank. Even a person who has just opened a bank account does not entail himself to be a customer unless he waits for sometime for completing a few transactions and be familiar with the bank.

Duration Theory

As Sir John Paget was emphasising duration and the subsequent transactions after opening a bank account, the definition was popularly known as Sir John Paget's "Duration Theory".

This duration theory came into existence when Justice Baihache pronounced his famous judgement in the case of *Ladbroke v. Todd* (1914). According to his judgement, the relationship between banker and customer begins as soon as the first cheque is paid in and accepted for collection. This view was confirmed in another English case *Commissioner of Taxation v. English Scottish and Australian Bank* (1920).

In *Mathews v. William Brown and Company* (1894) 63 L.J.Q.B 494, it was held that in order to constitute a person as a customer of bank, he should have some sort of an account with the bank but that the initial transaction in opening the account did not set up the relation of banker and customer, and there has to be some measure of continuity and custom. The dealings which are banking in nature would be established over a period of time.

The Kerala High Court, in the case of *Central Bank of India Ltd., Bombay v. Gopinathan Nair and others* (1970), observed that "Broadly speaking, a customer is a person who has the habit of resorting to the same place or person to do business. So far as the banking transactions are concerned he is a person whose money has been accepted on the footing that the banker will honour his cheques up to the amount standing to his credit, irrespective of his connection being of short or long standing".

In a nutshell, even a single transaction may make an individual a customer. Frequency of transactions is not essential to constitute a person as a customer but the transactions should become frequent in the future. The dealings must be of a banking nature.

If a person goes to a bank in order to pay the telephone or electricity bill or to deposit valuables for safe custody or to obtain change for a hundred rupee note, he cannot become a customer of the bank because the transactions are not of a banking nature but relate to casual services rendered by banks.

Therefore, a person who has a bank account in his name and for whom the banker undertakes to provide the facilities as a banker is considered to be a customer. It is not essential that the account must have been operated for some time. But a customer is presumed to have dealings regularly with his banker in future. It is essential that the dealings must be of a banking nature. A customer may be an individual, partnership firm, or a body corporate. In case of fixed deposits, the banker does not usually make enquiries of the type he makes when opening a current account like reference or introduction. Hence, it is contended that there cannot be banker–customer relationship when a person makes fixed deposits with the bank. But Sir John Paget regarded fixed deposit holder as a customer of the bank. Therefore, the relationship between a banker and customer is the foundation on which mutual duties, liabilities, and privileges depend. A thorough understanding of these terms is essential.

Under the provisions of Section 6 of Banking Companies Regulation Act of 1949, in addition to the business of banking, a banking company may engage in any one or more of the following forms of business, namely:

(a) Borrowing, raising or taking up of money; lending or advancing of money either upon or without security; drawing, making, accepting, discounting, buying, selling, collecting and dealing in bills of exchange, hundis, promissory notes, coupons, drafts, bills of lading, railway receipts, warrants, debentures, certificates, scrips and other instruments, and securities whether transferable or negotiable or not; grant or issue of letters of credit, travellers cheques and circular notes; buying and selling and dealing in bullion and specie; the buying and selling of foreign exchange including foreign bank notes; acquiring, holding, issuing on commission, underwriting and dealing in stocks, funds, debentures, bonds, obligations, securities and investments of all kinds; the purchasing and selling bonds, scrips or valuables on deposits or for safe custody or otherwise; (f) the providing of safe deposit valuables; (g) the collecting and transmitting of money and securities.

(b) Acting as agents for any government or local authority or any other person or persons.

(c) Contracting for public and private loans and negotiating and issuing the same.

(d) The effecting or insuring, guaranteeing, underwriting, participating in managing and carrying out of any issue, public or private of State, municipal or other loans or of shares, stock, debentures or debenture stock of any company, corporation, or association and the lending of money for the purpose of any such issue.

(e) Carrying on and transacting every kind of guarantee and indemnity business.

(f) Managing, selling, and realising property which may come into the possession of the company in satisfaction or past satisfaction of any of its claims.

(g) Acquiring and holding and generally dealing with any property or any right, title or interest in any such property which may form the security or part of the security for any loss or advance or which may be connected with any such security.

(h) Undertaking and executing trusts.

(i) Undertaking the administration of estates as executor, trustee, or otherwise.

(j) Establishing and supporting or aiding in the establishment and support of associations, institutions, funds, trusts, and conveniences calculated to benefit employees or ex-employees of the company or the dependents or connections of such persons; granting pension and allowances and making payments towards insurance; subscribing to or guaranteeing money for charitable or benevolent object or for any exhibition or for any public, general, or useful object.

(k) The acquisition, constitution, maintenance, and alteration of any building or works necessary or convenient for the purpose of the company.

(l) Selling, improving, managing, developing, exchanging, leasing, mortgaging, disposing, or turning into account or otherwise dealing with all or any part of the property and rights of the company.

(m) Acquiring and undertaking the whole or any part of the business of any person or company, when such business is of a nature enumerated or described in this subsection.

(n) Doing all such other things as or incidental or conducive to the promotion or advancement of the business of the company.

(o) Any other form of business which the central government may, by notification in the Official Gazette, specify as a form of business in which it is lawful for a banking company to engage.

According to Section 6(2) of Banking Companies Regulation Act, no banking company shall engage in any form of business other than those referred in sub-section (1).

Section 7(1) explains who can use the word "bank", "banker", "banking", "banking company". No company other than a banking company shall use as part of its name (or in any of the connection with its business) any of the words like bank, banker, banking, banking company. Section 8 deals with prohibition of trading – notwithstanding anything contained in section (6). Section 19 places restrictions on nature of subsidiary companies.

According to section 49A only a banking company can accept deposits and withdrawals by cheque.

Section 9 of the Banking Regulation Act (BRA), 1949, prohibits a banking company from holding an immovable property except for its own use.

General Relationship between Banker and Customer

Debtor–Creditor Relationship

When the banker receives deposits from a customer, the banker is a debtor and the customer is a creditor. The customer continues to be a creditor so long as his account shows credit balance. Once his account shows debit balance, the customer becomes a debtor. Therefore, the relationship between the banker and his customer is governed by the contract between them. Based on Sir John Pagets statement, the following points reflect the nature of relationship between a banker and his customer.

- The money deposited with the banker becomes bank's property and is absolutely at its safe disposal
- Instead of the money being set apart in a safe room, it is replaced by a debt due from the banker
- The banker is the debtor of the customer with additional obligation to honour his customer's cheque drawn upon his balance.

When the banker receives money from a customer, he does not hold it in a fiduciary capacity. Once money is deposited the money is lent to the banker and the banker is obliged to repay the debt wholly or partly when it is demanded by the customer.

A banker is a privileged debtor. He need not give any security for receiving the deposit from his customers. A customer is an unsecured creditor and does not get any charge over the assets of the bank even when the bank goes into liquidation. However, the Deposit Insurance Credit Guarantee Corporation (DICGC) minimises the risk of the depositor to the extent of INR 1,00,000 which can occur due to bank failure or bankruptcy.

The privileges enjoyed by a banker are as follows:

(a) Payment Place or Locality – In the case of ordinary commercial debt, the debtor can repay the money to the creditor at any place. But, in the case of a banking debt, the demand by the creditor must be made only at the particular branch where the account is maintained. It was held in *Clore & Co. v. Dresdner Bank* (1915) 2 K.B 576, that locality is an essential element in a banking debt and the banker should pay the money only when the demand is made at the branch where the account is maintained.

(b) Importance of Time – Time is important in the case of bank debt, the demand for repayment by the customer should be made only during the banking hours of business which are statutorily laid down. In *Arab Bank v. Barclays Bank* (1954) 2 All E.R. 226, AC 495, it was held that a banker is liable to honour a cheque provided it is presented during the banking hours.

(c) Express Demand in Writing – The creditor, that is, the customer must come to the banker and make an express demand in writing for repayment of the money. According to the decision given in *Joachimson v. Swiss Banking Corporation* (1921) 3 K.B 110:125 L.T 338 an express demand by a customer in writing is essential to get back the deposit money.

(d) Time-Barred Debt – In the case of ordinary commercial debt, the debt becomes time barred after three years as per the Limitation Act, 1963. However, in the case of a bank deposit, the time for filing a suit for the recovery of money deposited with the banker, if refused by the bank, is three years from the date of demand. Normally, a banker will pay the money on fixed deposits after the expiry of the term. Provided the Fixed Deposit Receipt (FDR) is duly discharged. If the demand for money is made after unreasonably long period, there may be some practical difficulties to return the amount as the commercial banks would have returned such unclaimed deposits to RBI, if they are not operated for 10 years.

(e) Right to Combine Accounts – A customer cannot combine his accounts while issuing a cheque for payment. For the purpose of computation of balance in his account, the customer cannot expect the banker to adjust from any other account maintained by him in the same branch or in any other branch. For instance, a customer has two accounts in his name in the same bank having a balance of INR 20,000 in one and INR 10,000 in another. While making payment the customer cannot issue a cheque exceeding INR 20,000 in the first respective account and INR 10,000 in the second respective account anticipating the banker would take into consideration the total of both accounts. If he does so, his cheque will be rightly dishonoured by the bank. In the case of *State Bank of India v. Samba Murty* (1988), it was decided that the customer cannot combine account for the purpose of withdrawal.

However, the situation on the banker's side is different. The banker can combine several accounts for the purpose of collecting his due from his customer. If there is overdraft (OD) in one account, the banker can collect the dues from another account showing a credit balance after fulfilling the following two conditions, that is, the banker should give notice to his customer of his intention to combine the accounts, and there should not have been any specific arrangement at the time of opening accounts to keep the accounts separately. Although the banks have a right to combine the account, a banker cannot combine a customer's personal account with joint account of the customer and another person (*Radha Raman v. Chota Nagpur Banking Association Ltd.* (1921), 8 PAT 413). The bank can only combine the account for an existing debt and not for a contingent debt. Both the accounts of the customer must be in the same right. The same right means that the capacity of the account holder in both or all the accounts must be the same. For example, the funds in a trust account are deemed to be in different rights, and therefore the debit balance in a personal account cannot be set off against the credit balance in the trust account in the customer's name.

(f) No Right to Close the Account – A banker cannot close the account of his creditor at any time without getting his prior approval.

(g) A Banker as a Creditor – The debtor–creditor relationship holds good in the case of deposit account. But in the case of loan, cash credit, and overdraft, the banker becomes a creditor and the customer assumes the role of a debtor. Again, a banker is a privileged person, because he is acting as a secured creditor. He insists upon the submission of adequate securities by the customer to avail of the loan or cash credit facilities. The Law of Limitation will also operate in such cases from the date of the loan unless it is renewed. The banker has the implied right to charge interest on loans given to the customer because when a banker grants loan to a customer, he becomes a creditor and the customer, a debtor. The normal practice followed by the bankers is to debit the customer's account periodically with the amount of interest due from the customer. In some cases, the agreement between the banker and the customer may, on the other hand, stipulate that interest may be charged at compound rate also.

(h) A Banker as a Trustee – A trustee is one who holds the money or assets of the beneficiary and performs certain functions in the interest of the beneficiary. A banker does not act as a trustee while receiving deposits. The customer is only a debtor and cannot have any lien over the assets of the bank. He is only a general creditor of the bank. The position of a banker as a trustee or debtor depends upon the particular circumstances of each case. If specific instructions are given at the time of deposit of money, the banker is taken as a trustee for the money and not as debtor. For example, when a customer pays into his bank a cheque drawn upon another bank, such a cheque is received by the bank as a bill for collection; the customer, therefore, is entitled to claim the cheque, provided the collecting bank fails before the bank has collected it and proceeds of the cheque, credited amount to his account. If on the other hand, the deposit has been made for a specific purpose, the banker stops the payment before applying it to such purpose, and the depositor cannot claim the money paid and must content himself with his right of proof as a general creditor. If before collection of the cheque or bill, the bank goes into liquidation, such instrument will not be available for distribution among the creditors of the bank.

In a case where a person had a deposit account with a banker, and asked the banker to buy certain securities out of the money which the banker agreed to do, but the banker failed before he did so, it has held that this agreement did not make the bank a trustee for the amount in deposit (*The Official Assignee of Madras v. The society for Providing Christian knowledge, 8 M.L.t. 52*).

(i) A Banker as a Bailee – During certain occasions, a banker becomes a bailee. It happens when he receives gold ornaments and other valuables or important documents for safe custody. In that case, he cannot make use of them to his best advantage because he is bound to return the identical articles on demand. Moreover a banker cannot acquire any title in respect of stolen articles. A banker does not allow any interest on these articles. It is only the customer who has to pay rent for the lockers. So a banker acts as a bailee only when he receives articles for safe custody and not, when he received money on deposit account. In general, banker is not a bailee. The banker is not liable to pay the identical currency notes and coins deposited with him by the customer. If the banker were the bailee, instead of paying interest on the customer's money held by him, he would have charged the customer for keeping money with himself belonging to the customer. When the banker is performing the function of bailee he must safeguard the customer's (bailor) articles in the safe deposit lockers by every means in his power.

(j) Banker as an Agent – Section 182 of the Indian Contract Act, 1872, defines an agent as one employed to do any act for another or to represent another in dealings with third persons. Under certain circumstances, the banker is acting as an agent of his customer. The agent–principal relationship is said to exist between a banker and his customer, when the banker buys and sells shares, collects cheques, bills, dividend warrants, coupons and pays insurance premia, subscriptions, etc., on behalf of his customer. So, when he executes the will of a customer, he is acting as an executor and when he administers the estate of a customer, he is regarded as an administrator. This kind of relationship does not exist when he receives deposits from a customer. He is not regarded as an agent of his customer. If he acts as an agent, he should use the deposit money according to the instructions of his principal (customer). He is also entitled to get a remuneration for this agency service.

The scope of the duty a bank owes to its customer, is highlighted in the *Keshari Chand v. Shillong Banking Corporation Ltd.*, (1965 AIR SC 1711; 35 commercial cases 514) where the court observed that the banker is also bound to exercise reasonable skill and diligence in presenting and securing payment of the cheque and crediting the proceeds to the customer's account. The court further observed that the banker should also take such other steps as required in the interests of the customer.

Special Relationship between a Banker and Customer

The special relationship between a banker and the customer includes banker's obligation to honour the cheques, consequences of wrongful dishonour of cheques, banker's lien conditions to be fulfilled to exercise lien by the banker, the conditions where the banker cannot exercise lien, banker's duty to maintain secrecy of customer's account, and his rights in respect of combining accounts.

Obligations to Honour Cheques

When a customer opens an account, there arises a contractual relationship between the banker and the customer, by virtue of which, the banker undertakes an obligation to honour his customer's cheques. This obligation is a statutory obligation. Section 31 of the Negotiable Instruments Act specifically compels a banker to do so. Section 31 is as follows:

"The drawee, of a cheque having sufficient funds of the drawer in his hands, properly applicable to the payment of such cheque, must pay the cheque when duly required to do so and in default of such payment, must compensate the drawer for any loss or damage, caused by such default".

Even though law compels a banker to honour all cheques, he cannot blindly honour all the cheques. The obligation is not absolute but qualified. The statutory obligation to honour cheques is limited in the following ways.

(a) The Availability of Money in the Account of the Customer

A banker's obligation to pay a cheque is subject to the availability of the amount in the deposit account. If there is no sufficient balance, the banker is justified to stop payment on the cheque. At times, this obligation may be extended to the extent of OD or cash credit sanctioned by the banker. If there is a prior arrangement for OD, the banker is bound to honour the cheque.

(b) The Correctness of the Cheque

The obligation to pay a cheque depends on the correctness of the cheque. All the required particulars like date, name of the payee, amount in words and figures and signature of the drawer, etc., are correctly filled in the cheque. Otherwise the cheque is liable to be returned unpaid.

(c) Proper Drawing of the Cheque

The cheque will be honoured only when it is drawn according to the requirements of law. It must be drawn on a printed cheque form, supplied by the banker and it should not contain any "request" to pay the amount.

(d) Proper Presentation

The banker will honour the cheques provided they are presented at the branch where the account is maintained and during the banking hours. If the cheques are presented after six months from the date of issue, they will be treated as stale cheques and will not be honoured.

(e) Proper Application of Funds

The banker will honour a cheque only when the funds are meant for its payment. For instance, if trust funds are withdrawn by cheque for private use, the banker will not honour it.

(f) Reasonable Time for Collection

A customer cannot impose on the banker a condition that the latter should pay his cheques blindly, even when, they are drawn against cheques sent for collection before they are collected. In *Underwood v. Barclays Bank* (1924) 1 KB 799, 1131 LT 271, it was held that in the absence of an express or implied agreement, giving the customer a right to draw cheques against uncleared items of credit, a banker is entitled to return such cheques with the remark "effects not cleared".

(g) Existence of Legal Bar

A banker is relieved from his statutory duty of honouring his customer's cheques if there is any legal bar like Garnishee order attaching the customer's account.

Consequences of Wrongful Dishonour of Cheques

A banker must deal with the payment of cheques carefully. His position is quite precarious. If he honours a cheque by mistake, the money is lost and at the same time, if he dishonours the cheque without sufficient reasons, he is to compensate the drawer for the loss suffered by him (*Marzetti v. Williams* 1830).

The following are some of the reasons for wrongful dishonour of cheques:

(a) Failure to credit deposits made by the customer.
(b) Failure to send the cheques/bills for collection.
(c) Faulty computation of balance in the customer's account.
(d) Negligence on the part of the banker.
(e) Posting the wrong amount/posting the correct amount in the wrong account.
(f) Payment made against countermanding order.
(g) Wrong debit in the customer's account.

According to section 31 of Negotiable Instruments Act, if a banker wrongfully dishonours a cheque, he has to compensate for any loss or damage suffered by the customer. The words "loss or damage" do not merely refer to the monetary loss that a customer may suffer, it also includes the loss of credit or business reputation. If the cheques are wrongfully dishonoured, the customer may be awarded reasonable compensation (*Rolin v. Steward*). In *New Central Hall v. United Commercial Bank Ltd.* AIR 1959 Madras 153, MLJ 28 it was held that where a banker having sufficient funds of a customer in his hands fails, even by mistake, to honour cheques issued by the customer, the customer has a right to claim damage. It may be noted here that the amount of damage will not depend upon the amount of the dishonoured cheque. As a matter of fact, the damage to his credit may be greater if the cheque is for small amount than it is for a large amount. In case the customer whose cheque is wrongfully dishonoured is a non-trader, he can claim only nominal damage unless the damage was alleged and proved as special damage. Under the following two circumstances special damage can be claimed:

(a) An action brought forth for breach of marriage.
(b) An action brought forth by a businessman having sufficient funds for the wrongful dishonour of his cheque. A banker is primarily concerned with the second case. A trader customer is supposed to suffer more in credit (reputation) if his cheque is dishonoured than a non-trader. If the dishonour of the cheque is willful, the banker is liable to pay vindictive damages. Thus, a customer can proceed against the banker for wrongful dishonour on the following grounds:

- breach of contract
- negligence
- libel.

Hence, the words 'loss or damage' as per Section 31 imply the following:

- damage to the drawer's general business
- damage to the negligence of the banker
- damage for the breach of the contract to pay cheques and
- damage to the general reputation and credit.

Case Law Illustrations

(a) In the case of *Canara Bank Ltd. v. Rajagopal* (1975) TLNJ 67, the customer, Mr Rajagopal issued a cheque for Rs 294 from his personal account with Canara Bank to his company, being the collection made by him as representative of a company, where he was employed. The company endorsed his cheque in favour of telephone department. When the cheque was dishonoured by mistake, the telephone department disconnected the company telephone, leading to the dismissal of Mr Rajagopal from the company where he was working. When the matter was taken to the court, the High Court upheld the damages to the extent of INR 14,000 for the loss of reputation and mental agony. This shows when a non-trader proved the substantial damage suffered by him, heavy compensation was payable to him.

(b) In another case of *Sterling v. Barclays Bank Ltd.*, the customer issued a cheque for £ 215.80. This cheque was dishonoured by mistake. The plaintiff was awarded £250 compensation, as he was a trader.

(c) In *Gibbons v. Westminister Bank* (1939) 2 KB 882 All E.R. 577, Mrs Gibbons, a non-trader had issued a cheque for a sum of £ 9.16 in favour of her landlord towards the rent. Owing to a mistake, it was dishonoured. The court awarded only a nominal damage of 40sh, since she happened to be a non-trader.

(d) In *Sterling v. Barclays Bank Ltd.*, the banker had wrongfully dishonoured Mrs Sterling's cheque. Though Mrs Sterling was a trader, the court awarded only nominal damages on two grounds – she had two cheques dishonoured previously, and people of that trade did not worry about their cheques being dishonoured.

It is evident from the above case law illustrations that the damage will be assessed on the basis of loss to one's credit or reputation, irrespective of the fact whether he is a trader or non-trader, although non-traders are not generally entitled to claim special damages.

Modern bankers, even though there is no statutory obligation to honour the bill of a customer, undertake the duty of paying the bills on behalf of their customers. When a customer accepts a bill and makes it payable at his bank, it is called "domiciliation of bill". If a bill is so domiciled, the banker should pay it on the due date. Bankers generally do not render this service unless they are appointed to do so by their customers. A customer should have made prior arrangement with his banker to honour such domiciled bills. Otherwise, it will be taken as a precedent and banker will be expected to do so in future also. The banker should keep in mind that the statutory protection extended to cheques under Section 85 of the Negotiable Instruments Act is not extended to the payment of bills. So in his own interest, he should demand an indemnity bond from his customer, for whom he renders this service. This bond safeguards the banker against possible losses that may arise on account of the payment of the bill.

In spite of the above-mentioned safeguards, a banker should observe the following additional precautions:

(a) Whether all the particulars in the bill are correctly filled in.
(b) Whether it is adequately stamped.
(c) Whether it is due for payment.
(d) Whether the signature of customer on the bill is genuine.

A Banker's Duty to Maintain Secrecy of Customer's Account

The relation between banker and customer is regarded as confidential. The banker should not disclose information regarding the customer's financial position to others. Such disclosure may harm the credit, reputation and business of the customer. This was firmly rooted in a leading case, popularly known as "Tournier's case" (*Tournier v. National Provincial and Union Bank of England Ltd.*, 1924 KB 461). In the above case, the banker had disclosed to a third party, the customer's connection with a certain book-maker. It resulted in loss of employment to the customer. It was held by Justice Bankes that there is a qualified contractual duty which has been acquired by the bank in the obligation of the banker not to disclose information concerning the depositor. In this case, it was not so and hence the bank was held liable to compensate for the loss suffered by the customer. Professional ethics demand that a banker should not reveal the nature of his customer's account to a third person.

According to Sir John Paget, secrecy should be maintained even after the account is closed and after the death of the customer. It is immaterial whether the account is in debit or credit. It extends to all transactions that go through account. But a banker cannot maintain cent per cent secrecy at all times. There may be certain reasonable grounds, under which he can justifiably disclose his customer's account on the following occasions:

- where disclosure is under compulsion of law
- where there is a duty to the public to disclose
- where the interests of the bank require disclosure
- where the disclosure is made by the express or implied consent of the customer.

Disclosure under the Compulsion of Law

A banker is obliged to disclose the information relating to his customer's account when the law specifically requires him to do so. His duty to the law of the country is more important than the duty to his customer. There are various provisions in the law compelling the banker to disclose information relating to his customer's account. The following are some of the important statutes enforcing the banker to reveal the details relating to customer's account.

Under Reserve Bank of India Act, 1934

The RBI is empowered to collect credit information from banking companies. The Act also provides that the credit information supplied by the Reserve Bank to the banking companies should be kept confidential.

Under Banking Regulation Act, 1949

Every bank is compelled to submit an annual return of deposits which remain unclaimed for ten years.

Under the Indian Companies Act, 1956

When there is a dispute in the company, the central government appoints an inspector under Section 138 to investigate the affairs of the joint-stock company. In such case the company should (a) produce all required books and papers to the inspector, and (b) render the inspector all assistance in connection with the investigation.

Under Income Tax Act, 1961

Income Tax should be payable by every individual or any body corporate to the central government according to Income Tax Act, 1961. The income tax authorities are responsible for collecting income tax. According to Section 131, the income tax authorities have the powers for enforcing the attendance of any person including any officer of a banking company and examining on oath; compelling the production of books of accounts and other documents; and issuing commissions.

Section 133 empowers the officers of income tax authorities to:

(a) Call for necessary information from any bank for the purpose of assessment of bank's customers.
(b) Compel a bank or any officer of the bank to furnish information or statement useful to the tax authorities.
(c) Under Section 285 of the Indian Income Tax Act, a banker is asked to advise the income tax officer, the names of those who have earned

INR 5,000 or above as interest on deposits during any financial year. Moreover, the officials have free access to the books of accounts kept in the bank.

Under Section 4 of the Bankers' Books Evidence Act, 1891

A banker may be asked to produce a certified copy of his customer's account in the ledger. This certified copy is admitted as evidence of the matters, transactions and accounts related to customer's account.

Under Section 3 of the Gift Tax Act, 1958

The Gift Tax Officer can examine the banker on oath and compel him to produce the books of accounts.

Under the Exchange Control Act, 1947

The Government has the power to gather information about the financial position of a customer who is suspected of violating the provisions of the Act.

Under Criminal Procedure Code

Section 94(3) compels a banker to produce a customer's account books before the police for the purposes an investigation. However, a court order is essential in this case.

Under Foreign Exchange Regulation Act FERA, 1947/1973

Most of the commercial banks in India are dealing with foreign exchange transactions as they are authorised by the RBI. The directorate of enforcement and the RBI are empowered to inspect the books and accounts and other documents of any authorised dealer, and also examine on oath such dealer or its director or officials in relation to business.

Garnishee Order

When a garnishee order is received, the banker must disclose the nature of the account of a customer to the court.

Disclosure in the Interest of the Public

Following are some of the situations when the banker reveals the secrecy of customer's account:

(a) Disclosure of an account where money is kept for extreme political purpose.

(b) Disclosure of the account of an enemy in times of war.
(c) Disclosure of an account for an unlawful association.
(d) Disclosure of an account where sizeable funds are credited.
(e) Disclosure of an account of a revolutionary body or terrorist organisation to avert danger to the state.
(f) Disclosure of an account where the bank's books reveal that the customer is contravening the provisions of law.

Disclosure in the Interest of the Bank

When his position is at stake, a banker may be compelled to ignore his oath of secrecy. Any prudent banker will safeguard his position before fulfilling his obligations. The following are the instances for disclosure in the interest of the bank:

(a) When the banker finds it difficult to collect the loan from his customer, he may take the matter to the court for settlement. In this connection he may have to reveal this to his guarantor.
(b) It is a common practice among the bankers to exchange information about the customers with fellow bankers for the sake of common courtesy. It is so, because later on, he may also be in need of such information for which he has to approach his fellow banker. The banker will disclose his opinion based on the financial records with him without taking into consideration the rumours about the customer.
(c) As a defence of past action, disclosure can be made. In *Sunderland v. Barclays Bank* (1938) 5 LDAB 163, the banker had dishonoured the cheque of Mrs Sunderland drawn in favour of a tailor. In fact, she had asked the banker to give proper reasons for the dishonour of that cheque to her husband. To defend his past action (dishonour) the banker had to reveal the fact of her having drawn cheques in favour of book-makers without the knowledge of her husband. After having honoured the last cheque drawn in favour of a book-maker, the banker had to dishonour the cheque in question for want of funds. Mrs Sunderland could not tolerate this disclosure to her husband, and so, she sued the banker for unwarranted disclosure. It was held that the banker was not liable because the banker had to disclose the fact in his own interest. Besides, there were supposed to be no secrets between a husband and a wife. Moreover, she had permitted the banker to give proper reason for the dishonour of her cheque to her husband.

Disclosure under the Express or Implied Consent of a Customer

With the willingness of the customer, the banker can reveal the accounts of the customer in the following cases:

(a) If a customer has given the name of his banker for trade reference, then the banker would be justified in answering the same.

(b) The banker should also answer the enquiries made by the proposed surety regarding the account of the customer as the guarantor would be anxious to know the financial position of the customer for whom he intends to give guarantee. The banker is expected to reveal the exact position, neither more nor less. It would be good if the banker gives his general opinion about the customer's account without mentioning the figures.

(c) For the purpose of getting visa to go to a foreign country, the customer may ask the banker to furnish the financial statements. In this case also, the banker can give the exact details about cash balance as on date and other relevant financial information available on record.

General Precautions

In disclosing the state of the account of a customer, great care should be exercised. If the banker is careless, he is liable to pay damages. The banker should follow certain general precautions while disclosing customer's account.

(a) At any cost, the banker should not be negligent in giving the information.

(b) Information should be given only after getting the express consent of his customer.

(c) Information should not be conveyed over telephone.

(d) The banker should give only general information, but not disclose the actual position of the customer's account.

(e) The banker should give his opinion or statement based on the records available with him, ignoring the rumours about the account without mentioning the actual figures.

(f) As far as possible, the banker should supply the information only to a fellow banker.

(g) On no account should he disclose to the holder of a cheque, the exact balance in a customer's account.

(h) The information should be given in such a way that he may avoid any liability in future. While supplying credit information, bankers should add a clause stating "This information has been given in strict confidence and without any liability on our part". The information was given without "prejudice" and in "strict confidence".

(i) The banker should give the information honestly and without any bias.

(j) While sending information to the customer through an agent, it should be put in a closed or sealed cover.

Banker's Lien

A lien may be defined as the right to retain property belonging to a debtor until he has discharged a debt due to the retainer of the property. The banker's lien refers to the right of the banker over such of his customer's securities as may come into his possession in the ordinary course of business. There are two kinds of lien: a) particular Lien and b) general Lien.

a) A particular lien confers right to retain goods in respect of a particular debt involved in connection with a particular transaction. b) A general lien confers a right to retain goods not only in respect of debts incurred in connection with a particular transaction but also in respect of any general balance arising out of the general dealing between the two parties. It is to be noted that a banker's lien is a general lien (Section 171 of the Indian Contract Act, 1872). A banker has a general lien on cash, cheques, bill of exchange, and securities deposited with him. A banker has his right to lien as long as it is not expressly excluded. The banker has a general lien on all securities deposited with him by a customer, unless there is an express contract to the contrary or the specific circumstances clearly reveal an implied contract inconsistent with the lien. Banker's lien is an implied pledge. An ordinary lien does not imply a right to sale, but a pledge entitles a right to sale.

In *Brando v. Barnett* (1864) case, it was held, "Bankers, most undoubtedly, have a general lien on all securities deposited with them, as bankers, by a customer, unless there is an express contract, or circumstances that show an implied contract, inconsistent with lien".

Conditions Required for the Banker to Exercise General Lien

(a) The securities and goods must come to his hands in his capacity as a banker.

(b) The banker should have obtained the possession of the securities and goods lawfully.

(c) The goods or securities should not have been entrusted to the bank for a specific or special purpose.

(d) The goods and securities held by the bank shall stand in the name of borrower only and not jointly with others.

(e) There must be no arrangement, either express or implied, which is inconsistent with the banker's right to lien.

Circumstances in which the Banker can Exercise his Lien

(a) Cheques, bills etc., deposited for collection.
(b) Specific securities left with him after the repayment of the specific loan.
(c) Dividend and interest warrants sent for collection.
(d) The credit balance of the firm.
(e) Securities not taken back after the repayment of the loan/loans.
(f) Goods and securities standing in the name of the borrower.

Case Law Illustrations

Lien cannot go beyond the agreement.

(a) In the case of *C R Narasimha Setty v. Canara Bank* (1990), it was held that a banker could not exercise his lien on the vehicle in respect of the cash credit dues of the firm. Since the hypothecation deed did not give any right to the bank to seize the vehicle for the dues of the firm. Thus, it is evident that a lien cannot go beyond the terms of the loan agreement.
(b) In the case of *K Jagadishwar Reddy v. Andhra Bank* (1988), it was held that the banker has no right to lien on the gold ornaments deposited for a loan in respect of another debt due by him as a guarantor since there is no contract by the customer offering the gold ornaments as a pledge for the debt due by him as guarantor.
(c) In *Syndicate Bank v. Vijaya Kumar* (1992), it was held that the bank has a general lien on Fixed Deposit Receipts (FDRs) which were given along with a special agreement giving to the bank, the liberty of adjusting proceeds to any loan or overdraft.
(d) In *Vysya Bank Ltd. v. Akkam Mallikarjuna Reddy*, the customer had obtained two gold loans and one crop loan. When the gold loan was repaid, the banker refused to give the jewels, exercising lien on them for the amount due under the crop loan. But the customer pleaded that the banker could not exercise his general lien on the jewels, since, the crop loan had been already waived under the waiver scheme of the government and the jewels were deposited specifically for the gold loans only. It was held that the bank can exercise his general lien on the jewels because:

- the waiver scheme is not applicable to private banks, and
- there is an agreement "to retain the gold ornaments for all monies now owing or which shall at any time thereafter be owing to the bank in any capacity whatsoever".

Banker's Lien as an Implied Pledge

The banker's general lien conferred upon him the right to retain the borrower's property until the loan is repaid with interest. It is clearly revealed in various cases that banker's lien is described as an implied pledge, which gives the banker not only the right to retain the property but also the right to sell after giving reasonable notice to the borrower when he does not take any steps to repay the bank's loan.

According to Lord Campbell, "A banker's lien is regarded something more than an ordinary lien and it is an implied pledge. This gives the right to sell the goods. He can sell the goods on default if the time is fixed for repayment of the loan. If time is not fixed, he can sell after requesting the customer to pay the loan and giving a reasonable notice of his intention to sell".

In another case *Deverges v. Sandemani*, the judge was of the opinion that one month notice was a reasonable time.

Cases under which the Banker cannot Exercise his Right of Lien

Money Deposited for a Specific Purpose

If money is deposited or some credit balance in the account is earmarked for a specific purpose, for example, payment of insurance premium or purchase of securities, the banker cannot exercise his right of lien over it. It is necessary for the customer to communicate his intention clearly through a proper notice.

Safe Custody of Deposits

When a customer deposits his securities, documents, ornaments, and so on, with the banker for safe custody, he entrusts them to the banker as a bailee or trustee with the sole purpose of ensuring safety from theft, fine and so on. The banker cannot exercise any general lien over them as there is contract contrary to the right of general lien.

Instruments Left for a Specific Purpose

Where a cheque or bill has been deposited with a banker with clear instructions to utilise the proceeds for any specific purpose, the banker cannot exercise his right of general lien on the proceeds of such cheque or bill for a debt other than the one indicated by the customer.

When a Customer has No Title

The banker cannot exercise lien over the properties of a customer, when the customer has no title over such properties.

Security for a Particular Debt

General lien cannot be exercised in the case of property of a customer pledged as security for a particular debt.

Before Grant of Loan

Where some goods and securities have been deposited with a bank for raising a loan, the right of lien cannot be exercised till the loan is actually sanctioned.

Securities Left Negligently

Where some documents or title deeds of a property have been left with the bank by mistake or negligence, the right of lien is not available over them.

Securities of a Partner for the Debts of the Firm

The banker cannot exercise his right of lien over the securities of a partner against the debt of the firm.

Securities Held in Trust

The banker cannot exercise the right of general lien over the securities deposited by the customer as a trustee in respect of his personal loan.

A Banker's Lien is Not Barred by the Law of Limitation Act

A banker has a right to retain the security for any number of years till the loan is repaid.

Negative Lien

It is otherwise called non-possessory lien. In the case of a negative lien, the securities are not in the possession of the creditor. But the debtor gives an undertaking that he will not create any charge on those securities in question without prior permission of the creditor. Such a letter of understanding must be duly stamped. Thus, under negative lien, the possession of the security is with the debtor himself who promises not to create any charge over it until the loan is repaid.

Banker's Right to Set-off

Set-off is the right of the debtor to adjust an amount due to him from the creditor as against the amount payable to the creditor when determining the net sum due to the creditor. For example, a banker has allowed an OD to Mr X amounting INR 20,000 and Mr X's savings bank account shows a credit balance of INR 10,000. In case X fails to pay the OD, the banker can exercise his right of set-off by combining both accounts by which the banker can claim the net difference of INR 10,000 from his customer. The mutual adjustment of debit and credit balances is called "set-off". The banker can exercise the right of set-off like any other debtor.

Conditions for Exercising the Right of Set-off

(a) The debts are certain and are due. The right cannot be exercised against future debt/contingent debts.
(b) There should not be any express or implied agreement to the contrary.
(c) The debit and credit balances be of same person in the same capacity. A bank cannot claim to set-off a partner's credit balance against a debit due by his firm.
(d) The banker cannot exercise his right of set-off against the guarantor if the liability of the guarantor is not determined. The exact liability of the guarantor can be determined only when the principal debtor fails.

A banker has the automatic right of set-off in the following cases:

(a) On insolvency of a firm or winding-up of a company.
(b) On receiving a notice of assignment of a customer's credit balance.
(c) On receipt of notice of a second charge over securities mortgaged.
(d) On the receipt of a garnishee order from the court.
(e) On the death, insolvency and insanity of the customer.

Banker's Right of Appropriation

A customer may open one or more accounts with a bank. Similarly, he may also take one or more loans from the bank. When money is deposited with the bank, as a general rule, the debtor who makes payment to his creditor shall have the right to say to which account he is making the payment. This right is provided to the debtor according to Section 59 to 61 of the Indian Contract Act, 1872. A debtor can appropriate the payment by an express intimation or under circumstances implying that the payment is made for a particular debt.

In case a debtor has not indicated the account to which the amount sent is to be adjusted or there are no circumstances to believe to which debt the amount is to be applied, then the creditor can decide as to which debt it should be applied. If neither of them indicated the appropriation, then the payment shall be applied in the order of time.

Banker's Right to Charge Compound Interest and Commission

The banker has the right to charge compound interest on amount due to him from the customer with half-yearly results. The banker is also entitled to claim "incidental charges". These charges may be the services they render to the customer or on the accounts which are un-remunerative. However, banks in India, to encourage banking habit among people were not charging their customers for un-remunerative accounts. However, the scenario has been changing fast after the banking sector reforms and after the entry of private sector banks. Now both nationalised and private sector banks charge the customers for different services and also to maintain un-remunerative accounts.

Law of Limitation

Bankers, businessmen, and even common men and women are dealing with loans and advances. As per the provisions of the Limitation Act, 1963, a debt will become a bad debt after the expiry of three years from the date of the debt. The implication is that the debtor need not legally pay the debt once three years are over, provided there was no contact between the debtor and creditor. But the banker is exempted from the Limitation Act. According to Article 22 of the Part II of the Schedule to the Limitation Act, 1963, the period of limitation for the refund of bank deposits is three years with effect from the date of a customer making a demand for his money. Section 26 of the Banking Regulation Act, 1949, has prescribed ten years to consider a banking debt as a bad debt. In the case of fixed deposits, a period of ten years will be calculated from the date of expiry of such fixed deposit. This is an advantage to the customer. However, in the case of overdraft the period of three years will commence from the date on which it is made use of by the customer. In the case of safe custody deposits, the Law of Limitation period commences from the date of demand.

Obligations while Closing Customer's Account

Closing of account means severance of relations between banker and his customer by the withdrawal of the customer's balance in the hands of the banker, either by the customer's own act or at the request of the banker. The customer can easily close the account and return the unused cheques. But the banker should not close the account of a customer without giving sufficient notice. Otherwise, the customer may draw cheques against his account which will be dishonoured, causing an irreparable damage to the credit and reputation of the customer. Hence, the banker should not close the customer's account without proper notice. Moreover, the amount standing to the credit of the customer does not become due unless it is demanded and banker should not pay it off.

16
Special Type of Customers

Introduction

An account can be opened by any person: (a) who is capable of entering into a valid contract, and (b) requests the banker in the proper manner, that is, the proposed customer follows the procedure laid down by the banker and accepts the terms and conditions as per bank rules. The banker has to be very careful about the character, capacity, and competency of his customers at the time of opening and operation of their accounts. The banker should deal with them differently according to different situations. Accounts of the following types of customers are minors, lunatics, illiterate persons, married women, agents, bankrupts, joint Hindu family, drunkard, partnership firms, joint-stock companies, local authorities, executers and administrators, trustees, joint account, non-trading organisations. The special type of customers and their legal holders, the precautions that the bank should take in case of opening of accounts are as follows.

Minors

According to the Indian Contract Act 1872, a person who has not attained the age of 18 years is a minor. If a guardian is appointed on behalf of the minor by the court, in such a case, the person should attain the age of 21 years in order to become a major. According to English law, individuals below the age of 21 years are minors.

The Indian Contract Act declares that every agreement with a minor is a void agreement, as minors do not have capacity to enter into contracts. Even after attaining the age of majority, a void agreement of the minor, cannot be ratified.

A banker should take the following precautions while dealing with minors, since minors are incompetent to enter into contracts.

(a) A banker may open savings account, but not a current account, in the name of minor in any of the following ways:

- in the name of minor
- in the joint name of the minor and his/her guardian
- in the name of guardian (for instance, Mr X, the guardian of minor Y).

(b) The date of birth of the minor as given by minor or guardian is recorded in the bank books. On attaining majority, the account of the minor which is in the name of the guardian should be closed and the balance should be transferred to a new account in his own name.

(c) In case of death of the guardian, before the minor attains majority, the balance should be paid to the minor on his/her attaining majority, or to a person appointed by a competent court as guardian of the property of the minor.

(d) A minor may draw, endorse or negotiate a cheque or a bill and pass on good title to holder. The holder can receive payment and enforce his rights under the instrument against any party but not against the minor. The minor cannot be sued in respect of a bill accepted by him, during his minority.

(e) Although the minor cannot enter into contract, there is no obligation if he acts as an agent of another who is competent to contract. The principal in such a case is bound by all the dealings made by the minor with the banker. A written authority from the principal should be obtained by the banker specifying the powers and extent of authority entrusted to him in this regard. The banker should see that the minor agent does not exceed such delegated powers.

(f) There is no risk in allowing operation of an account solely with the minor so long as the account shows credit balance. If the account is overdrawn by mistake, the bank has no legal remedy. Even a guarantee given by the third party to secure the debt of a minor becomes invalid, because a debt against the minor cannot be legally enforced. Similarly assets pledged by the minor with the banker as a security for the advance, are not legally available to the banker because such pledge is void. Such assets in the possession of the banker have to be returned to the minor.

(g) A minor cannot be a partner but can be admitted to the benefits of a partnership with the consent of all partners but he will not be liable for the losses or debts of the firm. If the minor is made a partner in a firm, the partnership deed is invalid not only as against the minor but also against all other partners. Within six months from the date of attaining majority, he should exercise his option to continue or not to continue with the partnership as partner.

Lunatics

"Lunatics" are persons of unsound mind. According to Section 12 of the Indian Contract Act, 1872, persons of unsound mind are disqualified from entering into a valid contract. However, his disqualification does not apply to contracts entered into by lunatics during the period of sanity or contracts which are ratified during such periods. A banker should take the following precautions while opening an account in the name of lunatics:

(a) Once the banker comes to know of such problem in a person, it would be good for the bank to avoid such a customer.
(b) The banker should confirm whether the applicant is a lunatic or not. He should not be carried away by rumours or gossip.
(c) In the case of existing account holder, the banker can act in the usual manner as long as he has no knowledge about his insanity.
(d) An existing customer may become insane. In such a case, the banker should be very cautious. He cannot presume that a customer is insane. The banker should get an official proof of his insanity. Once he gets the official confirmation, the banker should immediately stop paying his orders.
(e) If the customer has recovered from his mental illness, the banker must obtain a certificate from two medical officers certifying his mental soundness before resuming operations on the account.

Illiterate Person

Illiterate persons cannot sign their names but they can affix a thumb impression. A savings account or a fixed deposit account could be opened by the banker in the name of an illiterate person after proper introduction and photograph of the concerned person. A photograph should be affixed on the account opening form and duly authenticated by an authorised official. Withdrawals from the savings bank account of an illiterate depositor should be allowed only if the depositor concerned is present in person to the bank and produces his or her pass book.

Married Woman

A banker may open an account in the name of a married woman. Like any other customer, she has the power to operate her account herself and the bonafide dealing with the account cannot be questioned. But there was a time when married women were allowed to open accounts only after getting the consent of their husbands. Moreover, all her properties became the properties of her husband on her marriage. She was not allowed to hold property in her own name. So, the position of a married woman was far from satisfactory in those days.

The Present Position of a Married Woman

The present position of a married woman is as follows:

(a) Now the position of a married woman has considerably improved. She can open and operate an account even without the consent of her husband.

(b) She can now own properties in her own name even after marriage. According to the Hindu Marriage Act, 1956, the Indian Succession Act, 1925, and the Married Women's Property Act, 1874, a Hindu married woman can have properties in her own name.

(c) Even though she can own properties, in certain cases the properties would have been settled in such a way that she can enjoy only the income from those properties and the ownership would not have been transferred. If a banker was to lend under those circumstances, he could not attach the property for non-payment of the money.

(d) But, under certain circumstances, she can make her husband liable for the overdraft enjoyed by her. These are:

- if she borrows money for the necessities of her life
- if she borrows for the necessities of her husband.

However, the husband can escape from his liability if he proves that he has already supplied her with the necessities of life and household and he has never allowed her to act his legal agent.

(e) Further, a married woman enjoys certain privileges under law. These are:

- she cannot be imprisioned for non-payment of a judgement debt, and
- she cannot be made as insolvent, unless, she carries on some trade or business.

Banker's Duty

(a) A banker can very well open an account in the name of married woman. A banker is safe as long as her account shows a credit balance.

(b) But in case she applies for an overdraft, the banker should see that she owns separate property in her own name. In addition to this, he must see that her husband is also made liable for the repayment of the loan for which he should obtain his consent.

(c) In the case of illiterate women, their left-hand thumb impression should be obtained on the account opening form.

Pardanashin Woman

The Indian Contract Act does not provide the definition of a *pardanashin* woman. A *pardanashin* woman observes complete seclusion in accordance with the custom of her own community. She does not deal with the people other than the members of her own family. As she remains completely secluded, a presumption in law exists that:

- any contract entered into by her might have been subject to undue influence, and
- the same might not have been made with her free will and with full understanding of what the contract actually means.

Thus, a contract entered into by a *pardanashin* woman is not a contract free from all defects. The other party to the contract shall have to prove that the contract with her was free from the above-mentioned defects in order to enforce the same. The banker should, therefore, take due precaution in opening an account in the name of *pardanashin* woman. As the identity of such a woman cannot be ascertained, the banker generally refuses to open an account in her name.

Drunkards

A drunkard is an intoxicated person who is not capable of understanding the implications of his actions. He is not in a position to form a rational judgement while he is drunk. Hence the contract entered with the drunkard is void. If the banker finds the applicant under the influence of liquor, he should refuse to open an account.

Just because a person consumes liquor, he is not to be treated as drunkard. It is when he loses his mental balance, the banker should be careful. When such a person presents a cheque for payment, to be on the safer side, payment can be made in the presence of a witness.

Bankrupt

A banker should not open an account in the name of an undischarged bankrupt. If a banker comes to know of an existing customer becoming bankrupt, he is expected to stop all operations of the account and inform the official assignee appointed by the court.

Agent

An agent is a person who acts on behalf of another person. He can open an account and this account should be considered as the personal account of an agent. He can enjoy all privileges meant for any other person unless he is guilty of breach of trust. If a person is authorised to act on behalf of the principal, by a power of attorney, the banker should carefully presume that the documents confirm the powers conferred on the agent. On receiving notice of the principal's death, insanity or bankruptcy, the banker must suspend all operations on the account.

Joint Account

A joint account is one which is opened by two or more individuals. While opening a joint account, the banker must get a clear mandate in writing containing instructions as to how the account is to be operated. Generally, a mere authority given to draw money on a joint account does not extend to withdrawal of safe custody articles. It does not extend to overdraft. Hence, the banker should get specific instructions regarding the operation of the account and the nature of powers delegated to the authorised person. In the absence of a mandate, all joint account holders must jointly operate the account. The banker has to obtain the signatures of all, while opening a joint account along with clear instructions about the extent of authority of each person to operate the joint account.

Death of Joint Account Holder

The authority given to joint account holder gets automatically revoked on his death, insolvency, or insanity of the person giving the authority. Whenever the banker gets a notice of such revocation, he should act immediately.

In case of death of a joint account holder, the general rule is that survivors get entitled to any balance in the joint account. The banker should not honour the cheques issued by the deceased, once he gets notice of the death of the joint account holder. In case of death of all joint account holders, the balance in the joint account will become payable to the legal representatives of the person who dies last.

Debit Balance in Joint Account

If the joint account shows debit balance at the time of death of a joint account holder, the banker should close the account and open a new one in order to avoid the operation of the rule in Clayton's case and apply the rule of survivorship. The banker should get a fresh mandate for the operation of the account. In the case of bankruptcy or insanity of one of the joint account holders, the banker should stop the operation of the account. He should act according to the instructions given to him by the solvent/sane person along with official receiver of the court asked as the case may be.

Husband and Wife's Joint Account

When husband and wife hold a joint account, it is advisable for a banker to receive written undertaking from them regarding the disposal of balance in the case of death of either husband or wife. Otherwise, in the case of death of the husband, the wife as a widow cannot claim the balance.

In the case of *Guram Ditta v. Ram Ditta* (AIR 1928-Pc-172) the husband opened a bank account with his own money in the joint names of himself and his wife, with the instructions for either or survivor. On the death of the husband, the court held on the presumption that the husband did not intend to gift the money to the wife on his death.

In another case *S K Panikar v. Travancore National and Quilon Bank Ltd.* (AIR 1942 Mad 251) it was held that a deposit by a Hindu husband in the name of himself and his wife payable to either or survivor must, in the absence of evidence to contrary, be presumed to belonging to the husband. But if the wife dies first, irrespective of whether the intention of the partner is clear or not, the banker is justified in paying up the balance to the husband.

Joint Hindu Family Accounts

A Joint Hindu Family (JHF) consists of all persons linearly descented from a common ancestor and includes their wives. All the male members are copartners of the Joint Hindu Family. Every male member acquires interest in the joint property by birth. The affairs of the family are contributed by the senior-most male member called the *kartha.* The banker is expected to take the following precautions while operating an account of Joint Hindu Family.

(a) The banker should obtain the signatures of all adult members while opening the account.
(b) The *kartha* is alone entitled to operate the account. He can create charges over the ancestral property only in the interest of the family in general and ancestral business.
(c) In case of borrowings, the banker must take absolute precautions to find out whether it is borrowed for the benefit of the family.
(d) There is proper introduction of the account.
(e) The bank should ensure that the *kartha* has obtained authority from all the other copartners to operate the account.
(f) It is advisable for the bank to see that the documents are executed by the *kartha* and the copartners, whenever loan is given to *kartha.*
(g) A joint family letter should be signed by the copartners who have attained majority and the names of the members of the family including the minors should be submitted to the bank. In case there

is a change in the constitution due to death or birth, it should be brought to the notice of the bank.

(h) In case, the bank receives a notice from any copartner of the JHF regarding a dispute, it is advisable to put an end to the operations of the account till the court gives a directive.

(i) The joint family letter should contain an indemnity clause to protect the bank against the acts of the *kartha* and all are liable for all loans and advances taken by him.

Non-Trading Organisations

Clubs, societies, and charitable institutions are non-trading organisations formed for the purpose of doing service to the society. In case a society or an institution such as school or a hospital wants to open an account in its name, the banker should take the following precautions:

(a) These institutions should be registered in accordance with the Societies Registration Act, 1860 or Companies Act or the Cooperative Societies Act. Only registered societies will have separate legal existence and have the power to enter into a valid contract. Unregistered institutions will not have such power. Hence, accounts should be opened only for registered institutions.

(b) The banker should obtain copies of the constitution and by-laws of such institutions. These documents will give the banker, the broad objectives of the organisation, internal management of the society and the powers, functions of the persons managing the society.

(c) The banker should also get a certified copy of the resolution passed by the managing committee of the society stating his appointment as banker, the persons empowered to operate the society's bank account, and the names of the persons who are authorised to sign cheques and obtain loan from bank, on the security of the assets of the society. The copy of this resolution should be filed in the records of the bank.

(d) In the event of death, lunacy of the customer who is entitled to operate the account, the banker should stop the operation of the account. He should continue the account only after getting a fresh mandate as to who will operate the account from the managing committee of the society.

(e) If the society approaches for a loan, the banker should read the constitution, to find out the extent of society's and office bearer's power to borrow and create charge on the assets of society and the procedure to be followed for such borrowings and the purposes for which money can be borrowed.

(f) In case an office bearer of the society also has his personal account with the bank, the banker should not credit such account with the cheques belonging to the society without making proper enquiries. If the banker is negligent in this regard, he may be held liable for society.

Trusts

According to Section 3 of the Indian Trusts Act 1882, a "trust" is an obligation annexed to the ownership of property and arising out of a confidence reposed in and accepted by the owner or declared and accepted by him for the benefit of another, or of another and the owner. The person who reposes the confidence is called author of the trust and is known as "trustee".

The person for whose benefit the trust is created is called the "beneficiary". A trust is usually formed by means of a document called the "trust deed".

A banker should take the following precautions while having business dealings with the trustees.

(a) Before opening a current account in the name of the trust, a copy of the trust deed should be obtained and it should be compared with the original trust deed. The trust deed contains the names of the trustees, their powers, the details of the trust property, and other terms.
(b) The banker should obtain a duly certified copy of the resolution passed by the trustees to open an account with the bank.
(c) In case of several trustees, all trustees must act jointly unless the trust deed provides for delegation of powers to some of the trustees.
(d) The banker should carefully see that the applicant or applicants are authorised to open the account. It is advisable for him to inspect the order of appointment or instrument of trust through which the applicants derive authority. The order of appointment shall be court order where there is compulsory liquidation and the resolution of shareholders or creditors, if it is a voluntary liquidation.
(e) When the trust accounts are opened in the personal names of the trustees, the banker has to be very cautious not to mix-up trust funds with personal money.
(f) Power of trustees to borrow and pledge or mortgage any of the trust properties depends strictly on the provisions of trust deed. Therefore, it is necessary to get the reference for ascertaining the authority.
(g) If one or more of the trustees die or retire, the authority vested in the remaining trustees depends upon the provisions of the trust deed. On receipt of notice of the death or retirement of one of the trustees, the banker should ascertain from the trust deed whether the remaining trustees can operate the trust account or a new trustee is appointed in the place of the deceased or retired ones. If the trust deed empowers

the remaining trustees to operate the account, the banker may allow this to be done. However, the banker should suspend the operation of the trust account till a new trustee is appointed if this has been mentioned in the trust deed. When all the trustees are dead, new trustees may be appointed by the court.

(h) The insolvency of one or more trustees does not, in any way, affect trust property, since it cannot be utilised for payment of the personal debt of the trustee.

(i) The trustees cannot delegate their powers to an outsider. All of them should act together.

(j) A married woman can be appointed as an executive (executrix). But she cannot bind her husband for her acts, unless he interferes in her duties in the capacity of executrix.

(k) A banker should clearly differentiate the trust property with the personal account of a trustee. Both should not be mixed at any time. He should be very careful in protecting the beneficiaries. When he comes to know that trust funds are misused, a banker will be justified in dishonouring a cheque drawn by a trustee. Similarly, when trust money is deposited in the personal account of the trustee, the banker should question the reasons for it. A cheque payable to the trust account should not be collected and credited to the personal account of the trustee.

Executors and Administrators

Executors and administrators are both persons appointed to settle the accounts of a person after his death. An executor is appointed by the deceased himself, before his death. The person appointing him is called "testator". The executor has to act according to the directions given in the "will". However, he must get the official confirmation of the will, technically called as "probate" from the court.

The "Administrator" is appointed by court in those cases where the deceased has not given the name of the executor in his "will" or person named as executor has died or has refused to act. He disposes off the assets and makes payment of the liabilities of the deceased as per the directions given in the will or in its absence in the letter of administration, issued by the court appointing him as Administrator.

The following precautions should be taken by the banker while opening the account in the name of executors and administrators:

(a) The banker should keep in mind that the executor's account is nothing but the deceased's estate account.

(b) An account in the following style may be opened in the name of executors and administrators. "PQR executors (or administrators) of the estate of the deceased".

(c) If more than one person is appointed as executors, in such a case the banker should be very careful. He should get clear instructions about the nature and power delegated to each of them. In the absence of such information, the banker should take a mandate signed by all the executors as to how cheques and bills are to be signed and endorsed, holding all the executors jointly and severally liable for any overdraft.

(d) The executors may borrow money for discharging some urgent obligations of the deceased. The executors or administrators are personally liable for such loans unless the banker has given loan on the specific assets of the deceased. They cannot exercise the power of mortgage or pledge the property unless the letter of probate gives permission.

Local Authorities

Local bodies and authorities are trustees for the public funds under their control. Hence the banker has to take maximum care in the dealings of local authorities.

In case of local bodies, the name of the bank may be specified in the Act itself. If the statute does not mention any such name, the banker should insist on a resolution being passed by the governing board and a true copy of such resolution signed by the chairman, president, or chief executive should be produced while opening an account. The officials who are authorised to sign the cheques should also be provided either in the statute or resolution. The banker is expected to be aware of the borrowing powers of the authorities and the limits up to which they can borrow as per the statute.

Partnership Firm

Section 4 of Indian Partnership Act, 1932, defines partnership as "the relationship between two or more persons who agree to share the profits of a business carried on by all or any of them acting for all".

A general trading firm cannot have more than 20 persons, while for a firm carrying on banking business, the number is limited to 10. Each partner is the agent of the other and that of the firm and transaction entered into by him is binding on the firm if the transaction is related to the normal business, done in the firm's name and under express or implied authority to execute.

The following precautions should be taken while opening an account in the name of the partnership firm:

(a) The banker should ensure that the firm's account is opened only in the name of the firm and not in the names of individual partners. The banker has to ensure that all the partners of the firm have signed the application for opening the account, although the application for opening the account is made by one of the partners.

(b) A partnership is formed generally on the basis of the partnership deed. The banker has to carefully examine the original partnership deed. The deed contains the objects of the organisation, terms and conditions governing the partnership. He should also ensure that the number of partners should not exceed the maximum as prescribed by the Act. If the number exceeds, such association becomes an illegal association and the banker should not open an account in the name of illegal association.

(c) To open an account, the banker should insist that all partners join together, they all sign, except if any of them is out of the country. He should obtain their specimen signatures for purposes of record.

(d) One partner may be authorised by all other partners to operate the bank account. Such authority can be withdrawn by any one of the partners by giving a notice to the bank. Similarly, any one partner may stop the payment of a cheque issued by another partner on the firm's account.

(e) A partner has the implied authority to borrow money on behalf of the firm, for the purpose of carrying on the firm's business and such debt is binding on the firm. This will not hold good in case the partner is not a managing partner or the partnership deed expressly limits his powers.

A partner does not enjoy implied authority in the following cases:

- to open a bank account for the firm in his name
- to submit a dispute relating to the business of the firm to arbitration
- to compromise or relinquish any claim by the firm
- to acquire or transfer immovable property on behalf of the firm
- to enter into partnership on behalf of the firm
- to admit a liability or withdraw a suit on behalf of the firm.

(f) The firm has to be reconstituted with a new account in the following cases:

- on admission of new partner
- on retirement of a partner
- on insolvency of a partner
- on the death of a partner.

In these circumstances, the banker should close the account of the old firm and start a new account in the name of the reconstituted firm.

The liability of the partners of a firm is unlimited and every partner is liable to pay the debts of the firm to an unlimited extent. But if debts are due from the firm and partners are on dissolution of the firm, then Section 49 of the Indian Partnership Act, 1932 shall apply. Firm debts shall be settled out of the property of the firm and the surplus, if any, shall be available for private debts of the partners. Personal assets of the partners shall be applied first to meet claims of their individual creditors and the surplus if any, shall be available for debts of the firm. If partners sign a loan document individually as well as jointly, then the creditors of the firm can recover their debt simultaneously from the assets of the firm and the partners.

Rule of Clayton's Case

While dealing with accounts, a banker should always keep in mind the Clayton's principles. This case deals with appropriation of payments. Appropriation arises when a customer has borrowed different loans on different dates. When he makes payment, the question arises, as to which debt should be cancelled first.

As a general rule, the customer is given the first option to decide the account to which the amount should be credited. He should exercise his option at the time of depositing money and he can ask his banker to credit this amount to an account which is already showing a credit balance, instead of account which is showing a debit balance.

If the customer fails to indicate his choice, then the banker has every legal right to credit the amount in any one of the accounts of the customer. He can even cancel a time-barred debt or reduce an unsecured loan by exercising the right and inform the same to the customer. The appropriation is deemed to be completed as soon as the information regarding such appropriation is given to the customer.

In case both of them do not exercise their option, then the rule given in the Clayton's case will apply for appropriation of payment.

Clayton's Case

The rule in Clayton's case was laid down in an important case *Deveyanes v. Noble* 1816 Mes 529 35 E.R. 767. The principle in this case is of great significance to the banker, particularly in the case of running accounts like current account and cash credit account.

The rule is:

(a) Where the account goes into debit, the first item on the debit side is cancelled by the first item on the credit side, that is, appropriation takes place in the order of time.

(b) Where the account goes into credit, the first item on the credit side is extinguished by the first item on the debit side and so on. In other words, appropriation takes place in a chronological order.

The rule in Clayton's case is so important that it has been incorporated in the Indian Contract Act. 1872 Section 59 of the Act deals with the option of the debtor. Section 60 gives preference to the creditor and Section 61 contains provisions in respect of the above rule. This rule is applicable only to a running current account with overdraft facility because the question of appropriation of payment arises only in this kind of account. If the account is not allowed to run and a new account is opened, then this rule will not apply to the old account. So the banker, as a creditor, should exercise his option by closing the running account to safeguard himself from any loss. In savings and fixed deposit account, a customer cannot overdraw his amount. A banker should always bear in mind the rule laid down in Clayton's case and close the running account on certain events like insolvency, insanity, death, etc., otherwise, he will be liable personally for the loss incurred to the bank.

Joint-Stock Company

A joint-stock company is an artificial person created by law having perpetual succession and common seal. Once incorporated, a company can own property, carry on lawful business, incur liabilities, and can sue and be sued in its own name. The company generally is incorporated as a limited company. The liability of the member is limited to the extent of the unpaid value of the shares. The company is different from its members. Such a company is registered under the Companies Act of 1956 with separate legal entity. The company is managed by elected directors who constitute the managing board and these directors act as agents of the company.

The banker must know the legal aspects of the company before opening its account. He has to verify the following documents.

Certificate of Incorporation

This is a document issued by the registrar of joint-stock companies as a proof that the said company has completed all the formalities to come into existence. The banker should examine this document before opening the account of such company.

Certificate for Commencement of Business

Private limited companies need not obtain this certificate to commence business but public limited companies must obtain this certificate to start business operations.

Memorandum of Association

This is the basic document of the company filed by the promoters with the registrar of joint-stock companies. In this document, the name of the company, its place of business, objectives, capital, the types of shares and their information is given. This information is essential to the banker.

Articles of Association

These are the internal rules and regulations formed for the purpose of running the day-to-day business of the company. The banker, by inspecting this document, should pay special attention to the following provisions:

(a) The powers of the directors and the procedure for obtaining loans and the limits imposed on them.

(b) The powers of the directors to mortgage the assets of the company for obtaining loans.

(c) Procedure and powers relating to the issue and endorsement of cheques but any other documents on behalf of the company.

(d) Along with the application to open a bank account in the company's name, the banker must be given a certified copy of the resolution passed by the Board of Directors of the company, appointing the bank concerned as the banker of the company, and the names of the persons authorised to operate the account, persons who are authorised to execute documents, enter into mortgage and advance payments on behalf of the company.

(e) In case of existing companies opening their account, the banker should also obtain their previous two or three years' profit and loss account and balance sheets for the purpose of ascertaining their financial conditions.

(f) If the directors of the company have their personal accounts in the bank, the banker should not credit such accounts with the amount of the cheques belonging to the company without making proper enquiry. If a banker is negligent in this regard, he may be held liable to the company for "conversion".

(g) While granting loan on the security of the assets of the company, the banker should ensure that such charge is registered with the registrar of the joint-stock companies. He must also inspect the register of the charges to ascertain whether there are prior charges on such assets.

(h) While sanctioning loans of the company the banker should ensure that such loans are written in the ceiling prescribed in the Companies Act. The banker should carefully ascertain the power of the Board of Directors to obtain loans. He must also obtain the copy of the Board of Directors' resolution that such loan comes within the ceiling prescribed by the Companies Act. The banker should also ensure that the proposal of such loan is covered by the objects of the company in accordance with its Memorandum of Association.

(i) The banker should be very careful in advancing loans to a private limited company which has recently been incorporated by conversion of business of sole trader, as sometimes such conversions are made with a view to defraud their creditors. The banker should, therefore, make necessary enquiries to avoid such a situation. The banker should ensure that the sole trader settles all the old debts of the business before he converts the business into a private limited company and asks for a loan for the company.

Garnishee Order

Garnishee order refers to the order issued by a court attaching the funds of the judgement debtor (i.e. the customer) in the hands of a third party. (i.e., the banker). The term "Garnishee" refers to the person who has been served with the order.

The Garnishee proceedings comprise of two steps. As a first step, "Garnishee order Nisi" will be issued. "Nisi" means "unless". In other words, the order gives an opportunity to the banker to prove that this order could not be enforced. If the banker does not make any counter claim, this order becomes an absolute one. This "Garnishee order absolute" actually attaches the account of the customer. If it attaches the whole amount of a customer's account, then the banker must dishonour the cheque drawn by that customer. He can honour his cheques to the extent of the amount that is not garnished. Hence, the banker should go through the terms of the order very carefully.

If the order is vague or if it gives a wrong description of the party, it is not effective (*Koch v. Mineral are syndicate*). A Garnishee order issued against a husband's account cannot attach a joint account in the name of the husband and wife (*Hirschhorn v. Evans* (1938) 2 KB 801, 3AU ER 491). If the order is so worded as to attach two accounts in different capacities, then it attaches both the accounts (*Plunkeett v. Barclays Bank Ltd.* (1936) 2 KB 107, All ER 653; 154 LT 465). A Garnishee order in the name of a firm, attaches both the firm's account and the private accounts of the partners. A cheque in favour of a judgement debtor cannot be attached by the order, because, the cheque is not the property of the payee until the money is paid to him. The proceeds of sale of shares, stock, etc., are not attached, if they are not received by the bankers on the date of the order. The order cannot attach cheques paid into the account of the judgement debtor but not yet collected. However, in case where a cheque is sent for collection by one bank (principal bank) to another (agent bank), the moment the cheque has been realised by the agent bank, that realisation is deemed to be a realisation made by the principal bank itself, and as such it could be attached as was decided in the case of *Gerald C.S. Lobo v. Canara Bank (1991)*. The fact that the realisation slip was received by the principal bank at a later date was considered immaterial in the above case.

Foreign balances are not attachable. If this order is sent to the head office, then a reasonable time should be given for communicating this order to the concerned branch. In India, this provision is contained in Order 121, Rule 46 of the Code of Civil Procedure, 1908.

NRI Accounts

Non Resident Indian (NRI)

For exchange control purposes the term Non-Resident Indian (NRI) means, an individual, being a citizen of India or a person of Indian origin residing outside India. A person is deemed to be Indian origin if:

(a) He or either of his parents or any of his grandparents was a citizen of India, by virtue of the Constitution or the Citizenship Act, 1955.
(b) He, at any time, held an Indian passport.
(c) Nationals of Bangladesh and Pakistan shall not be deemed to be of Indian origin.
(d) A spouse (not being a national of Bangladesh or Pakistan) of a person of Indian origin shall also be deemed to be of Indian origin.

Non residents fall generally into the following two categories.

(a) Those who stay abroad for employment or for carrying on a business or vocation or for any other purpose indicating an indefinite period of stay outside India, and
(b) Indian citizen working abroad.

Facilities for maintaining bank accounts are available in India to persons of Indian nationality or origin living abroad. The exchange control procedures relating to these facilities have been greatly simplified.

Various Types of NRI Accounts

The present menu of bank accounts for NRI has the following four categories.

- Ordinary Non-Resident Rupee Accounts (NRO Accounts)
- Non-Resident (External) Rupee Accounts (NRE Accounts)
- Non-Resident (Non-Repatriable) Rupee Deposits (NRNR Accounts), and
- Foreign Currency (Non-Resident) Accounts (Banks) Scheme (FCNR (B) Accounts)

NRO and NRE accounts can be kept in the form of current, savings bank, recurring deposit, or term deposit accounts. Deposits under NRNR and FCNR (B) schemes can be kept only in the form of term deposits ranging from six months to three years.

Procedure and Practice to Open and Conduct of NRI Accounts

NRO and NRNR Accounts (Acceptance of NRNR deposits stand discontinued) can be opened by all non-resident individuals/entities. NRE and FCNR (B) accounts can be opened only by Non-resident individuals of Indian nationality or origin (NRIs), overseas corporate bodies (OCBs), and overseas trusts. OCB's are defined as overseas companies, firms, societies, and other corporate bodies which are owned directly or indirectly to the extent of atleast 60 per cent by NRIs, while overseas trusts are defined as those in which atleast 60 per cent of the beneficial interest are irrevocably held by such persons. Accounts can also be opened in the names of individuals, entities of Pakistan/Bangladesh nationality/ownership. Opening of such accounts, however, require prior approval of RBI.

All the four categories of accounts can be opened with specified branches of authorised dealers (Banks authorised to deal in foreign exchange) in India. NRO and NRE accounts can also be opened with authorised cooperative/commercial banks. All the major scheduled commercial banks including foreign banks and a few corporative banks are authorised dealers in foreign exchange. In addition, state corporate banks, certain urban cooperative banks, and small scheduled commercial banks have been given authorisation to maintain NRO and NRE accounts of NRIs. Besides, post offices can also maintain savings bank account in the names of persons resident outside India.

Funds held in NRE and FCNR (B) accounts are freely repatriable. Interest accrued on NRNR accounts from 1 October 1994 is eligible for repatriation. From the financial year 1996–1997 (April–March) the entire interest earned on NRO accounts is eligible for repatriation. Principle amount held under NRO is not normally repatriable. Funds laid in NRNR accounts as the name itself indicates, is also non-repatriable. NRO and NRNR accounts may be jointly held with residents. NRE and FCNR (B) accounts cannot be held jointly with residents but residents holding powers of attorney (POA) may operate these accounts for local payments and investments in India permitted by RBI. Resident power of attorney holder cannot, however, repatriate the funds outside India under any circumstances.

Remittances from abroad in freely convertible currencies and dividend/interest and sale proceeds of investments, etc., made in India which are of a repatriable nature can be credited to any of these accounts. Legitimate local dues in rupees to the account holder, viz., rent of flat/building, sale proceeds of investments held on non-repatriation, etc., can be credited to NRO accounts.

NRO accounts allow debits for local payments in rupees including investments, provided the account holder has given the undertaking at the time of opening the account that the investment/disinvestment would be covered either by general or special permission of the RBI.

NRE/FCNR (B) accounts allow debits for:

(a) Local disbursements/payments in rupees
(b) Remittances abroad
(c) Transfer to NRE/FCNR accounts of the same account holder, or of any other persons eligible to maintain such accounts
(d) Investment in shares/securities/commercial paper of Indian companies or for purchase of immovable property in India provided such investment/purchase is covered by the regulations made, or the general/special permission granted, by the RBI
(e) Any other transaction, is covered under general or special permission granted by RBI.

NRNR accounts allow debits for:

(a) Local payments/disbursements in rupees, and
(b) Repatriable interest accrued on the deposit.

Interest rates payable on NRO, NRE and FCNR(B) deposits are determined by the RBI. Banks are free to determine the rate of interest payable on NRNR deposits.

When an NRI returns to India with the intention of residing in India for an indefinite or uncertain period, his/her accounts are designated as resident accounts. However, NRE and FCNR(B) accounts may be converted into Resident Foreign Currency (RFC) accounts at the option of the account holder, provided he/she is eligible to open and maintain such accounts. A Resident Foreign Currency (RFC) account is a foreign currency bank account opened with a bank in India. Persons of Indian nationality or origin, who have been residing outside India for a continuous period of not less than one year and have returned to India on or after 18 April 1992 are eligible to open and maintain RFC accounts in a freely convertible foreign currency. The accounts can be opened with any authorised dealer in India.

Loans and Advances Against Security of Deposits

NRE/FCNR/NRNR accounts holders can themselves take loans/overdrafts from their authorised dealers for purposes other than investment in India. These advances have to be fully served by term deposits and regulations relating to normal margin, interest rate, etc., to be complied with. The account holder can repay the loan either by adjustment to the deposits or by fresh remittances in foreign exchange from abroad. The loan can also be repaid out of local rupee resources held in the NRO accounts of the borrower subject to condition that the loan repaid from local resources would be charged interest at the commercial rate in force at that time.

NRE/FCNR account holders can take loans/overdrafts in India for purposes of making direct investment in India. The investment can be made on non-repatriation basis by way of contribution to the equity of Indian firms/compliance with certain conditions. The companies in which the account holders desire to invest, should be engaged in manufacturing/ industrial activities, export oriented trading activities, hospitals, hotel of three star or higher grades, shipping, development of computer software, and on exploration services.

NRIs can also take loans against their NRE/FCNR(B) deposits in India for the purpose of acquisition of flats/houses in India for their own residential use subject to certain conditions. If an NRI borrower desires to repay the loan from local resources held in the NRO account, he is charged commercial rate of interest.

Resident individuals/firms/companies in India can take loans/overdrafts against collateral or fixed deposits held in NRE/FCNR (B) accounts by NRIs subject to certain conditions. In addition to the condition that the period of loan should not exceed the unexpired period of maturity of the fixed deposit that there is no direct or indirect foreign exchange condition for the non-resident depositor pledging the deposit for the resident borrower. Premature withdrawals are permitted subject to prescribed penalties which are usually in the form of interest loss.

There is no tax exemptions on interest earned on NRO accounts. Interest earned on NRNR accounts is free of Indian income tax. NRNR deposits are exempt from gift tax for one time gifting (in the case of NRIs only). Interest earned on NRE/FCNR accounts is exempted from income tax. Balances held in NRE/FCNR accounts is exempted from wealth tax and gifts made from these accounts to close relatives in India are free of gift tax.

17
Paying Banker

Introduction

When a customer issues a cheque, it is an order to the banker directing him to pay according to his mandate. It is a statutory obligation on the part of the banker to honour customer's cheques. The position of a paying banker is a very sensitive. If he honours wrong cheque, he will lose money. If he dishonours cheque wrongly, he may have to pay substantial damages. As "Tannan" rightly said, "the banker is between the devil and the deep sea". Hence, the paying banker must be very careful before honouring the cheques and he should take several precautions before he decides to honour or dishonour the cheque.

This chapter discusses the duties and responsibility of a paying banker, the precautions a paying banker should take before honouring the cheques, circumstances under which a paying banker can refuse payment of a cheque, the precautions to be taken by paying banker in the case of crossed cheque and the statutory protection provided to a paying banker.

Section 31 of the Negotiable Instruments Act, 1881 says, "The drawer of a cheque having sufficient funds of the drawer in his hands properly applicable to the payment of such cheque must pay the cheque when duly required to do so, and in default of such payment, must compensate the drawer for any loss or damage caused by such default".

The bank is always the drawer of the cheque. The cheque must be presented for payment by the customer at the branch at which the customer's account is opened and is in operation. The banker is not bound to pay unless the cheque is in proper form correctly signed, endorsed by the payee and presented at the proper time and place.

The paying banker should take the following precautions before honouring a cheque, namely making payment on the cheque when it is presented for payment.

(a) The banker should see whether the cheque presented at the counter is the one which he had supplied to the customer. The banker can refuse payment of any cheque drawn otherwise. If a cheque form supplied to another customer is used, the banker may not be justified in refusing payment. The banker is not obliged to honour payment when the customer orders payment on a piece of paper.

(b) A banker should see whether a cheque has been properly dated. If it is a post-dated cheque, he should not pay it. He may ask the customer to prescribe the cheque on or after the date appearing on the face of the cheque. But if it is a stale cheque, he may return the cheque. In case the cheque bears no date, the banker may return the cheque as he is not sure of the date of issue of cheque.

(c) He should see whether the cheque is crossed. If it is an uncrossed cheque, payment may be made through the counter. If it is a crossed one, he should advise the customer to present it through his account.

(d) A cheque should be drawn in a language understood by the banker in India, cheques are drawn in English or in the local language. If the banker is not able to understand the language, he may refuse the payment.

(e) The banker should ensure that sufficient balance is in the account of the customer. The amount drawn should not exceed the overdraft limit. If the funds are not sufficient or the amount drawn is beyond the overdraft limit, the cheque cannot be honoured.

(f) The amount in words and in figures should agree, where there is discrepancy between the amount in figures and in words, as per law, preference will be given for the amount in words and the amount in words is payable (Section 18 of the Negotiable Instruments Act, 1881). But in practice, the banker may refuse the cheque stating that the figures and words differ. The banker gets confirmation from the drawer and after getting the necessary correction, the banker will honour the cheque.

(g) The amount of the cheque should not be written in pencil or by rubber stamp. Even though there is no clarification in the Act in this regard, it is for the safety of the customer and in his own interest, he should avoid writing the amount with pencil as there will be ample chances of erasing and attesting the figures that cannot be deleted later.

(h) Cheques must be properly endorsed. In case of a bearer cheque, endorsement is not necessary legally. But in case of an order cheque, endorsement is necessary. Before honouring a cheque, the paying banker should see that the endorsements are regular.

(i) The cheque should not be mutilated. A cheque is mutilated when it is cut or torn or when a part of it is missing. There should not be overwriting either of figures or words. There should not be symptoms of erasing on the cheque. In the case of mutilation, where it is accidental, the banker may honour the cheque after getting the confirmation from the drawer.

(j) If there is any material alteration on the cheque, it must be confirmed by duly affixing the full signature of the customer for the bank to honour such a cheque. In case of more than one person who have signed the cheques, then all persons must fully sign on the cheque for confirmation of material alteration.

A material alteration is one which varies the rights, liabilities, or legal provision of the parties as ascertained by the deed in the original state, or otherwise varies the legal effect of the instrument as originally expressed, or which may otherwise prejudice the party bound by the deed as originally executed (*Selthia v. I E John, 1977 379, 394*).

Examples of Material Alteration are:

- alteration of place of payment
- alteration of the date of the cheque
- alteration of the amount of the cheque
- alteration in the names of the parties or the relationship between them or that may affect their legal status
- substitution of the word bearer in place of the term order.

(k) The payee must be named clearly and unambiguously, for example, Indian or order is not clear.

(l) The customer or his authorised agent must sign on the cheque. The signature on the cheque should tally with the specimen signatures in the records of the bank. The banker cannot honour an unsigned cheque or a cheque where the signature is not tallying with the specimen signatures.

(m) The cheque must be presented on a working day within the banking hours.

(n) The cheque must be drawn with great care and scope and should not be given for fraud. For example, if space is provided while writing the amount in figures or words on the cheque, someone may insert some figure or word to alter the amount of the cheque. It may not be possible to detect the fraud and in such a case the banker cannot be made liable.

(o) In case of crossed cheques, the paying banker should not pay a cheque in a manner inconsistent with the directions contained in the crossing. The duties of paying banker regarding crossed cheques are laid down in Sections 126, 127 and 129 of the Negotiable Instruments Act of 1881.

According to Section 126 of the Negotiable Instruments Act, 1881, where a cheque is crossed generally, the banker on whom it is drawn shall not pay it otherwise than to a banker. Where a cheque is crossed specially, the banker on whom it is drawn shall not pay it otherwise than to the banker to whom it is crossed, or his agent for collection. According to Section 127 of the Negotiable Instruments Act, 1881, where a cheque is crossed specially to more than one banker, except when crossed to an agent for the purpose of collection, the banker on whom it is drawn shall refuse payment thereof. According to Section 129 of the Negotiable Instruments Act, 1881, any banker paying a cheque crossed generally otherwise than to a banker, or a cheque crossed specially otherwise than to the banker to whom the same is crossed or his agent for collection, being a banker, shall be liable to the true owner of the cheque for any loss he may sustain owing to the cheque having been so paid.

(p) The existence of legal bar like garnishee order limits the duty of the banker to pay a cheque.

(q) A paying banker should look into the following minor details also before honouring a cheque.

- he must see whether there is any order of the customer not to pay a cheque.
- he must see whether there is any evidence of misappropriation of money. If so, the cheque should be returned, for example, breach of trust.
- he must see whether he has got any information about the death, insolvency, or insanity of his customer. Failure to note those instructions will land him in trouble.

(r) The banker should also verify whether there is any countermanding order from the customer. A countermanding order is an instruction or request from the customer to stop payment of the cheque. The banker should note the following in this regard:

- the order should be in writing and should include the payee's name, amount of the cheque, cheque number, and other particulars, if any
- in case of telegraphic or telephonic countermanding, the banker can postpone payment but cannot refuse payment. The banker has to wait for the written confirmation
- the banker should not accept countermanding order from the payee of the cheque. It is only the drawer who has the right to countermand. Therefore, the payee should contact the drawer in case the cheque is lost or stolen. However, depending on the status of the payee, and other circumstances, the banker must postpone the payment.

Circumstances under which Banker can Refuse Payment of Cheque

Stop Payment Order

The stop payment order may be given by the drawer either orally or telephonically or in writing.

On the Death of the Customer

On the death of the customer, the title to his bank balance passes to his legal representative. Hence, as soon as the banker comes to know about the death of the customer, he has to stop payment of the cheques presented by him after the death. It was held by Supreme Court in *Limited Bank of India v. Smt Kannan Balo Devi and others*, that notice about the death of a customer to one branch is not notice to the other branches. Hence, such notice should be given to other branches also where the customer holds the account.

Defect in Title

If the banker comes to know of any defect in the title of the party presenting the cheque, he can refuse payment.

Breach of Trust

In case of a trust account, if the banker comes to know that the customer intends to use the funds in breach of trust, he can refuse payment of the cheques.

On Receipt of Notice of Insolvency

When the banker receives notice of the insolvency of the customer he has to stop the account of the customer. After an order of adjudication is made, the property of the insolvent gets vested in the hands of official assignee or the official receiver.

Notice of Insanity

When the banker receives notice of insanity of a customer, he should stop the account of the customer. If the customer is removed to a lunatic asylum, or when a court by an order declares the customer is incapable to manage his affairs, the bank will be justified in dishonouring the customer's cheques.

Notice of Assignment Receipt

When a person transfers a right, property, or debt (existing or future) to another person, it is called assignment. The person who assigns such right, property or debt is called the assignor. The person to whom assignment is made, is called assignee. On receiving the notice of assignment of the customer of the credit balance, the banker can refuse payment of a cheque. The assignment takes effect only after the bank has received an express notice in this regard.

Countermanding Order by the Drawer

The drawer of the cheque may, in writing, instruct his banker to stop payment on a particular cheque giving particulars of the number of the cheque, date, and payee. A banker should make a note of the instructions and refuse payment on that cheque when presented. He cannot debit the customer's account with the amount of the cheque, which is countermanded. A bank could be sued as much for failing to honour a cheque as for cashing a cheque that had been stopped.

Notice of a Garnishee Order

As the banker and customer have debtor–creditor relationship, the credit balance in a customer's account represents a debt due to him from the banker. When a person obtains a decree as the judgement creditor from the court against the customer, he can attach the debt in execution. The banker (in the position of debit to the customer) on whom such an order is served is called the garnishee order. The banker has to comply with the court restraining him from paying the money from a customer account. Once the garnishee order is received, the banker must refuse payment of the cheque presented.

By Injunction

When there has been a dispute relating to certain funds, an injunction may be passed to freeze a bank account till such time the matter is settled.

Notice of Closure of Accounts

When the customer intends to close his bank account, he may send a notice specifying a date on which he would close the account with the bank. The notice is given to the bank to enable the holder of cheques to encash them before such a date. The banker should not pay any cheque presented on or after the date given in the notice. In the same way, the banker will also close an undesirable customer's account after giving a reasonable notice. No cheques should be honoured after this date. If the customer fails to close his account within a reasonable time from the date of notice, the banker can close an account and send the balance, if any, to the customer.

Reasons to be Given for Refusal of Cheques

When the banker decides not to pay a cheque presented to him for payment, he has to give a reason as to why he does not honour the cheque and some of the reasons may be as follows:

(a) Endorsement Irregular (EI)
(b) Words and figures differ (WXFD)
(c) Refer to drawer (RD)
(d) Not sufficient funds (NS)

(e) No Account (NA)
(f) Payment stopped by drawer
(g) Account closed
(h) Drawer deceased
(i) Irregularly drawn
(j) Drawer's signature incomplete/differs
(k) Exceeds arrangement
(l) Alteration indicate/figures/words requires drawer's signature.

Double Crossing and its Effects

When a cheque is crossed specially to more than one banker, except when crossed to an agent for the purpose of collection, the banker on whom it is drawn shall refuse payment thereof (Section 127 of the Negotiable Instruments Act, 1881).

If a cheque crossed specially to a bank is returned unpaid for any reason and is presented again through another bank, it may be honoured only when the crossing in favour of the first bank is cancelled in a proper way. The mandatory practice of cancelling a banker's rubber stamp on a cheque is to write, "All our stamps cancelled" and such writing should carry his signature.

Effect of Forged Endorsements

While making payment of a cheque, the banker has to see whether the endorsements on the cheque are regular. If the endorsement is forged, the banker is protected from forged endorsement. In the case of forged signature of the customer, the banker is expected to verify the signature of the customer with the specimen signature of the customer available in the records of the banker, but the banker cannot be expected to know the signature of the endorsee and hence he is protected against forged endorsement.

Legal Effect of Material Alteration

Section 87 of the Negotiable Instruments Act of 1881 says "Any material alteration of a negotiable instrument renders the same void as against anyone who is a party thereto at the time of making such alteration and does consent thereto, unless it was made in order to carry out the common intention of the original parties. Any such alteration, if made by an endorsee discharges his endorser from all liability to him in respect of the consideration thereof".

In case of crossed cheques, it is the duty of the paying banker to see that the cheque is paid only to a banker, otherwise he would not be deemed to have made the payment in due course. Where a banker makes such an irregular payment, he would be responsible to the drawer for any loss the drawer may suffer. The banker in such a case will not get the statutory protection under Section 128 of the Negotiable Instruments Act, 1881 because the payment is not made in due course. The banker making payment, ignoring the directions of the drawer by means of crossing, will be liable to compensate the true owner of the cheque to the extent of the loss he may incur owing to the cheque having been so paid.

If the drawer cancels the crossing saying "crossing cancelled, please pay cash" affixing his signature in full, then such process is called "opening of the crossing" and the bank may pay the cheque but even then the banker should be very careful, because he is in a vulnerable position and he will be liable to the true owner who took the cheque in a crossed condition.

Statutory Protection to a Paying Banker

Section 85 of the Indian Negotiable Instruments Act 1881, offers protection to the paying banker in India. "Where a cheque payable to order, purports to be endorsed by or on behalf of the payee, the drawee is discharged by payment in due course". To claim protection under Section 85 the banker should have fulfilled the following conditions:

- he should have paid on order cheque
- it should have been paid in due course
- such a cheque should have been endorsed by the payee or his order.

The statutory protection has been extended to the order cheque. An order cheque consists of "Pay to A or order", words on the face of the cheque. Endorsement is a must for an order cheque.

Protection Will be Given to the Order Cheque

The cheque should be endorsed properly by the payee or any person authorised by him to obtain payment. If a cheque is not endorsed by a payee or any third party the banker will not get any protection. The banker must see the regularity of endorsement before the payment of a cheque. Payment must be in good faith and without negligence. Payment must be made to a person who is in rightful possession of the instrument. There should not be any circumstances that may give scope of doubt that the holder is not entitled to receive the payment.

Protection to a Crossed Cheque

With respect to crossed cheques, Section 128 of the Negotiable Instruments Act, 1881 provides, "where the banker on whom a crossed cheque is drawn has paid the same in due course the banker paying the cheque, and (in case such cheque has come to the hands of the payee) the drawer thereof, shall respectively be entitled to the same rights, and be placed in the same position in all respects, as they would respectively be entitled to and placed in if the amount of the cheque had been paid to and received by the true owner thereof".

When the banker is making payment of a crossed cheque, he is given protection provided he makes payment taking care of the following two requirements:

(a) He has made payment in due course in good faith and without negligence and according to the apparent tenor of the cheque (Section 10), and
(b) The payment has been made in accordance with the requirement of crossing (Section 126).

Protection to a Bearer Cheque

Protection has been extended to a bearer cheque also under Section 85(2) which reads as follows:

"Where a cheque is originally expressed to be payable to bearer, the drawer is discharged by payment in due course to the bearer thereof, notwithstanding an endorsement, whether in full or in blank offering thereon, and notwithstanding that any such endorsement shall purport to restrict or exclude further negotiation. Thus if a bearer cheque is paid in due course, the banker is entitled to get protection" under Section 138 of Negotiable Instruments Act, 1881.

Protection to Draft

A bank draft is an instrument drawn by one office of a bank on another office of the same bank. Bank drafts are also treated as cheque for the purpose of providing statutory protection.

In the case of *S N Shukla v. the Punjab National Bank Ltd.*, it was observed that a draft cannot be drawn by a private individual like a cheque and it cannot be easily countermanded. Further, bank cannot stop payment of its own draft. Section 85A states "Where any draft, that is an order to pay money, drawn by one office of a bank under another office of the same bank for a sum of money payable to order on demand, purports to be endorsed by or on behalf of the payee, the bank is discharged by payment in due course".

Protection to a Materially Altered Cheque

Section 89 of Negotiable Instruments Act, 1881 gives protection in the case of materially altered cheque provided:

- the banker is liable to pay
- such an alteration is not apparent and
- the banker has made payment in due course.

In the case of *Tanjore Permanent Bank Ltd. v. S R Rangachari* (1959) 2 MLJ 196, the banker was not entitled to get statutory protection on the ground that the alterations were material and apparent and they were not authorised by the drawer.

In another case of *Brahna Shun Sherjung Bahadur*, the banker was granted statutory protection on the ground that the alterations were not apparent.

Statutory protection is available only when a banker acts as a paying banker and not as both paying and collecting banker.

Opening of Accounts in a Bank

A banker has to enquire carefully about the character, capacity, and credit position of the customer before opening an account. He has to ensure that some one who is already a customer of the bank or a member of staff in the bank knows the applicant, namely the proposed customer. The proposed customer has to furnish necessary information to the banker at the time of agreeing for opening an account. After carefully pursuing the information and making necessary enquiries from the references given by the new customer, the banker ascertains whether the person wishing to open an account is a desirable customer. If the banker fails to make reasonable enquiry about the new customer, the banker may be deprived of the statutory protection given to him under Section 13 of the Negotiable Instruments Act, 1881. The banker is said to act negligently if he does not make enquires that an ordinary and prudent man should make if he were to open an account for the customer. It is prudent for the banker not to accept a person as a customer without proper introduction or some reference except in case of parties personally known to an officer of the bank. If the bank is satisfied with the identity and standing of the applicant, it agrees to open the account in the name of the applicant. A banker has the right to refuse to open an account if the applicant appears to be an undesirable person. Some respectable person who has an account in the same branch or some member of the staff of the branch who knows the applicant personally should give introduction of the applicant. The full address of such person should be recorded in the account opening form along with his specimen signature. The signatures of the person introducing the customer should tally with his signatures on record and the same should be verified.

Proper introduction of the new customer has the following advantages:

(a) It serves as a precaution against fraud.
(b) It is safe ground in case of an inadvertent overdraft.
(c) It may absolve the banker from charges of negligence for conversion.
(d) It helps the banker to give proper and correct confidential opinion regarding the standing or credit of his customer to other banks under common courtesy.

In the case of *Bapulal Premchand v. Nath Bank Limited AIR (1946 Bom 482)*, it was held that, it was not obligatory upon a bank to make enquiries as to the responsibility of a customer in order to avail itself of the protection given under Section 131 of the Negotiable Instruments Act. The safe and prudent course for the banker would be to obtain references before opening a new current account in the name of a person not known to him.

Specimen Signature of the Customer

Every customer is required to supply the banker with two or more specimen signatures. These are taken on a bank account opening form. This form is to be filled and preserved carefully by the banker. When a cheque issued by the customer is presented to the bank, the signature on the cheque is compared with that of the customer provided on the specimen signature card and only when the signature tally, the cheque is passed. In the case of joint account, the specimen signature of the other person also should be obtained by the banker.

Anyone who intends to open a savings bank account should submit an application in a particular format with the bank which is available to the customer free of cost from the bank. Normally, the application contains the following particulars:

- name of the applicant or applicants (joint account)
- age and date of birth
- father/husband's name
- profession
- address: office and residence with telephone number
- name and address of the referee
- specimen signature
- nomination details
- two passport size photos to affix – one in the application form and the other in the pass book
- other important information required to the bank.

Documents necessary while opening account in a bank by various types of customers:

- mandate in favour of age
- power of attorney
- partnership deed in case of a partnership firm
- memorandum and articles of association of a company
- certificate of incorporation and certificate of commencement of business

- debenture trust deed
- trust deed
- standing order, rules, by-laws of associations, clubs, and so on, and registration certificates
- certain statutes relating to local authorities
- transfer forms
- insurance policies
- certificates of shares, stocks, and debentures
- mortgage deed
- guarantee bond
- valuation report of properties
- bill of lading, dock warranties, ware house keeper's certificate, delivery order, etc.
- consular invoice and certificate of origin
- probate and letters of administration
- balance sheet, and profit and loss account.

The banker should get from his customer a mandate, if the latter intends to operate on his account by another person. The mandate should clearly state the powers delegated to the mandatory. Specimen signatures of the persons authorised to operate on the account should also be given in the mandate and entered in the books of the bank.

The following are the risks in opening accounts without reference:

(a) The banker should take adequate care while opening accounts for new customer, otherwise, an unscrupulous person may open an account in someone else's name, steal his cheques, and deposit them in the account for collection.

The following case explains the risks faced by the bank.

In *Guardians of St. John's Hampstead v. Barclays Bank Ltd. (1923)*. In this case, a customer opened a fictious account, giving his real name as the referee. He gave an impressive introduction. When the problem about the conversion arose, the banker lost the statutory protection due to his failure to follow up the reference given by the applicant.

(b) The RBI has given directions to all the commercial banks, through a circular, directing them to get introduction while opening new accounts to check the black money in operation. In the absence of getting introduction, persons may open many accounts in different names. In case the bank grants personal loan without security, recovery may also be difficult.

(c) There is a risk of misusing the cheques by unscrupulous person after purchasing goods from different shops which becomes bogus cheques.
(d) In the case of minor's account, the account is to be operated by the guardian. In the absence of getting introduction about the guardian, the banker faces services risks.
(e) In the absence of introduction a person may open an account in the name of undischarged insolvent and persuade the bank to grant him overdraft, cash credit or loans, later on the banker may not be able to recover the funds.

When the banker is satisfied with the particulars given in the application, he allows the applicant to make the initial deposit (not less than the minimum balance prescribed to open the account) after filling the pay-in-slip which is a printed slip with perforated counterfoils available at the bank. This slip is filled up showing the account of notes, coins, bills, cheques which are paid into the account of the customer. This slip contains information relating to the party depositing the money, nature of account, date and signature of the depositor. This slip is signed by the cashier and the counterfoil is retained to the deposits which is a proof of deposit and retained by the depositor.

After having deposited the money in the new account, account will be opened in his name and the amount is credited to his ledger account. A passbook is a diary like book in which the banker records the transactions related to the customer's account for the latter's use. This passbook passes frequently between the banker and customer. The customer has to verify the entries and compare with the ledger account. In case of any discrepancy, the customer should bring it to the notice of the banker, and the banker alone can make entries in the passbook. A businessman prepares a bank reconciliation statement with the help of passbook. Some banks issue statement of accounts in the place of passbook to all customers.

Features of a Passbook

The following are the features of a passbook:

(a) It is issued by the banker.
(b) It shows the transactions that have taken place for a given time period.
(c) It is an authenticated copy of the customer's account in the books of the banker.
(d) Only a banker is authorised to make any entry or correction in the passbook. The customer cannot make any correction or entry in it.

(e) It contains the rules and regulations governing the savings bank/current account.
(f) It contains the initials of the banker. A computer generated statement supplied by the banker to the customer do not require any initials of the banker.
(g) It is a primary document to be used for preparing bank reconciliation statement.
(h) It is updated by the banker from time to time, normally when the customer present it for entries and is also to be produced every time the customer wishes to withdraw cash from the bank. If the cash is withdrawn through cheque, the pass book need not be produced.

According to Sir John Paget, "the proper functions which the pass book ought to fulfil is to constitute a conclusive and unquestionable record of transactions between the banker and the customer, and it should be recognised as such". After full opportunity of examination on the part of the customer, all entries at least to his debit, and to be subsequently final and not liable to be subsequently reopened, at any rate detriment to the banker.

Thus, Sir John Paget, an authority on banking strongly feels that entries once made in the passbook are supposed to be authentic conclusive evidence and the questionable record of transactions enabled by the bank and the customer is supposed to be bound by the entries.

Anyone may make a mistake and a banker is not an exception. If entries are made correctly in the passbook, no dispute arises. The problem arises only when the passbook contains wrong entries which may be favourable either to the customer or to the banker.

Effect of Entries Favourable to the Customer

"The pass book belongs to the customer and the entries made in it by the bank are statements on which the customer is entitled to act". (*Akrokerri (Atlantic) Mines Ltd. v. Economic Bank* 1904).

The passbook may show a favourable balance for the customer because of duplication of credit entry, entering higher account for such entries or omission of a debit entry or entering lower amount for a debit entry. Relying on the higher balance shown in the passbook, when a customer issues a cheque, the banker is not entitled to dishonour it. If he dishonours such cheques, he will be liable for damages. (*Holland v. Manchester and Liverpool District Banking Co.* (1909) 14 Com. Case 241). However, this does not mean that a customer can hold the banker liable for dishonouring cheques issued before he received the pass book written up with erroneous entries (*Smith v. Cox & Co.* (1940) 2 KB 568 3AER 546).

In *Canara Bank v. Canara Sales Corporation and Others* (1964) 44 company cases 6, the Chief Accounts Officer of the Corporation forged the signature of the Managing Director of the Corporation on many cheques between 1957 and 1961 to more than INR 1,26,000. When it was discovered by the Corporation in March 1961, the Corporation sued the Bank. But the Bank replied that the Corporation did not have any objection at the appropriate time even though the monthly statements were supplied to them regularly. It was held that the bank was liable because there was no binding on the part of the customer to examine his passbook and report the discrepancies to the bank.

Effect of Entries Favourable to the Banker

The passbook may show a favourable balance for a banker because of duplication of debit entries, entering lower amounts for such entries, omission of credit entries or entering higher accounts on credit side of the passbook. In this case, it is very difficult to define with accuracy to what extent the customer is bound by them. A passbook is written by the banker or his agent. Hence, a customer cannot be made to accept this against himself.

In the case *Chatterton v. London and Century Bank*, it was held that the return of the passbook by the customer to the banker did not constitute a binding acknowledgement of the accuracy of the entries even when he had placed tick marks against them. However, a signed acknowledgement of the accuracy of the entries might operate against the customer. The customer has every right to sue the banker for mistakes or forgery. The bank can escape liability only if it can establish knowledge to the customer of the forgery in the cheque. Forgery conveys no title. Mere silence, omission or failure to act is not sufficient ground to establish a case in favour of a bank. The customer has every right to file a suit in a court of law. The banks do business for their benefit. Customer also enjoys benefit. Banks survive and prosper by creating confidence in the minds of customers. There is always an element of trust between bank and its customer.

Sometimes, a customer pleads forgery and the bank, in turn pleads that the customer had returned balance confirmation letter duly signed by the customer. The customers are advised to acknowledge the correctness of the entries and confirmation of balance and return the letters after they are being signed. Banks follow this practice in order to avoid risk under the law of limitation and also to avoid any dispute with the customers in future regarding the liability. In the case of *Indian Bank Limited v. ESRa/smail*, the Kerala High Court observed that there should be evidence to show this practice indicate the settlement of accounts.

Closure of Accounts

It is the privilege of the customer to close his accounts whenever he chooses to do so. The banker cannot unilaterally close the account of the customer without giving notice, as this action may harm the interest of the customer. The following are the circumstances in which the banker may close the account of the customer.

Notice of Closure by Customer

When the customer gives notice to the banker stating his decision to close his account, the account can be closed. On closure of the account, the banker pays the balance in the account. If it is an account with a cheque book facility, the banker has to obtain a cheque from the customer for the balance duly signed by the customer made payable to "self to close the account".

In Case of Death of a Customer

Once the banker receives the notice of death of the customer, he must stop the operation of his account and cheque payment should not be entertained. The notice of the death of the customer cancels the authority of the bank to pay cheques.

If the Customer Becomes Insane

The banker's authority to honour the cheques of the customer will be revoked or cancelled only when the banker receives a notice of insanity of the customer. In other words, the authority of the banker to act as his customer's agent gets automatically terminated when he gets the notice about the insanity of the customer.

If the Customer Files an Insolvency Petition

When the individual customer files an insolvency petition or the corporate customer gets into liquidation, the credit balance of the customer account is to be transferred to the official receiver of the insolvent customer.

If the Court Orders for Closure of the Customer's Account

When the banker receives court orders prohibiting the payment of a certain sum from the account, the banker has to honour the court order.

Notice of Closure by Bank

The banker has to give adequate reasonable notice to the customer before he closes the customer's account. The banker has to honour the cheques drawn by the customer if the cheques have been issued before the receipt of the notice (*Buckingham v. London and Midland Bank* (1895) 12 TLR 70).

Dormant account is also called inactive account. If the customer does not make any transaction for a prescribed period of time in an account, and the banker is unable to contact a customer inspite of using the available means of communication channels, the account is called dormant account.

Collecting Banker

Collection of customer's cheques has been an important service rendered by the bankers to the customers and this service has been one of the prime source of revenue to the banker.

A collecting banker is one who receives payment of a crossed cheque on behalf of the customer. Although collection of cheques is not a legal duty of the banker, and yet banks generally act as collecting bankers to their customers for bills and cheques. This is important because crossed cheques can be collected only through a banker. Legally, a banker is not bound to collect amount on cheques for his customer, cheques drawn on the bank once he accepts an open or uncrossed cheque from his customer for collection and pays the amount to him before the cheque is collected, his position is that of a holder for value.

Collection of a cheque takes certain amount of time, especially in case of outstation cheques; for example, A in Chennai who has an account in the Indian Bank receive a cheque from B of Mumbai having an account in the Bank of Maharashtra. B draws a cheque on Bank of Maharashtra in favour of A. A deposits the cheque in Indian Bank at Chennai. It takes some days to clear the outstation cheque. Here, the Bank of Maharashtra is the drawer bank and Indian Bank is the collecting bank. When the Indian Bank allows A to draw the amount on this cheque, before it is cleared, then the Indian Bank will be regarded as holder in value. Hence, if a banker allows the customer to draw the amount before it is cleared, the banker will be regarded as holder for value.

Collecting Banker as Holder for Value

(a) When he pays cash to the payee before the cheque is collected from the drawee bank.
(b) When he allows the customer to draw against cheques paid into his account but not yet collected.
(c) When he collects customer's cheques to repay in full or in part an overdraft in his account.

In collecting cheques as a holder for value, the collecting banker is taking risk as there is possibility of the cheque being dishonoured.

Collecting Banker as Agent

If a banker credits the customer's account or pays the customer after collecting the cheque, he acts as an agent of the customer.

The relationship between the customer and bank is that of principal and agent. The bankers while collecting cheques belonging to other persons, are exposed to tremendous risks. If the banker collects a cheque to which his customer has no title, the banker can be held liable to the true owner for "conversion". Conversion is defined as "unlawful taking, using, disposing or destroying of goods, which is inconsistent with the owner's rights of possession".

According to *Hart's Law of Banking* (pp 606, 4th edition) "Conversion means wrongful inter-meddling with the goods of another for the purpose of taking them away from party entitled to them".

Goods include bill of exchange, cheque or promissory note. Conversion may be committed innocently. Conversion is a mistake that renders the person committing it personally liable. This liability exits even when a person acts as an agent.

A banker may be charged for conversion for wrongfully collecting cheques to which his customer was not having title or was having a defective title. The rightful owner can recover the property from anyone who takes it without his authority and in whose hands it can be traced.

When a banker acts as an agent of his customer, while collecting the cheques of the customer, the banker may be charged with conversion and he cannot escape from the liability from conversion. The true owner has a restricted right and he cannot exercise his right in case the property reaches the hands of one who: (a) receives in good faith (b) for value, and (c) without the knowledge that the other party had no authority thereon.

Duties of the Collecting Banker

Presenting Cheques Within a Reasonable Time

The collecting bank should present the cheques collected from the customer to the drawer bank within a reasonable time. If this is not done, the banker is liable to the customer for the loss suffered by him due to such delay.

Reasonable Care and Diligence

A collecting banker as an agent of the customer is duty bound to protect the interests of the customer, by acting with due care and diligence and he is not supposed to be negligent while discharging his duty as the agent of the banker. For example, he must present the cheque within a reasonable time. What is reasonable time depends upon the nature of the instrument, usage of trade and special circumstances of each case (Section 84(2)).

Notice of Dishonour

In case the cheque is dishonoured, the collecting banker should give notice of dishonour to the customer by returning the cheque with a covering letter and enclosing the objection memo which contains the reason for dishonour. If the collecting banker is holder for value, he has to give notice to all parties to the cheque apart from the customer. The notice of dishonour may be given verbally or in writing. It may be given in person or by post within a reasonable time.

Collection of Local and Outstation Cheques

The collecting banker receives the cheques from the customer along with the pay-in-slip containing the details of the cheques. Generally, he fixes a specific time period for receiving the cheques for collection and on cheques received after that, he gives his remarks regarding delay on the pay-in-slip such as "late for day's clearing". The realisation of out station cheques takes more time than that taken by local cheques and it is the duty of the collecting bank to see that the outstation cheques are realised at the earliest. The outstation cheques should be cleared without abnormal delay.

Banker Owes Duty to Customer

In the process of collection, either the banker himself collects a cheque or hands it over to some other party (banker) to clear it as the agent of the bank concerned. While collecting cheques himself, or through his agent, the banker will not get protection under the act unless he acts without negligence while collecting the cheque. Negligence arises where there is a duty to take care. The banker owes such a duty to his customer and not to anybody else. Under the act, he also has a duty to the true owner of the cheque collected by him.

Appointment of Sub-Agent and Legal Consequences

The bank being the agent of the customer, may appoint sub-agent. Sub-agents are liable only to the agent (*Mercantile Bank of India Ltd. v. C. Bulchand, AIR 1930 Sind 247*).

When a customer asks his banker to forward a cheque or bill to a specified banker for collection, the latter bank may be treated as the agent of the customer and not the sub-agent of the collecting banker.

For example, If A asks his banker X to collect a cheque through Y bank, then Y bank is the agent of A and not the sub-agent of X bank. X bank will not be liable to A for the negligence of Y bank (*Indo-commercial Bank Ltd. v. Bhoogalingam, AIR 1961 A 346*).

Statutory Protection for Collecting Banker

A banker is given protection under Section 131 of Negotiable Instruments Act, 1881, while collecting crossed cheques. According to Section 131 of Negotiable Instruments Act, 1881, a banker who has, in good faith and without negligence, received payment of a cheque crossed generally or specially to himself shall not, in case the title of the cheque proves defective, incur any liability to the owner of the cheque by reason of having received such payment.

From the above section, it is observed that the banker receives payment of a crossed cheque for a customer, notwithstanding that he credits his customer's account with the amount of the cheque before receiving payment thereof.

Another observation is, it is the duty of the banker who receives payment based on electronic image of a truncated cheque held with him, to verify the *prima-facie* genuineness of the cheque to be truncated and any fraud, forgery or tampering apparent on the face of the instrument that can be verified with due diligence and ordinary care (Negotiable Instruments (Amendment) Act, 2002).

Thus Section 131 protects the collecting banker when he collects a cheque bearing a forged endorsement or in respect of which the customer has no title or a defective title. It may be noted here that to claim protection, the collecting banker must comply strictly with the provisions of the section which are as follows.

The Collecting Banker Should Act in Good Faith and Without Negligence

A person is deemed to have performed in good faith when he performs honestly. The banker is not only to act honestly but also without negligence. In case of dispute, a collecting banker has to prove that he has acted without negligence in order to come under the purview of Section 131, the term negligence is based on the facts of each case and the term has been widely interpreted by the courts. Negligence may also bc stated as the omission to do something which a reasonable man guided upon the considerations which ordinarily regulate the conduct of human affair would do, or something which a prudent and reasonable man would not do. At this point, Lord Sankey's observation will reveal clearly the position of the bank. "In my view a bank can not be held liable for negligence merely because they have not subjected an account to microscopic examination. It is not to be expected, that the officials of banks should also be amateur detectives. It is difficult to define the degree of negligence which would render them liable. Many factors have to be taken into consideration, the customer, the account and the surrounding circumstances".

Crossed Cheque Only

Statutory protection can be claimed by a collecting banker only for crossed cheques. It is so because, in the case of an open cheque, it is not necessary for a person to seek the services of a bank, and so, a banker while collecting an open cheque in which his customer has no title, becomes liable for conversion. Protection can be claimed only for those cheques which are crossed before they reach the hands of a banker. Protection under Section 131 cannot be claimed because it cannot be called a crossed cheque.

The Protection Under Section 131 is Available Only in the Case of Cheque

If the signature of the drawer is forged, then the instrument is worthless and the instrument is not a cheque as per the definition of Section 6 of the Negotiable Instruments Act.

Banker-Received Payment

Receiving payment by the banker means the bank has performed function of collection of cheques and covers all such acts related to collection both preceding and ancillary acts. In case any of the acts relating to collection and if it amounts to conversion, the banker may be charged with negligence.

Customer's Cheque – Cheque should be collected for the customer and if it is not collected for the customer, the banker cannot get protection under Section 131. Where banker takes a cheque as an independent holder, he can claim protection. For example, if the collecting banker pays cash across the counter, and collects the cheque later on, then the banker is receiving payment of the cheque as a holder for value, and he cannot get protection under Section 131. But it is to be noted that this rule has no application where the banker credits the amount of a cheque to the customer before receiving the proceeds actually.

Liability of Collecting Banker

The collecting banker is liable for "negligence". What is negligence depends on the facts and circumstances of each case. Several legal decisions in the courts of law also provide us some insight on the term negligence. The following are some examples of negligence and the collecting banker does not get any protection under Section 131 in case of negligence. Thus, each case mentioned below becomes a case of liability of the collecting banker.

(a) The banker did not make proper enquiries at the time of opening the account of the customer. Had he been vigilant and taken due care to the time of opening the account, he would have prevented a fraud.

In *Bharat Bank Ltd. v. KC Chella Ram, 1954 24/Comp Cas 67; AIR 1955 Mad 402*) it was held that negligence in opening of the account would be relevant under Section 131, if the opening of the account and deposit of the cheque were really part of one scheme.

For example, where the account is self and is opened with the cheque in question or where it is deposited into the account soon after opening of the account, so much so that it gives the impression that it is part of it, then negligence in the matter of opening the account must be treated as negligence in the matter of realisation of cheque.

In the case, *Lad Broke v. Todd (1914) 111 LT 43*, a thief opened an account with a stolen cheque after forging the endorsement of a payee, the bank collected the cheque. The thief withdrew the amount. The bank lost the statutory protection because no introduction was obtained for opening the account.

(b) The banker should also enquire and record the name and nature of profession or business or other particulars of the employer of a customer while opening the account, as he may be held negligent, if he collects for him cheques payable to his employer (*Savory X Co. v. Lloyds Bank Ltd., 1932*).

Two clerks working in Savory X Co., stole bearer cheques belonging to the company. They drew cheques payable to third parties. One clerk was having an account in his own name and the other in his wife's name. The stolen cheque were deposited in these accounts. "Savory X Co". charged the bank to conversion on the following grounds that the bank did not make proper enquiry about the customer's employment particulars, and the customer's husband's name and employee's name at the time of opening an account.

(c) The banker, without making proper enquiry, collected in the personal account of a partner, a cheque where the payee was the firm (*Baker v. Barclays Bank Ltd.,* 1955 WLR 822).

(d) The amount on the cheque was unusually high and till then a cheque for such large amount did not come from the customer for collection (*Brahma S Jung Bahadur v. Chartered Bank AIR 1956 Cal. 399*).

(e) The banker, without proper enquiry, collected in the personal account of a trustee, a cheque where the payee was the trust or beneficiary and it was in the banker's knowledge.

(f) The banker, without proper enquiry, collected in the account of an individual, a cheque drawn in favour of a public authority.

(g) If the surrounding circumstances give reason for suspicion and warrant an inquiry, the collecting banker should make enquiries before collecting cheques.

(h) The collecting banker should verify the regularity of endorsements on the cheques collected by him. In case of stolen cheque collected with irregular endorsement, the banker would be held liable for conversion.

(i) The banker should collect cheques for the true owner. The banker has to be very careful while collecting cheques as the possibility of collecting cheques for others are more. Dealing with partnership account, cheques belonging to a firm may be collected for the active partner.

(j) In the case of special crossing, the banker whose name appears on the crossing alone is authorised to collect the cheque. If some other banker collects the cheques negligently without taking note of such crossing, he would be liable for conversion and for having acted negligently in collection of forged cheques.

The collecting banker may receive three lists of defective instruments. These are:

- where the drawer is signature is forged
- where the payee's signature is forged
- where the amount of cheque is raised or altered.

The banker has to be careful in all these cases. Although Section 18 of Negotiable Instrument Act, 1881 suggests, in dealing with them the banker will return such cheques in normal practice.

18

Secured Advances – Mode of Creating Charge

A secured advance is one which has been granted against some tangible securities, the value of which is more than the amount of loan granted. Secured advances are safer than unsecured advances because in the event of default by the borrower, the banker can sell the securities and appropriate the sale proceeds towards his loan account. Even then a banker should be careful, because certain securities have some inherent defects. The borrower might offer certain securities over which he may not possess any ownership at all. Such securities cannot be enforceable. Again, some others are not easily marketable. A good security must possess certain qualities.

Principles of Good Banking Security

Free from Encumbrances

The borrower should have an absolute title over the property offered as security. In other words, the security must be completely free from prior charges. If the borrower's title is defective, the banker cannot obtain a better title.

Easy Marketability

The security offered must be such that, it is easily marketable without loss in its value. In other words, it must possess the quality of liquidity. In the event of default, if the securities cannot be sold in the market, there is no point in accepting these.

Durability

The banker must see whether the security possesses the quality of durability. Durable goods alone can be stored for a reasonable period. Perishable goods cannot be stored for long, and hence, they are not accepted as good banking securities.

Easy Storability

The security should not pose a problem of storage to the banker. For example, certain goods like timbers, inflammable articles, etc., require huge and special storages which are costly. Securities like documents of title to goods, shares, consumer goods, etc., can be stored without much difficulty.

Easy Ascertainment of Value

The security must be capable of being valued without much difficulty. For example, daily market reports are available for certain securities like gold, silver, stock exchange securities, etc. But, in the case of securities like land and buildings, such reports are not available, and hence, their valuation becomes a difficult task.

Free from Price Fluctuations

An ideal security is one which is free from price fluctuations. When the price of the security falls suddenly, the value of security becomes lesser than the amount of the loan granted. Hence, there arises a necessity of demanding further securities or reducing the amount of loan already sanctioned. It involves additional burden on part of the banker.

Free from Disabilities

Certain securities are crippled with certain disabilities and a banker should avoid such securities. For example, partly paid-up shares, a life insurance policy where the age has not been admitted, etc.

Earning Income

Again, a good security must be capable of earning income. Such incomes can be appropriated towards the loan amount. For instance, stocks and shares of well-established companies earn a steady dividend. Such securities are preferable to a banker.

General Principles of Secured Advances

Although secured advances are safe from a banker's point of view, any negligence in creating a charge on the security or any ignorance about the nature of the security will put him in trouble. Therefore, a banker has to observe the following general principles for secured advances:

(a) Nature of the security.
(b) Validity of the title of the borrower.
(c) Free from defects.
(d) Documentations, that is, terms and conditions of the loan sanctioned.
(e) Margin = (Value of the security – Amount of loan granted) which is a provision for safety.

The margin for gold and silver may be 10 to 15 per cent. In the case of stock exchange securities the margin varies between 25 and 40 per cent, depending upon the market for the shares and debentures.

In the case of government securities, a low margin is justified. In the case of durable goods and essential goods like rice, wheat, etc., a low margin is sufficient. For perishable goods and luxury goods, high margin is required. While fixing the margin for various securities, the banker should also take into account the RBI's directives, issued from time to time, regarding the margin requirements.

Modes of Creating a Charge on Security

A charge is a right over some tangible assets of the borrower. It is a legal transaction as a result of which the lender is conferred certain rights and the borrower is refrained from dealing in them as specified. There are several modes of creating charge over tangible assets. They are: (a) Lien (b) Pledge (c) Hypothecation and (d) Mortgage.

Lien

Lien is defined as a right in one man to retain that which is in his possession belonging to another until certain demands of the person in possession are satisfied. It is given by law and not by contract (Halsbury's *Law of England*, vol. 20, 2nd Edn., p.552, para 695). It is a right to retain possession of specific goods or securities or other movable property of which the ownership lies with the debtor. The possession can be retained till the owner discharges the debt. Lien is of two types: (a) Particular Lien (b) General Lien.

Particular Lien

According to Section 170 of Indian Contract Act, 1872, where the bailee has, in accordance with the purpose of the bailment, rendered any service involving the exercise of labour or skill in respect of the goods bailed, he has, in the absence of the contract, to the contrary a right to retain such goods until he receives due remuneration for the services he has rendered in respect of them. For example, a tailor has a particular lien over the clothes stitched by him until his tailoring charges are paid.

General Lien

According to Section 171 of Indian Contract Act, 1872, bankers, factors, wharfingers, attorneys of high court, and policy-brokers may, in the absence of a contract to the contrary, retain as a security for a general balance of account any goods bailed to them; but no other persons have a right to retain as a security for such balance, goods bailed to them unless there is an expressed contract to that effect. The holder has a right to retain the goods until the payment is made out but he does not carry the right of sale to secure the debt or indemnity (*Alliance Bank of Simla Ltd. v. Ghamandilal Gainilal*) 40 CLJ 223 AIR 1925.

Features of General Lien

The possessor of lien has a right to retain possession until the whole debt or balance in the account is paid. A lien does not require any agreement, oral or written, but arises by operation of law provided the following requirements are fulfilled.

(a) That the creditor should have come into possession of goods, etc., in the ordinary course of bankers.
(b) That the owner of goods and securities owes a lawful debt.
(c) That there is no express or implied contract to the contrary.

Pledge

A pledge arises when goods or documents of title to goods are delivered by one person (called the pledger) to another person (called the pledge) to behold as a security for the payment of a debt or for the discharge of some other obligation, upon the condition that the subject matter of the pledge is to be restored to the pledger as soon as the debt or other obligation is discharged.

Section 172 of the Indian Contract Act, 1872, defines pledge as "The bailment of good as security for payment of debt or performance of a promise". When a collateral security, for example, stocks, shares, bonds, etc., is delivered to a bank as security for loan, the delivery constitutes pledge for the payment of debt. Pledge involves the transfer of its custody to the lender.

Essentials of a pledge

The essentials of a pledge are the following:

(a) Delivery of possession of goods is necessary.
(b) There should be a bailment of goods.
(c) The objective of such bailment is to hold the goods as a security for the payment of debt or the performance of a promise.
(d) In case of pawn/pledge agreement, the person who offers goods for pawn/pledge is called pawner/pledger and the person who receives the goods is called pawnee/pledged.
(e) Ordinarily, goods may be pledged by an owner or any person with owner's authority, that is,
    - pledge by mercantile agent
    - person in possession under voidable contract
    - seller of goods.

Rights and Duties of the Pawner/Pledger

The rights and duties of the pawner/pledger are the following:

Right to repay the loan: The pawner/pledger should repay the loan and interest as per the agreement and take back the pledged goods from the pawnee in time.

Right to receive the goods: The pawner/pledger has the right to receive the goods in the same condition when he parted with the goods, after discharging his contract. But if, by any chance, he makes default in the promise or fails to pay back, the pawnee may arrange to sell the goods after giving due notice to the pawner. The pawner has the right to redeem his goods before any sale is made. However, in the meantime, if any expenses had been incurred by the pawnee, these expenses can be reimbursed from the pawner.

Right to receive any increase in the goods: In case of any increase in the asset, the pledger will be entitled to receive the same from the pledgee.

Right to retain: The pawnee/pledgee has the right to retain the goods till the performance of the promise or the repayment is made including the interest thereon. He can also recover all reasonable expenses incurred by him on such goods pledged.

Right to retain goods for subsequent loan: In case the pawnee/pledgee lends subsequent advances on the strength of the goods already pledged, the pawnee (as a banker) has the right to retain such goods for the subsequent loan also unless there is an agreement contrary to this effect.

Right to receive payment of the debt: The pawnee/pledgee has the right to receive payment of the debt including interest.

Right to extraordinary expenses: Section 175 of the Indian Contract Act provides for the right to the pawnee to receive from the pawner any extraordinary expenses incurred by him for the maintenance of the goods pledged with pawner.

Right against the true owner: A pawner/pledger might have obtained the goods under voidable contract, that is, by fraud or undue influence, etc. When he pledges such goods with the pawnee, if the voidable contract had not been rescinded, the pawnee acquires good title to the goods, provided he acts in good faith and without notice of the pawner's defect of title.

In case of failure to pay the debt by the pawner/pledger, the pawnee/pledge has the following options before him.

(a) He can retain the pledged goods, until such time the debt is paid back.
(b) He can file a suit against the pawner for the debt.

(c) He may sue for the sale of goods and the realisation of the money due to him.
(d) He may sell the goods after giving due notice. He can recover any balance from the pawner if the proceeds of the sale is inadequate to meet his claim. Similarly, if there is surplus, the pawnee should repay the pawner.

Precautions

Although pledge is the most satisfactory method of creating a charge, a banker has to take the following precautions:

Ensure ownership: First of all, the banker should ensure that the pledger is the real owner of the pledged goods. A valid pledge can be created only by the owner of goods or mercantile agents in possessions of goods or any other pledgee.

Take reasonable care: The pledgee banker must take a reasonable care of the pledged goods, in such way that, an ordinary man would take of his own goods.

Exercise full control: The banker should exercise full control over the pledged property. For this purpose, he must make periodical inspections and check the goods. It would prevent the creation of any subsequent pledge in respect of the same goods.

No unauthorised use: The banker should not make any unauthorised use of the pledged property. If he does so, the pledger has every right to terminate the contract and to claim damages for the unauthorised use.

Put up sign boards: The banker should put up sign board at the place where the goods are kept, prominently showing that the goods are pledged to the banker. It prevents creation of any subsequent pledge in respect of the same goods.

Draft the agreement carefully: The banker must carefully draft the agreement, while creating a charge by way of pledge. The contract of pledge must incorporate all safety clauses for the banker and the banker must check whether the partners are competent to enter into the contract of pledge.

Hypothecation

According to Dr Hart, "Hypothecation is a legal transaction whereby goods may be made available as security for a debt without transferring either the property or the possession to the lender".

The change by way of the hypothecation is created by an instrument in writing known as 'Letter of Hypothecation'. Except for immovable property, all forms of assets may be covered under a hypothecation arrangement. The securities which are covered under hypothecation are goods, machinery, fixtures, and book debts.

The asset hypothecated remains under the possession of the borrower and he is free to deal with it. Since the banks do not obtain actual or constructive possession of the goods, the borrower has ample opportunity of dealing with them fraudulently.

In *Bank of Baroda v. Bachubhai Hirabhai and others* AIR 1987 Gujrat, it was clearly established that the bank is not liable to compensate the injured passengers when a vehicle hypothecated to it is met with an accident, since under hypothecation, neither ownership nor possession is transferred to the creditor.

In *Jagadeesan v. State Bank of India, Karur*, it was held that, "if there is a breach of contract on the part of the bank for violating the conditions of the hypothecation agreement, only a civil suit lies against the bank".

Features of a Pledge

The following are the features of a pledge:

No transfer of possession: Under hypothecation, the physical possession of goods always remains with the borrower. Actually, the banker gets only the constructive possession, that is, the borrower agrees to give possession of goods, when called upon to do so by the banker. For this purpose, he executes a document called "Deed of Hypothecation" (*Gopal Singh, Hira Singh v. Punjab National Bank* and Anr. AIR 1976 Delhi 115).

No transfer of ownership: There is also no transfer of ownership of goods to the banker. The ownership always remains with the borrower.

Obligation to repay a debt: Under hypothecation, there is an obligation on the part of the borrower to repay a debt. In the event of non-payment, he agrees to give the physical possession of the goods to the banker. It is this obligation which constitutes the real security for the loan.

Right of sale through court: In the event of non-payment of money, the banker has to file a suit and obtain a decree either to recover the money or to sell the security. If the agreement provides for the sale of the security in the event of non-payment of the debt, the banker can do so without the intervention of the court (*State Bank of India, Hyd. v. S B Shah Ali, 1994*).

Drawbacks

Hypothecation has the following drawbacks:

Double financing: The borrower may hypothecate the same stocks of goods with different banks and get different loans, since, there is no necessity of physically transferring the goods to the banker.

No right of sale: In the event of non-payment, the banker cannot sell the goods without the intervention of the court. Again, it is very difficult to realise these, since, most of the goods are in the form of raw materials or used vehicles, etc.

False stock statements: The borrower may give false and inflated stock statements, against which he may enjoy overcredit facilities. In fact, some of the stocks may contain even obsolete items.

Least control over the security

The banker has the least control over the security. Both ownership and possession of the hypothecated goods remain with the borrower. So, he can very easily indulge in fraudulent activities.

Precautions to be taken by a banker while granting loans on hypothecation

Even though the hypothecation agreement gives power to banks to enter into the premises of the defaulting borrowers and take possession of the goods hypothecated with the bank. But it is a fact that the bank will not be in a position to possess the goods without the consent of the borrower. Since the goods are with the customer, he can sell the goods or hypothecate the same goods with another bank. Hence, the following precautions should be taken by the banker in order to safeguard his interest although granting loans under hypothecation is quite risky.

Apart from taking the normal precautions – safety, liquidity, profitability, three Cs of the customer – capacity, character, capital, spreading risk, etc., the banker should take certain additional precautions. These are:

(a) The banker should make the customer sign the hypothecation agreement bringing in all the causes advantageous to the banker.
(b) It is essential that the goods be insured against theft, fire and other risks, etc.
(c) An undertaking should be obtained from the customer that he will not simultaneously hypothecate the same goods or borrow from any other agency on the strength of the same hypothecated goods.
(d) In case the customer has hypothecated the goods to another bank, he should be asked to earmark his stocks for identification. It is advisable that the borrower maintains separate record books to identify stocks hypothecated to different banks.
(e) The banker should arrange to get periodical return relating to the stock position in the godown and the drawing limit should be calculated accordingly.

(f) The banker should arrange for periodical checking and surprise checking of the stock.

(g) The banker should arrange to fix up a name plate in a conspicuous place of the godown with the words "Hypothecated to Bank", in the case of vehicle loan. These words should be clearly written on the vehicle.

Pledge v. Hypothecation

The basic distinction between pledge and hypothecation is that in the case of a pledge, the actual control of goods remains with the pledgee, whereas in the case of hypothecation, the actual control remains with the borrower. For a banker, in both the cases, the ownership is not transferred.

Mortgage

It is a method of charging which can be created only in respect of immovable properties like land and buildings.

Definition

According to Section 58 of the Transfer of Property Act, 1882, "A mortgage is the transfer of an interest in specific immovable property for the purpose of securing the payment of money advanced or to be advanced by way of loan, an existing or future debt, or the performance of an engagement which may give rise to pecuniary liability".

The person who transfers the interest in property is called a "mortgager" and the person to whom it is transferred is called "mortgagee". The document by which the transfer is effected is called the "mortgage deed".

Salient Features of a Mortgage

Salient features of a mortgage are the following:

Transfer of interest: It is the transfer of an interest in specific immovable property which indicates that some of the rights passed on to the mortgagee and some still are retained by the owner.

Identification of property: The property must be such that it can be properly identified. Complete postal address should be furnished for easy identification.

Transfer not essential: Actual possession of the property may or may not be transferred.

Object of transfer of interest in the property: The object of transfer of interest in the property must be to secure a loan or to ensure the performance of an engagement which results in monetary obligation.

Retransfer only after repayment of loan: Mortgager obtains retransfer of interest in property after the repayment of the loan amount and interest thereon.

Right to Recover: The mortgagee gets, subject to the terms of mortgage deed, the right to recover the amount of loan plus interest due thereon out of the sale proceeds of the mortgaged property.

Kinds of Mortgage

There are, in all, six kinds of mortgages:

- simple mortgage
- mortgage by conditional sale
- usufructuary mortgage
- english mortgage
- mortgage by deposits of title deeds
- anomalous mortgage.

Simple mortgage: In a simple mortgage, the mortgager binds himself to pay the debt personally, and agrees that in the event of his failure to pay the mortgage money, the mortgagee shall have the right to cause the property to be applied so far as may be necessary by means of a decree for the sale of property. If the mortgage property is not sufficient to discharge the debt, the mortgagee can bring a personal action against the mortgager and obtain a decree which, like any other money decree, can be executed against other properties of the mortgager. Thus, the mortgagee cannot sell the property himself. In case of default in payment, he will have to file a suit in a court of law for sale of the mortgaged property. In simple mortgage, no right of possession or foreclosure is available to the mortgagee.

Mortgage by conditional sale: In this case, the mortgager ostensibly sells the mortgaged property to the mortgagee with any of the following conditions:

(a) That the sale shall become absolute if the mortgager fails to pay the mortgage money before a certain date.

(b) That the sale shall become void if the mortgager pays the mortgage money.

(c) That the buyer shall re-transfer the property to the seller if the latter makes the payment of the mortgage money on a certain date.

Usufructuary mortgage:

(a) The mortgagee is authorised to retain the possession of the property till the loan is repaid.

(b) He is also authorised to recover the income like rents and profits arising from this property. It is appropriated towards the loan amount.

So, the liability of the mortgager is gradually reduced under this type.

(c) In the event of non-payment, the mortgagee can sue neither for the mortgage money nor for the sale of the property. Even the right of foreclosure is not available.

(d) The only remedy available is to retain the possession of the property, and receive the income arising from it till the loan is settled.

(e) However, if the mortgager fails to redeem the property within 60 years, the mortgagee becomes the absolute owner.

English mortgage: The mortgager binds himself to repay the mortgage money on a certain date and transfers the mortgaged property absolutely to the mortgagee. The condition, however, is that the mortgagee will re-transfer it to the mortgager on payment of the mortgage money as agreed.

Mortgage by deposits of title deeds or equitable mortgage: Under this type, there is a mere deposit of title deeds to property. The intention of the deposit is to secure loan. The usual practice is that the mortgager delivers title deeds to the mortgagee and also possesses a promissory note in his favour against which the mortgagee advances the money. In case of non-payment, the mortgagee sues for sale but he cannot foreclose the mortgaged property. Document of title would apply to any document that provides some evidence that the mortgager has title to the property. Under Article 62 of the Limitation Act 1963, the period for enforcing the payment of money secured by a mortgage is 12 years.

Mortgages can be classified into: (a) Legal Mortgage (b) Equitable Mortgage.

In the case of legal mortgage, the mortgager transfers his legal title in respect of the mortgaged property to the mortgagee. This transfer of title is effected only by a registered deed if the mortgage money is INR 100 or more. When the mortgage debt along with interest due thereon is fully paid, the title on the property is re-transferred to the mortgager. This involves a heavy stamp duty and other expenses of registration.

In case of equitable mortgage, the mortgager deposits the documents of title to the mortgaged property with the mortgagee for the purpose of creating an equitable interest of the mortgage in the property.

Salient Features of Equitable Mortgage

The salient features of equitable mortgage are as follows:

(a) Mere deposit of title deeds

(b) Intention to secure a loan

(c) No registration of documents

(d) **Authorised places:** This type of mortgage can be created in India only in cities like Mumbai, Kolkata, Chennai, or any other towns which the state government may notify from time to time in this behalf

(e) **Existence of Debt:** The creation of Equitable Mortgage requires the existence of a debt. The debt may be an existing one or a future one

(f) Re-transfer of Documents

(g) No right of sale without the intervention of the court.

Advantages of Equitable Mortgage: The following are some of the advantages of an equitable mortgage over the legal mortgage.

No registered deal is required: In case of equitable mortgage, no registered deal is required to evidence the transaction unlike legal mortgage. There are savings in expenses such as stamp duty, etc.

Legal sanctity: Equitable mortgage is more or less equal to legal mortgage under Section 96 of the Transfer of Property Act, 1882.

Takes care of borrower's interest: The information regarding equitable mortgage remains confined between the banker and the customer by which credit of the borrower is not effected.

Prompt sanction of loans: Customers in need of money urgently can be granted loans without delay by the bank through all equitable mortgage, as it does not require the compliance of formalities like registration.

Operational convenience: In case of adjustment of mortgage debt, title deeds are returned to the mortgager. He can redeposit the same for raising new loan. In the case of legal mortgage, a new deed and registration is necessary as the time of every mortgage.

Disadvantages of Equitable Mortgage

The disadvantages of Equitable Mortgage are as follows:

(a) Existence of prior equitable mortgage

(b) Existence of subsequent legal mortgage

(c) No right of sale.

The banker should take the following precautions while dealing with mortgage by deposit of title deeds or equitable mortgage.

(a) **Existence of ownership:** The title deeds should clearly establish the ownership of the borrower. The banker should obtain the original title deeds and legal opinion should be sought before accepting the offer of mortgage for loan.

(b) **Created at restricted Places only:** The banker should keep track of the places notified by the state government in the official gazette where an equitable mortgage can be created.

(c) **Check who is authorised to keep the documents:** Authority to the title deeds of the property must be deposited by the owner of the property or his duly authorised agent. In case of joint owners, a letter of authority in favour of one of them must be executed by the owners by depositing the title deeds. If the borrower is a limited company, a resolution, delegating the power to one of the directors must be passed by the Board of Directors. Letter of authority and the copy of resolution should be kept with the documents.

(d) **Insurance:** Adequately the mortgaged property should be insured against risk of fire etc.

(e) **Ownership:** Evidence of ownership documents like payment of property tax to municipal authorities.

(f) **Obtaining Permission:** Obtain permission of the competent authority like Urban Land (Ceiling and Regulation) Act, 1976 which is necessary.

(g) **Anomalous Mortgage:** If any mortgage does not come under any one of the 5 mortgages discussed above, it is a case of Anomalous Mortgage. In real practice, it usually takes the form of a combination of any two mortgages.

(h) **Reverse Mortgage:** A reverse mortgage is the exact opposite of a normal mortgage transaction but restricted to a housing property. A normal mortgage transaction involves the home being pledged by the buyer to the lender as a security for the loan. Interestingly, the borrower does not have to repay the money. The loan is settled on the death of the borrower and his spouse or when they cease to occupy the home as their principal residence.

In the year budget (2007–2008), the Finance Minister P. Chidambaram, introduced reverse mortgage product which is now fast liberating the senior citizens from that conservative parental mind set, putting at par with his European or American counter parts. Reverse mortgage loan (RML) is essentially for the benefit of senior citizens above the age of 60 years against the security of their self-occupied, self-acquired houses. The loan is usually paid off by the legal heir of the borrower or is recovered by the sale of the house.

A reverse mortgage loan need not be repaid by the borrowers during their lifetime. They will also continue to stay in the houses during their lifetime. Thereafter, an option is available to the legal heirs to repay the bank loan and redeem the property. If this option is not exercised, the bank will sell the property and liquidate the loan and surplus, if any, will be passed on to the legal heirs. The budget report of 2007–08 states "The old, who are otherwise deprived or enjoying a tour or making a purchase due to non supportive children or any other commitment, can now avail of a loan, and that too, without bothering about repayments in their life time".

Assignment

When a party to a contract transfers his right, title, and interest in the contract to another person or other persons, he is said to assign the contract. Then assignment is transfer of a right in favour of another person. The transferor is called the "assignor" and the transferee the "assignee". In banking, the subject matter of assignment are "actionable claims" which include book debts, supply bills and life insurance policies.

There are two types of assignments: (a) Legal (b) Equitable. A legal assignment is an absolute transfer of actionable claim and not by way of charge only. It must be in writing and signed by the assignor. A written notice of assignment containing the name and address of the assignee should be given by the assignor to his debtor. In case the assignor fails to do so, the assignee should himself serve a notice on the debtor of the assignor. An equitable assignment is one which does not fulfill the above requirements of a legal assignment. For many reasons, a banker always insists on legal assignments while lending. Assignment of debt is not considered a good security for bank advances as it suffers from many drawbacks. Realisation of the assigned debt depends on the integrity and credit worthiness of the debtor of the assignor (i.e. borrower). If there happens to be a breach of contract between the assignor and his debtor, it will prejudice the bank's interests. In view of the above problems, banks grant advance against assignment of book debts only to partners of good standing and repute. Advance against assignment of life insurance policies is however more common in banks.

Advancing of Loans

Generally banks advance money against certain securities. These securities may be broadly classified into two, viz., personal and tangible. Advances against personal securities are in the form of unsecured advances, wherein, the customer simply executes a promissory note or accepts a bill of exchange. To safeguard his interest, the banker insists upon some guarantees of respectable third party. This guarantee constitutes a personal security. Tangible securities, on the other hand, refers to those securities which can be realised in times of need. It may also be called collateral securities. Collateral securities are those securities deposited by a customer to secure a loan.

Principles to be Observed by a Banker while Granting Advances

While granting advances the following principles should be observed by a banker.

Reasonable Margin

A banker should not lend up to the full value of the security. He must keep sufficient margin against possible price fluctuations in prices, shortage, and depreciation in storing and for interest.

Marketability of Securities

Advances are made by the banks for short period because their deposit resources are repayable on demand or at short notice. If a customer defaults in making payments, the banker has to liquidate the security. Hence it is essential that the security offered by the borrower maybe disposed off without much delay. A banker should not accept such securities which are not easily marketable.

Documentation

Documentation means necessary documents like agreement of pledge or mortgage, which are prepared and signed by borrower at the time of securing a loan from the bank. The documents contain the terms and conditions on which a loan is sanctioned by the banker.

Advances against Goods

Advances against goods constitute a very important part of the bank's portfolio. Goods are mainly divided into two types:

(a) Natural products of agriculture and mining.
(b) Manufactured goods which have undergone some mechanical or industrial process. Under natural products of agriculture, food stuffs like paddy, wheat, millets, etc.; fibres like cotton, jute, coir; oil seeds like linseed, groundnuts; hill produce like tea, coffee, rubber, etc.; forest produce like timber and sandalwood; spices like pepper; minerals like gold, silver, coal, etc. Manufactured goods include things like textiles, woollens, iron and steel, paper, etc.

Advantages

Advances against goods have the following advantages:

Tangible Security

Goods are tangible securities, and so, they are better than guarantees. They can be sold in the market when the borrower makes a default.

Seasonal Business

Advances against goods are granted for a shorter period, as the goods are likely to deteriorate in quality over a long period of time. Generally, these advances tend to be seasonal for the purchase of raw materials for processing or ready-made goods or agricultural products.

Easy to Create a Charge

A charge over goods can be created very easily and with minimum formalities. It does not require any registration of documents, payments of stamp duty, etc., as in the case of real estate.

No Price Fluctuations

The prices of most of the goods which constitute the necessities of life, are more or less steady.

Short-Period Advance

Advances against goods are always given for short periods because, most of the goods cannot be stored for a long period. They satisfy the principle of liquidity.

Valuation based on Market Quotations

Valuation of these goods is easy because of regular market quotations of these goods.

Large Volume Business

Business community prefers to have advances from banks on the security of goods for working capital purposes.

Disadvantages

The following are the disadvantages of advances against goods by the banker.

Storage of goods

The banker has to properly store the goods which he receives as security, otherwise the commodity may lose value. These may be deterioration of commodities in quality. The storage costs in terms of money and space will be higher. Physical deteriorative goods should not be accepted.

Risk of Fraud

There are greater risks of fraud as regard to quantity and quality. Goods of good quality may be mixed up with inferior quality. Again, the contents of packages or bags alleged to contain certain goods may not actually contain them. Moreover, there is a possibility for shortage of goods, in each bag. It is humanly impossible for a banker to check each and every bag.

Transport

Transport of goods from the businessman's premises to the bank's godown in the case of certain goods, excessive transportation costs.

Fluctuations

In case of certain goods, the fluctuations in prices are wide. The banker runs the risk in case of falling prices.

Risk of Prior Charge

Prior charge may exist in respect of the same goods. In such a case, the banker will lose his security. For example, the godown keeper may enjoy a prior lien over the goods in his godown in respect of the godown charges due to him.

Security

Storage becomes difficult in the absence of adequate storage facilities. The banker is not supposed to invest and construct godowns. Just for the purpose of receiving goods as security, "the central warehousing corporation" and "state warehousing corporation" are mitigating the inconvenience. Still there is shortage of approved warehouses. In view of the above problems, a banker should be very cautious while granting advances against goods. He should take the following precautions.

(a) *Ensure proper storage facilities:* Necessary care should be taken to see that the pledged goods are properly stored. The goods must be fully protected from damages due to rain, fire, theft, dampness, etc.

(b) *Reject the old stocks:* Old, damaged, rejected and otherwise unsatisfactory stock should not be accepted by the banker.

(c) *Adequate insurance:* All goods subject to a charge must be insured up to the full market value of the goods. They must be insured against all possible risks. The policy and the premium receipt should be kept by the bank.

(d) *Verify and value the stocks from time to time:* A bank official should verify at the outset that goods tally with those mentioned in relative invoices and are in order with regard to quality, grade, quantity, etc. Comfortable margin must be maintained at all times.

(e) *Knowledge of the borrower:* A banker should have thorough knowledge of the customer. He must see whether the borrower is a dealer in the goods commodity and possesses necessary license. The three Cs of the customer – character, capacity, and capital may be ensured. The banker should examine his own previous experience with the customer. In case the borrower had financial dealing with other bank/ banks, the banker should be extra cautious. He should enquire with other banks about the customer's financial dealings.

(f) *Title of the borrower:* The banker should ascertain whether the borrower has a genuine title to the goods. This can be done by verifying the invoices or cash receipts.

(g) *Nature of goods:* The banker should not encourage lending against perishable commodities. He may lend against essential goods due to certain advantages like stability in price, easy saleability, and wide acceptability.

(h) *Prices in different markets:* The prices prevailing in different markets will have a tendency to affect the prices in the local market. Hence, while regulating the margin, the banker should take into account, the prices prevailing in other markets also.

(i) *Short-term loans:* The banker should see that he lends only short-term loans for a period of 3–6 months to provide working capital for the business. In case funds are locked up for a long period, the bank may face liquidity crisis. The bank faces only lesser risk in case of short-term loans.

(j) *Periodical inspection:* The banker should conduct periodical inspection to see that the quality and quantity of goods in stock tally with the records maintained by both the banker and the customer. If there is any discrepancy, the borrower should be put to task.

(k) *RBI's directions:* The RBI often issues directions, prescribing margins on various goods. These margins and other stipulations in connection therewith, should be carefully followed by banker, while lending against goods.

(l) *Take delivery of goods:* The banker should take delivery of the goods before granting any loan. The borrower may repay the loan in installments, in such a case he should ensure that the goods released are only in proportion to the amount of loan repaid. Each release must be directly supervised by a responsible officer.

Advances against Documents of Title to Goods

Documents of Title to Goods

According to Section 2(4) of the Sale of Goods Act 1930, "Document of title to goods includes a bill of lading, dock warrant, warehouse-keeper's certificate, wharfinger's certificate, railway receipt, warrant or order for the delivery of goods and any other document used in the ordinary course of business as proof of the possession or control of goods, or authorising or purporting to authorise, either by endorsement or by delivery, the possessor of the document to transfer or receive goods thereby represented". The following are the important documents of title to goods:

- Bill of lading
- Railway receipt/lorry receipt
- Dock warrant

- Warehouse-keeper's certificate
- Wharfinger's certificate
- Delivery order.

Features of Document of Title of Goods

The following are the features of document of title of goods:

(a) Most of the documents are issued by the transport authorities acknowledging the receipt of goods on board and undertaking to deliver the goods to the person named in the document.

(b) These can be transferred by endorsement and delivery. Since, they possess one of the qualities of a negotiable instrument, some authorities call them as "Quasi Negotiable Instrument".

(c) A transfer of this document represents a symbolic transfer of goods. Hence, it can be offered as a good banking security.

(d) These documents, except for the warehouse-keeper's certificate, carry a right of ownership to goods represented by the document.

Advantages

The following are the advantages of document of title of goods:

Reliable Security

Since pledging of a document amounts to pledging of goods, it serves as a reliable security.

Convenient Security

It can be handled conveniently. The person, who is in possession of this document, can transfer the goods to any person by mere endorsement and delivery without the necessity of any physical transfer of goods.

Less Formalities

It can be easily transferred without much formalities. Since it is a Quasi-Negotiable Instrument, it can be transferred by mere endorsement and delivery.

Disadvantages

The following are the disadvantages of document of title of goods:

Risk of Faud

There are greater risks of fraud with regard to the contents of packages. Generally, the carrier of goods does not give any guarantee as to the contents of packages. There is ample scope for dishonest and unscrupulous persons to indulge in fraudulent activities.

Bogus Documents

There is a tendency among borrowers to deposit bogus railway receipt or lorry receipt with a view to defraud the banker. These documents do not have any backing of goods.

Delivery of Goods without Documents

There is a possibility of taking delivery of goods without surrendering the document. The owner of goods can take delivery of the goods by executing an indemnity bond. This is permitted when the document is lost. Some unscrupulous persons can misuse it.

Forgery of Endorsement

In case the endorsement on the document happens to be a forged one, the bankers cannot get any right of ownership to the goods covered by the document, since the rule is "forgery conveys no title".

Right of Unpaid Vendors to Stop Goods in Transit

Under the Sale of Goods Act, the unpaid vendor has a right to stop goods in transit, provided the buyer has become insolvent and the goods have not yet been delivered to him. In such a case, the banker cannot take delivery of the goods by producing the document and his security is lost.

Precautions

The following precautions should be taken by a bank while lending against document of title to goods:

(a) The banker should verify whether the goods mentioned in the documents of title are insured.
(b) Since documents of title to goods is only an additional security, the banker should fully rely on the integrity and honesty of the borrower. He should examine whether the borrower is dealing in the type of goods for which he surrenders the documents of title.
(c) The banker should examine the contents of the documents of title carefully and see whether it is genuine. He must check whether it contains any adverse conditions or remarks which are prejudicial to the banker.
(d) In the case of loans against delivery orders, the banker should see that the document is transferred in the name of the bank.
(e) The following documents should also be obtained in case of lending against documents of title.
   - copies of invoice
   - insurance policy

- all copies of bill of lading
- certificate of packing.

(f) The banker should inform to the issuing authority concerned about the creation of a charge on the document. This will prevent the borrower from taking delivery of the goods by executing an indemnity bond on the plea that he has lost his document.

(g) The banker should also obtain a memorandum of charge duly signed by the borrower. This gives the banker the necessary power to sell the goods, in case the borrower makes a default.

(h) The banker should also see whether the goods covered by the bill of lading have been issued against all marine losses and the marine policy has accompanied the bill.

(i) In the case of warehouse keeper's certificate, the banker should inspect the warehouse often to see that the goods are in good condition and proper storage facilities are available.

(j) In the case of dock warrant, the banker should inform the dock company about the creation of a charge in the goods in the dock house. It would prevent any unauthorised delivery of goods.

Bill of Lading: A bill of lading is a document issued and signed by authority of ship's captain, acknowledging that the goods mentioned in the bill have been duly received on board and undertaking to deliver the goods in the like order and conditions received, to the consignee or to the order or assignee provided that the freight and any other charges specified in the bill of lading have been duly paid. It is prepared in triplicate and duly stamped. One of the copies will be retained by the captain and the other two are handed over to the consignor. The consignor along with other documents, sends one copy of the bill of lading to the buyer who can take delivery of the goods in his place.

Railway/Lorry Receipt: A railway receipt is also a document of title to goods issued by the railway authorities for transporting goods from one destination to the other. Though it is not a negotiable instrument, it can be transferred by endorsement and delivery. Hence, the consignor insures the goods during the transport against fire, loss, or damage. The endorsement on railway receipt does not confer on the endorsee the right to the railway for short delivery or non-delivery of the goods as the goods are transported at the owner's risk.

Dock Warrant: It is a document given by dock company, warehouse keeper or wharfinger in charge of goods deposited. The document discloses the goods, acknowledges the receipt of them and undertakes to deliver them to the order of the depositor.

Warehouse-Keeper's Certificate: It is a document given by a warehouse-keeper certifying that the goods are held by him and awaits instructions from the person to whom the certificate is addressed. It is a deposit receipt only and hence not transferable. In India warehouse-keeper's receipts is covered by the definition of document of title to goods contained in Section 2(4) of the Sale of Goods Act, 1930.

Wharfinger's Certificate: This is a certificate which is a mere acknowledgement of goods issued by the owner of the wharf which is a landing stage along the shore for loading and unloading vessels. For giving delivery of goods, separate delivery is needed. When Wharfinger's certificate is produced for a bank loan, it must be obtained in the name of the bank.

Delivery Orders: A delivery order is a document issued by the seller addressed to the warehouse-keepers to deliver the goods mentioned therein or part there of to the person mentioned therein. Either the owner himself or his assignee may fill in the name of the person who is authorised to take delivery of the goods. A delivery order is recognised as a document of title to goods.

Advances against Real Estate Property

The term "Real Estate" includes immovable property like land and buildings, factory premises, etc. Generally, bankers are very reluctant to grant loans against real estates, since, it suffers from many drawbacks and legal complications. Nowadays bankers have come forward to accept real estate just like any other security and extend loans and advances against it.

The following are the difficulties and legal complications while advancing loans against real estate property.

Assessment of Value

To assess the correct value of property is a difficult task. The banker in most of the cases is unable to assess the correct value of the property and will have to seek the services of experts, surveyors, architects, and engineers.

Title to Ownership

It is very difficult to ascertain the title of the borrower. The title can be ascertained by verifying the title deeds. Even experienced lawyers find it difficult to go through and understand the contents of the title deeds to properties. The law of succession varies from religion to religion and from state to state. Further, the banker has to see whether the property is free from encumbrances. It involves much expense and time.

Less Liquid

Generally, advances against real estates are long term in nature. A banker cannot lock up his funds for a long period, since most of his deposits are repayable on demand. Hence, advances against real estates are always less liquid.

Time-Consuming and Cumbersome Formalities

While granting loan on mortgage, expenses like stamp duty, registration charges, court fees, and so on have to be paid by the mortgagee. The bank has also to spend a lot of time in completing the formalities of registrations, etc. If such loans are not being paid on the due date and when the bank has to seek the help of the court to sell the property, which is cumbersome, advances against real estate are likely to be locked up over long period affecting liquidity.

Difficulty in Creation of Charge

Generally, a charge is created on this security by way of a legal mortgage. Though equitable mortgage is there, a banker prefers only legal mortgage. Creation of legal mortgage is always costly and cumbersome. The borrower has to pay stamp duty and registration fee. Further, the mortgage deed has to be executed.

Precautions

When a banker decides to grant advances against real estate, he should, then take the following precautions:

(a) The banker should ascertain whether the borrower has got a clear and absolute title to the property. For this purpose, he must ask him to produce all documents. He can even consult experienced lawyers for this purpose.

(b) Since real estates involves a lot of risks, it is advisable to grant loans only to customers who are financially sound and who are men of good character.

(c) It is essential to see that the property is unencumbered. If there is any prior charge, the banker's interest will be much affected. Hence, the banker must ask the borrower to produce an unencumberence certificate for the period immediately preceding 13 years. It can be obtained from the registrar's office.

(d) Once the loan is granted on mortgage, periodical repairs are to be undertaken to maintain the property in good condition. An insurance policy should be taken against risks of fire, further value of property irrespective of the value of loan given.

(e) Real estate is not easy to sell and if the building is being occupied by a tenant, it will fetch a lower price than a vacant building because of the protection given by rent control legislation in certain states which are unduly in favour of tenants. Therefore, banks should insist on a high margin which may be up to 50 per cent of the value of the property.

(f) The banker should also verify whether the property tax has been paid up to date to the local authorities. If not they can attach the property at any time and they will have a preference claim over the banker's claim. The banker should also verify the latest tax/revenue receipt and ensure that there are no dues to the government. In case the value of the mortgaged property exceeds INR 50,000, a certificate from the income tax officer should have been obtained stating that there are no arrears of income tax from the borrower.

(g) The banker must secure the first mortgage on the property, because a second and subsequent mortgages rank only next to the first one. Moreover, title deeds to property will not be available to the second and subsequent mortgage.

(h) Where an equitable mortgage of the property has been taken it is always advisable for the banker to get a memorandum of deposits from the borrower, in addition to the deposit of title deeds.

Thus, the banker should take utmost care when they are offered real estate as security for advances.

Loans against Life Insurance Policies

A life insurance contract is a contract between an insurance company and a person called assured, whereby, the insurance company agrees to pay a certain sum on the happening of a certain event, viz., death (in the case of whole life policy or after expiry of a fixed period or death whichever is earlier (in the case of endowment policy). The consideration for this contract is that the assured agrees to pay a certain sum either in one lump sum called annuity or installments called premium.

A whole life policy is one wherein the amount is payable at the death of the insurer. In a endowment policy, the amount will be payable to the nominee at the death of the insured or at maturity to the insured whichever is earlier. This type of policy is very popular. Endowment policy is issued by "Life Insurance Corporation of India" "with profit", or "without profit".

The main objectives of taking life insurance policies are to make a provision for dependents in cases of untimely death of the insured, to make a provision for old age and retirement and to obtain a loan from LIC for construction of house by the policy holder. At present, the LIC grants loans on its own unencumbered policies up to 90 per cent of the sum assured value, if the premiums have bean paid at least for a period of two years.

Advantages

The advantages of life insurance policies are as follows:

Highly Liquid

The life insurance company is always ready to pay the surrender value at any time. Hence, the policy can be converted into cash immediately at the discretion of the holder.

Tangible Security

Life policy is better than guarantees, since, it is a tangible security, the banker need not worry about this security.

Increasing Value of the Policy

The surrender value of the policy continues to increase on account of payment of subsequent premiums and declaration of bonus. The banker need not worry about the fall in value of the life policy at any time.

Easy to Ascertain the Title

Generally, a policy is taken by a person on his own life. So it is easy to find out the title of the borrower.

Not Many Legal Formalities

The policy can be assigned in favour of the banker very easily by means of giving a notice of assignment to the company. The banker is able to get a good title without undergoing much formalities.

No Price Fluctuation

The value of the security is not subject to price fluctuation as in the case of stock exchange securities. Hence, a banker need not worry about the price movements.

Disadvantages

The disadvantages of life insurance policies are as follows:

Default in Payment of Premiums

The validity of the life policy depends on the regular payment of premiums. In case the insured stops paying premium on the appropriate dates, the policy gets lapsed. Consequently, the banker may not even get the surrender value.

Risk in Case of Suicide

Life policies, in certain cases, may include a "suicide clause", which may prevent the payment in case the insured commits suicide.

Absence of Insurance Interest

One of the essential conditions of a life insurance contract is that, there must be insurable interest at the time of taking out a policy otherwise the contract would become void. Mere love and affection will not constitute insurable interest.

Non-disclosure of Material Facts

All insurance contracts are contracts of "uberrimae fidei", that is, "maintainance of utmost good faith". It means that the assured should have disclosed all material facts affecting his life, at the time of taking out a policy. Otherwise, the policy would become void. A banker cannot find out whether the insured has disclosed all material facts or not.

Chance for a Duplicate Policy

There is a chance for the borrower to obtain a duplicate policy from the company stating that he has lost his original policy. This duplicate can be obtained from another bank. Thus, there is possibility for double financing.

Precautions

The banker has to take the following precautions while advancing loans against life insurance policies.

(a) The banker should examine the conditions of the policy. Conditions such as restrictions on assignment of the policy may prevent the banker from lending against such securities.

(b) It is absolutely necessary that the age of the policy holder should have been admitted by the LIC. Till such time, the LIC does not ensure any liability. Hence, the banker should get the age admitted by the LIC either by a separate letter or by an endorsement on the policy, if not done earlier.

(c) The financial position of the insurance companies should be sound. A number of private sector insurance companies have entered the market in a big way, For example, Tata AIG; ING Vysya; ICICI Prudential Life Insurance Corporation of India, Royal Sundaram, etc., which are financially very sound. LIC is no longer a monopoly organisation.

(d) Once a banker grants loan on life policy, he should monitor the repayment of the loan and regular payment of premium. In case the borrower fails to submit the premium receipt, the bank should check with the company for regularity of payment of premium to ensure that the policy is kept alive.

(e) The banker should lend only to the extent of the "sum assured value" of the policy. If the banker lends more amount than the "sum assured value" of the policy, he may be the loser in the event of default on the part of the borrower.

(f) The existence of any prior charge on the policy would effect the banker's interest. Hence, he should ascertain from the company that there are no encumbrances on the policy. Sometimes, the company itself would have granted loans on the policy. It can be found out by making an enquiry with the company.

(g) Between a whole life policy and an endowment policy, the banker should prefer an endowment policy, because it matures within a stipulated period. Even among endowment policies, he should prefer endowment policies with profit, because bonuses are added every year to the policy amount.

(h) The banker should also ensure that the borrower has an insurable interest. There is no problem if the policy is taken on his own life. But if it is taken on the life of a third party, the banker must be very careful. Generally, in business, one partner can have insurable interest on the life of another partner. Creditor has an insurable interest on the life of the debtor.

(i) Even though a charge can be created by equitable mortgage, the banker is advised not to grant loans on the basis of equitable mortgage. The policy is deposited with the banker with a letter of undertaking that it shall be assigned when asked for by the banker on repayment of the advance. The policy should be assigned to the borrower and reassignment registered in the books of the insurance company. If there is no response, the policy may be surrendered to the corporation. In case of death of the insured, the banker will have to produce a death certificate from the proper authority of the corporation.

Advances against Stock Exchange Securities

The term stock exchange securities represent securities dealt in the stock exchange of our country. The securities traded on the floor of the stock exchanges are:

(a) Securities issued by the central and state governments like loan bonds, treasury bills, etc.

(b) Securities like debentures and bonds issued by the municipalities, etc.

(c) Shares and debentures issued by joint-stock companies. Stock exchange securities have been very popular due to the development of the capital market in India.

Advantages of Securities

Advantages of securities are as follows:

These are Reliable

These are reliable because a banker advancing money against these gets some tangible assets. Since these are on the active list of recognised stock exchange, sale and purchase can be made in large bulk and without any difficulty. Then those securities are easily marketable.

Easy Marketability Automatically Ensures Liquidity

They can be disposed off more quickly. In case, the banker does not want to dispose off the securities, he can revise the loan by pledging them with the RBI.

It is Easy to Verify the Title of the Holder

They can be transferred easily and their prices can be easily ascertained. Government and corporate securities pledged with the bank yield income by way of interest or dividend. The income can be used against loan. On discharge of the loan securities can be easily re-transferred and registered in his name without much of expense and formalities.

Creation of Charge

The formalities connected with the creation of a charge on those securities are very simple, one has to simply execute the transfer form in the case of registered securities. Other securities can be transferred by a mere delivery. So it does not involve much expenses and also much complicated problems.

Securities like bearer securities, share warrants, our government promissory notes are fully negotiable. They can be transferred by mere delivery and their transfer does not require any stamp duty. Hence the banker can get a good title than that of his customers, provided he acts *bonafide*.

Generally, the prices of good companies shares do not fluctuate very much. The guilt edged securities are not very much affected by business cycles. Hence, they are considered as safe securities.

Disadvantages

There are certain risks in advancing money against stock exchange securities. They are as follows:

Partly Paid-up Shares

A share may be partly paid-up, the facts of which are not indicated on the face of it. A partly paid-up share is considered to be a very risky security because:

(a) If the borrower fails to pay the calls, the shares will be forfeited.

(b) There is no market for such shares, since they will not be quoted in the market.
(c) The banker will have to pay the calls, in case he has already transferred it in his favour.
(d) The issuing company will generally reserve the right of prior lien over the shares, in respect of the calls money due, by means of its Articles of Association.

Duplicate Share Certificates

It should be noted that duplicate share certificates are also issued by the companies. It is possible that the same certificate could have been pledged with other banker of lenders. If the shares are registered in the name of the bank with forged signatures of the shareholder although a bank has acted in good faith, it is bound to compensate the loss suffered by the company.

Market Quotation

All stock exchange securities are not quoted in the market. If the shares are not quoted, it is very difficult to find out their market value. Moreover, such shares cannot be easily disposed off in the market, since, nobody prefers an unquoted share.

Private Companies

Normally banks do not follow shares of private companies. It would be impossible for the banker to judge the financial position of the company as private companies are not bound to publish their balance sheets.

Forgery

In the case of registered securities, if there is any forgery in the transfer certificate, the banker cannot acquire a good title. The rule is "forgery conveys no title". It is very difficult to distinguish between a genuine share certificate and a forged one.

Bogus Share Certificates

There is a possibility of producing bogus share certificate and obtain a loan. It is very difficult to distinguish between a genuine one and a bogus one.

Restriction of 1949 Act

Under Section 19(2) of the Banking Regulation Act of 1949, a bank cannot hold shares of any company as pledge, mortgage or absolute owner of an amount exceeding 30 per cent paid-up capital of the company or 30 per cent of its own paid-up capital and reserves whichever is lower. In the case of block loans, the banker should verify his records and see that he does not exceed the limit.

Precautions Taken by a Bank while Lending against Shares/Debentures

The following precautions should be taken by a bank while lending against shares/debentures:

Ascertain the True Ownership of the Securities

The banker should ascertain whether the securities are held in the name of the borrower or in the name of some other person. The securities should be held in the name of the borrower in his personal capacity and not in his official capacity. For example, if a person is holding shares in a company as a trustee, the banker should not accept these shares for granting a loan to the person.

Knowledge of Stock Market Trends

The banker should have knowledge of the stock exchanges, the factors that affect the prices, the mechanism of selling the securities, etc. the Banker should ensure that the shares were fully paid up. Otherwise for non-payment of balance on shares which are pledged to the bank, the company may forfeit the shares and the banker will lose his security and bear the loss.

Creation of Charge

While advancing loans, a charge over securities is created in favour of the banker. Such a charge may be either a legal charge or equitable charge. The banker should always prefer a legal charge.

Written Agreement

Although it is not required by law, the banker should enter into a written agreement in respect to the pledge of the securities. In the event of having a written agreement he will have provisions which favour him.

Reputation of the Company

The banker should see that the shares are of a reputed company. He may make an analysis of the financial strengths of the company, its reserve position over the market price of its securities. If the fluctuations of the price of the share are too wide, the banker may have a greater margin.

Security Amount

The banker should find out whether the securities offered are secured or unsecured. If they are secured in the event of winding up of the company, the banker will be able to get the full amount of the securities. If the securities are shares, the banker should prefer preference shares because they carry with them a preference in respect of dividend and return of capital.

Short Period Loan

While granting loans on stock exchange securities, the bank should arrange for short-term loans. Investment for longer periods would be against the principles of lending in commercial banks. The advances should be need based and considering the net worth of the borrower.

RBI Approval

If the advance exceeds INR 5 lakhs, the repayment schedule should be approved by the RBI. Normally the repayment schedule should not exceed two years.

Clearance of Loan

Unless the loan is fully cleared, the bank should not part with the securities.

Default

The banker should never accept shares of private companies as, in the event of default of the borrower, he cannot sell these to anybody. There is a total restriction on the transfer of such stocks.

Own Shares

As per Section 20 of the Banking Regulation Act, 1949, a bank cannot accept its own shares as security. It is so because in the event of liquidation of banks, such securities becomes valueless. Hence, the banker should comply with this restriction.

Notice to the Company

The banker should give a notice to the company informing that he has charge over the securities, particularly in the case of equitable title. Such notice will prevent the company from issuing a duplicate certificate.

RBI Directions

The RBI is issuing directions from time to time regulating the advances against shares. Such directions must be duly complied with, while granting advances against shares.

Speculation

Loans and advances shall not be considered for speculative purposes. Loans can be granted for meeting contingencies and need of personal nature and for subscribing to rights/new issues of shares and debentures.

Margin of Safety

The bank should keep a margin of safety as the prices of shares/debentures may fall at certain times. Banks prefer to have 25 per cent margin on preference shares and 40 to 50 per cent on equity shares.

Advances against Fixed Deposit Receipts

Fixed deposit receipts are issued by the banks for the deposit made by the customers for a specific period ranging from 15 days to five years or more. These are popularly known as FDRs among the business circle. The rate of interest varies depending upon the terms of deposit. The interest allowed by the bank is higher than interest allowable in other types of accounts. The longer the period of deposit, higher is the rate of interest. The rules governing the fixed deposits are printed on the reverse side of the FDR.

The bankers favour FDR as a security, as these are issued either by themselves or by their counterparts (other banks). In case the customer needs money prior to the due date, although he may not be able to withdraw strictly from fixed deposit account, he can obtain a loan from the bank on the strength of the FDR. The banker sanctions the loan depending on the requirement of the borrower subject to a minimum margin of 10 per cent to meet unforeseen contingencies.

Advantages

These are the following advantages:

(a) The banker is aware of the maturity date of the FDR. Hence, he can be sure of the term of the loan and the exact date of repayment of the loan.

(b) FDR is transferable.

(c) There is no valuation in the value of security as in the case of other securities.

(d) As the banker knows the customer, he will be satisfied with the title of his own FDR as a security.

(e) The loan is granted only against his own liability or any other bank. Hence, realisation or adjustment of accounts will only be a formality at the end.

(f) The lending procedure is not complicated and inexpensive. It is a simple method of getting financial assistance from the bank. Similarly, the banker would feel that the lending procedure is very easy and inexpensive.

Precautions Taken by a Bank while Lending against Fixed Deposit

These are the following precautions:

(a) The banker should make an advance to the same person or persons in whose name the receipt is issued. If the receipt is issued in the name of two or more persons and the loans are desired by one of them, all the depositors must sign a letter of authority authorising the bank to grant a loan to one of them on that security of the receipt.

(b) In case the deposit stands in the name of the third party, the fixed deposit receipt duly discharged by the depositor should be obtained, along with the letter of authority, authorising the bank to allow the loan to the person named in the letter against the receipt and to apply the proceeds of deposit towards payment of advance.

(c) According to the RBI directions, the interest chargeable on a loan against a fixed deposit receipt should be at least 2 per cent above the interest payable on such deposit, if the deposit is in the name of the borrower only an advance against deposits, including fixed deposits, a margin of not less than 25 per cent shall be maintained by the bank.

(d) The bankers should grant only short-term loan against the FDRs. He should prefer to lend on FDRs which would be maturing for payment within the next six months. Borrower can also be advised to deposit the matured amount with the bank after maturity.

(e) Whenever a loan is granted against FDR, the interest payable on deposit should be credited to the loan account.

(f) Loans against minor deposits can be granted after satisfying that the loan can be used for the benefit of the minor. A declaration should be signed by the father, guardian and should be certified by the branch. Even in the case of where mother is taken as guardian for the minor, father alone can exercise the loan papers if he is alive.

Advances against Book Debts

Book-debts are debts receivable from different debtors. They may represent money due to the firm on account of credit sales or service rendered to some persons or money paid on account. The bankers accept book debts only as a last resort and not as principal security as the banker might face the trouble of collecting such debts from unknown persons. The procedure is lengthy and cumbersome. Book debts are normally permitted only to joint-stock company, small-scale industry, and trading and commission agents. The advances made against book debts are treated as clean advances.

Advantages

These are the following advantages:

(a) Book debts can be assigned as per the law. Section 130 of the Transfer of Property Act 1882 permits the assignment of debt to anyone except to a judge, a legal practitioner or an officer of a court of justice. Hence, there is a legal transfer in favour of the bank.

(b) The chance of failure to pay back the debt by all debtors is very remote. In fact, by lending against book debts, the banker has reduced his risk among many.

(c) The assignment of debt gives the banker all powers to recover the amount directly from the debtor. The banker can file a suit against the debtor for recovery of the dues.

Limitations

These are the follwing limitations:

(a) The banker's duty does not stop with getting assignment of debt in his favour but also to give a notice of assignment to the debtor. The banker would be safe only where a separate contract is entered into when the debtor agrees to pay the money to the banker directly.

(b) From the banker's point of view, the debtors are only third partners. The banker may not know about the financial position or financial dealings of the debtors.

(c) The debtors may have a counter claim with the customer. The banker may not know anything about this. Where a list of debtors is given to the banker without thorough checking enquiries and confirmation, if money is lended to the customer only on the strengths of book debts, there may not be a legitimate claim from the debtors. This would create a serious problem for the bank while collecting debts from the debtors.

(d) The bank should check when the book debts had arisen. Sometimes, goods would have been sold by the customer to the debts long time back. In case of long overdues, it would be difficult for the bank to collect the money. Moreover, some debts would have become time barred as per Limitations Act 1963. The banker should also keep in mind that the law of limitation can be exercised by the debtor in his favour if the book debt is due for more than three years.

Precautions

The precautions are as follows:

(a) The banker should be satisfied with the validity of the claim and must enquire about the reputation of the debtors about which the banker does not know. Hence, the banker should ask his customer to list the transactions between him and his debtors. This will enable him to understand the nature of transactions between them. He will be able to judge whether a particular loan or debt is a time-barred one or not.

(b) Advances should not be made against book debts outstanding beyond 90 days. In exceptional cases, book debts outstanding up to 180 days may be considered after obtaining special sanction from the head office.

(c) The banker should arrange for registration of the charge with the registration of joint-stock company.

(d) The assignment obtained by the banker should be for the whole amount as not a part of it.

(e) Legal assignment should be obtained by the banker. The assignment must be in writing in the presence of witness preferably at the office of the bank in the prescribed format. Assignment is an order addressed to the debtor by the customer directing him to pay the debt to the bank straight away.

(f) The banker should send a notice of assignment to the debtor and get an undertaking from the debtor assuming that he would pay money directly to the bank.

(g) In case the banker has taken book debts as a collateral security, book debts statement should be submitted to the head office once in six months, that is, March and September.

(h) In case of corporate borrower where general power of attorney is executed and charge on book debts is registered with the registrar of companies, branches need not obtain letter of authority.

Advances against Supply Bills

Banks are sometimes approached for advances against bills for goods supplied to government departments or agencies. Businessmen, who supply goods to those departments or agencies on the basis of previously submitted tenders, and contractors on partial or complete completion of contract, submit a bill for the amount of goods supplied or the contract work done in accordance with the terms and conditions of the contract. Such bills are referred to as supply bills. These bills are passed for payment by the appropriate authority only after verification that the goods supplied conform to the terms of the contract. The procedure, however, of checking and passing the bills takes a couple of months and some times even longer. During this period, the parties approach bank for advances against such supply bills.

Supply bills are not bills of exchange, they do not, therefore, enjoy the legal status of negotiable instruments. A supply bill, however, represents a debt arising out of a *bonafide* supply of goods, or contract of work done. Such bills are endorsed for payment to the bank and have to be receipted on a revenue stamp. They are also accompanied by a separate letter of authority addressed to the concerned government department or agency by the supplier or contractor to pay the amount directly to the bank.

In law, there can be valid equitable assignments of future debts, and such debts cannot be attached by another creditor to the detriment of a prior creditor who may have advanced money on their security (*Hindustan Commercial Bank Ltd. v. Union of India and others, AIR 1965. Allahabad 474*).

The banker incurs the following risks in granting loans against supply bills.

(a) Usually the government might pay the amount directly to the creditor unless the assignment is registered with the debtor, and the debtor undertakes to pay the amount only to the assignee.
(b) Generally, the payments of such bills are made by the government departments after a long time because of procedural delays.
(c) The amount may be reduced or payment refused if there is a default in observing the terms of contract by the supplier/contractor.
(d) The security available to a banker is by way of arrangements of debts represented by supply bills. It suffers from the usual drawback of assignment of debts or security. There is always the possibility of a counter claim or set off against the debts.

Precautions

The banker should take the following precautions:

(a) Advances against supply bills should be granted only to honest suppliers or contractors, having a long experience in the business.
(b) The banker should thoroughly scrutinise the terms of the contract between the supplier/contractor and the government.
(c) The banker should ask the supplier/contractor to execute an irrevocable power of attorney in his favour, authorising him to receive the amount of the bill. The power of attorney should be filed with the department to which the supply bill is submitted.
(d) The banker should ask the supplier/contractor to give an undertaking to repay the amount received by the latter directly from the government department in respect of the bill entrusted to the banker for collection.

Advances against Debentures

A debenture is a document issued by a company acknowledging its indebtedness to the person to whom it is issued. Debentures carry a fixed rate of interest payable at given periods. Interest is payable whether the company makes a profit or not. Debentures may be secured either by a fixed charge or a floating charge on the company's assets. If there is no such charge, debentures are clean or unsecured, these are sometimes called naked debentures. Debentures are accepted by banks as security if they are readily marketable. Their marketability, however, depends on their safety and yield, the reputation and profits of the company and the public opinion about the integrity and capacity of company's directors. In considering the value of a debenture as security, it is necessary to know the terms on which it has been issued and the manner in which it has been secured. Unsecured debentures may be accepted by a bank as security only when the credit worthiness of the borrowing company is very good.

When considering debentures as a security against advances, the banker should take into account the following factors.

(a) Financial position of the company.
(b) Popularity and marketability of debentures.
(c) Regularity in the payment of interest.
(d) Date of redemption, if debentures are redeemable.
(e) Company's powers to issue debentures and restrictions on such powers if any.
(f) Whether debentures are secured or unsecured.
(g) Study of the debenture trust deed. A debenture trust deed is a registered mortgage deed which is executed for the purpose of securing a charge on the assets of the company, against the specific security of which the debentures are issued. The names of the trustees are mentioned as mortgages in the debenture trust deed. The trustees hold the property in trust for the debenture holders. A margin of 15 to 25 per cent is usually maintained, provided that the debentures are marketable.

Advances against Gold Ornaments

Advances against gold ornaments are profitable and at the same time dangerous too. Banks were restricted to lend against such security under the Gold Control Act of 1968. Now the restrictions are relaxed and banks lend against gold ornaments liberally.

Accepting the security, on the part of the banks, requires certain precautions:

(a) Loans should be given only to customers. The honesty and integrity of the customer should also be considered. Non-customers who want credit facility should be properly introduced. This is absolutely necessary because advances are granted on the basis of the borrower's declaration of *bonafide* ownership of the ornaments.

(b) The banks should verify whether the pledger is the absolute owner of the jewels. The borrower may be questioned directly for this purpose and he may be demanded to produce a certificate to this effect.

(c) As far as possible stone studded ornaments should be avoided. Ornaments bearing the initials other than those of the borrower should never be accepted. These are the indications that the ornaments do not belong to him. Of course, jewels with initials of the makers are acceptable.

(d) Sufficient margin should be retained. Generally 25 per cent margin is kept on this security.

(e) A demand promissory note is to be obtained from the borrower in addition to the ornaments pledged.

(f) On repayment of the loan, security pledged are to be returned to the borrower. A banker should get an acknowledgement to the effect that the ornaments were returned intact.

(g) Jewels can be returned to third party on repayment of the loan. A banker should obtain a letter of authority with a suitable undertaking. This undertaking may be in the form of a bond of indemnity.

(h) Failure to repay loan empowers the bank to put the security to auction. If the sale proceeds fall short of the outstanding loan, the bank can proceed against the borrower on the strength of the demand promissory note.

Banker's Receipt (BR)

Commercial banks have to fulfill many statutory obligations. As such obligation is to maintain Statutory Liquid Ratio (SLR). It means that the banks have to maintain a certain percentage of their deposits in permitted securities. These securities include Government of India securities, state government bonds, and securities of certain other government agencies like port trust, electricity companies, etc. Hence, every bank has to necessarily trade on securities for liquidity purposes as well as for earning profits.

A banker's receipt is a statement issued by a selling bank to a buying bank declaring that it has received payment for certain securities already in its custody and promising to deliver them within a certain period. Since the physical delivery of securities is not possible immediately after the deal is over, the selling bank gives an assurance that the securities would be delivered within a fixed period of time mentioned in the contract by means of issuing a BR. The period fixed cannot exceed 90 days. The BR transactions between one bank to another and brokers who arrange for the transactions only get commission. This BR is non-negotiable security. But, in practice, bankers have made them negotiable by issuing BRs against BRs.

As per the RBI guidelines, BRs could be issued only in the case of trading in state government agencies. As regard to the central government securities, the RBI has the exclusive possession. The Public Debt Office (PDO) of RBI keeps a complete record of all trades in those securities in its Subsidiary General Ledgers (SGL). In that case, the selling bank has to issue only SGL notice to the buying bank, which will lodge it with the RBI for necessary records.

Risks associated with BRs Banker's Receipts

Non-negotiable Document

A BR is a non-negotiable instrument. Hence, the buying bank cannot acquire any better title than that of the selling bank . Moreover, a buying bank cannot endorse the BR to some other bank nor can it issue a fresh BR against an old one.

Issue of Fake BRs

A BR is always issued against the backing of sufficient securities. It is possible that a BR may be issued by a selling bank without holding the necessary securities to back the BR. In such a case, the BR is called a fake BR and it is a fraudulent one.

BR in Favour of Brokers

A BR transaction is made between one bank and another bank only. But, sometimes, there is possibility to issue BRs in favour of brokers also. There cannot be any direct dealing with brokers by means of issuing a BR in his favour.

Short Life

A BR has a life period of only 90 days or even less depending on the contract. If physical delivery of securities does not take place within this period, the BR becomes valueless.

Misuse of BRs

The rampant misuse of BRs was the main cause for stock scams. BRs can be issued without security backing to generate liquidity. Again, there is a bad practice of issuing a BR against another BR.

Precautions

(a) The banker should note whether the BR has been issued in the presented format. Again BRs should clearly reflect whether the trading transactions have been carried out through brokers.

(b) The banker should pay attention to the period of the BR. Since its life is short, the buying banker must take physical possession of the securities traded, represented by that BR, within that period.

(c) Generally, BRs are issued on mutual trust and confidence. However, the buying bank should ensure that the BR has been issued against the backing of adequate securities. If any BR is issued without any security backing, it is a fraudulent transaction.

(d) The banker must also see whether the BR has been issued against state government bonds and securities of other government agencies. If it is related to central government securities, he should not accept it. In such a case, he should demand SGL notes only.

Index

A

acceptance market, 108
accommodation bill, 394–395
adequate cash reserves, 52
advancing of loans, 506–507
  against banker's receipt, 530–532
  against book debts, 525–527
  against debentures, 528–529
  against document of title to goods, 510–514
  against fixed deposit receipts, 524–525
  against gold ornaments, 529–530
  against goods, 507–510
  against life insurance policy, 516–519
  against real estate property, 514–516
  against stock exchange securities, 519–524
  against supply bills, 527–528
Agricultural Development Banks, 164
Agricultural Finance Corporation Ltd. (AFCL), 94
Agricultural Refinance and Development Corporation (ARDC), 164
agriculture banks, 4–5
Akrokerri (Atlantic) Mines Ltd. v. Economic Bank, 483
Allahabad Bank Limited, 2–3, 84
All-India Industrial Development Banks, 164
allonge, 409
ambiguous instrument, 395
ancient banking system of India, 117–118
Andhra Bank Limited, 3, 85
annuity, 516
Annuity Deposit, 42
appellate tribunal, 262
Arthasasthra, 1
assets of commercial bank
  cash balances, 42
  fixed assets, 44
  investments, 43–44
  loans and advances, 44
  money at call and short notice loans, 43
  short-dated treasury bills, 43
assignments, 506
Associated Chamber of Commerce and Industry of India, (ASSOCHAM), 288
authorised capital, 40
Automated Teller Machines (ATMs), 17, 28, 359–360, 366
Auto Renewal Plan facility, 20
average rate of return (ARR), 67

B

Baker v. Barclays Bank Ltd, 491
balance sheet of a bank, 37–40
bancassurance
  benefits for a bank/insurance companies, 385–386
  challenges, 386–387
  definition, 385
  objectives, 385
  success of, 387
bank drafts (demand drafts), 26, 400
banker, characteristics of a, 427–428. *see also* paying banker
  banker's lien, 444–445
  banker's lien as an implied pledge, 446
  conditions for exercising the right of set-off, 448
  conditions under which banker cannot exercise lien, 446–447
  as a creditor, 433
  disclosing customer's account, 440–443
  duty to maintain secrecy of customer's account, 439–443
  precautions while disclosing customer's account, 443–444
  privileges enjoyed by a, 432–433
  relationship with customer, 431, 435–438
  right of appropriation, 448
  right to charge compound interest and commission, 448–449
  as a trustee, 433–434
Bankers' Books Evidence Act, 1891, 441
Bankers' Industrial Development Company, 7
banker's receipt, 530–532
banking, definition of, 269
Banking Commission (1972), 117
Banking Companies (Acquisition and Transfer of Undertaking) Ordinance, 1970, 96
Banking Companies (Acquisition and Transfer of Undertakings) Act, 1969, 96
Banking Companies Act, 1949, 2, 34, 248, 427
Banking Companies (Regulation) Act, 1949, 94, 429
banking in England, 6–7
banking in Germany, 7–9

banking institutions in India
  classification, 5–6
  evolution, 1–3
  types of, 3–5
banking ombudsman
  appointment and tenure, 375
  awards passed by, 379–380
  banks covered by the scheme, 381–382
  customer relations (grievances – redressal), 376
  definitions, 374
  grounds for complaint, 376–377
  powers and duties, 376
  power to call for information, 378–379
  procedure for filing complaint, 377–378
  qualifications and remuneration, 375
  rejection of a complaint, 381
  and review authority, 380–381
  secretarial staff, 376
  settlement of complaint, 379
  territorial jurisdiction and location office, 375
Banking Regulation Act (BRA), 1949, 209, 248, 294, 431, 440, 521
banking union, 214
Bank of Baroda Limited, 2, 84
Bank of Baroda v. Bachubhai Hirabhai and others, 499
Bank of Bhutan, 317
Bank of Bikaner, 2
Bank of England, 1
Bank of Hindustan, 1
Bank of India Limited, 2, 84
Bank of Indore, 2
Bank of Jaipur, 2
Bank of Maharashtra Limited, 3, 84
Bank of Mysore, 2
Bank of Patiala, 2
Bank of Venice, 1
bank rate policy
  annual policy for, 2007–2008, 287–288
  Hawtrey's view, 282
  highlights of RBI's mid term review, October 31 2006, 286
  influencing factors, 285–286
  Keynes's view, 282–286
  limitations of, 288–289
  liquidity ratio system, 283–284
  monetary measures of RBI, 284
  RBI regulations, 283
  repo rate hike signals, 286–287
bearer instrument, 394
bear *(mandiwala)* speculator, 149
Bharat Bank Ltd. v. KC Chella Ram, 491
bill market scheme, 130–132
  advantages, 132
  Dehajia Committee Report, 131
  disadvantages, 132–133
  features of the new, 131–132
  old, 131
bill of exchange, 392–394
  vs cheque, 400
Bombay Stock Exchange (BSE), 155
Brahma S Jung Bahadur v. Chartered Bank, 491
branch banking system, 9–12
Brando v. Barnett, 444
break-even analysis, 65–66
break-even point, 66
brokers, 148
Budhayana, 1
bull *(tejiwala)* speculator, 149

C

call money/call loans/overnight money market, 107–108, 110–111
Canara Bank Limited, 3, 84
Canara Bank Ltd. v. Rajagopal, 438
Canara Bank v. Canara Sales Corporation and Others, 484
capital/asset ratio, 65
Capital Issues (Control) Act, 1947, 142, 160
capital markets. *see also* stock exchange
  access to international capital markets, 160
  challenges to, 158–159
  corporate securities market, 138–140
  developments in India, 140–142
  efficiency of, 135
  features of the Indian, 137
  government securities/gilt-edged market, 137–138
  important reforms in India, 160–161
  stock exchanges. *see* stock exchange
  structure/composition of, 135–137
capital of a bank, 40–41
cash budget system, 77–78
Cash Certificates, 42
cash credits, 58
cash flow analysis, 66
cash flow ratio, 65
cash reserve ratio (CRR), 25, 110, 292–293
Central Banking Enquiry Committee (1931), 16
Central Bank of India Limited, 2, 84
Central Bank of India Ltd., Bombay v. Gopinathan Nair and others, 429
central cooperative bank (CCBs), 210–211, 216
  defects of, 215
  functions of, 215
  loans and advances, 214
  mixed, 214
  progress, 215
  pure, 214
  share capital of, 214
  types, 214
Central Land Development Bank (CLDB), 220
Central Land Mortgage Banks, 165

Certificate Deposits (CDs), 125–126
chain banking system, 14
charge, 495
Chatterton v. London and Century Bank, 484
cheque. *see also* paying banker
  acceptance of, 419
  a/c payee crossing, 406–407
  amount to be paid, 401
  banker's, 402
  crossed, 402
  dating of, 401
  dishonoured, 419, 437–439
  double crossing, 407
  eligibility to cross a, 407–408
  endorsement of, 408–409
  essential features, 396–398
  forms of, 398–399
  general crossing of, 403–404
  issue of, 401
  making of, 419
  marking of, 419
  material alteration, 399
  MICR of, 399
  mutilated, 399–400
  not-negotiable crossing, 405–406
  opening of crossing, 408
  payee's name, 401
  signature of customer, 402
  significance of marking, 420–422
  special crossing of, 404–405
  transfer of, 408–409
  vs bill of exchange, 400
cheque truncation, 368
Chidambaram Group leasing company, 1973, 192
chit fund company, 182
Chore Committee report on cash credit system, 73–75
clean instrument, 395
Clearing Corporation of India Ltd. (CCIL), 173
clear instruments, 395
Clore & Co. v. Dresdner Bank, 432
closing of account, 449, 485–486
Code of Civil Procedure, 466
collateral loan market, 108
collecting banker, 486
  as agent, 487
  duties of, 487–488
  as a holder for value, 486
  liability of, 490–492
  statutory protection for, 489–490
commercial banking, 1, 4, 136. *see also* modern commercial banks
  vs non-banking financial companies (NBFCs), 183–184
Commercial Bank Limited, 3
commercial bill market, 109–111, 126–127
Commercial Paper (CP), 125
commission agents, 148
Commissioner of Taxation v. English Scottish and Australian Bank, 428
common systems of banking, 9–18
Companies Act of 1956, 202
complete instrument, 395–396
computerisation in banking, 351
  Automated Teller Machines (ATMs), 359–360, 366
  batch updates, 366
  at branch level, 352
  charged cards, 361
  cheque truncation, 368
  core banking facility, 356–358
  credit cards, 360–361
  debit cards, 362
  digital signature, 372–374
  e-banking, 369–370
  e-commerce, 367, 370–371
  electronic banking, 358
  electronic payment system, 359
  foreign exchange transactions, 365
  hardware requirements, 358
  Internet banking, 366–367
  local area network (LAN), 353–354
  member card, 362–363
  mobile banking, 367
  multi-user networking, 352–353
  networking requirements, 358
  note and coin counting machines, 368
  online banking, 367
  online updates, 365–366
  personal banking facility, 364–365
  real time gross settlement (RTGS) system, 371–372
  remote banking facility for corporates, 364
  signature storage and retrieval system, 368
  smart card, 362–364
  software requirements, 358
  stand-alone systems, 351–352
  tele-banking services, 365
  uninterruptible power system (UPS), 355–356
  wide area network (WAN), 354–355
cooperative banks, 5–6, 209
  categories of, 223
  constraints on, 222–223
  differences with commercial banks, 211–212
  policy measures, 223–224
  regulatory control, 223
  structural reforms, 224–226
cooperative credit institutions in India
  aim of, 209
  institutions chart, 211
  Maclagan Committee recommendations, 210
  major concerns of, 210

three-tier structure of, 210–211
Cooperative Credit Societies Act, 1904, 210
cooperative credit societies in India, 209
Cooperative Land Development Banks, 221
core banking facility
benefits of, 356–357
business components of, 356
business process re-engineering (BPR), 357
creation of primary data centre, 357
disaster recovery site (DRS), 357
specialised consultancy, 357–358
Corporation Bank Limited, 3, 85
correspondent banking, 15
Credit Analysis and Research Ltd. (CARE), 173
credit cards, 360–361
credit creation
by demand deposits or cash deposits, 47
formula of, 50
illustration, 48–50
investments in securities, 46
limitations of, 52–53
methods, 45
money at call and short notice, 46
multiple credit contraction, 51
nature of business conditions and, 53, 62–68
via bills discounting, 46
by way of loans and advances, 46–47
Credit Information Bureau (India) Ltd. (CIBIL), 317
credit management, 78–80
Credit Monitoring Management (CMA), 80–81
Credit Rating agencies, 155, 158
Criminal Procedure Code, 441
C R Narasimha Setty v. Canara Bank, 445
current ratio, 64
customer
agent, 454–455
bankrupt person, 454
Clayton's principles, 462–463
definition of, 428
drunkard, 454
effect of entries favourable to, 483–484
executors and administrators, 459–460
garnishee order, 465–466
illiterate person, 452
joint account, 455–456
joint hindu family (JHF), 456–457
joint-stock company, 463–465
local bodies and authorities, 460
lunatics, 451–452
married woman, 452–453
minors, 450–451
non-resident Indian (NRI), 466–469
non-trading organisations, 457–458
pardanashin woman, 454
partnership firm, 460–462
trusts, 458–459

D

debit cards, 362
debt-equity ratio, 65
Debtor–Creditor relationship, 431–435
deemed exports, 252
Deferential Interest Rate (DIR) loans, 68
deficit financing, 99
demand draft, 400
demand instrument, 394
demand loan, 57–58
dematerialisation, 152
Dena Bank Limited, 3, 84
deposit banking, 15
deposit expansion, 54
Deposit Insurance and Credit Guarantee Corporation, 37, 41
Depositors Act, 161
depository participant (DP), 153–154
depository system, 153
deposits, 41–42
deregulated interest rates, 61
derivative
amendments, 152
definition, 152
types of, 152–153
development banking
concept of, 162
definition of, 162
features of, 163
functions of, 163–164
in India, 164–166
operational environment for, 166
structure, 165
term financing institutions, 165
Development Financial Institutions (DFIs), 136, 162–163
Deverges v. Sandemani, 446
Differential Interest Rates (DIR) scheme, 101, 237
direct financial assistance, 168–169
Discount and Finance House of India (DFHI), 110, 127–128, 168
district central cooperative banks. *see* central cooperative bank (CCBs)
District Central Cooperative Banks (DCCBs), 209
documentary instruments, 395
domestic banks, 6

E

e-banking, 369–370
e-commerce, 367, 370–371
Education Plan, 42
electronic banking, 358
Electronic Data Capture (EDC), 363

Electronic Fund Transfer at Point-of Sales (EFTPOS), 17, 364
Electronic Fund Transfer (EFT), 18
endorsement, 408–409
assignment *vs*, 410
blank, 410
by clubs and other non-trading association, 417
by companies, 416–417
conditional, 412–413
correct spelling, 415–416
by deceased person, 415
definition, 409
effects of forged, 476
endorsee, 409
endorser, 409
endorser's liability, 414, 419
by executors and trustees, 417–418
facultative, 413
by firms, 416
by impersonal payees, 418
by joint payees, 418
kinds of, 410
partial, 411–412
per pro, 412
by public authority, 417
regularity of, 414–415, 418
restrictive, 411
"sans frais," 413
"sans recourse," 413
significance, 409–410
special or full, 410–411
by women, 415
endowment policy, 516
Enforcement of Security Interest Act (ESI), 382–385
English mortgage, 503
Entrepreneurship Development Institute of India (EDII), 174
Equipment Leasing Companies, 182, 190–191
equitable mortgage, 503–505
escrow bill, 396
Europay, 362–363
European Payment Systems Network (EPS), 363
exchange banks, 5
Central Banking Enquiry Committee recommendations for, 247–249
defects in the working of, 246–247
deposit with RBI, 248
exchange department, 250
export department, 250
foreign remittance department, 250
functions of, 244–245
import department, 250
meaning of, 244
minimum capital requirement for, 249
number operating in India, 249–250
public sector banks as, 250
RBI regulations for granting licenses, 248
role in financing foreign trade, 245–246
social control measures, 248–249
Exchange Control Act, 1947, 441
Exim Banks. *see* Export-Import Bank of India (Exim Bank)
export factoring, 337–339
Export-Import Bank of India (Exim Bank), 133, 165, 173
assistance for export bids, 252
capital and resources, 252–253
finance for export-oriented units, 252
functions, 251–252
fund assistance, 251
medium of exchange, 253
non-fund assistance, 252
Export-Import Development Banks, 164

F

factoring services
advance, 333
advantages of, 335–336
advisory services, 332–333
bank participation, 333
collection of receivables, 331–332
confidential and undisclosed, 333
credit control and sales ledger administration, 332
credit protection, 332
financing receivables, 331
in India, 336–337
international, 336
limitations of, 336
maturity, 333
mechanics of, 334
non-recourse, 333
and pricing of various services, 335
recourse, 333
supplier guarantee, 334–335
feasibility of a project
commercial, 67–68
financial, 63–64
socio-economic viability, 68
technical, 63
fee-based non-banking financial companies, activities of, 319
fictitious bill, 396
Finance Corporation for Industry Ltd. (FCI), 7, 162
Financial Companies Regulations (FCR) Act, 2000, 189–190
financial intermediaries, 319
financial lease, 191
financial service sector
area of, 319–322
fee-based, 318

fee-based non-banking financial companies, 319
fund/asset-based, 318
First Ranga Rajan Committee Report on Bank Mechanisation, 351
Fixed Deposit Receipt (FDR), 20, 41, 432, 445, 524–525
fixed exchange rate, 255
fixed or long-term capital, 4
flexible exchange rate, 255
floating exchange rate, 255
floating rate of interest, 61
Food Corporation of India, 16
foreign banks, 6
foreign bill, 395
Foreign Currency and Convertible Bonds (FCCBs), 152
foreign exchange. *see also* international payments, methods of
definition, 253
Foreign Exchange Management Act, 1999 (FEMA), 258–261
Foreign Exchange Regulation Act, 1973 (FERA), 256–258
Foreign Exchange Reserves, 2008, 253
kinds of exchange rates, 255–256
market, 253–254
penal provisions, 262
powers of the RBI, 261
regulation and management of, 261
Foreign Exchange Management Act, 1999 (FEMA), 258–261
Foreign Exchange Regulation Act, 1973 (FERA), 250, 256–258, 441
Foreign Institutional Investors (FIIs), 136
foreign instruments, 395
forfeiting, 319
forward contract, 153
forward exchange rate, 255
fund flow analysis, 66
future contract, 153
future time instrument, 394

G

garnishee order, 441
General Insurance Corporation (GIC) of India, 165, 177, 197
German Credit Banks, 8
Gibbons v. Westminister Bank, 438
GIC Griha Vittha Ltd, 168
Gift Tax Act, 1958, 441
Global Depository Receipts (GDRs), 152
Gopal Singh, Hira Singh v. Punjab National Bank, 499
Gouthama, 1
Great Depression of 1930s, 6
group banking system, 14
Guardians of St. John's Hampstead v. Barclays Bank Ltd., 481

H

Hart's Law of Banking, 487
hedging, 330
Hire-Purchase Finance Companies, 182
hire-purchase finance company, 193
Hirschhorn v. Evans, 465
holder of a negotiable instrument
in due course, 422–423
privileges, 423–425
for value, 425
Holland v. Manchester and Liverpool District Banking Co., 483
housing finance company, 193–194
hundis, 1, 109, 117–118
hypothecation, 498–501

I

IDBI – Principal Asset Management Company Ltd., 173
IDBI Trustee Services Ltd. (ITSL), 173
IFCI Act of 1948, 168
Imperial Bank of India, 2, 311
inchoate instrument, 395–396
Income Tax Act, 1961, 41, 234
Indian Banking Companies Act, 1949, 19
Indian Bank Limited, 2–3, 84
Indian Bank Limited v. ESRa/smail, 484
Indian Companies Act, 1956, 339
Indian Contract Act, 1872, 434, 450–451
Indian Financial Network (INFINET), 18, 371
Indian Overseas Bank Limited, 3, 84
Indian Partnership Act, 1932, 460
Indian Stock Index Future Market, 155
Indian Trusts Act 1882, 458
indigenous bankers
characteristics of, 118
different names for, 117–118
distinctions with moneylenders, 122
functions of, 118–119
future of, 121
problems of, 119–120
RBI guidelines, 120–121
suggestions for reforms for, 120
Indo-commercial Bank Ltd. v. Bhoogalingam, 488
Indo-Nigerian Merchant Bank Ltd., 317
Industrial and Commercial Finance Corporation Ltd., 7
of England (1945), 162

industrial banks, 4
Industrial Credit and Investment Corporation of India (ICICI), 132, 164–165
activities of, 178–179
facilities from, 180
financial position as on 31 March 2008, 181
management of, 179
objectives of, 177
performance and progress, 179–181
sanctions and disbursements, 179
shareholding pattern, 179
Industrial Development Bank of Canada (1944), 162
Industrial Development Bank of India (IDBI), 4, 110, 164–165, 177, 197
amendments, 173
central role of, 172
details of sanctions and disbursements of (1998–2002), 176
functions of, 174–175
ISO 9001:2000 certification, 173
ISO 9002:1994 certification, 173
objectives of, 172
performance and progress, 175–177
range of products and services, 173–174
resources of, 173
shareholding of, 173
short-term strategies, 176–177
total business (2010), 176
training institutions, 174
Industrial Development Banks, 164
Industrial Finance Corporation of India (IFCI), 4, 162, 164
advisory services, 170
ancillary services, 170
basic challenges, 171
corporate philosophy of, 167
credit of promoting institutions, 168
criteria for financing new projects, 169
economic contribution of, 167
functions of, 168
management, 166
objectives of, 167
performance and progress, 171–172
promotion of organisations, 168
schemes for promotional activities of, 169–170
Industrial Reconstruction Bank of India (IRBI), 164
Industrial Reorganisation Corporation (IRC), 162
Information Technology Act, 2000, 372
inland instrument, 395
Insurance Regulatory and Development Authority (IRDA), 136
Integrated Rural Development Programme (IRDP), 101
Interactive Voice Respond System (IVRS), 207
Inter Bank Participation (IBP) Certificates, 124
internal rate of return (IRR), 67
International Bank for Reconstruction and Development (IBRD), 263
International Monetary Fund (IMF)
achievements of, 267–268
establishment of, 262–263
functions of, 264–265
and India, 265–267
objectives of, 263
shortcomings of, 268
stipulations, 263
structure and management of, 264
international payments, methods of
bill of exchange, 254
drafts and cheques, 254–255
mail transfer (MT), 254
telegraphic transfer (TT), 254
Internet banking, 366–367
investment banking, 16–17
investment banking in Germany, 8–9
investment company, 182, 194
investment policy principles
Character, Capacity, and Capital of the borrower, 34–35
liquidity, 33
margin of safety, 36
national policy and objectives, 36–37
nature and location of business, 35–36
principle of diversification of risks, 35
profitability, 33–34
purpose of loan, 34
safety, 31–33
issued capital, 40

J

Jagadeesan v. State Bank of India, Karur, 499
Japan Bank for International Cooperation, 202
Jawaharlal Nehru Institute of Development Banking (JNIDB), 174
Joachimson v. Swiss Banking Corporation, 432
jobbers, 148

K

Kannan Committee recommendations on credit monitoring, 81
Keshari Chand v. Shillong Banking Corporation Ltd., 435
KFW, Germany, 202
K Jagadishwar Reddy v. Andhra Bank, 445
Koch v. Mineral are syndicate, 465
Konsortium, 7

L

Ladbroke v. Todd, 428, 491
land development banks, 5. *see* primary cooperative agriculture and rural development banks (PCARDBs)
Law of Limitation period, 449
Laxminarayan Committee recommendations on working capital lending, 81–82
L C Gupta Committee, 1998, 155
leasing company, 191–192
lending principles, 54–57
  aspects of priority sector, 60–61
  Chore Committee report on cash credit system, 73–75
  credit appraisal, 62
  credit monitoring, 75–81
  guidelines to the follow-up of bank credit, 69
  Laxminarayan Committee recommendations on working capital lending, 81–82
  Nayak Committee recommendations regarding sanctioning, 75–77
  RBI guidelines, 59–60, 68–72
  Shetty committee recommendations for consortium advances, 82
  style of extending bank credit, 70–72
  trends in rates, 61
  turnover method of assessment, 82
letters of credit, 5, 30, 77, 79, 174–175, 178, 250, 259–260, 313, 430
liabilities of a bank, 37
LIC Housing Finance Ltd, 168
LIC Mutual Fund, 133
lien, 495–496
Life Insurance Corporation (LIC), 110, 136, 165, 177, 197, 207–208, 516–519
Limitation Act, 1963, 384, 432, 447, 449, 503
limited liability, principle, 2
liquid ratio, 64
Loan Companies, 182
loan company, 194
loans and advances, 54. *see also* advancing of loans
  bills discounted and purchased, 58
  cash credits, 58
  demand loan, 57–58
  hire purchase advances, 59
  overdraft, 58
  working capital credit, 59
local area banks (LABs), 18
local area network (LAN), 353–354
London money market, 103

M

Magnetic Ink Character (MICR) of cheques, 399
magnetic strip cards, 364
mail transfers, 26
managerial competence, 68
markets for corporate securities. *see* capital markets
marking on a cheque, significance, 420–422
Marzetti v. Williams, 437
Mathews v. William Brown and Company, 428
Maximum Permissible Bank Finance (MPBF) method, 62
Mercantile Bank of India Ltd. v. C. Bulchand, 488
merchant banking, 27
  in corporate advisory services, 346
  as debenture trustee, 347–348
  definition, 344
  functions of, 345–348
  in India, 345
  as lead managers, 350
  in loan syndication, 346
  main function, 345
  in management of issues of securities, 346
  in marketing and underwriting of public issue, 347
  objective, 344
  obligations and responsibilities, 349–350
  in off-shore banking, 346
  portfolio management services, 347
  in process of mergers and acquisitions, 348
  in project counselling services, 347
  in providing venture capital, 347
  role in promoting mutual funds and stock option schemes, 348
  SEBI's legal framework, 349
  SWAP arrangements, 348
  in United Kingdom, 345
Metro Area NetWork (MAN), 207
miscellaneous non-banking company (MNBC), 182, 195
mixed banking system, 16
mobile banking, 367
modern bank, features of, 19–20
modern commercial banks
  anywhere banking, 29
  bank as an agency, 25–27
  bank as a referee, 28
  cash credit, 22
  cheque system, 25
  corporate banking, 30
  creating credit, 23–25
  credit card, 28–29
  current account, 20–21
  debit card, 28
  discounting bill of exchange, 23
  E-banking, 29
  electronic fund transfer system (EFT), 29
  fixed deposit accounts, 20
  foreign exchange transaction, 30
  gift cheques, 28
  home savings safe account, 22

Internet banking, 29–30
investment policy, 31–37
letters of credit, 30
loan advances, 22–23
loans, 23
methods of transfer of funds, 26–27
miscellaneous services, 30–31
overdraft, 23
recurring deposits, 22
safe custody facilities, 25–27
saving bank account, 21–22
tele-banking, 29
teller system, 28
monetary policy in India
Chakravarthy report and recommendations, 299–302
Narasimham committee report and recommendations on banking sector reforms, 306–309
Narasimham committee report and recommendations on financial sector reforms, 303–306
period 1951–1987, 298–299
RBI macro-economic and monetary developments in 2007–08, 309–310
Money Credit and Commerce (1923), 1
money in circulation, quantity of, 52
moneylenders, 121–122
distinctions with indigenous bankers, 122
importance in rural finance, 123–124
operations of, 122–123
money market. *see also* indigenous bankers; moneylenders
acceptance market, 108
bill market scheme, 130–133
call money/call loans/overnight, 107–108
Certificate Deposits (CDs), 125–126
collateral loan market, 108
commercial bill market, 109–111, 126–127
Commercial Paper (CP), 125
committee recommendations, 116–117
features of developed, 103–105
illustration, 107
Indian, 112–116
Inter Bank Participation (IBP) Certificates, 124
objective of, 102–103
participation certificates (PCs), 111
participatory notes (p-notes), 111
RBI definition, 102
RBI guidelines, 134
Repos and Reverse Repos, 127
structure of, 105–107
system of Primary Dealers (PDs), 133
system of Satellite Dealers (SDs), 133–134
treasury bill market, 108–109
treasury bill of different maturity periods, 124–125
money market funds, 329
Money Market Mutual Funds (MMMFs), 129–130
mortgage
definition, 501
features of, 501–502
kinds of, 502–505
loans, 154
multiple credit contraction, 51
multiple exchange rate system, 255–256
Mumbai money market, 103
mutilated cheque, 399–400
Mutual Benefit Company (MBC), 182
Mutual Benefit Financial Company (MBFCs) – *Nidhi* company, 182, 195
mutual fund industry, 136–137, 142, 155, 157
advantages and disadvantages, 327–329
asset allocation (December 2000), 329
balanced fund, 327
closed-ended schemes, 327
and economy, 326
export factoring, 337–339
factoring services, 330–337
future of, 329
growth fund, 327
hedging, 330
income fund, 327
mutual fund, definition, 325–326
Net Asset Value (NAV), 330
open-ended schemes, 326
sector fund, 327

N

Narasimham Committee Report, 232
National Association of Securities Dealers Automated Quotation (NASDAQ), 155, 157
National Bank of Agriculture and Rural Development (NABARD), 164–165, 214, 217, 222
establishment of, 226–227
functions of, 228–230
micro-financing schemes, 230–231
NABARD-GTZ, 231
objectives of, 228
organisational set-up, 227
policy initiatives (1998–1999) for RRBs, 242–243
role in Self Help Promoting Institutions (SHPI), 231
SDC (Swiss Agency for Development and Cooperation) collaboration, 230
sources of funding, 227–228
National Cooperative Development Corporation (NCDC), 222
National Credit Council (NCC), 93–94
National Institute of Bank Management, Mumbai, 85
Nationalisation Bill, 96
nationalisation of banks, 2–3

achievements post, 98–101
aims and objectives of, 97
arguments against, 89–91
arguments for, 86–89
Nationalisation Bill, 96–97
objectives of the government's decision, 86
pre-nationalisation developments, 94–95
National Securities Clearing Corporation Limited (NSCCL), 160
National Security Depository Ltd. (NSDL), 173
National Small Industries Corporation (NSIC), 164
National Stock Exchange of India Limited (NSE), 155–156, 168, 173
Nayak Committee recommendations regarding sanctioning, 75–77
negative (non-possessory) lien, 447–448
Negotiable Instrument Act, 1881, 395, 492
negotiable instruments
bill of exchange, 392–394
cheque. *see* cheque
classification of, 394–396
essential features of a promissory note, 391–392
features of, 389–390
holder, 422–426
presumptions to, 390
role of, 388
specimen form of demand promissory note, 391
type of, 390–391
Negotiable Instruments Act, 1881, 388, 390–392, 394, 396, 398, 400, 403–406, 411, 419, 422–423, 425, 427, 437, 470, 473, 476
Nepal SBI Bank, 317
net present value method (NPV), 67
net profit ratio, 65
New Bank of India Limited, 3, 85
New Central Hall v. United Commercial Bank Ltd., 437
New York money market, 102
New York Stock Exchange (NYSE), 177
non-banking financial companies (NBFCs), 61, 160
commercial banks *vs*, 183–184
Companies (Acceptances of deposits) rules, 196
companies under, 182
form of lease transaction, 191–192
functions of, 182
limit on public deposits, 188
measures of the amended Act, 186
measures to protect the depositor's interests, 185
norms observed for accepting/holding public deposits, 187–188
principal business of, 182
RBI's control over, 186–187
reasons for the rapid growth of, 183–184
regulatory and supervisory framework of, 186
salient features of amendments, 185
services rendered by, 184
types of, 190–191
Vasudev committee recommendations, 188–189
non-banking sector, 181
non-negotiable instrument, 531
non-performing assets (NPA), 82–83
non-scheduled banks, 5
North Eastern Development Finance Corporation Ltd., 173
NRE/FCNR (B) accounts, 467–469
NRNR accounts, 467–469
NRO accounts, 467–469

O

officers of enforcement, 262
The Official Assignee of Madras v. The society for Providing Christian knowledge, 434
opening an account, 479–480
open market operations of RBI, 289–292
operating lease, 191
opinion contract, 153
order instrument, 394
Oriental Bank of Commerce Limited, 3, 85
Over the Counter Exchange of India (OTCEI), 155, 157, 168

P

Paget, John, 19
Participant Interface (PI), 371
participation certificates (PCs), 111
participatory notes (p-notes), 111
passbook, features of a, 482–483
payback period, 67
paying banker
circumstances refusing a cheque, 474–476
countermanding order, 473
double crossing and its effects, 476
effect of entries favourable to, 484
effect of entries favourable to the customer, 483–484
effects of forged endorsement, 476
features of a passbook, 482–483
material alteration, 472, 476–477
particulars of specimen signature, 480–482
precautions before closure of account, 485–486
precautions before honouring a cheque, 470–473
precautions before opening an account, 479–480
statutory protection to, 477–479
payment due, under a negotiable instrument, 425–426
Pension Plan, 42
People's Bank of India Limited, 2
Personal Identification Number (PIN), 360
pledge, 496–498
features of, 499
vs hypothecation, 501
Plunkeett v. Barclays Bank Ltd., 465

20-Point Programme, 37
portfolio management, 325
premium, 516
Presidency Banks, 2
primary agriculture credit societies (PACS)
  grants, 216
  measures for financial support, 216
  share capital and liabilities, 216
  shortfalls, 216
primary cooperative agriculture and rural development banks (PCARDBs), 219–220
  functioning of, 221–222
  two-tier institutions of, 220
  working capital of, 220
primary credit societies (PCSs), 210–211
Primary Dealers (PDs), 133
Primary Land Development Bank (PLDB), 220
primary (urban) cooperative banks (PCBs)
  aspects of, 217
  degree of control of RBI over, 218–219
  entry point norms for, 218
  Madhava Rao Committee recommendations, 218
  monitoring of submission of statutory returns, 219
  performance of, 218
  RBI sanctions, 217–218
  schemes, 217–218
  standing advisory committee, 218
prime lending rate (PLR), 61
Prime Minister Rozgar Yojana for educated unemployed youth (PMRY), 101
Prime Minister's Integrated Urban Poverty Eradication Programme, 101
priority sector advances, 60–61
private sector banks, 6
Public Debt Office (PDO) of RBI, 531
public sector banks, 5
Punjab and Sind Bank Limited, 85
Punjab National Bank Limited, 2–3, 84
Punjab National Bank Ltd. v. the Bank of Baroda Ltd., 422

R

Radha Raman v. Chota Nagpur Banking Association Ltd., 433
RBI Act, 1997, 185
reducing balance method, 61
Regional Rural Banks Act, 1976, 232
Regional Rural Banks (RRBs), 222
  branch expansion programme, 238
  "CAMELS" approach, 243
  Dantawala Committee report on, 241–242
  differences with scheduled commercial bank, 234–235
  difficulties in deposit mobilisation, 237
  establishment of, 232
  functions of, 235
  governance issues and procedural rigidities, 238
  growth in loan business, 237
  issued/paid-up capital of, 233–234
  James Raj Committee recommendations, 242
  loan losses, 237
  mindset of stakeholders, 237–238
  NABARD policy initiatives, 241–243
  Narasimham Committee recommendation, 232
  objective of, 233
  progress of, 235–236
  RBI regulations, 234
  staff attitude, 239
  suggestions for commercial improvements, 239–241
  unviable business policies, 238
Re-Investment Plan (RIP), 42
Reserve Bank of India Act, 1934, 440
Reserve Bank of India (RBI), 2–4, 18, 21, 52–53, 110. *see also* monetary policy in India
  Banking Regulation Act, 1949, 270–272
  bank rate policy, 281–289
  consumer credit regulations, 295–296
  control of transactions, 296
  curbing of speculative activities, 295
  direct action control method, 297
  functions of, 275–280
  methods of credit control, 281–293
  moral suasian (persuasian), 296–297
  net liquidity ratio system (NLR), 289
  objectives of, 274–275
  open market operations, 289–292
  organisation and management of, 272–274
  publicity as an instrument of credit control, 296
  RBI Act of 1934, 269–270
  selective credit controls, 294–298
  variable portfolio ceiling, 295
Reserve Fund, 41
Resident Foreign Currency (RFC) accounts, 468
residuary non-banking company (RNBC), 182, 195
respondent bank, 15
return on cost of capital, 66–67
return on investment, 66
reverse mortgage loan, 505
Revilpout, 1
Risk Capital Foundation (RCF), 168
Risk Containment Measures (RCM), in stock exchanges, 155
Rolin v. Steward, 437

S

safe banking
  assignments, 506
  general principles for secured advances, 494–495
  good banking security, 493–494

modes of creating charge over tangible assets, 495–505
principles followed in granting advances. *see* advancing of loans
safe custody deposits, 27
safe deposit locker facilities, 27
Salary Saving Scheme (SSS), 207
Satellite Dealers (SDs), 133–134
Satellite Financial Management System (SFMS)., 371
savings bank, 4
savings bank account, 21–22
Savory X Co. v. Lloyds Bank Ltd., 491
SBI California, 317
SBI Canada, 317
SBI Cards and Payment Services Ltd. (SBICPSL), 317
SBI Factors and Commercial Services Private limited, 339
SBI Gilts Ltd. (SBGL), 317
SBI International (Mauritius) Ltd., 317
SBI Life Insurance Company Limited, 317
SBI (subsidiary banks) Act 1956, 312
SBI (subsidiary banks) Act, 1959, 2
scheduled banks, 5
Scheme for Urban Micro Enterprises (SUME), 101
scripless trading system, 152
SEBI, 348–350
Second Schedule of RBI Act, 1934, 5
secured advance, 493
general principles for, 494–495
Securities Contract (Regulation) Act 1956 (SCRA), 142, 152, 155
Securities Exchange Board of India (SEBI), 136, 154–155, 160–161, 173, 192
Securities Laws (Amendment) Act, 1999, 152
Securities Laws (Amendment) Bill, 1999, 155
Securities Management Trust, 7
Securities Trading Corporation of India Ltd (STCI), 168
securitisation, 382
Securitisation and Reconstruction of Financial Assets and Enforcement of Security Interest Act (SARFAESIA), 63
Securitisation and Reconstructions of Financial Assets (SRFA), 382–383
asset reconstruction, 383–384
securitisation of loans, 154
Security First Network Bank (SFNB), 366
selling mortgages, process of, 154
Seltbia v. I E John, 472
SFC (amendment) Act 1985, 202
Shared Payment Network Systems (SPNS), 18
Shetty committee recommendations for consortium advances, 82
short-term capital, 5
Shroff Committee (1954), 16
simple mortgage, 502
Sir John Paget's "Duration Theory,", 428–431
Small Industries Bank of India, 173
Small Industries Development Bank of India (SIDBI)
challenges for, 202
development of, 196
financials of, 200
functions, 198
future strategy of, 202
institutions of, 198
objectives of, 197
operational strategy of, 198
purpose-wise assistance by, 201
refinancing by, 201
relationship with department for international development, 202
role in promotion and development of SSIs, 197
sanctions and disbursement of, 199–200
shareholding pattern, 197
Small Industries Development Bank of India (SIDBI), 61, 133
Small Loans (cooperative banks) Guarantee Scheme, 1984, 217
Smith v. Cox & Co., 483
"social control"of banks, concept of, 92–94
Société Générale pour favoriser I'Industrie Nationale, 162
sources of bank funds, 44
spot exchange rate, 255
stag, 149
State Bank of Bikaner and Jaipur, 312
State Bank of Hyderabad, 2, 312
State Bank of India, Hyd. v. S B Shah Ali, 499
State Bank of India Act, 311, 314
State Bank of India (SBI), 2, 5, 197
achievements, 314
agricultural finance, 314
assistance to cooperative and allied institutions, 316
business prohibited under State Bank of India Act, 314
capital, 311–312
financing of small-scale industries, 315
financing through Self-Help Groups (SHG), 316
functions of, 313–314
and industrial finance, 315
Integrated Rural Development Programme (IRDP), 315–316
management of, 312
merchant banking division of, 316–317
objectives of, 313
subsidiaries and joint ventures abroad, 317
State Bank of India v. Samba Murty, 433
State Bank of Indore, 312
State Bank of Mysore, 312
State Bank of Patiala, 312

State Bank of Saurashtra, 312
State Bank of Sourashtra, 2
State Bank of Travancore, 2, 312
State Cooperative Banks (SCBs), 209
  capital, 213
  defects of, 213–214
  functions of, 212–213
state cooperative banks (SCBs), 210–211
State Financial Corporations (SFCs), 164–165
  capital resources of, 203
  challenges, 205
  Gupta Committee report, 205
  objective, 203
  provisions of Acts, 202
  sanctions and disbursements of, 204
  share capital of, 203–204
  terms and conditions of assistance, 204–205
State Industrial Development Corporation (SIDCs), 164–165
State Industrial Investment Corporation (SIICs), 164–165
State Land Development Banks (SLDBs), 165
Sterling v. Barclays Bank Ltd., 438
stock exchange. *see also* depository system; derivative
  approval of trading in stock indices, 154
  changes in the secondary market, 151–152
  definition, 142
  and foreign direct investment, 160
  and foreign institutional investors, 161
  important reforms in India, 160–161
  J R Verma Committee recommendations, 155
  listing of securities on, 143
  mutual fund regulations, 161
  obligations under a listing agreement, 145–148
  operators at, 148
  primary market reforms, 160
  procedure for dealing at, 149–151
  requirements with respect to listing of securities, 143–145
  role and functions of, 142–143
  screen-based trading, 161
  SEBI regulations, 160–161
  speculators at, 149
Stock Holding Corporation of India Ltd. (SHCIL), 155, 157, 168, 173
subscribed capital, 40–41
Subsidiary General Ledgers (SGL), 531
Sunderland v. Barclays Bank, 442
Super Saving Package, 42
Swadeshi movement, 2
SWAP, 348
swap contract, 153
SWIFT (Society for Worldwide Inter-bank Financial Telecommunications)
  authentication facility, 364
Syndicate Bank Limited, 3, 84
Syndicate Bank v. Vijaya Kumar, 445

T

Tamil Nadu Industrial Investment Corporation of India, 202
Tandan Committee Report, 62, 69–72
Tata Industries Ltd., 192
tax deduction, 41
telegraphic transfer, 26
Tournier v. National Provincial and Union Bank of England Ltd., 439
trade bill, 394–395
traveller's cheque, 26–27
treasury bill market, 108–109
  of different maturity periods, 124–125
Twentieth Century Leasing Company, 192
two-tier exchange rate system, 256

U

Underwood v. Barclays Bank, 436
underwriting, 339–340
  agreements, 342
  contingent, 340–342
  firm, 340
  in India, 343–344
  provisions of the Companies Act affecting, 342–343
  rights of underwriters, 342
  standby, 340
uninterruptible power system (UPS), 355–356
Union Bank of India Limited, 3, 84
unit banking system, 12–14
United Bank of India Limited, 3, 84
United Commercial Bank, 84
United Nations Monetary and Financial Conference, 1944, 262
Unit Trust of India (UTI), 110, 136, 165, 177
  advantages of, 206–207
  Deepak Parekh committee recommendations, 206
  governmental interference, 206–207
  objectives of, 205
universal banking system, 18
urban cooperative banks. *see* primary (urban) cooperative banks (PCBs)
urban cooperative banks (UCBs), 209
usufructuary mortgage, 502–503

V

variable reserve ratio (VRR), 292–293
Vaz Committee recommendations on lending, 81–82
venture capital financing
  definition, 322–323
  eligibility for, 323–324

BRIJ/SSN
01/05/2015

features of, 323
stages, 324–325
strategies of harvesting, 324–325
venture capital funds, 136
very small aperture terminal (VSAT), 18
Vijaya Bank Limited, 3, 85
virtual banking, 17–18
Vysya Bank Ltd. v. Akkam Mallikarjuna Reddy, 445

W

wide area network (WAN), 207, 354–355
work technologies, 351
World Bank, 177

Y

Yoga Keshemam Vahamyaham, 207